CW00932054

PUBLICATIONS OF THE
ARMY RECORDS SOCIETY
VOL. 28

WOLSELEY AND ASHANTI

Fighting in the Ashantee Forest by Louis Desanges (1874). Desanges shows Wolseley (centre) issuing orders to George Greaves at Odaso on 3 February 1874, with a skirmishing line of the Black Watch in the background. (Anne S. K. Brown Military Collection, Brown University).

WOLSELEY AND ASHANTI

The Asante War Journal and Correspondence of
Major General Sir Garnet Wolseley
1873–1874

Edited by
IAN F. W. BECKETT

Published by

THE HISTORY PRESS
for the
ARMY RECORDS SOCIETY
2009

First published in the United Kingdom in 2009 by
The History Press · The Mill · Brimscombe Port · Stroud ·
Gloucestershire · GL5 2QG

British Library Cataloguing in Publication Data
A catalogue record for this book is available from the British Library.

ISBN 978-0-7524-5180-0

Typeset in Ehrhardt.
Typesetting and origination by
The History Press.
Printed and bound in England.

Contents

Acknowledgements

Quotations from the Royal Archives appear by gracious permission of Her Majesty the Queen. Quotations from Crown copyright material in the National Archives appear by permission of Her Majesty's Stationery Office. I also wish to acknowledge my thanks to the following for allowing me to consult and quote from archives in their possession and/or copyright: The Earl and Countess of Wemyss and March, Henry Parker Esq., the Bodleian Library, the Trustees of the British Library Board, the Syndics of Cambridge University Library, the Centre for Buckinghamshire Studies, Devon County Record Office, the Kent Archives Office, the Killie Campbell Africana Library of the University of Kwazulu Natal, the Kwazulu Natal Archives Depot, the National Archives of Scotland, the National Army Museum, the National Library of Scotland, the National Maritime Museum, Nottinghamshire County Record Office, the Royal Marines Museum, the Royal Pavilion Libraries and Museums (Hove Reference Library), the William Perkins Library of Duke University, South Lanarkshire Council Museum, the Wiltshire and Swindon Record Office, and the Borthwick Institute of Historical Research of the University of York.

Particular thanks are due to the Countess of Wemyss and March; Zoe Lubowiecka of Hove Library; Pamela Clark, Allison Derrett and Mrs Julie Crocker of the Royal Archives; Louise Oliver of Royal Collection Enterprises; Michael Crotty of Duke University; Tessa Spencer of the National Archives of Scotland; Joanne Hawkins and Claire Nicholas-Walker of the British Library; Rebecca Jackson of the Staffordshire Record Office; Mike Bevan of the National Maritime Museum; Dr Alastair Massie of the National Army Museum; Andrew Crookton of the Wiltshire and Swindon Record Office; Aileen Anderson of South Lanarkshire Council Museum; Rachel Rowe of Cambridge University Library; Oliver House of the Bodleian Library; Captain P. H. Starling of the Army Medical Services Museum; Mrs J. M. Simpson of the Killie Campbell Africana Library; and Roger Bettridge of the Centre for Buckinghamshire Studies.

I am indebted to Dr Jim Beach, the secretary of the Army Record Society. I am also very grateful to Annie Jackson for her hard work as copy-editor, given the idiosyncratic nature of Wolseley's writing.

I. F. W. B.

Abbreviations

BL	British Library
Bodleian	Bodleian Library, Oxford
BPP	British Parliamentary Papers
CUL	Cambridge University Library
Duke	Duke University (William Perkins Library), North Carolina
Gosford	Gosford House, Longniddry
Hove	Hove Reference Library
KCL	Killie Campbell Library
NLS	National Library of Scotland
NAM	National Army Museum
NAS	National Archives of Scotland
NMM	National Maritime Museum
OIOC	Oriental and India Office Collections
RA	Royal Archives
SLCM	South Lanarkshire Council Museum
TNA	The National Archives
WSRO	Wiltshire and Swindon Record Office

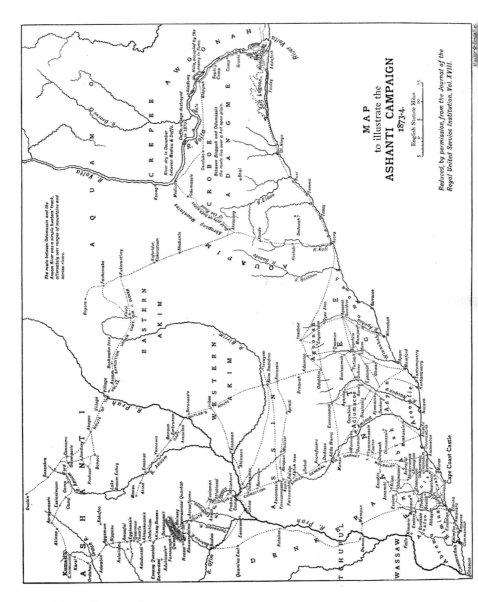

Map to illustrate the Ashanti Campaign, 1873–74, from Lady Glover, *Life of Sir John Hawley Glover* (1897)

Introduction

The Ashanti (Asante) War of 1873–74 was arguably the first Victorian colonial campaign to really catch the British public's imagination since the Indian Mutiny: *The Times* alone, for example, ran 415 articles on Asante in the second half of 1873 and first half of 1874.[1] It was certainly the first campaign of note in the post-Cardwellian period. Indeed, some including Edward Cardwell regarded it as a successful test of the new army system he had introduced through his military reforms as Secretary of State for War between 1868 and 1872, not least short service enlistment and the abolition of purchase.[2] In fact, success on the Gold Coast was actually accomplished with the tools of the old system in terms of officers who had largely purchased their commissions and battalions of long service soldiers from which younger, raw recruits had been weeded out before embarkation.

Asante was widely seen as a model campaign, won at modest expenditure in financial cost and in lives, indeed, a 'landmark' in proving white troops could operate effectively in the tropics.[3] As Garnet Wolseley's early biographer, Charles Rathbone Low, put it, compared to the achievements of the Conquistadors 'who fought in open country against an effeminate foe, and in a comparatively healthy climate', Asante showed that 'the country has no cause to lament the decay of the spirit that led our fathers to conquer India and colonise so large a portion of the globe'.[4] The campaign certainly dealt a heavy blow to the Asante, their kingdom being reduced to chaos by what the Fante termed the 'Sagrenti War' in a corruption of Sir Garnet.[5]

In the process, of course, it made a household name of the then Major General Sir Garnet Wolseley, the model for George Grossmith's portrayal of the 'very model of a modern Major General' in Gilbert and Sullivan's *Pirates of Penzance*.[6] Moreover, while the origins of the 'Wolseley Ring', or the 'Mutual Admiration Society' as its critics knew it, can be traced to the Red River Campaign of 1870, which earned Wolseley his knighthood, it was Asante that firmly established it. Redvers Buller, William Butler, John McNeill, Hugh McCalmont, and George Huyshe had all accompanied Wolseley to the Canadian North West, but in Asante they were joined by Evelyn Wood, Baker Russell, Henry Brackenbury, Frederick Maurice, Thomas Baker, Robert Home, Frederick Maurice, George Greaves, George Colley, and Lord Gifford. Huyshe died during the expedition to Asante, Home died as a result of service on the Bulgarian frontier delineation commission in 1879, and Gifford entered the colonial service in 1880: the remainder all reached general rank with Wood, like Wolseley, becoming a field marshal. Other officers who served in Asante were also to reach general rank such as John Brabazon, William Dalrymple, Fitzroy Hart, Arthur Paget, Edward Woodgate, and, in the case of Paul Sanford Methuen, that of field marshal. In wider terms, too, as the 'first serious British military venture into the tropical African interior', the campaign has been seen as a significant episode in the shifting dynamics of British policy towards West Africa in particular and towards empire and the projection of military power in general.[7]

Consequently, for all these reasons, the campaign is an especially significant one and it is the only one for which Wolseley's surviving campaign journal has not been published.

The background to the war

Britain had maintained coastal enclaves in West Africa since the seventeenth century, trading goods for slaves until abolition of the slave trade in 1807, then maintaining the coastal forts primarily as a means of suppressing the trade. In 1865 these outposts were at Bathurst in the Gambia, Sierra Leone, Lagos, and on the Gold Coast at Cape Coast, Dixcove, Anamabu, Winneba and Accra.[8] The Danes, Dutch, French, Portuguese, Spanish, Swedes and even the Grand Duchy of Brandenburg had maintained similar outposts at various periods in the past. The British also exercised a loose protectorate over the coastal Fante tribes 'which even experts did not understand' and an 'informal dependency' in the Niger delta.[9] The principal outpost on the Gold Coast, Cape Coast Castle, appears to have been settled originally and briefly by the Portuguese in the fifteenth century but the Swedes established a fort there in 1655. It was passed to the Danes in 1657, to the Dutch in 1659, back to the Swedes in 1660, and to the Dutch once more in 1663, before being taken by the English in May 1664.[10]

The Royal African Company and then the African Company of Merchants had administered the English and then British outposts on the Gold Coast successively from 1673 until 1821, at which point possession was transferred to the Crown and placed under the Governor of Sierra Leone. The principal threat was the powerful Asante kingdom, which periodically raided into Fante territory. Like other tribal groups in the region, both Asante and Fante were Twi-speaking Akan peoples who had migrated southwards towards the Gold Coast in the thirteenth and fourteen centuries. Benefiting from the acquisition of firearms traded for slaves, the Asante had conquered the Denkyira, Wassa, Assin and Akyem in the eighteenth century, Osei Tutu (ruled *c.* 1701–17) being the first *Asantehene* (ruler) and the real founder of an Asante empire. By the 1820s, the Asante had direct or indirect control over perhaps four million people spread over 150,000 square miles. A highly centralised state had emerged, drawing upon revenue derived from trade and tribute though it should be noted that few Asante were literate and, by 1873, the 'great roads' radiating outwards from the Asante capital at Kumase were far from being the well-maintained system of communications the title implied. Moreover, since the gold that had fuelled the growth of the state had been systematically traded over a long period of time for goods such as guns and powder, or turned into ornaments, specie was in critically short supply within Asante by the 1870s.

Nonetheless, though there was no standing army as such, Asante could raise a substantial force on a quota system once contingents from subject tribes were included, perhaps amounting to between 60,000 and 80,000 men in 1873.[11] By contrast, the Fante's own attempts at expansion had been halted by internal fragmentation. Asante and Fante had clashed directly only in 1765 and 1776 during the eighteenth century, but this was to be followed by frequent conflict in the nineteenth century: clashes occurred in 1806, 1811, 1814-16, 1823–24, 1826, 1863, 1869 and 1873–74 with others narrowly avoided in 1820, 1844 and 1853.[12]

The British had first come into brief conflict with the Asante in 1807 when the Asante had pursued two Assin chiefs through Fante territory and attacked the British fort at Anamabu.[13] Treaties to try to ensure peace and to cultivate trade with the Asante were negotiated by Thomas Bowdich in September 1817 and by Joseph Dupuis in March 1820, the first extending a degree of British protection over the Fante but the second recognising Asante sovereignty over the Fante, with the result that it was rejected by the British authorities and never ratified.[14] The Governor of Sierra Leone, Sir Charles McCarthy, then metaphorically and literally lost his head leading a small expedition into Asante territory in January 1824, the Asante having been provoked into an incursion by McCarthy's failure to comprehend that the *Asantehene* believed the British responsible for Fante actions when the Fante were regarded as Asante vassals.[15] Generally, the Asante expected tribute from subject peoples in the form of gold, slaves, livestock, and textiles and, as already indicated, also operated a quota system with respect to manpower required for the army.[16] Recovering from McCarthy's defeat – his head became a 'skull fetish' paraded through the streets for the annual *odwira* (Festival of Yams) – and assisted by tribal enemies of the Asante, the British defeated the Asante at Dodowa in August 1826 with the assistance of artillery and Congreve rockets.[17]

A treaty was then negotiated by George Maclean in 1831, by which the Asante abandoned their claims to sovereignty over the Denkyira, Assin and other former subjects, thus creating a kind of buffer zone between the Asante and Fante territory. In return for free passage to the coast and the former subject tribes engaging to eschew from 'insulting' their former masters, the Asante also agreed to submit disputes with the Fante to British arbitration.[18] Prior to 1826 the Asante had captured some of the 'notes' by which the Europeans had agreed to pay the Fante annual rent for possession of the coastal forts but, now, these were regarded by the British as being reclaimed by right of conquest. In any case, the interpretation of 'notes' varied, the Dutch having regarded them more as promissory documents relating to wages rather than tribute, which is how the Asante interpreted them.[19]

Crown control of the Gold Coast was relinquished once more in 1828 and vested in a Committee of Merchants, in whose interests Maclean acted as President of the Council at Cape Coast and self-styled Governor. British governmental control was revived in 1843, however, with Cape Coast once more becoming a dependency of Sierra Leone. A more formal protectorate was also established in place of the wholly informal influence maintained by Maclean, various local rulers of 'protected tribes', including those of the Denkyira and Assin, subscribing to a 'bond' that recognised British jurisdiction in March 1844. The Danes sold their coastal forts including Accra to the British in 1850, and Cape Coast was again made independent of Sierra Leone.[20]

Despite the treaty in 1831 the Asante had not actually forsaken their claims to sovereignty and new disagreements arose in both 1853 and 1863, primarily over fugitives seeking British protection since the Asante took the view that their return formed part of the treaty agreement, though no such undertaking had been committed to paper. The general problem was that while the Treasury resisted extension of British influence for reasons of economy, successive governors advocated such extension in the interests of countering the slave trade and advancing commercial enterprise: Lagos was annexed in 1861 in order to further restrict the slave trade. While trade with the Niger delta was worth about £1 million annually in the 1860s, trade with the Gold Coast was not much more than £80,000 a year and the settlements were costing about £300,000 a year. The revenue from the Gold Coast for the whole period of 1863–72, for example, was just £161,048 when the expenditure was £160,557.[21] Moreover, the extent of the protectorate was at best ill defined, stretching about 40–50 miles inland to the River Pra and between 200 and 300 miles along the coast. In 1873 it was considered to include the territory of the Fante, Assin, Akyem, Akwapim, Denkyira, and Wassa, as well as a few other small tribal groups.[22]

In 1853 a show of force dissuaded the Asante from more than a limited incursion into Assin but the response to the Asante incursion in 1863 was less resolute. The Governor, Richard Pine, was only reluctantly given the authority he demanded for a retaliatory advance on Kumase by a force based around six companies of West Indian troops. Matters were delayed by a lack of co-ordination between the Colonial Office, Horse Guards and the War Office and the whole venture was brought to a halt by the outbreak of disease, the expedition being abandoned in May 1864. In June 1864 Palmerston's government survived a censure motion proposed by Vice Admiral Sir John Hay, whose brother had died on the expedition, by just seven votes.[23] A Select Committee concluded in 1865 that any further extension of territory, assumption of government, or guarantees to tribes on the Gold Coast would be 'inexpedient' and recommended withdrawal from all but Sierra Leone once the administration could be realistically transferred to local African control.[24] In the event, the opportunity to offload the Gambia on the French collapsed due to pressure from British merchants. Commander John Glover, the Administrator of Lagos between 1866 and 1872 and a former naval officer, also pursued very much his own policy to expand its territory until he was dismissed.[25] Following the Select Committee report, the Gambia, Gold Coast and Lagos all came under the administration of Sierra Leone in 1866.

Under an agreement of July 1867, the British then switched some of their possessions on the Gold Coast with the Dutch, who were the only other power still involved in the region, a move intended to consolidate interests and save money. Transfer of territory or even outright purchase by the British had been under discussion for some years. The Dutch ceded Mouri, Kormantin, Apam and Dutch Accra to the British and the British ceded

Appolonia, Dixcove, Sekondi and Komenda to the Dutch. The newly agreed boundary on the Sweet River deprived some tribes of British protection. When the arrangement was announced in December 1867 some – the Komenda (a Fante tribe), Wassa and Denkyira – resisted the imposition of Dutch rule and also attacked Elmina, the principal Dutch possession whose tribal inhabitants were allies of the Asante. The Elmina were feared by the Fante because of their alliance with the Asante and they, too, joined in the blockade of Elmina. The Asante had possessed the rent 'note' for Elmina since capturing it from the Denkyira in the eighteenth century and the Dutch therefore had been paying them rent set at goods to the value of two ounces of gold each month though, by the nineteenth century, it was customary to pay periodically several years' arrears.[26] While the Dutch repulsed a Komenda attack on Elmina in May 1868, the Asante responded themselves by invading Dutch territory in November and December 1869, ostensibly in support of Elmina and the Dutch.

It would appear that an Asante thrust towards Cape Coast had been contemplated but in the event, action was confined to the small force led to Elmina by *Asantehene* Kofi Karikari's uncle, Akyampon Yaw, and another led by Adu Bofo, the *gyaasehene* or head of the *Asantehene*'s household attendants, who commanded the royal bodyguard and was head of the state bureaucracy. The latter headed towards the lower Volta, whose tribes such as the Ada, Awuna and Akwamu had been contesting control of the palm oil trade with the Asante since the 1860s. Neither expedition was conspicuously successful though Adu Bofo detained two German missionaries working for the Swiss Basel mission at Anum, Friedrich August Ramseyer and Johannes Kühne, together with Ramseyer's wife and infant son. A French trader, Marie-Joseph Bonnat, was also seized at his 'factory' at Ho and an African named Palmer, a British subject, was also detained.[27] Nominally acting as Asante ambassador, Akyampon Yaw then remained a menacing presence in Elmina until finally detained by the Dutch in April 1871. The opposition from the tribes, meanwhile, had convinced the Dutch to withdraw from the Gold Coast altogether and negotiations began with the British, linked to parallel negotiations on existing Anglo-Dutch agreements on Sumatra and the recruitment of British Indian labourers for Dutch Surinam. The Colonial Office reasoned that the acquisition of the Dutch territory comprising the settlements and forts of Elmina, Komenda, Chama, Butri, Dixcove, Axim, Beyin and Sekondi would not violate the 1865 policy since the aim was 'the maintenance of tranquillity and the promotion of peaceful commerce on the Coast'.[28]

When the Asante objected to the transfer of Elmina to the British, the Dutch insisted that their payments had been a present paid 'in the name of subsistence'. Moreover, an African envoy sent to the Asante by the Dutch, Henry Plange, returned in October 1871 with a document signed on 19 August – 'a certificate of apology' – apparently renouncing their claim to Elmina, though it would appear that the Asante were primarily interested in securing the payments they felt owed them.[29] Thus, when the Anglo-Dutch agreement, which had been signed in February 1871 and ratified in February 1872, came into effect on 6 April 1872, Elmina passed from Dutch to British administration. The purchase price was just £24,000 for stores and fixtures. In reality, however, the Asante had never regarded outstanding issues with the British as having been concluded in 1863–64. While the exchange in 1868 had seen their old enemies, the Denkyira, passed to the 'protection' of the Dutch – who had generally been acquiescent towards the Asante – the loss of Elmina to the British and the possibility of other former subjects combining with the Fante against them had led to the decision to attack Cape Coast. In fact, the Asante had taken a decision as early as January 1872 to go to war with the British.[30]

What has been described as 'the comedy of dissimulation' on the Asante part proceeded while they prepared for war.[31] John Pope Hennessy, the new Administrator in Chief of Sierra Leone and the West African Settlements, had been sent out in February 1872 to effect the transfer of the Dutch territory to British control. A controversial figure, Pope Hennessy, who had already been designated as Governor of the Bahamas, was only intended to occupy the post temporarily before the arrival of Robert Keate, who was delayed for several months. Pope Hennessy removed

Glover from Lagos and the Administrator at Cape Coast Castle, H. T. Ussher, before quarrelling with Ussher's successor, Colonel Robert Harley, over the nature of the Asante threat, which Pope Hennessy discounted. Indeed, one official in the Colonial Office noted in February 1873 that 'If all the officials with whom Mr Hennessy found fault began to justify themselves, a special department will have to be created for this business.' He has also been characterised by one historian as 'the worst colonial governor of the nineteenth century'. Pope Hennessy attempted to bargain for the return of the German missionaries, doubling the annual rent Elmina paid the Asante, lifting the long-standing embargo on trading firearms with the Asante, and releasing both Akyampon Yaw and also a son of Adu Bufo, who happened to be in custody at Cape Coast Castle.[32] The Asante simply played Pope Hennessy along and on 9 December 1872, the Asante army was again despatched from Kumase though one senior general, the *Anantahene* Asamoa Nkwanta, counselled against facing superior British firepower. Asamoa Nkwanta had led the army against the British in 1863–64 and was seen as an Asante 'Moltke'.[33]

The Asante had been ruled by a more aggressive court party since 1867 and, resentful of their exclusion from easy access to the coast by the Fante, they reacted strongly to the Fante attack on Elmina. The end of the European demand for slaves had made war less profitable and forced the Asante to try and develop an alternative trade in gold, palm oil and also kola nuts, for which there was a market in the Muslim north and east. There is some debate as to whether such adaptation was successful or otherwise, some interpreting increasing Asante aggression as an attempt to extend the tribute system by way of compensation. It has also been pointed out that the internal slave trade remained an important source of revenue. At the same time, it has been argued that abolition also undermined political consensus within the Asante polity, leading to the emergence of a 'peace party' favouring 'legitimate' trade without the restrictions of state monopoly, and an opposing 'imperial party' adhering to the military traditions of the past and to a 'mercantilist outlook', by which the state continued to regulate trade with the Europeans on the coast. The 'peace party' was associated with *akonkofo*, an emerging 'middle class' of commercial entrepreneurs.[34]

When the relatively moderate *Asantehene*, Kwaku Dua Panin (ruled 1834–67), died in April 1867 he wanted his successor to be his seven-year-old paternal grandson, Kwaku Dua Kuma. One former designated heir, Osei Kwadwo, had died or been killed in 1859 in the aftermath of what appears to have been a plot orchestrated by his mother, Afua Sapon, against her own brother, the *Asantehene*. Afua Sapon had either been executed or compelled to commit suicide. Many Asante found Agyeman Kofi unacceptable. It is unclear whether Kwabena Anin, Kwaku Dua's great nephew, who had replaced Osei Kwadwo as heir apparent, was still alive in 1867, but the *Asantehene* had certainly been highly suspicious of him and of his mother, Afua Kobi. The latter, indeed, who had replaced her own mother, Afua Sapon, as *Asantehemaa* (Queen Mother) in 1859, may have been the instigator of her mother's downfall in order to get her own son recognised as heir. If still alive, Kwabena Anin may also have been regarded as too peaceable. Accordingly, though he had not sought the throne, Kofi Karikari, Kwabena Anin's youngest full brother, who was aged about 30 and the candidate of the 'imperial' party, was 'enstooled' on 28 May 1867, the *Sika Dwa* ('Golden Stool') being the symbol of Asante nationhood.

Though he was to become more authoritarian, Kofi Karikari was initially more 'presidential' than his predecessors but, in any case, it would appear that the council of leading chiefs (*amanhene*), military notables (*nsafohene*), and the *Asantehemaa* played a substantial part in decision-making. The *Asantehemaa*, who might be the real or 'classificatory' mother or sister of an *Asantehene*, was effectively co-ruler in the Asante system. The *amanhene* of the union of states that comprised Asante also possessed a degree of autonomy and shared authority albeit countered by that of the *nsafohene* who stood apart from the matrilineal hereditary groups from which *Asantehene* and *amahene* were selected. In the case of Kofi Karikari, he and his mother, Afua Kobi, became dependent upon the *nsafohene* since his accession was long contested by his sister, Yaa Kyaa, on behalf of her sons. An additional difficulty for Kofi Karikari was that there were powerful rivalries between two of the *nsafohene*, Adu Bofo, the *gyaasehene*, and Amankwatia, the *bantamahene* and *krontihene*, who commanded the main metropolitan army and, on occasions, also the men levied from subject states. It is possible, indeed, that the internal rivalries within the Asante polity contributed to the determination of the Asante to prevent the kingdom being broken up, provoking the response to the perceived loss of sovereignty over the coastal tribes.[35]

Adu Bofo led one force of about 5,000 men against the Wassa and Denkyira while a smaller one led by Nantwi marched against the Akyem. The main army of between 30,000 and 40,000 men, commanded by Amankwatia, marched towards Cape Coast, crossing the River Pra, which marked the accepted boundary of the Asante kingdom on 22 January 1874. With the Fante unable to prevent the Asante advance despite reinforcement by a small force of 50 Hausa police under a British officer, Lieutenant James Hopkins of the 2nd West India Regiment, in March 1873, the Asante army dispersed the Fante and took Dunkwa on 14 April. It was now poised barely more than 20 miles from Cape Coast. The *Asantehene* now claimed not only Elmina but also the territories of the Akyem, Assin and Denkyira, all of which had been forsworn in 1831.

The Colonial Secretary in Gladstone's Liberal administration, the Earl of Kimberley, wished to avoid any greater entanglement in the affairs of the Gold Coast but an initial conference was convened at the War Office on 10 May 1873. It involved Kimberley, Cardwell, George Goschen (First Lord of the Admiralty), Robert Herbert (Permanent Under Secretary at the Colonial Office), and Colonel Sir Andrew Clarke. The former Director of Works at the Admiralty and the Governor-designate of the Straits Settlements, Clarke had appeared before the Select Committee in 1865 since he had served as a staff officer on the previous expedition. There had been only 171 West Indian troops on the Gold Coast at the time of the first Asante incursion, since reinforced by 100 more, there also being about 300 armed Hausa and Fante police and 250 assorted native volunteers.[36] Having succeeded Pope Hennessy, Keate had decided not to reinforce the garrison at Cape Coast but he had died within days of landing there to assess the situation and, taking over, Harley had sent for the additional West Indians. The meeting resolved to order the landing of 110 Royal Marines and to send for four West Indian companies from Barbados.[37]

Refugees were now flooding into Cape Coast, and though the Asante army was reported as suffering from smallpox and hunger, Captain Lionel Brett of the 2nd West India Regiment commanding at Cape Coast reported that it would be impossible to defend just the forts given the multitude of people seeking refuge in the surrounding towns. A War Office proposal for a counter-invasion of Asante led Kimberley to insist that, 'If we wish to weaken ourselves we cannot adopt a better course than to spend a few millions in conquering Ashantee, and establishing a West African Empire. It is to be hoped that no Govt. will be mad enough to embark on so extravagant an enterprise.'[38] With no further news received – due to the loss of two mail ships – the crisis appeared at an end but on 10 July came the unwelcome news that the Asante army had now moved to the south-west and the Fante had been defeated again at Jukwa on 5 June. In attempting to disarm Asante supporters at Elmina on 13 June the newly arrived marines, landed by Captain Edmund Fremantle RN from HMS *Barracouta* and commanded by Brevet Colonel Francis Festing of the Royal Marine Artillery, had opened fire and then come into conflict with some 3,000 Asante troops advancing on the town. Fremantle's ships bombarded the town and Festing was able to drive the Asante back about two or three miles. At Kimberley's insistence, a further meeting at the War Office on 15 July resolved on despatching another 200 marines and to prepare a 'wing of a regiment in England' for possible embarkation.[39]

Official policy was still that the Fante must do their best to defend themselves, albeit with what Kimberley termed 'cordial and active' British support. In 1871, indeed, a so-called 'Fante Confederation' had emerged, which Pope Hennessy and others felt was a practical means of advancing the aims of the policy of withdrawal. The government, however, had regarded it with some suspicion and it had been effectively broken by the arrest of its leaders. Nonetheless, Kimberley and Cardwell were moving towards a military response. Ironically, when Secretary of State for the Colonies back in 1864, Cardwell had pledged that white troops would never again be used on the Gold Coast due to the dangers of the climate. By contrast, however, while endorsing the Select Committee report in 1865, he had also amended it so that future action 'for the more efficient and economical administration of the settlements we already possess' was not ruled out.[40] Kimberley corresponded with Cardwell on 26 July in the knowledge that, while an Asante attack on the forts could be repelled, the prospect of an Asante army simply continuing to occupy much of the protectorate posed the far greater difficulties of the response of the British public to such a situation and the likely financial costs. As Kimberley put it, 'Are we to contemplate an attack on Coomassie and could we assemble a force sufficient enough for the purpose?'[41]

The two conferred on 28 July and, on 2 August, Kimberley also saw Commander John Glover, who had now offered his services though Kimberley was wary of employing him as a result of Glover's previous conduct in Lagos. Goschen had seen Glover after the news of the Fante defeat at Jukwa was received and asked him about the possibility of using the Pra in the event of a campaign. Glover had seen Cardwell a few days later, and then gone to a meeting at the War Office on 29 July attended among others by Cardwell; Clarke; the army's Commander-in-Chief, the Duke of Cambridge; the Adjutant General, Sir Richard Airey; the Quartermaster General, Sir Charles Ellice; and the First Sea Lord, Admiral Sir Alexander Milne.[42] Glover suggested raising the Volta tribes, a concept supported by Clarke. Having seen Kimberley on 3 August, on the following day Glover was authorised to raise the eastern tribes of the Volta region against the Asante with six officers appointed to his staff. The Cabinet had sanctioned Glover's operation on 2 August but, on 5 August, Parliament was prorogued for the summer recess.[43]

It was, therefore, without the formal sanction of either Gladstone or the Cabinet that Cardwell and Kimberley decided that much more was needed. As Cardwell was to explain to the Queen's private secretary, the Asante army remained threateningly close to the British settlements and they must either be abandoned or the Asante given a 'severe lesson'. Similarly, Kimberley emphasised that there were 'no such extravagant ideas as the formation of an African Empire'.[44] Accordingly, at a meeting at the War Office on 13 August, at which Glover was also present, Wolseley was appointed as Administrator and Commander-in-Chief on the Gold Coast. Cardwell subsequently distanced himself from the decision but he had sent Wolseley's first projected plan of operations, drawn up some time between May and July 1873 to Kimberley prior to the Cabinet meeting on 2 August.[45] However disingenuous Cardwell's role, Kimberley certainly favoured an expedition to Kumase, Wolseley later recording in his memoirs that, at one meeting, Kimberley had suggested he would resign if the expedition did not go ahead. According to a letter written by Wolseley in September 1902, Kimberley had 'abruptly & angrily settled' the question.[46]

Kimberley noted in his journal in September that he and Cardwell had first offered the command to Clarke, who had declined it, apparently on the grounds that it was not expressly stipulated that 'the country should be handed back to the native Government after the war was over'. In any case, Clarke's scheme was apparently far more limited than that of Wolseley, contemplating only the use of the existing force on the Gold Coast and negotiation. Clarke, indeed, had been a long-term opponent of greater involvement on the Gold Coast.[47] There had been speculation, and some support, in the press for the despatch to the Gold Coast of Colonel Charles 'Chinese' Gordon, then serving on the Danube navigation improvement commission, but this was never seriously contemplated. Indeed, though the Queen believed he should be borne in mind to succeed Wolseley if the latter was incapacitated, Gordon was encouraged to take up the offer in January 1874 from the Khedive of Egypt of Governor General of the Sudan.[48]

While decisions were being made in London, the Senior Naval Officer, Cape of Good Hope and West Coast of Africa, Commodore John Commerell VC, had arrived on 5 July but was badly wounded on a reconnaissance at Chama at the mouth of the River Pra on 14 August, and another naval landing party also attacked at Takoradi. The two attacks left four men dead and 35 wounded.[49] The fact that Harley and Commerell had quarrelled over the course to pursue was an additional factor in determining Cardwell and Kimberley to 'cut the knot' by sending out Wolseley, though the Duke of Cambridge had originally suggested sending out Major General John Jarvis Bisset, who had South African experience, to take over command.[50] Though the West Indian troops had arrived from Barbados on 6 July and the 200 fresh marines on 9 August, disease had soon begun to strike at the original marine contingent and the new reinforcements were not landed but kept offshore. Harley did proclaim a naval blockade of the Windward coast on 29 August to prevent weapons reaching the Asante but, receiving the news of Wolseley's appointment on 11 September, Festing resolved to suspend any further operations pending Wolseley's arrival though against the advice of Fremantle, who was all for action.[51] Wolseley sailed from Liverpool with 36 staff and special service officers on 27 September 1873 (see Appendix I).

At this stage, Gladstone was simply informed that Wolseley would utilise only those forces already available on the Gold Coast. The Prime Minister, indeed, had no clear conception of how the war had arisen and even Cardwell expressed himself at a loss to explain as late as September the precise reasons for the quarrel with the Asante, Gladstone counselling some care in presenting the government's case to the public.[52] In fact, the expedition was not fully discussed by the Cabinet until 4 October, two days after Wolseley had already reached Cape Coast. John Bright, the Chancellor of the Duchy of Lancaster, opposed the expedition altogether. Though Gladstone, whom Kimberley recorded as being 'aghast at the expenditure' counselled caution and was by no means convinced that any frontal assault on Kumase was necessary, it was, as W. D. McIntyre has put it, 'then too late to question the general's wisdom from London'.[53]

Wolseley

At the time he was given command of the expedition to Asante on 13 August 1873 with (from 6 September) the local rank of Major General, Brevet Colonel Sir Garnet Wolseley was Assistant

Adjutant General at the Horse Guards and had just turned 40 years of age. He stood some 5'7" tall and was usually characterised as handsome with a fresh complexion and clean-cut features though he was grey-haired from a relatively early age. He was a man of some charm, at least in public, Winwood Reade of *The Times* recording in his account of the expedition that Wolseley 'had the talent of giving commands in such a way that they gave a pleasure to those who received them, and his manner to young subalterns was inexpressibly gracious and kind'.[54] To Disraeli, who saw him on his return from Asante, Wolseley was 'a most intelligent man ... and winning from his modesty' and also 'a little man, but with a good presence, and a bright blue eye, holds his head well, and has a lithe figure'. To the Queen, to whom Disraeli presented Wolseley, he was a 'very smart, active, wiry-looking man, full of energy and calm and decided-looking'. Similarly, George Greaves, who was to be his chief of staff in Asante, later described Wolseley at this time as 'a man free from nerves, with clear, penetrating, observant blue eyes, spare, light frame, and brisk, active step' with a 'strong but suave voice'.[55]

Born at Golden Bridge House, Dublin on 4 June 1833, Garnet Joseph Wolseley was the eldest of seven children, four boys and three girls.[56] His father, an impoverished major in the 25th Foot, had left the army shortly after his marriage and died when Wolseley was just seven years old. The family was left in straitened circumstances and Wolseley's first commission as ensign in the 12th Foot on 12 March 1852 was secured through his mother seeking a direct nomination from the Commander-in-Chief, the Duke of Wellington, on the strength of his father's service. Prior to this, Wolseley had been educated in a day school in Dublin and had taken employment in a surveyor's office to improve his knowledge of draughtsmanship and surveying in preparation for a military career. At a time when many cavalry and infantry commissions were still purchased, Wolseley was to advance without benefit of money through sheer courage and determination, a conviction that his destiny was willed by God having been imbued in the young Wolseley by his mother's deeply held Irish Protestant religious faith. Determination to succeed was also fuelled by Wolseley having assumed the role of principal provider for his mother and two of his three brothers, George and Fred, and his awareness of the disadvantages of his lack of means. Having transferred to the 80th Foot, Wolseley soon distinguished himself in the Second Burma War (1852–53), receiving a serious wound in his left thigh that troubled him all his life. Promoted to lieutenant in May 1853 he was invalided home and then transferred to the 90th Foot in February 1854. In the Crimean War (1854–56), during which he was promoted to captain for his services, Wolseley was slightly wounded in the right thigh during the attack on the Quarries in June 1855, and then lost the sight of his left eye and suffered another wound to his right leg in August 1855. After further service in the Indian Mutiny (1857–58), where he served on Sir James Hope Grant's staff and earned a brevet majority and a brevet lieutenant colonelcy, Wolseley again acted on Hope Grant's staff in the Third China War (1860–61). Wolseley had thus emerged a brevet lieutenant colonel after just eight years' service.

Sent to Canada as Assistant Quartermaster General in January 1862 as a result of the *Trent* affair – when American federal officials boarded a British mail packet in November 1861 and detained two Confederate diplomats – Wolseley visited the Confederacy, writing memorably of his impressions of leading Confederate commanders such as Robert E. Lee and 'Stonewall' Jackson.[57] In Canada he became something of a protégé of the Commander-in-Chief, Sir John Michel, and the Adjutant General of the militia, Sir Patrick MacDougall, securing a brevet colonelcy in June 1865 and becoming Deputy Quartermaster General on Michel's recommendation in October 1867. Through the threat of Fenian incursions into Canada, Wolseley received command of camps of instruction and observation, handling large formations, albeit of militia and volunteers, for the first time. It was also Michel who recommended Wolseley to his successor as Commander-in-Chief in Canada, Major General the Hon. James Lindsay, for command of the Red River expedition in April 1870.

In the meantime, Wolseley had married Louisa Erskine ('Loo') in June 1867 and, at the suggestion of Sir Richard Airey, consolidated his military reputation in 1869 with the publication of a practical manual, *The Soldier's Pocket Book*, aimed at improving tactical efficiency. Though drawing upon ideas of those he had encountered in Canada such as MacDougall, Henry Havelock (later Havelock-Allan), and George Denison, it was the only guide of its kind to military organisation and tactical wisdom. The manual demonstrated Wolseley's instinctive understanding of logistics, knowledge immediately required when he was chosen to quell the rebellion by French-speaking *métis* (half-breeds) in the Canadian North-West. Wolseley forged through 600 miles of wilderness beyond Lake Superior with a force of 1,200 regulars and militia to re-occupy Fort Garry on the Red River and to return before the lakes froze.[58] As it happened the *métis* fled before Wolseley reached Fort Garry in August 1870, but it had been a triumph of minutely supervised organisation. Wolseley was created KCMG and CB and was both praised by Lindsay and eulogised by George Huyshe's semi-official campaign history, *The Red River Expedition*.[59]

Wolseley was then brought back to the Horse Guards as Assistant Adjutant General in the discipline branch in May 1871.[60] Initially, Wolseley found the limitations of his position frustrating.[61] The reforms of the army instituted by Cardwell were mostly completed before Wolseley returned to Britain. He fully supported their aims, however, and became identified with the cause of military reform through *The Soldier's Pocket Book* and also through his submission on field manoeuvres to the 1872 Wellington Prize Essay competition, in which he was placed second behind Frederick Maurice, whose own essay quoted Wolseley's manual. Wolseley also contributed articles to periodicals such as *Blackwood's Magazine* and *Macmillan's Magazine*.

Wolseley undoubtedly pressed for the appointment to lead the Asante expedition in 1873 and his organisational and logistic ability, his achievements on the Red River, his appointment of chief of staff to Major General Sir Charles Staveley's division during the 1871 autumn manoeuvres and his recent participation in the planning of the autumn manoeuvres in 1872, during which he was attached to the staff of Michel's 'southern army', were all doubtless recommendations in addition to his association with reform. Indeed, Wolseley had been offered the appointment of Military Secretary to the new Viceroy, Lord Northbrook, in 1872 but was compelled to turn it down through Loo's pregnancy. Moreover, it had been at Cardwell's insistence that Wolseley had been designated as chief of staff to Staveley in 1871.[62] It was also the case that despite his reforming reputation and later antipathy to the Duke of Cambridge, Wolseley enjoyed Cambridge's support at this time. Indeed, Cambridge had already suggested Wolseley's appointment as Adjutant General in India, only for the proposal to fall on Wolseley's lack of the required native language qualifications [**Documents 3 and 80**]. By the conclusion of the campaign, however, Cambridge had fallen in with the request of the Commander-in-Chief in India, Lord Napier, to avoid a 'rage' for reorganisation by appointing an old India hand. Clearly sensing the influence that Wolseley's pro-reform views might have in the public arena following his success in Asante, the Duke now believed Wolseley would be ideal for the newly created command of the Canadian militia as 'It would be a great advantage to get him away at all events from home, otherwise his head will be turned & he will do us harm.' Wolseley was duly suspicious but, in fact, the Governor General of Canada, Lord Dufferin, had specifically wanted Wolseley for the post.[63] In the event, Wolseley became Inspector General of Auxiliary Forces at the War Office in June 1874.

Despite his denial at one point [**53**], there is no doubt Wolseley was highly ambitious though he always expressed it in terms of his hopes for his country, writing, for example, in September 1882, 'To see England great is my highest aspiration, & that I might have a leading part in contributing to the attainment of that greatness, is my only real ambition.'[64] It might be noted that, like others of Anglo-Irish stock, he spoke solely of England and held the Irish in contempt. In other ways, Wolseley's extreme dislike for foreigners and for natives of all hues merely reflected contemporary convention [**20, 21, 61, 62, 64, 66, 67, 80**]. His contempt, however, was to extend increasingly to most party politicians, Wolseley later writing of the 'dirty dunghill sort of democratic wave ... now passing over the world', and also speaking of party politics as the 'curse of modern England'.[65] He was to develop a deep hatred for Gladstone in particular but, in 1873–74, rather as in his relationship with Cambridge, such views were expressed, if at all, in mild form. He has been accused of 'sinister Caesarism'.[66] Some of Wolseley's private comments – notably in his personal diaries – could certainly be extreme, as in December 1877: 'In all the old great republics a Dictator was appointed in times of danger and with us, the same plan should be followed, for it is really next to impossible for any party to retain power and carry on a great war.'[67] But, in reality, as examination of the Asante campaign makes clear, he always understood the restricted constitutional parameters within which the army existed and the requirements of his political masters. Indeed, referring back to the Asante campaign in April 1880, Wolseley wrote, 'I always make it a rule to serve the Govt. in power to the best of my ability & to help them to demolish their opponents who attack them on military matters with which I am concerned, for party purposes.' The only qualification would come if the government itself 'directly violated' a constitutional principle.[68] Consequently, while so frequently depicted as a dangerous radical by Cambridge and his coterie, and regarded by many Liberals almost as a colleague, Wolseley was deeply conservative in his politics. What made him appear radical was that he was a military reformer, and it is the case that his very professionalism was in itself sufficiently subversive to arouse the antipathy of military conservatives.[69]

Nonetheless, there was an egotistical side to his character and he consciously used his public utterances and writing, as well as his manipulation of the press, as he put it in February 1878, 'to keep my name before the public'.[70] In part, despite Wolseley's fatalism, deriving from strong religious views [32, 33, 53, 64, 102, 115, 117, 154], there was always a degree of uncertainty and a fear that opportunities had been missed. It is often there in Wolseley's correspondence, journals and diaries, especially in entries at the end of a year or on his birthday. In June 1877, for example, aged still only 44, Wolseley recorded, 'I shall soon be too old for good active work: when too old to be of any real use I shall be employed.'[71] Indeed, for all his achievements, the great European war in which he hoped to distinguish himself never came and, in a note in the draft of his unfinished memoirs, Wolseley was to convey something of his unrequited aspirations: 'How poor has been my life's work when compared to the lofty aspirations of my youth!'[72] Such thoughts, though, were mostly for the future and the fascination of the Asante journal and correspondence is to view Wolseley at an early stage in his more public career when some of the later traits had yet to develop fully.

Wolseley's journal and correspondence

The Asante journal and correspondence present the campaign through Wolseley's eyes at a number of different levels simultaneously, officially, semi-officially, and privately. In terms of Wolseley's private view of the campaign, there is a journal and family correspondence. Four other Wolseley journals have survived in the National Archives (formerly the Public Record Office) and all have been published. The journals of Wolseley's administrative role in Natal in 1875, of the campaigns in Zululand and against Sekhukhuni in the Transvaal in 1879–80, and of the Gordon Relief Expedition of 1884–85 were edited by Adrian Preston and published between 1967 and 1973. Preston, however, was an unsympathetic editor, who clearly intensely disliked Wolseley. The journal of Wolseley's administrative role on Cyprus in 1878–79 was edited by Anne Cavendish and published in a limited edition on Cyprus in 1991, Preston having previously published extracts in an article for the *Journal of the Society of Army Historical Research* back in 1967.[73]

According to Preston, the journal for Asante is incomplete but this is misleading.[74] As with his other journals, Wolseley sent batches of this journal back to Loo. In the case of the Asante journal as preserved in WO 147/3, it runs over the whole period of the campaign from Wolseley's departure from London on 11 September 1873 to his departure from Cape Coast Castle on 4 March 1874: the only natural break is a period between 14 and 19 November 1873 when there is one sparse entry covering all six days, coinciding with Wolseley being struck down with an attack of fever. This seems to have been a recurrence of the malaria he had suffered from since his early days in Burma. The journal was sent home in 17 batches – initially written on War Office foolscap paper in Wolseley's distinctive hand with a smaller size paper used from the end of December 1873 onwards – and there is, indeed, a gap between 8 and 25 January 1874, representing presumably the twelfth batch. There is an occasional overlap between batches so that Wolseley has two entries for 2 October and 2 February. There is no entry for 9 October or 26 February between batches, and no entries for 16 to 18 December as Wolseley recorded that he had been too busy to write it up [97].[75]

However, WO 147/4 contains a copy of the journal in the handwriting of Loo, which includes the missing section for 8 to 25 January. In comparing the two versions of the journal generally, it is clear that Loo corrected Wolseley's habitual misspelling on occasions and, in the process, incorporated mistakes of her own. She also altered the text in some very minor ways by occasionally changing the order of words in a sentence. For all practical purposes, however, the journal is complete. The copy was made primarily for circulation to Wolseley's mother, Frances, and to his immediate family including his brother, Richard, an army surgeon, and some of his sisters with the injunction that it must remain confidential and its contents not to be repeated beyond the family [19]. Loo later accused Wolseley in 1884 of consciously composing his journals too much with posterity in mind.[76] It was an accusation he denied at the time but there was one point during the Asante campaign that he regretted Loo herself had given up her journal because 'nothing affords the greater pleasure in after years than looking over its pages' [147].

Wolseley was certainly assiduous in keeping his records and he was greatly pained by a fire at the London warehouse known as the Pantechnicon on 13 February 1874 that destroyed many of his papers [167].[77] He was also certainly prone to philosophical musings on the nature of fame, which greatly irritated Loo, but at this stage of his career, the journal may have been no more than a sounding board although with the intention of providing an aide-memoire. Indeed, he instructed Loo not to make a copy of his intended Natal journal in March 1875 because it was too dull, this being, however, before he set out to South Africa.[78] It is also the case that the Asante journal is less overtly vindictive than later ones though it certainly makes clear Wolseley's views of his subordinates. As might be expected, these are generally favourable where Wolseley himself had picked them. There are also indications of Wolseley's concerns for those struck down by wounds like McNeill or illness, such as his ADC, the Hon. Alfred Charteris, who died of fever in November 1873 and Huyshe, who died in January 1874 [39, 104, 105, 134]. Wolseley was less charitable in the journal to those whom he had not chosen such as the one-armed Sir Archibald Alison, who was sent out to command the three British battalions in the last phase of the campaign. As Wolseley noted, 'I am very sorry for this as I don't care much for him & don't think he is the man I want' [87]. When he was so inclined and time permitted, Wolseley's writing could be highly descriptive [14, 20], but in general it had the immediacy of the moment.

Additional guides to Wolseley's more private thoughts are the letters to his wife and to other members of his family, of which those to his wife are the most extensive. Sir George Arthur published extracts from 12 of the 26 Asante letters from Wolseley to Loo in a heavily bowdlerised form in 1922.[79] The originals retained in the Wolseley Collection at Hove Reference Library are mostly intact though Wolseley's daughter, Frances, so heavily scored through a few passages as to render them unreadable. She annotated the collection as a whole presumably at some time after the death of Loo, from whom she had become estranged, in 1920 and after the letters were returned to her by Arthur briefly in 1922 before, in turn, they went back to the Royal United Service Institution to whom Loo had bequeathed them.[80] The annotations as to particular family connections or the identities of servants briefly mentioned are often useful but, irritatingly, the erasures are at points where Wolseley gives vent to his spleen as in that of 14–15 December 1873: 'that dreadful bore [name erased] has arrived.' It is possible, however, from a cryptic reference in the journal, to identify the individual as an army chaplain [90, 93]. Then again, from Wolseley's letter of 4 January 1874, Frances's sensitivities resulted in, 'This correspondent is a [erased] and has never been [erased]'. However, it is clear that this referred to the *Illustrated London News* correspondent, Melton Prior [118]. Unfortunately, none of Wolseley's surviving diaries relate to the Asante campaign.[81]

The letters to Loo were not intended for circulation within the family, Wolseley clearly regarding these as even more of a means by which to unburden himself of doubts, writing at one point that 'I feel a sort of relief and comfort in telling you in my letters that are for your own perusal only what I think and feel' [53]. As with the journal, the letters to Loo are free in their comment on individuals. Again, they tend to be favourable to those Wolseley picked himself and less so towards those imposed upon him. Frederick Maurice, however, is characterised at one point as 'certainly the worst man of business I have ever had anything to do with. He is like a woman, never in time' though Wolseley also found him a 'dear good fellow' and he had helped nurse Wolseley back to health during his bout of fever [93]. Adding to the private view to some extent are a few letters to friends such as William Earle, then Military Secretary to the Viceroy, and Robert Biddulph, then Private Secretary to Cardwell, though their relative positions at this time should be borne in mind, not least when Wolseley was still seeking to become Adjutant General in India. Indeed, a letter to Biddulph is preserved among Kimberley's papers and Cardwell told Wolseley he had seen another letter to Biddulph that has not survived.[82]

In terms of official despatches, Wolseley wrote to Loo in 1879 that he had advised George Greaves, his successor as High Commissioner on Cyprus, that 'it does not do to insert the whole truth in official correspondence' because 'unpleasant truths that can be made use of by the opponents of the Government you are serving should be reserved for one's private correspondence with ministers'. Significantly, Cardwell expressly thanked Wolseley for the 'moderate' tone of his despatches from Asante regarding government policy.[83] Fortunately, there are also a number of surviving personal letters from Wolseley to Cardwell and Kimberley. Interestingly, one such private letter to Kimberley provides an otherwise hidden insight into Wolseley's civil responsibilities with an account of a discussion within the Legislative Council at Cape

Coast Castle on the need to impose duties upon spirits and the separate problem of the water supply [**131**].

Perhaps more significantly, however, there is also a long run of private correspondence sent by Wolseley to the Duke of Cambridge. Willoughby Verner reproduced extracts from 19 of the 21 Asante letters in his biography of Cambridge but only the very first one of 3 September 1873 in full [**8**], the extracts (though accurate) becoming progressively shorter thereafter.[84] As already suggested, Wolseley was not as overtly hostile to the Duke as was apparent only a few years later though he did tell Loo that the correspondence he had to have with the Duke was 'rather a tax upon my time, as I have to tell him all sorts of fiddling little things' [**53**]. Nonetheless, it did give Wolseley the opportunity to expound on his views, such as the need to carefully select all those, but especially officers, sent on expeditions; to praise the abilities of those he had chosen; to expose what he saw as the deficiencies in the 2nd West India Regiment; and to aim a few blows at those such as Sir Andrew Clarke who had criticised Wolseley's operational plans prior to the expedition [**50, 55, 86**]. Together with the letters to Cardwell and Kimberley, this semi-official correspondence also enabled Wolseley to outline his case against Glover, of whose efforts Wolseley was increasingly critical [**82, 116**].

These semi-official letters, therefore, often greatly amplify the official despatches prepared for Wolseley's signature by his Military Secretary, Brackenbury, and his Private Secretary, Maurice, responsible respectively for correspondence with the War Office and Colonial Office. It should be borne in mind, however, that these were not formally printed for Parliament until some time after they were received and, in most cases, only in March and June 1874. Very occasionally, the original shows part of such an official despatch is in Wolseley's own hand.[85] Only one original is entirely in his own hand, a brief note in February 1874 denying that an earlier despatch in October had been intended to criticise the Admiralty for sending out marines to Asante too hurriedly some months prior to his own arrival without adequate preparation.[86]

Copies of these despatches are available in printed form in Parliamentary Papers, those for the main actions also being printed in the *London Gazette*, and in printed and original longhand form in various War Office and Colonial Office files as well as the Royal Archives.[87] There are very minor variations of spelling and grammar between printed and original versions and all official despatches seem to have been printed for parliamentary scrutiny, including Wolseley's sometimes caustic comments on suggestions from private individuals relayed to him by the Colonial Office. An example is the lengthy series of letters sent to Kimberley by Captain Knapp Barrow, a former officer of the 27th Foot who had served with the Gold Coast Artillery and acted as an ADC on the abortive 1863 campaign against the Asante. The Colonial Office itself noted of Barrow's lengthy warnings of impending disaster in October 1873 that, 'According to Capt. Barrow it would be almost as easy to get to the moon as to Coomassie'. Wolseley's view, as duly reported in the printed record was that 'each operation which I have undertaken has succeeded, precisely because in nine cases out of ten facts are the direct contrary of what they were represented to be by Captain Knapp Barrow'.[88]

Interestingly, however, the one exception to the publication of official despatches to Kimberley is a memorandum Wolseley wrote on 2 September 1873 before his departure from London on the viability of laying down a 30-mile-long railway line. After considering the advice of the Lieutenant Governor of the Royal Military Academy, Woolwich, Sir Lintorn Simmons, Wolseley considered this likely to shorten the duration of the campaign [7]. In the event, the railway, as Barrow had predicted, did prove impracticable and the railway material sent out was never landed at Cape Coast. The War Office did choose to print Wolseley's despatch of 13 October [40], in which he stated that the railway was not practicable but that it could have worked if there had been more time to construct it. The decision by the Colonial Office in February 1874 to merely file the earlier memorandum may be seen, therefore, as a protection for Wolseley since it was Kimberley's belief that the memorandum proved that the government itself should not be censured for sending railway material out.[89]

Generally, as the despatches are readily available, only those of particular importance are reproduced in this volume, primarily Wolseley's official instructions [9, 10, 11,17, 28, 78], his official requests for white troops [41, 49], some of his official correspondence with Kofi Karikari [39, 113, 126, 135, 144, 149, 151], one of his key official proclamations [57], and the treaty that concluded the campaign [159].

Official despatches naturally included Wolseley's official instructions to his subordinates, but, in addition, some semi-official correspondence has also survived between Wolseley and those subordinates. There is one brief early letter to Evelyn Wood in August 1873 that gives some insight on the now lost original campaign plan to move on Kumase by boat, a matter also alluded to in a letter to Wolseley's brother, Richard [1, 3]. To some extent, of course, this replicated the basis of Wolseley's success in the Red River campaign and was to be revived in terms of the Gordon Relief Expedition in 1884–85. It would appear from a letter Wolseley wrote in 1902 while compiling his autobiography that the original campaign plan memorandum was among those items lost in the fire at the Pantechnicon.[90] Principally, however, there are letters to Glover and to Archibald Alison. While private, they are still entirely formal in tone and, indeed, coldly so. As Wolseley recorded in December 1873, Glover had completely failed 'and is now desirous of throwing the blame on me, but fortunately I have not only his public letters but his private ones to me which will prove very differently' [108].

On the other hand, there is an almost effusive letter of concern sent to Edmund Fremantle, temporarily appointed as Senior Naval Officer on the West African Coast in succession to Commerell between August and November 1873, when Fremantle was wounded in the arm on a shore operation in October [43]. In reality, Wolseley considered the wound so slight that he was highly amused to see that Fremantle returned himself as 'severely wounded' when McNeill's wound in the same skirmish was extremely serious. He pointedly wrote to Cambridge that Fremantle's wound was 'not worth mentioning' [42, 45]. The reason for the letter, however, is plain from an earlier entry in the journal: 'He is just the man I want here. He is a gentleman, very anxious to do something to obtain a name, not talented, easily talked over to my way of thinking upon any point, and very obliging: anxious to assist in forwarding all military work. In fact I shall have my own way by a little "*rubbing down his back*" and making things pleasant to him' [38]. Indeed, Wolseley specifically asked for Fremantle to be allowed to remain rather than be superseded by Commodore William Hewett VC [45]. A rather exaggerated concern for a slight hand injury suffered by Alison is also apparent from the correspondence, albeit that Alison was one-armed [170, 171].

The journal and correspondence thus give detailed insights into the campaign as viewed from Wolseley's perspective. They can be supplemented by those views emanating from those within Wolseley's circle. Robert Home was filing reports for the *Pall Mall Gazette* and Frederick Maurice for the *Daily News*, as was another unidentified officer.[91] Based on his reports Maurice published *The Ashantee War: A Personal Narrative*. Moreover, Brackenbury penned a semi-official campaign history, *The Ashanti War* in two volumes and Butler an account of his part in the campaign in *Akim-Foo: The History of a Failure*.[92] Brackenbury had contacted Messrs. Blackwood even before embarking with Wolseley and wrote again in November 1873 indicating that Wolseley wanted an account based on all the official papers since press correspondents accompanying the expedition would all be writing their own and they 'know nothing of the main spring of action, or details of events except under their own eyes'. Wolseley also wanted the book to be the 'first in the field at all risks'.[93]

The approved view of the campaign, which Brackenbury had completed by May 1874, was thus well publicised though Brackenbury's version caused a number of problems, Alison particularly queried whether Brackenbury had clearance for any of the official documentation so liberally used.[94] It was to cost Brackenbury dear [179]. Wood also lectured to the RUSI on the campaign, though so did Glover, and Wood more or less reprinted his lecture word for word as the entry on the Asante expedition in his two-volume edited compilation, *British Battles on Land and Sea* in 1915.[95] Much later, Wolseley closed the second volume of his autobiography, *The Story of a Soldier's Life* in 1903 with an account of Asante.[96] One other special service officer on the expedition, William Toke Dooner, also published an account.[97]

There were other official reports on engineering and medical aspects of the campaign.[98] There is also some published correspondence of a number of those who served on the campaign, as well as later memoirs and biographies drawing upon private papers.[99] Recent attention has also been drawn to letters of participants printed in the provincial press.[100] An alternative and external perspective in print, often critical of Wolseley, was offered by the press correspondents who accompanied the expedition, Winwood Reade of *The Times*, G. A. Henty of *The Standard*, Frederick Boyle of the *Daily Telegraph* and Henry Morton Stanley of the *New York Herald*, all of whom published accounts.[101] Together with other unpublished correspondence in various collections relating to participants, it amounts to a rich coverage of the campaign that really made Wolseley's name.

Editorial methods

All documents are reproduced in full, with the exception of opening and closing familiarities. Grammar and spelling have not been changed, preserving Wolseley's sometimes idiosyncratic style with the exception of replacing the frequently used dash where it is clear that a full stop was intended. Customarily, for example, Wolseley omitted the 'u' in words such as honour, and invariably omitted apostrophes. It is commonplace to find names of places and individuals (particularly Africans) spelled differently within the same letter or entry. A glossary and a gazetteer are appended to identify different versions of place names and individuals (Appendix II). Any other editorial additions to the text are given in square parentheses. In introductory sections, as above, the use of a bold numeral in square parentheses refers to the identifying number allocated to a document.

The title accorded individuals at the top of each document on their first appearance is that borne at the time the document was written, later titles or ranks being indicated in the relevant footnotes or, for prominent individuals, in the biographical notes. Documents are arranged by date order and, where a letter covers more than a single day, it is deemed to be dated from the last day of its composition. In order to ensure that the campaign is viewed as it unfolded from Wolseley's perspective, the journal is integrated with the correspondence, letters of the same date being arranged after the relevant journal entry. For this reason, on occasion, a single allocated document number may include more than one day's journal entry.

The source of each document is given in full at the bottom. While the emphasis is upon unpublished documents, as indicated previously, a few key documents from existing printed sources have been included. For reasons of space, either because they date from Wolseley's voyage out to the Gold Coast, or add nothing substantial to the journal, a handful of Wolseley's letters to Loo have not been included (see Appendix III).

At a very late stage in the preparation of this volume, the National Maritime Museum acquired the papers of Vice Admiral Sir William Hewett VC, including nine letters sent to him by Wolseley between November 1873 and August 1874. Some of these have been included here as Appendix VI, added after the Notes.

I

Plans (August to September 1873)

As indicated previously there had been an initial conference at the War Office on 10 May 1873 following the receipt of the news of the Fante defeat at Dunkwa though it was only the news of the further reverse at Jukwa reaching London on 10 July that precipitated significantly greater preparations. In fact, long before Glover submitted his ideas to Goschen, Wolseley had drawn up a plan for a campaign sometime between May and July. In his memoirs, Evelyn Wood claimed that he found Wolseley at the War Office in May 1873 'poring over a Dutch map of Ashanti, and he told me, in reply to my question, that there was a King there who required a lesson to bring him to a sense of the power of England'.[1] Wolseley, too, later suggested that Cardwell had indicated at an early stage that he would be asked to lead any expedition and he had then privately submitted a plan to Cardwell.[2] No copy of this first plan has survived but, in keeping with Wolseley's Red River experience, it proposed taking a picked force of 1,400 European troops to Kumase by using boats on the River Pra [1, 3]. It would appear that it was this first plan that Cardwell sent to Kimberley prior to the Cabinet meeting on 2 August, Cardwell writing that Wolseley was 'now ready to capture Coomassie' with Kimberley expressing interest in the scheme.[3] As indicated in Wolseley's letters to Wood on 7 August and to his brother, Richard, on 15 August, this plan was rejected. Sir Andrew Clarke also submitted a plan of operations, similarly now lost, sometime prior to 11 August, which relied upon using only native levies and following the same line of operations as that intended in 1863–64. Captain Herbert

Thompson, the Inspector General of the Armed Police on the Gold Coast, had also submitted a plan to Kimberley, proposing to use just native levies.[4] Subsequently, presumably between 2 August and his appointment on 13 August, Wolseley prepared a second plan that he presented to ministers on 15 August [2, 3]. It was still intended to destroy Asante military power and to take Kumase, but now to advance by land. It preserved, however, the element of utilising a picked force rather than the battalions next slated for overseas service. As with the first plan, no manuscript copy survives but much of it is printed in Brackenbury's campaign history and it is that incomplete version reproduced here. Wolseley fully expected to be back in England by 1 March 1874 [3, 4, 19].

Wolseley's aim was to defeat the Asante army and take Kumase, echoing Charles Callwell's later characterisation of one of Wolseley's dictums that the object of a campaign should be 'the capture of whatever they prize most, and the destruction or deprivation of which will probably bring the war most rapidly to a conclusion'.[5] No major advance, however, could be contemplated prior to December 1873 though Wolseley anticipated clearing the Asante from the protectorate with the forces already available prior to this. Wolseley then intended to achieve a peace settlement and retire 'gracefully' [3]. It is clear that, from the beginning, Wolseley had serious doubts as to the utility of Glover's diversionary movement up the Volta with 1,000 Hausa and 10,000 native levies, particularly if this stripped Cape Coast of the available Hausa. Indeed, meeting with Glover and Kimberley prior to Glover's own departure from England on 19 August, Wolseley had objected to Glover getting all the Hausa. Wolseley claimed in his memoirs that he felt Glover's real object was 'to open out a new, an easy route for trade into the interior of Africa', a suspicion echoed at the time by Butler.[6] Glover's actual instructions as Special Commissioner to the Native Chiefs of the Eastern District, issued on 18 August 1873, were to raise levies from the tribes at Accra and advance upriver using a steamer and three steam launches to penetrate as far as possible. Since the condition of the interior was unknown, he should utilise any opportunities that arose to divert the attention of the Asante, though he was also to prevent his own native forces from engaging in 'barbarities'. As Kimberley had written to Gladstone on 13 August, Glover could spend up to £15,000 though it was 'provoking to have to spend such large sums of money on these savages'.[7] Kimberley was to make it clear that Glover, who left England on 19 August, was under Wolseley's command [17]. Given the Admiralty's sponsorship of Glover, Wolseley also claimed to detect Admiralty hostility to his own scheme in some of the subsequent meetings he attended with ministers after his appointment.[8]

It is also clear that, from the start, Wolseley believed that European troops would be required for the final advance, his plan going into particular detail on the composition of two picked battalions he wanted to raise rather than simply utilising the next two battalions slated for overseas service, these being the 2/23rd Foot and 2nd Rifle Brigade. Interestingly, in view of his general championing of the Cardwell reforms, Wolseley was clearly wary of taking the very kind of young soldiers that short service would increasingly bring into the ranks, stipulating that none with less than two years' service should be accepted. Despite his argument that forming complete companies from particular battalions would encourage *esprit de corps*, Wolseley's wish to establish what in effect was a special service corps for Asante should European troops be required was opposed by the Duke of Cambridge [2, 4, 8]. The Duke approved of Wolseley's plan generally, but believed firmly that forming two picked battalions would destroy regimental spirit and he also persuaded Cardwell that it would be an unnecessary early disruption of Cardwell's localisation scheme, whereby the number of battalions at home and abroad would be in balance with the battalion abroad supplied with drafts from its linked battalion at home. Cardwell, therefore, agreed with Cambridge that, if European troops were required, they would be the 2/23rd and 2nd Rifle Brigade since this would not disrupt slated Indian reliefs and, at worst, would bring them to readiness for overseas service simply earlier than intended. The Deputy Adjutant General, Major General James Armstrong, suggested readying only six companies of each battalion but it was agreed at a meeting attended by Cardwell, Kimberley, Cambridge, Wolseley, Ellice and Armstrong that both battalions be fully prepared.[9]

In drawing up Wolseley's official instructions, Cardwell limited himself to what he regarded as strategic considerations and measures affecting the health of any European troops committed, leaving it to Kimberley to convey to Wolseley the Cabinet's policy [9, 10, 11].[10] Thus, Wolseley was to avoid requesting any European troops if it was at all possible to conclude the campaign without them, though it is very evident that Cardwell never believed this realistic [8, 14]. Wolseley's own plan made it clear he expected to use Europeans and, indeed, while en route to the Gold Coast, he told Winwood Reade of *The Times* that he would need them, Wolseley's view according with Reade's own assessment.[11] Should Europeans be required then all suitable preparations must be made before they arrived, the expectation being that no major operations could begin before December. Kimberley, meanwhile, addressed the government's case for intervention on the Gold Coast [10]. This was necessary since, as well as divisions within the Cabinet, there was some wider hostility to the whole venture, extending to the Conservative opposition. Disraeli, indeed, had favoured giving up the Gold Coast altogether and was to try and make political capital out of the war in the February 1874 elections. His colleague, the Earl of Derby was also against the war, in view of 'the climate being believed to be the worst in the world, and neither gain nor glory attainable in the event of success'.[12] Even on the ship taking Wolseley and his officers to the Gold Coast there was some talk of the war being unjustified and it is noticeable that some of the published post-war accounts lay particular emphasis on the justification deriving from Asante aggression.[13]

In response to Asante aggression, Wolseley was to compel the Asante to withdraw, if necessary delivering them an ultimatum. The Fante must be forced themselves to act in their own defence and, should Wolseley judge that European troops were necessary, then he must present a clear case to the government. Wolseley had discretion in his dealings with the Asante, but there was a need for an Asante reaffirmation of the terms of the 1831 treaty, including guarantees on the security of the protectorate and the renouncing of any claims for tributes [11]. Wolseley was also to promote trade with Asante, and secure the release of the captive Europeans at

Kumase. As in 1831, it was suggested that the Asante be compelled to provide hostages against their future behaviour. As something of an afterthought, Wolseley was also to end human sacrifice in Asante if possible. Wolseley's only request for clarification was to ensure that John McNeill was designated as his second in command [15], this being agreed by the Colonial Office.[14]

Wolseley's instructions had resulted in some wrangling in London both before and after he set sail. Gladstone did not view the Asante practice of human sacrifice as a crime in the African context but the Queen most certainly did and Kimberley therefore had suggested that Wolseley be instructed to end such atrocities if possible.[15] Gladstone also believed that Wolseley had been given too much latitude in his military instructions from Cardwell, forcing the latter to emphasise that all final decisions rested with the Cabinet. Gladstone, indeed, believed that Wolseley should be instructed to negotiate with the Asante prior to issuing an ultimatum, which would be a last extremity. Gladstone was also worried by the growing expense, not least the preparation of a hospital ship and the provision of the railway, Cardwell again suggesting to the prime minister that nothing undertaken thus far could be regarded as 'pledging us to an expedition into Ashanti territory'. Gladstone, who appeared to be obtaining information on the preparations for the expedition from the press rather than his ministers, assumed the talk of a railway to be mere press fiction. Meeting at the War Office to approve the provision of the hospital ship and the railway, Cardwell, Kimberley, Goschen and Cambridge agreed on 22 September to seek Cabinet support. Back on 3 September, Gladstone had believed that there would be no need to discuss the expedition further until November but, by the end of the month, he had concluded that approval of War Office and Admiralty preparations was necessary. In the event, as indicated in the introduction, there was no actual Cabinet discussion of Wolseley's mission until 4 October, two days after Wolseley had reached Cape Coast.[16]

One aspect of the campaign, to which only a brief allusion is made, was the need to prevent further firearms reaching the Asante [10]. European firearms – albeit flintlock 'trade guns' – had long been traded on the coast, one factor in Asante success being that they were already plentifully supplied with firearms by 1700 and had prevented other tribes to the north trading in them. All the European powers had been involved in the trade, so-called 'Dane guns' being especially prized. The Birmingham Small Arms Company, established in 1861, exported somewhere between 100,000 and 150,000 trade guns to Africa annually from the 1860s until the 1880s, when Birmingham's supremacy was successfully challenged by Liège.[17] As already related, Harley had imposed a blockade of the coast on 29 August, Fremantle deploying four of his seven ships for the duty with a fifth continuing anti-slaving duties on the coast. These ships, however, had to cover 1,590 miles of coastline and, although there was often precise information on suspect vessels leaving British ports, it was felt that the blockade did not become effective until late October. To Wolseley's horror, it was then declared illegal by the government's law officers in November following representation by merchant interests, not least F. & A. Swanzy, the leading British trading firm on the Gold Coast, whose brig, *Bryn-o-Mor*, had demonstrated the determination of British traders to continue to land arms and ammunition. Difficulties were also encountered with French traders and it proved impossible to apply a blockade to the coast of the French protectorate west of the river Assinee. The blockade continued to cause friction, not least between Fremantle and Messrs Swanzy until finally lifted in March 1874.[18]

In preparing for the campaign, Wolseley had many ideas thrust upon him by those with much, some, or, indeed, no knowledge of the Gold Coast. Many were what Wolseley's contemporary biographer referred to as 'gloomy vaticinations', Henty also recording that one man's advice had simply been for all sent to serve on the Gold Coast to take their own coffin: Wolseley was to use the story in his speech to the Mansion House after his return from Asante [173]. Wolseley himself scorned 'prophets of evil' and later recorded, 'That dreadful creature, "One Who Knows," and those twin brothers, "The Man on the Spot" and "The Man who has Been There," all whined in chorus as dogs do at the ringing of a church bell.'[19] Wolseley himself anticipated conditions similar to those he had experienced in Burma.[20] Famously, therefore, his preparations included the designing of a special uniform for his officers and men, officers receiving a grey woollen homespun Norfolk jacket with grey pantaloons, gaiters, shooting boots and a cork helmet with an Indian puggree. It was worn for the first time when Wolseley and his staff went ashore at Sierra Leone on the voyage out to Cape Coast. The rank and file of those battalions subsequently sent to Asante similarly received grey smock-frocks and trousers, long boots and helmets. Neither too tight nor too loose, the uniform was admirably suited to keep men cool or warm as required. Officers were armed with a revolver and other ranks with a Snider breech-loading rifle, Wolseley changing his mind on his original recommendation of the Adams 1870 pattern six-shot double action rifled barrel .38-in. pin-fire revolver to suggest the shorter barrelled Thomas 1869 pattern .450-in. self-extracting revolver instead. All carried the saw-backed Elcho sword-bayonet, which had been developed by Lord Elcho in 1870: his son, Alfred Charteris, of course, was one of Wolseley's ADCs. Wolseley found it especially effective as a dual purpose tool [75].[21]

Amongst the advice Wolseley received before leaving England was the impossibility of animals living for long on the Gold Coast [4, 14, 173]. In the event, this proved unfounded, Cardwell ordering a cattle boat to be fitted out for 180 beasts to be brought from Madeira and Cape Verde. Wolseley's artillery officer, Rait, successfully trained a team of two oxen to draw a 12-pounder smooth bore mountain howitzer and it was belatedly decided also to obtain 150 mules, the cattle boat being sent back to Madeira and Cape Verde for this purpose.[22] Stanley suggested that elephants might also have been used but Brackenbury was to counter that they could not have been brought ashore through the surf at Cape Coast.[23]

Given the other initial advice that the land was level for up to 30 miles inland from the coast, Wolseley also accepted the idea of using a railway [7, 13]. At an estimated cost of £45,000, two 'steam sappers' and four tenders were made available, together with sufficient rails for up to eight miles initially, with a third 'sapper', four tenders, light trucks, ten trucks and up to 40 miles

37

of rail to be supplied subsequently if the line proved practicable. It was anticipated that half the cost could be recovered by selling off the rails at the end of the campaign. The initial material was ready at Woolwich by 7 October with the additional material being assembled by 27 October.[24] The 'steam sapper' was a versatile steam traction engine capable of running on road or rail, first produced by the Rochester factory of Aveling and Porter in 1868, but it weighed a little over four tons. Wolseley's chief engineer, Robert Home, indeed, never believed that the railway was a realistic proposition and presented Wolseley with a paper while they were coming out in the *Ambriz* outlining his objections. In the event the land was too uneven to lay rails and the gradients proved far too steep to use the steam sappers even as road engines since they could not zigzag to overcome them, and they could only be used as stationary engines for sawing wood and pumping water for their own consumption [45].[25]

As already suggested in the general introduction, Wolseley was evidently embarrassed by the railway affair, hence the publication by the War Office of his defence of the railway concept [40], but not that indicating his original enthusiasm [7]. Indeed, significantly, Wolseley made only the briefest mention in one letter (on 3 November) of an incident that appears to have occurred on 29 or 30 October when an Asante prisoner being sent with a copy of the ultimatum to Kofi Karikari was put on one of the steam sappers for its first road foray in the hope of impressing him: unable to cope with the gradients, the engine broke down after two or three miles [64].[26] Wolseley blamed the failure of the railway on those who had suggested the land was flat, but also suggested the idea had been forced on him by Sir Lintorn Simmons and Robert Home, which was clearly not so in the case of the latter [30, 36]. While the two steam sappers were landed, the rails were not and the failed scheme cost only £8,000, the rails subsequently being used eventually in England though there was also a request from Bermuda for the material in 1875.[27]

Another aspect of modernity was Wolseley's request for 180 miles of telegraph line to be erected on bamboo poles. Home again felt it unlikely to be of use and some suggested it would be simply pulled down by Africans but this proved unfounded, the Asante emulating it by stringing up white thread in the trees in the belief that it was a fetish token. The material having arrived on 9 December, the line was laid to Wolseley's advance camp at Praso by 24 January. The only difficulties, indeed, proved to be trees falling on the line, occasional earthing problems, and quinine-induced deafness among operators.[28] An extraordinary amount of stores were assembled by the Surveyor General's department, including 100 railway guard whistles and 30 fog horns, the latter presumably linked with the supply of 30 signalling books in case of inclement conditions. Indeed, the First Sea Lord opined that more equipment was being sent to the Gold Coast than had been sent to the Crimea.[29]

Inundated with applications from those wishing to accompany him, since all recent campaigns had been mounted by the Indian rather than by the home army, Wolseley's meticulous planning extended to the choice of his officers in what became the first real appearance of that remarkable grouping of military talent, the Wolseley or Ashanti 'ring' [5, 6]. Wolseley had become associated with some of his future leading adherents almost coincidentally during the Red River campaign since the choice of Buller, Butler, McNeill and Huyshe was dictated by those officers available in Canada, only Hugh McCalmont making his own way there to press his services. Wolseley, however, later wrote that he 'had long been in the habit of keeping a list of the best and ablest soldiers I knew, and was always on the look-out for those who could safely be entrusted with any special military piece of work'. There is some evidence of this, so that when Butler was proving troublesome during the Gordon Relief Expedition in December 1884, Wolseley wrote that he would 'drop him from my list'.[30]

Butler, Buller, McNeill, Huyshe and McCalmont, together with Assistant Controller M. B. Irvine, duly reappeared in Asante. Butler was still in Canada when he heard of the expedition on 30 August and immediately telegraphed Wolseley, booking the first steamer sailing from New York. Famously, indeed, his telegram read, 'Remember Butler. Will sail by first steamer.' He missed Wolseley's departure from Liverpool by just eight hours, the two ships actually passing each other off Holyhead. Wolseley, however, had left him a message to follow on and he was among those additional officers whose services Wolseley formally requested on 27 September. Butler finally arrived at Cape Coast on 22 October.[31] Buller, studying at the Staff College, was also abroad when the expedition was authorised, visiting the battlefields of the Franco-Prussian War, when he apparently dreamt that Wolseley wanted him and returned home to find the invitation awaiting him. In fact, Wolseley had initially recommended him to accompany Glover's expedition, but Buller could not be contacted. The Duke of Cambridge was apparently prepared to accept that Buller had graduated from the Staff College though he had not taken the final examination but, in the event, Buller was never granted the *psc* qualification.[32] McCalmont at least was readily available, writing to Wolseley as soon as he saw the announcement of the expedition in the press.[33]

Wolseley always claimed that he picked solely on merit and even his critics were to acknowledge that he had the knack of selecting able men. As he wrote in his memoirs of Asante, 'I felt that ordinary men could not be good enough for the work I had undertaken.'[34] Courage was one obvious recommendation and Wood, McNeill and the expedition's principal medical officer, Dr Anthony Home, had all won the VC while Gifford would win it on the campaign and Buller in 1879. McNeill was certainly 'the right sort' [53]. As it happened, Anthony Home had also been the surgeon of Wolseley's regiment in the Crimea and, having volunteered to go to the Gold Coast in June, had arrived at Cape Coast on 23 June.[35] As indicated above, Wolseley had already met Wood in the War Office. In their conversation in May, Wolseley had remarked to Wood, a former naval midshipman, that he would be happy to have him steer his boat on the Pra, a statement clearly recalled by Wolseley in August [1]. Wood was thus summoned by telegram on 12 September and, in turn, recommended the inclusion of one of his own subalterns in the 90th Light Infantry, Arthur Eyre. Wood arrived at Liverpool direct from the autumn manoeuvres.[36]

Wolseley also had a penchant for intellectual reputation. Maurice was an instructor in tactics at the Royal Military College and had won the Wellington Prize Essay competition in 1872.

Wolseley had been duly impressed at the time.[37] Brackenbury was professor of military history at the Royal Military Academy, and Robert Home had published *A Précis of Modern Tactics* for the War Office Topographical and Statistical Department in 1873. Wolseley already knew Robert Home while Brackenbury wrote to Wolseley after reading of expedition in the press and was surprised to be offered the post of assistant military secretary by return.[38] George Colley, whose services Wolseley was to request in October 1873 [**47**, **50**], was professor of military administration and law at the Staff College and widely recognised as one of the most brilliant military minds of his generation. Though he was not uncritical of the Staff College, Wolseley was to favour increasingly Staff College graduates on his campaigns for their potential adaptability, writing in 1884, 'My idea is to give every Staff College officer and everyone strongly recommended by a good commanding officer a chance in a subordinate position of showing what he can do and what he is worth.'[39] Of the first group of 27 officers who went out with Wolseley, eight had the *psc* qualification, namely Wood, Maurice, Robert Home, T. D. Baker, Captain William Dalrymple, Lieutenant Robert Gordon (93rd Foot), Dooner and Fitzroy Hart, the last three having graduated only in 1872. Dooner heard of the expedition from a colleague who had already volunteered on 24 August and, going up to London on the following morning, managed to see Wolseley.[40]

Of those special service officers sent out subsequently, another five were *psc*s: Colley; another 1872 graduate, Captain F. H. W. Miller (Royal Artillery); and three who had graduated only in 1873, namely Captain Charles Burnett (15th Foot), Captain Francis Russell (14th Hussars), and Lieutenant Harry Cooper (47th Foot). The brigade major sent out with the three white battalions in December 1873, Major Charles Robinson (Rifle Brigade), also had a *psc*. Wolseley's old friend, Augustus Anson, feared it was 'using the finest steel of our army to cut brushwood', while Edward Hamley, the Commandant at Camberley, remarked that it was 'cutting blocks with a razor'. Rather similarly, Major General Arthur Herbert thought 'these brutal niggers are not worth the life of one of our promising young officers'.[41]

On occasions in the future, Wolseley's choice of officers would be constrained but, for Asante, the Duke of Cambridge gave him a free hand. The one exception was the Duke's initial opposition to George Greaves, with whom Wolseley shared an office at Horse Guards, as his chief of staff, on the grounds that feeling in the army would be against '*two* Horse Gds officers going on so small an expedition as first & second in Command'. In the event, when McNeill was seriously wounded in October 1873, the Duke readily agreed to Greaves replacing him [45].[42] Wolseley, indeed, soon regretted he had not asked for 50 special service officers [14], requesting a further 12 to be chosen from 15 named, including Butler, in a despatch on 27 September.[43]

An interesting light is thrown on this list in the biography of the later Major General Andrew Wauchope. Then adjutant of the 42nd Foot, Wauchope had sent in his name but had not been initially selected. Captain George Furse of the 42nd, however, was chosen. Furse had been on the staff at Aldershot and 'was known to have an extensive acquaintance among army officers'. Thus, while on the voyage out to the Gold Coast, Wolseley gave Furse 'a paper bearing a long list of names, asking him at the same time to mark with a cross any name which he considered to be that of a good and efficient officer'. Having been instrumental in Wauchope's appointment as regimental adjutant, Furse ticked his name and Wauchope arrived at Cape Coast on 30 November 1873. Wauchope had journeyed out on the same steamer, the *Volta*, as Henry Wood, who was to replace Charteris as Wolseley's ADC. Henry Wood then mentioned Wauchope to Wolseley as having a good reputation as an adjutant, Wolseley remarking that they 'must look after that fellow'. Accordingly, Wauchope was briefly on Wolseley's staff before being posted to the native regiment commanded by Baker Russell, though he then returned to his own regiment when it arrived in Asante in December, acting as orderly officer.[44]

Wolseley reckoned his initial party a 'good lot of fellows'.[45] In subsequent campaigns, he was to continue to select those upon whom he felt he could rely instinctively and who were familiar with his working methods, hence the identification of the Wolseley 'ring' with Asante. Interestingly, Buller was to organise an 'Ashanti Club' in the autumn of 1874, designed to hold an annual dinner, of which the first would be in either central London or Greenwich, but for which all military and naval officers who had served in Asante in whatever capacity were eligible.[46] In many ways, Wolseley would become something of a prisoner of his early success, feeling it desirable to keep employing the same individuals lest his rejection of them might reflect on his earlier choice.[47] Both Dooner and Fitzroy Hart attracted Wolseley's criticism during the campaign [46, 51], but while Wolseley did not employ Dooner again, Hart continued to appear in Wolseley's campaigns. There were also to be a degree of vindictiveness towards non-ring members, of which the attitude towards Glover in Asante was an early example. One Colonial Office official, indeed, noted the tendency, writing in June 1874 that Wolseley 'never likes to commit himself too hastily to any approval of an officer not selected for his own expedition'.[48] It should be noted, however, that other 'rings' within the late Victorian army such as that surrounding Frederick Roberts were equally poisonous in their operation. The main potential disadvantage of the ring, as Cambridge understandably pointed out in 1884, was that 'if the same officers are invariably employed, you have no area for selecting others, and give no others a chance of coming to the front'.[49] In fact, the membership of the various rings within the army was more fluid than sometimes imagined.[50] In any case, new officers were brought in continually to Wolseley's circle, such as Herbert Stewart in Zululand in 1879, though Wolseley was not being entirely accurate when he wrote to Cambridge on one occasion of those whom he found wanting, 'As soon as I find I have made a mistake, I drop them remorselessly.'[51]

Another potential disadvantage was that Wolseley's command style was built upon the basis of individuals willingly filling specific roles in a kind of orchestrated military collective, with Colley or Greaves as chief of staff, Buller in intelligence, Brackenbury as military secretary, Butler in the field, and so on. ADCs were also frequently plunged into command positions as needed though McCalmont found little to do during his own brief service in Asante before fever struck him down since Brackenbury and Maurice did most of the administrative work.[52] Indeed, if an individual was not available Wolseley would often lament that the replacement was not as effective. Thus, Brackenbury proved a good secretary in Asante and on Cyprus but was a failure as chief of staff in Zululand when Colley was recalled to India. Given that Maurice was such a poor secretary in Asante [93], it is not perhaps surprising that he failed when pressed into this role again in South Africa in 1879. Wolseley, indeed, declared Maurice unsuitable either for staff duties or leadership in the field, keeping him on largely in gratitude for Maurice's nursing him when he was struck down by fever on the Gold Coast.[53] According to Charteris, the distribution of duties between Maurice and Brackenbury was not well defined, with unnecessary duplication, while Maurice's writing was so bad that Charteris had to copy out his despatches for him.[54]

Wolseley's secretaries not only dealt with the paperwork, drafting and transmitting orders and correspondence but, together with his chief of staff and field commanders, were what Preston has characterised as the 'central pivot' of authority, decision and power in Wolseley's system. Wolseley himself commented that few could imagine how much work fell on the chief of staff 'of a force such as that under my command'.[55] By contrast, on the Red River, he had minutely supervised the loading of every boat but he was to record further in October 1884 that he had no intention of attempting to undertake the routine administration devolving upon his chief of staff as 'it is a very stupid thing in any position in life to keep a dog and bark yourself'.[56] But Wolseley's chiefs of staff were not intended to share in decision-making, and Wolseley's system of close supervision militated against the development of initiative in his subordinates. The war correspondent, Alexander Forbes, was to write that, while Wolseley picked good men instinctively for the right roles and the 'gang as an aggregate' was 'a weapon of extraordinary and diverse force', if broken up its constituent elements would be 'but the withes of a faggot, with here and there a stick of exceptional stoutness'.[57]

Wolseley was respected rather than liked and had associates rather than friends and, as the members of the Wolseley 'ring' grew in stature and seniority, their willingness to work one with another for common goals became subordinated to their own ambitions. Moreover, while Wolseley was frequently successful in co-ordinating their diverse talents, his capacity to manage a personalised command system decreased in effectiveness in proportion to the growth in the scale of operations. Though Wolseley often employed larger staffs than many of his contemporaries, improvisation in the end was not an adequate substitute for a proper general staff system.[58]

The degree of careful preparation is apparent from the activity on board the *Ambriz* en route to Cape Coast. Half the saloon was covered with all the publications on the Gold Coast that could be obtained including Parliamentary Blue Books, the accounts by Bowdich and Dupuis of their respective diplomatic missions to Asante in 1817 and 1820, other visitors' accounts by William Hutton (1821), John Beecham (1841) and Richard Burton (1863), Major H. I. Ricketts's narrative of the 1824 war, and notes by the War Office Topographical and Statistical Department, which also produced a highly inaccurate map. Winwood Reade's *Savage Africa*, based on his travels in West Africa in 1861–62, was also consulted and as Reade, of course, was on the *Ambriz* he was quizzed by Wolseley [14].[59] Wolseley himself worked assiduously on the Blue Books [16, 20]. Since his personal staff monopolised the material available, Wolseley had Brackenbury and Huyshe lecture on the background to the war and what was known of the topography and tribes of the Gold Coast, the two lectures by Brackenbury and that by Huyshe being published subsequently [23].[60] Everyone, however, had been provided with an almanac with adaptations for the Gold Coast.[61] Wolseley also drafted out the ultimatum to be sent to Kofi Karikari [20, 39]. In exactly the same way, when preparing for his campaign to bring the Zulu War to a conclusion in 1879, Wolseley prepared using detailed notes he had compiled on his earlier mission to Natal in 1875 and, on the voyage out to Egypt in 1882, he dictated orders for every day of the campaign ahead.[62]

En route, some of Wolseley's officers were put ashore to begin the task of raising native levies or carriers and to bring them on to Cape Coast [20, 21]. Furse and Lieutenant Saunders were set ashore at Sierra Leone to go on to the Gambia to recruit among Muslim tribesmen of the Jolof and Mandinka as levies, and Robert Gordon to enlist Mandingo in Sierra Leone itself. Commissary Charles O'Connor of the Control Department, who was already well known to the natives, was similarly landed at Cape Palmas in Liberia to enlist Kru as carriers [22]. Instructions were also sent to get the collector of customs at Sherbro to recruit Susu as levies while Captain G. C. Strahan, who had taken passage out on the *Ambriz* to assume the post as administrator at Lagos, also undertook to send 150 Hausa.[63] In all, about 120 natives including 38 servants were taken on at Sierra Leone together with cattle and other provisions [22]. Charteris, for example, hired a cook, Davis, for Wolseley at £4 a month and a servant, George, at £2 a month.[64]

Even before the embarkation of natives and livestock, conditions on the *Ambriz* were extraordinarily bad [12, 14]. All accounts testify to the smell of new paint and foul bilge water, the rats and cockroaches, frequently flooded cabins, baths that did not work, drunken and inexperienced stewards, a truculent chief engineer, poor food and, according to Charteris, 'filthy wines'.[65] To compound the discontent, all were charged excess baggage as the shipping company had no government contract to convey officers and Wolseley and his officers then declined to sign a document to say they were satisfied with the ship.[66] Not surprisingly, there was an official report on the ship's condition. In mitigation, the company pointed out that the number of passengers expected had been increased from 12 when conveyance was first requested on 23 August to 20 on 27 August, to 25 on 29 August and to 34 on 1 September. Astonishingly, however, it claimed that complaints of wet paint and foul smells were entirely unfounded and, in any case, that 'the complaints came from the Newspaper Special Correspondents, who were grumbling before sailing at the best accommodation being allotted to the Military officers instead of themselves'.[67]

Mention of the press leads naturally to Wolseley's attitude towards war correspondents [14, 19, 20, 46, 53, 54, 118, 147]. He had described them in *The Soldier's Pocket Book* as 'those newly invented curses to armies' and 'a race of drones' who 'eat the rations of fighting men and do no work at all'.[68] Wolseley was certainly well aware that any failure in Asante would result in press criticism [46, 53, 62]. Henry Morton Stanley concluded that Wolseley must have been exposed in Canada to irresponsible reporters from 'the unclassic districts of Western America' since the 'representatives of the great London and New York dailies are of widely different material'. Consequently, he professed himself unoffended by the views that Wolseley and his officers seemed to share with regard to the press. There is a hint of tension, however, in Stanley's description of one conversation over dinner with an unnamed member of Wolseley's staff who remarked about the 'honour' of the press, 'Trust in his honour, by heavens! I would trust to nothing less than his back.' Stanley noted Wolseley's 'frigid reticence and chilling reserve' towards the press, but, at the same time felt Wolseley was trying to compete with the correspondents, pointedly noting that Brackenbury and Maurice were merely 'newspaper writers in military clothes'.[69] Charteris, describing possibly the same dinner as Stanley, remarked, 'We all agreed that we had never seen so offensive a snob. Pompous, vulgar, and not the least amusing. By tacit agreement no one alluded to the Livingstone business.' According to Charteris, after a second dinner, at which Stanley was even more offensive, Wolseley declined to have anything more to do with him. Buller, too, noted at one point in November that Stanley had yet to leave the environs of Cape Coast Castle and 'trusts entirely to fancy which will I should think suit the Yankees better than facts'.[70]

Hostility to Stanley may explain why he is not mentioned at all in either Wolseley's journal or letters and it was only in 1903 that Wolseley included an approving account of Stanley's conduct at Amoafo in *The Story of a Soldier's Life*, suggesting this had changed his opinion of Stanley: 'I can still see before me the close-shut lips and determined expression of his manly face which – when he looked in my direction – told plainly I had near me an Englishman in plain clothes whom no danger could appal.'[71] Stanley would not have appreciated being characterised as English, having failed to endear himself to Huyshe, who remarked on one occasion that they were fellow Welshmen, only for Stanley pointedly to say he was not Welsh but American.[72] In any case, Wolseley's contemporary view of the conduct of the correspondents that day is very different [147]. Apart from locating Livingstone in October 1871 at Ujiji on what would later become known as Lake Tanganyika, Stanley had previously reported the expedition to Abyssinia in 1867–68, as well as serving on both sides in the American Civil War.

In fact, Stanley – who brought his own steam yacht, the *Dauntless*, for use on the coast – did not arrive until 22 October, being a passenger on the same boat as Butler. Boyle, whom Wolseley characterised as a 'dangerous radical', did not arrive until 29 October [54]. Melton Prior did not leave England until 4 November. In Prior's case, the presence of an artist would certainly prove an advance on the entirely speculative sketches that had initially appeared in *The Graphic*.[73]

Only Winwood Reade and Henty went out on the *Ambriz*, Wolseley thinking little of either of them [14]. Wolseley later described Henty as an 'obese vulgarian without any pretension to be a gentleman, and a fearful coward'.[74] Henty had served in the Crimea with the Commissariat and had covered the Abyssinian expedition: later, of course, he would become a prolific author of adventure books for children. At least, therefore, he accorded with Butler's view that a former ranker was likely to prove a better war correspondent than someone like Reade, who appeared too intelligent for the role and thought in terms of what should be done rather than what had been done.[75] Reade had never covered a war before, but, like Boyle, who was in the same position, had travelled extensively in West Africa. Reade, indeed, had published *Savage Africa* after his first trip to West Africa in 1861–62 and *African Sketch-Book* after a second trip in 1868–69. Like Butler, he had also volunteered unsuccessfully to join the Livingstone Relief Expedition. Though characterised as 'debilitated' by Wolseley, 'cadaverous' by Charteris, 'fragile' by Brackenbury and 'not as good as some of the others' by Colley, at least Reade was always 'well to the front and probably saw more than any other'. When Paul Methuen arrived in December, he noted the correspondents 'sticking like vultures to the Headquarters Staff' and recorded,

'I believe they are a rotten lot, from what I hear.' He also suggested that Boyle was 'such a snob that other correspondents will have nothing to say to him'.[76]

On a day-to-day basis, however, whatever his private thoughts, Wolseley clearly took pains to cultivate a favourable impression among the correspondents. Melton Prior, for example, remarked that Wolseley, who was 'most jovial and kind to all ... appeared especially so to correspondents'. Henty, too, remarked on Wolseley's kindness and concern for the comfort of the correspondents. As will be seen later, Stanley was critical when Wolseley despatched a ship with just one telegram to Gibraltar to get home the news of the Asantes' freeing of the European captives and their promise to pay an indemnity as fast as possible, at the same time declining to send any despatches by correspondents. On at least one occasion, however, Wolseley arranged for some of Prior's sketches to be sent back to the coast with his own official despatch.[77] Wolseley also deliberately deceived the press correspondents with regard to his first real offensive operation on 14 October [38]. Stanley was then further exercised by Wolseley's apparent secrecy when advancing to the relief of Abrakampa on 6 November but, in fact, the move had been so hurried that Brackenbury later apologised for simply forgetting to tell Stanley who was living outside Cape Coast.[78]

There appears to have been no real attempt to control correspondents' access to the means of communication, however, and, in any case, all were dependent upon mail steamers carrying reports and despatches to Madeira to connect with the submarine telegraph cable to Lisbon, with consequent delay. Wolseley was frustrated by the unreliability of the mail steamers and when, on a later call at Cape Coast, the *Ambriz* left without waiting for his despatches he requested powers to detain ships, only for it to be deemed illegal. More frustration came with the breakdown of the submarine cable between Madeira and Lisbon in November 1873, which could not then be repaired until after the winter. It was agreed, therefore, to send out HMS *Vigilant* to run between Madeira and Lisbon with Wolseley's despatches and telegrams and, subsequently, it was arranged for an improved steamer service between Cape Coast and St Vincent. Both Wolseley's and

Winwood Reade's first despatches from Cape Coast Castle, for example, dated 2 October only arrived in London on 28 October, Reade's appearing in *The Times* next day. Indeed, it was the Asante expedition that prompted laying of the cable from Madeira to St Vincent in the Cape Verde Islands and serious discussion of extending the cable further down the African coast, but argument over the financial cost meant extension to West Africa was only accomplished in 1886.[79]

Certainly, the campaign was to be well reported in the press since apart from Reade (*The Times*), Henty (*The Standard*), Boyle, (the *Daily Telegraph*), Maurice (the *Daily News*), Home (the *Pall Mall Gazette*) and Prior (the *Illustrated London News*), there was also representation for the *Western Morning News*, *The Scotsman* and the *Manchester Guardian*. Reuter's appointed a coastal trader to send telegraphic despatches on their behalf, various medical journals sent reporters as well and, apart from Maurice, another officer was also filing copy for the *Daily News*. The latter is only referred to as attached to Baker Russell's regiment of native levies, which would mean Dooner, Hart, Gifford or Lieutenant Edward Townshend (16th Foot). Wolseley had been suspicious when it was rumoured on the *Ambriz* that Fitzroy Hart was acting as a correspondent for the *Daily Telegraph*, having Maurice write Hart a note that Wolseley 'had no objection to it whatever, but that he considered that I ought to have informed him of the act'. Hart, who had a poor view of the press, replied that he was not doing so and would not have done so anyway unless he had asked Wolseley first. Given Dooner's subsequent book, it is most likely that he was the additional correspondent.[80]

I

Brevet Colonel (Local Major General) Sir Garnet Wolseley[1] to Brevet Lieutenant Colonel Evelyn Wood, VC

7 August

[Holograph]

Adjutant General's Office

My scheme was too adventurous for the timid people who now rule us, so I fear there is no chance of my getting to Coomassie or of my having the very great pleasure of seeing you navigate your boat on the waters of the River Prah.

I shall only be too glad to forward your views in any way I can here, but pray do not imagine that my interest here is worth having. I wish I was to be with General Lysons[2] this year, for I look to him as one of the few Generals we have who is capable of and willing to instruct others during Manoeuvres.[3]

KCL, Wood MSS, KCM 89/9/22/1

2

Memorandum by Wolseley

August

[Printed extract]

The first object to be attained, as I understand the circumstances existing on the Gold Coast at present, is to free the Protectorate of its Ashanti invaders; and secondly, having accomplished this, to advance into the Ashanti territory, and, by the seizure and destruction of Coomassie, strike a decisive blow at the Ashanti power, not only directly by the loss and severe punishment inflicted upon its Government, but, by the moral effects of a great victory, to destroy for ever its military prestige and influence over the neighbouring nations. It is its great military reputation – giving it so much power and influence, and causing it to be so feared by all the surrounding tribes – that we must break up; and this can only be effected by inflicting a severe defeat upon its armies, and leaving our mark of victory stamped in the country by the destruction of the capital, Coomassie.

It has already been determined upon by Lord Kimberley to send Captain Glover up the river Volta, with a commission to raise a large native force, making use of a body of about 1000 trained Houssas[4] as a nucleus for that purpose, and, proceeding up that river as far as he can in small steamers provided for the purpose, carry war into the Ashanti territory lying on the right bank of that river. If possible, he is then to advance westward in the direction of Coomassie. It is hoped that this operation may have the effect of causing the Ashanti force now in the Protectorate to fall back behind the Boosemprah,[5] or at least act as a powerful diversion in favour of the force that is to advance from Cape Coast Castle, by drawing off, in the direction of the Volta, large detachments from the Ashanti army now in the Fanti country. I understand that Captain Glover's force is to be about 10,000 men, and that he takes out with him all the stores, guns, material, and munitions of war that he will require for his undertaking. I think it may be assumed that his expenses will be at least about £15,000 a month; arrangements will therefore be required for supplying him with that amount from the treasure-chest at Cape Coast Castle.

As this operation has already been determined upon, it is needless to discuss here its advisability in a military point of view, or to consider whether the best direction is thus being given to the best native troops (the Houssas) we have on the coast, and to the warlike tribes, the Accras and the Croboes,[6] who in the present condition of affairs are the most easily available, if not the bravest, natives that could be obtained for direct military operations against the Ashanti army now threatening our posts on the seaboard. In framing a plan of operations for the attainment of the two objects before mentioned, it is necessary, therefore, that it should fit into this operation already determined upon. Let us therefore consider the effect that Captain Glover's expedition may be expected to have upon the first object in view.

Captain Glover leaves England on the 19th inst., so he may hope to reach the Coast on the 10th September; so it may be, I think, assumed that he will have reached with his force the point on the Volta by the middle of November, from whence he will begin his march by land towards Coomassie. Of course, if the rains are over early this year, as Lord Kimberley informs me may be expected, he will be able to begin his march before that date.

It is to be expected that as soon as Captain Glover's force reaches Pong,[7] an effect will be produced upon the Ashanti army now operating near Cape Coast Castle, rendering it perhaps possible to attack it with whatever native tribes and black troops there may be available at this time.

Unless, however, the enemy's main body approaches near Cape Coast Castle, it cannot be hoped to strike any positively decisive blow at it until about the 1st December next; it would not, I think, be advisable to undertake any large operations until that date, for the climate and condition of the country after the rains would be very unfavourable. It would seem to me to be very important not to weaken our strength as regards Europeans by partial operations, returning to the coast after each, but to await our time until the conditions of the country and of the climate would admit of our advancing steadily day by day, with as great rapidity as possible upon Coomassie.

It may, however, be possible to clear the Protectorate of Ashantis at a much earlier date, and if that can be accomplished without undertaking any great operations in which Europeans are to be engaged, it should be done; for the final advance upon Coomassie would be immensely facilitated, if the Protectorate were freed from the enemy's troops for a few weeks before commencing an advance.

The first object is therefore either to be accomplished soon, say about the beginning of November, by minor operations in which the friendly natives alone should be employed, assisted by the moral effect produced by the rumours of Captain Glover's movement on the Volta; or if the Ashantis are not shaken by his operations, and if they are found to be too strong to be dislodged by the native tribes in our pay alone, then the first object can only be attained by the final operation against Coomassie; in fact, in that case, the two objects must be considered together.

In either case it will be necessary to have a force sufficiently strong to defeat in battle the combined armies that the King of Ashanti can bring into the field; and in the event of its being found possible to accomplish the first object before the final operations begin, that battle will take place north of the Boosemprah: but if the Protectorate is not cleared of the enemy before the final advance is made, the great battle will take place on the Cape Coast Castle–Coomassie road, probably in the neighbourhood of Mansu.

For this purpose, I think the following force would be required:–

	Men
2 Battalions of European Infantry of 650 men each,	1300
Detachment of Royal Artillery, with four mountain howitzers,	60
Detachment of Royal Engineers,	40
Administrative Services,	50
Total,	1450

This number to be exclusive of officers.

To act in conjunction with these regular troops, there should be about 10,000 of the best natives we can obtain, using as many Houssas as possible, and, with the exception of these Houssas, and any other disciplined police that may be available, all to be under their own kings – one British officer only being sent with each king to keep him up to the mark, and to inspire his followers with confidence.

If the enemy retire into their own territory early in November, it would be possible to have the bush cleared away at the various halting-places selected along the line of road from Cape Coast Castle to Prahsu for camping purposes, to sink Norton's tube-wells where required, and to make other arrangements for water-supply. Huts, which can in this country be constructed in a few hours, might also be erected.

It might also be possible, under these circumstances, to form a large depot of stores and supplies at Mansu (about 34 miles from Cape Coast Castle). If this were possible, the European troops might march the very day they landed. Under any circumstances it would not be advisable to land the Europeans until every arrangement that it was possible to make beforehand had been completed.

I may perhaps here remark that the composition of this European force is a point upon which too much stress cannot be laid. To detail any two battalions in the army for the service would not answer the purpose required, as it is essential that every officer should be carefully selected for such a service, as peculiarly suited for the work both physically and mentally; and to take any non-commissioned office or private, unless of the best constitution, would be merely to increase the difficulties of the operation.

I would propose, therefore, to obtain the number required in the following manner: To select 12 of the best battalions now at home, and having selected in each battalion the captain and 3 subalterns best suited for the work, direct him to obtain 109 volunteers of all ranks to form a company. That would give a total of 1308 non-commissioned officers and men, divided into twelve companies. To divide that number into two battalions, each to consist of six companies under the command of a selected lieutenant-colonel, having one selected major to assist him.

The detail of a battalion to be as follows:–

Lieut-Colonel,	1	Sergeant-Major,	1
Major,	1	Q.M.-Sergeant,	1
Captains,	6	Orderly-room Sergeant,	1
Subalterns,	18	Colour-Sergeants,	6
Adjutant,	1	Sergeants,	24
Medical Officer,	1	Corporals,	30
Quartermaster,	1	Buglers,	14
		Privates,	577
Total of officers,	29	Total N.C.O. and men,	654

In order to obtain the best men as volunteers (no men under two years' service to be accepted), I consider it would be necessary to give them extra pay at the following daily rates, to be in addition to free rations from date of embarkation to date of return to England:–

Sergeant-Major,	1s. 6d.
Q.M.-Sergeant,	1s. 4d.
Colour-Sergeants,	1s. 2d.
Sergeants,	1s. 0d.
Corporals,	0s. 8d.
Privates,	0s. 6d.

Every man to be medically inspected by the doctor, and none but the strongest to be accepted.

I feel convinced that the small force required, if obtained in this manner, would be in every way equal to twice that number if supplied by detailing whole battalions as they exist at present; and as the men of each individual company would all belong to one regiment, serving under the immediate command of their own officers, the *esprit de corps* in the whole body would, in fact, not be weakened but intensified.

The artillery and engineers required should in a similar manner be selected volunteers.

The extra pay thus given would, I am sure, be the most profitable item of expenditure in the total cost of the expedition.

The men should also be provided with a special kit at the public expense.

[The cost of kit in detail was added, as also a memorandum as to the detail of staff proposed for the expedition.]

Henry Brackenbury, *The Ashanti War: A Narrative* (Edinburgh: William Blackwood & Sons, 1874), pp. 117–23

3

Wolseley to Surgeon Major Richard Wolseley

15 August

[Holograph]

The Grove,

Kingston on Thames

I have just written to Mother[8] telling her that I am to be Governor, Commandr in Chief & I know not what else of the West African Settlements. We are to advance into the Ashantee territory, to capture and destroy the capital Coomassie (about 140 or 150 miles from Cape Coast Castle) and having struck the great King of that great Nation a severe blow we are to make peace with him and retire gracefully. The season for operations is December, January & February, when inland the climate is by no means bad. I hope at latest to reembark for England – if God spares my life – on the 1st March next. I believe I have to leave England next month, so my time will be well occupied until then, as I am going to give up my house here for Loo wont stay in it by herself, and moving with all our things is no easy matter. I believe I am to have temporary rank as Maj. General whilst employed. I am to day to lay my plan of operations before a meeting of Ministers. I propose about 20,000 men, about 2000 only being Europeans. Some time ago when this thing was first mooted I drew up a scheme for going to Coomassie with about 1400 picked English soldiers, making our way up the rivers which I know exist there, but the enterprise was considered to be too dangerous. In fact those who had to consider it, had no experience in "voyageur" work[9] and could not imagine boats going anywhere unless there was deep water, and they were like so many of our men in power timid from age and ignorance: I believe I would have settled the whole business for £150,000. Now there is no saying what it may cost. I must tell you in strict confidence that the Duke has recommended me (I never asked him to do so) to Lord Napier to succeed Thesiger as A.G.[10] There is a difficulty about my not having passed in the languages, but it is possible that it may be got over, either by ignoring the rule altogether, or by saying that I am to be appointed subject to my passing before a certain date. If I get this I shall have to leave for India almost immediately upon my return to England. Goodbye my dear Dick. I shall write to you and Mother frequently when I am away: As you are so continually on the move I shall always [send] my letters to you to [send] under cover to Mother so that she can read them & send them on to you. Fred[11] is off to Ireland to night: Mary is I am glad to say much better for her trip.

Hove, Wolseley MSS, 163/4/22

4

Wolseley to Lieutenant Colonel the Hon. Augustus Anson, VC, MP[12]

18 August

[Holograph]

[Adjutant General's Department headed paper]

Just a line to thank you for your very nice, kind note. You cannot wish more than I do that you were well enough to go with me: There is no one in the Army I would sooner have with me as second in command. Although the Ashantees can bring about 100,000 men at least into the field, the enemy that I have most to dread is the climate although I believe that is given a worse name than it deserves.

I have undertaken the "job" on the condition that I return home *at once* when I have done my work: I shall have a small force of picked English Soldiers about 1,400 formed into two battalions, the officers to be carefully selected as well as the men, and all to be volunteers for the undertaking. The men will be well paid, but I suppose the officers must content themselves with glory, if any of that commodity is to be had. I have to raise a large native force under their own Kings & Chiefs and with this Army to advance upon Coomassie the Ashantee capital. It is about 145 miles from Cape Coast Castle. There is nothing broader than a sheep track through the dense jungle. No animals (transport animals) will live at Cape Coast Castle so my only beasts of burden will be men and women carriers. If all goes well, I hope D.V.[13] to leave the coast for England about the 1st March next, when I shall look forward to telling you of all my doings. Many thanks for your kind offers of assistance should I want anything finished here when I am away, and I shall gladly avail myself of your offer should circumstances require it.

Gosford, Wemyss MSS, 'Letters about Alfred'.

5

Wolseley to Richard Wolseley

21 August
[Holograph]
War Office

Many thanks for your nice note. I have already thought of the Quinine and proposed it as part of the daily rations.

I have noted McTaggarts[14] wish but I cannot hold out any hope to him. I have already such a host of Volunteers. Don't mention it to anyone, but tell me who is the best Capt. and the 3 best Subs in your Battn who would you think wish to go out?[15] I am worn out writing notes on this subject.

Hove, Wolseley MSS, 163/4/23

6

Wolseley to Lord Elcho, MP[16]

30 August
[Holograph]
Horse Guards, War Office

I am much obliged to you for your little pamphlet[17] which I read yesterday with the greatest interest. If I may be permitted to express an opinion on it, I consider it admirable. The unit cannot henceforward be too small, for henceforward individuals must be far more highly instructed than in days gone by. And that is the reason why the value of the Volunteer Force is I think much greater now than it was when the movement was first initiated.

I had a note three days ago from Augustus Anson asking me to take your son as an ADC with me to the Coast of Africa. I replied that I should be very happy to do so provided, that your son was really anxious to go, for I believe that one volunteer is worth any two men ordered out, and provided that it met with your approval. I have just had an answer from Anson telling me that both conditions have been fulfilled, so I have sent his name in and it will be duly notified to his Comd. Offr. I shall take great care of him, and if I find that he does not stand the climate I shall send him back by an early steamer. I intend leaving by the mail that starts on the 12th prox. but as I have another ADC[18] he can follow by the mail that leaves ten days later. I would advise his going by the second mail, for he will then get out in a better season, and I do not expect to do anything for about six weeks after my arrival at Cape Coast Castle.

Gosford, Wemyss MSS, Drawer 39, Bound Volume, 'Alfred'.

7

Wolseley to the Earl of Kimberley

2 September

[Holograph]

From all the information supplied by recent reports from the Gold Coast, it would seem that very little reliance is to be placed upon men as carriers, and the experience of the operations conducted in 1863–64 shews that the Coolies employed near the Coast are unreliable.

I would therefore suggest that the proposal made by Governor Nactglass[19] in his memorandum upon the operations necessary to bring the Ashantees to reason should be carried out: viz – That a narrow Gauge Rl. Road should be laid down for at least 30 miles from Cape Coast Castle towards Coomassie.

Sir Linthorn Simmons,[20] who has written to me on the subject, and who has had considerable railway experience believes there would be no difficulty in arranging with a Contractor in England for the construction of an 18 inch Rl. Road at the rate of about £3000 a mile, say £100,000 for 30 miles.

The more I consider the nature of the operations to be undertaken the more convinced I am of the importance of the Rl. Road. Sir L. Simmons says there would be no great difficulty in having the line in working order by about the 1st December. It would shorten the duration of the operations and would render the execution more sure.

TNA, CO96/103; Bodleian, Kimberley MSS, MS. Eng. c. 4112, ff. 27–8

8

Wolseley to Field Marshal HRH George, Duke of Cambridge

3 September
[Holograph]
Horse Guards

I feel deeply sensible of the honor done me by Your Royal Highnesses letter of the 1st instant,[21] and by the Privilege accorded to me of writing direct to Your Royal Highness during the progress of our expedition, a privilege of which I shall gladly avail myself.

The proposals I put forward relative to the formation of Battalions for this service, were based upon the belief that our Infantry at present – so unlike what it was in days gone by – being so largely composed of growing lads was unfitted for the fatigues of a tropical Campaign, it would be necessary to draft into any whole Battalion selected for the work, so many volunteers from other Corps, that the Regimental spirit – the backbone of Her Majestys Army – would be swamped.

The theatre of operations is a dense forest, where fighting can only be conducted by small units, as we found in Burmah and in New Zealand: my idea was therefore to use strong Companies selected from Battalions, according to the ability of each to furnish either one, two or three. I thought by this means to preserve the Esprit de Corps, in fact to intensify it by the encreased rivalry that would thus be called into play. This Expedition being of a peculiar and novel nature, I thought that perhaps its requirements might be better met in a special manner, especially as it would have been thus possible to have carried out the principle of selection as regards officers, a point that in bush fighting is of such vital importance.

I have thus stated the reasoning upon which my proposals were based in order to explain to Your Royal Highness why I made them, and not from any wish to reopen now, a question that has been decided by Your Royal Highness, a decision to which as in duty bound, I at once bowed when I was informed that my proposals did not meet with Your Royal Highnesses approval.

I am sincerely grateful and flattered by the confidence reposed in me by Your Royal Highness and I hope and trust that I may be enabled to fulfil the high opinion so graciously formed of me: if I fail to do so, it will not be from want of energy. The expression of Your Royal Highness's sentiments towards me is an additional incentive to exertion on my part.

If I possibly can attain the objects in view without landing European soldiers, I shall certainly endeavor to do so, as I am most anxious to avoid exposing the lives of more than are absolutely necessary, to the baneful influences of such a climate. If after arrival at Cape Coast Castle I write home requesting the despatch from England of the Troops now being prepared for service there, Your Royal Highness may rest assured that I have been most unwillingly constrained to ask for them, not seeing my way to fulfilling the objects of my mission without their assistance. Two months will elapse between the date of my asking for them and of their arrival on the Coast under any circumstances, and it is quite possible that events in that time may have changed so that even when they arrive, I may not require them. If so, of course I shall send them back to England without landing them at all.

Cambridge MSS, RA VIC/ADD E/1/7191

9

Edward Cardwell to Wolseley

8 September
[Printed]
War Office, Pall Mall

I have the honour to inform you that the Command of Her Majesty's Land Forces on the Gold Coast has been conferred upon you during the present troubles with the Ashantees, in combination with the Civil Administration of that Settlement.

The objects, with which this arrangement has been made, have been communicated to you by the Secretary of State for the Colonies. My duty is to give you such general instructions in respect to your Military Command, as may be necessary to convey to you the views of her Majesty's Government in that respect.

The difficulties, with which you will have to contend, are not such as are to be encountered from an enemy formidable in the field. They are the far more serious difficulties of contending with a climate peculiarly fatal, especially at particular seasons of the year, to the constitution of European soldiers; and in a less degree, of all soldiers recruited anywhere else than upon the Coast itself.

In determining what reinforcements it may be necessary to send you from time to time, Her Majesty's Government will be greatly influenced by the reports they will receive from you, after your arrival on the Coast; when you will have had time to communicate with those whose experience on the Coast, and knowledge of the immediate circumstances of the case, will best enable you to judge what measures you ought to adopt in order to give effect to the views of Her Majesty's Government, as conveyed to you by the Secretary of State for the Colonies, and what means it is necessary to employ for that purpose.

The Force at present upon the Coast appears, by the latest reports, to be fully adequate for the defence of the British Settlements themselves against the attacks of the Ashantees. It will be for you to consider what military measures will be necessary to free those Settlements from the continual menace of such attacks, and to accomplish the further objects of your mission.

In arriving at a judgement on the subject you will not fail to bear in mind the following considerations, viz:–

1 That European soldiers ought never to be exposed to the influence of that climate, when the service required can be performed by Houssas, or by Native Auxiliaries, or by any other Force indigenous to the country.
2 Nor unless the service is one of paramount importance to the main object of your mission.
3 Nor unless it can be accomplished with a rapidity of execution which may render the exposure to the climate very short.

For this reason, if the employment of Europeans shall become a necessity, every preparation should be made in advance, and no European force should be landed on the Coast until the time for decisive action has arrived. The period when the risk of loss from climate is at a minimum, appears to be that comprised within the months of December, January, February, and March; and it is consequently of much importance that your decision should be arrived at as soon after your arrival on the Coast as you may be enabled to form it with sufficient knowledge of the circumstances, and with satisfaction to yourself.

You will be able to judge what prospect Captain Glover has of raising a Local Force so as to make a decided impression upon the invaders by his movement upon the Volta and how far it is possible to organise that not inconsiderable body of natives of whom Colonel Harley speaks as available, when supplies of food shall have been placed at your disposal for their use.

You will also be able to judge what assistance native attendants will be able to render to the European troops, if you shall eventually find that you are compelled to employ Europeans in order to effect the purposes which Her Majesty's Government have in view.

The reports just received by the "Himalaya"[22] give an account of the sickness of the Marines employed upon the defence of the Settlement before the arrival of the West Indian troops, and of the West Indian troops themselves, which Her Majesty's Government have received with great concern. It is true that the season in which your operations will be carried on will be much less exposed to the hazards of the African climate than that which has just passed; and there seems good reason to believe that those hazards are greater upon the seaboard than in some favoured parts of the interior; but it is to be remembered, on the other hand, that service on a march is exposed to trials of its own, which do not affect men living on board ship or in quarters.

I have thought it right to state for your guidance these general considerations, because nothing but conviction of necessity would induce Her Majesty's Government to engage in any operation involving the possibility of its requiring the service of Europeans at the Gold Coast. But it is far from my intention to fetter your judgement in the responsible and arduous duties which have been entrusted to you; and no one, I am sure, will be more sensible than yourself of the cardinal importance of the considerations to which I have invited your attention, or more desirous to spare to the utmost of your power the exposure of European soldiers to the climate of the Gold Coast.

TNA, WO 106/285; WO 147/27; CO 879/6; CO 96/107; BPP, Cmd. 1891, pp. 140–1

10

Kimberley to Wolseley

10 September
[Printed]
Downing Street

Her Majesty's Government having determined, in consequence of the critical state of affairs on the Gold Coast caused by the Ashantee invasion, to unite the chief civil and military command in the settlement in the hands of an officer of high reputation and experience, I have the honour to acquaint you that Her Majesty has been pleased to approve of your appointment to administer the government of the Gold Coast Settlement, and I transmit to you herewith Her Majesty's Commission as Administrator.

2. You will, as Administrator, correspond directly with this office, and not through the Governor-in-Chief of the West African Settlements, who will be instructed during your tenure of office to abstain from all interference in the affairs of the Gold Coast.

3. The circumstances which have led to the present position of affairs on the Coast appear to be briefly as follows:–

4. The King of Ashantee, as you will find on reference to the document dated 19th of August 1871, which is printed at page 34 of the correspondence presented to Parliament on Gold Coast affairs in February 1872, disclaimed any pretension put forward in his letter to Mr Ussher, No. 24, of the 24th November 1870, that Elmina was his by right; but in his letter to Colonel Harley of 20th of last March, the King again asserted that the fort of Elmina and its dependencies are his, and it seems beyond a doubt that one

of the main objects of his mission was the assertion of Ashantee supremacy over Elmina.[23]

5. But, independently of Elmina, it must be remembered that peace had never been formally re-established with the Ashantee kingdom since the war of 1864, and that a petty warfare had from time to time been carried on between the Ashantees and the border tribes.

6. It has been asserted that Mr Plange,[24] the messenger sent by Mr Hennessy to Coomassie, did not faithfully deliver the friendly messages with which he was instructed from the British authorities to the King; it is, however, a remarkable fact that almost up to the time of the news arriving of the invasion, the Gold Coast Government was in apparently friendly communication both with the King of Ashantee and his ambassadors at Cape Coast, and that the Administrator was in daily expectation of hearing that the captive missionaries had been released, and that amicable relations had been permanently established with the Ashantee kingdom.

7. No indication had been given by the King of Ashantee that he had any serious ground of quarrel with the British Government, whether as regards Elmina or any other matter; and no opportunity was afforded to the Administrator to endeavour to remove peacefully any cause of complaint which the King might allege against the British Government or against the tribes in alliance with Her Majesty.

8. The statement in a letter from Mr Salmon,[25] then acting Administrator, to Mr Hennessy, dated 8th of November 1872, that the Ashantees were at that time and had been purchasing very large quantities of ammunition, guns, gunpowder, and lead bars, seems to show that the invasion had been deliberately planned, and that it was not the result of a sudden outbreak of savage violence, on account of any supposed affront or neglect on the part of the British authorities. It is to be observed, moreover, that in the letter to Colonel Harley to which I have referred above, the King of Ashantee by no means limits his demands to Elmina, but calls upon the Administrator to restore the Denkerahs, Akims, and Assins, to their former position as his subjects, in direct contravention of the treaty of 1831, in which it is stated that 'the King of Ashantee

has renounced all right or title to any tribute or homage from the Kings of Denkera, Assin, and others formerly his subjects.'

9. I need scarcely say that Her Majesty's Government cannot for a moment listen to such preposterous demands, nor can they allow the territories of the tribes in alliance with Her Majesty to be devastated, the inhabitants butchered or driven away into slavery, and all progress and commerce stopped on the Coast by hordes of barbarians.

10. At the same time, Her Majesty's Government have never had any desire to prevent the Ashantees from peaceful intercourse with the Coast; on the contrary, they have always been anxious in every way to foster and encourage such intercourse; and one of the advantages which they anticipated from the possession of the forts at Elmina was, that through the friendly connection between the Elminas and the Ashantees, increased facilities would have been afforded for trade with the latter.

11. On your assuming the government, or as soon after as you may think advisable, you will address a communication to the King of Ashantee, summoning him to withdraw his forces from the territories of our allies within such a period as you may fix, and to make adequate reparation for the injuries and losses which he has inflicted upon our allies, and give securities for the maintenance of peace in future. I have in another despatch indicated to you generally the nature of the conditions which Her Majesty's Government would consider equitable.

12. You will intimate to him that active measures are in preparation against him, and that if he refuses to comply with our demands, or delays to withdraw his forces within the time named, he may rest assured that means will not be wanting to compel him to do so, and to inflict such a defeat upon him as will effectually deter him from repeating his aggressions.

13. Colonel Harley has been instructed to invite the principal kings and chiefs of the friendly tribes to meet you on your arrival at Cape Coast, and you will of course lose no time in endeavouring to collect and organise any native force which you may judge to be necessary for conducting any operations which may appear to you certain, or in a high degree likely, to be undertaken.

14. You should state to the native Kings that the Queen, on learning the calamitous position in which her allies are placed by the invasion of their country by the Ashantees, and their inability, without further assistance, to repel the invaders, has sent out specially an officer of high authority and experience, uniting the chief civil and military command, for the purpose of rendering them that assistance.

15. You should explain to them that while Her Majesty's Government are prepared to take such measures as may be found expedient on your advice to aid them in carrying on the war against the Ashantees, they expect the native tribes to use their utmost efforts to defend themselves, and to place their resources unreservedly at your disposal.

16. The native tribes undoubtedly made considerable efforts at the beginning of the war; but since their last defeat, they appear to have been unable to rouse themselves to even the most necessary exertions for their own protection. The reports received by Her Majesty's Government show that at Cape Castle the natives have not even taken steps to clear away the bush which endangers the safety of the town, and that nothing has been done by them to obtain trustworthy information of the movements of the Ashantees. You will intimate plainly to the native kings that it is impossible to help those who are unwilling to help themselves; and that unless they unite together cordially in their own defence, and show themselves prepared to make every sacrifice in their power to maintain themselves against the invader, they must not look for aid to Her Majesty's Government.

17. Her Majesty's Government are unable to give you more precise instructions as to the measures which should be taken in order to bring the war to a speedy and successful termination, without further information than they at present possess. Much will depend upon the amount of co-operation which you may be able to obtain from the friendly tribes, the position and force of the Ashantees, concerning which but imperfect intelligence has hitherto been received, and upon the opinion which you may form after examination of the state of affairs on the spot as to the practicability of an expedition into the interior, and

the number and composition of the force with which you might recommend that such an expedition should be undertaken. It may be that you will find the forces at your disposal upon the Coast sufficient for the accomplishment of any object which you may think it proper to undertake But if you should find it necessary to ask for any considerable reinforcement of European troops, I have to request that you will enter into full explanations as to the circumstances in which you propose to employ them, and the reasons which may lead you to believe that they can be employed without an unjustifiable exposure, and with a well grounded anticipation of success.

TNA, CO 879/6; CO 96/108; BPP, Cmd. 1891, pp. 141–43

11

Kimberley to Wolseley

10 September
[Printed]
Downing Street

Her Majesty's Government wish to leave you a large discretion as to the terms which you may think it advisable to require from the King of Ashantee, but I may point out to you that the treaty which was concluded with Ashantee in 1831, and of which I enclose a copy for your information, seems to afford a reasonable basis for any fresh convention.

2. It would certainly be desirable to include in such a convention an explicit renewal by the King of Ashantee of the renunciation contained in the treaty of 1831, of all claim to tribute or homage from the native kings who are in alliance with Her Majesty, – and further, a renunciation on his part to supremacy over Elmina, or over any of the tribes formerly connected with the Dutch, and to any tribute or homage from such tribes, as well as to any payment or acknowledgement in any shape by the British Government, in respect of Elmina or any other of the British forts or possessions on the Coast.

3. The King should also, for his own interest no less than with a view to the general benefit of the country, engage to keep the

paths open through his dominions, to promote lawful commerce to and through the Ashantee country, and to protect all peaceful traders passing through his dominions to the coast; and it might be expedient that a stipulation should be made that a resident British consul or agent should be received at the Ashantee capital, if Her Majesty should think fit at any time to appoint one.

4. You will of course be careful to avoid as far as possible anything which may endanger the lives of the European missionaries and their families who have so long been held in captivity at Coomassie, without any fault of their own so far as Her Majesty's Government are aware, and you will use every effort to secure their safe release.

5. You will also endeavour to procure the surrender of all the prisoners taken by the Ashantees from the tribes in alliance with Her Majesty.

6. It is a usual practice with the native tribes to demand hostages for the faithful performance of treaties of peace. This was done in 1831, when two hostages of high rank were delivered over to the British Government by the King of Ashantee.[26] If you should find it advisable to make a similar demand on the present occasion, you will bear in mind that the hostages should be men of high rank and position in Ashantee.

7. It would be reasonable to exact from the King the payment of such an indemnity as may be within his means, which are said to be considerable, for the expenses of the war, and the injuries inflicted on Her Majesty's allies.

8. Lastly, the opportunity should not be lost for putting an end if possible to the human sacrifices and the slave-hunting which, with other barbarities, prevail in the Ashantee kingdom.

TNA, CO 879/6; BPP, Cmd. 8901, pp. 143–44

12

Wolseley Journal, 11–12 September

Thursday 11 September

Left London by 5. p.m. train from Euston Square: many friends to see us off – Augustus Anson amongst the number. Had a saloon carriage and travelled very comfortably. Fred put an envelope into my hand just as the train was moving off. It contained £500 and such a nice note from him. I do not intend keeping the money however except £50. I shall send him back the remaining £450 from Liverpool tomorrow. Train was delayed near Stafford owing to the number of special trains running in all directions from the neighborhood of Cannock Chase where the great march-past has taken place to day, attended they say by at least 150,000 people. Put up at the North Western Hotel at the Rl. Rd. Station where we had good rooms and a very good supper.

Friday 12 September

Told to be on the floating landing stage at 1. p.m. Found upon arrival there that a deputation from the Mayor and Corporation wanted to see me.[27] They "interviewed" me and expressed the Mayors regret that he was prevented by domestic affliction – his brother having just died – from paying his respects to me before I embarked. We were kept waiting for over an hour previous to getting off by the Steamship Co. people who of course were not ready. At last got off by a tender and embarked in the S.S. "Ambriz" belonging to the African S.S. Compy., 1360 tons register (1900 tons) Capt. Smart, master.[28] It was blowing hard as we embarked. These steamers are only in the habit of taking out a few passengers, consequently having to prepare for 28 officers in addition to the ordinary traffic necessitated putting up a number of new cabins. The smell of paint in them was intolerable and most sickening. She is the dirtiest craft I have ever been on board. The stench of bilge water in my cabin is most offensive. She was only purchased recently from the White Star Line and this Company has not yet had time to get her in order – everything is at sixes and sevens; the stewards of the lowest and dirtiest class of Irish Liverpool ruffians, whose filth and diseased appearance is very loathsome. Feeding on board extremely bad. Sent letters ashore by the pilot.

TNA, WO 147/3

13

Wolseley to Louisa Wolseley

12 September
[Holograph]
Noon

Just before going on board just a line. I found upon counting over the notes given me by Fred that the amount was £500 instead of £400 as I told you last night. I am keeping £50 and sending him back £450. Your note just to hand – so glad to get it – cheer up little woman and remember that all our – certainly my happiness in life depends upon you.

I am glad you are taking your Pal[29] down with you to the Grove as it will be pleasant for you both. It is blowing very fresh here, so we shall have a good tossing about before night is over. I am afraid that we shall be very crowded on board. I was told before leaving yesterday that I should be given the Railway I asked for. Old Storkes[30] quite melted over me: indeed I have received from all the authorities every possible support, and kindness. Good bye my dear little woman. Never forget to say your prayers both night & morning & repeat the little hymn I taught you.

Hove, Wolseley MSS, W/P 3/1

14

Wolseley Journal, 13–19 September

Saturday 13 September
At sea. A fine day – many however ill.

Sunday 14 September
Breeze freshening. Divine Service at 10.30 a. m. read by the Captain who is a nice fellow quite a redeeming feature in this horrid ship.

Monday 15 September
Blowing very hard, and the ship rolling most uncomfortably – remained in my berth until dinner – very few at table, and I do

not feel at all well although not yet actually sick. Lat 46°4' north. Long 9°. 24' west.

Tuesday 16 September
The day better and weather becoming warmer. Sir H. Storkes the day before I left town read me a private letter or rather part of one that he had received from Mr Cardwell;[31] alluding to me, Mr C said, "It only remains now to hope that he will have the moral courage, if there be impossibilities in his way, to look them fairly in the face, to report them accurately, and leave us to take upon ourselves the responsibility of dealing with them. Bad as such a conclusion would be, yet if it be based upon *truth*, it must be accepted." When going to bed, a rat ran over my feet in my cabin. Had a hunt for him but lost him. I hear that some hundreds of dozens of rats were killed on board a few days before we embarked. Lat 42°. 39' north. Long 10°. 48' west.

Wednesday 17 September
A fine day, wind dead aft: ship rolling but still the weather is very enjoyable – all those who were ill, on their legs again, and up to their food. Another rat in my cabin & succeeded in killing him. Cockroaches are making their appearance. Deep in my blue books for several days past. Hope to reach Madeira on Friday forenoon. This is the worst managed ship I have ever had the misfortune to make a passage in. All the men with me are now well, and a heartier or a cheerier lot I never met. Baker Russell is a host of jolliness in himself. Lat 39°. 11' north. Long 12°. 44' west.

Thursday 18 September
A fine lovely day. Light clothing is being got out by everyone and men talk already of sleeping on deck. The cabins are most offensive. Two newspaper correspondents on board, Mr Windwood Reed for the Times & Mr Heinty[32] for the Standard: besides them, Lt. Maurice R.A. is to write for the Daily News, Major Home R.E. for the Telegraph, so we shall be well represented in the press. Lat 35° – 42' north. Long 15° – 19' west. 202 miles from the anchorage at Madeira. Windwood Reed is a wretched whist player and it is

amusing to see how everyone tries to get away from the parties that he happens to be playing with. He is a most cadaverous looking man, with curious deep thoughtful eyes and a very small mouth with black beard and whiskers. He reminds one of a debilitated mute, not suffering however from the disease which belongs to that interesting class, viz. drink. He is the author of "Savage Africa" and the "African Sketch Book". I can recommend you to read the latter as it is told in a finished manner and is very interesting. It gives a good deal of information about the West Coast of Africa, not so much however about the Gold Coast as about the Gaboon & Gorilla Country. He showed me a letter to day which he has written to Mr Delaine[33] giving him a brief outline of his views regarding our position on the Gold Coast and the Ashantee question in particular. He says that the riches of the country are inexhaustible and that the great object we should have in view is to open out the interior of Africa to our trade. To this the Ashantees are opposed tooth and nail, as they fear that the tribes to their north, once in possession of fire arms would no longer be under their power as at present. He says therefore that a hard blow struck firmly at the Ashantee power is indispensable for our interests; it is essential that we should make our power known in this part of Africa, so as to avoid the recurrence of wars. He goes on to say that the only way in which a palpable hit can be made against the Ashantees so as to be recognized generally is by the taking of Coomassie, and that in order to accomplish that object, the use of a small force of Europeans (he says about 2000 men) is necessary. He does not believe in the unhealthiness of the climate as he has been himself for months in the interior without injury to his health. I am glad that he has taken up this line for his Times letters. Mr Henty the Standards man is a fat jolly looking man without any pretence to being a gentleman: he began life in the Purveyor's Dept during the Crimean War, and has since he left that branch of the Military service, he has turned his hand to all sorts of things: he is very dirty and is not at all a man to stand the climate of the Coast if all the accounts of it that I have heard are true. He is a good whist player; smokes strong tobacco in a strongly smelling pipe all day. He was the Standards correspondent during the Abyssinian War.

Our other civilian passengers are, a nigger, a consul going out to his post somewhere on the Congo River: a little cockney merchant bound for the same part of the world,[34] and a youngish man en route for Cape Ct Castle where he has been promised a civil berth by Col. Harley. He goes out just to find his patron removed, but as he has been in the Indian Navy and seems strong, I dare say that I shall be able to find work for him to do. Now that I have started, I shall never cease to regret that instead of asking for 20 officers for special service with this expedition that I did not ask for 50. I know I shall have to ask for more when I arrive, and they will be a long time on the way before I can make use of their services.

Friday 19 September
Reached Madeira & anchored in Funchal Roads at 11 a.m. We had a fine calm night, and to day the temperature before we landed was delicious, as we coasted along the Island. The town is very picturesque when viewed from board ship. Of course there is a large Church (built in this instance of a stone of a burnt amber color) and then there are old fashioned but effective looking (from an artistic point of view) forts. The governors house is distinguished by being colored yellow. One wing, by far the best was built by Marshal Beresford[35] when he was Governor here in I think 1806 or 1807, the central portion is under repair having apparently recently tumbled down with the sun. It stands on the beach and is surrounded by houses. In its rear facing landwards as we afterwards saw, it is enclosed with high bastioned ramparts having embrasures for guns: what the object of this arrangement could have been except to exclude the air I have no idea. As you look towards the town from the ship on the left hand stands a high rock jutting abruptly out of the sea crowned with batteries & forming a striking and picturesque feature in the view. I believe we hanged one of our soldiers there when we held the place for striking or stabbing an officer. Looking directly towards the centre of the town, one is puzzled to know for what purpose a high stone pillar like a factory chimney in height, or rather more still like an Irish round tower, except that the diameter of the pillar is much smaller, could have been intended. Upon enquiry I found that it was built to act as a

75

sort of Derrick so that boats coming in laden at high tide could have their cargoes lifted out and hoisted directly into the highest stories of the warehouse standing back from the tower some few yards. Unfortunately and curiously to relate as soon as built, a violent storm ensued which altered the beach so much that the pillar was left standing high and dry on the shingle the sea having receded from it several yards. Its history and fate puts one in mind of the tower of Bable.[36] I never was in a country that looked more burnt up than Madeira as a whole does to day: the beds of numerous watercourses can be traced here and there, but not a drop of water is to be found in them. No rain has fallen since May, and as there is no dew at night, it is hard to understand how the vines and sugar canes grow so luxuriantly. Before landing the usual formalities of the health officers visiting us was gone through, then a swarm of Custom House officials surrounded us; boys in boats, some naked; others very nearly so calling out as in Malta for sixpences to be thrown into the water for them to dive for: these boys however are not so keen as those of the Mediterranean for they would not deign to dive for pennies. There is a constant heavy swell here, so that boats coming along side carelessly are apt to be very much knocked about. Mr Reed the principal Hotelkeeper came off and Charteris ordered dinner for 12 to be ready at 4.30 p.m. so that we should have ample time to get back on board to sail at 7 p.m. We went ashore in strong heavy boats that have to be beached every time they take people ashore: as we neared the beach, we went right about turn, and watching a wave went up the beach stern foremost as far as the wave would carry us: the beach was composed of round shingle each stone being about the size of a turkey's egg from that to a cricket ball, there was no sand nor did there seem to be any stones of a smaller size. Directly from the landing place, which is at the Governors house, an avenue of trees about 150 yards long leads up to the Alamada: we went directly to the hotel which is also on the shore, and had some fruit & Madeira for luncheon. We were supplied with very fair horses – small but some very fair, and all had the look of having been well cared for and well fed. One of the remarkable objects that attracted the eye as we examined the place from the sea, was a church some 1500 feet above the town. To this place we bent our steps. All the streets and paths are very neatly paved with round stones such as I have said constituted the beach: there are no foot paths, but as there are no wheeled conveyances this does not matter. The means of conveyance are in very neat looking hammocks having hoods slung on poles & carried by two men, and sledges drawn by bullocks, except just along the beach the paths and roads are so steep that wheeled carriages could not be used with safety, and the pavement is so good and even that the runners of the sledges go smoothly over it. Produce that is not carried on mens backs is conveyed from place to place on long sort of traineaux like toboggins drawn by oxen. None of these traineaux or sledges have the runners shod with iron. A piece of hard wood is placed along them, and is renewed from time to time when worn out. The paths we ascended were in some places excessively steep and it was wonderful how our little horses managed to keep their footing. Each horse was accompanied by a man who toiled along at our sides, perspiring at every pore, and although unable to speak a word of English communicating very intelligently to us that they wished for something to drink whenever we halted for a few minutes to rest and breath our horses, such halting places were invariably alongside of a nice house. On our road which was never more than 12 or 14 feet wide we passed the numerous villas filled every winter by the consumptive people from England. What a dreary life they must lead here, for I know of nothing more wretched than residing in a place where there is no level land, but where in order to take exercise you have to be continually either going up or going down hill. On each side of you as a rule is a high wall over which is a trellice work supporting vines, from which myriads of grapes were pendant. Now and then one caught glimpses of the gardens inside these walls, where flowers of every bright color made a pleasing effect. Gyraniums of the deepest red and pink and so double that they resembled roses, fuchsias covered with flowers and many varieties of evergreen plants that never would thrive in that magnificent conservatory of ours at the Grove. All the halting places that I have alluded to were so situated, that a fine view was to be obtained from them, and certainly the views were lovely.

On every side, gullies and valleys where stunted oaks grew abundantly, and several descriptions of pine were dotted about. The large leaves of the plantain with their light green coloring formed a good contrast to the dark shade of the fir trees. Below was the sea of the deepest blue, not green as with us, but really blue, where lay our steamer and the few other craft that were discharging cargo. Upon reaching the church, or convent as it is called, although there are neither monks nor nuns there, the climate or rather I should say the temperature was superb. It is quite dry, not a tinge of moisture in it, and although below the day had been very warm on the terrace in front of the Church the air was delicious. The English Consul subsequently told me that this has been a most unusual day, as the Sirocco[37] has been blowing, an event that only takes place a few times in the year. He looked thoroughly washed out and quite exhausted from this hot wind. We went over the Church, nothing to see except the usual amount of daubs in the way of pictures and a wax figure of the virgin that would have done for Madam Tusseau's.[38] I never saw such determined beggars as these Portuguese, no, not even in an Irish village: we were annoyed by a pack of the dirtiest of dirty children to give them something, and lazy looking men bothered us to try their wine and spirit. We had dismissed our horses as the correct thing to do is to return in a basket sledge, the roads being too steep for laden horses in descending. We started off two or three in each sledge and to each sledge two men who held on behind to two drag ropes to prevent the sledge from running away and becoming unmanageable and to guide it. These men also occasionally pushed or standing with one foot on a runner, pushed with the other to encrease the speed when the pace was not *dangerous* enough to please the mad Englishmen. The danger of toboggining was nothing to it, for had we turned over nothing could have saved our bones from being broken against the walls that bordered each side of the road; however there was no upset, and we found our horses waiting for us at the foot of the mountain & riding through the town returned to the Hotel after a very pleasant excursion. A bath, and a barber to cut our hair as short as possible, giving us upon our return to the ship the appearance of convicts, and then a stroll to make purchases. Russell and I went in search of embroidery, and I daresay were well fleeced: I think we laid out about £8 a piece, and it is very probable that the same things could be obtained in London for one half the price. The woman who sold the embroidery spoke French. The woman who sold us lace was an Englishwoman who kept a shop where all sorts of *hot* writing table ornaments were exposed for sale, also books stationery etc etc. She had an exhausted, washed out looking appearance that did not speak well for the climate as a place of residence all the year round. We had a very fair dinner, and the champagne when mixed with soda was not bad. Wicker work chairs is a staple manufacture in the place, and as we assembled on the beach a little before 7 p.m. to go back to our floating prison, it was amusing to see each man with one of these chairs either on his head or carried by a boy behind him.[39] We did not entirely get under weigh until 8 p.m. Col. Wood brought a grey or rather a white horse from the Governor paying £30 for it: altogether for embarking charges for hay during the voyage (hay is very dear here) it will stand him exactly in £47.3s. 9d. As he goes to Elmina it is just possible he may live for a few months there as bullocks thrive there although they will not do so at Cape Coast Castle; however as he is not a rich man I think he was not wise in trying such an expensive experiment. We had not left more than about half an hour when the mail from the Coast passed us. It was very provoking that she did not arrive a couple of hours earlier as the news would have been very interesting. The date of the last news we obtained was the 20th August from the Coast telling us of Commodore Commerells wound[40] and of the attack upon Dix Cove. I am very sorry to lose him, for I am sure that I should have got on very well with him, but in one sense it will do this expedition good, as it will arouse public attention to the war, and show clearly that the Ashantees mean fighting the English as well as the Fantees. I believe that Capt. Hewitt was named to succeed Commerell before we left home so I hope he may be sent out with the least possible delay. I have met him some years ago somewhere, I forget where, and I am told that he is a right good fellow all round. The best dressed people I saw at Madeira were the priests who as usual looked sleek and well to do.

The Governors salary at Madeira is £400 a year. So much for Government pay in Portugal.

TNA, WO 147/3

15

Wolseley to Kimberley

19 September
[Signed holograph]
On board the Steam-ship Ambriz
Madeira

I have the honour to acknowledge the receipt of your Lordships letter of 10/9/73 informing me that Her Majesty had been graciously pleased to appoint me to administer the Government of the Gold Coast settlement and transmitting to me Her Majesty's Commission as administrator.

I have to report that in conformity with your Lordships instructions I left Liverpool on September 12th ultimo by the West African Company's steam-ship Ambriz.

I desire to call attention to a point of some importance in which the Colonial regulations do not appear to carry out your Lordships instructions that during the continuance of the present critical state of affairs on the Gold Coast the Civil administration should at no time be separated from the military command.

An officer of standing and experience Colonel McNeill V.C. C.M.G. was appointed with your Lordship's concurrence to accompany me as Colonel on the staff and second in command so that in the event of any death or illness the civil administration should be in competent hands. I find however that by the rule laid down on page 173 of the Colonial "Rules and Regulations" if an administrator should from any cause whatever become incapable of acting, the Government devolves upon such officer or person as may have been designated for that purpose in the Governor's commission. As no one is named in my commission as my eventual successor the collector of customs or some other member of the Legislative Council would I believe succeed to the administration of the colony in the event of my death or illness.

I have therefore to request that your Lordship will be good enough to furnish me with an authority that I can lay before the Legislative Council at Cape Coast Castle informing the members that in the event of the office of administrator becoming permanently or temporarily vacant from any cause whatever it would devolve upon whosoever happened to be for the time being the senior combatant Military Officer on the spot.

I also beg to request that Colonel McNeill V.C. C.M.G. may be appointed a member of the Legislative Council. It appears to me desirable that in the event of his succeeding to me he should have been previously aware of anything that may have taken place in that body.

TNA, CO 96/110; BPP Cmd. 892, p. 9

16

Wolseley Journal, 20–22 September

Saturday 20 September

Lat. 30°. 35' north. Long. 16°. 39' west. Our course S. b' east. Distance run 134 miles 143 miles from Grand Canary at noon. A fine day: sea calm: temperature very enjoyable but the sun hot. Had a deck awning spread for the first time. I forgot to say that Mr. Ashbury was at Funchal in his yacht, a fine large steam craft. He called upon me, but I missed him – he intends coming on to the Coast in his yacht in the hopes of seeing something of the war. He has Lord Neville – (who the devil is he) on board and one of Lord Stanhopes sons on board with him. He is I have always been told that he is the most arrant of snobs, having been blackballed for the Rl. Yt. Squadron and several other clubs.[41]

Sunday 21 September

Was awoke at a little before 6 a.m. by a gun being fired on board and upon going upon deck saw we were in the roadsted at Los Palmas, a town of Grand Canary – a large town without trees: the houses built with flat roofs and as if constructed of card board. On the hill above the town an old fort having detached works on both flanks as we looked at it from the sea. There is a fine church built of dark brown stone. The hills all round are bare and destitute of vegetation, a most dreary and burnt up looking locality. All landings prohibited as these wretched Spaniards (and Portuguese also) who keep their towns in a filthy state regardless of all sanitary laws delight in a strict system of quarantine: some time ago, someone in Liverpool was reported to have died of cholera and consequently all vessels from England are put in quarantine here. The consequence is that no mail steamers anchor here: they remain under weigh until they have delivered their mails. No one scarcely seemed up in the town, so that it looked as if it were a city of the dead. Cochineal is one of the chief articles of export. I am told that there is plenty of corn and fruits grown in the valleys that are said to be very fertile – but from what one sees from the sea it looks like a desert place, the general tint being that burnt up looking appearance that India has in the hot season. A lovely day: left again at about 7.30 a. m. divine service at 10.30 on deck. Lat. at noon 27°. 23 N. Long 15°. 40' W. Distance from Grand Canary to Sierra Leone 1380 miles.

Monday 22 September
A lovely day with a refreshing wind blowing making one feel quite chilly in light clothing. Saw a flying fish this morning – the first I have seen this voyage. Captain Strachan R.A. the Governor of Lagos, or rather going out to be so, is on board: he is a very nice fellow, and has the smallest and best shaped hands I have ever seen with a man. His father was the man implicated in the Strachan, Dean Paul swindle.[42] Spend all my time reading up the Blue books relating to the Gold Coast, very dry work especially as they have been put together so carelessly and without any apparent order or method, that they are most confusing and difficult to follow. Lat. 23°. 40 N. Long 16°. 59. W. – distance run 234 miles. Dreamt all last night of my mother.
TNA, WO 147/3

17

Kimberley to Wolseley

22 September
[Holograph copy]
Downing Street

I have had under my consideration the question of the mode in which the correspondence of Captain Glover with this Department should be conducted.

2. Referring to the instructions to Captain Glover, copy of which was enclosed in my Despatch No. 410 of the 18th ultimo, I have to acquaint you that in all matters relating to the military operations or general conduct of his Expedition I shall address Captain Glover through you, from whom he will take his orders, and under whose general supervision he will conduct his operations. But as the Colonial Office is to be the Accounting Department of Her Majesty's Government for the expenditure incurred by Captain Glover, and on account of which that officer will be directly responsible to me, it will be more convenient that he should correspond all purely financial details direct with this Department. Copies of Captain Glover's Despatches to me on this subject should however be forwarded to you by him, and I shall in like manner furnish you with copies of any communications which I also may find it necessary to address to him.

3. If in any matter of emergency where delay prejudicial to the public service would be caused by communicating through Cape Coast, Captain Glover should find it necessary to write direct to me, or I shall find it necessary so to address him, copies of such communications will of course be sent to you for your information.

4. Although I think it necessary to provide for this emergency, I do not anticipate that it will be found necessary to deviate from the course laid down in the second paragraph of this Despatch.

5. I have to request that you will instruct Captain Glover accordingly.

CUL, Glover MSS, RCMS 131/12; BPP, Cmd. 1891, pp. 211–12

18

Wolseley Journal, 23 September

Tuesday 23 September

Lat 19°. 54' north. Long 17°. 51 W. distance run 231 miles. Several small birds caught by strings, and some pigeons lit on the yards: the sea has lost its blue and is now green as we are only about 30 miles from the shore.

TNA WO 147/3

19

Wolseley to Frances Wolseley

23 September

[Holograph]

On board the steamer Ambriz

Lat 19 . 54 North

Long 17 . 51 West

I avail myself of a fine smooth day to scribble you a few lines. I dreamt of you all during the night the night before last – woke up several times and then dreamt of you again. I hope you are well my dearest mother, for the longer I live the more I feel how necessary to my happiness is the knowledge that you are in the enjoyment of good health. Believe me when I say that no tie I have is so dear to me as that, that unites me to you. You may think this strange perhaps when I see so little of you, but I always live in the hope of your being before I die, located somewhere near me, where I might be able to see you daily. I send Loo home the journal that I keep day by day: she has to enter it into a book and then send it on to you for perusal: remember that there is much in it that is very confidential, it must not therefore go out of your hand or be read by anyone excepting brothers and sisters, nor is anything I say there about public affairs or about individuals to be repeated beyond our family. Please be very careful about this. We hope to reach Madeira next Saturday morning when I shall post this to you. Although to day we are in the tropics, there is a pleasant breeze, and the temperature is by no means unpleasant or oppressive. I hope you will take in the Times & the Standard & the Daily News whilst I am away, as we have special correspondents from all these papers with the expedition and I am sure that their letters will interest you. I have a very difficult task before me, far more difficult than most people have any idea of, and my reputation as a soldier hangs upon succeeding in it. I know my dearest mother that I shall have your morning and evening prayers for my success, and as I shall not spare myself, and have a capital set of officers with me. I hope with Gods assistance to bring my mission to a successful termination before the 1ˢᵗ March next, so as to [be] back in England by the 1ˢᵗ April. I am glad to know that dear Fred has made you so comfortable. His kindness to me before I left was everything that it could be. I hope and trust that he may never have to return to Australia, or should it be necessary for him to go there, that it may only be for a spell to finally arrange his affairs there. Please give all my best love & ask them all to write to me for although I shall have no time for private letters yet to read those from home will always be a great treat to me. Goodbye now for the present my dearest and best of mothers. The motion of the screw makes writing very difficult.

Hove, Wolseley MSS, W/W 4/1

20

Wolseley Journal, 24–27 September

Wednesday 24 September

Lat 16° – 1' North. Long 17°. 40' west. distance 233 miles – 78 miles from Cape de Verd. A very warm day. Sighted the revolving light on Cape de Verd at 6.45 p.m. It was about 18 miles distant. This is the region said to be one of perpetual rain & calms. It did not rain with us.

Thursday 25 September

A tornado of wind and rain at about 4 a.m. It only lasted a few minutes. It cooled the air for a little, but the heat set in again at breakfast hour. I have corrected the final draft of my ultimatum to the King of Ashantee. It is in accordance with my instructions and is only really meant for the English public, as it is not expected that even an answer will be sent to it. I have had to be very careful therefore in the words selected, so that it shall maintain the dignity of England by its firmness & decision, without going too far so as to cut off the King from all possibility of acceding to my demands. I feel that if it does not meet with public favor, the Government will throw me over and say that I am to blame. Lord Kimberley in his instructions on this point has left me – I suppose in order to save his own skin should the document meet with disfavor in the newspapers – the widest latitude on this subject. I was wrong in saying that Major Home had undertaken to correspond with the "Telegraph" newspaper. He is only to write occasionally for the Pall Mall, so unless a man is sent out specially for the purpose *"The largest circulation in the world"* will have no news from our Force. Lat 12°. 18. North. Long 17°. 14' distance run 224 miles.

Friday 26 September
A very warm night last night a violent tornado of wind and rain. Two sharks, one a very large one seen alongside this morning. Also some Gulls for the first time: they are not like, except in color, those we have at home, their heads, tails & wings are much more pointed and from tip to tip of wings is I should say quite twice as many inches as those that we are accustomed to. Lat 9°. 41' North. Long 15°. 26' West. distance run 206 miles; 148 miles from Sierra Leone Cape. Finished the last of the Blue books that I have been engaged in so deeply since I embarked.

Saturday 27 September
Reached Sierra Leone at 6.45 a.m. A fine morning, and everything looked green and refreshing and we slowly steamed into the harbor passing the wreck of the SS "Negretia" still sticking on the Carpenter Rock.[43] Her captain when she was lost was our first officer. Very few ships in the place: a small steamer from Woolwich with stores for the Gold Coast and the Government Yacht, the "Sherboro" and a few others constituted the shipping of the port. We carried an Ensign at the "fore" showing there was a Governor on board. The Governors barge came off for me and we went ashore

in it about 8 a.m. There is only a very small detachment of troops and there are no serviceable guns mounted so I had only a guard of honor furnished by the Military Police and no salute. There was a large crowd of black people at the landing who followed us as we walked up to Government House, along a street with trees on each side: the trees were umbrella, and mangrove trees. The day was unusually hot and oppressive no air in the morning, the consequence was that our walk of only some five or six hundred yards surrounded by a howling crowd of niggers, who smelt high and completely shut out all air from us, was no agreeable exercise before breakfast. Not knowing the hours kept by the English at the place I and my personal staff had landed without breakfast, having only had a cup of coffee about day break. We did not get our breakfast until nearly 11 and although it was an admirable one, most of us felt sick from emptiness of stomach before we had it: I felt squeamish all the day in consequence, for there is nothing so injurious or so dangerous in these colonies as to take exercise, or in fact even remain for any time awake without having the stomach well supplied with food. The Governor's house stands on high ground overlooking the town and sea below, the Barracks being behind it on a still higher position: the house is an old Battery converted into a dwelling house: the lower walls are consequently about four feet thick. In front is a terrace formed by the position upon which the parapet of the battery had stood: In plan it is bastioned: below the escarp is a plot of enclosed ground that might be and ought to have been converted into a garden, but which is allowed to remain waste. There is a stable attached to the house but no horses as none will now live in the settlement although they formerly throve tolerably well. There is a large market house in the town near the landing that was built originally as an exhibition building: near it, is the English Cathedral, an unpretending looking Church of very ugly proportions. There is also a public reading room not yet quite finished I believe called the Wilberforce Institution so named after the great friend to this African race:[44] I cannot say that I partake of the feelings that actuated that worthy philanthropist. I have seen the slaves in the South before they were emancipated, and I have seen something of negroes in many parts of the world, and now that I have seen them en blogue,[45] I feel convinced that to be in slavery until they become properly educated in civilization is their true place: Slavery carried out under stringent laws to protect the slaves from cruelties or from the separation of domestic ties etc. etc. is the only position that the negro in his natural condition is fit to occupy. Here at Sierra Leone as one looks round at the hills clothed with brush and trees, one feels how different would be the appearance and prosperity of the place if the black inhabitants were held to labor for their subsistence: it is monstrous to think that such naturally productive localities should be given over to waste and consequently as become breeding beds for the propagation of malaria, because the people who are supposed to own the soil are too lazy and worthless to till the soil, and I cannot believe that the Creator intended there should be races left on the face of the earth to vegitate in sensual idleness, without laboring for their daily bread. The Governor Mr George Berkeley is a little man of about 52 or 53 years of age, with rather a red face and a quite manner.[46] He has not the ease of deportment that generally marks the high bred gentleman, but there is nothing in the least about him to which exception could be taken. He was very kind to us all and did everything he could to make our visit pleasant and in his official capacity, all that he could to further the object of our expedition. Capt Kendall, the Colonial Secretary was very anxious to go to Cape Coast Castle in a civil capacity: a Mr Moylan also who has supplied the Times with all the letters that have hitherto appeared in that paper regarding Cape Coast affairs, was desirous of doing so also. I asked Mr Berkeley regarding both.[47] The former he said was of no use to him and indeed he was anxious to get rid of him, so far as he was personally concerned he would be very anxious that he should go with me, but that if I asked his opinion about him he felt bound to say that he would be of no use to me whatever – as regards the latter he was he believed an Irish Fenian and a very objectionable character. He gave me the Govt. steamer to take Captain Furze & Lt Saunders to Bathurst for the purpose of raising recruits there.[48] He also sent on to Mr Loggie C.M.G. at Sherboro a proposition I made to send on that gentleman to the Coasu tribe to raise from five to eight thousand fighting men from those people.[49] He also caused proclamations to be sent round the town and neighborhood of Sierra Leone requesting recruits. I left an officer, Lt Gordon[50] there to look after this duty, and before I left in the evening, some 40 had already come forward. Captain Strachan (Administrator of Lagos) remained behind with the Governor at his particular request to await the next steamer for the purpose of talking over the affairs of his new Government. We dined at 5 p.m. and went on board ship at 7 p.m. and steamed slowly out of the harbor.

TNA, WO 147/3

21

Wolseley to Louisa Wolseley

27 September
[Holograph]
Sierra Leone

Just a line to say we have arrived here: this is a very pretty place, so green but with what Mrs Russell would call plenty of "rank vegetation. The Governors House, where I write this is an old Battery situated behind the town on high ground overlooking the harbor. I landed in state, but as there [are] only a few soldiers here, and no service with guns, I had to dispense with a salute which I know you will regret very much. I had a guard of honor of armed police who met me on the landing and the "population" were there in great force who followed me as an howling mob from the sea beach to Government House. I steamed into Harbor having a Union Jack flying at the foremast which it appears is the right of a Governor, and the Government steamer dressed immediately with all her flags. A large barge came off for me & I felt quite like a Royal personage for the first time in my life, my feeling being also partly that I was a showman or acting a part upon a stage. The Governor, Mr Berkeley, is a nice gentlemanlike little fellow of I should say 55 or more years of age; his appearance is not commanding, but he has been very kind to us since we arrived. We had an admirable breakfast and are to have an early dinner at 5 p.m. after which we reembark and proceed on our voyage. I find that I shall have great difficulty in obtaining the recruits I had hoped to obtain here and elsewhere. I am dropping one officer here to recruit. I am sending two others from here in the Governors steamer that he has placed at my disposal to the Gambia to do the same, and I intend leaving another at Cape Palmas also. The heat here is nothing like what it is in India, but it is of a steamy sort, making one feel as if in a turkish bath at times. The thermometre as I write with all the windows & doors open is 82 in the room. That is more than it will be at Cape Coast Castle. The negroes are just like so many monkies & one feels as one looks at them that they ought to be slaves, they are fit to be nothing else, as they are a lazy good for nothing race, no matter what Exeter Hall may say to the contrary.[51] I hope you will write me long long letters: with best love to the Elders, ever my dearest child your fondly devoted husband.

Hove, Wolseley MSS, W/P 3/4

22

Wolseley Journal, 28–30 September

Sunday 28 September

Divine Service on deck: the sea rather rough and unpleasant. Heavy rain at night.

Monday 29 September

Quite a cold day: reached Monrovia, the capital of Liberia about 7 a.m. A showery morning. This is a miserable place although sounding very grandly as the metropolis of a "*Republic*". I believe that the Govt. exercise no real authority over the wide extent of coast claimed as territory, except at Monrovia & Cape Palmas. The Kroos[52] scarcely acknowledge the presidents authority. After the American War between North and South a large number of liberated slaves were deported to this place. On the point upon which the lighthouse stands there is a Mission establishment, and the surf breaks along the rock below in an angry manner. A small river flows in here with a bar at the mouth. We sent in our mail bag and were soon again under weigh. Most of the Sierra Leone servants that we took on board there have been sea sick and look very wretched. Poor devils, although we pay £2.10s.od each for their conveyance to Cape Ct. Cast. they have no sleeping place except the deck, where they are exposed to the very heavy showers of rain that we have had very frequently since they have been on board; their food is poor and the only water they are given is from the condenser and is never allowed time to become cold. They are a cheery lot however for upon the first glimpse of fine weather, they laugh and jabber like so many monkies in the Zoological gardens:– in the evening they play schoolboy games of forfeits, where the forfeit is always to be hit on the hand with a knotted handkerchief by all the others, and they lay on their blows as hard as they can. They also sing psalms and sing well in concert.

Tuesday 30 September
Reached Cape Palmas at 10.30 ock. a.m.: landed Mr O'Connor[53] of the Commissariat with a crew of Kroomen hoping to raise a body of carriers for service at Cape Coast Castle. He took an iron treasure chest with him, which before putting into the boat he had fastened by a very long line which was again fastened to the boat, so that in the event of being upset in the surf, the boat would serve as a buoy to the treasure to enable its recovery. Here was the wreck of the "Negretia"[54] also of this line of steamers; she had just anchored and as she swung round to her anchor, she struck an unknown rock badly and nothing remained to be done but to run her full power at the beach where she is now stranded. This Company lost three steamers in the short span of about six weeks. At this place the nautical surveys have been made very imperfectly, and there are said to be numbers of rocks not yet laid down. We were surrounded by canoes during our short stay there: they are dug out of one tree and are gracefully modelled something like a caïque in profile, but of course very narrow. The largest did not hold more than a dozen men, but most of them had only two Kroomen in each: fine athletic looking savages, none with more clothing than a breech cloth and some even without that attempt at decency. They are very expert at diving for pence, and also for biscuits and rolls of bread, which did not appear to their tastes to suffer from immersion in salt water. There are evidently no sharks

here as these men seem to be as much at home in the water as fish could be: many of them had their heads completely shaved whilst others had their curly wool shaved into patterns so that some looked as if their hair had been neatly parted with a comb. We rolled most uncomfortably all the time we were at anchor there, giving us a fair idea of what life must be on board ship when anchored for any length of time off this coast. We left again at 11.45. The coast has been very low and ugly wherever we have seen it since we left Sierra Leone, covered with a dense forest in which cotton trees palms & cocoanut seem to abound.

TNA, WO 147/3

2

Assessment (October 1873)

No sooner had he landed at Cape Coast Castle than Wolseley appreciated fully the difficulties facing him and was soon in the midst of a busy daily routine [**24**, **27**, **32**, **33**]. For one thing, there was an acute shortage of available manpower, something illustrated by the fact that the guard of honour from the 2nd West India Regiment that greeted Wolseley when he landed then had to double off to perform the same function at Government House.[1] Some 700 men from the 2nd West India Regiment were widely scattered across eight different posts with only 400 or so ready to hand at Elmina, Akrofo, Cape Coast itself and two outlying improvised strong points. That named Abbaye, presumably named after the Egyptian campaign of 1801, was about four miles north of Elmina and that named Napoleon was about four miles north of Cape Coast. Moreover, there were only 13 officers from the West India Regiment available for duty. The only other organised force consisted of just ten armed native police under the Inspector General of Armed Police, Captain Herbert Thompson of the 2nd Dragoon Guards (Queen's Bays).[2] That there were any outlying defensive works at all was largely due to the exertions of Lieutenant Alexander Gordon of the 98th Foot, the Adjutant to the Armed Police, who had also begun to clear the road towards Manso so that it would be wide enough for the passage of artillery. With rumours abounding, Gordon, whom Wolseley immediately took on as a special service officer, had also verified that the main Asante army of about 40,000 men was now at Mampon only some four or five hours' march from Cape Coast.[3]

With none of the anticipated preparatory effort having been made to enlist any Fante levies,[4] Wolseley was particularly exercised by the way in which Glover had been allowed by Harley to take all the Hausa away from Cape Coast [35], a point emphasised in his first despatch to Kimberley on 2 October.[5] Moreover, Wolseley claimed that, though there was an abundance of ammunition, there were only 19 rifles left in the armoury at Cape Coast and that stores of all kinds were in such short supply that there was enough food for only four days. Wolseley immediately took 300 rifles destined for Glover off the steamer *Gertrude* [25, 34].[6] He also called for 150 Hausa to be released to him from Lagos in return for 50 West Indians and, on 9 October, appealed urgently for the despatch of the 1st West India Regiment to Cape Coast [35].[7] Harley disputed Wolseley's version of the state of the stores at Cape Castle and the Duke of Cambridge also expressed surprise since Wolseley had seen the official returns before he left England and should have been aware that stores were kept deliberately low in tropical climates. The Duke also opined that Wolseley must also have known that there would be relatively few officers available in the 2nd West India Regiment.[8]

Of course, Wolseley's request for an additional 12 special service officers had already been sent to London and was readily agreed. The possible need for the 1st West India Regiment had already been anticipated and Wolseley's request for them would also meet with approval despite thereby denuding the West Indies garrison.[9] The regiment would not arrive, however, until December. Fortunately, although he had been ordered by the Admiralty not to risk putting seamen and marines ashore unless there was a direct attack upon Cape Coast, Fremantle readily agreed to exceed his instructions. Indeed, on 13 October, he issued orders for a landing party of 346 officers, seamen and marines drawn from eight ships of his squadron to be held in constant readiness for action ashore with an allocation of 70 rounds per man and two days' provisions each. To accustom them to wearing boots all seamen and marines were ordered to wear them on board from 0900 to 1600 daily.[10]

Despite his lack of immediate manpower resources, however, Wolseley began to have the defences of Cape Coast improved and a government presence pushed further forward towards Mampon [23, 25]. With Wolseley and his staff in Government House, and the artillerymen, engineers and commissariat officers in Cape Coast Castle itself, Baker Russell and the six officers initially allocated to him – Dooner; Fitzroy Hart; Gifford; Captain Charles Bromhead of the 24th Foot, elder brother of Gonville Bromhead of Rorke's Drift fame; Captain Algernon Godwin of the 103rd Foot; and Lieutenant Edward Townshend of the 16th Foot – were located at Prospect House, which was put into a state of defence. Meanwhile, Evelyn Wood and four officers – Lieutenant James Graves of the 18th Foot; Eyre; Lieutenant Richard Richmond of the 50th Foot; and Lieutenant Edward Woodgate of the 4th Foot – went to Elmina to ensure its defence [23]. Stores were being landed with Robert Home, assisted by three more engineer officers who arrived on 10 October, supervising the erection of the prefabricated huts sent out on *Ambriz* to accommodate them, as well as helping to plan defences. The necessary survey work and map-making of the roads beyond Cape Coast was begun by Huyshe and Fitzroy Hart. Gordon of the 98th also pushed forward small reconnaissance parties as far as Fante Nyankomase.[11] Buller also began to organise an intelligence service, obtaining information from traders, paying for information, finding interpreters and endeavouring to recruit Assin who could speak Asante as spies. Curiously, when serving in the same capacity in Asante in 1896 Robert Baden-Powell found himself given the nickname 'Bully', as he was using a compass, which the natives had never seen before Buller used one and which had been thus invested with magical powers.[12]

Whatever his intentions with regard to sending for European troops, Wolseley had to follow the spirit of his instructions by going through the motions of raising Fante troops. Accordingly, Fante kings and chiefs were summoned to 'palavers' on 4 and 6 October [23, 24, 25, 26, 27, 32, 34, 35]. On the first of these colourful occasions, held in crowded and stifling conditions in a marquee outside Government House, Wolseley apparently displayed 'great tact'. The message, however, was clear: namely that the Fante must act in their own defence and raise fighting men for Wolseley. In return, the kings and chiefs would receive a subsidy at a rate of

£10 per month for every 1,000 men provided. The native levies would receive a pint of rice and a quarter pound of salt meat per day and, until such provisions were landed in sufficient quantities, 4½d. a day in lieu. Daily pay would be 3d. The kings and chiefs would be required to accompany their own men in the field and Wolseley promised to attach one of his officers to each. There was also an exhortation to avoid 'barbarous practises' such as killing prisoners and mutilating the dead. Each king and chief was then set on his way with the customary present of gin.[13]

Though almost certainly predisposed to his conclusions, Wolseley, who knew his own Control officers were offering carriers 1s. od. a day, found the kings and chiefs 'greasy', 'grasping', 'cowardly' and 'unreliable' [24, 25, 26]. Ultimately, he came to believe that the Fante were not worth fighting for: indeed, they were only fit to be slaves of the Asante [55, 61, 62, 64, 66, 67, 80]. Most other European observers formed a similar view of the Fante. Henty certainly believed that the kings and chiefs felt there was not enough money on offer and that the replacement of the prevailing rumours that the Asante were in retreat by rumours that they were advancing was a ploy to increase pressure on Wolseley to offer more. Equally, Winwood Reade detected a feeling among Wolseley's audience that the Asante would soon leave Fante territory in any case, removing any need for them to act at all. Fremantle thought them simply despondent.[14] At the second palaver, to which the kings and chiefs were summoned to give their formal responses to Wolseley's demands, they did indeed complain that 4½d. a day was not enough for subsistence. Wolseley promised food in lieu of money and again reiterated his intention to send officers to assist each king and chief [27, 32, 35]. The assembled kings and chiefs then promised to bring their fighting men to a rendezvous at Dunkwa in two days' time. Some kings and chiefs had not appeared at either of the palavers and letters were despatched urging them also to appear at Dunkwa.[15]

In addition to the formal palavers, Wolseley had a series of other meetings that were not mentioned in his journal though they were recorded in his official correspondence.[16] These included a meeting with 'ladies of colour' on 13 October, one result of which was to encourage the revival later in the month of the local custom of the women parading through Cape Coast naked and shaming their men to enlist as fighting men or carriers by 'beating' them out of their homes [**48, 64**].[17] Others were with the kings of two Akan states neighbouring on Fante territory, Winneba and Gomoa, on 18 and 19 October respectively, and all the Fante kings and chiefs once more on 21 October. Wolseley also met the 'Captains' of the Cape Coast Volunteers on 10, 13 and 16 October. The latter were local Fante commanded by merchants, nominally with a strength of eight companies. There were considerable doubts as to their effectiveness, and Wolseley soon had them moved to the outposts of Napoleon and Abbaye, considering their current location at Prospect Hill as too close to 'home' to ensure their effectiveness. Ultimately, some were incorporated into a company of the native regiment commanded by Evelyn Wood.[18]

Wolseley did not have enough of his own officers available to send to each of the principal Fante kings and chiefs. Therefore, as well as taking Bromhead and Godwin from Baker Russell's command and Graves from Wood's command, he also pressed into service Brevet Major James Lazenby of the 100th Foot, who had been acting as Brigade Major at Cape Coast prior to Wolseley's arrival, and Sub Lieutenant Clavell Filliter of the 2nd West India Regiment. Wolseley also borrowed a marine officer and three naval officers from Fremantle, these being Lieutenant Parkins Hearle of the Royal Marine Light Infantry, Lieutenant George Pollard of HMS *Simoom*; and Sub Lieutenants Charles Corkran and Conyers Lang of HMS *Barracouta* [**31, 35**]. Lazenby was sent to King Kwasi Edo at Mankessim; Godwin to King Ammono at Anamabu; Bromhead to King Tshibu Dhahon of East Assin at Dominassie; Hearle to King Kwesi Kyei of Denkyira at Dominassie; Filliter to Chief Thomas Salomon of Dominassie; Pollard to King Anfo Oto of Abura at Dunkwa; Lang to King Assano at Yamolanza; Corkran to King Quasi Ancasia at Asebu; and Graves to King Akinny at Accomfie.[19]

Other naval officers having already been landed for special duties, however, Fremantle felt unable to lend yet another officer to Wood as it would not leave him with sufficient cover for commanding potential landing parties.[20] Those sent to the kings and chiefs were to use every effort to persuade them to turn out their fighting men. Captain Thompson was also sent off in HMS *Merlin* to Dixcove to raise the Wassa and encourage them to march a fighting force to Praso, while he was also to communicate with the Ga. When Captain James Nicol, the elderly adjutant of the Hampshire Militia, arrived at Cape Coast as a volunteer on 10 October, he too was sent off recruiting to the Bonny River.[21]

Few of these efforts, however, bore any real result with the native rulers procrastinating and frustrating Wolseley's officers at every turn and the number of tribal levies increasing only slowly [**44**]. Indeed, by the end of October, there were only about 1,400 native levies with the kings and chiefs. Lazenby was the most successful in eventually bringing in about 1,100 men by November but Lang got only 488, Godwin only 421, Bromhead only 276, Filliter only 217, Nicol only 157, Thompson only 63, Graves only 54, and Hearle only 45 while Corkran secured virtually none. Those officers who had been dropped off en route to Cape Coast to raise fighting men for direct recruitment into the intended two native regiments also began to appear with their recruits and, again, numbers were disappointing. Through the efforts of Gordon of the 93rd, first 66 men arrived and then another 120, while Lieutenant Henry Bolton brought in 94, but Furse and Saunders recruited only 100 men between them and O'Connor managed to find only 100 Kru as carriers.[22]

In the end, Wood had about 500 men arranged in four companies, comprising respectively Fante from the Cape Coast Volunteers – 'educated men of colour, and the merchants' clerks and storekeepers' according to Henty – and Elmina, Hausa and Susu though the Hausa, characterised as the sweepings of Lagos, were then replaced by men from the Bonny and Opobo rivers. None could speak the language of the others and Wood utilised a divide and rule system of getting men from one company to carry out the disciplinary punishments to be inflicted on others. Baker Russell's regiment was somewhat larger and consisted of six companies drawn from Hausa, men from Sierra Leone, 'Mumfords' drawn from the coastal town of Mumford, Winneba, Opobo from the Niger Delta, and Anamabu.[23] Wood and Russell's regiments generally were clothed in white smocks though the Winneba refused to wear them. The Susu, who had a particularly bloodthirsty reputation, declined to fight with anything other than swords and so were issued with cutlasses, while the Opobo, whose kingdom the British had recognised as independent of Bonny in 1873, were supposedly cannibals and feared by all the others [86].[24]

Wolseley's artillery officer, Captain Arthur Rait, was given Hausa exclusively for his seven-pounder 'Abyssinian' mountain guns, these being the steel Mark II seven-pounder rifled muzzle-loading guns introduced in 1868 and designed for use with pack-animals. The gun shortly to be used in action at Esamano was carried on a bamboo base by some Kru but, generally, the closeness of the wheels to the guns enabled them to be dragged along narrow paths though it was felt the axle trees got in the way where wheeled traffic was not required.[25]

Wolseley was also contemplating an attempt to recruit the Western Akyem, being conscious that Glover would be raising the Eastern Akyem [26]. As yet Wolseley was unaware that Glover was experiencing his own difficulties in raising men on the Volta, and was anxious to avoid Glover advancing into Asante territory prematurely. In any case, he felt both his and Glover's operations might yet be stayed by the Asante accepting terms [25, 34]. Accordingly, Wolseley issued strict instructions to stay Glover's hand.[26] Glover had intended to recruit an additional 1,000 Hausa around Accra but, in attempting to cut out the role of the local Ga chiefs in recruitment and in the distribution of arms and ammunition to the interior tribes by negotiating directly with the Akyem and Akwapim, Glover found that the native rulers and other slave holders on the coast had put their Hausa slaves into irons to prevent them joining his expedition. His existing Hausa then caused difficulties by trying to free men from the King of Accra's prison and coming into conflict with the inhabitants. Indeed, Glover was compelled to pay £5 for every slave who volunteered for his force in order to restore relations, to which the Colonial Office soon took exception as condoning the buying of slaves. The Ga, however, had little intention of confronting the

Asante, seeing the opportunity to punish instead their old enemies, the Awuna, who were allies of the Asante. Worse, the King of the Eastern Akyem used the money Glover had given him to provide carriers to buy salt instead.[27] Consequently, Glover was exercised by Wolseley's intention to recruit the Western Akyem to whom he himself would have looked for additional men.

As it happened, Wolseley devised a ruse concerning Glover's expedition as cover for his intention to attack the Asante in order to instil some confidence in the Fante, spreading a rumour that Glover was under pressure at Adda and he would go to his assistance [31, 38]. In *The Soldier's Pocket Book* he had suggested just such a means of misleading the press 'and thus use them as a medium by which to deceive the enemy'.[28] The target was Esamano, a short distance north west of Elmina, and the nearby villages of Ankwanda, Eguafo and Ampene from which the Asante were drawing supplies. Wood had been instructed to issue an ultimatum to the local chiefs to desist and appear before him but they had ignored him in the belief that the Europeans would not dare venture into the bush. Indeed, they sent to the Asante army at Mampon for help. As Wood recorded, the King of Ankwanda declined to appear before Wood saying, 'I have smallpox today but will come tomorrow', and fled to Mampon, while the chief of Esamano replied, 'Come and fetch me, white man no dare go bush.'[29]

A force of 138 Hausa arrived at Cape Coast from Lagos on 11 October and Wolseley embarked with them on HMS *Bittern* to run down to Elmina [38, 45], the men being given elementary instruction in the use of the Snider on board by Brackenbury, Charteris and Maurice, a process then continued at Elmina by Woodgate and Richmond.[30] Having let Wood in on the plan, Wolseley returned to Cape Coast to consult with Fremantle, who agreed to provide one landing party for the defence of Cape Coast and another for the expedition itself since all available West Indian troops were to be used. Keeping the secret from all but McNeill and Irvine, Wolseley then embarked his force on HMS *Barracouta* and HMS *Decoy* on 13 October [38, 42, 45]. Difficulties were encountered in getting the men ashore at low tide in a heavy surf early on the following morning but the advance on Esamano got under way at about 0430. Figures given for the strength of Wolseley's force differ but the official despatch gives it as 29 sailors with a seven-pounder gun and a trough for nine-pounder Hale's rockets, 149 marines, 205 West Indians, 126 Hausa, 10 armed Fante police, 30 axe men, and 270 carriers. There was a brief but intense firefight at Esamano, which was burned, and then Wolseley's force moved on to the other villages, which had already been bombarded by the ships and which were also set on fire. The force had covered some 21 miles by the time it was picked up by the ships, water, claret and brandy being landed to revive that part of the force that went on to burn the villages.[31]

In theory, the operation had been under Wood's command but, with little to do, Wolseley's personal staff 'ventured their lives freely' as did Wolseley himself, Wood recording that, while this excited his admiration, it 'caused some uneasiness to those who reflected on the nature of the void their fall might create'. Charteris certainly recorded Wolseley as 'shouting, threatening, encouraging and directing' while he, Buller, Brackenbury and Fremantle were all also to the fore.[32] It was not clear how many Asante or their allies were killed since only a few dead bodies were found at Esamano together with an abandoned child. Wolseley's casualties comprised just one Hausa killed and 16 wounded, three carriers wounded, two seamen and two marines wounded, and three of his officers wounded: in addition, Buller had his compass case smashed by a bullet.[33] Of the officers, Fremantle was slightly wounded in the same volley in which Buller's compass case was hit, but McNeill had his wrist shot through [42, 43]. According to Wolseley's later account, McNeill appeared saying, 'An infernal scoundrel out there has shot me through the arm', with the muscles, tendons and sinews of wrist standing out 'like strands of an unravelled rope's end'.[34] It proved a serious wound, prompting Wolseley to request that Greaves be sent out to take over as Chief of Staff with Wood being designated as Wolseley's own replacement in the event of him becoming incapacitated [45, 50].

Wolseley drew particular pleasure from the demonstration that Europeans could indeed operate successfully in the bush, believing it to have a powerful moral effect on the Asante commanders at Mampon.[35] Indeed, this first success, small as it was, attracted the government's congratulations.[36] Not everything, however, had gone entirely to plan. Marines had been landed without sufficient rations [43], Wolseley's critical report causing Fremantle some difficulties.[37] According to Fremantle when the rockets were fired, some younger marines had also thrown themselves on the ground, Wolseley remarking in a fairly obvious echo of Wellington, 'Well, I can only say if it frightens the enemy half as much as it does our own people it is doing good service.' The seven-pounder had been delayed coming into action when the key to unscrew the plug in the shells could not be located. Water had also generally been in short supply, fresh supplies as well as the fortifying claret being landed from the ships as the force reached Ampene. The greatest problem, however, had been the perceived unreliability of both the West Indians and the Hausa. Though Woodgate felt the Hausa had done reasonably well considering they were under officers they had never seen until two days previously, none spoke English and the only interpreter was soon put out of action, Wolseley and most others felt they had been undisciplined and had fired wildly, the latter a criticism also made of the West Indians. The action also suggested to Wolseley that more officers were needed to control troops in dispersed bush warfare [42, 45].[38]

Wolseley used the performance of the Hausa and West Indians to justify his call for two battalions of European troops but his request to London was actually dated the day before the action at Esamano [35, 41]. His request for a third battalion as a reserve, to be raised from picked volunteers and commanded by Colley, was written on 21 October though dated three days later [46, 47, 49, 50, 53]. As it happened, however, through the vagaries in the steamer service, both requests went back to London together on 27 October.[39]

Of course, it had always been Wolseley's intention to send for regiments from home and, as early as 9 October he warned Kimberley to expect a formal request by the next mail.[40] This crossed with fresh instructions from Kimberley but actually drafted by Gladstone indicating the Cabinet's reluctance to commit

European troops and the need to reserve judgement on any final advance since the main object was to clear the protectorate and the government would be satisfied now with an honourable peace [28]. The instructions derived from the Cabinet discussion on 4 October, to which attention has already been drawn and at which Bright attempted to halt the expedition. Kimberley felt these new instructions 'seemed to satisfy those who hope to get out of the war by doing nothing but which really changed nothing in former despatches'. Indeed, the Cabinet 'swallowed this extremely nauseous pill without many wry faces'.[41] Wolseley's requests for the three battalions only reached London on 17 November but the Cabinet had met on 10 November in anticipation and Cardwell had already authorised the dispatch of stores for 1,500 men. Over-riding Bright's opposition and showing what Kimberley characterised as a 'proper reluctance', the Cabinet agreed within five hours of Wolseley's requests arriving to send three battalions. HMS *Tamar* and HMS *Himalaya* sailed from Plymouth for Queenstown with the intention of setting out for West Africa between 19 and 21 November and arriving by 11 December. Gladstone still hoped for peace and worried that there might not be anyone with whom to negotiate a settlement if the Asante were completely crushed. As a result, there were the further instructions that Wolseley should limit the use of the European troops as much as possible, impose a peace without occupying Kumase unless absolutely necessary, and warn the Fante that they could have no future claim on British protection [78].[42]

Kimberley had originally urged Wolseley to compose his request for troops carefully and, according to Lord Aberdare, the Lord President of the Council, the Cabinet was duly impressed with Wolseley's apparent moderation as he 'judges things most calmly not seeking by brilliant enterprises to earn some brilliant name, but anxious to bring the war to an end as soon as he can'.[43] The Duke of Cambridge was somewhat less impressed by the request for a third battalion and Wolseley's attempt thus to resurrect a special service battalion. However, he had already complied with Wolseley's earlier request for additional special service officers, subsequently sending out a further 20 officers and assuring Wolseley that 'generally the selections have been made with great care and an anxiety to let you have the best men'. The Duke also agreed to allow Colley to go out with the European regiments in order to help organise the transport system.[44]

In his request for white troops, Wolseley had been at pains to downplay the risk that would be run from the climate if they were only committed between December and March, and for no more than six to eight weeks. As Wolseley noted in December 1873 he seemed 'always to be condemned to command in expeditions which must be accomplished before a certain season of the year begins', in this case before the onset of the rains [95, 117]. Of the 110 marines landed in August 1873, only 14 would still be serving in December and, of the first batch that landed in June, two were dead and 87 invalided within six weeks.[45] The 1830 Select Committee had recommended reducing the European presence in garrison and using the West India regiments instead in the 'White Man's Grave'. Indeed, a survey of the army's mortality rates between 1819 and 1836 suggested that the annual death rate in Sierra Leone was 483 per 1,000 of those serving. In fact, European troops had been largely withdrawn in 1819 and their brief redeployment from 1824 to 1826 had again been costly. But the West Indians, too, had succumbed to disease, those committed in 1863–64 suffering 83 dead per 1,000. Malaria, yellow fever and gastrointestinal infection were the main threats, of which malaria and yellow fever were by far the most deadly.[46]

It was only in the early twentieth century that it was widely accepted that malaria and yellow fever were borne by mosquitoes and the suggested precautions varied from 'expert' to 'expert'. 'Seasoning' fever was to be expected and would not generally be severe and 'intermittent' fever could usually be treated with quinine and emetic but 'remittent' fever might well prove fatal. Wolseley himself took quinine and agreed with his principal medical officer, Anthony Home, that the dangers were probably exaggerated [23, 25, 32, 62]. Quinine had become commercially produced in Britain in the 1820s and had become standard issue for the Royal Navy in the tropics in the 1850s. Home, however, who lectured to the special service officers on 6 October, did not believe in the efficacy of quinine. Indeed, he held that damp, cold and miasmas issuing from the earth were the main cause of fever and he recommended a man avoid draughts when hot, but also suggested a good and varied diet. On the voyage out, presumably influenced by Home, Huyshe had recommended wearing flannels day and night, suggesting also 'that cold tea is unanimously allowed to be the best thing to work on'. Healthy exercise, moderation and avoiding unnecessary exposure to the sun were most important. According to Stanley, most of Wolseley's officers resolved while wearing cholera belts, flannel next to the skin, bathing twice a day, exercising moderately and avoiding late dinners and suppers, to 'live generous' by consuming quantities of beer, claret, and wine. Charteris, who also tended to believe the risks exaggerated, certainly believed in the beneficial effects of claret and champagne. When Paul Methuen arrived in December, he found Wolseley's officers drinking quantities of champagne as a means of remaining healthy and a general aversion to taking quinine until the onset of fever in the belief that a daily dose would otherwise negate its subsequent impact: Methuen himself resolved to avoid quinine and not to wear a respirator.[47]

In what Henty regarded as a swindle, insurance companies had compelled Wolseley's officers to pay high additional premiums for annual cover and it was not long before they began to go down with fever. Fitzroy Hart went down on 18 October with 'seasoning' fever and Dooner on the following day. Buller, who got a touch of fever on 25 October and actually fired shots at his Fante bearers in his delirium, reckoned the doctors on HMS *Simoon* taking temperatures were competing with one another: 'I think the chap that scored the highest temperature scored something, perhaps a drink; nothing else could have made them so keen.' Buller was to get fever again on the way back from Kumase and continued to suffer bouts after he got back to England.[48]

Home's estimate was that 30–40 per cent of a picked European force would become ill in six to eight weeks but that actual mortality would not be high. This depended, however, upon proper preparations being made.[49] As it happened, such preparations had already been begun with a comprehensive list of sanitary instructions drawn up during the summer under the direction of Surgeon General Sir William Muir, head of the Sanitary Branch of the Army Medical Department, the latter itself newly organised in 1873. As already related, a hospital ship, the *Victor Emmanuel*, formerly HMS *Repulse*, had been fitted out in September 1873 at a cost of £38,000: it could accommodate 240 patients and was equipped with such special features as forced-air ventilation, steam boilers for disinfecting used linen and cooking utensils, night lighting, patent water closets, an ice machine, and its own surf boats. Sailing from Portsmouth on 30 November, it was to arrive off Cape Coast on 1 January 1874.

Arrangements were also made for the two troops ships and the hired steamer taking out the European troops, HMS *Himalaya*, HMS *Tamar* and the *Sarmatian*, to remain on station at Cape Coast to receive sick and wounded. In addition, HMS *Simoom*, to be supplemented if necessary by the steamer *Manitoban*, was sent off to St Vincent in the Cape Verde Islands to receive those evacuated from Cape Coast when there was some suspicion that infection was spreading among the patients on it at Cape Coast. Patients would be evacuated to Cape Verde in four warships designated to carry despatches but would also be put on steamers passing Cape Coast and, similarly, steamers passing Cape Verde would be expected to transfer patients from there to Liverpool, Southampton or Gibraltar. In order to facilitate this, contracts were made with the Union Steamship Company, the Royal Mail Brazilian Steam Packet Company and the British and African Steam Navigation Company. A liner, the *Ilione*, would also be available as an isolation ship in the event of an outbreak of yellow fever: it would be despatched to a cool climate immediately with its European crew replaced by Kru since it was assumed Africans were immune.

In fact, there was an outbreak of yellow fever in Sierra Leone and on the Bonny river earlier in 1873 and the *Ambriz* was also to have 13 dead on board from it when returning to Cape Coast from Luanda in November 1873, leading to its quarantining and that of other vessels arriving from the Bonny River. In December Maurice reported that the captain, engineer and doctor of another steamer from the Bonny River, the *Benin*, passing Cape Coast, were all dead from yellow fever. Ships' captains tended to try and conceal outbreaks of fever and one vessel, the *Biafra*, was to evade the quarantine with fatal results for two naval officers embarked on her [58, 64, 66, 102]. Smallpox was also prevalent at Cape Coast but all troops were vaccinated and additional smallpox vaccine was sent out. Since it was assumed bad water also spread disease, the precautions on land were to include water condensers, distilling water and the use of both chemical testing and Norton tubular pumps to draw water from deeper down in the soil. In the event, boiling and filtering even with additions such as alum or potassium permanganate simply improved the taste rather than killing bacteria. Indeed, simply avoiding where the Asante army had camped did as much as anything to reduce risk. It was less easy to do much about the fetid conditions of Cape Coast beyond a superficial clean up.

In all, 73 out of the 270 European officers who eventually advanced on Kumase were medical officers with an additional 264 personnel from the Army Hospital Corps. In the event, of 2,587 Europeans who had landed at Cape Coast by May 1874, only 71 died from all causes, with 53 of the dead being from the European battalions: 40 of the deaths were from disease and just 13 from enemy action. Of 1,271 West Indian troops landed, only 35 died with 34 of these being to disease. Of the European deaths from disease, 52.5 per cent resulted from fevers or sunstroke and 37.5 per cent from gastrointestinal infections, while in the case of the West Indians, 50 per cent were gastrointestinal infections and 26.5 per cent from fevers. The overall mortality rates from disease were extraordinarily low at 8.7 per 1,000 per month among the Europeans. However, 1,018 Europeans had been invalided, representing 43 per cent of the white personnel. Thus, although the sickness rates were high, the medical achievement was still considerable.[50]

In fact, it was not just Wolseley's force that was affected by disease for it was increasingly clear that the Asante army at Mampon was suffering from smallpox contracted from the Fante and dysentery, both exacerbated by hunger and fatigue. In the subsequent advance on Kumase, indeed, Asante prisoners were kept isolated from the European troops for fear of 'famine fever'. Indeed, as many as 20,000 Asante may have died from disease in the course of 1873 including Amankwatia's son. Though it is sometimes suggested Akyampon Yaw also died of disease, he actually succumbed on 16 October to wounds received in the naval bombardment of Asante-held townships around Elmina.[51] It was disease, then, rather than the action at Esamano that led to the Asante breaking up their camp, the news of which reached Wolseley on 25 October by way of an escaped female Fante slave.[52] It was important, however, for Wolseley to follow up the Asante retirement for maximum effect and he felt he needed to inflict a defeat on them though he feared that this might mean he would not have anyone to negotiate with, and it might not actually be in the British interest to destroy Asante power entirely [51, 52, 74, 80]. Accordingly, Wolseley issued what Reade called a stage 'screamer' and he himself acknowledged as a bombastic proclamation to the Fante urging them to pursue the Asante though he also intended to show his existing European marines and seamen as prominently as possible [53, 55, 57]. It had, however, no appreciable impact.[53]

It would appear that Amankwatia had wanted to retreat before but Kofi Karikari had declined to allow it, being angered by the appearance of Wolseley, and the former advocacy of an invasion of the protectorate by both Amankwatia and Adu Bufo, whose army also wished to retreat from Wassa territory. Indeed, the King had insisted that the army should not retreat until the chiefs who wanted war had reimbursed its cost. In the event, the King authorised a retreat on 19 October. Storm damage to buildings in Kumase on 26 October, including even some to the King's stone palace, was then felt to be an ill omen. Having initially wanted to retreat, however, Amankwatia apparently now regretted it and, a notorious drunkard, took to the bottle.[54] Amankwatia had also been accused of exceeding his authority by communicating with Wolseley.

What had happened was that Amankwatia had intercepted Wolseley's ultimatum of 13 October to Kofi Karikari to quit Fante territory within 20 days [39, 45 and 46]. Two more copies had been sent on 17 and 18 October, one with the Asante prisoner who was given the (unsuccessful) demonstration of the steam sapper previously mentioned, and another with an escort of two Fante police, who were themselves treated to a review and marching display of the Asante army. The drafting of the original had itself been delayed, as, according to Maurice, 'no proper written representation of the Fantee or Ashantee dialect existed'. Rather similarly, Buller had found it difficult to interpret intelligence reports when the language seemed to have no written characters and 'as many patois as there are inhabitants'. Conceivably, Amankwatia had detained the messages as it was the Asante custom that the messenger must travel to the King only on the 'high road' to Kumase and Wolseley now had outposts on it at Dunkwa and Manso. In any event, Amankwatia chose to reply to Wolseley, claiming that the purpose of the invasion had been to punish the Assin, Denkyira, Akyem and Wassa and that he had no quarrel with the British. In the end, Wolseley's ultimatum only reached Kumase on 1 November, by which time the period specified had already elapsed and no reply was sent until 25 November.[55]

Amankwatia prepared to strike at Wolseley's outposts as a means of freeing the main route back to Kumase: it should be noted that, though the 'great roads' linking Kumase to the coast and to trading centres to the north were generally kept clear of trees, roots and other vegetation, they were still no more than narrow paths cut through the bush and forest.[56] Meanwhile, Wolseley ordered Wood to advance from Elmina on 25 October while he moved forward himself towards Asebu intending to go on to Dunkwa. Accordingly, the Fante levies and a large number of women carriers were assembled with what Butler described as considerable noise and 'general buffoonery', only for them to show marked reluctance to close with the Asante once on the march. Mampon was found to be deserted and Festing was then ordered to undertake a further reconnaissance from Dunkwa towards Assanchi on 27 October with 100 West Indians and 1,400 mostly Abura, Assin and Anamabu levies. Near Iscabio he ran unexpectedly into an Asante force moving on Abrakampa, where Baker Russell had a garrison of 890 men, but including only 60 marines and seamen and 100 Hausa. Wolseley, who had again chosen to keep his plans secret from the correspondents and had switched his objective from Dunkwa to Abrakampa, had intended to link up with Festing at Assanchi. But, with no sign of Festing, he pulled back to Abrakampa. Festing, who had fought off the Asante with the assistance of his two seven-pounder guns and a rocket trough, was wounded as were four other officers, Godwin of the 103rd Foot suffering a very serious wound to the groin [**54, 55**].[57] The performance of the Fante had again frustrated Wolseley [**54, 55, 58, 62**]. Indeed he was to complain to Kimberley in an official despatch that he was left in a 'somewhat humiliating' position in not being able to attack an enemy within reach of his outposts.[58]

23

Wolseley Journal, 1–5 October

Wednesday 1 October

A fine clear warm day, the water smooth. I forgot to mention that at my request Brackenbury gave an admirable lecture on Monday upon the causes of this war and upon the history of our dealings with the Ashantis and the protected tribes, bringing down the subject to the beginning of the war we had at Cape Ct Castle in 1863–64 that very nearly resulted in turning out the Government then in office. Yesterday, Huyshe gave a lecture upon the topography of the "theatre" of war, that is to be and the manners & customs of the inhabitants. To day Brackenbury finished his subject by another lecture giving all particulars of the events that have taken place up to date of last intelligence from the Gold Coast. I thought that these lectures would be very interesting to everyone and most useful to all who are taking part in this expedition. I shall have them printed for private circulation amongst the officers when I land.[1] At noon to day we were only 169 miles from Cape Ct Castle, so we hope to reach Elmina tomorrow morning at daybreak and there to land Col. Wood and his officers[2] & then go on to our final destination: I have begun to dose myself already with quinine hoping it may prove to be a prophylactic against fever, but upon going ashore I shall put myself at once in Homes hands, & will do as he says, for I am determined to give myself every possible chance that science can dictate to keep my health, and with Gods help I hope to escape all illness of every sort during my stay ashore.

Thursday 2 October
Reached Cape Coast Castle & anchored about 6 a.m. We did not go to Elmina as the Captain thought that by arriving so early at the former place he would be able to get off again this same evening. Capt. Freemantle came on board about 7 a.m.: he is the Senior Naval Officer here now – no news. His ship saluted me at 8 a.m. I am to leave this ship, the Ambriz at 4.30 p.m. & to land in state. More by next steamer.

2 October continued
Left the S.S. Ambriz at 4.30 p.m. Landed easily under the Castle walls where I was received by a Guard of honor and a salute fired from the Castle. There was a considerable number of people gathered together to see the fun: the streets were lined to Government House where I was met at the bottom of the steps by Col. Harley. He is a pompous Paddy given to fine speeches, that have much more sound than meaning. If I had been in his position, I should have met my successor on the beach with a hearty welcome. I was then sworn in before a large crowd of officers and the European and half-cast merchants. Govt House is a fair building but stands in the centre of the native town; it has a small garden and a good water tank in it. A very fine day, no news.

Friday 3 October
Walked with McNeil to Connors Hill from whence there is a good view. It is used as a Sanitorium and on it the Governors House ought certainly to stand. It is now occupied by a few huts used as a Sanitarium with a Detachment of the 2nd W. I. Regt. The sanitory condition of the town is horrible and the heaps of filth and the stench at some points is in my opinion calculated to breed a pestilence. Read official papers all the morning. Went by appointment to see Harley with McNeil. Spent the day with him going over all sorts of matters. His information is very meagre and is imparted in such a very pompous manner that it is slow work transacting business with

him. He accuses the Military of having done nothing. Paid Home a visit who is living in the very room in which poor L. E. L. was found dead with a bottle of poison in the hand.[3] I find that it is a mistake to imagine that she was poisoned: the true and very sad story I believe to be as follows. She was a woman of strong passions and poetical & romantic ideas. When very young she was seduced by a man called, as well as I can remember Jordan or Jurdan, who was the Editor of some Magazine.[4] She afterwards had other affairs and I believe was too intimate with Lord Bulwer Lytton or whatever his title was – I mean the man who wrote novels. By him & Lady Bulwer Lytton[5] the match was made up very quickly between L. E. L. & Mr Maclean who had just been appointed Governor of the Gold Coast: she had always expressed a great desire to see Africa & gladly accepted Maclean. They lived very unhappily together and the morning of her death, a letter just received from a former lover was opened by the husband: in it were expressions that satisfied him that his wife had not led a virtuous life prior to marriage. To cover up her shame & remorse she is supposed to have put an end to herself – a sad ending for a woman of her abilities. Home dined with me.

Saturday 4 October

A very fine day. I met all the assembled Kings and Chiefs under a couple of marquees placed side by side in front of the house. I harangued them telling them that the Queen would only help those who helped themselves and asked them what they were prepared to do towards promoting this war which I impressed upon them was not H.M. war but their own. I am afraid that my offer of money was not considered sufficient they are such a set of lowminded beggarmen. I gave them until 3 p.m. on Monday to consider what I had said & to give me an answer. Harley paid me a visit after it was over & we walked with him to see the Distillery apparatus put up at the salt pond. I had written to him in the morning saying that as I had obtained from him on the previous day all the information he had to impart that I hoped he would go home whenever it suited his convenience to do so. I wrote to him in the *blandest* of terms thanking him for all his kindness. Festing dined with me. He is very like Mr Donald Smith, the Gov of the Hudson Bay Compy.[6]

Sunday 5 October
McNeil & I walked about 2 or 3 miles along the Dunquah road – it is in very good order but I hear that at some places the gradients are so steep that I shall not be able to use the traction Engines on them. If this turns out to be the case it will be a great blow to me. Upon our return to Govt House I found that the mail had arrived & would leave again for England in a couple of hours. Harley goes home in her. Harley came here after breakfast to say good bye and I walked with him to the beach where I had ordered a guard of honor to do him all honor. He embarked under a salute of guns from the Castle & when his ship weighed anchor for England, the Fleet saluted him also, so he cannot say I failed in any way to do all I could to show him every respect, for he was not really entitled to any of this attention. Went to Church at 11 a.m.: Mr Maxwell the Colonial Chaplain officiated: he is a black man from Sierra Leone. A lovely day: walked in the evening to see Russels party who are established in a nice airy house on a hill to the north of the town. Festing, Freemantle & McNeil went with me. I selected a site where I intend placing a defensible post and a small Battery in case the King of Ashante really does mean to pay us a hostile visit. Fremantle dined with me. Glover is unwell. I sent off a letter to him explaining my views to him.
TNA, WO 147/3

24

Wolseley to Louisa Wolseley

5 October
[Holograph]
Cape Coast Castle
I have only a moment to write as the mail steamer is just in and will leave in about 1½ hours. My former letter will go by this same vessel. I have not had time since I landed even to keep my journal, but I hope on tuesday to have some breathing time & do something

for myself. The climate here for a man worked as I am is capital: I have no time to be ill. I take a walk for health sake every morning & evening. I am up with the earliest lark & to bed very early. I have a nasty job before me that looks uglier the more I look at it. The papers will tell you all about my meeting with the Kings yesterday: a greasy lot – some of them fine men. Baker Russell is still idle as I have not yet got him any men, so he has plenty of time for writing, so do not compare my letters with those he sends his wife. Love to the elders. I am looking forward anxiously to the next mail. Goodbye: God bless you, ever my dearest Loo.

Hove, Wolseley MSS, W/P 3/7

25

Wolseley to Cambridge

5 October
[Holograph]
Cape Coast. Government House

I arrived here on the 2d. inst. all those with me being well and in high spirits. As Your Royal Highness may imagine I have not had much time for writing since I landed and merely begin this now as the mail steamer has just arrived and will start again in about a couple of hours.

Having had long conversations with Colonel Harley, and heard all he had to say, and learnt all the information he had to convey, I have told him that he may go home whenever it may suit his own private convenience to do so: he talked yesterday evening of starting to day if the steamer arrived, but as I have not yet seen him this morning, I do not know whether he intends going by to days mail or waiting for the next which is also due. The arrival of the steamers from England is very fairly punctual, but the dates when those bound for England reach this place, are very uncertain.

A few of the Kings and chiefs were here awaiting my arrival, so I thought it best to see them at once, which I did yesterday. I had previously consulted with Colonel Harley and others who ought to know the native character, as to what I should say to them, and the terms I should offer. I shall not attempt to give Your

Royal Highness in this hurried note an account of what I said, as I was surrounded by reporters who will give what I said, I have no doubt, word for word in their newspaper letters. I made great use of Her Majestys name throughout as if my instructions had come to me direct from Her, as in dealing with people like them, the Queens name has great weight, and they do not understand or appreciate the messages from Ministers.

I endeavored to impress upon them that this war was theirs and not Her Majestys war, and that She could only help those who helped themselves. I am to see them again tomorrow to hear their answer. They are difficult people to deal with and those at this place being somewhat more civilized than the Chiefs in the rural Districts, have much weight with the others for that reason: they are a very grasping set, and may induce the well disposed Kings of the distant provinces to hold out for more money. The Commissariat are giving their carriers here 1s/ a day, and it is just possible that the Kings may say that their men will not accept my offer when they can get a shilling here as carriers. My answer will be – yes, but then those carriers are regularly enlisted, and have nothing to do with you the Kings or chiefs – They are my servants, and I shall be prepared to enlist as fighting men for six months, some thousands of your best warriors if you will give them over to me entirely, to be commanded by English officers: this I know to be what they dread most, as it would take all power and authority out of their hands, destroying their prestige for ever with their own people. This question of obtaining men will be my great difficulty, for their argument is that the war is an English war, having been brought about by the cession of Elmina and that consequently, it is our duty to fight the Ashantees.

The road is now, through the untiring energy of Lieut. Gordon 98th Regt.,[7] made as far as Yancoomassee, about 26 or 27 miles from here. It is practicable for Artillery. I have a post at Accroful about 15 or 16 miles from this on that road, consisting of 50 men of the 2nd W.I. Regt. and some Fantee police. I am having a large clearance made at Dunquah (22 miles on same road from this) where I shall construct a fortified post and will then push on the men I now have at Accroful to it. My next stage from thence will be Mansue, and when I get there I shall have within a protected radius so much ground that I shall be able to look about me and see what I can do towards clearing the Ashantees out of Mampon where their main camp has been for a long time.

I am sure that Your Royal Highness will be horrified to learn that upon enquiry of how our supplies of provisions and arms stood here, I find that we had yesterday only provisions for the Regular Troops on the Coast for *four days*!! That the only arms are 19 Sneiders in the Imperial, and 400 Enfields in the Colonial store.[8] There are also a few Dutch Sneiders but there is no ammunition for them. I did not expect to find any large body of troops raised here, but I *did* expect to find our magazines brim full of arms and provisions. This cripples my actions very much, for now I shall not be able to do anything until the Arms I demanded before leaving England arrive, and Your Royal Highness is aware, that the ships hired by Government for conveying stores are not usually quick sailers.

I have sent Lt. Colonel Wood to Elmina with some officers to see what can be done there towards raising troops. I have sent Captain Furze 42d. Highlanders & Lieut. Saunders R.A. to the Gambia on a similar mission. I left Lieut Gordon 93rd Highlanders at Sierra Leone to raise men there, and I have sent Lieut. Bolton 1st W.I. Regt[9] to Accra and Winnebah to do likewise. If I can obtain even 2000 men from places at a distance from Cape Coast Castle, I shall be to that extent independant of the people here, who seeing that I can obtain men without their aid, will perhaps feel then more disposed to come forward.

Captain Glover is getting on as well, but I fear that his original project of operating from the Upper Volta cannot be carried out, and that he will have to move through the Protectorate. I am most anxious that he should not do anything rash, as I hear privately that he talks of pushing on almost immediately to Coomassie. Now any check experienced by his Force would be most prejudicial to the common object that we both have in hand, and as in accordance with my instructions I have to communicate with the King of Ashante before I undertake any serious operation I have written to Glover telling him this and forbidding him to undertake any extensive operations until he hears from me.[10]

Dr Home the *P.M.O.* here tells me that he has sent home to his own Department a full report upon the possibility of using Europeans for an expedition into the Country, only landing them when every arrangement had been made for them and never halting anywhere for any length of time until they returned and reembarked for England. He tells me that he has gone deeply into the question, & that he sees no risk whatever in undertaking it. He like most, I might say everyone of those here who have deeply considered the matter is of opinion that this war can never be finally settled without English soldiers. He says that as he is the official upon whom the responsibility of giving an opinion upon this question must rest, he cheerfully accepts that responsibility and stakes his reputation upon the truth of his views. As Your Royal Highness is aware, he is about the ablest man we have in the Medical Department after Sir Wm. Muir:[11] he has had great, and very varied experience all over the world, so his opinions will I trust carry with them the weight they are entitled to, and will serve I hope to relieve the public mind of the dread and superstitious horror entertained regarding the West Coast of Africa as a theatre for military operations. I have been in India, Burmah and China, and have never experienced in any of them more charming weather than yesterday. The filth and dirt of this place is dreadful, and that Europeans should be able to live here at all astonishes [me] more than that any should die.

All the officers who came out with me are in good health – I have found it necessary to ask Mr Cardwell for twelve additional officers which I hope will meet with Your Royal Highnesses sanction and approval. Without officers I cannot expect to do anything here. The post is closing, so I have to crave your Royal Highnesses' indulgence for this hurried and very informal note, and have the honor to be Your Royal Highness'es obedient and very faithful servant.

Cambridge MSS, RA VIC/ADD E/1/7201

26

Wolseley to Commander John Glover

5 October
[Holograph]
Cape Coast

I am very sorry to learn from Captain Freemantle that you have been unwell and I trust that when this reaches you, your health may be again everything that you could wish it to be. I am sending down for the Fantee police now at Accra for I find myself so weak here, that if the rumor reported in your letter about the King of Ashante having taken the great oath to attack this place be true I have really only the fleet to depend upon. The 2nd W. I. Regt is detached all over the place, so that I practically have no one to fight. I saw some of the local Kings and Chiefs here yesterday, but they are a poor lot who want only to get money: tomorrow morning I am sending off to the Kings of Western Akim to assemble on the Prahsu, Cape Coast Castle line. I should of course have liked to have had the Kings and Chiefs also of Eastern Akim, but as you have already entered into communications with them I shall do nothing with them hoping they may join you cordially and well. Please tell Captain Sartorius[12] to confine his negotiations to Eastern Akim, as I want to cross a force eventually from the Akim country at Swaidroo into Ashantee territory, should Coffee Calculi not comply with the demands I am ordered to make upon him which I see no likelihood of his doing. However the delay thus entailed upon us allows of better preparations being made by us both. What I want to effect is that you should cross the Prah at the points you indicate, when I do the same at Prahsu and Swaidroo. I find that all the maps are wrong as regards the position of Coomassie which is really in the meridian of longitude of Anamaboe, and not as shown in maps to the westward of Cape Coast Castle: I also find that Prahsue is at least eighty if not ninety miles from Coomassie. So that where the Swaidroo road (Swaidroo is on the Berim River) crosses the Prah is nearer the Ashanti Capital than Prahsue, and that your points of crossing are still nearer. I cannot get any men here, and am trying now what I can do along the Coast, and in

Western Akim. I find that this place is destitute of arms and provisions so I have nothing but money to give these Chiefs here, who are besides a cowardly and unreliable lot of land sharks. I have sent on home your demands received to day, although I did not understand what it was you required when you ask for Blasting a road for 60 miles.[13]

When you mention the right bank of a river do you do so with the Naval or the Military meaning attached to the term?

I shall have an answer to my palaver with the Kings tomorrow and will let you know should I be able to come to terms with them. Would you kindly let me know by the ship that takes this letter what terms you have agreed upon with the various Kings and Chiefs that have acceded to your requests. I have been so busy for the last three days that I have not had time to write at all [:] by and bye however I hope to keep you acquainted with all my doings, as I beg and trust you will do with me as regards your doings & intentions, for I look upon unanimity in action as essential for the success of both of us, and when once on the Prah all our onward progress should be always in concert. Hoping that I may have the pleasure of shaking you by the hand either in or near to Coomassie.

CUL, Glover MSS, RCMS 131/6

27

Wolseley Journal, 6 October

Monday 6 October

Walked with McNeil to pay the Chief Justice, Mr Marshall, a visit.[14] Did not see him as he was still in bed. Walked up to the lighthouse from whence I had a capital view of the surrounding country – & chose my line of defence in case of attack. Had a second meeting with the assembled Kings & chiefs here who came to give me an answer to the proposition I made them on Saturday – practically they have accepted my offer and I have promised to each King to send with him an English Officer to assist in collecting his people and then in marching them to Dunquah where I intend forming a large camp and to push on from there as soon as I can to the Prah. Walked in the evening with McNeil to the Castle & so along the Morree Road to a point I have selected for defence in case of attack. The roar of the surf as we walked along the beach was very grand. The natives in their persons seem clean as they are always washing themselves and some of them even at this late hour in the evening were disporting themselves in the Surf. There are no sharks here, so the natives swim about and seem as much at home in the sea as they are on land. I feel worn out every night and can barely crawl to bed at 9 p.m., where I sleep like a top – I have no rest for a moment for body or mind from 6 a.m. until I get to bed.

TNA, WO 147/3

28

Kimberley to Wolseley

6 October
[Printed]
Downing Street

The preparations which had been made by the Military and Naval Departments to place you in full possession of all the means necessary for success in your important mission, have given rise to very numerous conjectures and speculations as to the intentions entertained by Her Majesty's Government.

It is not necessary for me to warn you against being misled by expressions which will not fail to reach you, of these unauthorised anticipations, and to insist again upon the cautions which have been conveyed to you in former despatches. Her Majesty's Government are confident that you will avoid engaging in any desultory operations which can lead to no serious result if successful, and may give an opportunity to the Ashantis of inflicting losses which, though not in themselves considerable, are magnified into serious disasters to the British arms. At the same time they desire to impress upon you that they would be most reluctant to sanction any expedition which would require that European troops should be sent from this country to the Gold Coast. Previous instructions have given you authority as to the immediate use of the forces now under your command with a view to a speedy peace, or to striking an effective blow at the Ashantis.

A satisfactory state of things will be attained if you can procure an honourable peace, or can inflict, in default of such peace, an effectual chastisement on the Ashanti force. Unless, and until one of these objects shall have been gained, you will understand that the primary purpose of military operations will be to drive the enemy from that district of country, their presence within which endangers, or seriously menaces, the security of the British settlements upon the Coast.

To procure their withdrawal from the large and ill-defined territory which may be included within the loose designation of the Protectorate, is an object which, however desirable, is distinct from the former one. The pursuit of it by military means must depend upon a variety of considerations, among which a main one is the union and force of the tribes who inhabit that country. This question should be reserved for the determination of Her Majesty's Government.

Her Majesty's Government desire that the views I have thus stated should be present to your mind in framing any recommendation which you may find it necessary to submit to them.

But this will, of course, not preclude you from reporting your opinion in favour of any course of action which, with the knowledge you will have acquired on the spot, you may conceive that the circumstances demand.

TNA, CO 879/6

29

Wolseley Journal, 7 October

Tuesday 7 October

Took a long walk with McNeil through the bush where it was very hot and as we lost our way several times it was hard work pushing our way through the bush where there was no path. We passed a number of graves in various places which we afterwards ascertained were those of people who had died of smallpox. I am very much bored every day by Freemantle the Senior Naval Officer who comes off from his ship and pays me unconscionably long visits at about 4 p.m. He never seems to think that I am hard worked & that his presence in my room prevent me from getting through my work: he also forgets that I want to have a walk for health sake about 5 p.m. He is a very good fellow so much so that I trust no one senior to him may be sent here whilst these operations are being carried on. Walked down to the Castle in the evening.

TNA, WO 147/3

30

Wolseley to Cardwell

7 October
[Printed]
Government House, Cape Coast
I have the honour to inform you that from the reports which I have received as to the features of the country surrounding this station, I am of opinion that no railway, except one on Mr Fell's principle,[15] would be capable of being laid and worked within the time at my disposal.

The country which had been represented as being flat, is, so far as I have explored it, covered with rounded hills (mamelons) and intermediate deep ravines, so that the conditions as regards the laying down a railway are very different from those which I was led to expect.

TNA, WO33/26; WO147/27

31

Wolseley Journal, 8 October

Wednesday 8 October
A man was hanged this morning for a cruel murder. The whole population seemed to think it great fun. I was sitting near a window writing about the time when I knew the execution was to come off, and I suddenly heard a howl of delight in the adjoining street, men and women clapping their hands, and staring towards the lighthouse where the gallows had been erected. I looked out towards the lighthouse & found that the howl of pleasure was because the poor wretch had just been sent to eternity and these

cruel savages were enjoying the spectacle as one affording them intense pleasure.[16] I walked in the evening to Connors Hill where the 2nd W. I. Regt moved into Camp yesterday. It is a fine airy healthy spot and is where Governors House ought to be. I have to day sent off about 7 officers to assist the Native Kings in their work of assembling their fighting men. If I can obtain 5000 men from this I shall consider myself fortunate. I intend before many days are over having a brush with the enemy and am now making all my arrangements in secret with that object in view. I am like the Irish gentleman at the fair "spoiling for a fight" as I require a success to re-impose confidence which I find has fallen here to the lowest ebb.

TNA, WO 147/3

32

Wolseley to Louisa Wolseley

[6–]8 October
[Holograph]
Government House
Cape Castle

My hurried note to you of yesterday was written under such pressure as regards time that I intend now supplementing it by a longer one as there is another mail expected here to day for England. I am looking forward most anxiously to the arrival from home of the next mail, as it will bring your first letters to me and thus on I shall be in weekly communication with you. My child I am worried from morning to night. I have to see everyone & think over everything both civil & military here so that except when asleep I know no rest: I bend all my thoughts and energy upon the task before me, and I do not yet see my way to accomplish what I desire. Need I say that notwithstanding all I have to do and think of, that my thoughts turn constantly to you. I picture to myself what you are doing; what are you doing now at 3 p.m.? I often wonder as I pray for you every morning & every evening if you too are at the same exact moment praying for me. Tell me when you write that you do not forget me in your prayers: I always beg of God to bless you and by means of His Holy Spirit to turn your thoughts more and more to him every day that you live, and that you may learn to love Him & to serve Him more and more, and thank Him for all the blessings you enjoy. Do you mind my telling this? Or do you think my preaching out of place? I am to see these wretched Kings and Chiefs again in half an hours time & to receive their answer to my proposition. I shall enclose in this a copy of my letter to the King of Ashantee it is for Holmes perusal.[17] *No* one else is to see it or know that I have sent it. I hope you & he will approve of it. Please tell the Bushby family[18] that I have handed over the parcel for Commerell to the Senior Naval Officer here who will forward it to him by the first opportunity. I sent home the Madeira Lace & the Babas[19] frock etc by Colonel Harley to be left at St Georges Place for you. I hope you will like it. I think the lace was 1/3d a yard for the narrow & 2/ or 2/6d. a yard the broad the frock was £1.17.0d & I forget the price of the embroidery. Let me know if you think this cheap for I then can get you more on my way home.

I have seen the Kings and they seem well pleased, but they say they have no power over their men. I shall not get much out of them until I have had a success somewhere over the enemy. I shall write home for the European Troops almost immediately for I have seen enough to show me that I can do nothing without them.

My mode of life here is as follows. The Gun fires at 5 a.m. when it is quite dark. At 5.30 a.m. I have a biscuit, a cup of chocolate and a quinine pill: dress & am out walking with McNeil at 6 a.m. Walk for an hour or 1½ hours: return very hot take off my things which are then saturated with water from my body, & when I am cool I bathe: breakfast at 8.30 – have something light to eat at 2 p.m. & dine at 7 p.m. & crawl worn out to bed at 9 if no one is here & never later than 10 p.m. I have not felt so well for a long time as I do now, and please God I hope to keep my health all through. Col. Festing who is a careful man and who came out with the marines before the worst of the season was over & has been here all through it, has never been ill for a day. The Chief Justice – a one armed man named Marshall – has been here for 3 months & never a day ill. All those I brought out are still as well and jolly as they were at home.

8th October. The second steamer has not yet arrived. I fear she has been either lost or is brokendown, so this may not go home yet for a couple of days. We had a man hanged here this morning. He was hanged from the lighthouse tower on Fort William so all [the] world could see the execution & all the town was on the green were as seemed as well pleased as if a balloon had been sent up for their amusement. The man had murdered a poor slave girl in the bush for something trifling she had about her, so I do not pity him, but as usual the execution was a bungle as the bolts could not be drawn and the poor devil was consequently kept waiting for some minutes standing on the drop. A pleasant breeze blows here at all times, so that one is never stifled with heat. I expect the mail from England tomorrow. Where are you located? I am so glad to learn from Russell that Casey his servant is to be with you & your Pal whilst we are away. I enclose a cheque for £50 on Cox: you must get it cashed at a Bankers as it is crossed. I know that you will always be comparing the length of my letters with those of Baker Russell, and you must be aware that I never can hope to compete with him. At present he has nothing to do, and although by and by he will have work to do still he will.

10 p.m. 8th Sept [sic]

Steamer for England just arrived. As will leave at daybreak so I must finish this: God bless you my own dear child and ever believe me to be your attached husband.

Hove, Wolseley MSS, W/P 3/8

33

Wolseley to Frances Wolseley

[7–]8 October
[Holograph]
Cape Coast Castle
Government House

I landed here on the 2nd instant with all the guards of honor & firing of cannon to which my *exalted* rank now entitles me. The streets were lined with troops up to the Government House & here I am now duly installed trying to do what I can towards carrying out the objects of my mission. If you will read the Times, the Standard & the Daily News you will see long reports of my doings for I am surrounded by newspaper correspondents who will of course keep the world well acquainted with all that goes on here. I am sure my dearest mother that you will be glad to hear that I am enjoying the very best health; indeed I am better & feel stronger than I have done for some time, for office work in London never agreed with me. Here I am worked like a galley slave: I never have a moment to myself even when writing a note such as this I am interrupted over and over again before I can get through it, having to decide all sorts of matters both civil and military. I have to day to sign a death warrant for hanging a man tomorrow amongst my other pleasing functions.

8th October 10 p.m.
The steamer for England has just arrived [;] she will leave again at daybreak in the morning so I must close this. Please give my best love to all my brothers & sisters. My dearest mother I have all my life long prayed in my prayers for you and prayed that God might grant you long life in this world and that as a family we might all meet in heaven. I hope you all pray for me constantly and for my success in this enterprise, for it is of a nature that I can only hope for success through the goodness of God and I have the strongest faith in the efficacy of prayer. So I beg of you to pray for me. Goodbye my dearest and best of mothers and always believe in the affections of your eldest son.
PS Please give my best and fondest love to dear Aunt Wolseley and ask her to write to me.[20]
Duke, Wolseley MSS, XVIII-H

34

Wolseley to Glover

8 October
[Holograph]
Cape Coast
I am very much distressed at having detained the Gertrude so long; had I known that the Captain would not have been able to

have found the 300 arms at once, I should have sent her on and asked you to send me back that number. However she is now off and will be with you tonight. I have sent off your letter about Addah to the Senior Naval Officer to see what can be done about complying with your request and if it can be done you shall have a man of war for the service you consider necessary. I am sending Major Stevens[21] from here to relieve Mr Goldsworthy at Accra in accordance with the wish you expressed in a recent note to Colonel Harley.[22] This will I hope help you: Major Stevens was the only man I had available for the place, for of course none of those I have brought here would consent to take up a civil appointment and remain there whilst operations were being carried on in the front. I am afraid that I cannot make much of these Kings and Chiefs here. They want money and have little or no authority over their people. As soon as they can collect their men I hope to establish a camp at Dunquah about 21 miles by road N.E. from this on the road to Mansue. I shall then try and follow your example in clearing out the coast line to windward of Elmina of any Ashantis there may be there, for I know that the monster Adjiempon is in the neighborhood of King Blays town,[23] and that that worthy and loyal man has been hard pressed to hold his own against the Ashantis and the Coast people who are in arms in their favor.

I am also very anxious to obtain some little success at a cheap cost so as to give life to these weak hearted Fantees, who are thoroughly cowed and with whom I do not expect to do much.

Since beginning this letter, I have seen Lieut. Bolton who has shown me some correspondence he had with you with reference to his mission to Accra to obtain a few artificers. I told him on no account to interfere in any way with your arrangements, & he has assured me that he had your consent to his enlisting 22 artificers upon the same terms that you were giving yours. As regards the terms that I – after due consultation with Colonel Harley – have found it necessary to offer the Fantees Kings. What I have done is as follows I have promised each King £10 a month for every *1,000 fighting* men that he will furnish, the men to be accepted as able bodied men by myself. To each fighting man I have promised pay at the rate of 3d a day, as I understand from the conversation I had with you in presence of Lord Kimberley that such was the amount you intended giving to those whom you hoped to raise. I have also promised them a simple ration of 1 pint of rice & ¼ lb. of salt meat or until I can give them this ration 4½d a day in lieu thereof. I give them no clothes or blankets & their rations & the ammunition that I shall give them are to be carried by their own carriers without any payment whatever from me from Cape Coast Castle to their troops wherever they may happen to be. At the outside I do not expect to obtain more than 5,000 men in this way. I am endeavoring to raise at various points along the Coast between the Gambia and Winnebah an enlisted force of 2,800 (two thousand eight hundred) men upon the Houssa principle, officering them with English Officers as far as I can do so. These men are to be regularly enlisted men for six months & if I succeed in obtaining them (at present I do not ever see any prospect of obtaining half that number) I shall give to each a blanket, a march frock, arms & accoutrements (when those articles arrive from England) and pay them at the rates given to recruits raised for the W.I. Regts. The 2nd W. I. Regt is now recruiting along the coast and I had to give the same terms as they [the] men obtained for it were given, except of course that I cannot promise them the gaudy uniform worn by those Corps. I have sent a mission to the King of Wassaw, and with him I have dealt as I presume you will have to do with the many independant Kings on the Volta who are removed from the demoralizing influences of civilization: that is I have promised him £100 for every thousand *fighting* men that he brings into the field, one half to be paid to him when he takes the field and begins operations, the other half when the war is over.

Such is briefly the substance of my promises to the native potentates, winding up upon all occasions, that if they loyally cooperated with me, I would guarantee to them that I could inflict such a blow upon the Ashanti power that, for all time to come peace might be secured. I have carefully refrained from mentioning any intention of going to Coomassie, but said that if necessary I would pursue the Ashantis into their own territory. This I consider this an essential point, for as in accordance with the instructions I have received from Lord Kimberley with reference to the peace that I am eventually to make with the King of Ashanti, our operations, both yours and mine, may at any moment be stayed, by his accepting the terms I am authorized and desired to offer him.

Should it become necessary for us to make an advance hereafter upon Coomassie I sincerely trust that our operations may be so well timed and made so thoroughly in concert, that we may both arrive before that place at the same time. This I consider to be essential in the public interests and for the purpose of securing a happy issue to our undertaking and for properly giving effect to the policy of our Government.

I am deeply distressed to find by the last sentence of your note that you are again suffering from fever, but I trust that you may have shaken it off completely before you require to move. I shall keep you constantly informed of what I am doing & I am sure you will do the same with me as regards all your operations & intended movements.

CUL, Glover MSS, RCMS 131/6

35

Wolseley to Cambridge

9 October
[Holograph]
Cape Coast

Since writing to your Royal Highness on the 5th instant I have again had an interview with the Kings and Chiefs here, and the result has been more satisfactory than I had anticipated. They asked for more money on the score of the high price now charged everywhere for provisions, but this demand I countered by saying that if they did not approve of the rate I had proposed for subsistence – viz 4½ a day per fighting man, I would be prepared to issue rations in kind. This stopped them, for they like money better than supplies. Nearly all the Kings have now started for their towns where they hope to collect their men. They impressed upon me their want of power over their people and implored me to assist them in their efforts to get their fighting men together. I have therefore sent with each King, one

English officer, an Interpreter and two native police with this object in view, and I expect good results from this arrangement. I am woefully short of officers but through the kindness of Captain Fremantle the Senior Naval Officer who as a temporary measure has lent me three naval officers and four marine officers I am able to tide over my present difficulties: I must however look forward a few weeks, when I am sure to have some of those I brought out with me, incapacitated from fever: when my numbers are thus reduced, I shall be at my wits ends to do, or rather to carry on the work & the arrangements already begun. The expense of sending out subaltern officers is small, and the guinea a day allowed to them from the date of their joining this command is money well expended. I know that England teems with active young officers at present, longing for active work in the field. The more of them that your Royal Highness can send to me, the better able I shall be to bring this business to an end. The staff I have with me I can assure your Royal Highness is worked at a high pressure: I never saw men work harder or more willingly. The amount of clerical work got through daily is immense, as all officers going on Special Missions to Native Kings, require to have written instructions. Everything has to be created, for I found *nothing* in working order when I arrived. The sanitary condition of this place was deplorable – no one seemed to do more than write minutes deploring the sad state of filth the town was in, but no one moved actively to try and abate the nuisance. I am having all refuse heaps buried, and as the clearances of bush or of grass round the town progress, I have the stuff so cut down burned in heaps.

My official letters to Lord Kimberley and to Mr Cardwell will afford Your Royal Highness full information upon most of the points of interest, so I shall not go over here the same ground. I found upon arrival that Colonel Harley had quite misinterpreted the meaning of Lord Kimberleys instructions on the subject of withdrawing all the Houssas from Cape Coast and the numerous Forts and Detachments in its vicinity. Colonel Festing urged upon Colonel Harley the necessity for retaining even 100 Houssas, but Col. Harley felt bound by the tenor of Lord Kimberleys letter to send every man. The consequence is, that at present, there are so many small Detachments of the 2nd W.I. Regt. at various posts along the Coast, that I could not turn out here with 100 effective bayonets from that Regt. These detachments were made previous to my arrival to replace the Houssas withdrawn from the forts and posts referred to. It would be a great matter if the 1st W.I. Regt could be sent here at once, for when I leave the Coast for the field I shall have to leave small garrisons in the Forts for their protection, especially at Elmina, and the posts to the westward of it, where the population is generally hostile to us. I shall also have to keep open my line of communications and must have detachments along my line of route, especially at Prahsue, if I cross into Ashante territory. Even a wing of the 1st WI Regt would help me greatly in accomplishing these objects. If the Houssas had not been taken away, all this would have been unnecessary, for I could have done all this work with them.

I am loath to give an opinion so shortly after landing here upon such a serious subject as the necessity for employing Europeans upon this expedition, but the conviction forces itself upon me more and more every day, that to carry out my mission economically and efficiently, the services of the two Battalions of Infantry, of the Detachments of Royal Artillery and Royal Engineers that I originally asked for, will yet have to be made use of. At present I am incurring great expense in my endeavors to raise a native force that I can have no great confidence in, and that may probably desert me and the few officers I have with me in the first serious encounter I shall have with the enemy. The Fantees have lost all heart: they are thoroughly cowed by the defeats they have had, and they are one and all individually *afraid* of their enemies. Your Royal Highness will therefore easily understand my anxiety to have with me a reserve of English soldiers not only for the protection of the officers who have volunteered for this Expedition, but also with a view to inspiring confidence in my own ranks, and a corresponding dread amongst the Ashantees. As I have always said, Your Royal Highness may rest assured that I shall only land the European Contingent when everything is ready for them, and that I shall take every possible care of them from the moment I land them, until I can again send them on board ship. Next week I hope to be in a position to address the Secretary of State for War officially on this subject. All my party continue to enjoy excellent health. I have written this in a hurry as the steamer only waits for this letter to be off.

PS I enclose a road sketch made by Captain Huyshe & hope by next mail to send home some good plans of country.

Cambridge MSS, RA VIC/ADD E/1/7203

36

Wolseley Journal, 10 October

Friday 10 October

The S.S. "Elmina" for England in: left again at [Blank]. The S.S. "Roquelle" from England arrived at noon bringing letters from Loo the first I have had since leaving England.[23] As I anticipated the news of Commerells being wounded has "*blooded*" the English people and drawn more attention to this war. I find from the nature of the country that to be of any use a Rl. Rd. is out of the question in the short time at my disposal. The gradients on the road are so steep that traction Engines cannot be used – both the Rl. Rd. and the traction Engines were pressed upon me by Major Home & Sir L. Simmons, both belonging to that theoretical but very unpractical Corps, the Rl. Engineers. I asked for them after my original requisition for stores had been submitted, and against my better judgement. Capt. Strachan Administrator of Lagos arrived. I told him that I was very anxious that he should let me have Captain Lees[24] to collect my customs here as soon as he could spare him, as I wished him to act in my absence & carry on the Civil Government of the Country. It is great promotion for him, and as he is a very good man for the place I shall be fortunate in having him. Strachan dined here – took him for a walk before dinner to see Russells quarters on Prospect Hill & then up to Connors Hill where I introduced him to the well-known Major Bravo. That worthy is a regular Mantilini, highly perfumed, does not like work & is no soldier.[25]

TNA, WO 147/3

37

Wolseley to Glover

10 October
[Holograph]
Cape Coast

I am very glad to learn from your note that you are all right again. Col McNeill will send you an official by this mail telling you that I approve of your proceeding to organize Eastern Akim & of clearing out the Volta districts so that your base may be safe and secure from attack when you are in the interior. I am very much obliged to you for sending the guns etc to Swaidroo for I have none here to give away: the only arms I have worth anything are the 300 Sneiders that I got from your ship: with them I hope to arm as many men here. At present owing to the various detachments made from here to replace the Houssas sent to you I could not at this present moment turn out 100 bayonets from the Hd. Qtrs of 2nd W. I. Regt.

Of the Fantee police here I have no opinion: I am not a strong man but I think I could polish off a herd of them with my umbrella. In fact if I am attacked here, my reliance must be upon the 150 Marines & whatever bluejackets the S. Nl. Officer can land for the defence of the place. I should be much obliged if you would kindly tell me what amount of presents you give to such Kings as those of Eastern Akim: it is very advisable that our presents should be equal in value as it does not do that we should unknowingly outbid one another either in terms or presents. I am horrified about your report regarding the Sneider Ammunt.[26] I have ordered the remainder of that I have in store to be examined, for ammunition of such a sort would be nearly as disastrous to the army depending upon it as the vermicelli supplied to Sir C. MacCartney upon whose red & bluecoats your friends at Accra swear with an earnestness that cannot be very gratifying to the shades of that worthy man's tailor.[27]

CUL, Glover MSS, RCMS 131/6

38

Wolseley Journal, 11–13 October

Saturday 11 October

"Roquelle" proceeded on her journey to the South. At 1 p.m. Capt. Freemantle paid me a visit to say that H.M.S. Argus stationed at Elmina had signalled to him that an attack was expected to be made during the day upon that place. H.M.S. Bittern arrived with 138 Houssas from Lagos. I have given them Sneiders here. I went on board of her at 2.30 p.m. & we steamed away for Elmina. She is very slow. We did not get ashore there until about 4.30 p m. Walked to Fort St. Iago[28] & had a cup of tea in the Castle before reembarking. It was dark before we got on board. Elmina looks to me far more unhealthy than Cape C. Castle, for although the country is flatter and more open, the place generally is more offensive. Did not get back here until nearly 8 p.m. Nearly all my party very sea sick. I myself rather squeamish. Had a good dinner & turned in at once. A little light rain fell during the day. I have made all my arrangements for my first fight, to come off on Tuesday next the 14th inst. at daybreak. I keep the thing here a profound secret, and shall begin to spread false news on Monday by announcing that I have recd. a despatch from Capt. Glover saying he is hard pressed at Addah by the hostile tribes from the Rt. Bank of the river Volta: I shall go off to see the Senior Naval Officer during the day, confide to him my project & ask for his cooperation. I intend moving with everybody available to a place called Essaman 4 miles N W from Elmina where there is a force of Ashantees. I shall attack the place & burn it down: then turning southward by a back road to the coast do the same by Ampinee a village on the sea beach. I anticipate with Gods assistance a complete success, and if so it will do more than I can possibly do here to re-kindle enthusiasm and pluck amongst these wretched Fantees.

Sunday 12 October

Slight rain this morning. Held a Legislative Council at 10 a.m. and considered rules for the Quarantine Ordinance I passed at my first meeting of Council.[29] Went on board the Barracouta at noon &

paid my official visit to the Senior Naval Officer, Capt. Freemantle. He is just the man I want here. He is a gentleman, very anxious to do something to obtain a name, not talented, easily talked over to my way of thinking upon any point, and very obliging: anxious to assist in forwarding all military work. In fact I shall have my own way by a little "*rubbing down his back*" and making things pleasant to him. Lunched on board all the Captains of the other ships being present. I told Freemantle I wanted to have private conversation with him. He said after lunch. He got rid of all those present except Capt. Peile[30] who being a Post Captain was I suppose too great a swell to ask to leave. I talked of different other matters & did not enter upon my projected operations as I am sure from the look of Peile, he could not keep a secret. When leaving the Barracouta I asked Freemantle to come ashore with me & I then told him in my own room what my plans were. I wanted 170 Marines & conveyance from here to Elmina during the night of the Detacht of the 2nd W. I. Regt. now here etc etc. He was delighted & I swore him to secrecy. I announced at Breakfast this morning that I had had bad news from Glover, that he was hemmed in at Addah by hostile tribes from right bank of the Volta, and that it was possible I might have tomorrow to run down in a man of war to help him: that I expected another letter from him tomorrow, that would settle what I intended doing. All were taken aback and the news spread everywhere. McNeil & Irvine[31] were in my confidence but all the rest of my officers were kept in ignorance. I have written to Col. Wood now commanding at Elmina telling him my plans & directing him to tell no one. He writes back that no one shall be allowed to sleep in his room lest he should divulge it in his slumber. I attach the greatest importance to secrecy in this my first operation first because I want to be completely successful, and I have such a small force to act with, that if the Ashantees knew of my intentions they might move down such a large force to defend these villages, that I should not be able to do anything with them, and secondly, because secrecy and surprise has a demoralizing effect upon all troops that are attacked especially upon savages. The enemy has been accustomed to obtain most accurate information of all we do, whilst on our part, the authorities have always been ignorant of the Ashantee doings or whereabouts. This surprise will show them that a new era has begun in military operations.

Monday 13 October
Announced to my staff that I had again heard from Glover: that he was hard pressed at Addah & that I intended going there. At 3 p.m. sent orders to the 2nd W. I. Regt to embark all their available strength (about 90 bayonets) on board H.M.S. Decoy for conveyance to the Volta. Sent off about 200 carriers to Elmina with ordinary stores so as not to attract attention with orders to Wood to have them all locked up for the night in the Castle there upon their arrival in the evening. Embarked with all my personal staff except Huyshe & Maurice on board H.M.S. Barracouta at 9 p.m.: 40 sailors were landed to occupy the Castle here during absence of the 2nd W.I. Regt from here.

TNA, WO 147/3

39

Wolseley to King Kofi Kakari

13 October
[Holograph copy]
Government House Cape Coast
The Queen of England has heard with profound concern of your recent doings by which you have directly violated the treaty concluded in 1831 between Governor Maclean and the late King of Ashantee.

Her Majesty's successive governors were engaged in peaceful negociations with you for the deliverance of strangers whom you had wrongfully seized and were holding captive: yet during the continuance of these negociations when friends of the prisoners had consented to pay the sum demanded by you for expenses incurred on their account, whilst Your Majesty's envoys were still at Cape Coast, suddenly without warning given or cause alleged you invaded the territories of Her Majesty's allies and still continue to occupy them. You have killed or driven into slavery all upon whom you could lay hands. You have even attacked Her Majesty's forts.

All this you have done whilst professing to the last a desire for Her Majesty's friendship.

It were but justice therefore that summary punishment should be at once inflicted upon yourself and upon your people.

But the Queen of England as She is strong is patient. Her Most Gracious Majesty is willing to believe that evil advisers or it may be unfaithful messengers have deceived you. She wishes only well to the great Ashantee people as to all the peoples of Africa. She would be glad to know that peace and happiness were enjoyed by all. She is most anxious for the permanent establishment between your nation and Her subjects and allies of those commercial and friendly relations which are so essential to the well being of all and of which in a happier moment your Majesty once wrote that they are "the best support of nations and the principal care of the wisest".

She wishes that all misunderstanding or imaginary cause of grievance that may exist in your Majesty's mind should be removed.

She has sent me therefore reposing in me all Her fullest and most gracious confidence to arrange with you for the establishment of a lasting peace. As however it is not the custom of our country to discuss terms of peace with one who persists in an attitude of aggression I have to require as preliminaries to negociation

1st That by the 12th (twelfth) of November next you withdraw all your forces from the territories of Her Majesty's allies.

2nd. That you surrender up at once all men women and children of every tribe and people at present in alliance with Her Majesty whom you have captured.

3rd. That you give guarantees for the payment of ample compensation to all whom you have ill-used.

If you will in good faith consent to these conditions I shall be ready to treat with you in a friendly spirit and to consider any reasonable proposals you may make.

But if within 20 days I have not received from you an assurance of your readiness to comply with Her Majesty's wishes or if you have not within the date already mentioned withdrawn all your forces into your own territory beyond the Prah river, having given such guarantees as may satisfy me for the fulfilment of the above-mentioned terms, I hereby warn you to expect the full punishment which your deeds have merited.

Rest well assured that power will not be wanting to that end. I can scarcely believe that you do not know how unequal would be the struggle which you invite.

Her Majesty's dominion reaches far and wide over the earth. Against you or your forefathers she has hitherto never found it necessary to employ more than an insignificant part of the special forces which guard this petty corner of the vast realms which own Her Sovereign.

When you recently assailed Her forts they were held only by a handful of men. Yet your people were repulsed with loss. How then when Her Majesty puts forth Her might against you [,] can you hope to resist Her. [?]

Be warned in time lest in refusing to attend to my summons you prepare misery for yourself and for your people.

I entreat your Majesty to be careful that the exact terms of this dispatch are accurately conveyed to you.

I beg you to have it read to you on two different occasions by two different persons neither of whom is present while the other reads. In this way I hope that you may avoid any risk of such misunderstanding as to the exact nature of the message sent to you as I fear may have occurred on some previous occasions.

I am Your Majesty's well-wisher.

Cambridge MSS, RA VIC/ADD E/1/7208; Brackenbury, *Ashanti War*, I, pp. 201–3.

40

Wolseley to Cardwell

13 October
[Printed]
Cape Coast Castle.

I have the honour to inform you that I have this day requested Her Majesty's Consul at Madeira to forward to you the following telegram.

'Country unsuitable for railroad and traction engines. Do not send them out.'

I have the honour now to confirm the above telegram, and to request that the traction engines may not be sent out, and that no further steps be taken to provide a railroad, as I find that the difficulties of the country are much greater than I had been led to expect; and as I am now of opinion that neither could a railroad be laid, nor traction engines worked with the means, and within the time at my disposal.

TNA, WO33/26; WO147/27

41

Wolseley to Cardwell

13 October
[Printed]
Cape Coast Castle

I have the honour to request that the troops (strength as per margin) which, before my departure from England, I requested might be held in readiness for service in the Ashanti Expedition, may be despatched to this station at the earliest possible date after the receipt of this letter.

2 Battalions of Infantry, 650 each	1300
Detachment R.A.	60
Detachment R.E.	40
Administrative Services	50
	1450

The above number is exclusive of officers.

Two subalterns (but no captain) to be sent with the R.A., also a double proportion of non-commissioned officers to take charge of small-arm ammunition.

In making this request, I bear fully in mind the instructions which I had the honour to receive from you before leaving England; and I do not make this demand hastily, or without having freely communicated with those who have experience on the Coast, and knowledge of the immediate circumstances. On the other hand I remember your desire, that my decision as to the employment of European troops should be arrived at 'as soon after my arrival on the Coast, as I might be enabled to form it with sufficient knowledge of the circumstances and satisfaction to myself'. I have therefore consulted all those whose experience and knowledge was at my disposal, and I have studied the question in its various bearings.

From these consultations and this study, results my firm conviction of the necessity for the employment of European troops, and of the perfect feasibility of employing them without undue risk, for those purposes which your instructions specify – namely, 'to free these settlements from the continued menace of the attacks of the Ashantis, and to accomplish the further objects of my mission'.

There is, Sir, but one method of freeing these settlements from the continued menace of Ashanti invasion; and this is, to defeat the Ashanti army in the field, to drive it from the protected territories, and, if necessary, to pursue it into its own land, and to march victorious on the Ashanti capital, and show not only to the king, but to those chiefs who urge him on to constant war, that the arm of Her Majesty is powerful to punish, and can reach even to the very heart of their kingdom.

By no means short of this can lasting peace be insured; one truce after another may be made, but they will again and again be broken, for the Ashantis have learned to believe that they may with impunity invade and lay waste the protected territory, and dwell there unmolested by the white man, till they arrive under the very walls of our forts.

If the history of former wars with the Ashantis be examined, it will be found that every sign of weakness, and every unsuccessful effort of ours, has been followed by renewed hostilities on their part; and on the other hand, that the show of military strength alone has brought peace.

It was thus that the Ashanti advance to Annamaboe in 1807 was followed by the invasion of 1811; this again by the advance to Cape Coast Castle in 1817, when the Ashantis were bought off; and this by the insult and invasion of 1823. The sad failure of Sir Charles Macarthy's expedition in 1824 brought the enemy to the walls of our forts, and again, in 1826, they renewed their attacks. Now for the first time they were not only defeated but routed; and the signal victory of Dodowah freed the country for many a long year. The King of Ashanti sent to say 'that he found it was no use fighting against white men', and the truce was declared which ended in peace in 1831.

For 25 years – almost the time of a generation – this lesson had its effect. But in 1853 the restless chiefs again urged on the king to war, and the perpetual dread of invasion was renewed. Though happily staved off by the judicious measures of Governor Hill, and a show of strength, the invasion was kept hanging over the heads of the protected tribes; and the unmeasured threats of the king led to the expedition which was undertaken in Governor Pine's rule, when a detachment of our African troops marched to, and encamped upon, the Prah, and were left there inactive to suffer and to die, till the wreck which remained were recalled at the expiration of five months, three months of which had been passed in a severe rainy season.

From that day to this there has been no peace between the Ashantis and England. No strength has been shown by England, except defensive strength when our forts have been actually attacked. Our Fanti allies, who fell back before the enemy, have disbanded and become demoralised. They have lost their confidence in the English power of protection; and in proportion the Ashantis have grown bold and confident. Their forces lie in security within nine miles of our forts, and for six months they have lived on the produce of the land said to be protected by us.

Her Majesty has confided to me the task of insuring a lasting peace. Past history, the experience of those who have watched the condition of the Coast, and my own observation of the actual state of affairs, alike convince me that by no method but such signal chastisement as I have described, can such peace be insured, and that such punishment cannot be inflicted without the assistance of British troops.

It cannot, I think, be doubted, that under the influence of civilization and European protection, the Fanti tribes have grown less warlike and more peaceful than formerly. Yet even in their best times they were no match for the Ashantis. When left alone they were conquered and overrun; and when, later, English officers cast in their lot with them, they could not be induced to turn out their whole strength; for I am able to state that the numbers reported as having taken the field are enormously exaggerated, and that there were never 10,000 men present under arms. Sir Charles Macarthy was outnumbered by the cowardly defection of his native allies; and the success of the earlier actions of this present year, and the presence of English officers failed to induce the natives to stand firm. On one excuse or another they retreated from before the enemy, whom they now believe to be too strong for them, and against whom they are evidently very reluctant to fight.

I have held interviews with the kings. I have seen the greedy mercantile spirit in which the war is viewed by them, and the excuses made to delay their departure for the field. They tell me they have little influence in raising their men; that their men prefer trading to fighting, and have gone to far countries to hide. The Cape Coast people actually claim the privilege of being the *last* to turn out to fight the invaders of their country.

In the face of these facts, ignorant as I am as yet of the force which may be raised by the officers employed in recruiting along the coast – whether it is to be counted by thousands or by tens only – ignorant as I must also for some time be as to what force the surrounding kings will produce – and the hour having arrived when on account of the advancing season my decision as to the need for European troops must be made, it is impossible for me to say that my purposes are such that I dare undertake to carry out my mission with native forces only; nor would the Government or the country hold me excused were the valuable lives of the British officers who have volunteered for this expedition sacrificed, and the prestige of our country lowered, by the desertion of these native forces – a result which I foresee is too likely were I to rely solely upon them, and give them no nucleus of first-rate material to set them an example, and afford them a point on which to rally.

Under no circumstances, it appears to me, could I rely on such native troops alone to pursue the war into the enemy's territory. Nor would their presence serve to show the power of Her Majesty as would that of a body of English soldiers.

I am by no means the first high official in this colony who has seen the necessity for the employment of thoroughly disciplined troops to stop these perpetual Ashanti invasions.

In 1824, after Sir C. Macarthy's disaster, M. Dupuis[32] wrote as follows:–

'Government will see the necessity of now doing what ought to have been done long ago. Unless 3000 to 4000 men are sent out to beat these savages out of hand, they will keep the country agitated until they effect the total subjugation of the Coast.'

In 1853, Governor Hill[33] wrote:–

'A disciplined force should be sent here, as I am perfectly satisfied that 1000 men from the West India Regiment, with their bayonets, would do more than ten times that number of natives imperfectly armed and disciplined.'

And in 1863, Governor Pine[34] said:–

'That his earnest desire is that a final blow should be struck at Ashanti power, and the question set at rest for ever as to whether an arbitrary and a sanguinary monarch shall be for ever permitted to insult the British flag and outrage the laws of civilisation.'

He goes on to recommend, 'that a force of 2000 disciplined soldiers should be transported to these shores, so that, combined with a native force of upwards of 50,000 men, it might march straight on Coomassie'.

With these forcible opinions in support of the necessity of trained and disciplined troops, and with your instructions before me, I consider it my duty to state that, in my opinion, the desired effect cannot be obtained by the employment of West Indian Regiments alone. In the first place, the morale effect of their presence upon the Ashantis is not to be compared with that which a similar number of Europeans would exert; and, in the next place, they are not physically by any means as capable of withstanding the climate, still less exertion and fatigue.

It is a well-known fact here that Europeans suffer from the climate less than black men from other localities.

The medical reports on the expedition of 1864 say that 'Black troops have none of the hardihood and spirited endurance of the white man. They suffer more from the effects of the climate on their arrival than white men do. They are not accustomed to very onerous duties, which they had to perform on this occasion.'

And you will find that Captain, now Sir A. Clarke, in his Report of 1864, strongly advocates the substitution of an European force for a West Indian Regiment, owing to their suffering less from the climate, having more power of endurance, and being able to do the same work with fewer men. I might also refer you to the opinion of Colonel de Ruvignès,[35] that 'the West Indian troops are worse than useless, and are constantly embroiled with the natives'.

I have no wish to deprecate the West Indian Regiments, but I could not enter upon my task with that confidence which is so necessary for success were I not supported by some of Her Majesty's English troops.

I consider therefore, Sir, that (1) the service required cannot be performed solely by any force indigenous to the country; and (2) that the service for which I require these troops is of paramount importance to the main object of my mission, – viz., the establishment of a lasting peace with the Ashanti nation.

But, Sir, I should still not apply for these troops, and I should even prefer to tell you that the mission intrusted to me is incapable of thorough accomplishment, were it not that I am convinced that the service for which I demand the European soldiers can be performed by them without undue risk. I believe, indeed, that the evidence upon this point is irresistible.

Two months, or nearly two months must elapse before the troops can arrive off Cape Coast Castle. In that time the road, which is now complete to Yancoomassie, will, unless the Ashantis have been more successful than hitherto in preventing its construction, be complete at least as far as the Prah; the native troops will have attained such organisation as I can give them; the transport will be prepared for an advance; and I may even hope with the aid of the Houssas and these forces to have cleared the country on this side of the Prah.

I may therefore say, that on the arrival of the troops in these roads about the middle of December, all will be ready for their immediate advance into the enemy's country, and that they shall not be kept inactive for one single day.

I would here again refer to the medical reports of 1864, which say – 'The effects of the climate depend to a great extent on the season of the year.' Now the weather at this present season is totally different from that experienced during the rains. It is now bright and fine, without excessive heat, and it may be expected to improve from week to week. The troops would arrive soon after the commencement of that season of the year, which your instructions describe as the most healthy – viz., the months of December, January, February, and March; and as I guarantee that the operations in which they would be engaged would not last more than about six weeks, or at the most two months, they might re-embark on board ship by the beginning or middle of February, and under no circumstances would they be required to remain on shore after the commencement of the unhealthy season.

In regard to the risk to European troops of a march up country at this season of the year, there appears to me to be a very strong probability if not a demonstration, that the country becomes more healthy as the coast is left.

Colonel Bird,[36] then Acting Governor of the Gold Coast, speaks thus of the expedition in 1853:–

'Hitherto we have been led to believe the inland districts were too unhealthy for the European constitution This expedition has proved the fallacy of the belief. During the last two and a half months the officers who have been engaged on this expedition have enjoyed better health than they have been accustomed to do on the coast, and that in spite of exposure to sun and rain, great bodily exertions and privations, which a roving camp–life such as theirs has been necessarily entails.'

I would also refer you to the memorandum of Lieutenant-Colonel de Ruvignès, dated 25th April 1873, wherein he says: 'I have to observe that many officers, myself amongst the number, served without detriment to their health or constitution for long periods in West Africa. I can safely say that it was only during periods of utter inaction on the coast that I suffered from illness; though when in the interior, in the thick bush of the Fanti country bordering on Ashantee, or in the forests of Akim and Ashantee, with privations and long marches, sometimes 30 miles a–day, living in mud huts at one time, at another in open forests, I felt no ill effects, neither did any of the officers who served under my command.'

I might multiply similar evidence, but I am unwilling to increase the length of this despatch, for there are other points to be dealt with of great importance.

The ill–health of the troops engaged in the expedition to the Prah of 1864, and the sickness of the Royal Marines who were engaged in the early part of the present year, have, I submit, produced an exaggerated alarm as to the general influence of this climate upon European health.

If the conditions of the expedition of 1864 to the Prah be examined, they will be found so exceptional as to afford no grounds whatever for the belief that the unfortunate results of that affair would be repeated in such an expedition as I propose. The medical reports of 1863 give the strongest proof of this.

From these reports we learn the following facts: –

The troops composing the expedition were remarkably bad subjects: they were not only West Indians, but they were from many cases, shown in these reports, specially unfit for any severe work. They had landed at the worst season of the year; they had been attacked by fever and dysentery immediately on their arrival at Cape Coast, and had not wholly recovered when marched up country.

They had everything against them; heavy duties to which they were not accustomed, no excitement or interest of any kind, no enemy before them; but they had worse food than usual; they were encamped on the banks of the Prah in extremely low and marshy ground. Yet even under these conditions they were reported in March 1864 as in good spirits and fair health, busily employed in erecting stockades, completing huts, and constructing a bridge.

But the subsequent *inaction* did its work. Depression ensued and the men became ill, though not till the rains commenced, which set in early and were very severe. The camp became a swamp; and for three months longer were the troops kept inactive in this deadly spot.

The hospital accommodation was of the worst description – men lying on the wet ground with pools of water under them.

Under such conditions is it not to be wondered at that a single man escaped alive? and is it not clear that this expedition affords no grounds for supposing that similar sickness would attack picked European troops actively employed on the line of march during the healthy season?

As regards the detachment of Royal Marines who came out in H.M.S. Barracouta, and were sent home in the Himalaya, I have in the first instance to observe, from personal inspection, that the accommodation provided on board that ship (the Barracouta) for their transport, was not in any respect what European soldiers should be provided with in a voyage to the tropics. There was no light and but very little air. The condenser, which was constantly at work, was on the same deck, and in the same compartment with the troops. The heat and smell from the steam-engine had free access to the place where they were berthed.

I should not consider this proper accommodation for troops going even to a cold country; and I have good reason for saying that the men landed in an exhausted condition.

The principal medical officer, Dr Home, C.B., V.C., has investigated the question of the sickness of these marines, and he informs me that he believes their sufferings were exceptional.

They landed at the worst season and without preparation. They were crowded together in unhealthy dilapidated barracks at Elmina.

It was the tornado season and tents could not be pitched, and the medical officer at that time did not consider it desirable to expose troops to the rain, though Dr Home is now of opinion it would have been better to do so than to have so crowded them together. They were exposed, immediately on landing, to the fatigue of a long night-march. They fought a very distressing action at Elmina, and suffered privations of food and rest for some time after the action.

But far more potential in producing sickness than all these causes was the fact that they were drenched with surf on landing; and that the boats containing the party which left Cape Coast to be quartered at Elmina grounded on a sand-bank, from which cause the men were detained for two hours under an excessively heavy downpour of rain, most of them, it is believed, afterwards sleeping all night in their wet clothes.

These conditions are then, I submit, as in the case of the expedition of 1863–64, so exceptional, as to afford no grounds for the belief that similar sickness would attack picked troops actively employed on the line of march during the healthy season.

I have no desire to underrate the risks to health caused by a prolonged stay in this climate, but not only do I find a remarkable unanimity of opinion here as to the possibility of undertaking a march of limited duration into the interior under such conditions as I propose, but I think the existing conditions of health of the troops on this station show that such an expedition does not involve great risk.

I would here remark, that notwithstanding all the unfavourable conditions reported as regards the Royal Marines, Dr Home remarks that their entire non-effective list, all casualties included, was on the thirty-first day after landing only 17 per cent, the remaining 83 per cent being thoroughly effective.

In my despatch No. 26/73 MS., I drew your attention to the remarkable healthiness of the troops in camp at Napoleon and Abbaye, as compared with those in barracks at Elmina.

On the 11th instant, Dr Home reports as under of the troops at Cape Coast and Elmina:

'The health of the troops in the command has improved with the partial cessation of the rains and morning mists (locally called smokes). At Elmina the sick-rate per cent of strength is 6.76; at Cape Coast Castle 11.51 (West Indians in both cases). There is less sickness amongst the European officers.'

I have now before me the weekly return of sick of the Abbaye detachment of 100 men, from 4th to 10th October. It is blank. There was not one case of sickness. The surgeon in charge reports the detachment, in camp now from four to six weeks, as quite healthy.

These facts prove clearly the fact that while sickness is diminishing throughout the whole coast, by reason of the improving season, it is far less in the camps inland than in the barracks on the coast.

Since arriving here, I have received a letter, of which I enclose a copy, from Captain Thompson, Queen's Bays,[37] in which he withdraws the opinion he had expressed to His Royal Highness the Field-Marshal Commanding in Chief, before leaving England, that Europeans could not live in the bush.

But, Sir, still more strong is the report of Dr Home, V.C., C.B., the principal medical officer, my responsible adviser on sanitary questions.

I beg to refer you to his despatch to the Director-General of the Medical Department, by which it will be seen that he is of opinion that European troops may be employed without extraordinary risk, under those conditions which I propose – viz., that the men be landed the day they are to march, that every recognised sanitary precaution be taken, as far as possible, and that the longest time the men will remain in the country is two months.

It now remains for me only to repeat my request, that as soon as possible after the receipt of this despatch, the troops above specified may be embarked for this station, and to add that I attach the greatest possible importance to the men being selected for this service, and to good accommodation being provided for them on board ship, so that they may arrive here in thoroughly healthy condition.

Should my request be complied with, and the troops be despatched, I undertake not to land them, if, in the time which must elapse before their arrival, circumstances should induce me to consider that the object of my mission can be accomplished without their aid; and further, I undertake, should it seem possible to do with any smaller number, not to land one man more than I consider absolutely necessary, to the success of my expedition.

TNA, WO33/26; WO106/285; WO147/27

42

Wolseley Journal, 14–15 October

Tuesday 14 October

The Barracouta under weigh about 1.30 a.m. dropped anchor off Elmina, began disembarking the Marines (about 170) in number) and the Detacht. of 2nd W. Indian Regt at 3 a.m. There was a little moon but the naval people were wrong about the tide which we expected to be full. The consequence was that all the boats carrying the troops were grounded on the bar at the mouth of the river, & some were there for over an hour: some were nearly swamped and all more or less wet, some had to have their ammunition changed when we landed. This retarded my movement as I had hoped to have been at least a mile on my road before the first streak of daylight at 5 a.m. I shall not attempt any account of our fight. Is it not written in the columns of the Times & Standard? Essaman the first village attacked was about 5 miles N.W. from Elmina: the enemy were completely surprised and we destroyed it. I am sorry to say that poor McNeil was badly wounded & I fear I shall be deprived of his invaluable services for at least 6 weeks. Having halted for about an hour we then turned nearly south and came out on the Coast at Amquana – destroyed it and marched upon Akimfoo & Ampinee which shared the same fate after a little skirmishing, the blue jackets & marines having landed from H.M.S. Argus & Decoy to cooperate. We had a hard days work, but the result was most satisfactory. The distance marched was a good 20 miles for those who marched back to Elmina. I embarked in H.M.S. Decoy at Ampinee and came back by water to Cape Coast Castle, being in time for dinner at 8 that I had left orders to have ready for us. McNeill was housed in Elmina Castle for the night, Dr Home remaining with him. I am very well pleased at the result of the days work. I have learnt a lesson that if I am to get to Coomassie, I must have Europeans as the natives even the Houssas are unreliable. The Houssas have heaps of pluck but they are wild to a degree and expend their ammunition in a way that is dreadful to contemplate, as for the W. I. troops they are of little use in the bush under the present organization.

Wednesday 15 October
McNeil arrived here in a cot having been carried from Elmina: he is still in fearful pain poor fellow. It is a cold blooded thing to say perhaps, but when he was wounded his blood poured out over my coat, trousers & waterbottle so that for a moment I thought I must really have been hit myself without knowing it. I hear on all sides the best reports of the effect this fight has had here. The people now recognize that their Governor is not only an administrator but a soldier who will go into the field and fight their enemies. Since Sir C. McCarthys days they have never been led into the field by their Governor, so I believe that I shall establish for myself amongst them that military reputation which is a more powerful leaver when used with barbarians than it is even with civilized soldiers. The loss yesterday was 1 offr severely wounded 2 slightly wounded, 1 houssa killed & 22 men wounded mostly slightly. As a rule the wounds will never be more than slight in this war for the Ashantee powder is bad & their slugs do not hurt much beyond 40 yards. I am rather amused in looking over the list of casualties to see that Capt. Fremantle has had himself returned as "*severely* wounded". Walked on the beach in the evening with Brackenbury & saw Raits Houssa Gunners at work firing at a target out at sea.
TNA, WO 147/3

43

Wolseley to Captain Edmund Fremantle, RN

15 October

[Holograph]

I am very sorry to hear that your arm prevents you from writing but I trust that in a short time you may be able to use it as usual. McNeil came here by road. He is still in great pain but is cheery and looks well. Acting upon the Doctors recommendation, he is going to the Sanitarium on Connors Hill this evening where we shall be able to see him constantly and cheer him up.

I have written to you officially thanking you for your kind assistance yesterday and I now avail myself of this opportunity of doing so privately.

I have also written to you with reference to the Marines having been landed, many of them without their rations: this is a very serious matter and I hope you do not think that I am travelling out of my proper sphere when I ask you to have the circumstances enquired into, so that the man who is really responsible for this neglect may be duly pitched into by you. I shall make no allusion to this in my official report however, but in case it should get into the newspapers, I think that no time should be lost in fixing the blame upon him who should justly bear it.

NMM, Fremantle MSS, FRE/109

44

Wolseley Journal, 16–19 October

Thursday 16 October

The steamer Warree[38] arrived during the night with some stores for us, and more for Glover. The weather is now becoming warmer than when we arrived at first. At 2.45 p.m. as I write this the thermometer is 82° Faht. in the shade in my room. The Cape Coast Chiefs have been at work for some days past trying to get their fighting men together; this evening they formally announced to me that they had collected 760 men & have promised to hand over about half that number tomorrow morning to Russell, nous verrons. McNeil going on well: he was removed to Connors Hill this morning, walked in the evening with Freemantle to see him: found him very irritable which is not a good sign.

Friday 17 October
100 Houssas from Elmina arrived: they go on tomorrow morning to Abrakrampa, where I intend forming a fortified post, that will I think before long bring on a fight with the Ashantees now encamped at Mampon. These Houssas are unshod, and their feet have suffered greatly even from our short operations of tuesday last. I have given them shoes here, but our shoes will not fit them: this distresses me a great deal. The Cape Coast Companies have turned out and mustered some hundreds strong this evening at Russells place. They are a miserable lot and each Company wants the others to go out first.

Saturday 18 October
Have issued a proclamation about our tuesdays affair. It is rather high falutin but bombast goes a long way in such matters here. McNeil was a little agueish yesterday so the Doctors thought it necessary that he should go on board ship; we sent him on board H.M.S. Simoom this morning at 6 a.m. He looks well and cheery. Arranged that the Captains of Nos. 1 & 7 Companies should go to Napoleon.

Sunday 19 October
Started at 5.30 a.m. for Napoleon, took Charteris & 20 armed police with me. Did not say where I was going until the last minute. Reached that place in 1½ hours: found it to be a weak redoubt too large for its present garrison. It is a pretty but a very unhealthy position having a great deal of marsh and flooded land in its vicinity. The Ashantees frequently forage close to the place & now & then catch an unfortunate beggar, and generally cut his head off. When looking out of my window on Friday, I saw some savages hawking about the street a head of an Ashantee that had just been cut off. We had breakfast in the Redoubt, the relief of the Detacht 2nd W. I. Regt. took place when I was there, so were

for the once sufficiently strong to have given a good account of any Ashantees that might [have] attacked us. Every other day I am bothered by men coming to say that Abbaye, Napoleon, this place, etc etc is to be attacked that night. The last scare was Napoleon, so upon arrival there I found that the officer in command had been up nearly all night. We had divine service under a tree there the W.I. troops attending. Lieut. Stephens[39] who commands at the place had a small harmonium on which he played the psalms. Charteris read the morning service & he & I sang the psalms lustily, the men following suit. The effect was impressive but it certainly was not harmonious, my *"sweet voice"* is more suited for howling at soldiers in action than for singing. We got back to C. C. Castle about 2.30 p m. having passed a crowd of people from here going out there to be enrolled into companies. A scare in the evening from Napoleon the o.c. there sending in a special messenger saying that for some hours he had heard severe volley firing in a N E direction. I presume it is a false alarm at Abrakrampa, but as Huyshe is there and says he can hold out against attack I am easy in my mind upon the subject.

TNA, WO 147/3

45

Wolseley to Cambridge

[15–]19 October
[Holograph]
Cape Coast

I am glad to have it in my power to give Your Royal Highness some good news from this place. Ever since my arrival I have been most anxious to strike a blow, no matter how small, provided I was as morally certain as any one can be at any time in war, of a complete success. It was absolutely necessary in my position here: Around me were these dispirited and demoralized Fantees, without confidence in themselves or faith in us:– they did not believe we were in earnest. We had been for a long time saying to them, "go on", but they wanted to have, "come on", addressed to them. Since the Commodores misfortunes on the Prah and in its neighborhood, the tribes to the westward of Elmina have one by one declared against us and joined the enemy, receiving detachments from their main army at Mampon, and supplying it daily with food and stores purchased in Elmina and even at this place. Until the Houssas from Lagos (138 strong) had joined me I was unable to undertake anything, but as I knew tolerably accurately when they would arrive, I made my plans accordingly, having selected the hostile villages west of Elmina as the point I intended for the blow. I directed Colonel Wood, Commanding there to summon the chiefs of those places to appear before him to account for their conduct: they flew to the Ashantee Camp for advice, and after deliberation with the Ashantee Generals and Captains they refused to obey. They were told that although we were brave, the Ashantees were still braver and that we would never dare to attack them in the bush; that if we attempted to do so, they the Ashantees would move from Mampon to their assistance. The Houssas arrived on Saturday: they were armed with Enfield rifles: I issued Sneiders to them, and set some officers to drill them all day in the use of their new arms. They are a fine wiry looking set of men, and seem to take a great pride in being soldiers. I went with them to Elmina the day they arrived, and explained to Col. Wood what I intended doing, telling him that he was to have command of the column, but that I meant to accompany it for political reasons. On Sunday I announced publicly that I had received bad news from the Volta that Captain Glover had been attacked at Addah etc etc etc. I went on board H.M.S. Barracouta during the day and took Captain Fremantle into my confidence telling him my plans and requesting his co-operation. He entered into all my views, promising to keep everything secret.

On Monday I announced that I had received still further news from Captain Glover: that he was hard pressed and that I intended embarking in the evening en route for the Volta. The whole strength of the 2nd W.I. Regt. every guard and orderly being dispensed with was about 100 men (a little under 100) I sent these on board H.M.S. Decoy at 6 p.m., 40 Bluejackets from the squadron being landed here to take the guards. At 9 p.m. I went on board H.M.S. Barracouta everyone being still under the impression that I was bound eastward. News of our doings is quickly spread here, and the Ashantees are kept well informed of all that goes on in these coast towns. As my force was very small, and the quality of the main body of it unknown to me, I was most anxious to keep my real intentions secret from the enemy, lest he should have met me with too large a force to be dealt with. I desired also to show him that I could surprise him, for a well executed surprise has always a very demoralizing effect upon uncivilized troops: once make them feel that they cannot rely upon the information they receive, and that we are evidently well informed of *their* doings, and then hit them a hard blow suddenly where they do not expect it, and I believe that one has then laid the first stepping stones to further successes.

I shall not attempt to enter into details as to the manner in which I prevented my intentions being known, but the secret was so well kept, that even when we got under weigh between 1 and 2 a.m. on the morning of Tuesday the 14th instant, most even of my own staff still believed that we were bound for the Volta. We landed at Elmina at 4 a.m. but as the tide was low, all our troops boats grounded on the bar at the mouth of the river, and so delayed our movements a little. The official report of the operation is contained in the letter to the Secretary of State for War by this mail, I shall not therefore weary Your Royal Highness by recapitulating here an account of our proceedings. The days work was a complete success, and its effect has already galvanized these people with a new life. Colonel McNeill's severe wound has deprived me of an officer that I cannot replace here. Of course we cannot make war or obtain any good results without casualties, but it is most unfortunate that in a minor operation like that of yesterday, that a fluke shot should strike down the second senior officer out here. He was hit in the left wrist, and the shot has torn away all the tendons there, making a very large and horrible looking wound. In writing thus to Your Royal Highness I need not hesitate to say that it is a *very serious* wound, the danger being lockjaw: the pluck with which he bore it at first, making light of it, was all that would be expected from [a] man of his stamp: two arteries were cut, so that his blood deluged all of us that were near him: this weakened him very much making him feel faint especially as the pain must have been excruciating. He came in here this morning, and I am having a good hut prepared for him on Connors Hill where he will be made as comfortable as possible. Dr Home thinks this a better arrangement than sending him on board ship, as the Simoom rolls very much and would be a very dull quarter for him, whereas as long as he is on shore we can all see him daily and help to cheer him up. Since our arrival he has worked like a slave at all hours by day and by night, and I now feel that without him is like being without my right arm. Dr. Home tells me that if all goes on well with him, he may expect to be again fit for duty in six weeks or two months: the mail that is to take this is not expected here until the 22nd instant by which time Dr Home will be able to give a more positive opinion. As I have myself suffered from a severe wound in a tropical climate I know how uncertain the recovery of even the strongest men must always be, and this causes me great anxiety both for himself as my friend and for the result that his loss may have upon the Expedition. If, when the mail leaves this on the 22nd instant, Dr Home cannot give me a most promising account of his condition, I shall telegraph to the S. of S. for War in Cypher requesting that Colonel Greaves may be sent out forthwith. I sincerely trust that Your Royal Highness will allow him to come: I have the greatest confidence in him, and his abilities as a Staff Officer are well known to Your Royal Highness. No ordinary officer could do the work here: he must have great physical power as well as clearness of head and business-like habits, and I know of no officer in the Army who combines so many of the requisite qualities as Colonel Greaves does.

The experience we have all gained from our little operation of yesterday is very great, and the lessons it has taught us are most important. The Houssas although led by two of the officers I brought out with me, were uncontrollable. They fired away their ammunition at nothing, mostly in the air. Every man employed had 70 rounds of ammunition (60 in pouch & 10 in haversack), these were soon expended by the Houssas. The tremendous fusilade unsteadied the 2d. W.I. Regt. and had an effect even upon the Marines, and the utmost exertions were necessary on the part of all officers – the Staff working even harder than the others – to prevent this firing at nothing becoming general from front to rear of the column. In this bush work one cannot have too many officers, nor be too careful even in selecting the best officers and the best men. Success must always be cheaper than failure, and in such a country it is only with the very best and steadiest soldiers that success becomes as much a certainty as can ever be counted upon in war. The bush is so thick that one quickly loses control over the component parts of a column: Officers & N.C. Officers must therefore act upon their own responsibility to a very large extent, and if the officers are not good, there is great risk of panic. This was made very clear yesterday: in writing thus privately as Your Royal Highness has kindly permitted me to do, I need not hesitate in saying that the officers of the 2nd W.I. Regt. are as a body of very little use: there are a few exceptions, but beginning with Major Bravo the large majority are not what they should be. Captains Brett and Fowler[40] did very well and exerted themselves to their utmost, but some were worse than useless. I am sorry to write thus about men wearing Her Majesty's uniform, but I think it well that Your Royal Highness should hear this from me before it reaches home through other channels as it is certain to do, for so many people saw what took place yesterday, that private letters to friends in England are certain to refer to the subject. An indifferent officer is an incumbrance to me, for I have to feed him, and the question of supplies is a very serious matter.

I am sending home a tracing by this mail to the S. of S. for War, showing the result of our surveys. I regret that time does not permit of its being copied for Your Royal Highness here, but a copy can be made of it in a few hours in the topographical Department. Although not one of the officers I brought out with me has yet suffered in the least from the climate, and all are consequently fit for work, still the pressure of work is very great, and I do not see any chance of it's becoming lighter. I fear therefore that I shall never be able to send home more than one tracing from each of our surveys. I am now in communication with Mansue, and hope soon to have the road *cut* as far as that place. I am sorry to say that the traction engines will be of no use to me, as the gradients on the road are too steep for them at many places. Neither should I be able with the time and means at my disposal to utilize the railway that I learn is being prepared for this expedition.

The day after tomorrow I shall move the Houssas from this to the front. On the 18th instant I intend sending them under Lieut. Gordon 98th Regt. to a village called Abrakrampa – about 3 miles to the west of Akroful where I now have a fortified post occupied by 50 men of the 2nd W.I. Regt. I intend making Abrakrampa very strong, and moving the Detachment from Akroful there. As soon as I have collected about 5000 native levies at Dunquah and its neighborhood, I shall try what can be done against Mampon, for before I advance beyond Mansue, I must clear the country between the coast on the South, the Prah river on the west, and Bosumaprah on the north. As soon as I have done so, I shall begin collecting a large magazine of stores at Mansue. The steamer Warree has just arrived: tomorrow morning the 16th we begin unloading her: she then goes on to Captain Glover with stores for him.

Nearly all the 30 huts I brought out with me have been put up and enclosed within a wattle fence, where I can keep a large quantity of stores until I am ready to send them to the front. I am very sorry to hear that Captain Freemantle is to be superseded by a senior officer. He and I get on so smoothly together, that if it is not yet too late I would beg of Your Royal Highness to have him retained here as Senior Naval Officer.

Colonel Festing is a very good officer and will be of great use to me in the field. He has had no staff experience however and although a good soldier, I feel bound to tell Your Royal Highness that I do not consider him – worthy and gentlemanlike as he is – to be a sufficiently able man to act as second in command. He has not had any experience in organizing a scratch Force as ours must be, and he does not I think carry sufficient weight to assume command of this expedition in the event of my death from any cause. Colonel Harley had wild views of attacking the Ashantees at Mampon with a few hundred white men and some native levies that never could be got together. He urged Colonel Festing to embark in the undertaking who most *wisely* I think declined the attempt: had he been weak in this matter a serious disaster would have been the result.

I trust that Your Royal Highness will pardon the informality of my letters, but I believe that I can in this manner convey more information than I could ever hope to do in an official form.

16th October – Colonel McNeill goes on well, and is very cheery. Captain Fremantles wound is not worth mentioning. I enclose a copy of the ultimatum I addressed to the King of Ashantee in accordance with my instructions: I trust that it may meet with Your Royal Highness's approval: I have had much difficulty in arranging for it's [sic] despatch to him, but I have succeeded in sending him three copies, by three separate messengers and hope that at least one may safely reach it's destination.

Sunday. 19th October. I have at last succeeded in moving these Cape Coast Chiefs to do something: Two companies are now assembling at Napoleon, and I hope soon to have more of them there, as I want to be strong at that point and yet do not like keeping any of the 2nd W.I. Regt at it, as they are always ill there. I was there this morning at 7 a.m. (it is under 5 miles from this) and even at that hour a fog hung over the river, and the smell from the marsh was offensive and I should say most injurious to health. The Ashantees frequently come close to the redoubt, and a prisoner is occasionally taken: On Friday I saw some natives carrying an Ashantee head past Government House that had been brought from the neighborhood of Napoleon. When I attack Mampon – I hope to be able to do so in about a fortnight – my present intention is to advance with all the available strength of Elmina from Abbaye, with the Cape Coast people from Napoleon, both those advances being more as diversions to the principal column with which I shall be myself, that will move from Abrakrampa westward upon Mampon. I shall not attempt it unless I can count upon a success, for having only 150 Marines makes me nervous about operating in the bush against large forces of the Ashantees. However I believe that our late success has scared them somewhat, and we may not perhaps find them as formidable as we expect. If I had a Battalion of well selected officers & men, I would very willingly go straight at them tomorrow. I have now a small party at

Mansue and the road will soon be practicable for Artillery to that place. I shall however do little beyond there until I have cleared the enemy out of Mampon.

I am afraid that Your Royal Highness must expect a large number of officers to be wounded, for in this bush fighting the leaders must necessarily be very much exposed, and the enemy lying concealed naturally fires upon those whom they see leading others. I do not however anticipate having many killed, for the enemys powder is poor stuff and their slugs do not hurt much over fifty yards. The news from posts to the westward is encouraging: Adjiempong the notorious Ashantee Captain is said to be dead, and I have reason to believe in the truth of the report. He was the most cruel of all the enemys chiefs.

Cambridge MSS, RA VIC/ADD E/1/7207

46

Wolseley Journal, 20–23 October

Monday 20 October

Heavy rain during the night & a little in the morning: did not get any usual morning walk in consequence. Wrote McNeill a nice letter regarding himself and manner in which I appreciate his services, advised him to go home & return with white troops. He says in reply he will do whatever I like, so I shall go off tomorrow morning & see him and arrange this. I am sending home by the mail expected here on 22nd inst requesting Greaves may be sent out at once. Reports just in say that Adjeampon is dead. I believe the rumor. Weather getting hotter every day. Walked to see Russell in the evening – found that Hart had gone on board Simoom ill with fever, especially funk: Dooner in a funk and complaining but striving to fight against it. Lord Gifford looking ill but sticking to his work. All Russells party go out in the sun too much & more than is necessary. A very pleasant evening. Walked from Russells place to Connors Hill, found Mr Sarbah (a black merchant)[41] at drill with his volunteer company. I hope to send them to the front on Saturday. The Bonny[42] with stores for us arrived.

Tuesday 21 October

Roused up at midnight by alarming letters from the front of the Ashantee movements: one must not forget the cry of Wolf, but at the same time I enjoy treating these rumors with contempt. Went off at 7 a.m. with Home & Charteris to the Simoom to see McNeil. He is pulled down a great deal but very jolly. The Drs. had a consultation over his wound & it was agreed that at present he could not go home, but Home tells me *privately* that there is no chance of his again taking part in this expedition. Walked in the evening to see Russell who is a little seedy, but will not confess it. I have asked him to oblige me by going on board ship for a couple of days so he has consented. He goes to-morrow evening. Wrote to the S. S. for War asking for a third Battn as a reserve.

Wednesday 22 October

Mail of 30th from home just arrived. I begin to dread all the flattering things that are said of me in the newspapers lest I should prove to be a miserable failure: I wish they would reserve their praise until the war is over. Thermometer in my room at noon only 82°. I have heard that my letter to the King of Ashantee was received in Camp at Mampon & opened by the Chiefs there. I hope soon to hear of what they thought of it. I believe that the large bulk of the Ashantee Army is still at that place. I sent Russell into the boat going off to the ship. He resented being sent there very much. Late in the afternoon the two policemen that went with the Ashantee messenger to Mampon returned with three Ashantees bringing me a letter from Amanquartier the Ashantee General in command of all their troops in the Protectorate.[43] There is nothing in the letter worthy of note except that he says his quarrel is with the Assins, Akyus, Wassaws, & Denkiras who chalenged his own King to fight: that he has done so, and beaten them six times and that now they have flown to me for protection. His letter shows that our action of the 14th inst. has had an effect, and that there is a disposition to negotiate. Amanquartier gave my two policemen £2. 4s. od. between them in gold dust. Heavy rain at 5 p.m.

Thursday 23 October

McNeill going on very well. I have sent back the Ashantees to Mampon with a letter to Amanquartier saying that my letter was for the King & not for him and I request that it may be sent at once on Coomassie (I know that it has already been sent there) also that I can not negotiate with [him] as long as he continues to occupy the territory of H.M. allies, reminding him that the four tribes that he claims as his masters slaves were specially mentioned in the treaty of 1831 as owing no further allegiance from that date to the King of Ashantee. All quiet along the road as far as Mansue.

TNA, WO 147/3

47

Wolseley to Brevet Lieutenant Colonel George Colley

[23] October

[Printed]

Just a line to tell you I have asked for a third battalion, in addition to the two which are already under orders. I have again opened the question of how it is to be raised, and have implored that it may be formed as I originally wanted all to be – i.e. of six companies, one to be taken from a battalion, the best captain in six battalions to choose his own subaltern and call for 109 volunteers, so that the six companies would number in all 650 men, besides officers.

I have asked that if my proposal is granted, the command of the battalion should be given to you; so you had better see somebody at the Horse Guards that you know well, to see how things go on.

If this is acceded to, select some good captains and brevet-major and urge their appointment. We have had a very successful little affair here on the 14th inst., and the result has already been very beneficial; the only drawback is losing the services of McNeil, who is, I am sorry to say, very severely wounded. His pain must have been excruciating, but he bore it like a true soldier and made no fuss about it.

I have learnt several lessons from my recent fight, not the least being that a selected officer is worth two sent out in the ordinary way of duty according to the roster.

I hope all this can be managed. I have written privately to H.R.H. on the subject and it is possible that my arguments may have some weight with him.

Will tell you all about the kit required. I hope to see you here.

Sir William Butler, *The Life of Sir George Pomeroy-Colley* (London: John Murray, 1899), pp. 89–90

48

Wolseley Journal, 24 October

Friday 24 October

No mail in yet. It is very provoking that the very important letters I have for England should be so long delayed: I had hoped to have got these letters off a week ago. If I had done so I believe that my stay on the Coast would have been shortened by that number of days. Went to Connors Hill in the morning to inspect Captain Sarbahs Company. 60 men were in the ranks all more or less the educated natives of the place. They have still much to learn, but I hope in another week they will be fit to be sent to the front. I sent round a notice yesterday informing "all men" that 4 p.m. to day I should have every man arrested of the three Companies now supposed to be at Napoleon who were found in town at that hour. I intend on Monday calling upon the women to go round and beat all the skulkers. Their fashion is to go round the town naked when employed upon this noble and patriotic duty. The Chief Justice[44] called upon me in the evening & expressed his horror at the arrest of men for not turning out: he said it was contrary to English law: I told him I had ordered it at the request of the Chiefs as it was in accordance with their law. He replied English law not native law ruled here. We were standing on the steps of Government House at the time, so I said, Well, judge if English law holds good here, pray go into that house, & into that house & into that and liberate the slaves in therein. He had nothing to say: he begged I would release them at once; I positively refused but said Come in & have a cigar, which he did. The fact is now that we are here he has nothing to do, and although he is a very lazy fellow, like Conolly[45] he wishes people to think he is full of business, & Major Baker in carrying out my orders for the arrest of these men had not consulted him: it was a question of dignity: he is a goose.

TNA, WO 147/3

49

Wolseley to Cardwell

24 October

[Printed]

Cape Coast Castle

I wrote on the 13th instant, urging the despatch of the two battalions of Infantry, and the detachments of Artillery, Engineers and administrative services which, before leaving England, I had requested might be held in readiness for service in this expedition.

Since the date of that letter eleven days have passed, pregnant with facts of vital importance in relation to the conduct of this war.

I have seen the days pass by since I held a reception of the native Kings and Chiefs, and no native levies of any importance have taken the Field; apathy, if not cowardice, seems to have enveloped the people of these tribes.

I had hoped to raise large native levies from other parts of the coast; but a few scores of men from each tribe, amounting altogether to only a few hundreds, seem all I am likely to obtain.

I have seen the danger of depending upon ill-disciplined levies in bush warfare.

I have learnt that the 2nd West India Regiment, on which I had relied as an effective battalion, is unable to furnish more than about 100 bayonets for the field.

All the evidence which I have collected shows the Ashanti capital to be further from the coast than we had supposed.

On the other hand, each day has shown me that the climate is not, at this and a later season, by any means so injurious to European health as I had imagined. The health of my officers has been excellent: one or two have had slight attacks of fever, but none have been seriously ill.

I have seen that after a night without rest, a long and fatiguing day's march can be made by Europeans in this climate, without as much evil effect from sun and fatigue, as I have often known follow a march of less duration under less fatiguing conditions, on a summer's day in England.

I have fought an action in the bush, which has convinced me more strongly than any opinions of others could have done, that it is quite practicable for European troops to best the natives in bush fighting, and that the only troops by which this war can be satisfactorily ended, are highly disciplined men under highly trained officers.

Under these conditions, in spite of the difficulties of transport involved, and with a full sense of the responsibility I incur, I have, after mature deliberation, decided that it is my duty to request you to despatch an additional battalion of the same strength as the two now under orders to join this expedition.

I make this demand because I foresee that it is highly probable I may have, at an early date after the arrival of the English contingent, to fight an action in which the losses both of officers and men may be heavy; and that though the losses from climate will I trust be less, the losses in action may be greater than I had supposed.

I must have a reserve in hand to meet the losses which I am likely to experience, and to ensure that my force shall at no time be reduced below the original numbers asked for, which I have always considered the least with which I could operate at a distance from the Coast.

By no means, except the despatch of an additional battalion from home, can I obtain a reserve worthy to be trusted, and I earnestly hope that if you accede to this request, the question of the composition of the battalion may be re-considered, and that this battalion may be formed of selected officers and men, according to my original proposal – one company of volunteers, with volunteer officers, being taken from each of six selected battalions.

If this is done, I trust the command may be given to Brevet Lieutenant-Colonel Colley, 2nd Queen's, an officer in whose abilities I have the greatest confidence, and who is very anxious to serve on this expedition. Care should be taken that no officer senior to Colonel Greaves should be sent out.

Should you accede to my request for this third battalion, I hope that the despatch from England of the two battalions now under orders may not be delayed until the third battalion is ready, for I am urgently in want of troops here, not having at this moment a force sufficiently strong to take the field for the purpose of driving the Ashantees out of Mampon.

My furthest post from this is now at Mansue, and I cannot under any circumstances advance beyond that place until the country between the Prah on the west, the Coast on the south, and the Mansue meridian of latitude on the north, has been cleared of the Ashantees.

TNA, WO33/26; WO147/27

50

Wolseley to Cambridge

24 October
[Holograph]
Cape Coast

Although I have already written a long letter by the mail that will also take this home, I think it necessary to incur the risk of wearying Your Royal Highness by another, for since the date of my other letter I have felt it my duty to ask the Secretary of State for War for a third Battalion. I have given at length in the official application my reasons why I felt constrained after long thought to take this step, so I shall not repeat them here as of course my official letter will be laid before Your Royal Highness by Mr Cardwell. In it I have presumed to reopen the subject of how this third Battalion should be formd: I am therefore anxious to explain why I have done so. But having given my opinion for what it is worth, I beg to repeat what I have always said in writing on this subject, that I desire to be guided in it entirely by Your Royal Highnesses wishes. The experience I gained in our recent little fight has shown me practically the importance of having carefully selected officers for this bush fighting: at one moment during the action of the 14th instant a general stampede appeared to be imminent: the ammunition carriers had thrown down their burdens, the Houssas were streaming back having fired away all their ammunition, the detachment of the 2ⁿᵈ W.I. Regt had become very unsteady, and the Marines were excited, firing wildly, many of them firing in the air; for some moments things looked unpleasant, and a panic was prevented and only just prevented by the exertion of all the officers about me, and those attached to Colonel Wood. There could be no confusion between the usefulness of these *selected* officers and of those *belonging* to the Marines and to the 2ⁿᵈ W.I. Regt. Troops engaged in the bush quickly lose all formation and the fight resolves itself into knots of men led by officers – the result depends upon the manner in which those officers do their work. The fire of the native troops is so very bewildering to all but the very steadiest troops, that panic can only be prevented by the soldierlike qualities of the officers engaged. Owing to the difficulties of transport the number of English soldiers that can be employed in this war must be small, but in my opinion every soldier employed should be a volunteer of good health and strong physique, and every officer should be *carefully selected*, so that the small force engaged should be the elite of Her Majesty's Army, a result that cannot in my humble opinion be secured by sending out any one formed Battalion.

In minor operations such as we are here engaged in the peculiar difficulties to be encountered can only be successfully met by specially devised plans of operation carried into execution by troops specially formed for the occasion. I humbly submit that the rules and Regulations of our Army are not calculated to meet the exigencies of a little war like this, and it is because I feel this strongly, that I presume to suggest to Your Royal Highness a peculiar though by no means a novel plan for the formation of the third Battalion that I have been obliged to ask for. If I failed to give Your Royal Highness the result of my recent experience here, I should be wanting in my duty, and I have to ask pardon if in doing so, I have in anyway presumed too much upon the liberty of personal correspondence with Your Royal Highness that has been so graciously accorded to me.

Should these views by approved of, I hope that Your Royal Highness will allow Lt. Colonel Colley now at the Staff College to come out in command of the third Battalion, as he is very anxious to serve here and he is an officer that I have every confidence in. It is very essential that the Seniors should be officers qualified to take command of the expedition should any untoward accident at any time dispose of those appointed by Your Royal Highness as first and second in command. In this bush fighting, no matter what care one may take to prevent the senior officers from unnecessary exposure, it is impossible to say whether the junior Ensign or the Commandg Officer may be the first knocked over. If Colonel Greaves is sent here the seniority of the officers serving in the expedition will be, Lt Colonel Warren[46] Rifle Brigade, Lt Col Mostyn 23rd Fusils.,[47] Lt Col. Festing R.M. Artillery, Lt Colonel Wood. With the exception of Col Festing I know them all well having served with them for years, and although they are all good soldiers, I consider that Colonel Wood is the only one that it would be wise to entrust with the command of this expedition: I hope I am not in the wrong in thus stating my private opinion.

Dr. Home has just informed me that Colonel McNeill will not be sufficiently recovered in time to resume his duties with this force: this sad news has been kept secret from Colonel McNeill, lest it should interfere with his recovery. I had hoped that it might have been possible to have sent him home by this mail, but the doctors consider that he cannot be safely moved at present. Major Baker carries on the duties of Chief Staff Officer *ad interim*, and does his work well, but I fear he will break down as it is too much for one man. Captain Buller looks after the Intelligence work, and I hope soon to have an efficient machinery at work for obtaining constant information of what goes on in the enemys camp. I believe that the bulk of the great fighting Ashantee Army is still at Mampon – about 15 or 16 miles from this place. If I had the English troops now here I would attack it at once, but until they arrive I do not expect to be in a position to carry out the movements against Mampon that I briefly sketched out in my last letter. It would be most unwise to run any great risk now, as the little life that I have succeeded in instilling into these wretched Fantees would be destroyed by any reverse in the field.

WOLSELEY AND ASHANTI

My leading post is now at Mansue (MANSUE) where I have had a strong fort constructed and have taken the liberty of naming it Fort Cambridge after Your Royal Highness. I shall not go beyond that place until I have cleared the Ashantees out of Mampon, for even at Mansue, my position is against all military rules, and is only justified by political exigencies. I want to appear strong although I am very very weak. I regret very much that before leaving England I did not ask for another W.I. Regt., for although owing to the quality of their officers such a Regt is of no great value in the field for active operations, yet for the occupation of fortified posts along the road, they would be invaluable. When Captain Glover arrived all the Garrisons along the coast consisting of Houssas were withdrawn by Colonel Harley and their place taken by detachments of the 2nd W.I. Regt reducing the available strength of that Corps so low that I could not now get together 100 bayonets from it without calling upon the Navy to find garrisons for Cape Coast Castle and for Elmina.

I sincerely trust that the two Regts. of Infantry, the Detachments of RA and RE and of Army Service Corps already under orders for this place, may be sent here without any delay, when this mail reaches England. It is a trying position to be placed in, that of having an enemys Army within 16 miles of our Head Qrs and yet to be without the means of attacking it.

Cambridge MSS, RA VIC/ADD E/1/7217

51

Wolseley Journal, 25–26 October

Saturday 25 October

Went on board "Simoom" & breakfasted. McNeill very cheery and well: he is still in pain. The doctors say he may go to Madeira by next mail but one. Buller went on board yesterday far from well, but he talks of returning tomorrow: he is one of the right sort, whereas Hart (31st Regt) the Army List mans son[48] is a funkstick as regards his health and remains on board although he is quite fit for service ashore. Another case of illness with him & I will send him home. Very good & reliable information in from Mampon that the enemy is breaking up his Camp, there sending off his army in Detachments with the intention of retiring behind the Prah. This we hear on the authority of several, but our best information is from a pretty girl the mistress of an Ashantee Chief. She is a Fantee and a slave and made her escape last night. I have ordered reconnaissances to be made tomorrow from Abbaye & Napoleon.

Sunday 26 October
Sent for Russell at daybreak & told him to be ready to move with 100 of his best men at 1 p.m. to Assayboo (10 miles from here). I go there later myself with 250 marines & bluejackets. Yesterday, I sent off Capt. Rait with 2 7 pdr. guns & 50 men of 2ⁿᵈ W.I. Regt. They push on to Dunquah today, where I have now about 800 native levies. All the fighting men of Cape Coast Castle not employed as carriers have now gone out to Napoleon. Large parties left yesterday evening for that place, but they are a poor lot of chicken hearted people. I shall be away from here for about 3 or 4 days, returning here most probably on Thursday next and re-embarking the marines & blue-jackets the same day. I do not want to prevent the Ashantees from retreating, but if possible to give them a kick behind as they go over the golden bridge that I build for their retreat. I shall thus if all goes well create the impression that I have driven the Ashantees out of the country & so encrease the confidence now gradually gaining ground amongst the natives here. I leave this behind to go by the mail of which we have as yet heard nothing.

Sunday 26 October continued
Left Cape Coast Government House at 3.30 p.m. There was such difficulty in collecting carriers that the convoy of camp equipment, ammunition etc etc did not get off until late. I started in the Governors Buggy drawn by four men & two others pushing behind. We soon came up with the rear of the column of marines, the blue-jackets having of course pushed on regardless of everyone else to Assayboo. I left the buggy at several steep hills & gave it up altogether at 6 p.m. walking in the last four miles. Huyshe makes the total distance 10 miles but I should say

that it is good eleven. Reached Assayboo about 7.30 p.m. very tired. A very bad camping ground, most of the tents pitched on the road. A fearful state of confusion; the crowd of niggers all jabbering. Five of us slept or rather tried to sleep in one tent. I never perspired so much in my life. I was in a bath all night and had not an hours refreshing sleep.

TNA, WO 147/3

52

Wolseley to Colonel Robert Biddulph[49]

26 October

[Holograph extract copy]

Cape Coast

Now once we have beaten the Ashantees badly beyond the Prah, the advance upon & occupation of Coomassie would be merely a triumphal walkover. But it might so destroy the King's Govt. & power, as to leave me no one to treat with: this is really the great evil that I dread, for nothing would induce me to keep English troops inactive beyond the Prah whilst I was casting about for some Ashantee potentate sufficiently important to treat with. If Coomassie is taken by force of arms it is most probable either that the King will commit suicide or be deposed in the General anarchy that is sure to follow the taking of their capital. Now what I want is to give the Ashantees a severe beating without destroying the Ashantee power, so that I may have a recognized Govt. to negotiate with; to make a treaty, the best I can, and to return with the least possible delay to the sea coast, embark the English troops, send them home, disband the native levies, holding the Prahsue–Cape Coast road with detachments of Houssa police so as to keep it open for trade.

Now if these views are approved of, believe me that some more binding instructions should be sent to Glover than any yet sent to him. He should be positively forbidden to cross the Prah, without my orders for him to do so. Once across the Prah, he should be positively forbidden to advance upon Coomassie without my orders.

His success would be my success, so it is no petty jealousy that gives rise to these views. I am as anxious as Glover can be for his ultimate success, but from what I know of his character & of his former doings on this coast, I believe that if left to himself, success, unrestrained success on his part would be another word for anarchy in the Ashantee Kingdom.

The Fantees by their arrogance & insulting messages to the King of Ashantee, & their ill treatment of his messengers & traders have brought on this war: They have neither the power nor the courage to bring it to a conclusion, but I verily believe that if all dread of Ashantee was removed, by the utter destruction of King Koffee's Kingdom, our own position here for the future would not be in any way improved. It is not our interest that the Ashantee power should be destroyed. If this is the opinion of the Govt. then Glover's acts should be restrained by positive & binding orders for him not to cross the Prah etc etc (as I have said above) except in concert with me in accordance with the instructions I may send him. These are my views, & I give them for what they are worth. They may be wrong, but they are honest, & given frankly in what I believe to be the true interest of the present Administration at home, whose Agent I consider myself to be here.

Bodleian, Kimberley MSS, MS. Eng. c. 4112, ff. 29–31.

53

Wolseley to Louisa Wolseley

[17–]26 October

[Holograph]

I enclose my journal as usual. I begin this to day although no mail for England is expected to leave here before the 22nd or 23rd instant. I have written such long despatches about our fight, and so numerous will be the newspaper accounts of it, that I shall not weary either you or myself by going over the story here. It was a complete success, but poor McNeils severe – I may add dangerous, wound throws a damper upon the affair that is most unfortunate. He bled so profusely that my clothes & waterbottle were died [sic] with his blood: he is a man of the right sort, for he took his wound like a soldier, although the pain was excruciating. He is going on well and hopes to be able to be about again in six weeks. The danger is that lockjaw may ensue, as all the tendons of his left wrist have been torn away. It is hard luck that such a good officer should have been struck down in such a trifling affair, but "God is Great" as the Moslems say, and we must not cavil at his decrees. My child war brings one to think more seriously than when sitting at home at ease & makes me reallize how dependant we are upon him for everything. Our life is a frail affair, the cord of which is easily and rapidly snapt at all times whether at home or abroad. I trust that God will spare me to carry this war out to a successful end, although I tell you candidly, that I have no great desire to live long myself: even my ambition of which my very heart was at one time so full lies in a great measure died out within me, and candidly I have often at times of late, wished most sincerely that I was in heaven. Don't rate these gloomy thoughts, I never was in better health or in better or higher spirits *outwardly* than at present, but I feel a sort of relief and comfort in telling you in my letters that are for your own perusal only what I think and feel.

I enclose you some visiting cards. Only fancy *ladies* with cards here: their complexion varied – the women not the cards – from the color of an old saddle to that of a Ysamiard. One Miss Jessie Cruikshank[50] is really a very good looking girl, and is now sitting in her verandah of which I command a view as I sit writing to you. Her slaves are busily employed in the same verandah doing up my shirts, as Madame la Mére is our washerwoman. The three ladies paid me a visit yesterday, all got up in swell hats, that looked like Bond street. Please tell your pretty Pal that her Baker is in first rate condition, *"as fit as a cat"* and working away like a good soldier, and you know that is the highest compliment that I can pay any man in the language that I think and write in. I wrote B. J.[51] a letter yesterday that will go home by this mail, not that I care for her, but because I wish to please Holmes for whom as you know I entertain the warmest feelings, and I know that he likes her to have letters to her. I am anxious to hear how you and the Pal get on at the seaside. I am sorry to hear that the poor little Baba missed McCort[52] for I am sure no one else in our *great* establishment grieved at her departure. I hope the new nurse may be a comfort to you. I enclose you a note from General the Honbl. R. Rollo C.B.[53] as it refers to you. I have answered it & said that I would let you know of *her* kindness in asking you to pay them a visit. She is a nice woman, but there is something wrong in their marriage that I never was able to fathom. At times my child I feel very lonely here. Things go on so slowly that I feel depressed now and then. I do my best and work hard, but one feels exhausted at times, and then I feel low and put out. Need I say that my thoughts at such moments always turn to you. [Sentence erased.]

Some of the *noble*!!! people for whom we are about to make war have just gone by the house carrying the head of an Ashantee in triumph. They wanted to bring it here to show me, but I sent down word to say that if ever I caught a man bringing in a head here, I would have him flogged.

18th October. I keep up a very lengthy correspondence with H.R.H. which is rather a tax upon my time, as I have to tell him all sorts of fiddling little things. McCalmont has been laid up for some days past, but not from the climate: as you know I told you before I left that the doctors said he was not strong enough for the job, and I fear what they said proves true. He has been on board the Simoom for the last five days and he does not get well as rapidly as he ought. I wish he would go home for an ailing A.D.C. is the devil.[54] My other A.D.C. is as strong as a lion. I never met a finer fellow in every way: he works hard all day and feeds us very fairly: he is the stuff for a soldier and has a good head on his shoulders. The best thing we get to eat is the fish, which in the morning at breakfast is excellent: the best sort is a herring the flavor of which is very good. The sheep are so small that a common dish is the haunch and both legs in fact the whole animal minus the head & shoulders, and when served up to table it is about the size of a very large hare, not having often as much meat as a good hare. Dear Huyshe has started this morning for the front to a place where I am forming a new post. It is marked on the map Abracampah – a little to the east of north from this place

Monday 20th October. I enclose you for Holmes information the copy of a proclamation[55] I have issued with a view to striking terror into my enemies. It is penned in a fine Bombastes Furioso style of literature. McNeill will go home by the mail that takes this. If you want to write to him, his Club is "The United Service Club, Pall Mall". I wish I had something to send you home by him, but there is nothing to be had here except horrid looking gold rings, and I know you would not care for them.

Tuesday 21st October. I have just returned from the Simoom when I went to see McNeill: Dr Home went on board [with] me for the purpose of finally examining the wound and determining whether he could be moved by next mail. He tells me that it is out of the question; he says it is a dreadful wound, and he wound up by telling me confidentially that he would not be able to take part again in this war. This grieves me very much because I know that it will be a sad blow to McNeill and I shall feel his loss beyond measure. He is not to be told this until the last moment. I am writing for Greaves by this mail but I cannot have him here for at least two months. This is all very disheartening to me, for there never was a place where if you want anything done, you must do it yourself, more than here. I have asked for three Battalions instead of two. I wonder what the Ministers will think of that!! I wish I had them here now, for at present I am too weak to do anything in the fighting line. I shall send B. J. a copy of the proclamation so keep the one I enclose.

22nd October. The mail just in bringing me your letter of 28th Sept & one from Holmes dated 29th. I am so very [passage erased]. Butler has been here to breakfast; and delivered to me your parcel – many thanks my little woman for the *specs* and the *nose* wash: the former now ornament my trunk as I write this, so you see they have been taken into immediate use. Russell has been a little seedy but don't tell Pal unless she has heard of it from himself. I have insisted upon his going on board ship for a couple of days to restore himself. He takes no care of himself and will go out too much in the sun. Thank God I am still flourishing & never felt better. In reading your note, I have been thinking of what we had best do when I return, and I think that the best plan for us will be to take very good lodgings in London for a month after my arrival. I shall be able to give you at least a fortnights warning before I return home myself, so you could run up to town from the sea side leaving the Baba there for a couple of days and take some *good* lodgings for a month. I shall be a little flush of money, so I would prefer taking really good ones, or what would be still better if you could arrange it getting a couple of bedrooms, a dressing room & a sitting room at the Alexandra [palace erased] Hotel: I should not mind giving £10 a week for the rooms and attendants & you might arrange for the grub as an extra, so much a meal or so much a day. What do you say? Let me know by return. I shall want to be in London for a month or at least for a few weeks when I return: after that I should like to run abroad for a month – think of the best place for us to go to, and how you can dispose of young lady during our absence: would Eyty[56] take care of her? I like to think over all our schemes, although when I think that two months must elapse before I can have the troops here with which I am to fight, my heart sinks within me. If I only had them here now I could do so much. You must allow that I have written you a long letter this time. I enclose you a little note just received from Ben Stevenson:[57] see how nicely he alludes to "laurels" at the end. Have you seen a bad poem although very flattering to me regarding my name Garnet in the Punch of Sept 27[th58] I feel so uncomfortable when I read all this "*high talk*" about myself in the newspapers & have a sinking within me, when I think how coarse would be the abuse of the same writers if I prove a failure here: war is an uncertain trade, and no matter how hard I may work – I still may fail and if I do, only a cabbage garden in a remote country district where I can hide myself should I ever return after failure will be my lot: but my trust is in God, and I have faith in Him that he will crown this undertaking with complete success, no matter what may be my own individual fate.

23rd October. The women here were [wear] the funniest looking bustles made I believe – I have not yet personally inspected one – when I have time I shall do so – of rolls of cotton stuff upon which the baby sits a–stray legs, a cloth being fastened round the little beggars back so that nothing is seen but its head & sometimes its arms. It sometimes gets round so as to suckle the very long breasts of the mother. The women wear their hair in spikes twisted round with string thus [Figure 1]. It is really far from unbecoming especially as their hair is more like wool than hair and they have not much of it. In the Graphic of Sept 27th there is a likeness of Princess Marguerita (wife of heir apparent of King of Italy)[59] that I consider is very like you. Look at it & tell me if you agree. It is in the same number with dear old Jock Mackenzies likeness.[60] This infernal mail for England that I am most anxious to get off is still due. It is a serious matter for me as my letter asking for the European troops goes home by it. McNeill is going on well.

Figure 1. 'The women wear their hair in spikes twisted round with string thus' [**53**].

25[th.] No mail for England in yet. It is too provoking. I went on board the Simoom this morning and breakfasted there. McNeill very cheery & going on admirably. The doctors say he may go to Madeira by the next mail but one. Russell is at work as well as ever. I walked up yesterday evening to see how his Army was getting on and found him jolly and well as usual. I enclose you the form of prayer that has been printed for use in the churches here – perhaps you will say it sometimes when you think of me here.

Sunday 26th October. I am off to Dunquah for a few days to see what the enemy is really about there: I take with me 250 marines & bluejackets. Russell goes with me with 100 of his best men. I hope to get back here on Wednesday or Thursday before which time the mail for England must surely be in. So I close this for the present. Goodbye my dear child. Pray without ceasing for my success, and think of me always as your fond husband.

Hove, Wolseley MSS, W/P 3/9

54

Wolseley Journal, 27–30 October

Monday 27 October

Started at 6.30 a.m. for Abrakrampa: tried to travel in a cot, but the road was so bad I had to walk distance nearly 4 miles through thick forest and high grass. Reached Abrakrampa at 7.45 a.m.: a large village. Had an interview with King Abra and started him off with all his fighting men with Lt. Pollard R.N.[61] and 20 Houssas to beat up the Ashantee quarters at Abamoo & Inacodayo, the latter is on the Sweet River. I intend if all goes well beating up the Ashantees in the neighborhood of Assanchi tomorrow morning Col. Festing from Dunquah marching upon the same place. I don't want to head the enemy or prevent his defeat. Festing from Dunquah moved out this morning by my orders along the Haunted Road: he had only gone a few miles when he came upon an Ashanti encampment which he surprised and destroyed. The enemy bolted into the bush, and Festing remained in action with them for several hours pitching in shot shell and rockets into them besides vollies of Sneiders – towards evening he returned to Dunquah. Five officers were wounded all slightly but one, Captain Godwin (103rd Regt.)[62] who has had a bullet in his groin – a very nasty place. The enemy are now retreating, they have broken up their camp at Mampon and intend going back into their own country behind the Prah.

Tuesday 28 October

Had made all arrangements for moving at 5.30 a.m. but of course the King of Abrah was not ready so it was 6.30 a.m. before we got off. I sent the King & his men on a head under Lieut. Pollard R.N. Russells men & the Houssas behind them then the marines & blue-jackets – we took a rocket tube with us – marched upon Assanchi – took a few prisoners & had one man wounded: remained at Assanchi until noon & then marched the sailors & marines back to Abrakrampa leaving the Houssas at Assanchi until Pollard should return who I had sent on to open out communication with Col. Festing whom I had ordered to move out again to day along the same road. It poured with rain on us during our return – we were all drenched to the skin in a few minutes. I was very angry with the Marines on the return journey who got up several alarms, all I believe owing to a duffer of a fellow named Crease[63] who commanded them. Towards night I became nervous about Pollard who is a reckless sort of a sailor & one who would push on regardless of consequence, especially as I heard later from Festing that the native levies at Dunquah who had been engaged the day before, positively refused to march this morning so that his movement towards Assanchi to meet us was impossible. Late at night Gordon with the Houssas returned saying that he had advanced as far as Escabio where he met all the Abrakrampa men running in, & reporting that Pollard had been stopped by the Ashantees & was working round them to Dunquah. This made me still more uneasy, but about 2 a.m. a runner came in from Akroful saying that Pollard had reached that place in an exhausted condition with 6 men, who had carried him for the last few miles as he was unable to walk.

Wednesday 29 October

Scouts out in all directions – a few prisoners taken – difficult to keep the Fantees from taking off their heads. Pollard returned: says that King Abras men behaved very badly; they bolted from him when the first shot was fired & he was very nearly surrounded: it was only by the great local knowledge possessed by a head man that stuck to him well that he succeeded in getting out [of] the Ashantis clutches. Left 50 marines & blue jackets at Abrakrampa. The rest marched at 3 p.m. for Assayboo: I walked there myself where I found my "*carriage*" and was drawn into Cape Coast by six men. I find that on the bush roads it is out of the question using a hammock as the paths are so narrow that the bearers cannot go two abreast and they have not sufficient intelligence to carry a cot as the Indians do on their shoulders one man behind the other: the consequence is that I shall knock up if this goes on, for my leg feels very bad to day. In future I shall stick to the main road where I can be either in a buggy or carried comfortably. Reached Cape Coast Castle at 6.15 p.m. McNeill going on well.

Thursday 30 October

Busy all the morning writing: a fine day. Mr Boyle correspondent for the Telegraph arrived by last mail: dined with us – a violent radical – I should say a would be republican. Enemy still in full retreat, and in a great funk I should say. If these cowardly Fantees would only now close round his scattered columns, not a man of his army ought ever to get back over the River Prah, but these chicken-hearted rascals will do nothing. Whilst at dinner a gun was fired showing that the mail was in for England, so this must go home in the morning.

TNA, WO 147/3

55

Wolseley to Cambridge

30 October
[Holograph]
Government House
Cape Coast Castle

Since the date of my last letter (the 24th October) the position of affairs here has changed for the better. The results of our fight at Essaman have been far greater than I could have anticipated: finding that white men attacked them in front, and were also established in their rear at Abrakrampa, Akroful, Dunquah and Mansue, the enemy became uneasy, and resolved upon retreating. For some time back there have been two parties in the camp at Mampon, one, the elder chiefs being in favor of remaining in the Fantee territory, the other, composed of the younger chiefs being anxious to return to their own country. At the head of the former party was Amanquartier, the General Commanding in Chief. He was afraid lest his head should be taken off if he returned without receiving his recall from the King, and a similar dread was felt by most of the principal Captains. Our success on the 14th instant seems to have turned the balance in the younger partys favor, and as far as I can make out, they began to send their sick away two days after that date, and since then have been moving off by detachments, of from one to several thousands. Their camp at Mampon that has been for so many months past a standing menace to Elmina & Cape Coast Castle is now deserted, and their retreating columns are endeavoring to find their way to the Prah, in the vicinity of Prahsue. I am not strong enough to attack their larger columns, but hope to harass their smaller bodies, and whilst taking care not "*to head*" them anywhere, to do my best to give to their retiring movement all the semblance of the compulsory retreat of a beaten army before a victorious one. I am obliged to play this game of brag and bombast in order to give confidence to our allies. It is very distastful to me, but it is the only thing left to me to do, unless I sat down here and acted the part of the Civil Governor alone, doing nothing at all in the Military line.

The enemy owe a great grudge to the King of Abrakrampa,[64] and have declared their intention of marching through and destroying it during their retreat. The position it occupies is of great importance as a protection to the main road to Mansue. I have roughly dotted down on the enclose[d] piece of paper, the relative position it occupies with reference to Assayboo etc etc for your Royal Highnesses information. For some time past I have had an officer there as a Commissioner to the King, and recently I had it regularly placed in a state of defence sending 100 Houssas there and occupying Akroful by a detachment of 50 men of the 2nd W.I. Regt. as a support to Abrakrampa. On Saturday last the 25th instant having ascertained positively that the retreating columns of the enemy were in the neighborhood of the Sweet River, west and north west of Abrakrampa, I determined upon moving out myself to that place with the Marines, in the hopes of being able to fall upon some one of the enemys columns if I could find one sufficiently weak to authorise me to attack it. I left here late in the afternoon of the 26th instant and marched with 250 Marines and bluejackets to Assayboo, and pushed on the following morning to Abrakrampa, having sent an order to Col. Festing Commg at Dunquah to march out with all his available force westward along the haunted road with a view to clearing out some of the enemies camps known to be in the vicinity of Escabio. Upon arriving at Abrakrampa I pushed out a strong reconnoitring party of native levies and Houssas along the Abonum road, ordering it to turn off the Effootoo road at that place if it was found unoccupied towards Quacodayo on the Jooquah road, where I expected a column of the enemy would be met with. I held my force in Abrakrampa ready to move at a moments notice upon any point where its assistance might be required, but I felt unwilling to fatigue my white men by marching any further that day unless their aid was absolutely required. I heard every half hour from this strong reconnoitring party who picked up a few prisoners from time to time but met with no resistance. Quacodayo was unoccupied except by stragglers; I sent the party on to Ainsa from whence it returned in the evening. The prisoners taken all told the same story: the enemy was in full retreat but intended *en passant* to take

and destroy Abrakrampa against the King of which Amanquartier
had an especial grudge. I heard from Festing in the evening: he
had surprised an Ashantee force and dispersed it. Unfortunately
his native allies of which his force was almost entirely composed,
behaved very badly: some would not fight at all, and even the best
of them had not only to be led by our officers, but to be *driven*
by them with sticks into action. I am very anxious that all our
skirmishes with the enemy should invariably end by a general
charge (with a great cheer) for even fifty yards towards the enemy,
but there was no charge possible with the native allies. As usual
where all the chief fighting has to be done by the English officers,
several were wounded, but their wounds are only scratches,
for these Ashantee arms do not hurt much at 50 yards. Captain
Godwin 103rd Regt is the only one really hurt; he was hit in the
groin by a slug, and I do not yet know whether it still remains in
his body. I never can have too many officers here, for these Fantees
will do nothing without they have an Englishman with them, and
between slight wounds, and slight touches of fever we always have
a number on the sick list. The young officers I brought out with
me work like slaves, and my difficulty is to prevent them from
knocking themselves up by overwork: I cannot replace them here,
for as I have told Your Royal Highness in a previous letter, the
officers of the 2nd W.I. with a very few exceptions are useless for
war purposes of an active nature.

On Tuesday the 28th instant I moved to Assanchi, ordering Col.
Festing to repeat his movement of the day before, I picked up a few
prisoners at that place but found no body of the enemy. I remained
there until noon having sent out patrols and scouts in all directions,
and then returned to Abrakrampa. I sent 100 of the native levies
under Lieut Pollard R.N. along the Dunquah road with orders to
open out communications with Col. Festing, and left the rest of
the Kings men & all the Houssas at Assanchi in support to remain
there until Mr Pollards return: When Mr Pollard got near the
Ashantees who had been dispersed the day before and who were
there in the bush near Escabio, his men bolted leaving him with
only 6 followers who behaved well: these men took him by a cross
road through the bush into Akroful where he communicated with

Col. Festing at Dunquah. Col. Festing had not been able to carry out his instructions that day as the native allies positively refused to move. These are the people we are fighting for!!

The more I see of this business, the more I am convinced that it is essential we should so end it, as to prevent for ever the *possibility* of another war. The people are not worth fighting for, and to promise them protection is merely to relieve a quarrelsome, worthless and cowardly race from all the responsibilities of a war, that they are certain to bring down from time to time upon their country.

Not seeing any immediate prospect of being able to use the sailors & marines with advantage I sent them back to their ships, leaving 50 of them until Saturday next the 1ˢᵗ November at Abrakrampa, when they will also return to Cape Coast and reembark. The moral effect of showing these white men along the road is good and gives the enemy an exaggerated idea of our strength. I am anxious to show them as often as possible and in as many places as I can, but to really use them as seldom as possible, carrying on the skirmishing necessary with the retreating enemy by means of the native levies. I have issued a bombastic proclamation calling upon the whole Fantee country to rise and follow up and crush the retreating enemy. I do not yet despair of getting some of the Allied Kings to do this, and of being able by their means to inflict severe damage upon the enemy before he gets back across the Prah. If I had my European troops now, I could crush him. The mail has just arrived and will leave early tomorrow for England. Reviewing my position at present it is far better in some respects than I could have hoped, but in some ways it is worse, for although I never expected to have a good practicable road made to Mansue & protected by strong fortified positions by the end of October, and to have forced the enemy to retreat by that date, still I had hoped that there would have been more zeal and pluck displayed by those in whose cause we are fighting. A terror of the Ashantee name has struck deeply into the hearts of all this Fantee race, and it does not seem as if it ever can be eradicated.

Your Royal Highness will be glad to find that all the nonsense talked by Sir A. Clarke, R.E. about the impossibility of English troops marching in this climate has been shown up in its true light by our recent movements. Our men although fat and unaccustomed to marching, did well, each man carrying 70 rounds of ammunition (60 in pouches & 10 in haversack). Sir A. Clarke said that Englishmen could not march here, that every man must be carried. Never was there a wilder statement made by an unpractical man. An officer marched in here from Dunquah yesterday heavily laden with pistol, ammunition, water bottle and field glass, a distance of 20 miles, without halting anywhere for food. The marines and bluejackets marched in here this morning from Assayboo (10 miles) arriving at 8.15 a.m. and marched past this house with as great regularity as they would at Aldershot. I trust that these facts may set to rest all dread regarding the use of English soldiers for a short spell in this country, for without their assistance I do not believe it is possible ever to inflict a serious blow upon the Ashantee Army.

I trust that all my movements will meet with Your Royal Highnesses approval. My task here is no easy one, but its burden will be lessened considerably, should my actions be approved of by Your Royal Highness.

Cambridge MSS, RA VIC/ADD E/1/7222

56

Wolseley to Fremantle

30 October

[Holograph]

I shall have to send an officer to Accra in a few days, so perhaps it is better to postpone deciding about sending a vessel to Glover until then. I am glad to hear that your arm is not the worse for our march out. Although we had no fighting, I believe that our parade through the country has already done great good and will do more by and bye, as it serves to scare the Ashantees who hear of European soldiers being on their track.

I am very sorry to hear such bad news of the Commodore: I am glad however that he is out of the tropics.

Unless something unforseen occurs I intend withdrawing the Marines & bluejackets from Abrakrampa on Saturday; if I have to change this, I shall let you know tomorrow.

NMM, Fremantle MSS, FRE/109

57

Proclamation by Wolseley

30 October

[Printed]

To all the Kings, Headmen, Chiefs and Tribes on the Gold Coast, allies of Her Majesty the Queen of England, greeting.

I desire that you should know that immediately after the attack made upon Essaman and Ampinee, and the destruction of those places by the English troops under my command, your enemies broke up their encampment at Mampon. Finding that they were unable to contend with us either in the open or in the bush, they are now in full retreat endeavouring to return to their own country by Prahsue; one of their retreating columns has been attacked and dispersed by my troops near Dunquah.

They are trying to carry with them in their flight all the goods of which they have robbed you, all the wives and children whom they have stolen from you.

Men of the Gold Coast will you allow this?

Will you let the hours slip by whilst your wives, your sons, and your daughters, are being driven off to slaughter by the flying enemy?

Will you not pursue them?

Now or never is the time to show that you are men.

I for my part shall hold no man as the friend of Her Majesty, or as the friend of this country, who delays for one moment.

You have nothing to fear, I hold the whole road from here to Mansue, so that they cannot assail it. Gather upon my strong forts of Dunquah, Abrakrampa, and Mansue. No one will venture to attack these points. Thence press onwards to the Prah, and oppose your enemies as they are endeavouring to re-cross the River. If you now act quickly and with vigour, the fall of your enemy and the peace of your country will be secured.

TNA, WO32/7638, WO33/25, 26; CO 96/102

58

Wolseley Journal, 31 October

Friday 31 October

The mail for England arrived last night, so I was up early getting my letters ready intending to go on board to see McNeill off when the steamer was starting. I sent Charteris on board Simoom to arrange matters for McNeill. Before long I received the most alarming news. The mail steamer had yellow fever on board: four men had died of it on the voyage & Capt. Lees coming here from Lagos to serve on the Colonial Staff has landed ill as Dr Home declared with yellow fever. There was the devil to pay. The steamer was put in quarantine & those who had landed were sent off to Prospect Hill where I had them surrounded by a cordon of Police. The first Ordinance I passed as Civil Governor here was that establishing quarantine, so the law now comes in most opportunely. I am in great hopes of this alarm being a false one, but still it will serve to keep everyone up to the collar in their exertions to keep disease from this place. Our patrols have been into Mampon and burnt it. The enemy still declare their intention to attack Abrakrampa: I sincerely hope they will do so. Russell commands there, so it would be grand fun for him. If I only had one good English battalion now, not a man of this retreating army should ever get back into their own country. Owing to the yellow fever on board, of course McNeill did not go home. I have walked too much in the bush: my leg is bad.

TNA, WO 147/3

3

Marking Time (November 1873)

As the Asante army attempted to regain the main route back to the Pra to secure its line of retreat so Wolseley probed forward trying to locate it. Wood was advanced towards Beulah while Baker Russell sent out parties from Abrakampa and Festing from Dunkwa, Wolseley hoping to disrupt Amankwatia's ability to forage and force him into attacking one of his outposts since his own force was not sufficient to attack the Asante [**59**, **60**, **62**]. On 3 November a reconnaissance in force by Festing ran into an Asante force. Festing was leading 80 West Indians, eight Hausa with a rocket trough, 12 Fante police and just over 1,000 native levies. The levies, however, promptly fled, leaving Lieutenant Eardley Wilmot of the Royal Artillery, who had pushed on ahead, isolated with the Hausa he had been training and some of the West Indians. So badly wounded in the arm that it would have had to be amputated, and in considerable pain, Wilmot fought on until shot dead through the heart at close range. Lieutenant Osborn Jones of the 2nd West India regiment was hit trying to reach Wilmot and Festing was also hit in the hip as he retrieved Wilmot's body. Wilmot, who was engaged to be married, was the first of the *Ambriz* contingent to die and his funeral at Cape Coast was a solemn affair, Wolseley overhearing someone say, 'That is the first of us' [**61**, **63**, **64**, **66**].[1] Lord Gifford and Lieutenant Gordon were trampled when the levies suddenly fled during Wood's advance and Eyre had to threaten to shoot them to get them even to pass bodies of dead Asante.[2] It did little to improve Wolseley's opinion of the worth of the Fante [**61**, **62**, **64**, **66**, **67**, **80**]. Others also took the view that they were simply cowards, Butler later remarking that the Akyem, too, were 'a hopeless lot of craven beggars'.[3]

Wolseley, however, soon got his wish that the Asante would attack one of his outposts for Amankwatia had determined to punish the Abura at Abrakampa before he left the protectorate. Wolseley had come to discount the possibility of an attack on Baker Russell at Abrakampa and had actually ordered some of the seamen and marines there withdrawn to the coast on the very morning the attack began. Fortunately, the post had been well fortified – initially by Gordon and then by Robert Home, Pollard, Huyshe and Buckle – with loopholed buildings, shelter trenches, an abattis, the conversion of the brick-built Wesleyan chapel into a small fortress and, most significantly, the bush cleared around the settlement for between 70 and 120 yards. Baker Russell had eight officers, 50 seamen and marines, 100 Hausa, 93 West Indians, 100 Susu, 64 levies from Sierra Leone, 114 Fante, and the King of Abura with about 500 of his followers. There was also a rocket trough and 'Nelly', an old Dutch 1½-pounder that had been used previously as a yacht signal gun at Cape Coast Castle and was now supplied with bags of bullets and scrap iron as improvised langridge. Warning of an attack came on 3 November through an escaped Fante female slave of the Asante and it finally developed on the afternoon of 5 November, continuing through much of the night until the following morning and resuming in the afternoon of 6 November. According to Reade, who like Boyle had made his own way up to Abrakampa, the attack was 'feeble in everything but noise', accompanied as it was by horns, drums and shouting. Though estimated at about 10,000 strong, the Asante could not get close enough to do any real damage since the slugs fired by their muskets – a mixture of odd bits of lead and iron, limestone and even sea shells – were not really effective beyond about 50 yards. Indeed, only two Europeans were wounded, together with one West Indian and 18 levies.[4]

The ineffectiveness of the Asante attack, however, was certainly not apparent to Wolseley when he received Baker Russell's request for assistance in the early hours of 6 November. Wolseley hastened to order forward Wood and sent Brackenbury to round up as many seamen and marines as Fremantle could spare, taking out 22 officers, 303 seamen and marines and some rocket troughs himself in relief of the post [**65, 66, 67, 68, 80**]. Pushing as fast as possible through the heat of the day, when the marines had no proper sun helmets and the seamen only white covers for their caps, Wolseley's force suffered enormously. About a third fell out from exhaustion and Wolseley had to supplement them with 50 marines from the garrison at Asebu en route as well as halting at one point for four hours. Warm chocolate was handed out to those who got to Abrakampa to refresh and cool them but many of the marines were to become 'pallid, languid and listless' as a result of the march. Wolseley finally arrived on the evening of 6 November. It took Wood some 14 hours to get to Abrakampa, largely through the unwillingness of the Fante to move quickly enough and his guides deliberately misleading him, and he only arrived on the morning of 7 November.[5]

When the attack was not renewed on 7 November, Wolseley attempted to organise a pursuit but chose only to try to do so with the levies, who could not be induced to move forward even when driven by the Susu and the free use of sticks and umbrellas by Wolseley's officers. Indeed, according to Wood, one officer 'used so much persuasion towards a Chief as to spoil a strong umbrella'. Shortly after, indeed, Wolseley decided to disarm many of the levies including the Cape Coast Volunteers and turn them into labourers. The Asante, however, had gone and Amankwatia, who was said to have been wounded in the leg and carried away drunk in a blanket, left behind on the field his carrying chair, his bed, his sacred cock and chickens, his fetish implements, and his war drum: the latter was subsequently presented to the Royal United Service Institution. It was also said that a brother of Kofi Karikari had been killed.[6]

Reade and Henty were both critical of Wolseley for not using the seamen, the marines or the West Indians to pursue the Asante but Wolseley himself was to report that he did not feel able as yet to risk Europeans in the interior 'both on the ground of the risk to health, and of the expenditure of labour involved in supplying them'. It may also be the case, however, that Wolseley was already affected by the fever shortly to overcome him. Indeed, Reade had noticed that instead of posting a seven-pounder pointing towards the Asante position, Wolseley had 'pointed it towards the Esseboo Road, and there he sat with his staff eagerly gazing in the opposite direction from the enemy'. On the other hand, Fremantle, who together with Baker Russell had urged Wolseley to pursue the Asante, believed that it was not fever that prompted Wolseley's inaction but a fear of securing a major success too early that might encourage the government to prevent a march on Kumase.[7]

Fever was beginning to take its toll of the Europeans, with both of Wolseley's ADCs, McCalmont and Charteris, stricken down and invalided [**59, 64, 72, 73, 74, 75**]. Like others, Charteris had refused to admit he was ill but had exhausted himself running a mile with a message on 28 October. Sent on board the *Simoom*, which left for St Helena with other wounded and invalids including McNeill, Godwin and Graves on 21 November, Charteris died at sea on 23 November [**104, 105, 142, 158, 169**].[8] By 15 November, indeed, of 64 white officers who had arrived at Cape Coast since 2 October, 29 had been hospitalised at one time or another, seven being invalided, and two had died, Wilmot having been killed and Assistant Commissary J. Harrymount having died of dysentery on 8 November. The *Barracouta* was also sent to sea on 23 November to give those seamen and marines suffering from sickness the chance to recover.[9]

Wolseley himself had suffered from his bad leg in having to walk much of the way to Abrakampa as there were too many creepers across the route to accommodate a travelling chair or hammock. In retrospect, he also felt he had set out too quickly to return to Cape Coast on 8 November and fever struck that same day [**62, 64, 69, 70, 71, 74, 77**]. Anthony Home reported it as 'ardent fever' deriving from the forced march and exposure to the sun but Wolseley himself believed it to be a recurrence of the 'Burma fever' – presumably malaria – from which he had suffered periodically ever since 1853. Either way, having subsided to some extent on 10 November, the fever returned on 12 November with Wolseley's temperature exceeding 104 degrees. With T. D. Baker, who had been acting as chief of staff since McNeill's wound, taking on much of the resulting workload [88], Maurice nursed Wolseley until he was sufficiently recovered to resume his duties on 20 November. Wood for one had not expected Wolseley to recover and, in his memoirs, Wolseley was to give a graphic description of how his fevered mind wandered, dictating in his mind a letter of resignation to Cardwell and even working up a scheme whereby the sea could be harnessed to powering Lancashire mill machinery.[10]

In the meantime, all knowledge of the whereabouts of the Asante had been lost, this remaining the case for three weeks after Abrakampa. Indeed, there seemed so little activity that Stanley and Henty steamed down to Accra in the *Dauntless* to report on Glover's progress, not returning to Cape Coast until mid-December.[11] Glover professed to be in want of funds [**77, 84**], but also felt that his attempts to raise more of the Akyem was being thwarted by the mission with which Wolseley had charged Butler on 2 November, namely to raise the Western Akyem [**60, 64, 82**]. In turn, however, the ultimate failure of Butler's mission was attributed by Wolseley to Glover having given so many inducements to the Eastern Akyem, while Butler himself felt that Glover was far too interested in pursuing his own course on the Volta than crossing into Asante territory.[12] Wolseley's intention was that Butler should contact the supposedly more warlike kings, Kobina Fua and Kofi Ahinkora, and cross the Pra on 15 January 1874 with a substantial Akyem force some 30 miles upstream from where Wolseley would cross with his main force at Praso. Butler, who was soon wracked with fever, encountered innumerable difficulties in his attempts to generate action on the part of the Akyem such as finding Kobina Fua intent on going 'in all the pomp of Negro buffoonery' to Accra rather than towards the Pra. Indeed, Butler returned to Manso at the end of November to report his failure before determining to return to the Akyem in December to try and fulfil Wolseley's intention. He was accompanied on his second attempt by Captain John Palmer Brabazon, formerly of the Grenadier Guards, who had joined the expedition as a volunteer; Captain Arthur Henry Paget of the Scots Fusilier Guards; Lieutenant Robert Stuart MacGregor of the 50th Foot; and Surgeon Robert Whittington Lowe of the Army Medical Service. Subsequently, Wolseley was to be particularly impressed by Brabazon's contribution [122, 158]. In all, Butler calculated he had walked over 900 miles between November and January. An Akyem force was gathered but, in the event, refused to cross the Pra on the appointed day so Butler duly invaded Asante territory with just MacGregor and Lowe – Brabazon and Paget were both ill – and six Fante police [116, 121, 134]. So far as Reade was concerned, it was 'dangling a weak body of men as bait' to draw off the Asante.[13]

Wolseley's own evolving plans depended upon completing the arrangements to ensure that his white battalions were able to march to the Pra in the best possible conditions to preserve their health [76, 80, 82]. More reconnaissance would be carried out and a 'flying' bridge thrown across the river. Moreover, there would be a series of staging posts and supply depots at approximately ten-mile intervals between Cape Coast and Praso, to which the troops would march by detachments, leaving Wolseley to cross just 60 miles of Asante territory beyond the Pra to Kumase. Praso, 73¾ miles from Cape Coast Castle, would be a major base capable of accommodating 2,000 Europeans while each of the other depots would be able to accommodate 400 Europeans and a garrison of 50. In the end, the seven chosen locations – Inquabim, which was seven miles from Cape Coast; Akrofo, which was 13¾ miles out; Fante Nyankomase, which was 24¼ miles out; Manso, which was 35¾ miles out; Suta, which was 46 miles from Cape Coast; Assin Nyankomase, at 58¼ miles' distance; and Beraku, 67¼ miles out with Manso also doubling as a large magazine – were slightly different from the original list. This had included Amponsie Quantah and Dansame but they were dropped and Assin Nyankomase and Beraku substituted. However, having inspected Suta, Wolseley then decided it was also unsuitable and chose Ata Insu instead, this being 4½ miles further on, though it is not actually clear if this was put into effect [85]. Troops would be accommodated in huts each 60' x 17' and intended for 50 men with walls of split bamboo, roofs thatched with palm leaves, and bamboo or palm stalk sleeping platforms off the ground. At each station, there was to be provision for 35 sick and wounded, with a hospital at Praso capable of dealing with 100 casualties and another at Manso with 60. Each post would have 35 hammocks or cots, with six bearers allocated to each in order take men back to the next, while the main column would be accompanied by 85 cots or hammocks with their allocated bearers. Anthony Home had also worked out a detailed daily ration for the Europeans of 1½ lbs of bread and 1½ lbs of salt meat supplemented by rice, peas, potatoes, tea, sugar, sausage, cheese, and chocolate plus half a gill of rum and an ounce of lime juice a day. For water, each post would be equipped with Crease water filter tanks. There would even be bakeries at the staging posts. Not all was ready by the time Wolseley's advance began in January but there was judged to be sufficient hospital capacity for 45 per cent of the whites and 20 per cent of the West Indians with 7 per cent reserve capacity.[14]

The scale of the preparations required was considerable, the work falling to Robert Home and his engineers and labourers. Not only was there the need to prepare the staging posts but Wolseley also wanted a 12'-wide dry route all the way to the Pra, requiring swamps to be drained, and bridges and causeways constructed: 237 bridges were eventually built, some streams being 60' wide and 13' deep. Gordon had roughly cleared about 25 miles of the route by the time Wolseley arrived in October but it was impossible to push the road beyond Manso until after the Asante retreated, at which time the 'little rains' were swelling many of the streams [86, 87]. It took 12 hours to bridge one 6' wide stream at Manso while the Fante frequently tore up newly constructed bridges for fuel. The huge size of the tree trunks that had to be cleared was also a problem and, calculating that he needed at least 1,200 labourers to accomplish his task, Home still had only 250 in early November with the result that Wood's regiment was pressed into service as additional labourers on 27 November.[15]

Wolseley still hoped he might catch the Asante before they crossed the Pra but they slipped past Lieutenant Colonel Webber and his West Indians at Manso, of whom Wolseley was critical [85, 86, 117]. Then Wood, who was ordered up to instil some energy in the advance on 22 November, ran into the Asante at Fesu on 27 November [81, 82, 83, 84]. The carriers with Wood's force fled, unnerving his Susu and Hausa who fled in turn, forcing Wood to order a retirement. Temporarily back from his mission to the Akyem, Butler moved forward from Suta to reinforce Wood with an improvised force of 12 West Indians and 60 Cape Coast Volunteers. The Asante pursuit, however, stopped after about four miles when, according to Butler, they came across the delights of an abandoned Fortnum and Mason hamper that appear to have totally mystified them: 'never before had such a prize been taken by an Ashanti army. Fancy the face of Amonquatier, as he dipped his fingers into the jam, and flourished a Bologna sausage over his head in his camp at Faysoo. Truly were these things trophies of victory over the white man.' Wood had been forced back some seven miles and many of his carriers had fled over 15 miles from Manso back to Fante Nyankomase but the action appears to have had an impact upon the Asante as well, who continued their own retreat. Indeed, Ramseyer and Kühne were told that 'such a battle as that at Fusuwei had never been fought by the Ashantee'. Kofi Karikari, amid much festivity, represented it as a great success until the arrival of a deputation at Kumase from Amankwatia on 18 December, announcing the losses sustained in the campaign, brought 'a cry of distress ... which rolled like a wave through the whole town'. Bonnat, too, adjudged the losses heavy, the chief of Bekwae alone having lost over 1,000 men and another 'company' being reduced from 700 to 200. In reality, the Asante hacked a way through to the road beyond Wolseley's posts and reached the Pra without further molestation. As Brackenbury was to comment on the conduct of the Asante retreat, 'the army of a civilised nation need not have been ashamed'.[16]

59

Wolseley Journal, 1–2 November
Saturday 1 November
I sent all the Cape Coast levies about 800 men from Napoleon to Bulah this morning: the Judge or Chief Magistrate as he is officially called, went with them to encourage them: they found it unoccupied by the enemy and have established themselves

there. I am sending Lt. Col. Wood to command there. I shall then have Amanquartiers main army between two fortified posts – Bulah & Abrakrampa: if I gradually draw a cordon of posts round the enemy, and so restrict his foraging ground that I may succeed in forcing him to attack one of them. Charteris seedy. Home declares he has dysentery and says he must go on board ship. Charteris declares he never felt better, but I can see that he is drawn about the face, so I shall order him on board to morrow if he is no better. All these officers I have with me being selected men seem to think it necessary never to give in. There is a medium in all things, and obstinacy in confessing to be ill in such a climate as this is may lead to serious consequences. One of them Capt. Godwin (103rd Regt.) came in from Dunquah to day with a very nasty wound: the slug has penetrated into his groin & gone down under his thigh bone, yet when I saw him he declared his wound was a mere nothing & that he would be all right in a few days. I hear that the O. Cg. at Dunquah had great difficulty in making him come in here & that he would walk about to make people believe he was all right. Dr Home tells me it is a bad wound & that his services are lost to me for this war. It is of such stuff that heroes are made.

Sunday 2 November

Wood came here from Elmina & left again for Bulah where he is to assume command. The Africa[1] with English mail of 11th Oct. arrived in the morning. Went to morning service at the Church. No important news from the front. Charteris very seedy: took him on board the Simoom very much against his will in the evening: McNeill going on well, but still suffering pain at night. Godwin very jolly, but his wound is a very nasty one. The Simoom is a horrid place for sick men as the ports are so small and she rolls infernally.

TNA, WO 147/3

60

Wolseley to Glover

2 November
[Holograph]
Cape Coast

I have at last succeeded in getting a man for Accra: Dr Moore R.N.[2] who will go down to you in a ship of war tomorrow. In it, I also send Captain Butler on a mission to Western Akim: I thought it best to send him via Accra as, I heard from the King of that place the other day and he said he was going to Accra. I hope therefore that Captain Butler may meet him at Accra and return with him to his capital: I set great store by his mission for in the present state of affairs here, he is the only King that I can hope for assistance from in my endeavors to harass the retreating enemy: If I only had a Battalion of Houssas or of any men who did not funk the Ashantis & who would go in straight at them I believe that I might now destroy Amanquartiers Army, but I have nothing except a few West Indian troops and a few hundred sailors & bluejackets & do not therefore feel strong enough to attack Amanquartiers main body: I engage all his detached columns whenever I can find a favorable opportunity but my officers are so reduced in number already, from being wounded in trying to get these cowardly Fantees to go on, that if I go on at our present rate of casualties, I shall shortly have none left. I had 5 officers wounded the other day (the 26th October) in one trifling little skirmish, and one of them I am sorry to say is very badly hit. However I believe that the Ashanti Army that has so long been the dread of the Protectorate is now in a bad way, and that its leaders view their present position with alarm. They wish to go north via Prahsue but as I hold Dunquah & Mansue they are perplexed how to act: I want if possible to force them to attack one of my posts, where I should have a chance for inflicting a serious loss upon them. I have asked Capt. Freemantle to send you on the war vessel that will take Moore to Accra, to help you for a week should you require any assistance at the mouth of the Volta. Please do not forget to communicate with me by every opportunity and hoping that this may find you quite free from fever.

CUL, RCMS 131/6, Glover MSS

61

Wolseley Journal, 3 November

Monday 3 November

Russell was not attacked as many believed he would be. He sent out several reconnaissances in one of which Lord Gifford was nearly killed, as all his men bolted. This young fellow Gifford is a trump: he works like a slave, and although a delicate man is always to the fore and ready for anything: Woods reconnaissances from Bulah were very successful and he picked up a few prisoners at Esseecroom on the Sweet River. Festing marched out from Dunquah & engaged the enemy to the west of that place. He was in action with them for some hours but almost all his native allies ran away. Most of his officers were slightly wounded in trying to make the natives fight & I regret to say that poor Wilmot R.A.[3] was shot by a bullet right through the heart: He died almost immediately in Festings arms, Festing being hit on the hip when carrying him out of fire. Wilmot had been hit early in the skirmish, but like a good soldier had gone on leading his men. It is hard that a fine young fellow should be sacrificed I may say by a cowardly lot of niggers who won't fight for their own country.

TNA, WO 147/3

62

Wolseley to Richard Wolseley

3 November

[Holograph]

Govt. House Cp Ct. Castle

Fred and you have been as yet the only ones at home who have found time to write me a line. This is a most depressing climate & a very depressing place in every way, so a home letter is more acceptable here than at any place where I have ever been before.

The thermometer as I write this at 12.10 p.m. only stands in my room at 84° and yet I am bathed in perspiration just as if I were in a turkish bath. Quarts of liquid must pass off in the twenty four hours through one's skin, and I believe it is that constant sweating that keeps me alive. I take a pill of 2 grains of quinine every morning before 6 a.m. when I have a piece of toast and a cup of coffee. Until my last return from the bush I always had a walk before breakfast, but I knocked up in my bad leg from the hard walking I did through the bush, and am now giving it as much rest as I can. Thank God everything has turned out most fortunately for me since I landed. My little fight of the 14th ultimo was although it [is] I who say it well conceived & well carried out, and it has had an effect far beyond my most sanguine hopes, for its immediate result has been the breaking up of the Ashantee camps that have so long been the standing menace to Cape Coast Castle & to Elmina, & if I only now had some reliable troops I should be able to destroy the whole Ashantee Army in the Protected States. But at present I am a General without an Army. I hope that what I have done may be approved of at home. What I dread most is inaction, and that if I am forced to do nothing for some couple of months that the press may turn round and abuse me as roundly as it had previously lavished unmerited praise upon me. Wounds and slight fevers deprive me of the services of officers whom I cannot spare, for these cowardly niggers will do nothing unless led or rather *beaten* on by a white officer. This week will be a critical one here, for the Ashantee Army can not remain long in its present position: what I am trying to secure is to force it to attack one of my fortified posts, for I am not strong enough myself to attack it. I am glad to hear that Mother has moved into her new house – please tell me the address when next you write, for at present I do not know where to send my letters to her. Best love to all. Ever your fond brother.

Hove, Wolseley MSS, 163/4/24

63

Wolseley Journal, 4–5 November

Tuesday 4 November

Went over the Episcopal schools here. They are a disgrace to the place. The little black parson who as Colonial Chaplain draws nearly £600 a year and really does nothing for it beyond reading the service on Sunday to about thirty people in church. Poor Wilmot was buried here at 5 p.m. As I heard a young fellow say when they were filling in the grave "*that is the first of us*". Whose turn will it be next? All quiet in the front. The enemy lost so severely yesterday that he has broken up his camp and is said to have decamped northwards towards the Prah.

Wednesday 5 November

My leg has been troubling me, so I have been giving it rest. Walked in the evening with Baker & Freemantle to the Light House and had a fine view of the surrounding country. Russell still expects to be attacked at Abrakrampa, so I have arranged with Freemantle that the 50 sailors and marines there are to remain until further orders. At dinner Home R.E. gave 50 to 1 in shillings that no attack upon it took place.

TNA, WO 147/3

64

Wolseley to Louisa Wolseley

[3–]5 November

[Holograph]

Govt. House C.C. Castle

Your letter from St Leonards of the 10th and 11th October reached me here yesterday and I am glad to think that you and the Pal are now comfortably settled at Folkestone: I know how glad you will be to [Passage erased]. To me here, your mode of life although very monotonous to you sounds from your description to have so much repose and peace in it, that it seems like a vision of Heaven to one in the fiery furnace below, but as a far wiser man than I am once said we all praise the lives passed by others and envy the existence of those following exactly opposite pursuits to our own. I went on board the Simoom yesterday to see McNeill. He is getting on well: walks about the deck and tries to look jolly although I know at his heart – apart from the body pain he suffers at times – that there is a knawing disappointment that he cannot take an active part ashore. For a soldier such as he is, I know of nothing more trying. I once had during the Siege of Sebastopol to go on the sick list from dysentery: I was as weak as a cat and stuck to my work as long as I could, but at last the doctors said I must go away. I was sent on board ship outside the harbor of Balaclava for a fortnight.[4] As I sat on the deck in the evening and heard the booming of the Guns at the front, I used to become sometimes so excited that more than once I felt inclined to jump overboard and swim for shore. The feeling that I was skulking in safety whilst others were doing my duty was too much for me: it horrified me into a good state of health so, that at the end of [the] week, I went ashore and astonished my friends by returning to work when my leave was only half spent. I can see this same feeling in McNeills face every time that I visit him, and I pity him from my heart. I am sorry to say that Charteris had to go on board ship yesterday, being really taken there by force: he has been unwell for several days but kept his illness secret which is foolish although I can fully enter with the reasons he had for doing so: he has diarrhoea and is much pulled down, but I hope that a few days sea air may set him up all right: I am badly off for an A.D.C. now for McCalmont (the King as he is universally called here) [5] has been on the sick list ever since he left England: he is a delicate little fellow and will have to go home I fear. If he does I shall take a Captain Lanyon (2nd W. I. Regt) [6] to replace him, who is a very nice fellow & accustomed to personal staff work. I often wonder if you would laugh if you saw the deference with which H. E. is treated here by everyone. A Governor General in Canada is nothing to it, for being a General Commandg an Expedition in addition to my civil powers makes me a little swell and of more importance than any ordinary Governor of a colony such as Canada. I have had too much walking whilst away in the bush and have had to nurse my wretched leg since I returned to this place.

It is much better to day, and I hope to have it as well as usual in a couple of days and I shall take more care of it in future. I was very much amused at the notion of the French plums coming out by Captain Hewitt. It was very good of Holmes thinking of sending them to me. The next time anything is sent to me let me have a box of *good* cigars *not Manillas* as they don't answer in this climate, but really good Havana cigars. If this reaches you before Col. Greaves leaves England please send me out a box or two, for so many sailors come to see me and dine with me here that they make large hauls upon my tobacco & I make three or four cigars myself every day & find they agree with me. I expect every moment to hear from Baker Russell as we hope he may have been attacked this morning. The great bulk of the Ashantee Army is close to his post and the Ashantee Commander in Chief has declared his determination to take it: If he really does carry out his intention seriously it will be a grand thing for Russell and may be one of the best things done in the war, but it would be so fortunate that I shall not believe in the rumor until I hear that the attack has really taken place. Before this goes off I shall be able to give you further news. The bulk of the men are now cleared out of Cape Coast, leaving the women behind: these ladies now daily parade the streets dancing and singing their bodies daubed over with white and very scanty clothing on to hide their charms. When they meet a man they set upon him some of them denuding themselves of even this scanty clothing to put him to shame. One of our traction Engines is now at work here to the utter astonishment of the natives who had never heard of such a thing before. The day before yesterday I sent a letter to the King at Coomassie by an Ashantee prisoner: in order to impress him as much as possible I sent him out of this [place] for a short distance along his road in a waggon drawn by the Engine. I should like to hear what his description of this screaming monster will be when he reaches his destination.

I enclose a cheque for £50 please acknowledge by return & do not fail to get more from Holmes if you want it.

4th November. My heart is sick this morning in a way that I cannot account for: last night in the midst of dinner, or rather just after our fish a scrawl was put into my hand saying "Poor Wilmots remains go to Cape Coast with this note – please have a coffin ready for them: nearly all our officers wounded" – I need scarcely add that I did not eat much dinner: I had several people dining with me but of course I kept the news to myself. Later on I received a letter from Col. Festing giving me an account of his skirmish: Wilmot was badly hit early in the fight, but like a gentleman went on with his work fighting like a good soldier and striving to get these cowardly Fantees to fight, until he was shot through the heart: he died almost at once in Col. Festings arms, Festing being hit by a slug in the hip when bearing him out of fire. It is now so long since I have seen men killed in action that this poor fellows death has upset me. Gods will be done, but to me a sinful man, it seems hard that a fine young soldier should lose his life in trying to make a cowardly race fight for their own country. The more I see of these Fantees the more I feel convinced that they ought to be the slaves of the Ashantees, who no matter how barbarous and cruel they may be have at least one manly virtue, the brightest of all virtues namely, courage. A brave man may be converted into a good man but a coward is fit for nothing and is capable of nothing good.

Let me turn from these gloomy thoughts and look at the bright side of things. Our affairs go on well, and I am in a much better position now than I expected to have been on this date when I first landed. The first object of my mission has been accomplished that is Her Majesty's possessions on the Coast are now free from danger, and are no longer menaced by large hostile camps in their neighborhood. The 2nd object of my mission, that of clearing the so-called Protectorate of Ashantees is being accomplished for the enemy are retreating & I have frequent skirmishes with his retreating columns. The 3rd object, that of inflicting a severe blow upon the Ashantee power I can only accomplish as I have already reported home with the aid and assistance of European troops. I have sent Butler off on a mission into Western Akim where I hope he may be able to raise the people who are a better race than these Fantees: if he succeeds in doing so, I may yet be able to inflict great loss upon the enemy before he gets back behind the river Prah. Send this sheet no 3 to Holmes to read as it may interest him. If I only had one Battalion of English soldiers in addition to what I have I would go in at these fellows and smash them up.

5th Novbr. In reading the psalms this morning I came upon a verse that brought back my early days most vividly. I think I have often told you that my father having been so very unfortunate in the Service did not wish any of his sons to become soldiers: I was reared as a child with the idea of entering the Church, and as a little boy always said that I should have for the text of my first sermon the last verse of the 27th psalm. I remember it by heart still as given in the Bible version: "Wait on the Lord, be of good courage and He shall strengthen thy heart, wait I say on the Lord".[7] I quote from memory as I have no Bible with me, & the prayer book version is not nearly such a good motto for a soldier. The mail is not yet in, but is hourly expected. McNeill, McCalmont and Capt Godwin all go home by the first steamer that arrives with a clean bill of health, for I am sorry to say that many of the vessels coming from Bonny & ports to the South bring with them men suffering from infectious fevers – so much so, that the first Ordinance I had passed here by the Legislative Council was one instituting a Quarantine. It is very difficult my dear child to find anything to write about in this horrid place that would interest you, for I know you don't care to hear about quarantine regulations or military affairs. The room I sit in nearly all day is my bedroom it is about 27 feet long by about 17 broad, here is a plan of it (W stands for window) [Figure 2]. My bed is a big four-poster of iron. My front windows look out upon the sea. The window where I sit all day writing looks out into the street where niggers jabber away like so many garrulous old monkies. Women naked down to [the] waist troop along it, carrying their babies on their bustles behind, the child being prevented from tumbling off by means of a cloth passed round the child's back and round the mothers stomach. The old women are very nasty to look at, their breasts hanging down like black udders. The young ones are really very well made and their figures are generally very good. I enclose a letter for my mother – please send it to her as I do not know her new address. I must now close this, God bless you my dearest child – such is the constant prayer of your fond husband.

PS Baker Russell is well and jolly – not a man on the sick list where he is – my best love to the Pal.
Hove, Wolseley W/P 3/10

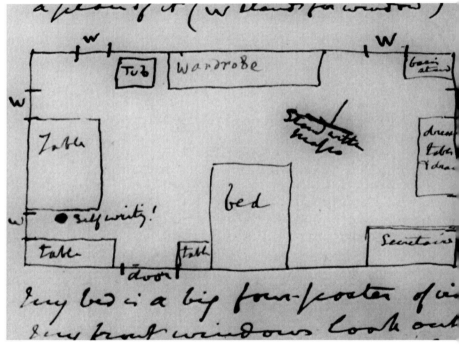

Figure 2. 'The room I sit in nearly all day is my bedroom ... here is a plan of it (W stands for window)' [64].

65

Wolseley Journal, 6 November

Thursday 6 November

At 1.30 a.m. last night I was roused up by a messenger from Russell saying he was attacked by thousands and that the action was still going on: sent off Brackenbury to the Senior Naval Officer & asked him to land every available man so that we might at once move to Russells assistance. 300 sailors & marines landed and started about 7 a.m. I left at 9 a.m. A very hot march – nearly 100 men fell out, en route received an official report from Russell of his day's work yesterday. He gave the enemy toko[8] and has killed a number of them. His report was very modest and good. Upon reaching Assayboo (10 miles from C. Ct. on Prahsue road) received another message from Russell saying that the attack had been renewed seriously and that he was nearly surrounded and wanted assistance – my men were done by their march, but of course under the circumstances it was necessary to do something. I took on at 4 p.m. 140 of the freshest of the 300 men & the garrison of Assayboo (50 marines) and a large supply of ammunition, rockets, a rocket trough and plenty of food. I had in the morning in anticipation of this move ordered 60 of 2d W.I. Regt. from Dunquah to Akroful, ordering the O.C. at the latter post to move as soon as these 60 men reached him, with his own Detachment of about 50 men to a point on the Akroful–Abrakrampa road [which] joins the Battyan–Abrakrampa road & to await my arrival there. I had early in the day sent on 180 of the Assayboo levies under an English officer to that same point. I had so much ammunition & stores with me that I wanted to avoid having to fight my way into Abrakrampa if possible and therefore did not attempt to move by the direct Assayboo–Abrakrampa road as I knew the enemy had patrols on it, and it was quite possible he might be on it in force close to Abrakrampa. All turned out as I had hoped. We reached our destination before dark being cheered on the road by the sounds of heavy firing as we neared Abrakrampa. Russell met me just outside the village – found him jolly but very very tired. All his people had been up all the previous night, and indeed I may say that off and on they had been fighting for

36 hours. My reinforcement was just what they wanted: my staff took over command of the outposts etc for the night to let Russell & his officers have a nights rest. The enemy ceased firing shortly after sun down. I had ordered Col. Wood with all his force from Bulah to make a reconnaissance in force via Esseecroom upon the enemys rear. The vile Cape Coast Castle people were afraid to do this & mizzled after they had reached Essecroom – that village I had intended occupying as a fortified post, but there are so many dead bodies (Ashantees) lying about that I cannot carry out this intention. Instead of leading him towards the enemy, the Guides took Wood far away from their vicinity and brought him out upon the main road at Assayboo: I ordered on all the Cape Coast people for the evening to Battyan.

TNA, WO 147/3

66

Wolseley to Cambridge

[4–]6 November
[Holograph]
Government House: Cape Coast

The condition of affairs continues to improve: when I last wrote to Your Royal Highness – on the 31st ultimo – I had been led to hope that the enemy would have carried out their avowed intention of attacking Abrakrampa, but whether it was that they learnt of its being occupied by an English force, or of the large clearances made round it, they have not carried out their intention. Yesterday I directed that reconnaissances in force should be made from all our advanced posts in the enemys vicinity, native forces being alone made use of. Two of these reconnoitring parties came upon the enemy, and in both instances our native levies behaved most disgracefully, running away in crowds, sometimes by whole tribes, notwithstanding the great exertions made by the English officers I have attached to each King and Chief. As usual several of the English officers have been wounded & I sincerely regret to add that one, Lieut. Wilmot RA was shot dead. He behaved like an English Gentleman throughout the skirmish, having been badly hit when it began, but continuing to do his duty notwithstanding, until an unlucky bullet went through his heart: I enclose the copy of a short private letter received from Colonel Festing on the subject,[9] and his official report will be sent to the Secry. of State for War. These will place Your Royal Highness in possession of all the facts of the case. I have done all that lies in my power to put some courage into these wretched Fantees. I began by boldly going straight into the bush with a handful of white men and a few W.I. soldiers to attack the Ashantees in their own selected positions. I showed them how easily we beat the enemy. I gave them arms and ammunition: at their express desire gave to each Chief an English officer who did his best to organize and discipline them: I have appealed to their love of country and their desire for money: but all in vain: They won't fight: when driven into action by the pistols and sticks of English officers they bolt *en masse* when taken under fire. They are only fit to be the slaves of the Ashantees, and when once we have vindicated our honor here by giving the enemy one good sound thrashing, we shall be justified in studying our own interests only when deciding upon the terms we should make peace upon. A people who will not fight for their own liberties & for their own country are unworthy of any consideration. I have felt it to be our true policy as I stated in my last letter to Your Royal Highness to do all the work to be done by the native levies, reserving the sailors & marines lent to me occasionally by the Senior Naval Officer for any serious work that I might at any time feel necessary to accomplish. Indeed I keep even the 2d W.I. Regt. in reserve also employing them almost entirely in the defence of the various posts I have established for the protection of stores and of my communications. Colonel Festing does not however set much store upon the services of these W.I. troops who are really more suited for the defence of posts than for active work in the field. Your Royal Highness will see from Colonel Festings letter that his opinion on this point accords with that I expressed in my letter written after our little fight at Essaman. I deplore deeply that so many officers should be hit, but it cannot be helped: the native levies will do nothing unless led by us, and to lead them well, officers must expose themselves considerably. These constant attacks upon the retreating enemy already begin to bear fruit: they cut off their means of supply and tend to spread demoralization amongst them. This is already evinced by the increased number of prisoners now taken daily. I believe if I did nothing at all, the enemy might be so encouraged as again to settle down in some camp on this side of the Prah, and I am not strong enough to fight him.

Everything has taken place most fortunately for us since our arrival, and I am now in a far better position than I expected to be at this date. Of course the two drawbacks have been, first the serious one that I find it to be impossible to get these cowardly Fantees to face the Ashantees, and secondly, (resulting from the other) that my loss in wounded officers has been greater than I had anticipated. I hope that Your Royal Highness may be able to send me out some more, for I know that there are numbers of good men anxious to see service here, and much experience is to be gained by young officers in a war of this nature. Our health continues to be good: of course a few are occasionally laid up with slight fevers, but they are seldom more severe than a bad cold or influenza at home. Our men and officers are always better when in the bush than when at Cape Coast or Elmina. I have just had a note from Major Russell, Commanding at Abrakrampa saying that out of the 50 Marines and bluejackets there not one was on the sick list. These men return here tomorrow much against their will, as they hate living on board ship, and enjoy being in the bush very much. The Marines out here do not fairly represent that fine Corps, for I hear they are the rejected ones left behind in garrisons at home, when the men were selected to form those splendid Battalions that took part in the manoeuvres at Dartmoor in the Autumn. I know that Your Royal Highness will be glad to hear that my relations with the Navy continue to be of the most cordial nature: Captain Fremantle does everything I ask him, and would tomorrow land 400 marines and sailors to assist me, if I felt myself justified in attacking the enemys main body.

5th November. The enemy it appears suffered so severely on the 3rd instant near Dunquah that they broke up their camp there and began to retreat towards the Prah cutting paths through the bush to facilitate the movement. I am very sorry that some of the medical officers here return officers and men as severely wounded, when really they are but little hurt. I have called Dr. Homes attention to this, and he fully concurs in what I say, and has written to all the doctors on the subject. Only two officers have been as far as I have yet heard badly wounded, viz, Colonel McNeill and Captain Godwin 103rd Regt. Both of those officers will go home by the first steamer for England that comes in here with "a clean bill of health": I am sorry to say that most of the mail steamers coming from Bonny and posts to the south have bad fevers on board, so that really my means for sending home invalides are few and far between.

I am writing officially to the Secry. of State for War by this mail regarding Lieut. Gordon 98th Regt – upon my arrival I found that everything that had been effected previously had been carried out by that most energetic officer. It was by him that the outposts had been established. Whatever progress had been made with the road towards the Prah was owing to his personnel exertions, and the little that was known of the enemys doings and whereabouts was through his reconnaissances. He has been over thirteen years in the service and he is an officer that I have no hesitation in recommending strongly to Your Royal Highnesses' consideration.

6th November. The enemy attacked Abrakrampa yesterday afternoon: their attack was continued during the night. Major Russell has there 50 marines & bluejackets whom I did not withdraw owing to the threatening aspect of affairs, with a small gun and a rocket trough – about 90 Houssas – 100 of the 2nd W.I. Regt – 108 Koosoos (armed with Sneiders) – 213 Winnebales etc armed with Sneiders and of the native allies he has about five or six hundred of whom about 150 are armed with Enfield rifles. With this force in a well fortified village he can hold out against any number of Ashantees. Behind him at Assayboo, is a fortified post with 50 marines & some native allies, at Akroful is a post of 50 of the 2d W.I. Regt: this post is strongly fortified. I have moved down about 60 more of the 2d W.I. Regt from Dunquah to this latter post, & I am now starting myself with about 300 sailors &

marines for Assayboo. It is now 7 a.m. I shall be guided by the position I find affairs in these as to what I shall do in the afternoon, as it may be necessary for me to push on to Abrakrampa. I am very glad the Ashantees have attacked that place. Their loss will be so great that it cannot fail to have a considerable effect upon them. I shall write again this evening as the mail is not yet in.

Cambridge MSS, RA VIC/ADD E/1/7227

67

Wolseley Journal, 7 November

Friday 7 November

Had a quiet night: a small dropping fire at daybreak from the enemys piquets. The enemy have lost great numbers and have expended a great deal of ammunition without doing us much harm. Several officers have been hit by spent slugs, but no blood drawn. A sailor lost his eye yesterday & about 20 or 30 of the native levies have been killed and wounded. Cape Coast people arrived in the morning. I told their chiefs that they must make an attack this afternoon upon the enemy. They said they wanted guns: I replied that I would not give them any more until I saw how they behaved in a fight. They paraded at 2 p.m. and were with difficulty got into line in the open & driven by the officers sticks and umbrellas into the bush, the Koosoos driving them on before them with their cutlasses. I never could have believed it possible that humanity could contain such a set of cowards, the chiefs were as bad if not worse than the men. At any rate the bush was unheld by the Ashantees, so I pushed on the King of Abrahs men & the Houssas direct towards the enemys camp, which they surprised with a rearguard in it. I believe they nearly captured Amanquartier, for rumor says he was drunk and so remained behind to have his drink out. We took his sedan chair and his bed, chairs, drums, sacred cock & his fetish implements. We started off all the natives in pursuit, but it was no use, Houssas and all did nothing but plunder: the road for miles was strewn with plunder and these undisciplined blackguards could not be induced to stick to the enemys tail. Number of prisoners taken, & a considerable number of slaves set free: most of these poor devils had one wrist fastened to a log by means of an iron staple driven into the log round the wrist. One man I saw with a most ingenious instrument of torture round his neck: indeed I cannot fancy how the poor devil ever slept except in a sitting position. One good looking woman and baby had a miraculous escape: she had been taken by the Ashantees near Commendah and had been for months slave to some monster of a Captain. When the attack was made upon the camp her master had to bolt & ordered her to be off also – she did not display all the alacrity she might have done so this fiend proceeded to cut her throat and was engaged in this noble action when one of our bullets shot him through the head. She certainly had a fearful gash in her throat & she had no object in trumping up this story. All prisoners describe the Ashantee Army as thoroughly demoralized from defeat short of powder and as having lost immensely in these two days affairs. I intend sending all the whites except the 50 marines the original garrison to various places along the road tomorrow.

TNA, WO 147/3

68

Wolseley to Cambridge

7 November
[Holograph]
Abrakrampa

The enemy have carried out their avowed intention of attacking this place. An official letter on the subject from Maj. Russell 13th Hussars who is in command here that I received yesterday whilst marching to this place will accompany a short despatch to the Secry of State for War by this post: from it Your Royal Highness will learn what had taken place up to a few hours previous to my arrival. I marched yesterday morning with about 300 sailors and marines from Cape Coast upon Assayboo. It was a very hot day so our progress was slow. At Assayboo I received a short note from Major Russell saying that the attack had just been renewed and requesting me to push on. My men were very tired but by taking the fresh garrison of Assayboo (50 Marines) & 100 of the freshest of the men I had brought with me I pushed on here via Battyyan (marked on the road survey sent home to War Office), the direct road being occupied by the enemys piquets, and arrived before dark. As Your Royal Highness may imagine, the last couple of miles of our path were made very rapidly, as the sound of firing in front was very heavy, and I received whilst en route another letter saying the men were very tired having been up all night. Soon after our arrival the firing died away into a few random shots. Our loss is trifling: no officer hurt, although many have been hit: one sailor badly hit in the eye, and a considerable number of the levies more or less wounded.

Everyone here has worked hard and Major Russell is certainly the right man in the right place. Lieut. Gordon 98th Regt has acted throughout as his Staff Officer, and as I brought his name to Your Royal Highnesses notice in my last letter, I need not add here anything further in his praise. I hope the enemy will renew their attack to day, for if they do I shall go out at them with a rush. As I have upon several occasions written disparagingly about the 2nd W.I. Regt I am glad that I can speak well of the Detachment here. Major Russell tells me that they yesterday formed a skirmishing line, and went in straight at the enemy in the bush: they did this he tells me in the pluckiest possible manner. Much depends upon the officer in their immediate command. I am well supplied with men, with food & with ammunition & could hold this place for ever against the Ashantis as long as I have supplies. The Ashanti loss has been very great, and their expenditure of powder has been enormous. If they will only go on hammering at this place for a few days longer, I cannot imagine how they can ever expect to get back over the Prah with a host of these native tribes hanging upon their flanks and rear. If our Allies had now any courage we might finish the business south of the Prah at this place. The enemy is about 10,000 strong here Amanquartier being still the Commander in Chief.

I wrote this in a hurry hoping to catch the mail for England that was overdue yesterday when I left. All here are well, and in the highest spirits.

Cambridge MSS, RA VIC/ADD E/1/7232

69

Wolseley Journal, 8–10 November

Saturday 8 November

Woke up feeling very seedy: one of my bad headaches coming on. By the time I reached Government House, I was in a high state of fever, the sun having been very hot and touched me up from having nothing in my stomach. Went to bed, but did not send for a doctor thinking I might be all right in the morning.

Sunday 9 November

Worse – my head feels as if I must go mad: I think of millions of subjects in a minute, work them out and then go on to others, there being no connection between any two subjects. Sent for Home, who took me up in the evening to Connors Hill.

Monday 10 November

A fearful night.

TNA, WO 147/3

70

Wolseley to Louisa Wolseley

10 November

[Holograph]

Cape Coast Castle

As well as I remember I wrote to you on the evening of the 7th from Abrakrampa telling you of all our great doings. The game being played out there I came back here the following morning. As bad luck would have it, one of those dreadful headaches accompanied by slight fever set in in the morning and I could not eat my breakfast. It was stupid my not staying there for a couple of days longer, but one has such a horror of its being suspected even that you are unwell here, that I did not like to countermand the orders I had given and so made a long march (not on foot remember) during an oppressively hot days sun and have been paying the penalty for my extreme stupidity ever since. As you may remember I had one of these attacks I think last June at the Grove. I have been subject to them ever since I was in Burmah[10] but the sun element brought to bear upon this one has made it the worst I ever had. I have gone into all these details because one is surrounded by newspaper correspondents who for wise purposes best known to themselves may describe me [in] their letters going home by this mail as half gone myself already. I reached Cape Coast just in time to send you a line enclosing a cheque for £50 as I had remembered that I had failed to enclose it in my previous letter in which I mentioned having done so. My head was in that state that I [do] not know what I was doing so I trust the cheque was en régle – please acknowledge its receipt.

The mail from home has since come in. I am so glad to think that you are both now comfortably situated. I have a number of letters to write and the mail may be in at any moment. Goodbye my dearest child.

Hove, Wolseley MSS, W/P 3/13

71

Wolseley Journal, 13–19 November

Thursday 13 November
Came on board H.M.S. Simoom. The Captain[11] gave me up his cabin. Maurice my Private Secretary has nursed me like a proffessional nurse. He has had a hard time of [it], up nearly all night sometimes.

Friday 14 to Wednesday 19 November
On board H.M.S. Simoom for the last few days. I have been quite well, with a good appetite, but the Doctors would not let me go ashore.

TNA, WO 147/3

72

Wolseley to Louisa Wolseley

17 November
[Incomplete holograph]
Cape Coast
I feel so well [to] day that I begin a long letter to you, unless indeed in the mean time the steamer for England arrives, when of course I shall have to close it and send it off wherever I may happen to be in my noration. I have had a nasty bout of it, and my head was so bad that during one whole night I thought not that I was going, but that I had gone mad. This has taken so much out of me that I am still a little weak in the loins, but a few more days will make that all straight. The new Commodore[12] has arrived a nice dapper – though stout little fellow looks about 30, but is I should say about my own age. I think we shall get on well together: I was very sorry to lose Capt. Freemantle as Senior Naval Officer, we got on so well; Freemantle being a gentlemanlike fellow but devoid of brains, suited me down to the ground for he always did whatever I asked him: However now that I have seen Hewett, – who has plenty of brains, I think I am just as well off and that he too will comply with all my wishes. This waiting for the English Troops to arrive is heartrending, I do not expect them here until the 1st January and we can do nothing until then. McCalmont has gone home ill. I told you that he had something the matter with his internals before he left England and that the Doctors said he would not stand: well they were right & he has left under the idea that he will yet be able to get back here in time for the Grand Coup. He went away crying poor little fellow. Should you by any chance ever come across him, speak of his illness as if you had heard it was the ordinary country fever. There is nothing serious the matter with him but he is delicate. My other A.D.C., poor fellow has been at deaths door – he is now very very ill and as weak as a baby: unable to sleep at night with this cursed fever on him. I have just come from him, and a sad sight he is. If he only could be transported to his mothers home to receive a mothers care, he would be right again bad as he is in a week. He is to go home in the steamer that will

take this letter. I have written to Lord Elcho telling him all the circumstances and informing him that the doctors have told me that if he comes back here, he is safe to have another attack, and that another attack seizing him perhaps beyond the River Prah at a distance from all comforts or means of quickly sending him to sea, would probably be fatal. Taking him all round I think he is one of the finest young fellows I have ever known and a thoroughly straight forward English Gentleman: one that would be incapable of an underhand meanness who if he struck you, would strike you openly and straight in the face. He is a first class A.D.C., and if he sticks to the Army is sure to rise and make a name for himself in it. I have already replaced McCalmont by a Captain Lanyon 2nd W.I. Regt. a very nice fellow. He has never joined that illustrious Corps having always been on staff employ since he was gazetted to it. I am getting out 15 officers by the next steamer and I shall wait their arrival before I make my choice.

I am still on board of H.M.S. Simoom, where the Captain has given me up his cabin. He is the most good natured of men, and in appearance, face & figure the image of your friend Mrs Bailiff,[13] so much so that I asked him one day if had not a sister of that name, knowing that her maiden name had been Peel and that his was pronounced the same. Since then I have learnt that his is spelt Peile, the oddest name I have met for a long time: it is pronounced as I have already said Peel. McNeill has made the most … [remainder of letter lost]

Hove, Wolseley MSS, W/P 3/14

73

Wolseley Journal, 20–21 November

Thursday 20 November

Charteris very bad: his life is in danger, nothing but his youth can pull him through: the Bonny that should have been here on the 14th instant has not yet come in; we had been counting upon her arrival to take home all those who are too ill to remain here: this Simoom has become so impregnated with fever that everyone who comes on board of her catches it, so much so that I arranged yesterday with Dr. Home, our P.M.O. that no more military invalides should be sent on board of her. Taking this into consideration and my great anxiety to get Charteris away, I wrote this morning to the Commodore telling him that the Simoom could not be of any further use as a Military Sanitarium owing to the fever then rife on board of her. Her doctor, a most invaluable man that has been so kind to me and to all who have had to live on board of her is now down very ill with fever, although he has only been a few times on shore. I apologized to the Commodore for making a suggestion but said that in my opinion she ought to be sent to sea, and that if he would order her to St. Vincent, she might there discharge all her invalides on board the Cape Mail bound for England. He at once acceded to my views, changing the destination from St. Vincent to St. Helena owing to the latter being so much nearer. She began taking in coal from the other ships at once, and is to start as soon as she has enough on board. I went ashore at 5 p.m. very glad indeed to be on terra firma once more.

Friday 21 November
The Simoom started at 3 a.m. and of course that infernal Bonny came in, in the morning. She will take this mail home. There has been a tornado threatening all day but it has not come down.
TNA, WO 147/3

74

Wolseley to Cambridge

21 November
[Holograph]
Cape Coast
Since my last letter to Your Royal Highness of 7th instant I have had a very sharp attack of Burmah fever, that completely prostrated me for several days. I am now however as well as I have ever been since I landed. I am very sorry to say that Mr Charteris of the Coldstream Guards one of my A.D.C.s has been very seriously ill: he has been worse than anyone else who have had the fever, and for two days he lay in a very dangerous condition. He has been for the last three

weeks on board the Simoom, and as fever seemed to have taken possession of that ship, the P.M.O. agreed with me that no more sick should be sent on board of her. Under these circumstances I addressed a letter yesterday morning to the Commodore telling him this, and throwing out a suggestion that she might with advantage be sent to St Vincent to meet the homeward bound mail from the Cape of Good Hope: the Commodore at once acquiesced, saying that owing to distance and shortness of coal he would send her to St Helena instead: she started for that place at 3 a.m. this morning having on board Col. McNeill, who has made a wonderful recovery, Mr. Charteris, Capt. Godwin 103rd Regt. The first named will stop at Madeira as he expects to be well enough to rejoin the Expeditionary Force when the English troops come out – the two last go to England, as neither can hope to return here.

I am now using every endeavor to collect large magazines at Mansue where I have had large storage accommodation constructed. Fort Cambridge there is very strong and commodious, so that I run no risk in doing this, although the main body of the enemy is still in its vicinity. We have had several reports that King Coffee is dead, but I do not believe them – his death would complicate matters very seriously, as it might leave me without anyone to treat with when I have given them a good thrashing. No answer has been received to my letter to the King, although there cannot be much doubt that at least one of the copies reached Coomassie safely. The greatest difficulty I have to face in this war is the question of carriers. The people are so naturally lazy, that even the promise of high wages will not induce them to work. I shall be obliged to put some pressure upon them for after all that England is doing for these people I cannot afford to allow the Expedition to come to a stand still through a too rigid observance of English laws, laws that are in every way unsuited to these nations.

I have good reason to believe that this Army of Amanquartia is the one great Army of the Ashantee Kingdom, and that if I now had the power to destroy it, that a march to Coomassie would be merely "*a walk over*". Captain McCalmont who was the senior of my two A.D.C.s went to Madeira by the last mail. I do not expect he will be able to take any part in this war. He has not suffered in any way from the climate. His illness was contracted in England. The rest of my staff are in excellent health.

Cambridge MSS, RA VIC/ADD E/1/7247

75

Wolseley to Elcho

[17–]21 November
[Holograph]
Cape Coast Castle
[17 November]

Your son goes to England by the steamer that will take this note. He has been very ill – indeed for one day I was very much alarmed, as he lay for some time in a very critical condition. A favorable turn has now succeeded and the doctors have to-day resolved upon sending him home: We expect a vessel in tomorrow by which all our bad cases both of wounds and fever are to go home. This will be a very great blow to your son. He hates the idea of leaving and like all true plucky fellows believes that if left alone he would soon be all right again. To me personally his loss is a very very heavy one. He is the best of ADC's: a charming companion, and such a good fellow all round that his departure will create a gap that I cannot expect to refill satisfactorily. Dr Home the Principl. Med. Officer, one of, if not the cleverest of the medical men in the Army who has been attending him, tells me that if he returns here, he is sure to have another attack, and if that attack should occur beyond the Prah when we shall be living a very hard life & without good means for looking after sick men, the consequences would most probably be fatal: Under the circumstances I feel it to be my duty to impress upon you the necessity for preventing him from coming back here. I had always looked forward to sending home my final despatch announcing peace by him as a messenger, but I must forego that pleasure hoping that if good fortune should ever give me command of a Force in a much more genial climate, that I may still be able to carry out this plan under more favorable circumstances.

I hope your son has told you that your sword bayonet is par excellence the weapon for this country: it cuts down bush better than any billhook or axe.

I hope that Augustus Anson is better the last account I heard of him was very unpromising; I am sure there is nothing for him but a long sea voyage to Australia and a stay of a year or so up country there.

[21 November]
I open the note I wrote to you on the 17th instant to say, that as the long looked for ship had not arrived I wrote to the Commodore yesterday telling him how very anxious I was about several invalids, but especially about your son, and requested him to send HMS Simoom to sea. He at once agreed, and it was settled that he should go to St Helena where she will pick up the homeward bound mail from the Cape on the 3rd of December. The Simoom started this morning at 3 a.m. I bid your son goodbye yesterday evening: he was delighted at the idea of getting away. Colonel McNeill who is on board with him will telegraph to you from Madeira upon arrival there if the line has been repaired by the date of their arrival.

Gosford, Wemyss MSS, Drawer 39

76

Wolseley Journal, 22–24 November

Saturday 22 November
Baker Russell came in here yesterday & spent the night. He returned to Abrakrampa to day. The Commodore, Captain Blake[14] & the flag Lieut. called here in the afternoon & at 5 p.m. we all walked up to Connors Hill to see the model Hut that has been erected there for Hospt purposes. A violent tornado came on & we just got back to Govt. House as it burst in a torrent of rain over the town. All the above mentioned naval Gentlemen remained to dinner & we prepared beds for them, but they went off about 9 p.m. to their ships.

Sunday 23 November

Went to church. I dislike doing so here very much, as I do not like the little black man that officiates. The congregation is small – the parson receives a salary of nearly £600, so he does nothing, but the Wesleyans who are in great force, are a thriving and earnest community with good schools: our schools are a disgrace. Walked with Baker to see Irvine. He is better – then took a turn to near the salt pond. 500 of the allies from Dunquah have just come in to carry back ammunition tomorrow. As they wont fight I have determined upon making them carry.

Monday 24 November

Heavy rain early this morning. Went on board the Commodores ship to pay him my official visit – a grand affair – was received on board by all the officers & a large guard of honor – breakfasted with him & left, the same ceremonies being gone through and a salute fired as I left the ship. I hate these marine excursions but the Navy are great sticklers for all this etiquette: took a good walk along main road in the evening with Baker.

TNA, WO 147/3

77

Wolseley to Glover

24 November

[Holograph]

Govt. House. C. C. Castle

I regret extremely that I cannot supply the money you have asked for, but I have asked the Commodore to help you, and he is now sending you £2200, of which £1200 is in silver. Lord Kimberley distinctly told me before I left England, that beyond the £5000 I brought out for you that I need not provide funds to meet your requirements.[15] I have sent on by the last mail your letter on this subject to the Colonial Office & I trust that money may reach you in time, for it would be sad if your operations were delayed a day from wants of funds: How is it that your Control Officer did not foresee your wants as regards money? If he had done so, the required sum might now be in your possession.

I am glad to say, that I am all right again: it was not this country fever but an attack of a fever from which I have suffered periodically ever since I was in Burmah in 1852.53. It completely prostrates me whilst it lasts. Wishing you every success in your trans Volta campaign & hoping to hear frequently from you.

CUL, RCMS 131/6, Glover MSS

78

Kimberley to Wolseley

24 November

[Printed]

I informed you, in my despatch of the 11th of November, that I should address you further when the statement which you proposed to send to the Secretary of State for War respecting the employment of a European force had been received.

2. You will have learnt from the Secretary of State for War by the last mail that, after consideration of that statement, it had been determined to despatch at once the troops which had been held in readiness, and that the further battalion which you had asked for would follow.

3. I have now to acquaint you with the views of Her Majesty's Government respecting the employment of this force, and the general limits within which, as far as circumstances may admit, your action should be confined.

4. You are aware, from previous despatches, both from the Secretary of State for War and myself, that Her Majesty's Government were most reluctant to send European troops to the Gold Coast. In the instructions conveyed to you in my letter of September 10, before your departure from this country, you were informed that, if you should find it necessary to ask for any considerable reinforcement of European troops, you were to enter into full explanations as to the circumstances in which you proposed to employ them, and the reasons which led you to believe that they could be employed without an unjustifiable exposure and with a well-grounded anticipation of success.

5. You have now given it as your opinion that a certain force of European soldiers is indispensable, not only for the purpose of

an advance into the enemy's territory, but also for the preliminary operations which you describe in your despatch to me of October 9,[16] and you state that you have satisfied yourself that they can be employed during the more healthy season in the manner you propose, without serious risk from sickness.

6. After carefully considering the arguments by which your proposals are supported, Her Majesty's Government had no hesitation in determining to comply with your request, and orders were at once given accordingly for the despatch of the troops.

7. Before the troops reach the coast you will, no doubt, so far as lies in your power, have made every preparation in advance, so that no European soldier may be landed until the time for decisive action has arrived; and Her Majesty's Government rely with confidence that you will not employ this force, especially in the interior, a day longer than the paramount objects of your mission may require. The limit of their employment is fixed by the continuance of the more healthy season, and Her Majesty's Government trust you may be able to re-embark the troops for return to England during the month of February, or at the very latest in March, before the end of which month, at all events, it will be absolutely necessary to withdraw them. This limit of time, which is imposed by the conditions of the climate, will, of course, of itself place a corresponding limit upon the operations which it will be prudent or possible for you to attempt. The nature and extent of the operations which it may, within this limit of time, be necessary to undertake in order to bring the war to a conclusion, must be left to your own judgement to determine; nor do Her Majesty's Government wish to fetter the discretion which must always be placed in the hands of an officer commanding a force in the field; but they desire that, in forming your decision, you will bear in mind the following considerations:–

8. You were informed in my despatch of October 6 that a satisfactory state of things would be obtained if you could procure an honourable peace, an effectual chastisement on the Ashantee force.

9. It is obvious that it will be the interest of the Ashantees to gain time by negotiation, so as to delay the progress of the operations

against them until the unhealthy season returns. They have abundantly proved their capacity for carrying on such illusory negotiations, and I have no fear that you will suffer yourself to be deceived by them. But it may be that the King of Ashantee, on learning the retreat of his army and the further preparations against him, will be ready to make reparation, and to conclude at once a peace on conditions acceptable to Her Majesty's Government, in order to avert the impending blow. Her Majesty's Government would view with much satisfaction such a termination of the existing difficulties.

10. But if it should be necessary to advance far into the interior of the country, and even beyond the Prah, it appears to Her Majesty's Government by no means to follow that it would be advisable to occupy Coomassie.

11. If you should inflict a severe defeat on the Ashantee army near or beyond the frontier, the occupation of the capital might, perhaps, be effected without much difficulty; but it is probable that the result might be a complete break up of the King's Government and power. In such an event, you might find yourself in possession of Coomassie without any government or ruler to treat with; and as it would be wholly out of the question to keep European troops in a state of inactivity in the interior, you might be compelled to return without having obtained a full security for the establishment of a lasting peace.

12. It seems probable that one of the main grounds of quarrel between the Ashantees and the coast tribes arises, as in other parts of Africa, from the impediments interposed by the latter to the free access and trade of the Ashantees with the coast. If the King of Ashantee were persuaded that our object would be to facilitate and protect the trade of the Ashantees, and that they might regard Elmina as in every respect as much open to them, now it is under our influence, as it was when under Dutch protection, or as it could be in any other circumstances, it is reasonable to suppose that it would effect a great change in his relations with the British settlements.

13. In any communication which you may have with the King, you should lose no opportunity to impress upon him that our object

is to promote, in every way, the intercourse of the Ashantees with the coast, and to protect the trade coming from the interior from interruption and annoyance. You cannot too strongly assure him that we desire to be on terms of friendship with the Ashantee nation, and that he has been completely deceived if he has been led to believe that our object in obtaining possession of the Dutch forts was to cut off his people from communication with the coast; that, on the contrary, if they come as peaceful traders, it is as much our interest as his that they should meet with no hindrance which it is in our power to remove.

14. I have further to observe that, whilst the violent aggression of the King of Ashantee upon the Protectorate, at a time when he was professing to be in friendly negotiations with the British authorities, cannot be overlooked, much less the ravages and barbarities by which the progress of the invaders has been marked, it must not be forgotten that there is a reason to believe that the Ashantees received some provocation from the tribes of the Protectorate, and in negotiating the terms of peace, you will be careful to give fair consideration to any complaints which the King may urge against these tribes; and if you should be of opinion that they are to any extent well founded, you will give due weight to them in determining the amount of reparation which you may require.

15. I may sum up by saying, that it is with the wish of Her Majesty's Government that you should conclude a satisfactory peace as soon as it can be obtained; that you should advance no further into the interior than may be indispensable for the attainment of such a peace; and that, after concluding, if possible, a Treaty with the King of Ashantee, you should return with the least practicable delay to the sea-coast, and send home the European troops, keeping on foot only such other forces as you may consider necessary for the service of the settlements, and for holding the road to the Prah, so as to keep the communication with the interior open to trade.

16. With respect to our relations after the war with the tribes of the Protectorate, considering that with some few exceptions the native tribes since their first defeats have made very little effort to defend themselves against the Ashantees, and that, practically, the whole burden of the war has fallen upon this country, it must be

understood that when the present operations have been concluded, Her Majesty's Government will hold that they have discharged their obligations to the protected tribes, and that they are entirely free to review their relations with those tribes, and to place them on such footing as the interests of this country may seem to them to require.

17. In desiring you, therefore, to leave the road to the Prah under the protection of such a force as you may deem necessary, they must not be understood as pledging this country to permanently maintain a force to keep the road open; and you will be careful not to enter into any stipulation with the Ashantees which may fetter the discretion of Her Majesty's Government in dealing hereafter with the relations between this country and the Gold Coast generally.

18. You will, of course, give such instructions to Captain Glover as will insure his conforming strictly to the views of Her Majesty's Government as indicated in this despatch.

TNA, CO 879/6

79

Wolseley Journal, 25 November

Tuesday 25 November

The Adile[17] arrived yesterday from the Volta. She left this evening with a Control officer on board for Cape Palmas & the various ports where Kroomen are to be had, as I am sadly in want of carriers and one carrier who is a stranger here is worth three belonging to the place who go off to their villages & hide. The marines at Abrakrampa & Dunquah have begun to suffer from fever, so I ordered them in: they will be distributed throughout the Squadron until the Simoom returns. Walked in the evening to Connors Hill.

TNA, WO 147/3

80

Wolseley to Colonel William Earle

25 November
[Holograph]
Govt. House: Cape Coast
Your note of the 18th August reached me here some time ago, but I am so busy and have so much writing to get through in the day that I shirk private correspondence as much as possible: however I shall now scribble you a letter giving you some news, although seeing that I am surrounded by correspondents, it will be no easy matter to tell you something that you do not already know. When I arrived here on the 2nd October last I found everything in a very unsatisfactory state: the authorities had established no intelligence Departmt. and litterally knew nothing of the enemys strength, doings or intentions. My first steps were directed towards this point and I was tolerably successful. The Fantees stand in such dread of the Ashantees that no sums of money would induce any of them to go into the enemys camp, so I was obliged to use the Elminas who were hostile to us and in alliance with the enemy as my chief spies. The outposts and the Forts along the disaffected coast to the westward of this took up so many men that my only available force consisted of 100 men of the 2d W. I. Regt. very badly officered and unsuited by their dress and training for bush fighting. I had long durbars with all the native Kings and Chiefs, who instead of being anxious to take the field against their hereditary enemies were only intent in driving a lucrative bargain with me regarding the terms upon which they would consent to fight for their own country. We came to terms and they were lavish in their promises. I sent English officers with them to assist in collecting their men. The Ashantee army between 20 & 30,000 fighting men occupied a position about 14 miles north of Elmina threatening that place & this. I was very anxious to find some detachment from it upon which I could pounce. I succeeded, having landed a few hundred sailors & marines & withdrawn my garrisons from this place & Elmina (that were temporarily occupied by sailors) I was able to muster about 180 of the 2d W. I. Regt. and 100 Houssas that I had

got from Lagos. Having intentionally spread false news that I was going to the Volta to help Glover who was reported to be hard pressed & kept the project from nearly all my own staff, I pounced down upon some villages occupied by the Ashantees – fought them in the bush, where they always boasted white men would never dare to go, gave them a good thrashing and returned to Elmina that night, our loss having been trifling – McNeill excepted who was very badly wounded & who I doubt much will be able to resume his work with this expedt. The effect of my fight exceeded my wildest expectations – the enemy broke up his camp two days afterwards & began the retreat towards the Prah. I am too weak to fight his main body, but I adopted the policy of establishing fortified posts in his vicinity in the hopes of inducing him to attack one of them. In this I also succeeded, and with all his army he attacked for two days & a night a village held by Baker Russell with 50 white men and some native allies. I made a forced march from here with about 250 sailors & marines & 50 of the 2d W. I. Regt. and took in a large convoy of ammunitn in safety on the evening of the 6ᵗʰ. It was very exciting the last few miles of our march. The rolling of the musketry ahead of us and every moment I expected to be attacked & to have had to fight my way in: however as I made a long detour I got in with only a few shots fired: the next day the enemy leaving lost severely in Chiefs & in men & being short of ammunition began their retreat which they conducted very skillfully. I made a grand reconnaissance in force of their position at 2 p.m. & found them bolting. I set all the native allies in pursuit; but the cowardly ruffians did nothing but pick up a few stragglers and loot the enemys baggage of which immense quantities were left behind. If I had had two British Battalions then I feel confident that I should have been able to have finished the war there and then. The Native allies are worse than useless, for whenever they are kicked into action by the English officers with them, they bolt *en masse* whenever they can, leaving their white officers to shift for themselves as best they can. This war can only be finished by English troops and when finished our Govt. must take care that under no circumstances whatever shall they ever again become involved in a war with the Ashantees. The Fantees are only fit to be slaves to the Ashantees, and it would be far better for us if the Ashantees had possession of this country – trade would encrease 100 fold, and we should have to deal with a fine warlike race instead of with the Fantees who certainly are par excellence the cowards of the world.

I have had a large number of officers wounded in my various skirmishes & reconnaissances but only two badly and one poor fellow killed. Of course you must break eggs to make omelets but it is most painful to lose any white man in a war such as this is, where those most concerned will not fight for themselves. The climate here is most peculiar, the sun is not as hot as in Burmah or India and yet the place is most enervating. The least exertion tires one, and every months stay here makes you less and less energetic. Constant fevers of no very serious nature reduce the strength – I cannot account for all this but merely state it as a fact. My advanced post is now at Sutah (marked on the topographical Dept map) and the road is cut to that place and will in a few days be in tolerably fair order to that point. To day I am pushing out strong reconnaissances from there to harass the enemy rearguard – These reconnaissances will hang upon the enemys rear until he has crossed the Prah, and when most of his force is over that river, may possibly be able to inflict some severe damage upon those crossing last. I want to get them over the river as quickly as I can, for my first care is the road – when completed to the river I shall go up there with about 300 sailors & marines & all the force I can muster and cross the river myself to establish a tete de pont, and perhaps a bridge over the river, if not a regular bridge, at least a flying one. The moment I cross I shall be attacked – this is what I prefer: if I can only induce the enemy to keep on attacking my tete de pont, I shall lose only a few men, I shall kill a number of the enemy & I shall have the comfort of knowing that each days fighting seriously reduces the enemys store of powder. I am now forming large magazines at Mansue, that is to be my entrepôt between this and the Prah. Of course as soon as I establish myself on that river I shall form large magazines there. I have selected positions for camps at every 8 or ten miles between this and my advanced post. These I have had cleared and am erecting huts for 400 men at each and a hospital at each for 30 men [,] a hospital at Mansue for 60 men. I am putting up large filters at these places and making every arrangement so that I can push on the English troops to the Prah by detachments in the greatest comfort, taking every precaution for their health. At Prahsu or rather near it, I shall construct a camp with huts for 2000 men & a hospital for 100 men. The Ashantees do not believe that we will ever dare to cross the Prah: their prisoners laugh when we ask them as to what they think the King will do when we take Coomassie: they cannot realize that anyone will ever dare to invade their territory. I summoned the King shortly after I arrived here proposing terms of peace. He has not answered my ultimatum as he cannot understand that we are powerful enough to punish him. It is very probable that the King and his principal ministers will blow themselves up when his army is completely defeated on their own territory. If they do so, it will complicate my position very much, as I shall have no one to treat with: indeed it will be the end of the Ashantee Kingdom, for it is so surrounded with deadly enemies especially on the North that if its military prestige is once destroyed its enemies will pour down upon it and wipe it out of the list of kingdoms. What I want to effect is to give the Ashantee Army a round thrashing on Ashantee territory & then to make peace with King Coffee, forcing him to pay a large sum as indemnity for the cost of the war. The terms made must be such as to preclude all possibility of another war – we must never have another war here, and the Home Govt. must be so protected that no Administrator or other local official shall ever be able to involve England in hostilities with the Ashantees. Judging from Mr. Brights speech at Birmingham[18] I think it is very probable that the Cabinet may determine upon giving up all our establishments on this Coast. Our position here is the most anomalous in the world: we have a Judge here who tries men & condemns them to death in accordance with English law, whilst at the same time we have domestic slavery all round us. At this present moment my clothes are washed by slaves the property of a woman living within a stones throw of this Govt. House. You can purchase a slave any day here, and we have a special court here for adjudicating in all matters and difficulties between masters & slaves, and yet, ye shades of Wilberforce this is all done by English officials under the British flag. This fact will I think influence the ministers in deciding upon the future of this country and in hastening its separation from England. We should have just as much trade with this country if we only had a consul here. A great difficulty in the administration of this country is in obtaining officials of a proper class. Few will come to such a country having such a deadly climate – men fall ill and then you have one official performing the duties of four of five others besides his own, and being overworked doing all badly. There is a great tendency, even amongst men whose birth and education ought to raise them above such practices, to dip the hands deeply into the public purse here – it seems to be looked upon as a natural course to pursue when you have the chance afforded. I have not much time to devote to the Civil Govt. of this place, but I have already put a stop to numerous abuses since my arrival. If I am to have a successor here as Governor I pity him for he will have his hands full. Of course I retire immediately that Military Operations are over: that was the only stipulation I made before accepting my present position: indeed I hope please God to be back again in England before the 1st April next. I wish there was any chance of my being then made A.G. in India to succeed Thesiger. I was working away hard at Hindostani when I was ordered here, but I need scarcely tell you that I have no time for such studies at present. H.R.H. was most kind to me in this matter and told me the last time that I spoke to him that he had recommended me for that post to Lord Napier. However I am looking forward too much: I have a very nasty and difficult nut to crack here first, and the nearer one approaches it, the uglier it looks. My transport question is one of our great difficulties: everything has to be carried on mens or womens heads (the load being 50 lbs) so that it is no easy matter to form large magazines in front, and without them all operations are impossible.

Please tell General Johnson[19] that I found the missing book regarding which I wrote to him. I had lent it to one of the Staff College professors, but having lent it to so many I had forgotten where it was when I wanted it. Prisoners just taken by some of my reconnoitring parties say that Amanquartia will not retire behind the Prah without the Kings permission. Yesterday he was at Faisoo with all his Army: this is a bore for me, for I have no force to compel him to retire & his halting on this side of the river prevents my completing the road to the river & establishing large magazines on it.

Pray Give my kindest remembrances to Lord Northbrook and give my love to Evelyn Baring.[20]

PS One of the young Windhams is here as a Sub Lieut. on board H.M.S. Active. He is very like Wilby without his teeth.[21]

Hove, Wolseley MSS, Autobiographical Collection

81

Wolseley Journal, 26–27 November

Wednesday 26 November

The enemy have left Sutah so my advanced post pushes on there to day: it is to be the first camping ground beyond Mansue. I am thinking of landing about four or five hundred sailors & marines & marching with them to the Prah to fall upon the rear of the enemy as he re-crosses that river. There are a great many pros & cons. The pros that I *might* be able to inflict a severe blow upon the enemy's rear guard, the cons are that I should retard the work on the road which is of the first importance and interfere with the collection of stores at Mansue where I am endeavoring to establish a large magazine, & finally the sailors & marines are so badly equipped for work ashore that I fear we should lose large numbers of them from the sun. Helmets & puggarees are indispensable in this climate & they are unprovided with them. Walked in the evening with the Commodore to see the condenser.

Thursday 27 November

Mail for England in. A fearful tornado last night accompanied by very heavy rain.

Thursday 27 November continued
Homeward bound mail arrived – our advanced post now at Sutah, to which place the road is cut. Requiring Hospital accommodation on shore now that HMS. Simoom is away, I have converted the Protestant Church temporarily into a hospital. The Commodore & Capt. Blake dined here. Irvine has been down with fever for the last few days: he is now much better.
TNA, WO 147/3

82

Wolseley to Cambridge

27 November
[Holograph]
Government House, Cape Coast
Nothing of any importance has occurred since I last had the honor of writing to Your Royal Highness on the 21st instant. Lt Colonel Webber 2nd W.I. Regt[22] whom I had placed in command of my most advanced post at Mansue has permitted all the Ashantee Army to pass close to his post without inflicting any damage upon them, and without harassing them in any way. My most advanced post is now at Sutah (marked on map) and the road is being cut in advance of that place. There has been a great deal of rain in the bush for the last ten days swelling the streams and swamps and retarding the work on the road considerably. These "later rains" as they are called here, last well on into December when the Harmattan winds begin. I have placed Colonel Evelyn Wood in command of the head of the road, and as he is a most energetic officer I hope to harass the retreating enemy when he is crossing the River Prah into his own country. It is just possible that I may myself move forward with 450 sailors & marines that the Commodore has kindly promised to place at my disposal with a view to engaging the enemys rear guard before it crosses the Prah. I should like to do this very much, but there are many reasons why I should forego it. First of all the marines & sailors that I should use are unprovided with helmets and would consequently I fear suffer severely from the sun. Then such an

operation requiring a large number of carriers for provisions, ammunition and sick & wounded men would interfere seriously with the progress of making the road and preparing the camping places for the English troops: to feed the concentration of so many men as I would operate with, would seriously reduce my stock of provisions that I have collected at Mansue (I intend making Mansue my great entrepot between this and Prahsue). I find that the Ashantee Army owing to the difficulties of finding provisions and of having only one very narrow path to move along does not do more than about four miles a day, so that it will be at least a fortnight before it can all be across the Prah. The news that I receive in the course of the next few days will enable me to decide whether I shall move forward with these sailors or not. The 100 marines (belonging to the Simoom) that I had distributed in two parties are at Abrakrampa, the other at Dunquah, I have ordered to reembark as several men had had slight fevers. They are a poor miserable lot of men, unfit for hard work of any kind. One of the N.C. Offrs of Rl. Engineers sent here is so far gone in consumption that it is doubtful whether he will reach England alive or not. I have directed the P.M.O to report to me officially on this case, with a view to bringing it officially before Your Royal Highness: if the other men of the Engineers have been as carelessly inspected by the Medical Officers in England, the result may be serious.

As the Native Allies will not fight, I am now using them in large numbers as carriers – 500 men are furnished daily from those collected at Dunquah who come in here in the evening in charge of an officer, and return the following morning, each man carrying 50 lbs. In this way I hope to have a large magazine soon at Mansue. The work at the several places selected as halting places for the European troops is going on rapidly. I am having huts constructed of bamboo (split) and thatched with palm leaves. In each is a guard bed, so that no man will have to sleep on the ground. The halting places selected are 1st Inquabim (about 7½ miles from this) 2nd Akroful, 3rd Yancoomassie 4th Mansue, 5th Sutah, 6th Amponsie Quantah, and 7th Damsamsue which is close to the Prah, all being short marches. At Damsamsue I shall have a hospital for 100 men, at Mansue one for 60 men & at all the intervening stations hospitals for 30 men each. At Inquabim (the 1st stage from here) I have a very large iron tank filter, and I hope to be able to get one on to Akroful.

As soon as the enemy are clear across the Prah I shall throw a flying bridge over that river and establish if possible a very strong tête de pont on the north bank. This will be the beginning of the 2nd phase of the war, for the Ashantees do not yet realize that we shall ever dare to cross into their territory. I had sent Captain Butler on a mission to the Kings & Chiefs of Western Akim with whom I opened out communications soon after my arrival here. I found subsequently that Capt. Glover had sent an emissary to those Kings before I arrived, so I ordered him to stop all further correspondence with them (he having only been commissioned to the eastern tribes) this he did at once most loyally, but unfortunately the evil had already been done; the Kings & Chiefs hearing of all the lavish presents that Captain Glover had dispensed so freely amongst the Kings & tribes he had been dealing with, did not feel inclined to join me, from whom they had only a regular stipend to expect, and only to receive that, when they brought their men into the field. The result has been that instead of Captain Butler being able to appear with some thousands of these Western Akims on the flank of the enemy as he was crossing the Prah, he has only received vague promises as yet. This is a sad disappointment to me, as I had been counting on the assistance of these Akims, said to be really a fighting people. The mails are most disgracefully irregular. Our last postal mail from England was dated the 17th October. I am writing by this mail to the Secrety of State for War, pointing out the necessity of having a very fast despatch boat sent here, so that the Govt may receive the earliest news of our doings when we advance beyond the Prah.[23] In the event of my having important intelligence to communicate, I should thus be able to send the despatch boat to Madeira, or should the telegraph not be in working order from there, to Gibraltar from whence I should be able to send a telegram to England.

Cambridge MSS, RA VIC/ADD E/1/7251

83

Wolseley Journal, 28–30 November

Friday 28 November

Wood who is now in command at the head of the road made rather an unfortunate reconnaissance yesterday: I had told him to keep the spur in the Ashantees & to keep them moving if possible – also directed that frequent reconnaissances should be made of their position but that he was to be careful not to run his head against the main body of Amanquartiers army. He moved out yesterday, with a few hundred men, towards Faysoo where the main body of the enemy was encamped – drove in their piquets taking a prisoner who told him that the main body of the Ashantees was immediately in his front. Instead of contenting himself with this he went in at the enemy – very nearly got surrounded. The Houssas bolted as did also the Koosoos, & he was merely saved from a disaster merely by the personal bravery & energy of the officers he had with him. He had a Houssa killed, and a few wounded. The enemy followed him for over 3 miles. Affairs of this sort are only injurious, as they revive the enemy's confidence and tend to demoralize our native troops. Even the very best of our native troops will only behave well when they feel they are on the winning side, but let them feel that our side is getting the worst in a fight, and they bolt *en massse*. I asked the Commodore to send up 50 sailors and marines to the head of the road as a moral support to Wood, they are to land to-morrow at 3.30. a.m. & to march at 4 a.m. doing the journey to the front by the regular stages told off for the white troops when they arrive. I have sent word to Wood that he is not to use these men for fighting purposes except in extreme cases. Russell & his Regt. I have also ordered to the end of the road, also Raits Artillery to Mansue as their Head Quarters from whence they can detach guns as required to Woods assistance. 106 Savages from Bonny that arrived here yesterday started under their Chief Prince Charles (Bonny Prince Charlie) [24] for the head of the road to day they are a fine looking lot of men. The judge dined with me: he has just come back from Accra and gives a very unfavorable account of Glovers success, but I would not give a farthing for his opinion upon any subject whatever. No mail in yet from England. We have not had one since that of the 17th Oct.

Saturday 29 November

I was to have gone up country tomorrow but have postponed my journey until Monday in the hope of receiving the mail. Walked to Connors Hill & went round the Hospital. There are two officers there not long for this world: one has consumption very badly, constant spitting of blood, as there is a frequent internal bleeding. He may die at any moment. The other has dysentery & Dr. Home has a poor opinion of his chance of recovery. The men are all doing well, having only slight fevers. There is one exception, a man with dysentery, and dysentery here is very fatal carrying you off very rapidly.

Sunday 30 November

The mail came in last night. 11 officers for me arrived by her: I have made one – Lt Wood, 10th Hussars my A.D.C.[25] This steamer was detained four days at Sierra Leone owing to the cargo being badly packed, so we ought to have another mail here on the 3rd or 4th. Four letters from Loo.

TNA, WO 147/3

84

Wolseley to Glover

30 November

[Holograph]

Govt. House.

My position here remains unchanged. My advanced post along the Prahsue road is now at Sutah within about 8 or 10 miles of Amanquartia and the main body of the Ashantee Army. Colonel Wood reconnoitered it the other day by driving in their outposts. Unfortunately the 100 Houssas he had with him took a panic & bolted back upon the Koosoos in [their] rear who joined in the panic and a disaster was only prevented by the courage of the English officers he had with him – none of them were wounded I am glad to say, and only one Houssa killed. I hear that Amanquartia cannot recross the Prah until he receives permission from the King to do so, and unfortunately I am not strong enough to attack him. I have some three or four thousand Fantee Allies in the field whom I pay, but they invariably run away: I am gradually reducing a large proportion of them to act as carriers, as I find them useless as fighting men. Please let me know what your success has been in raising the Eastern tribes & let me have a return of the numbers you have been able to collect. I hope they now prove to be a far better lot than what I have got together. I hope the £2200 sent you by the Commodore may be sufficient to keep you going until you receive the money that I presume you have long since demanded from England. The last time that I saw Lord Kimberley, it was clearly decided, that I was to provide only for my own monetary wants, so that I have no money to spare. An English mail is just in [,] the first we have had since that of the 17th October last. Pray write to me frequently & let me know how you are getting on trans Volta.

CUL, RCMS 131/6, Glover MSS

4

Crisis (December 1873)

Though Buller had organised a scouting force that was to be put under the command of Gifford, Wolseley was not entirely trusting of their ability as his forces neared the Pra.[1] Accordingly, two privates from the 2nd West India Regiment – Wolseley erred in describing them as NCOs – who could not speak Fante and, therefore, could not be misled by the natives, were sent forward 25 miles to the Pra to report on the situation. The two men, Privates Fagan and Lewis, fired their rifles across the river into Asante territory and left their names on a piece of paper pinned to a tree to prove they had been there before reporting back that there was no sign of the Asante [85, 86, 87]. They received a gratuity of either £2 or £5.[2] Wood and Russell's regiments were meanwhile busy improving the road towards the Pra.[3] The telegraph line was also being extended towards the Pra [97]. It was not always an easy process once the advance had gone beyond the low bush on the coast and into the forest: curiously, the first supply of wire sufficient for a distance of 20 miles had come out as part of Lieutenant Herbert Jekyll's private baggage, the remainder arriving in December in a slow transport, the *Dromedary*. Breakages in the line were frequent and fever hit several of the six men sent out as operators, the other 19 engineers under Jekyll being constructors. Nonetheless, the telegraph began operating on 22 December and reached as far as Akrofo beyond the Pra by 8 February: over the course of the whole campaign, some 3,000 messages were transmitted.[4]

There was also some unfinished business to conclude, Sergeant Hughes of the Cape Coast Volunteers with 630 levies and Wassa tribesmen being sent to punish Chama, the village at the site of Commerell's old ambush in June 1873 [**102**]. Fremantle had been refused permission to deal with the village at the time and that part of the coast and around Dix Cove was still not fully under control. Wolseley himself went down to see the start of the operation in HMS *Active*, and HMS *Encounter* and HMS *Merlin* were left on station to assist after Wolseley returned to Cape Coast. In the event, few Wassa turned up and Hughes's men fired off most of their ammunition and were soon withdrawn, seamen and marines burning down the village.[5] It is easy to lose sight of Wolseley's role as civil governor at Cape Coast and there is one relatively rare reference to Legislative Council business in December, Wolseley trying to re-impose a previous tax on spirits against the opposition of the chief magistrate, James Marshall [**90**]. It was a matter to which Wolseley returned in January, when he admitted to Kimberley that it was difficult to keep civil affairs in view and that potential improvements in living standards for the native population must await the end of the campaign [**131**].

All the preparations, however, were likely to be undermined by the increasing magnitude of the transport crisis deriving from the difficulty of both obtaining and retaining native carriers. The raising of carriers was the responsibility of the Control Department while Wolseley had initially concentrated on raising native levies. Since the Control Department was offering 1s. 0d. a day and Wolseley could offer only 3d. a day plus subsistence, this complicated raising levies, especially when the 2nd West India Regiment was also recruiting on the coast and to boot could offer a 'gaudy uniform' [**26**]. As already suggested, Wolseley also blamed Glover for promising too many rewards to the Volta tribes with a concomitant impact upon the demands of the Fante chiefs. Certainly, it appeared easier to recruit women since, Buller remarked, they were 'natural beasts of burden' and carried far better than the men.[6] According to Wolseley, all the problems derived from the deficiencies of the Control Department, an entirely civilian branch of the War Office established by Cardwell's immediate predecessor, Sir John Pakington, in 1867 in an attempt to ensure that transport and ordnance services did not become involved in combatant roles. Control was to be abolished in 1876 but the commissariat staff continued to be civilian until 1888. In his despatch to Cardwell on 15 December Wolseley remarked that handing over carriers to the Control Department was like 'pouring water into a sieve', a phrase first used in his journal on 14 December [90], and which was to be repeated no fewer than three times by Brackenbury in his history of the campaign.[7]

Wolseley had first expressed real concern in his letter to Cambridge on 21 November [74]. He similarly mentioned it to Earle four days later [80]. It remained a pressing problem [86, 111]. Surgeon Goldsbury was despatched to the Windward ports to find more men [97], while, at the same time, Dr O'Reilly was sent to Elmina, where he obtained an additional 700 men in just 10 days. Huyshe had earlier been despatched with Commissary Elliot to bring in labourers from Asebu, Abrakampa, Dunkwa and Manso and impose fines on native kings, while Lanyon had gone to disarm the tribes at Cape Coast to impress them as labourers. Criminals were also pardoned provided they volunteered. When the chiefs of the formerly disaffected tribes around Elmina had come in to sue for peaceful terms on 26 November, Wolseley had also demanded they provide carriers.[8] Another solution was to impress some of those enlisted as fighting levies as carriers especially if they had shown themselves unwilling to fight [76, 82, 89]. As he recorded in his journal, Wolseley also made what he called an appeal 'in quite an affecting manner' to the chiefs on 9 December and he threatened to send his white troops home [87, 90, 120]. In fact, the first troopship arrived prematurely on 10 December. The arrival of the ship was the first sign that the men were actually being sent out as it was only known from letters received that regiments were being prepared for service.[9] The ship had to be sent back to sea with Wolseley subsequently having to postpone the date of his planned advance across the Pra from 1 to 15 January [110]. Having arrived on 17 December, Colley was placed in command of the transport arrangements on 19 December and Wolseley allocated 17 officers to help him [97, 105], Cambridge having rightly assumed that transport problems might require attention and that Colley would be the man to effect improvements.[10] Such, indeed, was the case [138].

Colley was not entirely comfortable serving nominally under Irvine's command, but felt it necessary 'to oil the wheels of the machine' and eventually assumed complete charge of all transport, carriers and lines of communication. Colley soon felt that transport was 'melting round me' and, of his 16 subordinates, seven soon went down with fever. Colley himself was described by the end of the campaign as 'pale and worn of face, with cheeks hollowed by fever and fatigue, and eyes unusually large and lustrous, but still with every feature and fibre of face and frame betokening an immense reserve of resolution'. In January a further seven officers and seven commissaries were allocated to Colley.[11] Colley's first act was to issue a memorandum detailing a new transport organisation on 19 December, separating regimental from general transport, dividing the route to the Pra into four districts – to which particular groups of 500–800 men or women were permanently allocated – and allocating groups on a tribal basis. Receipts for delivery consignments would now be the sole authority for pay. A 'headman' was placed in charge of every 20 carriers and a superintendent for every 120, the latter receiving 2s. 6d. a day and headmen 2s. od. a day. Officers were also encouraged to use patience as well as firmness in dealing with the carriers and to refrain from 'frightening' them.[12]

The carriers, however, kept deserting, Wolseley recording on 4 January 1874 that the entire group intended for the 2/23rd's transport had deserted en masse [117, 122]. In despair at being completely 'in the hands of these lying, lazy and worthless Fantee carriers', Wolseley decided to convert the 2nd West India Regiment, the 1st West India Regiment – which had arrived from Jamaica on the *Manitoban* on 27 December with 24 officers and 554 men and had been disembarked two days later – and Evelyn Wood's irregulars into carriers [117, 122]. Volunteers from the 42nd were also pressed into temporary service for an extra 1s. od. a day and an issue of grog, 135 of them pulling carts for 10 miles.[13] Wolseley calculated that he needed 3,500 carriers to support the advance beyond the Pra to Kumase, while Colley calculated a requirement for 8,500 as a whole, with 2,500 for daily subsistence, 2,500 to provision the advance base at Praso and 3,500 for regimental transport, the intention being to take up to Praso 30 days' rations for a force of 6,500 men and 1.1 million rounds of ammunition.[14]

Having signalled the necessity to set aside the niceties of English law [74], on 6 January Wolseley informed Alison that everything was at a standstill and directed that every able-bodied native be seized [120]. He began to believe that it would not be possible to bring the 2/23rd up to the Pra at all beyond perhaps a token 100 men [122, 124]. Fortunately, matters eased by mid-January with Wolseley pardoning political offences in return for the supply of carriers, the situation transformed largely through Colley burning some villages and surrounding and raiding others for men [132, 138]. Indeed, what Boyle termed 'razzia' proved very effective.[15] As early as November 1873 Wolseley had got a resolution through the Judicial Assessors' Court to permit the arrest of those who refused to be conscripted for labour, and that they be forced to work without pay and be liable to flogging if they refused to work. This had not been thus far utilised but was now put into practise, Henty believing the influence of 'negrophilists' in Britain having prevented Wolseley from enforcing the order previously.[16] Marshall, however, continued to seem chary of punishing deserters among the carriers as severely as Wolseley wished [132]. Nonetheless, Wolseley intended to leave a request that several death sentences be commuted when he himself departed from Cape Coast.[17] Notwithstanding Colley's instructions, Methuen told his father that natives were flogged 'pretty often' though 'not unless they richly deserve it'. Once, however, the press correspondents were 'sticking like vultures to the Headquarters Staff' during the advance in January, it was done 'with discretion'.[18]

Alison was also involved in surrounding villages and seizing men and, with Wolseley's advice, [120] raised carriers' allowances from 3d. to 6d. a day and subsidies to the chiefs to £50 for every able man sent into the field, £10 a month for every 100 men and £6 a month for every 100 women. Alison wrote to his wife that he was spending money 'in a way that would make the hair of a War Office official stand on end, in any endeavour to procure carriers'. In fact, the pay on offer was far from generous by West African standards, the Kru receiving 1s. 6d. a day from the Royal Navy. Recognising that there was little on which carriers could spend their wages and that many were going hungry, Alison also endeavoured to find supplies of maize corn rather than the rice that had been supplied since many carriers would not eat it: at one point Colley was feeding carriers on 'pressured' meat. Robert Home also experienced desertions among his engineering labourers even when they were owed money as there was nothing on which they could spend it. An additional difficulty was that many of the pre-packed loads of rice, flour, biscuit, sugar and salted meat landed at Cape Coast were too heavy for the carriers.[19] In the end, Colley believed that it had been a near run thing with only five days' supplies left by the time the troops reached Kumase.[20]

The nature of the crisis was apparent to all in Asante. Alison, for example, confided to his wife that he believed Wolseley's staff had been too young and inexperienced to manage the transport properly and that Wolseley had made a mistake in going forward with his staff before the expedition had been properly assembled at Cape Coast. Similarly, Dooner noted on 9 December that the transport system was 'in a fair way of breaking down'. Methuen, who arrived in December, reported to his father that all would be on 'short commons' across the Pra, and he was equally critical of Wolseley's staff. Yet, to some extent, the true seriousness was successfully concealed, Colley suggesting in February that the press had no real idea of the crisis that had pertained.[21]

So far as the official version went, the despatches to Cardwell and Kimberley eventually published in March and June 1874, such as that to Cardwell on 15 December, made only oblique references to the real scale of the problems with the carriers. Only on 8 January did a despatch to Cardwell report on the problems of desertion, indicating severe measures had been taken and West Indian troops and irregulars pressed into temporary transport service.[22] As already suggested, in so far as any crisis was admitted, the blame was placed firmly on the Control Department. Wolseley's despatch on 5 February summing up the campaign after the fall of Kumase recommended that the lines of communication always be in the hands of combatant officers, something Wolseley then subsequently repeated to Cambridge [158].[23]

The press correspondents, too, were somewhat muted in their criticism. Boyle reported the desertions, but put the entire blame on the cowardice of the Fante. Stanley criticised the Control Department on 16 December but also implied that Wolseley should have been exercising closer supervision over it and should now seize every able bodied man. By contrast, however, he also noted the arrival of Colley, the increase in the number of carriers being obtained and therefore ended by congratulating Wolseley that the 'great difficulty of the hour has been tided over so rapidly'. In fact, Stanley had been absent for some time visiting Glover in Lagos so missed the worst of the crisis. Winwood Reade on the other hand was extremely critical not only of the Control Department, but also of Wolseley for not insisting that more Control Department personnel were sent out, for not bringing in elephants, mules and oxen from elsewhere. Indeed, Reade judged that while Colley did indeed bring order to chaos it was Wolseley who was culpable for the chaos in the first place. Interestingly, however, Reade suggested erroneously that Wolseley was not aware of the problem until early December. As it happened, there was an attempt to get 18 pack and riding mules from Lisbon but the order got muddled in transit and just nine poor specimens were received from Madeira, of which only two were serviceable: in the end, a few more arrived from Ascension and a total of eight were used in the advance beyond the Pra. Henty, who had first-hand experience of Commissariat work, was also critical, drawing a contrast with the efficiency of the transport arrangements in the Abyssinian campaign and suggesting Wolseley had been too slow to recognise the problem and too hesitant in introducing impressments. His criticism was mitigated, however, by his recognition of the deficiencies of the Control Department.[24]

In print, the response came from Maurice and Brackenbury. Maurice touched on the carrier problem in a number of his press reports, as on 27 November and 8 January, but on such occasions was quick to suggest that all possible measures had been taken to rectify it, and he declared the difficulty solved on 15 January.

The comment added in the later book based on Maurice's wartime reports indicated that Wolseley was aware of the problem from the beginning, had taken all the necessary measures as quickly as Stanley or anyone else might have wished, and could not have resorted to compulsion earlier without more officers being available to police the carrier system, and once Colley arrived it was only a matter of time before all was efficient. Brackenbury went into fairly exhaustive detail on the administrative and logistical arrangements and admitted the 'truth' of the problem having existed but naturally laid the blame firmly on the Control Department, indicating that it was not the 'business of the General in command to find the means of transport, as was done here'. According to Brackenbury, Wolseley could not have acted earlier because too few officers were available to allocate to transport duties, and the problem of desertion only became acute in mid December. Accordingly, once this was clear, an officer of rank and authority in the form of Colley was immediately put in charge to rectify the deficiencies of the Control Department.[25]

As already indicated, the immediate effect of the transport crisis in December was Wolseley having to send the first troopship to arrive, the *Himalaya* carrying the 2nd Rifle Brigade, back to sea on 12 December with instructions not to return until 31 December. The warship *Tamar* then arrived that same day with the 2/23rd and they were also sent back to sea on 14 December to return on 30 December. The 42nd appeared on the *Sarmatian* on 16 December [86, 87, 90, 93, 97]. Each battalion had been brought up to approximately 30 officers and 650 men, the 42nd requiring the addition of two officers and 169 men from the 79th (Cameron) Highlanders.[26] In addition, the ships also brought No 1 Battery, 17th Brigade RFA comprising three officers and 61 men; 28th Company RE consisting of four officers and 68 men; one officer and 42 men of the ASC; two chaplains; and two officers and 52 men of the Army Hospital Corps. There were also a further 41 medical officers and ten further special service officers. Wolseley now received Kimberley's instructions of 24 November on the employment of the white troops [78]. As Wolseley was to remark, they were too late to enable him to strike a decisive blow at the Asante before they retreated and too early for an advance on Kumase.[27] Wolseley chose to land only staff, special service officers and some engineers and ASC personnel, later criticism that all the engineers should have been landed being refuted by the fact that the number landed was by agreement with Captain Richard Buckle, RE. In fact, the men of the 28th Company RE were predominantly platelayers and engine drivers originally intended for work on the aborted railway. The artillerymen were not landed at all, leaving Rait to continue to rely upon Hausa gunners.[28]

Colley arrived with the troops, as did Greaves to replace McNeill, but rather less welcome was Archibald Alison sent out to command the white troops. Wolseley had expressed reservations as soon as he heard Alison had been appointed [**87**]. McNeill also thought little of Alison while Greaves subsequently told Wolseley during a conversation on Cyprus in August 1878 that, had Wolseley been incapacitated during the advance into Asante territory, he and Brackenbury had arranged with William Mackinnon, Anthony Home's successor as Principal Medical Officer, to 'put Alison compulsorily on the sick list' and to hand over the command to Colonel McLeod of the 42nd [**99, 105**]. Wolseley, who believed Alison a pedant too 'brimfull of maxims borrowed from Jomini and Montecuccioli' agreed that this would have been the best course. Wolseley's allusion was to the Swiss military theorist and sometime chief of staff to Marshal Ney, Baron Antoine-Henri de Jomini (1779–1869), whose *Précis of the Art of War* was published in 1838, and who was known for his rigidly mathematical approach to the principles of war, while Raimondo Montecuccoli (1609–80), author of *On the Art of War* and *Aphorisms*, both published posthumously in the early eighteenth century, was a notably cautious seventeenth-century Habsburg general. It is an interesting comparison given the fashion for Jomini in particular in the mid-nineteenth century in Britain, Europe and the United States and is an indication of Wolseley's natural adherence to the so-called 'imperial school' of British military thought that emphasised flexibility and practicality over the slavish imitation of continental practice.[29]

Alison himself recorded that he received a cordial welcome from Wolseley but was certainly aware of the hostility and resentment on the part of Wolseley's staff, finding it 'better to keep myself amongst my own people' though he suggested that he got on well with Greaves.[30] In fact, Alison and Greaves had started to co-operate on the third day of the voyage out to Cape Coast in drafting a series of tactical instructions, which were clearly the basis for the celebrated memorandum issued by Greaves in Wolseley's name on 20 December [100, 101]. McLeod also had sight of the draft on the voyage and agreed it.[31] The emphasis upon fire discipline in the final memorandum was particularly marked. Indeed, during the Zulu War, Melton Prior specifically contrasted Wolseley's injunction to 'Fire low, fire slow' with Chelmsford urging his troops at Ulundi, 'Men, fire faster, can't you fire faster?'[32] The concept of the section as the most appropriate tactical unit was also something of an innovation. A hundred copies of the memorandum were issued to the regiments in Asante and it was also widely circulated within the army as well as being publicised in the accounts of Brackenbury and others, the campaign in Asante generally providing many apt lessons for the doyen of the theorists of 'small wars', Charles Callwell, as well as his imitators such as W. C. G. Heneker.[33] It would suggest, of course, that Alison was not as rigidly Jominian as Wolseley later liked to pretend.

Some of the hostility to Alison was simply to a newcomer and Wolseley was anxious to achieve due recognition for those who had been there from the start such as T. D. Baker, Brackenbury and Rait [88, 91, 97, 102]. Indeed, Wolseley drew Cardwell's attention to the services of his officers on 15 December, the Duke of Cambridge subsequently agreeing that Wolseley's recommendations be accepted, notably in the case of Baker.[34]

At the time the transports arrived, Wolseley believed that he might not need to land the third battalion since he might not have to go all the way to Kumase. Consequently, the 42nd could be left on board as a reserve though Wolseley would take a small naval brigade beyond the Pra, the 2/23rd and the 2nd Rifle Brigade having been the original two battalions slated next for overseas service when Wolseley had made his request for white troops in October. Quickly, however, Wolseley changed his mind and decided to take the 42nd after all as a means of further shortening the campaign through a more decisive blow, leaving the 1st West India Regiment in reserve [**88**, **91**, **97**, **105**, **119**]. Alison told his wife that he had been instrumental in the decision to take the 42nd and leave the West Indians, the plan now being for three columns advancing some 60–70 yards apart, each cutting a path 12 yards wide. Three seven-pounders would be allocated to the centre column with three rocket troughs for each of the flanking columns. A Gatling and two howitzers would stay at the Praso base on the Pra.[35] Further problems soon became apparent, however, for as well as carrying the bulk of the telegraph wire the *Dromedary* also carried the short Snider rifles and Elcho sword bayonets for the 42nd and 2/23rd, only the 2nd Rifle Brigade being equipped with them already, the Short Snider issued to rifle regiments and sergeants of line infantry battalions having a barrel of 3¾ in. compared to the standard 36½ in.[36] It caused Wolseley to consider landing the riflemen first, issuing them with naval cutlasses and transferring their sword bayonets to the second battalion to be landed [**105**, **107**]. Commodore Hewett agreed to supply rifles and naval cutlasses but, in the event, the *Dromedary* turned up on 30 December and the rifles were landed the following day.[37]

A second problem was that when the *Sarmatian* returned from its enforced cruise on 27 December, one man had died from erysipelas ('St Anthony's Fire') on 20 December and three other cases had followed [**106**, **107**]. The ship had been taken up from the Canadian trade and was ill suited for transporting men in the tropics for want of air and light on the lower decks. It was felt desirable by both Alison and Surgeon Major Woolfreys to land the 42nd immediately rather than transfer them to the *Manitoban* as Wolseley wanted, since the latter ship was also considered not sufficiently well ventilated: Anthony Home had gone down with fever on 23 December and was temporarily replaced by Woolfryes until Mackinnon arrived on 29 December. The decision threatened to frustrate the plan to land the Rifle Brigade first but, as no more cases occurred, Alison and Greaves were able to comply with Wolseley's desire to see the Rifle Brigade ashore first after all, the *Himalaya* returning as scheduled on 31 December. It had been intended to land the 2/23rd after the 2nd Rifle Brigade but

Alison, who Wolseley had left in charge of moving up the white battalions [105], became aware that the expedition had not been a popular assignment in the 2/23rd and that resulting desertions had necessitated drafts to the regiment before its embarkation. As a result, he recommended that the 42nd join the 2nd Rifle Brigade ahead of the 2/23rd or, if Wolseley wanted all represented, then taking 400 men from each battalion. Wolseley, however, remained committed to taking all three battalions and some at least felt Alison had been largely motivated by the fact that he was himself a Scot. As it happened, many of the 2/23rd arrived looking pale and anaemic with some fever cases. In the event, when, as already indicated, the carriers intended to transport the 2/23rd deserted en masse on 3 January, only half the battalion had been so far sent on its way towards the Pra. Thus, with Mackinnon recommending that it could not remain where it was, it was promptly marched back to Cape Coast to be re-embarked, serving at least to reinforce Wolseley's threat to the kings and chiefs that he would withdraw if they did not provide more carriers [120, 122, 124].[38] Mindful of the 2/23rd's place ahead of the 42nd on the roster for overseas service, the Duke of Cambridge was particularly critical of the decision to land the 42nd first but was mollified to some extent by the subsequent participation of the token contingent of 100 men from the 2/23rd in Wolseley's eventual advance.[39]

Alison had been left in control at Cape Coast because, though expecting to receive some peace overtures from the Asante [88, 90, 91], Wolseley had set out for the Pra on 27 December [106, 108]. He was accompanied by eleven of his staff, four soldiers acting as orderlies and clerks, a bodyguard of 15 armed police, 26 servants and 78 carriers. The Naval Brigade left the same day, some 272 strong under Captain Hans Blake of HMS *Druid*, with the 2nd West India Regiment following on 30 December.[40]

As Wolseley was about to set out he had received further bad news from Glover on 22 December. Glover had already exasperated Wolseley by his demands for additional funds that had left Wolseley's own coffers bare [89, 97, 98].[41] His expectation that Glover would nonetheless cross the Pra on 15 January 1874 with between 11,000 and 16,000 tribesmen to coincide with his own planned crossing was now arrested by Glover's admission that it would take him another 40 days to make the Pra and he might muster only 700 Hausa and Yoruba at most. Exasperated, Wolseley peremptorily ordered Glover to safeguard his stores, cross the Pra on schedule and advance towards Dwaben – though not as far as Kumase – since the affairs of the Volta tribes were of no significance compared to the need to defeat the Asante [102, 103, 105, 108, 109, 110, 111].[42] Indeed, in a remark soon to be oft repeated by Wolseley, if he could not help then Glover might as well be in Abyssinia or on the Zanzibar coast.[43] Glover, all of whose correspondence Wolseley had carefully preserved, 'promised compliance, but declined responsibility for the result'. As one Colonial Office official noted upon receiving the news, 'I fear Capt Glover is rather a failure. His army of 40,000 dwindles to 700.' In the event, leaving Goldsworthy to continue operations against the Awuna on the east bank of the Volta, Glover crossed the Pra on 15 January about 45 miles south east of Kumase with 740 men [116, 133].[44]

85

Wolseley Journal, 1–7 December

Monday 1 December

Left Govt. House at 5.30 a.m. in my "carriage" drawn by six niggers. The carriage is an old Yankee buggy but having high wheels runs very lightly and is pleasant to travel in. We halted at Inquabim for breakfast. That is to be the 1st stage from C. Coast for the English troops: the huts are getting on well. Went on in the afternoon to Akroful, that is to be the 2nd stage. Here we slept having inspected the work in progress.

Tuesday 2 December

Inspected the Detchmt of troops stationed at Akroful – started at 8 a.m. after breakfast. I travelled in a cot to try and get some sleep as I scarcely slept at all last night. Capt. Lanyon the A.D.C. I have with me, had a wonderful contrivance in the way of a hammock made for me: I was to be carried in it by day & sleep in it by night.

I have the greatest possible horror of things intended for two purposes; "the bed by night, the chest of drawers by day" I never believe in, but as Lanyon had taken a great deal of trouble with this hammock, fitting it with mosquito nets etc etc I did not like to refuse sleeping in it. I accordingly got into it: the first time I turned from one side to the other one of the side pieces broke in two. I was stifled with heat and could not sleep, the consequence is I feel seedy this morning. We reached Dunquah at 10 a.m. My party consists of the Commodore whom I asked to come for the trip, Dr. Home the P.M.O. who is a capital fellow but who is always threatening to send me to Madeira if I say I have the slightest pain in my stomach. Most men are afraid to go near him lest he should order them on board ship, and everyone dreads that more than anything else. Dunquah is a very large clearance there being some three or four thousand natives encamped here – as they have been here for some time I would not have it as a halting place for English troops, but selected Yancoomassie (4½ miles from Dunquah). We were to have gone on there to encamp, but at Homes urgent request I remained at Dunquah for the night. The soil here is sand & the site is very dry: the water good & plentiful.

Wednesday 3 December
Inspected the Detachment of 2^d W.I. Regt here – a melancholy sight – some men without boots. The Regt. is rotten to the core & the officers are quite useless. A large majority drink hard, and none look after their men. Left about 8.30. I travelled in my carriage as far as Akukorbunnum Insue where we halted for luncheon about 9 miles from Dunquah. On our way there I carefully inspected Yancoomassie (the 3rd halting place). The engineers have only just begun to clear the ground & mark out the site for the huts – water very good. All the houses – or rather the ruins of them for the Ashantees have not left a roof on any one are mostly built of wattle & daub, the mud being put on thick & smoothed over, so that one would not know at first sight that there was any wattle at all – the roofs have very steep pitches, quite as steep as this [Figure 3]. Home, C.R.E. met me before we reached our halting place for luncheon. He is pulled down from his fever, but says he

is all right now: he thanked me several times for the letter I wrote pitching into him: I think I have taught him a lesson that will keep his bumptiousness down for some time to come.[1] The road beyond our luncheon place is only cut – it is very bad and wet all the way to Mansue. Colonel Webber who commands there met me en route & I was received by a guard of honor etc etc. Went round and inspected all the place: it does the Engineers & all concerned very great credit. The Fort (Fort Cambridge) is a very strong little Redoubt. I wish the Ashantees had tried its strength. There is capital bathing here in the Okee river, which has fallen several feet since yesterday. Fresh bread is issued here, but I am sorry to say that the bread is very bad. There is also fresh meat issued here from time to time, as cattle are now driven up the road.

Figure 3. 'The roofs [of the Asante houses] have very steep pitches, quite as steep as this' [**85**].

Thursday 4 December

We heard last night that the English mail had arrived. Unfortunately something has gone wrong with my letters: they were sent forward from Cape Coast in two large bags by a special runner, and have not reached me yet, although the ordinary post that left some hours after, announcing what had been done, has arrived safely. The lazy runner has most probably stopped to see some friends in a neighboring village. If this is so, I shall have his back well tickled for him. Inspected the Hd. Quarters of the 2nd W. I. Regt.: a pitiable sight. Colonel Webber the Officer Commdg knew nothing about his men: he confessed to me that they had not had daily parades. The mens clothes & accoutrements & the way they were put on were deplorable. I gave him my mind very freely.

4 December continued

I wrote my journal for the morning of to day: it went home in my letter that I sent Loo by the early post. After sending it off I received my English letters of 10th ultimo. It rained very hard between 4 & 5 p.m. This is I am sure an unhealthy place as the soil is an impervious clay, on which the water lies until evaporated by heat. Now Dunquah was just the reverse being a sandy soil where no water lay even after the heaviest rain. The huts are all ready here for the soldiers on their march to the Prah. Went round the Lines of the 2nd W. I. Regt. I believe that I am the first officer who has ever done so: nothing could be more disgraceful. They were like pigsties.

Friday 5 December

A dark cloudy morning: breakfasted and started at 8.15. Road very wet from yesterday's rain in many places. Reached Sutah at 12.10 p.m. Began to rain just as we got there. Sutah a horrid place and very badly selected as a camping ground. Soil impervious red clay. Showers during the day: it rains here every evening: I hope these rains do not continue all the year: all published accounts of the weather here say that we are now in the dry season when the Harmattan[2] wind ought to blow – flies very troublesome here & at

Mansue. Inspected the troops at 5 p.m. A party of Bluejackets & marines (50 in all), a few of Raits Artillery & 50 men of Russells Regt. on parade. Control arrangements very bad, everyone in front of Mansue short of provisions.

Saturday 6 December
Started at 6.30 a.m. a cloudy morning & good for travelling. A dense fog when I first got up a little after 5 a.m. Road very wet at first: better afterwards. 7¼ miles to Faisuwah. Breakfasted at Atah Insu, with Russell which is about 4½ miles from Sutah. A very nice camp on sandy soil. Inspected Russells Regt. at 11 and started again at 11.30 a.m. reaching Faisuwah about 12.30 p.m. Road very good, so came along at a good pace. Faisuwah a very nice camping ground on sand: water very good and air charming. Control arrangements wretched: not sufficient in camp to feed the force for tomorrow with complete rations. Resolved upon changing the camp from Sutah to Atah Insu, as I think the former unhealthy. It will add 4 miles to the march, but still I think it is better to do so than run any risks regarding health. Found Wood and all his party in the best of health and spirits. Capt. Furse had been pushed on this morning to Yancoomassie – about 4½ miles. Report says that all the Ashantee Army has crossed the Prah: Butler writes to say that his information is that it was recalled by the King to make head against an invasion of Ashantee by the Gamacas, a Mahommedan people lying to the North & North West of Ashantee.[3] I fear that this news is too good to be true. Several scouts came in this afternoon who affirm that there are no Ashantees south of the Prah except a few stragglers and sick scattered about in the bush. I sent out two men of the 2nd W. I. Regt who volunteered to go, with the scouts, ordering them to go to Prahsu.[4] There cannot be any collusion between the soldiers & the scouts as they can only communicate by means of signs. I shall thus be certain of hearing the truth which I never am sure of when I have to deal with scouts. Several officers want to go, but I don't want to run the risk. Butler will be there I know before a couple of days are over.

Sunday 7 December

Started at 8.23 a.m. for Yancoomassie (5 miles): the road as usual through a forest of magnificent trees, the highest as a lot I have ever seen in any part of the world. The bush is in consequence much less dense: indeed our skirmishers could get through it very well. For the first mile & a half the road led through the deserted Ashantee camp, an immense collection of very neatly made huts, so much more neatly made than ours are: their bedsteads are also well & ingeniously constructed. This is the camp that Wood reconnoitred on the 27th ultimo. Although he had to retreat, his attack so frightened the enemy, that they broke up their camp that same evening and bolted for the Prah. The working parties were on the road as we passed along it: they had *made* the road by evening to within 1½ miles of Yancoomassie. Horrid smells of dead bodies badly buried all along the road. One dead fellow I saw unburied, he had been shot by one of our shells. Reached Yancoomassie at 10.13 a.m.: Furse & Richmond of Woods Regt there, & Mr Bell, a drunkard of the 2nd W. I. Regt there in command of a Detacht. of his Regt.[5] They had made a good clearance: the site is good but far from good water. Inspected the troops: as usual found the 2nd W. I. Regt. in a deplorable condition, no officer looking after his men. Lunched there & left again for Faisoowaah (where I came from in the morning) at 2.13 p.m. & reached that camp at 4 p.m. A heavy thunder storm with rain in the afternoon.

TNA, WO 147/3

86

Wolseley to Cambridge

[6–]7 December
[Holograph]
Faisuwaah, about 25 miles south of the River Prah
I left Cape Coast on the 1st instant for the purpose of inspecting all the camps and posts along the line of road as far as it [is] cut. I halted one day at Mansue in order to make a careful inspection of the 2nd W.I. Regt. I had expected to find it out of order, but I was shocked to find it in the condition I did. I do not think there has

been a kit inspection for months, and there had not been for some time any daily parades. Some of the Detachments of the Regt that I had inspected on the road were in a similar condition: some of the men turned out with bare feet – there was every variety of costume; and the mens accoutrements had seemingly never been fitted to the wearers. It is a corps in which the officers take no interest in their men. Their lines were like a pigsty, all the Companies being mixed up without any regard to order. Colonel Webber has only recently joined and has had an attack of fever lately, so although I think he is very much to blame, I think it is more the want of system in the Regt. and the worthlessness of the officers as a body that is responsible for the deplorable condition in which I found them. I am making a report on this subject to the Adjt. General for Your Royal Highnesses information. In my last official letter to the Secrety. of State for War I gave a general outline of the halting places I intend establishing along the line of road to the Prah – so I shall not recapitulate them as Your Royal Highness will have seen that letter.

At this camp Lt Colonel Woods Regt is now in little native huts the officers being in tents. Both Russells and Woods Regts. are very fair, and will do good service when associated with English troops: by themselves, they lack confidence, but when on the winning side, will I think do us good service. Lt Colonel Woods Regt numbers in round numbers 430 men: Major Russells 540 men. They are composed of Houssas, Kossoos, men from the Bonny River, from Sierra Leone and some selected men from the best of the Fantee Tribes: they are armed with Sneiders. I have not yet tried the Bonny men, but of the others, the Kossoos are the best, their favourite weapon is the sword, so I have given a cutlass to each. Each of these tribes are kept intact in companies by themselves. The advanced post consisting of 230 men of Woods Regt is now at Yancoomassie about 5½ miles north of this [.] Our patrols have been into Amponsi Quantah 8½ miles from here: Our scouting parties have been to the Prah River yesterday, and report all the Ashantee Army across the river. I shall send a patrol there on Monday; Captain Butler who is my commissioner in Western Akim reports that the King of Ashantee sent to the Commander in Chief of the Army south of the Prah ordering him to return at once to Coomassie for the purpose of resisting an invasion by the Gamacas, a Mahommedan people to the north and north west of Ashantee who frequently make war upon King Koffee. This is such good news that I do not believe it, although it is possible & highly probable, for if the Gamacas have heard that Ashantee was about to be invaded from the south by the English, they would most probably take advantage of the position to strike a blow at their hereditary and implacable enemies the Ashantees.

7th December. I have just returned from Yancoomassie, where I inspected the men now there. The Detachment of the 2nd W.I. Regt. very badly looked after under a useless officer, Mr Bell, whom Colonel Webber tells me is a confirmed drunkard, and who when on board ship coming out here the other day drank so hard that the Captain of the ship at last ordered the Steward not to give him any more wine or spirits. I shall have him sent to his Regt. Hd. Qtrs as soon as possible, and I shall instruct Col. Webber to try him the first time he is found drunk. All the special service officers work so hard and have the success of this war so much at heart, that it is very trying to find the officers of the only Regular Regt. I have here, so indifferent to the interests of the service, & so careless about the welfare and comforts of their men. I have to ask your Royal Highnesses pardon for going into these particulars, but it is saddening to see a Regt. in the neglected state the 2nd W.I. Regt. is in at present. The men are good some of them very fine looking soldiers, and all most willing. There is no further news to day: I sent off two men of the 2nd W.I. Regt (who volunteered to go) last night with a couple of our scouts, with orders to go to Prahsue: the scouts tell such untruths that they take us in frequently, and say that they have been to places where they never have been. The scouts cannot make themselves understood by the men of the W.I. Regt. so there can be no collusion between the two soldiers and the scouts I have sent forward. I expect them back tomorrow night, and I shall halt here tomorrow to hear what they have seen. I hope to have the road cut to Damsamsue (a few miles from the Prah) by the 16th instant. I shall then push forward my magazine of stores from

Mansue to that place. I shall not undertake any serious operations north of the Prah, until I have 30 days provisions for the troops at Damsamsue. At present I have 50 bluejackets & marines at Sutah who I am bringing on here tomorrow. When I [am] ready in front, I shall ask the Commodore to land about 300 more Bluejackets & move them forward to the Prah. I shall push on all the available men I have to Prahsue, and I shall cross the river just before daybreak having strong batteries on the southern bank to cover the movement. Under cover of the men I take across the river, I shall construct a strong tête de pont,[6] and then throw my bridge across. I hope the enemy will attack me immediately as I cross, but if they do not I shall make myself very strong there and push on my road so that everything may be ready when I move forward the English Regts to attack the Ashantee Army wherever I may find it. Owing to the difficulty of obtaining carriers it is no easy matter to fix the day when I shall be ready to make my final advance, but I shall not land the English soldiers until I am ready to do so; as from what I have seen in the newspapers, and calculating that my despatch asking for English troops must have reached home by the 20th November; that a Cabinet Council met on the 22nd and that the troops sailed on the 25th November, I expect them to reach Cape Coast on the 16th or 17th instant. If my calculations are correct, I shall send them to cruise under easy steam, probably for ten or more days. They will have come too late for operations against the enemy South of the Prah, and too soon for operations to the north of that river.

The Commodore has accompanied me on this tour of inspection. He does everything in his power to help us. He has lent us a dozen carpenters from the fleet to assist in constructing the huts at the halting places for the English troops. He has also supplied us with all the available old canvas in the fleet to assist in making these huts – I am sorry to say that we still continue to have a great deal of rain in the bush; a day seldom passes without a thunder storm accompanied by very heavy showers: this retards the work on the road, as the laborers run for shelter, and it also causes the road to be very wet and deep. We are told that these "Little rains" ought now to cease & the Harmattan winds to begin – these winds are cold, pleasant to Europeans but trying to the natives, even to those belonging to this place.

I expect to be back in Govt. House at Cape Coast on the 10th or 11th as although I shall halt here tomorrow, I intend to go back by double stages. I return there with great reluctance as the air and the climate here is so very superior to Cape Coast. One feels quite a different man in the interior to what one feels on the sea board. I send this off now to be sure of catching the next homeward bound mail, but I shall write to Your Royal Highness again, when I return to Cape Coast Castle.

Cambridge MSS, RA VIC/ADD E1/1/7258

87

Wolseley Journal, 8–11 December

Monday 8 December

A thick mist at daybreak that gets even into one's tent and makes every thing very damp. I intend halting here to-day, hoping to have my scouts back this evening: or else to hear from Butler that he is at Prahsue. The road party pushed on under Home R.E. this morning to Yancoomassie. Home says he will have the road cut to the Prah by Saturday – I give him until Monday – The scouts & the two men of 2nd W. I. Regt that I sent to Prahsue returned at 8 a.m. These soldiers gave a very circumstantial account of what they had seen:– two canoes on this side & 8 on the north bank: a few dead bodies lying about upon both banks, but not a live one to be seen. I gave each soldier £1 as a present for having performed their work so well & so quickly. Started at 11 a.m. lunched at Sutah that now looks well as the weather has been dry for some days here, & pushed on to Mansue where we arrived a little after 7 p.m. There has been little or no rain at Mansue since we left – so I may assume that the "*little rains*" are drawing to an end.

Tuesday 9 December

Started at 7.10 a.m.: lunched en route at Yancoomassie, where the Sergt in charge had done wonders since I passed here before.

Reached Dunquah about 3 p.m. Had an interview at 5 p.m. with all the Kings & Chiefs there, telling them that I expected the English troops very shortly, but that I could not land them as I had not sufficient supplies for them at the front: I called upon them in quite an *affecting* manner to come forward, men, women & children to carry provisions to the Prah. They reserved their answer for tomorrow morning. I told them I would even then send all the troops back to England unless I received this necessary assistance from them. A fine day.

Wednesday 10 December
I received an answer from the Kings & Chiefs that they could only reckon upon 1200 carriers. They asked for police & officers to assist. This I promised. I had asked them to give me 5000 carriers. Left Dunquah at 7.15 a.m. Lunched at Inquabim (the first halting place) and reached Cape Coast Castle before 3 a.m. having heard en route that the Himalaya had arrived – Confound her – I shall send her for a cruise to St Helena to be back here again on 1st Janry. next. As I told H.R.H. in my last letter to him, they have arrived too late & too soon. If I had had them on the 10th November I am almost certain that I could have finished the war. Now that the enemy are all across the Prah, I must wait until I can collect a sufficiently large quantity of provisions at Prahsue before I begin my operations in Ashantee. Heard from the Horse Gds that Sir A. Alison is coming here as Brigadier General & second in command. I am very sorry for this as I don't care much for him & don't think he is the man I want. I am sure that McNeill will be back again by the end of the year & he will find that a senior officer has stepped into his shoes. I am very much annoyed at all this.

Thursday 11 December
Nothing new.
TNA, WO 147/3

88

Wolseley to Cardwell

11 December
[Holograph copy]

<u>Private</u>

Govt House
The mail that arrived this morning brought me your kind and very gratifying note of the 18th ult. I am so glad to find that you approve of what I have done, for that is the greatest incentive to further exertions on my part. I am very sorry that in my report to you of our little affair at Essaman I mixed up subjects that should have been reserved for a separate despatch.[7] I shall be more careful in future on this point. I intend sending the English Regts. to sea until the 1st Jany, for owing to the difficulties of transport, I cannot have a sufficient magazine of food etc etc at Prahsue before the 15th. of that month. As the reason for which I asked for the third Battalion exists now no longer, the enemy having retreated behind the Prah, I do not intend landing it. I shall however keep it in reserve at sea where I can always find it so as to land it any day, should the resistance I meet with beyond the River Prah, and the losses in action be such as to necessitate its employment, a contingency that I do not anticipate. My idea is that after one or two serious defeats in the neighbourhood of the Adansi Hills, the Ashantee Army will fight no more. This opinion is based upon what the Natives say here. I have also learnt that it will be necessary for me to make the first overtures for peace, and I shall consequently do so as soon as I have convinced King Koffee of his inability to stop our advance. Everyone here talks of my going to Coomassie, & I don't contradict them, but I shall leave no stone unturned to avoid having to do so, except with perhaps 1000 men as an escort to sign the treaty if I am fortunate enough to be able to make one. I could not take all my force there without making a road, and even then to feed it so far from my base on the seaboard, would be no easy matter with the uncertain material in the way of transport, that I must necessarily depend upon. I am above all things most anxious to

avoid keeping the English soldiers a day longer on shore than is absolutely necessary.

I have to thank you, Sir for the prompt manner in which all my requests have been complied with, and for the rapidity with which the English troops were despatched immediately that my despatch asking for them reached you.

As I consider that the first phase of this war is now over, the Protectorate being cleared of the Ashantee Army, I am writing you a despatch on the subject; for the men who have borne the heat and burden of the day, fighting against long odds, and working in this climate in a manner that none but carefully selected officers can ever be expected to do, deserve I think special consideration. Since the day that Colonel McNeill was wounded, Major Baker has acted as Chief of the Staff. He has worked indefatigably, up at all hours of the night: the amount of work he has got through and continues to get through in every twenty four hours, is astonishing: I am anxious to mention him now, for when Sir A. Alison & Colonel Greaves arrive he falls from the high position he has occupied so long and so efficiently, to be merely an Asst. Adjt. General.

I regard the work that the Regts. will have to do as child's play compared with what has been already done by the officers who came out with me. The Regts. will be landed and marched by easy stages to the Prah, every practicable attention having been paid to their comforts & every provision having been made for their wants. The officers who came out with me, have been detached many of them singly amongst the native tribes, & many have undergone privations of no ordinary kind.

Hoping that I may have the good fortune to continue to earn your approval of what I do, and thanking you sincerely for the manner in which you have acceded to my many requests.

Bodleian, Kimberley MSS, MS. Eng. c. 4112, ff. 69–72

89

Wolseley to Glover

11 December
[Holograph]
Govt. House: C. Coast

I have just returned from my most advanced posts, and send you by this mail a letter giving you the result of the information I have obtained during my trip along "*our road*", and giving you details as to the dates when I hope to be in a position to advance into Ashantee territory. I hope you will be able to combine with me in crossing the Prah, and that you may be able to collect a large force to operate with. Of the native levies that have come forward for me, I can say nothing in their favor: they won't fight, so I am gradually converting most of them into carriers, but they desert in hundreds, so that the transport question with me has become a very serious one.

I am sending you a doctor by this mail to Accra: please arrange for his joining you wherever you want him. I am getting out some more money by next mail and when it arrives my Controller tells me, he can afford to send you £1000. I am most anxious to help you in every possible way, but having been informed by Lord Kimberley before leaving England that I was not to have anything to do with supplying specie to you, I made no allowance in my demands on the treasury for your requirements. I hope that you may not require any more money from me, but if you do, I shall always do my best to assist you.

In sending me an account of how you intend moving to the Prah for the purpose of combining with me for a simultaneous advance into Ashantee, I should be much obliged if you would kindly send me a sketch map showing the routes to be taken by your columns, with the names of the places where they are to cross the Prah. Upon arriving at that river, I hope you will not lose a moment in communicating with me at Prahsue. I am anxiously awaiting news from you regarding your progress to the east of the Volta. Wishing you every success in your operations there.

CUL, RCMS 131/6 Glover MSS

90

Wolseley Journal, 12–14 December

Friday 12 December

A native rumor in the town that messengers are on the road from Coomassie to this place (Cape Coast) begging for peace. Started at 6 a.m. for Beulah where I had an interview with the Chiefs of Cape Coast. I harangued them & told them their men must be turned into carriers, as without carriers I could not collect sufficient provisions on the Prah & that unless I had large stores at Prahsue by the end of the year, I would not land the English troops that Her Majesty had sent out to assist the Fantees. Got back to Govt House at 1 p.m. having breakfasted at Beulah. Beulah is a very pretty place, indeed quite lovely at places. There was a very large mission (Wesleyan) station here, but it was burnt by the Ashantees. The garden of course is overgrown now but there are some very fine trees, although some of the best have been cut down when it was first occupied by us, for purposes of defence. A whip snake jumped off the branch of a mango tree beside which I was standing. It appears that all snakes here are very fond of the mango & several large ones have lately been killed when climbing up those trees. H.M.S. Tamar[8] arrived having 2/23rd Regt on board. H.M.S. Himalaya put to sea to return here on 31/12/73. I am over-run with Chaplains here – They are a great bore as I will not take them beyond the Prah. They eat and don't fight.

Saturday 13 December

I was to have had a meeting of Council to day to renew the tax on spirits, regarding which there have been so many rows here, but the Judge sent to say he could not attend being very seedy: this I know was all humbug. He did not want to come, because being an *official* member he has to vote as I direct – and I directed him to vote in favor of the tax, and I believe he has very foolishly inveighed against it out of doors. I postponed the Council & ordered him to attend tomorrow. This little story is sufficient to show what a farce these legislative councils are. A very violent rain storm accompanied by high wind at 10 a.m.: the heaviest rain we have yet had here. Private letters by the mail from Lord Kimberley, Mr. Cardwell & H.R.H. all very flattering about my operations here. Walked to Connors Hill in the evening.

Sunday 14 December

A deliciously cool night last night. I am worked very hard now: I hope the business may be soon over, as I cannot go on at this high pressure for ever – H.M.S. Tamar went to sea to return on 30/12/73. Buller returned from the Prah. He says the stench of the dead Ashantees near the river & for miles on this side of it is dreadful. There [are] a number of dead on both banks; the poor devils had crawled to the water, drank & died. I am becoming nervous about my transport which is in great confusion. I pour thousands of carriers into the Control Department, but I might as well pour water into a sieve.

TNA, WO 147/3

91

Wolseley to Cambridge

14 December

[Holograph]

Govt. House. Cape Coast

Your Royal Highnesses most gracious letter dated the 11th ultimo reached me on the 11th instant, and I have to offer my best thanks for the advice contained in it, advice that in future I shall strictly attend to.[9] It is not easy however to write readable letters to the Colonial Office without entering into some Military details, for at present there is little or nothing [of] political worth being reported. My advanced party is now on the Prah and I hope by tomorrow or tuesday evening to have a practicable road cut to it. My relations with the Navy have throughout been of such a cordial nature and I have from the date of my landing here received such unvarying assistance from everyone in the fleet, that I have felt myself compelled to avail myself of the services of a small Naval Brigade (250 in number) [.] I knew they expected it, and as whatever little I have been able to accomplish up to the present time, has been chiefly carried out by sailors and marines, I thought it but fair that those who had borne the heat and burden of the day, should also be allowed to share in the more brilliant operations that the use of English troops is now likely to enable me to undertake. They will act as a small Battalion of infantry, all the men and officers being carefully selected as the very best in the squadron now on this coast. I have sent the 2/23rd Fusiliers and 2nd Rifle Brigade to cruise at sea until the end of the month and intend doing the same with the 42nd when it arrives. The enemy having all recrossed the Prah before the Regts arrived, I had nothing for them to do on this side of that river, and owing to my very great difficulty about transport, I cannot have collected on the Prah until the 15th January a sufficient supply of provisions etc etc. I could not therefore avail myself of their services until that date, when if all goes well I intend to make my first days march into Ashantee territory. My present intention is not to land the 42nd Highlanders at all. I shall keep them cruising on and off the coast so that I can bring them to the front any day should I require their services. I am most anxious to expose as few Englishmen as I can to this climate, so if I can get on without using more than the two battalions originally asked for, I shall do so. I know that this will meet with Your Royal Highnesses approval. The reason that induced me to ask for a third Battalion exist[s] no longer, but still as it is here, I intend retaining it as a reserve in case of accidents. My present intention is to leave this [place] myself about the 27th instant, Sir A. Alison and a sufficient staff remaining behind to superintend the landing of the troops. I shall send on before me the sailors & marines, and mean to throw a force by surprise across the Prah on the night of 6th, 7th or 8th January to construct a tête de pont, and to cover the construction of a bridge over the river. I hope to have everything ready in this way for the final advance of the Force on the 15th January, as I intend to have the two English Regts. & the 1st & 2nd W.I. Regts concentrated on the South bank on the 13th of that month, giving them a halt to wash clothes on the 14th January. At present there is not an Ashantee to be seen on the North bank, but their dead bodies lie about everywhere on both sides of the river. They have I hear all gone to their homes, but until our scouts have come back from following them, I shall not know more of their movements – I think it is very possible that I may within the next ten days receive overtures of peace from Coomassie, it is their general practice.

As the first phase of this war is now over having been as I hope Your Royal Highness will consider satisfactorily brought to a conclusion, I have thought it but right to put on paper my appreciation of the manner in which the officers who came out with me have done their work. This I have done in a despatch to the Secretary of State for War and I take the liberty of recommending the officers named therein to Your Royal Highnesses favorable consideration.[10] They have borne the heat and burden of the day, whereas for the troops about to land early in the year, everything will have been provided beforehand, and they will not I hope be kept longer on shore than six or seven weeks, when they will reembark and start immediately for home. I feel especially for Major Baker who has so long done the work of Chief Staff Officer & who has worked night and day, never having been an hour unwell. After I lost the services of Colonel McNeill, I do not know what I should have done without Major Baker, whose knowledge of the service added to zeal and ability makes him an invaluable staff officer. Captain Rait who has been my Commandg Officer of Artillery, was selected by me as the very man for work out here: he has done all that man could do, and I need scarcely tell Your Royal Highness that it cannot but be very painful to him after all his hard work to be superceded [*sic*] by an officer who has never seen service and who is only a few months senior to him in the Army. I have therefore brought his name forward. All my staff have worked hard and well. Captain H. Brackenbury my Assistant Military Secretary is a most invaluable officer and relieves me of a vast amount of work: he is a staff officer of the highest ability, and only requires opportunity to rise to a high position.

Your Royal Highnesses wishes regarding Captain Williamson 2/23rd Fusilrs.[11] shall be strictly attended to. I am very sorry he has come out, for we all suffer more or less from the sun here, and if you have a weak spot in your head, the sun is certain to find it out – If he suffers at all, I shall get the Doctors to invalide him at once. He is an old friend of mine, as I knew him well in Canada.

The health of all my officers is very good – most have had fever more or less, but they are made of such stuff, that they will never confess to being unfit for duty.

Captain Glover is I hear at Whydah. I am very glad that more stringent orders have been sent him ordering him to conform to whatever instructions he may receive from me. I am sending a copy of my letter to him to Lord Kimberley by this mail, so Your Royal Highness will see it.

Again allow me to offer my best thanks for the kind advice contained in Your Royal Highnesses letters to me: the expression of Your Royal Highnesses approval of what has been done here, is most gratifying to me, and I trust that I may be fortunate enough to gain it all through this war.

Cambridge MSS, RA VIC/ADD E1/1/7263

92

Wolseley Journal, 15 December

Monday 15 December

Mail from the Cape just in. She came direct without calling at St Helena as her screw is damaged. This is an unexpected event, because our last advices from England informed me that the arrangement with the Cape Mail Steamers had fallen through. I suppose the question of a few thousand pounds. The ordinary steamers homeward bound are so very unreliable, that the Govt ought not to depend upon them for their mails from this place – penny wise, pound foolish.

TNA, WO 147/3

93

Wolseley to Louisa Wolseley

[14–]15 December

[Holograph]

Govt House: Cape Coast Sunday

This is Sunday, and as I have closed the Church to convert it into a hospital I have just been reading the morning service to myself.

The twelve oclock gun fired as I was doing so, and I immediately thought of you and pictured to myself Pal and you in church both the best dressed women there and therefore the envy of all others in the church – that dreadful bore [Name erased] has arrived: I feel that that little red headed – no offence to the Pal – little man is going to be a bore hanging on to my coat tails through life.[12] I have a dislike of deaf men and much as I love and admire red hair in a woman – deaf men annoy me as one has to shout at them. He is both deaf & red headed. On board the ship that brought him out there was a black (nigger) parson – the two holy men walked about constantly together and some wag on board dubbed them "Rouge et noir". I returned here on the 10th and on the 11th a mail from England arrived. I need scarcely tell you that the number of letters I receive by every steamer is large. They come in two large bags & it takes me some days to pore through them. To my horror there was no letter either from you or Holmes. I thought that perhaps you were ill and all sorts of gloomy thoughts raced through my head for it was the first mail that did not bring me a letter from both of you. However late in the afternoon yours was brought to me stamped over in many places as "*unpaid*" "not sufficiently paid" and other words to that effect, and this it was I suppose that caused the delay – please in future see that your notes are properly prepaid like a good child. I have had very nice notes from Mr Cardwell & Lord Kimberley, both of which I have sent to Holmes to be forwarded to you. They are about my first fight on the 14th October – please give the enclosed to Pal: it is about Baker, so I am sure it will please her. The Himalaya & Tamar have both arrived and as I am not yet ready to land the troops I have sent them to cruise at sea until the end of the year. They will land the first week in January next. I intend leaving this [place] for good about the 27th instant, and I hope to begin my campaign north of the Prah on or about the 15th January: by the end of that month all fighting will be over and please God I shall have so beaten King Koffee that he will gladly accept my terms. If all turns out well, all the European troops should be on board ship on their way home by the 1st March & I shall not be long behind them. As soon as you learn that I have defeated the King, buy me a nice dressing gown: You said you would work me a pair of slippers – send them to Rouse to have made up and have them ready for me when I return. I also want a set of evening studs – very small ones, so you can present me with a present if you like. Holmes could buy them for you, or perhaps you had better select them yourself when you go to London to await my arrival – no more than £5 to be given for them. I enclose you a lovely beetle as a charm to be hung round the Baba's neck. They are rare here and it was given to me the other day by a man who found it.

15th December. Mail for England just in, and will be off again at noon so I must finish this. I have always a great struggle at the last moment to get my letters off: my Military Secretary[13] who conducts the Military Correspondence with the War Office is a capital fellow & always up to time, but I have a Private Secretary who is certainly the worst man of business I have ever had anything to do with.[14] He is like a woman, never in time: puts me in mind of my sister Matilda[15] in that respect. He is a dear good fellow, and I shall never forget his kindness to me when I was ill here: he slept in my room for ten days and for the first week he never had an hours rest at night, as he was upon constantly giving me something to drink etc etc. Goodbye my dearest little woman. I am glad to learn that you think of your fond husband.

Hove, Wolseley MSS, W/P 3/16

94

Wolseley to Matilda Wolseley

15 December
[Holograph]
Govt. House.
Cape Coast Castle

Just a line before the mail leaves to tell you that I am flourishing, being very much pleased by the letters I have received from the home ministers conveying to me their congratulations upon my success of the 14th October last; two Battalions of the English troops have arrived & I hope D.V. upon this day next month to make my first march forward towards Coomassie beyond the River Prah. Before the end of January, all must I think be over either one way or the other. I have a numerous and and [*sic*] a brave enemy to contend with and a very small force to meet him with. However I am full of hope and with Gods assistance I hope to bring Mr. Koffee Calcali to his bearings before I am done with him. I still cling to the hope of being back again in England about the first week of April, and if all goes well I do not see why this hope should not be fulfilled. Please thank Fred for me for having sold my horse, but he has not charged me with the expenses attendant upon the sale & of taking him to Ireland. My best love to our dearest Mother and all at home. I am glad you have changed the name of your house to something less pretentious than Belgrave Hall. Ever my dear Matilda your fondly attached brother.

Hove, Wolseley MSS, 163/4/25

95

Wolseley to Louisa Wolseley

16 December

[Holograph]

I wrote you yesterday by the Cape mail that called in here by mistake: to day the regular African mail arrived and as she will call in at several other ports, it is not likely that this will reach you for many days after my letter of yesterday. I do not think there is any chance of another steamer going to England for a fortnight, so make up your mind to being without news of me for about two weeks after the date you receive this. I cannot tell you how I long for the next two months to be over: so much will be done in that time, for I must by the 16th of February have either failed or succeeded. Please God it will be the latter, and then I shall begin to turn my face towards England. I count the days over again and again. I seem always to be condemned to command in Expeditions which must be accomplished before a certain season of the year begins: In the Red River affair, I had to get to Fort Garry sufficiently early to admit of my getting back the Regular troops before the frosts set in, now I have to arrange so that I shall not be caught by the rains, and so that if possible I shall only keep the British Regts. on shore for about six weeks. We heard by the Cape steamer yesterday that Capt. Commerell is much better. He is now on his way to Madeira, where I believe he intends to spend the winter. He was able to walk about when the mail left. You would I am sure be amused if you saw the dignity and state that surrounds me here – I have people to dinner every day and sit in the centre of my table, my two A.D.C.s taking the head and the foot. I wonder when I shall do all this in a respectable climate where you can do the grande dame opposite to me. I had a note from Russell yesterday asking to send him a turkey for his Xmas dinner, which I shall do. Goodbye my dearest child. You are very dear to me and are constantly in my thoughts.

Hove, Wolseley MSS, W/P 3/17 .

96

Wolseley to Captain HRH Prince Arthur[16]

17 December
[Holograph]
Government House
Cape Coast

It is very gratifying to me to receive a letter from your Royal Highness, and I need scarcely add that I at once carried out your Royal Highness'es wishes with reference to Mr. Fitzgerald,[17] whose name appears in the days orders as extra A.D.C. to Sir A. Alison. The ships carrying the 42nd Highlanders arrived here last night having made an extremely fast voyage. I am sorry to say that owing to transport difficulties I shall not be able to land the English troops for over a fortnight yet. When they do disembark, they are to march in wings up to the Prah, where all the force rendezvous on the 13th January, to make its first march into Ashantee territory on the 15th of that month. I expect that all our fighting will be over by the end of January, but we have a brave and determined enemy to contend against, and all will feel that they are fighting in defence of their country, which feeling may intensify their courage.

Duke, Wolseley MSS, XVIII-H

97

Wolseley Journal, 19 December

Friday 19 December

I have allowed several days to pass without writing my private journal as I have been very busy and worn out every day with writing. I frequently begin my pen & ink work by candlelight in the morning, and often write again by the same light before I go to bed. My transport still worries me and the dread that I may not have enough provisions on the Prah by the 15th January nor enough carriers to enable me to move my force forward on that date preys upon me night and day. I am making every exertion to collect men & women from all quarters, & have put the whole transport arrangements under Lt. Col. Colley so that I hope at least to have some organisation & system imparted to those whom I have been able to collect: up to the present the Control Dept. has been unable to effect this. The S.S. Sarmatian[18] with the 42nd Highlanders and Sir A. Alison arrived on the [blank]. I have now determined upon taking all three Battalions with me across the Prah, leaving the 1st W. I. Regt. in reserve here and at Elmina. The 42nd is said to be in excellent order & to be by far the best of those Battalions sent out. All the tribes to the westward along the sea coast are now anxious to come in & be pardoned, they say that they never liked the Ashantis, but that as we could not protect them they were forced to join them: King Koffee has sent to his troops in and about Appolonia to return to Coomassie, and I hear that they are seizing men women & children to carry back as slaves from the tribes that have recently been in alliance with them against us – save me from my friends. I am sending off H.M.S. Argus tomorrow morning to the Windward ports carrying Dr Gouldsbury[19] as a commissioner from me to treat with these people & tell them that I am willing to pardon their *political* offences if they supply me with a large number of carriers – the numbers to be fixed by Gouldsbury. I am in hopes of getting thus nearly 1000 men & women. The mail that should have left England on the 24th ultimo still unheard of. Something must have happened to her. I have £15000 coming to me in her which if lost will inconvenience me a great deal. The mail that should have left England on the 30th will be due tomorrow. This irregularity in the mail service, especially in the arrival of the homeward bound steamers is most unfortunate & prejudicial to the public interests. H.M. Gunboat Decoy arrived yesterday evening bringing Mr Blisset,[20] the Control officer attached to Captain Glover with a letter to me asking for money: unless he gets £4000 at once, he will be unable to move. This annoys me very much, for I was told by Lord Kimberley that I need not make any arrangements for supplying Glover with money beyond the £5000 I brought out for him originally. The consequence is that I want all the money in the military chest for myself, and yet I do not like allowing his operations to be brought to a stand still from want of funds. I have therefore given him in silver £3,600 (the entire amount of his credit with the Crown Agents) on treasury bills, out of the Colonial Chest, leaving but little in it. The Commodore has also sent him £2000 in gold, so I hope he is now rich enough to co-operate with me across the Prah on the 15th of January next. Strange to say that Major Baker who has worked so hard as Chief of Staff since McNeill was wounded, has never been ill with fever, but now that Greaves has arrived to supercede him, a fever has taken hold of him. He is the most obstinate of men; won't confess he is ill, and won't go on board the Commodores ship for a couple of days for change of air. He is a splendid fellow and it is most fortunate for me that he remained well throughout until Greaves arrived. Mosquitoes are now beginning to be a little troublesome. The telegraph wire is now being put up. When all the wire has been landed & the gang of workmen are in full swing, the officer in charge of it[21] hopes to get on at the rate of 5 miles a day. If so I shall have it in working order before I cross the Prah on the 15th prox.

TNA, WO 147/3

98

Wolseley to Glover

19 December
[Holograph]
Govt House. Cape Coast

I am very distressed to find that you are short of funds: and to prevent any interruption in your operations, and lest want of money might prevent you from being on the Prah by the 15th January, I have nearly cleared out the Colonial Chest here (I could not help you from the Military Chest). I shall not therefore send you the £1000 I said I would, when the next mail [has] arrived from England, as I presume that the £3600 I have now sent you, will keep you afloat until you receive more from the Colonial Office.

Please send me a map showing where you intend crossing the Prah and let me know the distance your crossing places are from Prahsu. I presume that in order to make your first march into the country north of the Prah on the 15th January, that you will be actually in position there two or three days before. All my force is to be concentrated at Prahsu on the 13th although I shall not cross until the 15th Januy.

As I am crossing into Ashantee territory with a handful of native allies only besides my English Brigade I look to your advance in such imposing numbers, provided it is well known at Coomassie, to relieve me of some of the pressure that would otherwise be brought to bear upon me, but anxious as I am for your cooperation, I shall advance into Ashantee territory whether you are able to assist me or not. Please keep me constantly informed of your movements and of when you begin your advance towards the Prah. Wishing you every possible success in your trans-Volta campaign.

CUL, RCMS 131/6 Glover MSS

99

Wolseley Journal, 20 December

Saturday 20 December

We have had one or two showers of rain lately. It would seem that even in the dry season rain falls often. This can be accounted for by the great, vast mass of forest that covers the entire country & is always full of moisture. In my room as I write this at 11 a.m. the thermometer is only a little over 82° (faht). On the 18th inst. a strange letter from Home the P.M.O. was received by me: he has been suffering from fever lately and I fear that his brain has been affected by it. Brackenbury has been to see him to day and found him very desponding [.] Clever as he is, his disposition and temperament is of such a very melancholy nature that I wish to heaven he would go home. Heard from Baker Russell – some *kind* friend has written to [him] saying his wife is not well. Walked in the evening with Greaves to Connors Hill. Baker has the fever.

TNA, WO 147/3

100

Draft of Memorandum on Bush Fighting by Brigadier-General Sir Archibald Alison, Bt

No date [December]

[Holograph]

Bush Fighting almost always leads to the separation of companies and their removal from the eye of the Colonel & field officer. It also usually leads to the separation of the parts of a Company, and their removal from the immediate supervision of the Company commander. To meet the exceptional requirements of this mode of fighting the following arrangements must be made

1 Each Company must be divided into *four permanent* sections – the N.C. Officers & Men of which must be always kept together alike in the bivouac, on the march, or in action. The telling off of the Company must never be permitted to alter their section. The

men of them must as far as possible go on all duties together – the N.C. Officer in charge must never be shifted.

2 When in extended order for bush fighting, the men of a file must always act together. When the unit is open they should be in line about one pace distant from each other.

3 The men may fix bayonets or swords when commanders regard it advisable to do so.

4 As soon as a Company enters the bush the Captain must at once assume the entire direction of it. He must profit by any opening which may arise without it waiting for orders. He must exercise his own judgement on the manner in which it is brought into action, & handled in a section. But he must never forget that he is though an independent unit before acting in unison with other units towards common end, & he must thus take care always to unite his action with that of the other independent companies of his battalion.

5 In like manner as soon as a company goes into action the N. C. Officers in charge of sections must at once assume the command of their respective section, keep them well in hand & work them in unison with the other engaged sections of their Companies.

6 In taking a Company into action it will usually be advisable to extend only a single section in the first instance, prolonging the line to the right or left with the second & third sections only once the position and line of action of the enemy and weakening of enemy has been ascertained. But one section must always be held in reserve to meet any turning movement or unexpected rush.

7 The men must be specially warned to beware of clearings & never to form in them, but always when they have to cross them to do so with a rush & to plunge at once into the bush beyond. To halt in a clearing is to expose yourself as a target to enemies [*sic*] shot from the bush.

8 The greatest care should be taken never to throw away a shot. Wild aimless firing only encourages the enemy. It may sometimes be necessary to fire a few rounds into the bush, when no enemy is seen, but this must only be done to order.

Bodleian, Alison MSS, MS. Eng. lett. c. 450

101

Memorandum by Colonel George Greaves
20 December
[Printed]
Head Quarters,
Cape Coast Castle
The Major General Commanding has made the following notes for the information and guidance of the SOLDIERS and SAILORS about to take part in the operations north of the river PRAH.

Health
The climate is much better and more pleasant in the interior than on the sea shore, and if ordinary precautions are taken, there is no reason why any of the troops should suffer in health during the few weeks that they may have to remain in the country.

The officers must see that tea or chocolate, with a little biscuit, is provided for their men every morning before marching, and quinine will be served out by the medical orderlies.

During the heat of the day, or when marching late in the morning commanding officers may, at their discretion allow the patrol jackets to be taken off and carried by the men. These can be easily carried slung behind under the waist belt. Immediately that the march is over or if any long halt takes place, these jackets must be put on; for a chill, when the body is heated, is above all things to be avoided.

The following maxims should be impressed upon the men:
1 Never allow the body to suffer from a chill, and there will not be much chance of your ever being sick.
2 Never expose the head uncovered to the sun, and when halting or on sentry get into the shade, if possible.
3 When camping for the night, do your best to construct a raised sleeping-place even a few inches off the ground. (Examine the camps of the Ashantis on the road to the Prah, and copy their plan of making bedsteads; they are easily and quickly made, and sleeping off the ground is a great preservative of health.).

4 If any irregularity of the bowels is experienced, go at once to the doctor for a dose.

5 Never drink water until you have filtered it.

The operations beyond the Prah will last only a few weeks, and the Major General relies on the manliness of the soldiers and sailors to keep them out of hospital as long as they have strength to march. The battalion that is composed of the best men, and that is best looked after by its officers will send the fewest sick men to the rear.

Mode of Fighting

The theatre of operations will be a great forest of gigantic trees, with an undergrowth of bush varying in thickness. At some places men can get through the bush in skirmishing order, at others they will have to use their sword-bayonets to open paths for themselves. All the fighting will be in skirmishing order, the files being two, three, or four paces apart according to circumstances.

When once thus engaged in a fight in the bush, officers commanding battalions, and even officers commanding companies will find it difficult to exercise much control over their men. For this reason it is essential that the tactical unit should be as small as possible. Every company will therefore be at once divided into four sections, and each section will be placed under the command of an officer or non-commissioned officer. These sections, once told off, are not on any account to be broken up during the war, nor are their commanders to be changed except under extraordinary circumstances, and then only by order of the officer commanding the battalion. All details of duty will be performed by sections, or, when only very small guards or piquets are required, by half sections.

In action, as a general rule, three sections only of each company will be extended, and the fourth will form a support in rear of the centre of the company's skirmishing line, and at from 40 to 80 yards from it. Care must be taken that the support never loses sight of its own skirmishers, and that it conforms to their movements; but its commander must never allow it to become mixed up with the skirmishers, unless it be ordered forward by the officer commanding the company. The captain will always be with the skirmishing line exercising a general control over it; and, as the enemy only fight in loose skirmishing order, it will seldom be necessary to bring forward the support into the skirmishing line.

Fighting in the bush is very much like fighting by twilight; no one can see further than a few files to his right or left. Great steadiness and self-confidence are therefore required from every one engaged. The Ashantis always employ the same tactics. Being superior in numbers they encircle their enemy's flanks by long thin lines of skirmishers, hoping thereby to demoralise their opponents. The men engaged in our front line should not concern themselves about these flank attacks. They must have the same confidence in their General that he has in them, and depend upon him to take the necessary measures for meeting all such attacks either in flank or rear. Each soldier must remember that with his breech loader he is equal to at least twenty Ashantis, wretchedly armed as they are with old flint muskets, firing slugs or pieces of stone that do not hurt badly at more than 40 or 50 yards range. Our enemies have neither guns nor rockets, and have a superstitious dread of those used by us.

In action the two comrades forming each file must always keep together, and the officers and non-commissioned officers commanding sections will use their utmost endeavours to keep their sections from mixing up with those on their right and left.

If, during the advance through the bush, fire is unexpectedly opened by the enemy concealed behind cover, the men will immediately drop on the knee behind trees or any cover that may be at hand, pausing well before delivering their fire, and taking care to fire low at the spots from which the enemy were seen to fire. All firing against a concealed enemy should be very slow, and officers and non-commissioned officers in command of sections must spare no efforts to prevent the men from wasting their ammunition. It must be explained to the men that, owing to the difficulties of transport, the supply of ammunition beyond the Prah will be very limited; and that every shot fired which is not deliberately aimed, not only encourages the enemy, who would soon learn to despise a fire that did them no injury, but seriously affects the efficiency of the force, for, if ammunition were to run short, a stop would be put to our further advance. The Major General must rely upon the intelligence of the soldiers and sailors to husband their ammunition, without any efforts from their officers being required.

The advance will be made along narrow paths, where the men can only march in file, and sometimes only in single file; when an action commences, the troops on the centre path will deploy to the front into skirmishing order, either to the right or left of the path as ordered, upon the leading file; the rear section of each company will always form the support, and officers commanding companies will be careful to lead these deployments so that their front may always be as nearly as possible at right angles to the path they had been marching upon. All officers must remember that the front line will, as a general rule, face north by west, and when at any distance from the path, they must guide the direction of their advance by compass.

Officers Commanding battalions and companies will not order any bugle call to be sounded in camp or on the march north of the Prah, except to repeat those sounded on the main road by order of the Major General Commanding; and these, if preceded by any special regimental call, will be repeated only by the battalion concerned, and by any battalion that may be operating between the main road and the corps indicated by the call. When any call is not preceded by a regimental call, it will be repeated by every bugler within hearing, except those that may be on duty with the baggage guard.

Whenever the advance and double is sounded it is to be understood to order a general advance of the whole front line upon the enemy. The men will then advance cheering at a fast walk, making short rushes whenever the nature of the ground will allow of their being made. All such advances will be preceded by a heavy fire of guns and rockets.

On reaching a clearing in the course of an action, or when the enemy is in the immediate neighbourhood, the troops will not cross over the open space until the clearing has been turned and the bush on both sides of it has been occupied.

When once a position has been gained, it is to be held resolutely. In warfare of this nature there must be no retreats.

No village or camp is to be set on fire except by order of the Major General commanding. Officers and men are reminded of the danger and delay which occur if a village is set on fire, before all the ammunition and baggage have made their way through it.

All plundering and unnecessary destruction of property are to be strictly repressed. Officers are held responsible that when a village or camp is occupied their men are kept together, and prevented from dispersing to seek plunder.

The importance of kindness from all ranks to the friendly natives who are employed as carriers cannot be too strongly urged. If the carriers are ill-treated, the troops run imminent risk of being left without food and ammunition.

It must never be forgotten by our soldiers that Providence has implanted in the heart of every native of Africa a superstitious awe and dread of the white man that prevents the negro from daring to meet us face to face in combat. A steady advance or a charge, no matter how partial, if made with determination, always means the retreat of the enemy. Although when at a distance, and even when under a heavy fire, the Ashantis seem brave enough, from their practice of yelling, and singing, and beating drums, in order to frighten the enemies of their own colour, with whom they are accustomed to make war, they will not stand against the advance of the white man.

English soldiers and sailors are accustomed to fight against immense odds in all parts of the world; it is scarcely necessary to remind them that when in our battles beyond the Prah they find themselves surrounded on all sides by hordes of howling enemies, they must rely upon their own British courage and discipline, and upon the courage of their comrades.

Soldiers and sailors, remember that the black man holds you in superstitious awe; be cool; fire low, fire slow, and charge home; and the more numerous your enemy, the greater will be the loss inflicted upon him, and the greater your honor in defeating him.

NAM, Warre MSS, 8112–54–88

Wolseley Journal, 21–24 December

Sunday 21 December

Major Baker much better: the fever has left him, and he has some appetite. Went to service at 8.30 a.m. in the Wesleyan Chapel lent to us by the Missionaries. Mr. Patterson read the prayers & I was very much amused at his turning to the north during the Creed: poor little man he forgot that the Church ran north and south instead of east and west as in Episcopalian Churches, so he was rude enough to turn his back upon us & yet not fulfil the high church humbug of facing the East when he gabbled through the Creed. If ever I build a Church I shall have the Communion table at the end where the door usually is, so I shall avoid having to admire the backs of fat curates and oily looking rectors & deprive them of all excuse for at least one piece of popish nonsense. Walked to the Salt pond in the evening: the Commodore dined with me – no mail in yet. I am becoming nervous about the £15,000 I have on board of her. Heard of poor Lieut. Wells death: he died of yellow fever on board the Biafra before she reached Madeira.[22] The scoundrel of a master on board her, evaded the quarantine laws here & said he had no sickness on board: we ascertained after he left that this was a lie: that several people on board of her had died of yellow fever previous to her reaching this place. The master & the doctor on board ought to be hanged. The naval medical officer, who granted her pratique is away, but I expect him back tomorrow. When I hear what he has to say for himself, if I can have a case made out, I shall have the lying Captain arrested the next time the Biafra comes into these waters.

Monday 22 December

Nothing to relate.

Tuesday 23 December

Started at 5 a.m. from the shore and went on board H.M.S. Active that carries the Commodores broad pennant. I took half a dozen of my staff with me. She got under weigh at once & we steamed slowly for the mouth of the Prah – I have sent a small native force down to the lower Prah under Sergt. Hughes[23] an intelligent native who speaks English: his orders are to combine with the Wassaws and punish the Chama people who still harbor some Ashantees & who were the men that treacherously wounded Commodore Commerill. I had asked for two men of war to go to Chama yesterday & upon arriving off the mouth of the Prah, I found H.M.S. Merlin and Encounter there at anchor; we did not succeed in getting Sergt Hughes off until late as he was inland with his men about 8 miles. All arrangements were made for crossing his force over the Prah tomorrow at 7 a.m. He has he says nearly 1000 men with him. We then steamed into the Prah in a steam launch: we crossed the bar easily, but I did not think it was worth while to run any risk of being sniped from the bush on either bank as poor Commerell was, so we turned back after we had gone up a little distance. We got back here about 10 p.m. having had a most agreeable day. I forgot this disgusting place for at least one day.

Wednesday 24 December
Gunboat in from the Volta bringing me despatches from Capt. Glover saying that he cannot fulfil his engagement of being on the Prah on 15th January – Sent him back at once a positive order that he crosses the Prah on that date with all his disciplined men & the 11000 Akims he has in camp at Janketty. He won't like that. I told him that unless he was able to fulfil his previous engagement with me that as far as the Ashantee war was concerned we might just as well be operating in Zanzibar on the other side of the continent. The gunboat that carried my order to him is to wait for an answer. Ethiopia in from England with mail of 30th ultimo – nothing yet heard of Soudan since she left Madeira on 1st inst: she carries the mail of 24th ultimo & has £15,000 for me on board.[24] Walked in the evening to Prospect House to try our revolvers & the buck shot ammunition. The former is very good: the latter is a disgrace to Woolwich Arsenal. H.M.S. Encounter returned from Chamah having crossed over Sergt. Hughes & his 630 men to the west bank of the Prah: they soon burnt the town of Chamah and then engaged the enemy in the bush. They had started for a village about five or six miles inland when the Encounter left.
TNA, WO 147/3

103

Wolseley to Glover

24 December
[Holograph]
Govt House, Cape Coast

Your despatch of the 22nd instant just received has filled me with dismay. The English Govt. look to me to get the British Regts. away from this Coast with the least possible delay: next to beating the Ashantees or at least humbling them, this early withdrawal of the English troops from the Coast is I believe the object most desired at home. Unless you cooperate with me on the Prah I cannot let them leave until I have finally settled with King Koffee, whereas with you at Juabim, which place I believe you could reach easily in about eight marches, and could I believe get there without much, if any opposition and the enemy having been thoroughly defeated by the English troops near the Adansie Hill, I could make what terms I like. With the Ashantee Army beaten by my white troops, I should then if I thought it necessary to occupy or to destroy Coomassie be able to send you forward to that place from Duabim whilst I sent all, or at least the bulk of my Europeans back to England. To enable you to carry out your engagement, I have run myself tolerably dry as regards money here, and I am now compelled to use the authority confided to me, and to order you in the despatch that accompanies this letter to march all your disciplined troops to the Prah to cross that river on the 15th of next month with them and the 11,000 Akims now collected at Janketty. The quarrels between the tribes to the east of the Volta can be settled at any time, but the Ashantee War, to prosicute which both you and I have been sent to this country [for] can only be disposed of *now*: *it* won't wait, the Alroona business will. I speak at a distance from your theatre of operations, but I never believed that the Acras would join you on the Prah. Let them settle their own business on the Volta, or should you feel bound to remain with them to assist them, of course you can do so, but I must have your disciplined men and the Akims from Janketty across the Prah on the 15th prox^o. Unless you can accomplish this, no matter what may be your success with the Alroonas, you must clearly see that as far as this wretched war between England and Ashantee is concerned, you might just as well be operating on the Zanzibar coast of Africa as in the Alroona District. Having spoken thus plainly to you and told you my views as to the military exigencies of the moment, I shall rest satisfied that if you do not cross the Prah as originally intended, it is because you could not. From what I know of you, I feel that if what I require of you could be accomplished by any man, it will be so by you.

PS. Let me hear from you at once upon recpt. of this. Send the Gunboat back with your reply for much depends upon it.
CUL, RCMS 131/6, Glover MSS

104

Wolseley Journal, 25–26 December

Thursday 25 December
Christmas Day. Went to Church at 8.30 a.m. did not stay for Communion service because I was sitting near the parson & thought that I saw wafers on the table instead of bread. I found out afterwards that I was wrong. The Commodore, Rolfe,[25] his flag lieutenant, Lt. Windham & Col. Colley dined with us. Had turtle soup for dinner, having been sent a present of a turtle by Lt. Bolton who caught it himself near Anamaboo, not far from this place.

Friday 26 December
Sad news by the Amethyst: poor Charteris died a few days after he left this place: it will be a sad blow to his family. A long letter from McNeill saying that although his wound is nearly healed up that he is such a cripple he cannot dress himself and does not therefore expect to be able to rejoin the Force. My staff left to day: I start tomorrow at 6 a.m. to overtake them at Akroful the 2nd halting place, from here & so will begin our campaign. May God bless it.
TNA, WO 147/3

105

Wolseley to Cambridge

26 December
[Holograph]
Government House: Cape Coast Castle

The 42nd Highlanders arrived here on the 17th instant. It is such a fine Battalion that I have resolved upon landing it as well as the two others that arrived first, and to take all three with me across the Prah. My reasons for this change in plan are that the 1st W.I. Regt. that I had intended using north of the Prah requires in proportion to its strength as many carriers for the conveyance of the mens kits, as an English Regt. does – the W.I. soldiers also receive the same rations of food, so that in fact I should gain nothing by taking the 1st W.I. Regt instead of the 42nd and the services of one English battalion are worth that of two Regts of black soldiers. This arrangement will I hope enable me to deliver a more crushing blow to the enemy and so shorten the war, an object that is never absent for a moment from my mind. I trust that Your Royal Highness will approve of this.

I am sorry to say that Dr. Home the Principal Medical Officer has been very ill, and is to go to England upon the recommendation of a Medical Board. I have written to Madeira ordering on Dr. McKinnon[26] to take his place. Dr. Home's untiring energy, and the ability with which he has provided for the medical requirements of the Force about to move across the Prah, deserve the highest praise. I have written officially to the Secretary of State regarding him and I now avail myself of this opportunity of bringing his services to Your Royal Highnesses' notice. As a medical man, his ability is of the highest order, and his powers of organization are considerable.

My staff start to day for the Prah: they go on foot and will make the same marches as the troops. I leave tomorrow and will overtake them at the 2nd Halting Place (Akroful) tomorrow evening, as I travel in a hammock, my wounded leg unfortunately preventing me from marching like the others. I leave Sir A. Alison & his staff here, together with a D.A.Q.M. Genrl to superintend the disembarkation of the three English Regts. Unfortunately the short rifles of the 23rd and 42nd have not yet arrived, and I am in despair, for without a sword bayonet it will be impossible for a soldier to get through the bush. The ordinary bayonet in the bush is only an encumbrance: I have taken them away from all the native troops and purchased native knives for them instead. Every Ashante soldier carries one of these knives with which he is able to cut a path for himself as he goes through the bush: he could thus walk round the poor English soldier armed only with a bayonet.

Since the enemy's Army retired behind the Prah I have been unable to learn much of their doings, and until I push a force across the river I do not expect to obtain any really reliable information. I shall cross it with the Naval Brigade and some native troops about the 5th or 6th January for the purpose of making a bridge and a strong tête de pont to cover it. My scouts are now on the north side, but until I have some troops there also, they cannot be trusted to go far inland.

Sad news has reached me when writing this. Alfred Charteris, Lord Elcho's son died on board H.M.S. Simoom three days after she left this roadstead. When I bid him goodbye here, he was barely conscious, as his mind had been wandering off and on for some days, and I hear that for 24 hours previous to his death, his mind was so disordered that he sternly refused all sustenance. He was an admirable officer, brave, zealous and intelligent:– his death will be a sad blow to his family. I have also heard from Colonel McNeill who informs me that although his wound progresses most favourably, he is such a cripple, unable to dress himself, that he does not think there is much chance of his being able to rejoin me. I am glad to say that the weather has changed for the better: it is somewhat hotter but much drier. The Harmattan wind of which we have long heard so much has begun to make itself a little felt: It is cool and refreshing. Captain Glover wrote to me the other day saying that unless he obtained £4000 at once he could not fulfil his engagement to me to be on the Prah and to cross it on the 15th January. I therefore sent him £3,600 and the Commodore sent him £2000 more: Since then I have had a despatch from him saying that the Native Allies in whom he had been trusting so much had failed him so that he could not count upon being able to cross the Prah on the date previously arranged. He has become involved in the tribal quarrels of the people he has been subsidizing, and to aid them has begun operations to the east of the Volta River. As far as the approaching campaign against the Ashantees is concerned he might just as well be fighting in Abyssinia so I have peremptorily ordered him to go with, or to send all his discipline troops, numbering over a thousand men to the Prah at once, and with them and the 11,000 of the Eastern Akims that are now collected at Janketty on the Upper Volta (about 25 miles above Pong), to cross the Prah on the 15th January as previously arranged. I hope to arrange so that about 2000 of the Western Akims under Captain Butler (late 69th Regt.) and two other special service officers may cross on the same day at Prahsu-Akim, about half way between where Glover and where the Main Force will cross.

I have placed the Transport entirely under Lt. Colonel Colley, who will act under the instructions of the Depty Controller: I have given him 17 officers to help him and have placed the line of communications between this place and the Manoeuvring Force under his orders to prevent any possible clashing of authority anywhere: Colonel Colley has already done a great deal, so that I think I now see my way out of a difficulty that has weighed upon my mind for some time past. Lt Colonel Festing, I intend leaving with about 200 of the 2nd W.I. Regt at Prahsu to protect my bridge and magazines there.

Trusting that all these arrangements may meet with Your Royal Highness'es approval.

Cambridge MSS, RA VIC/ADD E/1/7276

106

Wolseley Journal, 27–28 December

Saturday 27 December

Left Government House, Cape Coast at 6.15 a.m. A lovely morning. Was awake at 3 a.m. so got up. I am sorry to say that of late I wake up too early and find that my only chance of sleeping subsequently is to get up and read or write. I read for an hour this morning & went back to bed where I was dozing when the 5 oclock gun fired. It is not daylight now until nearly 6 a.m. I soon heard the regular tramp of a large body of men under my window. It was the Naval Brigade that had just landed and was on the march to the Prah. I travelled in the "Carriage of the Sun" as usual,[27] and my six niggers were the best horses that I have had yet, so I got along well and reached the 1st Halting place, Inquabim at 8.15 a.m. where I found the Naval Brigade turned out to receive me: they had arrived half an hour before me & no man had fallen out during the march. I never saw a finer looking set of men. They are the pick of the fleet. As I was starting off they turned out again and gave me three cheers, a sound that has been heard here for the first time: as I looked at them & heard their cheer I could not help thinking that if the whole Ashantee Army was in front of that handful on passable ground, it would have bolted to a man from those cheers. There is nothing in the world like an English cheer, and whenever I hear one given by soldiers or sailors I always feel a sort of longing that [I] was leading them in a storming party. Reached Akroful at 10.35 a.m. found my staff there except Greaves and Baker who had started with me and who came up in a quarter of an hour after me. The telegraph is as yet only laid to this place: heard by it that the English mail is in bringing the mail that left home on the 6th instant and also the Soudans mail. That ship had broken down at Teneriffe. Both this place & Inquabim are very nice: every comfort provided for the men that was possible. Got our letters in the evening: all official letters from home very complimentary. Bad news from the 42nd. That Regt has come back from its cruise and I have had a report by telegraph saying that Erysipelas had appeared amongst the men. I may have to land them before the date fixed which will be very annoying.

Sunday 28 December
Starting a little after 6 a.m. for Yancoomassie (Fantee) where I found everything ready for the troops. Their progress to the Prah will be made with the greatest luxury, and I hope & trust without sickness. The P.M.Os report about 42nd Regt received. The first case of erysipelas was fatal. Three other men took it,

but they are now convalescent, and are on Connors Hill. The 42nd will consequently be landed first, and I sincerely trust that I shall hear nothing more of the disease. We had a slight tornado in the afternoon accompanied by a shower.

TNA, WO 147/3

107

Wolseley to Alison

28 December
[Holograph]
10 a.m. Yancoomassie

This news about the 42nd is very distressing. I hope it may not be as bad as it appeared in the telegram. Colonel Greaves telegraphed to you this morning on the subject. I am very, very averse to landing them, and – if the PMO agrees would like to transfer all or half or whatever proportion he considers necessary to the Manitoba and to the Victor Emanuel if she arrives today. Perhaps it would be advisable to send whatever ships they are transferred to, to sea – this the PMO should decide, but it is very bad to have men predisposed to any illness on board ships in the roadstead as all vessels roll so much there. If the worst comes to the worst the Regt must be landed in two detachments one going to Akroful the other to Inquabim. Under no circumstances would I hear of them being encamped if going into quarters at Cape Coast itself. It is so very essential that all the men to be employed beyond the Prah should have the sword bayonet, that I would prefer landing the Rifle Brigade first, in order to give time for the short rifles to arrive. If possible get the Rifle Brigade armed with cutlasses like the Navy. If the Commodore would do this it would be a mercy. The cutlasses should be sharpened. If you do this and no short rifles arrive before either the 23rd or 42nd leave to land, take away the bayonets from the first of those Regts to come on & give them the sword bayonet of the Rifle Brigade; if the police have any sword bayonets or there are any in store issue them as far as they will go. It does not matter in the least their not fitting the rifles as a fixed sword or bayonet in the woods in this warfare is neither useful nor ornamental. You are authorised to take away from the 1st WI Regt all the short rifles belonging to their Sergts – and I want this to be done if those from England do not arrive in time. Perhaps the Commodore could help you still further. Pray leave no stone unturned to obtain short rifles & sword bayonets for every man coming to the front. I cannot impress too strongly upon you this point. The naval swords are still better, so the more the Commodore could lend us the better. Please see him at once upon this point.

The Naval Brigade is a splendid body of men. I fear that our young soldiers will look a poor lot beside them. I hope you do not feel any ill effects from your slight attack of the sun the other day.

Bodleian, Alison MSS, MS. Eng. lett. c. 450

108

Wolseley Journal, 29–31 December

Monday 29 December

Left Yancoomassie Fantee at 5.45 a.m. for Mansu (about 11½ miles). Roads very wet at places where the trees are so high and thick that the sun cannot possibly get at the ground. Mansu is very complete. Inspected the 2nd W. I. Regt. in the evening: it is in much better condition than when I was here before, but even now it is not creditable to Lt. Col. Webber, and I told him so, *tout bonnement*. He is no use as a soldier on service. I wish he was going through the arduous duty of mounting Guard at St. James, instead of commanding a Regt out here.

Tuesday 30 December

Marched at 5.40 a.m. Road good to the Okee River but very bad beyond it: reached Sutah at 9.20 a.m. Everything in very good order here & ready for the reception of the European troops.

Wednesday 31 December

Last day of the year. I wonder where on earth I shall be this day [in] twelve months. Marched this morning at 5.45. Road very bad, so I had sent on my "Chariot of the sun" in which I travel to Atah Insu, after which I thought the road to Yancoomassie was tolerably good – I travelled to Atah Insu in my chair: the road mostly through swampy ground much cut up by traffic during wet weather: it is far worse than when I last went over it, although much has been done to improve it. At Atah Insu I got into my "chariot" but found the road so deep, and bad that I made very slow progress. We reached Yancoomassie Assin about 10.45 a.m. Received disagreeable letters from Glover. He has *completely failed* in the objects of his mission and is now desirous of throwing the blame upon me, but fortunately I have not only his public letters but his private ones to me which will prove very differently: the upshot is that instead of being able to cross the Prah on the 15th January (when I cross) with as he previously guaranteed at least 16,000 and most probably 30,000 fighting men, he can now only guarantee to cross at that date with about 700 Houssas & Yorubas. I have been throughout most careful in all my correspondence with him, and as copies of his and my despatches go home to the Colonial Office I have no doubt of the authorities at home being in my favor. Work still going on here at the huts, but all will be ready when the English Regts. pass through. We had a big fire in front of our huts in the evening in honor of the day, and some men & women amused us by dancing, the music being some boys singing clapping their hands & beating an empty wooden case as if it were a native drum, and so ended the year 1873.

TNA, WO 147/3

109

Wolseley to Commodore William Hewett VC, RN

31 December
[Holograph copy by Greaves]
Head Quarters
Camp Yancoomassie Assin
You were good enough to inform me verbally last week that if necessary you would undertake to make arrangements for the defence of the stores collected by Captain Glover at Addah on the Volta.

I have now the honor to forward for your information a copy of a part of a Despatch just received from that Officer written in reply to an order sent to him by me directing him to be on the Prah and be ready to cross that river on the 15th January.

As Captain Glover expresses great doubt as to the security of his magazine on the Volta I would feel much obliged by your adopting such measures as you may consider advisable with a view to their protection.

Captain Glover does not inform me how he intends disposing of the Armed Steamer and Steam launches he has on that river but should he have now withdrawn their crews from them they can be made use of on the Volta by whatever officers you may detail, should you be able to comply with this request for the protection of Captain Glovers magazines on that river.

CUL, RCMS 131/6, Glover MSS

110

Wolseley to Glover

31 December
[Holograph]
Camp Yancoomassie Assin

Your letters dated 28th December have just reached me, and I am sorry to find you take such a gloomy view of your prospects. I think however that when you reflect that *the object* for which all of us have been sent to this country, is to bring the King of Ashantee to terms, you will think better of our general position. My experience of these natives enables me to understand how it is that you have been disappointed in being able to begin your march towards Coomassie at the early date you anticipated when I arrived at the beginning of October last; and I am sure that no one who knows how hard you and the officers under your command have worked can ever think that the delay in beginning your operations is in any way attributable to your want of energy. The manner in which you and your officers have worked to try and bring the native tribes to act with you must be well known to Lord Kimberley, as it is to everyone here, and anyone who has had much experience with the people of Western Africa will know how little reliance there is to be placed upon their promises, and will therefore easily understand your present position.

I congratulate you sincerely upon your successful passage of the River Volta and the able manner in which you carried out that operation and the skirmish you had with the Alroonahs on the eastern bank. I am in great hopes that the loss you then caused them may enable Mr. Goldsworthy with the large force he has at his disposal to make short work of the Alroonah difficulty. I do not anticipate any danger to your magazines on the eastern bank for crossing such a river as the Volta would be no easy operation for the Alroonas who have neither steamers nor artillery, and – of course I speak without any direct knowledge of the Volta – that with your armed steamers and steam launches on it, assisted by the Commodore, your magazines ought to be perfectly safe. Nevertheless, even supposing that some risk is run regarding the safety of your stores on the Volta, it is well worth incurring it to accomplish the object for which you were sent here as Special Commissioner: that object is very clearly stated in para. 8 of your original instructions from Lord Kimberley of 18th August 1873.

As I mentioned in my last note to you, both of us have been sent here to bring this Ashantee War to an end, and as Europeans are to be employed in it, it is essentially necessary that all of them should be on board ship on their return journey to England at the very latest by the end of March: Every day is therefore of consequence – of immense consequence in this war, and indeed it has been a matter of extreme regret to me that owing to the difficulty of obtaining native carriers I was not able to begin my forward movements into Ashantee territory on the 1st instead of the 15th January. Pray leave no stone unturned to communicate frequently with me when you have crossed the Prah, as it is essential that I should be constantly informed of your doings, position and prospects. Hoping we may soon meet, and that through our united efforts we may be enabled to bring this war to a speedy conclusion.

PS. It may perhaps be possible for you to communicate with me at Prahsu Assin by means of a canoe on the Prah.

CUL, RCMS 131/6, Glover MSS

111

Wolseley to Edmond Wodehouse[28]

31 December
[Holograph extract copy]
Camp Yancoomassie Assin

If Capt. Glover only crosses the Prah with the 700 Houssas he mentions in his letters of the 28th inst. of course in a military sense his operations can have little or no effect upon the result of the battle that I must fight on the main road, but when that battle has been fought & he is by it enabled to push on without incurring any risk to Juabin his position there would have a great political influence upon the course of events in hurrying on the King in making peace. His main army being defeated, say somewhere in the vicinity of the Adansi Hill, and Capt. Glover being in the left rear marching upon Juabin and apparently upon his capital, he w'ld feel that his only chance for existence was peace; my only fear is that he may be driven to desperation. I am therefore very anxious to save both Coomassie & Juabin from destruction. In order to be certain of my instructions to Capt. Glover of this date reaching him, I intend sending him a duplicate copy of them from Prahsu by hand, the original having gone by sea to Addah. In this second copy I mean to add a postscript urging him to spare Juabin & protect it from his Houssas if he possibly can.

Our weather is improving daily, and so is the climate the further we go inland. The health & sprits of everyone is excellent. All are longing for the 13th proxo. and everyone is confident of success.

With the exception of our transport about which I am always in difficulties everything goes on well. Please tell Lord Kimberley that I look forward with confidence to being able to carry out the instructions he has given me both as regards measures & the time that he has laid down for me to accomplish them in.

BL, Gladstone MSS, Add. MSS 44225, f. 144

5

Advance (January 1874)

The first half of January was spent moving Wolseley's white battalions up to the Pra at about seven miles a day, half a battalion at a time. The second half saw them beginning the advance into Asante territory. On the eve of the first major action at Amoafo, Methuen described the situation as Wolseley and Kofi Karikari 'playing the same game – the former trying to gain time to get the supplies up, and the latter to get any army together, in which they have both succeeded'.[1] Wolseley, indeed, had reached the camp at Praso on 2 January and the bridge over the river marking the boundary of Asante territory was completed on 5 January though Wolseley himself did not cross until 20 January, five days later than originally planned [112, 116, 119]. The bridge had taken some 61 hours to complete, Home and his engineers overcoming manifold difficulties since only five 'Blanshard' pontoons had been found and sent out, the model having been deemed obsolete in 1870. Moreover, the 'Fowke' pontoons sent out had been largely eaten by ants and rats and the twelve 'Bainbrigge' trussed girders available could provide only half the roadway required. As a result a Canadian–pattern cribwork bridge was improvised [150].[2]

Led by Gifford's scouts, the native levies of Wood and Baker Russell began pushing up to the Adanse Hills, which were thought to be the most likely location for the Asante to fight. As Wolseley's men advanced, nine new fortified positions were constructed and supplies brought forward to them, these being at Essiaman, Akrofo, the Parakoome River, Moinsi, Adanse, Fomena, Ahkanknasie, Insafu, and Kwaman [119, 122, 125,

134, 138, 142].[3] There were occasional panics as on 17 January when some bullocks became frightened and so unnerved the Kru carrying for the Naval Brigade that their flight was only halted by officers firing revolvers over their heads. As it happened, the Naval Brigade also provided some simple amusement, adopting the son of a West India Regiment officer's servant, dressing him in naval uniform and calling him 'Mixed Pickles Esq.'.[4] All, however, were deeply touched by the death of the previously healthy George Huyshe on 19 January, fever setting in following dysentery: in his delirium, Huyshe sliced off his native servant's ear with his sword [**118, 127, 130, 132, 134, 137**].[5]

The halts imposed on the white troops in order to enable supplies to be brought up had a detrimental impact on the men's health and, with 214 men down sick by 25 January, Wolseley ordered up another 10 officers and 200 other ranks from the 2/23rd to supplement the garrison at Praso and on the line of communications. Alison was critical of what he saw as a tendency to play down the amount of sickness but Greaves rejected any criticism on the grounds that the home authorities should not be unnecessarily alarmed. Greaves further raised tensions by refusing to allow Alison's staff officers to receive the same allowances as special service officers.[6]

Apart from the on-going problem of transport and supply, which was not really resolved until mid-January, another aspect of Wolseley's campaign plan was also posing difficulties. As outlined to Cardwell on 15 December, Wolseley's advance into Asante territory was to be four-pronged. It was a plan some criticised but it was argued the main advance was strong enough to overcome any resistance and the other three prongs were merely diversions.[7] Apart from the main thrust across the Pra, there were to be the diversionary advances by Glover and Butler and, in addition, another from Wassa territory led by Captain William Dalrymple with the assistance of a fellow officer of the 88th Foot, Captain Hans Garrett Moore, a future winner of the VC.[8] As already indicated, neither Glover nor Butler crossed the Pra in strength on 15 January. Subsequently, Butler managed to increase his number of Akyem to about 1,400 but when faced with a supposed Asante force on 31 January, they simply deserted him when he was just 15 miles from Kumase and less than ten miles from Wolseley. Subsequently, Butler was to spend two months in Netley Hospital recovering from his ordeal.[9] Having begun his mission on 3 January, Dalrymple also failed to recruit the Wassa [121, 134]. Instead of the 15,000 once promised by the kings, Dalrymple had mustered barely 50 men by the end of January and, having 'wasted tact, temper and judgment in dealing with the hopeless inertness of the native character', abandoned his mission.[10]

Relatively little was seen of the Asante even by Gifford's scouts and one response appeared to be a reliance upon various fetishes to deter Wolseley's advance, including leaving a mutilated body, buried kid goats and white thread strung between the trees in imitation of the telegraph line being carried forward with the advance since the Asante assumed it was some kind of white man's fetish.[11] Gifford captured a Muslim fetish priest who confronted his scouts with curses designed to deter the advance. A Dafin scholar, Sulayman Kunatay, whose magical manifesto designed to stop the British was found on the Adanse Hills, was to be in one of the Asante deputations sent to Wolseley, of which more later. It has also been suggested that it was Muslim advice that the Asante should not defend the potentially strong position on the Adanse Hills as it might prove so strong that Wolseley would be forced to retreat and the Asante thereby deprived of the chance of surrounding him. Certainly from the Asante perspective, there were disturbing omens, an aerolite falling in the market place at Kumase and the fetish tree from which Kumase took its name falling down on 6 January [131].[12]

Another aspect of the Asante response, however, was to engage in diplomacy, a frequent activity among pre-colonial West African states. Indeed, the group that appeared at Wolseley's outposts on 2 January was led by a man routinely described in the contemporary accounts as the 'town crier' of Kumase. In fact, the man in question was an *esen* or *nsenieni*, better characterised as a court herald and, therefore, one of the principal agents of diplomatic communication.[13] The envoy carried with him two letters from Kofi Karikari addressed to Harley and dated 25 November and 26 December, both translated by the Fante interpreter, Joseph

Dawson, who had been detained in Kumase since having been sent there by Harley to interpret his own messages to Kofi Karikari in December 1872 [**112, 115**]. The first maintained that Amankwatia had been sent to attack only the Fante because Denkyira was to be taken from the Asante, and that the captive missionaries had not been released because the ransom demanded for them by Adu Bufo remained unpaid. The second suggested the Asante had defeated the British at Fesu when the army was attacked while returning home, and requested a reply to the first letter and an explanation for the British attack. Capture of the Fortnum & Mason hamper at Fesu was cited as evidence of the Asante victory. According to Dooner, the envoy maintained that the King had said, 'The white man may come to my market place. I will not fight with him.'[14] Implying that the Asante generals had misled Kofi Karikari and that there was no intention of cutting off Asante access to the coast, but that he was poised to invade Asante territory, Wolseley reiterated the need for the Asante to observe the 1831 treaty, to release the missionaries, to pay an indemnity, and to conclude a new treaty [**113**].

Before sending the envoys away with his reply, however, Wolseley resolved to impress the envoy and his escort with the preparations for the invasion of Asante territory, keeping them to see the bridge completed, demonstrating the Gatling on 4 January and then marching the Naval Brigade past them on the road when they were on their way back to Kumase on the following day [**112, 114, 115, 116, 117**]. The Gatling demonstration was not entirely successful. One of the two landed had already been left behind at Dunkwa when a practice shoot on 12 November had shown that it would not traverse properly. Now Rait and Lieutenant William Knox of the Royal Artillery had difficulty getting the remaining Gatling to work, probably through an empty cartridge case becoming jammed and stopping the drum revolving. Stanley heard one officer in the audience remarking it was a 'rotten arrangement'. In the end, however, Rait managed to fire a drum of ammunition up the river with pleasing effect in terms of the splashes of water and applause from Fante carriers though observers differed in their assessment of the impact upon the Asante.[15] On the night of 4 January one of the Asante, named by Brackenbury as Quamina Owoosoo (perhaps Kwame Owusu) and also said to be the brother of Esen Kwaku, committed suicide by putting a gun to his mouth [119]. Initially, the assumption was either that he was simply terrified by the power of the Gatling, or that he had incautiously proclaimed resistance to the British futile, remarks that his brother threatened to report to the king. Subsequently, it transpired that he had broken the Asante diplomatic code by observing that any white man who carried an ultimatum to Kofi Karikari would lose his head, a discourtesy to his hosts that he knew would cost him his own life once reported.[16]

The next round of the diplomatic exchange came on 12 January [125], Wolseley receiving a letter from the king dated three days earlier and carried by a much more senior envoy, Owusu Koko Kuma, son of a former *Asantehene*, Osei Tutu Kwame (ruled 1804–23). He was accompanied by one of the missionaries, Kühne, whom Kofi Karikari had decided to release after long deliberations with his advisers on 9 January: Ramseyer and Bonnat decided that Kühne should be the one to go as he was ill. Such a senior diplomat was empowered to negotiate but not to conclude any negotiations and, in any case, according to the missionaries, he carried an Islamic charm 'which with a mere shake of the hand was to have the effect of causing the governor [Wolseley] to go back'. Wolseley was enjoined to halt his advance, implying a readiness to negotiate. According to Kühne, the Asante army was dispersed and the king, who would not be able to afford an indemnity, unwilling to fight.[17] Wolseley refused to halt his advance, Buller taking back Wolseley's reply to the effect that Dawson could remain as an interpreter at Kumase as Kofi Karikari had requested, but that the remaining white captives must be released [125, 126, 128].

Kofi Karikari's reply of 21 January carried by Esen Buadi reached Wolseley two days later with the remaining white captives – the Ramseyers and their two children and Bonnat – arriving that evening [134]. Just as he had refused to see Owusu Koko Kuma, Wolseley also refused to see Esen Buadi, deputing Greaves to do so. Again pleading for Wolseley to halt, Kofi Karikari now indicated that Amankwatia would be required to pay any indemnity while Ramseyer and Bonnat confirmed that the king himself had paid the ransom demanded by Adu Bufo for their release.[18] Wolseley regarded the release of the remaining captives sufficiently significant to rush the news to London so that the government might announce it as part of the Queen's Speech at the opening of the parliamentary session, Wolseley believing it would be a 'grand coup' for the government [**134, 147**]. The telegram was sent off at 1800 on 23 January by runner then taken by an officer from Praso to the nearest telegraph at Beraku for transmission to Cape Coast where it was sent in cipher to both the Colonial Office and the War Office by way of the *Sarmatian* sailing for Gibraltar expressly for the purpose on the evening of 24 January. It appeared in the London press on 5 February. Smarting at Wolseley pre-empting their function, the correspondents calculated that the cost had been upwards of £7,000. The message showed Wolseley's flare for publicity as well as his care in eliciting the favour of his political masters, Gladstone having already expressed to Kimberley his continuing appreciation of Wolseley's political adroitness. As already indicated, Wolseley was to write in April 1880 in reference to Asante, 'I always make it a rule to serve the Govt. in power to the best of my ability & to help them to demolish their opponents who attack them on military matters with which I am concerned, for party purposes.'[19]

Unbeknown to Wolseley, however, Gladstone had announced to his Cabinet colleagues his decision to seek a dissolution on 23 January and a general election campaign was under way so that some supposed the telegram an electioneering ploy, if not a hoax. There had been some press speculation that a timely success might influence the prolonged election poll, which was held over the last week of January and the first week of February but, in the event, the news came too late to make any difference to Gladstone suffering defeat. Disraeli's Conservatives secured a majority of 52 seats. Gladstone's Foreign Secretary, Granville, had already predicted in January that the war 'might have been our death' but 'cannot be our life'. The announcement served, therefore, as Reade put it, to cast merely 'a brief and delusive gleam' over the last days of Gladstone's administration; Gladstone resigned on 17 February.[20]

As it happened, the release of the captives also fulfilled most of the remaining original purposes of Wolseley's expedition.

The Asante had left the protectorate even before white troops had arrived and, in effect, Kofi Karikari had now signalled an intention to comply with all demands. What then would be the purpose of continuing to Kumase? Reade believed that Wolseley had negotiated rather than pressing directly on to Kumase once across the Pra as he wished to build a reputation as a diplomatist. He felt, therefore, that Kofi Karikari went a long way to outwitting Wolseley by being prepared to make any concessions that would prevent Wolseley reaching Kumase. Yet, at the same time, a treaty without a clear-cut military victory would not satisfy British public opinion and Wolseley was forced to go on to Kumase. Thus, the fate of the captives was no longer of account and, in any case, they had 'no claim upon the British Government'.[21] Historians, however, have tended to conclude that Wolseley was always determined upon imposing a settlement by taking Kumase and, therefore, in response to the king's letter of 21 January, compiled a list of demands that he knew would be so humiliating as to be totally unacceptable.[22] The terms laid down on 24 January for halting the advance were the return of all native captives in Asante hands, an indemnity of 50,000 ounces of gold, of which half must be paid at once, and six hostages. If the conditions were met, a new treaty could be signed [**135, 137**]. Bonnat had already said that Kofi Karikari could not afford 50,000 ounces of gold,[23] but the real sticking point was the question of hostages.

Wolseley had indicated his intention to demand hostages to the Duke of Cambridge on 15 January [**130**], and it would appear that he had been advised by one of the African Medical Service doctors with the expedition, Dr James 'Africanus' Horton, an Ibo by birth, that a king's sons were not considered to be of royal blood in a European sense and that the Asante would not feel them sufficiently important hostages.[24] Thus, in addition to the *Asantehemaa* (Queen Mother), Afua Kobi, who had long opposed continuing the war, five heirs rather than sons were specified including Kofi Karikari's brother and designated heir, Mensa Bonsu. As Dawson wrote to warn Buller, any other hostages might have been acceptable but not these.[25]

Wolseley professed not to understand Kofi Karikari's policy and, though reassuring the Asante that a reconnaissance led by McLeod on 26 January should not have burned down a village, and still emphasising peaceful intentions, continued to advance [**134**, **139**, **140**]. There were certainly increasing signs that the Asante were gathering their army and preparing to fight [**139**, **141**, **142**]. When, therefore, two letters from Kofi Karikari dated 26 and 27 January and again urging Wolseley to halt were received on 29 January, with a coded message – an apt passage from the Bible – from Dawson suggesting Kofi Karikari was acting duplicitously, Wolseley felt fully justified in pressing on. Wolseley himself then engaged in some double dealing of his own, promising to halt for four days to allow the king to consider his options when in fact it was necessary to bring up further supplies [**143**, **144**].[26]

The illusion of preserving peace was generally held to have had one unfortunate result on 29 January when McLeod led a reconnaissance by force – 80 men from the 2/23rd, 223 men from the Naval Brigade, 58 levies from Baker Russell's regiment, and two rocket troughs – towards Borborasi where the King of Adanse's forces were thought to be located. Orders had been issued previously not to fire unless fired upon, so that the Asante should not be seen to have a fight forced on them. Captain James Nicol, commanding the Anamabu from Baker Russell's regiment, was shot dead entering the village, hit in the heart, lung and spinal column by three different slugs [**143**, **147**]. Accounts differ but most suggest that, in obedience to the order, Nicol had attempted to parley with the Asante and was thus, as Reade put it, a 'human sacrifice' to an order then rescinded. McLeod cleared the village of the Asante, capturing in the process the state umbrella of the veteran Asante general, Asamoa Nkwanta.[27] What made his death more poignant was that Nicol, the 46-year-old adjutant of the Hampshire Militia, had volunteered for the expedition as a means of earning additional money for his wife and children, and of conceivably re-entering the regular army. Maurice noted that Nicol had been living in 'penurious isolation' in trying to save as much of his campaign allowance as possible and Stanley had even found him panning for gold in one stream, misled by glistening sand. A fund was immediately started for the widow and children, raising about £80 and, subsequently, when the Grocers' Company of the City of London gifted Wolseley £250 for distribution to those who had suffered as a result of the campaign, half was given to Nicol's widow.[28]

The presence of Asamoa Nkwanta at Borborasi suggested that a major action was in the offing and, indeed, the old general and the King of Adanse were trying to draw Wolseley on to the main Asante army, which was holding a strong horseshoe-shaped defensive position on a ridge around the village of Amoafo above a swampy and heavily forested defile though the bush was dense everywhere. The expectation was to hold Wolseley there while the forces of the King of Dwaben or *Dwabenhene*, Asafo Agyei, broke into Wolseley's rear from the east and cut him off at the Pra. In the event, Asafo Agyei was diverted instead – apparently against his will – to oppose Glover though he may also have bridled when it appeared no frontal assault was intended against Wolseley, the Amoafo position being seen as purely defensive. With Amankwatia in some disgrace, supreme command was vested in the *Mamponhene* (King of Mampon), Kwabena Dwumo, who would usually command the army's right wing in battle. Buller got wind of the plan from one of his spies and Wolseley, who had hoped to fight close enough to Kumase to avoid more than one engagement, accepted the challenge on 31 January [**145, 146, 147**].[29]

Wolseley's own plan was to advance in a large hollow square formation, characterised by him as a 'parallelogram', in order to safeguard against the anticipated flank attacks.[30] The front face extending some 600 yards – 300 yards each side of the main path to Amoafo – would be formed by the 42nd with the support of Rait's two seven-pounders and with Gifford's scouts out ahead. Command of the 42nd was vested in Major Duncan Macpherson with Alison in overall command of the front face. Some 300 yards to the left of the path, McLeod would command the left face of the square, with half the Naval Brigade and Baker Russell's regiment with two rocket troughs under Lieutenant George Palmer at the left-hand front corner of the square. Some 300 yards to the right of the path, Wood's right face comprised the rest of the Naval Brigade and his own regiment, with another two rocket troughs under Lieutenant William Knox for the right-hand front. Wolseley and his staff would be at the centre with the 2/23rd contingent as reserve, while the 2nd Rifle Brigade would form the rear face of the square. Led by engineers with path-cutting squads of natives, McLeod and Wood would both strike out from the main route, initially cutting a new path at right angles then beginning to cut a path directly parallel to the main route. Baggage was to be left at Ahkanknasie under the guard of a company of Baker Russell's regiment and a detachment of West Indians and the field hospitals and reserve ammunition column located at Insafu with a guard of West Indians.[31] The whole force totalled 1,509 Europeans (134 officers and 1,375 other ranks) and 708 natives, the strength of both Wood and Baker Russell's regiments having been reduced by those detached to guard the new posts established on the line of communications.[32] The Asante were generally held to have numbered between 15,000 and 20,000.

Not unexpectedly, the action that followed, fought in dense and gloomy bush, was rather less structured than Wolseley's official despatch and Brackenbury's official account would suggest.[33] Henty perhaps captured the atmosphere best:

> It is impossible, indeed, to give a picturesque account of an encounter in which there was nothing whatever picturesque; in which scarcely a man engaged saw an enemy from the commencement to the end of the fight; in which there was no manoeuvring, no brilliant charges, no general concentration of troops; but which consisted simply of five hours of lying down, of creeping through the bush, of gaining ground foot by foot, and of pouring a ceaseless fire into every bush in front which might contain an invisible foe.

He also commented on the tremendous noise as the Asante used enormous powder charges in their old muskets and the trees broke up the sound so that 'the result was a strange and confused reverberation, mingled with the hissing sound rising from the storm of bullets and slugs mingled with that of the rockets'.[34] Other accounts also dwell on the noise of drums, cries, tom-toms and horns, which at least suggested the direction of the enemy, if not the elevation at which to fire, since few saw any actual Asante.

The Asante themselves invariably fired high and another common sensation was slugs stripping bark off the trees and, in the words of Prior, constantly bringing down 'leaves in a rustling shower suggestive of a gusty autumn morning in England'.[35] Given the nature of the action and the skilful way in which the Asante began to infiltrate the square, it was not perhaps surprising that there were subsequent accusations, particularly on the left and right faces of the square, that units had fired on each other as well as assumptions that one's own unit had been more hard pressed than others.[36]

While Gifford's scouts quickly took the village of Ejinasi, they soon encountered heavy resistance beyond it, and, committed company by company and fighting section by section from about 0800 onwards, the 42nd was soon seemingly swallowed in the swampy defile. Alison, who greatly admired the determination of the Asante – he called their flanking attacks 'beautiful' – described it as two hours of heavy fighting and, indeed, the heaviest half hour he had ever experienced, while veterans of the 42nd maintained that they had seen nothing like it in the whole of their Indian service.[37] Indeed, six of the eight companies of the 42nd were engaged by just after 0900 within what Alison described as 'a semicircle of hostile fire', causing him to call for support. Having committed a seventh company, Alison called for more support at 0930.[38] On the left, Captain Buckle was killed at an early stage, shot through the heart at close range while cutting the path. McLeod lost touch with the 42nd so, at about 1045, he began to cut a new path northeastwards to try and regain contact. On the right, too, Wood began to lose touch with the 42nd and came under such heavy fire that the Naval Brigade was forced to lie down to return fire. Wood himself was also wounded by a nail slug just below the heart and temporarily incapacitated.[39] Confronted with reports of difficulties on all sides and having already sent the 83-strong detachment of the 2/23rd forward in response to Alison's first message, Wolseley, now established with his staff at Ejinasi, could spare only one company of the 2nd Rifle Brigade for Alison rather than the half battalion he had requested. Another company was sent to McLeod and three to Wood. At one point, Asante, who had got in between the 42nd and the right flank, threatened Wolseley's headquarters itself from less than 100 yards away, until Commodore Hewett restored the position. Wolseley, who had refused to allow the village of Kwaman to be loopholed in order to demonstrate his confidence, and irritated by Alison's demands, adopted that studied determination to maintain his composure in the view of the press correspondents to which reference has already been made [**147**].

In the meantime, however, Rait had managed to get one of his guns forward over the swamp and up the path beyond in direct support of the 42nd, who were making slow progress. Fourteen or fifteen rounds of case shot at less than 50 yards' range did the trick and, by about 1220, Alison had reached Amoafo. Two more Rifle Brigade companies were extended to the northeast of Amoafo at 1315 and the firing appeared mostly over by 1345. Wolseley therefore ordered Colley to bring up the baggage to Amoafo from the rear but, at about 1500, a new Asante attack developed along the road back to Insafu. A company of the Rifle Brigade was despatched to relieve the pressure on the intervening village of Kwaman held by only 33 West Indians and Captain Charles Burnett of the 15th Foot, who rose from his sick bed to take command.[40] Insafu and Fomena, defended by just 25 men of whom many were sick and wounded, also came under attack. The Asante were driven off but, at about 1600, Colley's baggage column was then attacked as it approached Kwaman, the carriers panicking and sweeping Colley back with them to Insafu, from whence he was able to restore order through the night, not resting for some 19 hours. Wolseley sent back nine companies of riflemen and Highlanders to line the route on the following morning and the convoy came safely into Amoafo, maize and plantains found in the abandoned Asante position sustaining the force through the night.[41]

Considering the intensity of the firefight, there were astonishingly few deaths among Wolseley's force. Only four men had been killed, namely Buckle, two privates of the 42nd, and a Susu from Wood's regiment: one of the privates had been wounded and, caught by the Asante, beheaded. Fortunately, Asante slugs had little penetration unless fired at very close range, mostly causing only inflammation, but 21 officers and 173 other ranks had still been wounded. Captain William Baird of the 42nd, indeed, was to die from his wounds on his passage back to Britain. The heaviest casualty rate was in the 42nd, with nine officers and 104 other ranks wounded out of the 27 officers and 489 men who had gone into action. In all, the wastage rate from wounds and sickness amongst those Europeans from the 42nd, 2/23rd, 2nd Rifle Brigade and Naval Brigade landed at Cape Coast in December now amounted to 12 per cent.[42] On McLeod's recommendation, Wolseley put forward the names of Lance Sergeant Samuel McGaw, Private George Cameron and Pte George Ritchie, all of the 42nd, for the VC. In the event, only the recommendation for McGaw was accepted, the wounded NCO having continued to lead his section throughout the action. The Queen presented the VC to McGaw at Osborne on 20 April.[43]

Losses among the Asante had been far greater and they had been shocked by the power of the artillery and breechloaders. It was said, 'The white men have guns that hit five Ashantis at once.' The precise loss cannot be determined but may have amounted to anything between 800 and 1,600 dead though the Royal Engineers claimed to have buried over 3,000 corpses. Moreover, the dead included Amankwatia, shot by a soldier from the 42nd through the back of his ceremonial chair while he was being carried to the rear. Another prominent Asante, Apea Kyeame, was also killed and Kwabena Dwumo apparently wounded.[44] It was clear, however, that the Asante were not yet ready to yield.

112

Wolseley Journal, 1–2 January

Thursday 1 January 1874

Started at 5.55 a.m. Road very good and very pretty at places – travelled in the Chariot of the sun – reached Barraco at 9.15 a.m. A Detachment of 47 officers & men of Naval Brigade here – 3 on sick list, only one being ill from causes that can be attributed to the climate. Work going on here briskly and will be finished in time for troops. To my horror during the day the Doctor attached to my Head Quarters discovered that there was a dead body buried under his hut, which was a large one intended for 50 men. I am afraid that I shall have to leave it unoccupied.

Friday 2 January

Marched from Baraco to Prahsu Camp 6½ miles – road fair but merely cut through the forest, all large trees being avoided by going round them. In going down a hill rather quickly one of my "wheelers" fell and before the buggy could be stopped both front & hind wheel went over his body. He jumped up and wanted to go on, but as the wheels being American are very narrow I was afraid that he must have sustained some internal injury so I made him sit down & left my boy with him until the doctor should come up. I afterwards heard that he was only bruised, no bones broken or serious injury done. Prahsu is a very pretty spot, after the tunnel-like monotony of the road for nearly eighty miles (exact distance 74 miles) it was so refreshing to see a clear open space and a fine river flowing through it. The southern bank being 30 feet above the water encreased the beauty of the view. A vast amount of work has been done here, large open squares with huts all round them, the ground levelled, roads made etc etc. My own hut stands overlooking the river being on the bank. It has actually two rooms, one to sleep & the other to write and receive visitors in. Gave orders at once to go on with the bridge over the river: a few hours after my arrival messenger came in from the scouts on the north bank saying that messengers had arrived from the King & had been halted by them about 1½ miles away. They had letters for me from the King. I had them brought over the river and put under strict guard. The letters were apparently written by the King in complete ignorance of what has recently occurred here. My bridge will be ready for traffic on the forenoon of the 5th so I shall keep these messengers until the 6th so that they may cross by the bridge & see Russells Regt at Atobiasi and Essiaman & so that they will thus be able to announce to the King that the invasion has really begun. The weather is lovely, and the night cool & pleasant. Dined with Russell and had a capital feed.

TNA, WO 147/3

113

Wolseley to King Kofi Kakari

2 January
[Printed]

I have to-day received your Majesty's two letters of the 25th November and 26th December 1873.^{1} These are addressed to Colonel Harley, though written in answer to a letter from me, in which I had told you that Her Majesty the Queen of England had sent me as her General to command her troops on the West Coast of Africa, and also to be Administrator of the Gold Coast Settlements.

I must therefore inform you, that immediately upon my arrival Colonel Harley left Cape Coast Castle for England, and that I am the Queen's representative here.

2. In my letter of 13th October 1873, which has been read and interpreted to your Majesty, I stated the terms upon which Her Majesty the Queen of England would be prepared to enter again into friendly relations with your Government. They were as follows:–

(1)   That within a named time you should withdraw all your forces from all the territories of Her Majesty's allies.

(2)   That you should deliver up all men, women, and children whom you have captured from every tribe and people at present in alliance with Her Majesty.

(3)   That you should give guarantees for ample compensation to all whom you have injured.

Your Majesty has not complied with these terms.

3. Your Majesty acknowledges the treaty made between Governor Maclean and one of your predecessors in the year 1831, in which the King of Ashanti renounced all right or title to any tribute or homage from the Kings of Denkera, Assin, and others, formerly his subjects. Notwithstanding this, I find that you speak of the people of this country, who are allies of the Queen of England, as 'your own slaves', and that you ask me for an answer given back to your authority.

I must therefore inform you that Queen Victoria considers herself, as well as you, bound by the terms of Governor Maclean's treaty, and that under no circumstances whatever can I entertain your proposal, or give you back the tribes for whom you ask.

4. Your Majesty says that a message was delivered to you by Mr Henry Plange, that 'in four months' time the Administrator-in-Chief was to take your power away for Kwarkefram'. I have to inform your Majesty that no such message was ever sent to you, and that Mr Plange, if he said this, spoke falsely.

5. Your Majesty states that you sent to recall your army before my letter reached you, forbidding Amanquatia to attack our forts. But your army did attack Elmina, and was completely defeated. I have also to inform you that very soon after my arrival I wrote to Amanquatia, and sent him a letter for your Majesty, which he acknowledged and answered, saying that he had no quarrel with the white man. Nevertheless, after he had thus written, he attacked the town of Abrakrampa, where my white soldiers were.

6. In your Majesty's letter of 26th December, you say that your former letter was returned to Coomassie owing to an attack made upon your army on its way home at Faisoo, and that this attack pains you very much. Your Majesty must understand that Amanquatia having attacked my troops at Abrakrampa for two days, after he had received my letters addressed both to you and himself, I could only believe that your Majesty was desirous of continuing the war. I determined, therefore, to drive your army behind the river Prah, which I have done.

7. I do not think your Captains have told you the truth regarding the events which have taken place in this country since my arrival, and I believe they have concealed from your Majesty the numerous defeats they have experienced from small bodies of the troops under my command. When Amanquatia attacked Abrakrampa there were only fifty white men there; yet, after two days' fighting, he was forced to retreat in confusion with great loss; and many of your war-drums, chiefs' chairs, and other military trophies, besides much baggage, were captured by my troops.

As regards the attack upon your retreating army at Faisoo, it was made only by a small party of my undrilled black troops, who were ordered to fall back as soon as they found where your army was; yet it caused the whole of the Ashanti army to retreat in the utmost haste and confusion, leaving their dead and dying everywhere along the path.

8. The detention of the messengers sent by the Cape Coast authorities to your Court is contrary to the laws of all civilised nations; and as regards the white people now held as prisoners at Coomassie, I have to remind your Majesty that they are not either English soldiers or English officials, but strangers, who were treacherously seized by one of your chiefs in the territory of a king in alliance with the Crown of England, at a time when there was peace between England and Ashanti. Their friends had arranged to pay you a sum of money claimed by this chief for expenses; but whilst the affair was being arranged, your army invaded these territories of Her Majesty's allies, slaying and carrying off into slavery their inhabitants, and laying waste the country on every side.

9. For these crimes committed by your army the Queen of England has sent me as her General to demand reparation; and she has also lately sent a large force of her white troops, to render all resistance on your part hopeless.

I wish to impress upon your Majesty that hitherto your soldiers have only had to fight against black men, helped by a few Englishmen. If, however, you should now be so ill-advised as to continue this war, your troops will have to meet an army of white soldiers.

These white troops are now on their march from Cape Coast for the purpose of invading your territory to enforce compliance with my just demands, which I shall presently lay before you; and I warn you that I intend to invade your country by the Wassaw road, the Prahsu-Assin road, the Prahsu-Akim road, and the road leading from Bagoro in Eastern Akim direct to Juabin and Coomassie.

10. The Queen of England has placed ample forces at my disposal to crush the Ashanti nation; but, as I told you in my previous letter, she is as patient as she is strong.

Her Majesty is desirous that a permanent peace should be established between her subjects and the Ashantis. She is desirous to promote in every way free intercourse between your people and the towns of Elmina and Cape Coast Castle, and all other towns under her protection, with a view to the promotion of trade between the two nations, and the establishment of a lasting peace between them.

11. Your Majesty is completely in error if you believe that the Queen's object in obtaining possession of the Dutch forts was to cut you off from communication with the coast. She wishes that when your subjects come as peaceful traders, every protection should be afforded to them; and when peace is finally established, she will do all in her power to prevent all hindrance to trade between the two nations.

12. Her Majesty is still willing to believe that you have been deceived by designing people, as in the case of the fictitious message said to have been delivered to your Majesty by Mr Plange. She is anxious to avoid shedding more Ashanti blood, knowing how your army has already suffered. Yet she cannot submit to leave without redress such violent aggression as that lately perpetuated by your army upon her allies, at a time when you were professing to be engaged in friendly negotiations with the British authorities.

13. I shall therefore be prepared to make a lasting peace with you upon the following terms:–

1.   That you deliver up forthwith all the persons, both European and African, that you have wrongfully detained as prisoners at Coomassie, together with all the men, women, and children carried off into captivity from this country by your army.

2nd. That having unjustly forced this war upon the Queen of England, thereby entailing immense expense upon her, you will pay Her Majesty 50,000 ounces of approved gold.

3rd. That a new treaty of peace be signed at Coomassie, to which place I would proceed for that purpose with a sufficient force of white soldiers; and that previous to my going there, you deliver up to me such hostages for my safety as I shall name hereafter, when I learn that your Majesty has accepted the terms now offered.

14. This war has already entailed many defeats upon your armies. You have lost thousands of men in battle, and from want and

disease. I am well aware of all these facts. You are surrounded by hostile tribes who long for your destruction. Be warned in time and do not listen to the advice of evil counsellors, who for their own purposes might urge you to continue a hopeless struggle against an army of white men, a struggle that can only lead to the destruction of your military power, and that must certainly bring great misery upon your people and danger to your Majesty's dynasty.

15. As I am about to march into your territory to enforce, if necessary, the terms of peace here proposed, I have to request that the messengers whom your Majesty may send with the answer to this letter be ordered to carry a white flag plainly displayed at the end of a staff, in order that they may be known by my scouts to be friendly messengers.

16. Being most anxious that your Majesty should know the exact contents of this letter, I have to request that you will cause it to be read and interpreted to you at different times by two interpreters, neither of whom should be present when the other is interpreting the letter to your Majesty.

TNA, CO 879/6, CO 806/2

114

Wolseley Journal, 3 January

Saturday 3 January

Composed my answer to the King stating the terms upon which I was prepared to make peace with him & warning him that I was about to invade his territory from four points to enforce these terms if necessary.[2] The Naval Brigade marched in. No man of it has fallen out since they left C. C. Castle. The Ashantee messengers had been kept in one of the huts intended for the Naval Brigade, so when they arrived the messengers were marched across the Square to another hut passing as they did along the Naval Brigade that had deployed into line to make a good show. Everyone here in the best of health and spirits, very few on the sick list, and most of the sick are only slight cases.

TNA, WO 147/3

115

Wolseley to Louisa Wolseley

3 January
[Holograph]
Camp Prahsu

I wrote you a hurried line yesterday, and since early this morning I have been hard at work writing away but a man having caught an electric fish of which there are many in the river put me in mind of you, so I stopped my official letters to scribble a line to you. If this catches the mail for England I imagine that you will receive three notes by it from me, so you must allow that although my letters are dullness itself still their quantity is great. This is a very pretty camp and I have a comfortable hut with two rooms in it. I can see through the walls everywhere as they are merely made like a net, and I obtain occasional glimpses of the sun through my thatched roof, but still I feel in clover and if I had only less writing to get through I should be well off. Yesterday messengers reached me from the King at Coomassie: the principal man of the party[3] is the town crier: he had a plaque of beaten and imbossed gold as a sort of gorget and about 8 inches long by six wide. I have had to compose a very careful answer conveying to the great Koffee the terms upon which I am prepared to admit him to my friendship. I do not intend allowing him to go back to Coomassie until the 6th instant by which time my bridge over the river will be finished and Russells Regt will have invaded Ashantee and taken up a position in King Koffees Kingdom about 8 miles from this. As Colonel Wood has been in front lately I now send Russell forward to give him a turn and a chance of glory. I hope you read the account of the Abrakrampa affair in the Telegraph as it did Russell the most justice although written by a dreadful little man who regarding his own doings seldom speaks the truth. I am at present however under the impression that we shall have no more fighting, but that after all our great preparations for hostilities that he will give in when he finds that we really mean business. I wrote a note to B. J. the other day that goes home by this mail in answer to one I had from her – from what Holmes said in one of his letters I know that he likes the attention to her, and I have such an affection for him that I like to please him, much as I hate putting pen to paper. I have just had a note from Joey Hudsons brother who is a Lieut. on board the Tamar.[4] He wants me to get him appointed to the Naval Brigade ashore. The Tamar is a troopship intended for the conveyance of soldiers. I send you the picture they have on their paper and envellopes as I think it very amusing: a sailor carrying a soldier. I have just discovered that the mean authorities at home have stopped my half pay because the salary I receive here is four times the amount of my half pay. It will be a matter of £100 to me, and that is a serious sum to a poor devil who wants to have some amusement when he returns home. My child the time goes bye and every day brings me nearer to you, for this day [next] month I must have settled matters or at least be engaged in arranging finally with the King as to terms, then high for England with all speed. If all goes well what spirits I shall be in. I read a chapter of Thomas a Kempis every day.[5] I have got more than half way through it already, and like it very much. I dined with Russell last night and here was our bill of fare – good preserved soup – preserved salmon – preserved sausages: a fresh turkey & pair of boiled chickens & bacon curried fowl, plum pudding, rice pudding, preserved pears, cheese & plenty of Moselle – not bad that for the bush 80 miles inland!! I can't say that we have such dinners every day but we live very fairly: I am afraid that north of the Prah we shall not fare well, however the men I have with me don't care what I give them to eat if I will only lead them to Coomassie. All eager to go on and as bloodthirsty as any set of men well can be. I hope Miss Frances is flourishing. My best love to the Pal and always my dearest little perriewinkle believe me to be your loving husband.

Hove, Wolseley MSS, W/P 4/2

116

Wolseley to Cambridge

3 January
[Holograph]
Camp Prahsu

I arrived here yesterday morning having marched here by the stages I have fixed for the English Regiments. The Naval Brigade 251 men marched in here this morning, no man having fallen out during any of the marches between Cape Coast and this place. The men have been carefully selected volunteers from all the ships of the fleet; I cannot expect that the three Regiments will all be as fortunate, for the sailors have had very fine weather all through and as Your Royal Highness knows, heavy rain – that may come on here at any time – makes a great difference in the way that men march especially over unmetaled roads. We have to day 370 white men of all ranks in camp here and only 10 on the sick list, many of which cases are very slight, such as boils, a thorn in the leg, a blistered foot and so on. In other words, we have less than 3 per cent sick. I shall indeed be fortunate if I can keep the percentage of sick down to even ten per cent. This is a lovely and well situated camp. The tent I write in is on the bank of the river and is 30 feet above the water. When my first Detachment reached this place it was a tangled mass of brush wood; now there is a great clearance having a well situated and well laid out hut camp upon it, with regular streets and squares giving it the appearance of a prosperous native town. The whole place and for miles around is like an ants nest, swarming with workmen building and collecting materials. The Engineers under Major Home assisted by the sailors are now working at our bridge, and I hope it will be passable for troops by the forenoon of the 5th inst. The river is 62½ yards wide at the point selected for the bridge. The current is swift, and the river is still unfordable although falling daily. The bridge is being constructed upon pieces of cribwork after the mode so common in Canada,[6] a few trestles being used on the northern bank. I expect the first detachment of the English Regts to arrive here on the 8th & the last detachment on the 13th inst. and I hope to have everything fairly ready for my final advance into Ashantee territory on the 15th instant. My one great difficulty is transport, and I am very anxious on this subject, as the carriers sometimes without any known reason whatever desert by hundreds My advance beyond the Prah can therefore only be at a slow pace. As soon as the bridge is finished, I intend pushing across Russells Regt. and sending it forward about 8 miles to Atobiasi with an Advanced Guard pushed still further on to Essiaman (Your Royal Highness will find both of those places marked on the map). In this way I hope to have the road cut to the latter village before the 15th instant, and clearances made for our camps.

A few hours after my arrival here yesterday morning news was sent to camp from our scouts that they had met messengers from the King carrying a letter for me. The letter was in answer to the summons I sent him a few days after my arrival at Cape Coast, but was seemingly written in complete ignorance of the events that have taken place since I landed. I am now writing to him telling him the terms upon which I am prepared to make peace & I intend sending back his messengers with my answer on the 6th instant. I keep them here so long in order that they may go over my bridge and that they may be able to report to their master that the invasion has already begun and that my troops are actually in possession of the villages named above. If he means to fight, it is in my interests that he should do so as soon as possible, and as near to this place as I can induce his Army to come. I have ascertained that the country between the Prah and Quisah (to the north of the Adansi Hill) is a wilderness and devoid of inhabitants. This is a district that formerly was occupied by the Assins, but since that tribe left it, and came into our territory, & claimed our protection, it has never been inhabited regularly by the Ashantees.

I heard this morning from Captain Butler who is in Western Akim endeavoring to raise the people there for the purpose of invading Ashantee by the Prahsu-Akim route – : he writes rather hopefully, and I trust he may succeed: he is a very able and energetic officer – just the man for this work, and if he fails, I am sure no other man could have succeeded. Captain Glover is now on the march to Bagora in Eastern Akim, but I fear that instead of having with him when he crosses the Prah on the 15th inst. the 16,000 or 30,000 fighting men he had previously stated he could count upon having on that river by that date, he will not I fear have with him more than some 700 Houssas. This is a great disappointment to me, for I had always counted upon his large force creating a strong diversion in favor of the main column under my immediate orders should the King resolve to fight; or should he be undecided, I felt sure that the fact of the Ashantee territory being invaded by a large army in another direction than by the main road to Coomassie, would have exercised a strong influence upon the King in favor of peace. I know that it will be no fault of Captain Glovers or of those under his command if he fails to induce a large native force to accompany him into Ashantee territory, for he has worked hard as hard as any man could: he has been cruelly misled by native promises, having relied upon the oaths of a people ignorant of the value of time; and regardless of truth. He had become entangled in tribal disputes to the east of the Volta into which he had been partly led I imagine by his Native Allies, who wished to have their enemies the Ahoonas punished at little risk to themselves. Captain Glover has left Mr. Goldworthy with some 11,000 men in the Ahoona territory to settle affairs there, whilst he has himself started for the Prah. He has 11,000 Akims encamped on the Upper Volta at a place named Janketty and I am still in hopes of his being able to induce them to cross the Prah with him on the 15th instant. I trust that all my arrangements may meet with Yr. Royal Highness approval, and that I may be pardoned for any querlunousness [*sic*] there may be at times in my letters both private and official, for it is difficult here to write with eavenness of tone where there is so much to worry one, and where difficulties seem to crop up hydra like all the quicker from being rooted up.

Cambridge MSS, RA VIC/ADD E/1/7286

Wolseley Journal, 4 January

Sunday 4 January

The Head Qtrs of the 2nd W. I. Regt. arrived commanded by that duffer Webber. Read the morning service to myself. The men were too busy for church parades. Russell & Webber dined with me: dreadful news about the transport: all the carriers intended for the 23rd Regt. deserted in a body & still further desertion going on still. I am in despair. Have sent to stop the landing of the 23rd Fuslrs. until further orders. Ordered up 1st W. I. Regt. to Mansu & written an appealing letter to the Colonel[7] telling him the straights I am in & calling upon him to convert the whole of his men into carriers for the time being. I have done the same here with Woods Regt & with the 2nd W. I. as I cannot possibly advance until I have a further supply of food here. At present owing to the breakdown of the transport I have only 10 or 11 days food for 2000 Europeans & for natives in proportion in this place, whereas all my calculations were based upon the promise of my Depty. Controller who promised me at least 20 days, but he hoped it would be 30 days supplies for my whole Force to be here by the 15th inst the day I had therefore fixed upon as the date for the crossing of the Prah by Glover, Butler and myself & for the men moving to the westward by the Wassaw path to cross into Ashantee territory. This makes me all the more anxious to make peace without fighting, if King Koffee will but come to terms: to make peace without fighting at least one battle will be a sad disappointment to all my Force, but I cannot help that: everyone here is mad for a fight & if Koffee would but come down to meet me, so that I should be able to deliver my decisive blow near my supplies here, I also would hail the opportunity for a battle with the greatest pleasure but when I think of having to penetrate beyond Quisah to find him & fight him, I feel a sinking of my heart that is to me appalling, knowing how completely I am in the hands of these lying, lazy and worthless Fantee carriers. I have sent ships in every direction to obtain carriers elsewhere but with very partial success for what are a few hundred carriers when I require 3500 to move my troops ashore without provisions north of the Prah, and then I have to feed that host of nakid savages as well as my own fighting men. However I don't despond, I have a firm faith in the eventual success of this Expedition & I know that God will not forsake me now in my need. I have done all that my intelligence has enabled me to do to render the affair a success, & we have all worked hard to that end. In the Red River Expedition as here I had to work against time; there in order to finish the business so that I might be able to get back the Regulars before the lakes froze. Here where the climate is so fatal to Europeans I have to settle matters before the rains set in. This morning I had out the Ashantee messengers and showed them the Gatling and the roar of its fire and the precision of its aim seemed to impress them somewhat. A lovely day.

TNA, WO 147/3

118

Wolseley to Louisa Wolseley

4 January

[Holograph]

The enclosed drawing[8] worthy of Turner was scribbled yesterday whilst I wrote to you, and to my disappointment I have just found it in my blotting book having forgotten to put it in your envelope yesterday. It is a lovely sketch but I thought it would amuse you as showing the position of my hut on the top of the bank – not the top *end of the square*. I had the two senior officers of the Naval Brigade to dine with me last night: we dine under a shelter made of large plantain leaves the sides being all open, so that we get the air and are somewhat protected from the heavy dews. In the middle of dinner Huyshe arrived having travelled as quickly as possible from Cape Coast. Strange to say he is one of the very few who have escaped being ill since we landed. He is so thin that he has no internals like anyone and strange to say like many other extremely thin men he has an appetite like a wolfe. He has just given me some itineraries drawn up by himself, as he does the surveying for me. I enclose two – please send one to Holmes as

I think he would like one. We have the illustrated London News man[9] in camp so you are sure to see lots of sketches from him of this place. Please keep me all the drawings that appear of scenes out here: this correspondent is a [Phrase erased] and has never been [Passage erased]. He dined with me one evening at Cape Coast, and after dinner someone said to Greaves "How grey your hair has become lately" – whereupon this little [Word erased] who had never seen Greaves before called out "is [it] from drink or hard work". Greaves is not a safe man to ask such questions of, but he kept his temper laughed and replied most aptly "I see that you have *drawn* all the hair off the top of your head" Everybody laughed loudly and the [Word erased] said it was a hard hit at his profession. Goodbye, you owe this scrawl to my having forgotten to send you the enclosed valuable drawing.

Hove, Wolseley MSS, W/P 4/3

119

Wolseley Journal, 5–6 January

Monday 5 January

In the middle of the night was roused up by a shot fired close to me: heard the Guard over the Ashantees who are in a hut close to mine, all jabbering: sent to find out what had taken place and found that one of the Ashantee scouts had shot himself whether by accident or on purpose it is difficult to say. His brother who is with the party and the head man say he has been brooding over his position & believed we meant to kill him, so they all say that he did it on purpose. This is a disagreeable complication, as King Koffee may make out that we killed him. The transport difficulty increases on all sides. I am at my wits end about it. The bridge was finished at 4.30 p.m. & Russells Regt crossed partly by it & partly in canoes. The Ashantees requested permission to bury their companion on the north bank – this they did passing over the bridge. English mail in with letters from home of 12th December. They came by the "Thames". The Harmattan has now really set in; there is no moisture in the air, and the skin feels quite dry.

Tuesday 6 January

Tumbled about in my bed thinking of this dreadful transport question: sent back at daybreak a special messenger to halt the 42nd Regt until further orders. That Regt will to-day have reached Mansue & Yancoomassie Fantee. Their carriers to be used for bringing up food. I fear that many will desert, but I cannot help it. Instead of increasing we are diminishing our reserve here although we have as yet only the Naval Brigade. Lord Gifford with his scouts pushed on yesterday according to orders to Essiaman where he was fired upon by the Ashantee scouts who wounded one of his men: he killed an Ashantee & took a woman prisoner who says there are plenty of the enemy near him. I don't believe it. 100 men of Russells Regt from Atobiasi go on this morning to Essiaman to support Gifford. I sent the Naval Brigade across the river this morning & ordered them to go out about a couple of miles along the Coomassie road, so that the Kings messengers in going back should pass the Naval Brigade as if it was on the march to the front – as soon as they have passed, the Naval Brigade will return to camp here. I want the messengers to take back word to the King that they actually saw a European force marching towards his capital. This will hasten his movements whether he means to fight or make peace. Last night deliciously cold & in the early morning a great coat out of doors was very pleasant. The poor devils of natives are shivering & shaking with cold. I fear we shall lose more of them still by this cause. The Envoy was terrified when he passed through the Naval Brigade seeing them as he thought actually on the march towards Coomassie: he begged of Buller to ask me to stop all further advance until I received an answer from the King. He will lose no time in getting back to the King, or perhaps he will send my letter back by runners – at any rate I think the King will know it's contents by the 9th instant, so that it is quite possible I may have an answer back before the 15th instant I hope so.

TNA, WO 147/3

120

Wolseley to Alison

6 January
[Holograph]
Camp Prahsu
There is no organized force of the enemy between this and Coomassie, so that if I had stores enough here I might go forward at once without meeting with any resistance. Nothing of any importance can therefore take place for some time to come, especially as I *cannot* advance with more than a detachment on the 15th owing to the want of supplies. On the 18th I intend if possible to have the Naval Brigade and Russel's Regt at Quisah, to halt there, fortifying a position as a standing menace to the King in Coomassie. That is the outside of what I can hope to do for some time to come, and I believe I shall be able to accomplish that without any fighting. Everything is at a stand still owing to the desertion of the carriers, for instead of increasing the small reserve of stores I had collected here, I am daily reducing it. I therefore wish you to remain at Cape Coast for the present, and if this does not reach you until after you have started, I want you to return there, as it is indispensable that there should be an officer of rank there at present, especially until the return of Lees from Accra. I highly approve of all you have begun. Whatever measures you consider necessary to obtain carriers you may depend upon my supporting you in. You had better make a regular 'drive' in Cape Coast and seize every man you can & march them by the regular carrier stages up to Yancoomassie Assin under a strong police escort, guarding them at night & if necessary shutting any of them who attempt to escape. When once they have passed Inquabim – martial law does not actually exist in the town of Cape Coast, but once beyond Inquabim, the carriers must be treated as followers of the Army.

Send to Elmina & leave the same down there and all marched to Cape Coast for loads, to be marched to Yancoomassie Assin as the others. If Lieut. Bolton 1st W. I. Regt who has been for some time past engaged on special bde. service – is well enough please send him back with some police to his district to drive in if necessary by force any carriers he can obtain. Write to Major Brownell[10] the Civil Commandant at Saltpond tell him to do the same at once; tell these officers or any others you may employ upon this service that they are authorised to promise any King or Chief £10 a month for every hundred men they provide as carriers besides of course the pay of 1s a day and rations to the men themselves – that I will pay £6 a month for every 100 women they furnish. The Chiefs to come with their own men and remain with them. I state these amounts as a guide but you can increase them if you think it necessary. Money is now of *no* object but time is of vital importance. Keep the judge with you as he can assist you greatly in his position of Assessor. It would be well to collect all the canoes of Cape Coast & place them under a guard to stop all fishing for the present. Col Greaves is writing to you officially ordering the reembarkation of the wing of the 23rd as a temporary measure. Tell the people everywhere that I have done so because they have failed to assist me in carrying forward stores, and that unless they now come forward & help me as they promised that I shall reembark all my troops and hand over the country to the Ashantees who will make the Fantees slaves at once. I have already threatened them with doing so, but when they see that I have actually begun to carry out my threat, perhaps it may stir them up a little. Don't please leave the neighborhood of Cape Coast Castle until you hear from me that you are wanted here. I depend upon your energy and zeal in all things.

Bodleian, Alison MSS, MS. Eng. lett. c. 450

121

Wolseley Journal, 7–8 January

Wednesday 7 January

A deliciously cold night with a little fog in the early morning. Nothing new from the front – over 700 loads of provisions arrived here to day. Began the tete de pont. Naval Brigade employed morning and evening in clearing bush in front of it. I walked yesterday evening about a mile along the rivers bank up to where the Assin Camp was and was surprised at the numerous crossing places that had been used by the Ashantees. In some places the river was very nearly spanned over by the great trees on each bank being cut down opposite one another that stretched over when fallen in the water a considerable way across: these were supplemented by wooden rafts. At many spots they had stretched ropes made of Bamboo across the river by means of which rafts plied backwards and forwards. Taking everything into consideration I believe that about 40,000 souls must have crossed of whom at least half were fighting men. Mail for England leaves tomorrow so I close this for the present.

TNA, WO 147/3

Thursday 8 January
[Copy]

Camp Prahsu. We are now getting in here daily about 700 or 740 loads, so as it only takes 140 loads to feed all the men I have here and in front, I gain nearly 600 a day towards my reserve, that gives me for Europeans – if all the stores were for Europeans – 9000 rations a day added to my reserve. If I can keep this up I may still be able to have nearly 20 days supplies for the force I shall take over the Prah on the 15th or 16 inst. A letter from Glover giving better prospects as to the numbers of fighting men he will have on the Prah ready to cross by the 15th inst. Encouraging letters also from Butler & Dalrymple.[11] Gifford with his scouts has examined the road some distance beyond Ansah. His scouts have been to the Fumusu River where they say about 50 Ashantee scouts had slept the night before. They say that the enemy is in some strength at Akrowfumoo but that is only conjecture. Tête de pont nearly finished. We have only 3 per cent sick amongst the white men in camp & most of those cases are slight. Our mail made up for England to leave Cape Coast by "Manitoban"[12] on 10th inst.

TNA, WO 147/4

122

Wolseley to Cambridge

8 January
[Holograph]
Camp Prahsu

Nothing of great importance has taken place since my letter of the 2nd instant, beyond the still further desertion of carriers. Some whole tribes have run away, crippling the transport so seriously that I have had to order the 42nd and the Rifle Brigade to halt where they are on the road, and to reembark the one wing of the 23rd that had landed. It is quite possible that I may be able to dispense with the services of the 23rd altogether owing to the dispersion of the Ashantee Army to the mens homes. All my former calculations were based upon the understanding with the Control Department that I should have at least twenty and perhaps thirty days supplies here for all my force by the 15th instant, and as that is now impossible owing to the wholesale desertion of the carriers, my plans must be modified in consequence. This is very annoying, and naturally increases my anxiety considerably. In Your Royal Highness's letter of the 9th December Captain Brabazons[13] name is mentioned:– he is an excellent man for this work – full of energy, and willing and anxious to do anything or go anywhere. Previous to the receipt of Your Royal Highnesses letter about him I had sent him to act with Captain Butler in Western Akim. I have to day received a letter from that officer saying that Captain Brabazon was down with fever, and as they have no doctor with them, that he was coming in here for a few days to recover. This is such a very healthy place at this season that if it is only the ordinary fever he is suffering from, I have no doubt he will be back at his work ere many days elapse. In camp at present we have 426 white men of whom only 13 are on the sick list: these figures speak for themselves. My bridge is finished, and the tête de pont will be completed tomorrow. The road to Essiaman where Russells Regt is now stationed (about 13 miles to the front), will soon be cut, and practicable for guns. I am putting up a store house at that place, as it will be my first stage when I advance from here.

I had to call upon the 1st and 2nd W.I. Regts. and Woods Regt to act as carriers for a short time. All have responded like good soldiers. The nights and early mornings are now so deliciously cold that one might imagine oneself in England, but I fear that our native soldiers will suffer from the sudden change between the temperature at night and by day. I hear from the Volta that Captain Glover will be able to cross the Prah with a larger force than he had anticipated when he wrote to me announcing his having already begun his march in accordance with the orders I had sent him. My scouting party about 80 men under Lord Gifford is now at Ansah about 19 miles from this and will be tomorrow established on the Fumusu River with scouts thrown forward to Acrowfumu. Lord Gifford is one of the most promising young officers I have in my force, and enters heart and soul into his work: my only anxiety about him is that his zeal may urge him on too far; however he has a good head on his shoulders, and I must trust to his discretion. I send home by this mail surveys of this camp on a large scale, and [a] road survey on the ordinary scale of the road in advance as far as Essiaman.

Cambridge MSS, RA VIC/ADD E/1/7291

123

Wolseley Journal, 9–10 January

[Copy]

Friday 9 January

River has fallen nearly a foot since I came here on the 2nd inst. Naval Brigade employed night & morning in clearing bush around tête de pont. The Harmattan eased yesterday evening so the night was warmer than previously & my paper is again damp. I hope it has not left us altogether. No news.

Saturday 10 January

Road sketched by Hart as far as the Fumusu River. Scouts have been to Acrofumoo & say that it is held by a strong party of Ashantees. I hope to occupy it on the 16th inst. A small crocodile was caught on the bank at the bathing place yesterday. Last night the men of the 2nd W. I. Regt assert that they saw an elephant come down to the River to drink opposite their camp. Capt. Baker,[14] Inspct. Genl. of police arrived yesterday morning having walked from Cape Coast to Barraco (about 6 miles in rear) in three days, 68 miles in three days is not bad going for an Englishman in this climate. No harmattan. An idiot called March,[15] a commissary stationed at Yancomassie Assin, sent in here to-day 650 loads of ammunition; we have plenty of ammunition & I have been straining every nerve to collect a magazine of provisions here, yet I have been frustrated by this fool. I wish I could flog him. His fault is really criminal for it has lost me a day & that means keeping the English troops ashore a day longer than was necessary.

TNA, WO 147/4

124

Wolseley to Alison

10 January
[Holograph]
Prahsu

You may rest assured that when the two European Regts cross the Prah you shall be at their head. I calculate that you can easily make the journey from Cape Coast to this place in five marches. Captain Baker of the police who walked all the way came to Barraco (6 miles behind this place) in three days. Your route for 5 marches would be Dunquah 19¾ miles – Mansu 15¼ miles. Sutah 10½ miles, Yancoomassie Assin 12¼ miles, Prahsu 16 miles. Please be ready to start upon short notice. I highly approve of all you have done and am much obliged to you for the way you have worked. Strictly *entre nous* I do not think there is the slightest chance of my being able to bring up the 23rd. I am writing to you officially saying that in the event of the 23rd being kept back from want of carriers that 100 of the best men with Col. Mostyn are to [be] landed etc etc etc. I attach considerable importance to the reembarkation of the wing of the 23rd and was annoyed at the orders sent from here to Col. Mostyn etc not having reached their destination in time to have had their reembarkation carried out before. If anything will work upon the minds of these Fantees this reembarkation will.

Bodleian, Alison MSS, MS. Eng. lett. c. 450

125

Wolseley Journal, 11–13 January

[Copy]

Sunday 11 January

A warmer night & morning. Sky cloudy during day as if rain was coming up. I hope not. Transport question looking better.

Monday 12 January

Gifford has reconnoitred Akrofumoo: says it is only occupied by the Ashantees during the day, that they retire behind the village at night. In the evening received a letter from King Koffee, brought to my outposts by one of his family. He says my terms of peace accord with his views. Asks for an English officer to be sent to him to arrange matters. Sends back one of the European missionary prisoners & begs of me not to advance any further.

Tuesday 13 January

Mr Kühne,[16] a German missionary who has been an Ashantee prisoner since 1869 reached my Hd. Qtrs. He looks very ill has been for a long time suffering from lung disease, says there is no army between this & Coomassie. He saw 30 armed men near our outposts. Quisah & Fomanah beyond Adansi Hill are mostly inhabited & the Adansi Chief is in Quisah so perhaps he might be able to turn out some hundreds of armed men. Mr. Kühne says that he thinks they will retire without fighting if I push on. Russells Regt. occupied Akrofumoo to-day & 200 of 2nd W. I. Regt moved from this to Essiaman. Sent Capt. Buller away in the afternoon with my answer to the King. He will deliver it to-morrow morning to the Envoy – who is strictly guarded by Russells Regt. at Akrofumoo. On the evening of the 16th it will be in the King's hands. Of course I won't stop as he desires until he has complied with my demands. I think it probable that the other prisoners will be in my possession by the 21st or 22nd inst.

TNA, WO 147/4

126

Wolseley to King Kofi Kakari

13 January

[Printed]

I have to-day received your Majesty's letter of the 9th instant,[17] and Mr. Kuehne has also reached my camp. I am glad to find from your letter that your Majesty has resolved upon peace; but before I can enter into any negotiations whatever with your Majesty, it is essential that you should convince me of the sincerity of your intentions by at once sending into me the other prisoners now held by you. As your Majesty wishes to have an interpreter left with you while peace is being arranged, I have no objection to your retaining Mr. Dawson[18] at Coomassie for the present, but I must immediately have back all the Europeans besides the natives from Accra, Aquapim, Elmina, and the Fantee territory now held captive in Ashantee. The fact of your Majesty having already detained two messengers from the former Governor, prevents me at present from entertaining your request to have an English officer sent to you.

I stated in my letter of the 2nd instant, the general terms upon which I am prepared to treat with your Majesty, and until these terms are complied with, I cannot halt any of my four armies. The advanced guard of this army has already crossed the Prah, and the other three will shortly invade your kingdom at three other points, as explained in my last letter.

Her Most Gracious Majesty Queen Victoria is as anxious as your Majesty can be for the establishment of a lasting peace between England and Ashantee. But in order that peace may be lasting, it is essential that your Majesty and your people should learn that you can no more prevent an army of white men marching into your territory, whenever your Majesty's hostile proceedings make such a step necessary on our part, than you can stop the sun from rising every morning.

M. Kuehne is sending with this a letter to his brother German Missionaries, with silver coin to the value of six ounces of gold dust to defray any necessary expenses of their journey to my camp.

TNA, CO 879/6, CO 806/4

127

Wolseley Journal, 14 January

[Copy]
Wednesday 14 January
A very warm day. Huyshe laid up with dysentery. He is very weak.
A mail in from England by the "Sprite" but no home letters.
Stores coming up well. Telegraph only open to Sutah. Woods
Regt. & Raits Artillery march to-morrow en route for Acrofumoo,
upon arriving there Russells Regt goes on to Moinsey & to seize
the crest of the Adansi Hills.
TNA, WO 147/4

128

Wolseley to Glover

14 January
[Holograph]
Prahsu
My advanced post (one Regt) is at Akrowfumu (about 23 or 24
miles north of the Prah). On the 16th inst. I shall have a Regt
at foot of Adansi Hill with an advanced post holding the crest
of Hill, and another Regt at Akrowfumu, with a fortified post
in rear at Essiaman, and by the 26th instant I shall have all my
Force concentrated at Quisah and Fommanah holding the road
with advanced posts for about ten miles north of latter place.
My movements are slow owing to large desertion amongst
my carriers. I shall halt there for a couple of days to bring up
supplies. I do not expect to meet with any resistance as far as
that position.

One of the white prisoners, has been sent in (Mr Kuhne) and
I think that all the others will probably be sent to me about 22nd
instant. The King says he wants peace, but evades giving me a
positive answer as to whether he accepts my terms or not. He may
be trying to humbug me to gain time as he is very anxious I should
halt. This of course I have no intention of doing, and I shall push
on as rapidly as the carriers at my disposal will allow me. I give you

all this information so that you may be guided in your movements by a knowledge of my whereabouts for the next twelve days.

Please keep me informed *daily* of where you are & what you intend doing: also keep Captain Butler informed on these points: he will do the same to you regarding his movements & intentions. Wishing you every success.

CUL, RCMS 131/6, Glover MSS

129

Wolseley Journal, 15 January

[Copy]

Thursday 15 January

This is the day that I had fixed upon for the invasion of the Ashantee territory: circumstances enabled me to do so at an earlier date with my native troops, but the desertion of carriers has delayed the advance of English Regts. However I cannot complain as I now hold the Coomassie Road nearly to the foot of the Adansi hills & to-morrow I hope to have my advanced posts on the crest of that hill. Wood's Regt and Raits Artillery crossed the Prah to-day and marched to Altobiasi. Mail of 23rd in from England. Very hot day. Mr. Kühne the returned Captive missionary is still with us & evidently enjoys the good feeding of our mess after his lengthened captivity. I never saw a river so full of fish as this is, but they are very coarse. If we had nets great quantities might be taken.

TNA, WO 147/4

130

Wolseley to Cambridge

15 January

[Holograph]

Camp Prahsu

I have just had the honor of receiving Your Royal Highness'es letter of the 22nd December, and as the mail leaves this in an hour for Cape Coast to catch the steamer leaving the day after tomorrow, I hasten to send a few lines by it. I have written so fully to the Secrety. of State for War giving him officially an account of my doings and intentions, that I shall not repeat them here. I hope tomorrow to have my outposts on the Adansi Hill. If they are unopposed as I believe will be the case, I shall send the whole of Russells Regt to the crest of the pass to fortify it, having Woods Regt & Raits Artillery at Moinsey at the foot of [the] hill on [the] southern side, and 200 of 2nd W.I. Regt in support at Acrowfumu. It is probable that I shall again hear from the King on the 21st or 22nd instant, and he may then perhaps send me back all the prisoners. If he does so, I shall be inclined to believe his sincerity in saying that he wants peace. Of course I shall not halt or concede in any way to his wishes, until I have the heir apparent & some other persons of distinction in my hands as hostages.

As things look now there does not seem to be much chance of another shot being fired. The carrier difficulty is being got over tolerably well, and I hope to have 30 days supplies for all my force, (carriers included) by the 23rd instant, when everyone except the garrison for the tête de pont will have left this for the front. It is possible that I may push forward myself to Akrowfumu on the 20th or 21st instant, as I find it inconvenient to be so far away from my outposts whilst negociations are going on. There are some slight fever cases in camp but only one at all serious case, Captain Huyshe D.A.Q.M. General who suffers from dysentery; he is very weak to day. These slight fevers although very unpleasant are not dangerous, but dysentery is the one disease we have really to dread here. With the exception of Huyshe we are all in good health and spirits, longing to get to Coomassie and to settle the business quickly.

Cambridge MSS, RA VIC/ADD E/1/7300

131

Wolseley to Kimberley

15 January
[Holograph]
Government House
Cape Coast

Private

I am very much obliged to you for your very kind note of the 18th ultimo & for the assurance it conveys to me that you are satisfied with what I have done. The weakness of my force has compelled me to be very cautious, and to take care that in all I attempted, I was as certain of success as any man can ever be in military operations.

The encreased tax upon spirits ceases on the last day of this month. I have had to postpone the meeting of Council owing to the Chief Magistrates illness, but I shall have a council next Wednesday, the 17th instant, if necessary at Mr. Marshalls house, when I intend to reimpose the 2/6 a gallon upon spirits as a permanent tax: nothing is more injurious to the trade of a place like this than import duties imposed only for a few months, and I believe that the reason why so comparatively a small amount of spirits was imported under the 2/6 duty, was because the tax ceased at the end of the year. All the merchants with one exception – Mr Grant[19] who is a member of Council – gave up importing spirits, hoping in this way to force or to induce the Administrator at the end of the year, to go back to the old rates. When I have made the tax of 2/6 a permanent one, I believe that as much spirits as usual will be imported under it – and should my successor at any time find that he can dispense with it, he can give notice that it will cease in a year from that date: I think that a year should always elapse in these reductions of tariff to allow merchants to look forward and make their arrangements beforehand. There is a fine field here for an active minded man as Administrator: on every side that one turns, I see things that should be attended to, but with my military work, I am only just able to keep things going as I found them. The pay and allowances of all officials is a question that should be carefully gone into, and I think that all allowances should be consolidated, and the men well paid. This refers only to the English officials. I am of opinion that the existing system of allowances has a somewhat demoralizing effect upon them, and tends to peculation.

The first want of this town is good water and this is really easily procurable from the Sweet River where the Beulah road crosses it: ten miles of iron piping would suffice. When the war is over, I shall have a report made by one of our Engineers, and the necessary levels taken and a rough estimate prepared: the money required, I would propose borrowing here unless the Crown agents would supply it at 5 per cent interest.

This is the first great step necessary for the health of the people here. I was having large public latrines for both sexes constructed at several places, but as Captain Crease who was acting as Colonial Surveyor left for Ascension yesterday en route for England invalided, I fear that most of the sanitary improvements I have effected in the town will cease to act, and things will soon relapse into their ordinary state of filth. Small pox is still about, and one cannot effectually deal with it. Compulsory vaccination would be I know supported by all the educated natives & by the Kings & Chiefs. It would be easy to carry it out here and at all of our other settlements.

I start for the front about the 27th instant, and hope to make my first arch into Ashantee territory on the 15th January but all depends upon my transport. As I found that the Native Allies were useless as a fighting body I gradually absorbed them into the transport, retaining only a few hundred of the best as fighting men. I am diffident now from my past experience of the native character in giving an opinion regarding their promises, but I am still in hopes of being able to collect at Swaidroo on the Bernim River about 3000 men from the Western Akims: if I do so I shall move them by the Prahsu-Akim route into Ashantee: they will thus form a connecting link between me and Captain Glover to whom I have written recently as you will perceive by my despatches of this date.

Hoping that all my operations may continue to meet with your kind approval.

Bodleian, Kimberley MSS, MS. Eng. c. 4112, ff. 75–80

132

Wolseley Journal, 16–17 January

[Copy]

Friday 16 January

A very hot night. I sleep under a small mosquito net to prevent beetles spiders etc. etc. falling on my face from the roughly thatched roof. The consequence is that I am bathed in perspiration every night & wake up from its effects & the stinging of the prickly heat caused by it: I lie turning about sometimes until daylight & so do not get as much sleep as I should like. Mr. Kühne told me a very curious thing about Coomassie, that superstitious people like the Ashantees cannot fail to regard as an omen. The sacred tree from which the capital derives its name & which is very very old, fell with a crash in the street the day that I returned my answer (the 6th inst) to the King. It is esteemed so sacred that no one would dare to touch any portion of it. I hear privately that the correspondents find great fault with my combinations. Unfortunately they were told that I intended to cross the Prah on the 15th inst with all my Europeans, & because I have not done so, they imagine that I have failed in my intentions etc etc. As events have turned out, I invaded Ashantee on the 5th inst & on the 16th (to-day) hold the Coomassie road up to the Adansi Hill, a position that I never dreamt of occupying so early. Now, I have a road cut all the way to that hill, & have all the intervening rivers bridged, & large clearances made for my Europeans to encamp when I send them over the Prah en route for Quisah & Fommanah. When I calculated upon crossing the Prah on 15th inst I thought I should have had to fight perhaps immediately, & in my calculations as to time I did not expect to make more than about four miles a day, as that was the outside extent to which the road could be cut. If as I now expect I shall have my "army" concentrated at Quisah & Fommanah on the 26th inst it is about a day earlier than I had previously calculated upon being there crossing the Prah on the 15th inst. & marching very slowly & fighting at least once. I am glad to say that the carrier question is looking bright to-day. All the various ships I have sent to several places have succeeded fairly. I obtained over 800 men from the windward ports by pardoning all the political offences of the people & tribes there provided they supplied contingents of carriers. I obtained 1000 from the disaffected tribes of Elmina by the same means. I had sent detachments of troops into the district to which the deserters belonged, surrounded villages at night & seized every able bodied man. I am now quartering men of the W. I. Regts. in all the suspected villages so that the deserters cannot return to their homes. I sent Colonel Colley from Dunquah to the eastward of that place giving him a carte blanche to use coercion to any extent he liked short of shooting and he has done capitally. He began by burning a village that had ill treated some police sent to arrest deserters: he surrounded villages at night, beat them up at unexpected hours & the result has been most satisfactory. The men have now come forward in large numbers so that approximately speaking, I shall have between four & five thousand carriers over and above the 3000 attached to Regts. This makes my heart light again. The wing of the Rifle Brigade at Barroco were seedy a little, so I have ordered them in here to-morrow.

Saturday 17 January
The wing of the Rifle Brigade marched in from Barroco looking very well. Several of the officers look seedy. Carrier difficulty completely got over. Telegraph now into Yancoomassie Assin. Dunquah entirely cleared out of stores & Mansue very nearly so. This is good & all owing to Colley's energetic measures. Fear is the only motive force with these cowardly Fantees. The man tried the other day by the Judge at Dunquah for advising men to desert, has escaped from the guard house. I am very glad for [it] as I did not mean to hang him, he will now serve my purpose by running through the country to avoid capture & will thus spread abroad the news that he had been sentenced to death & only escaped hanging by running away. Apropos of his trial I was very much amused by the course pursued by the Judge. He is no lawyer & the weakest of mortals. No back-bone in his composition. He tried the man by my order, found him guilty but instead of sentencing him, sent me his notes & asked *me* what sentence he should pass on him. His letter was rambling – he said the man deserved to be hanged – that his

crime was far worse than murder etc etc & yet he recommended him to mercy in a shilly shally sort of manner. He wanted to shirk the responsibility of passing sentence "off his own bat", but he wrote to the wrong man in writing to me; I replied, reminding him that as he was the chief judicial authority so I was head of the executive power, & that for me to give him even an opinion upon a case then under his hands would be contrary to the spirit & practise of the law of England. I thought it rather fun to lecture a judge upon law. He then as he said upon reconsideration sentences the man to be hanged at such time and place as I might appoint. I intended to keep him under sentence of death in prison until the end of the war, as a living example of what would be done to deserting carriers & then commuting the sentence to a year's imprisonment. The man by escaping has solved all difficulty in the matter, but the news of his sentence has spread far & near, & he in his flight will carry the news to a distance, so the terror I wanted to spread amongst these deserters will have been well established. Huyshe holds his own but is still in a critical state. A hot sultry day.

TNA, WO 147/4

133

Wolseley to Glover

17 January
[Holograph]
Camp Prahsu

Your letter of the 10th instant dated from Kebbi has just reached me. In all your operations you must remember that you and Captain Butlers movements are only intended as diversions in favor of the main attack by the column moving under my immediate command along the Coomassie–Prahsu–Assin road. It is therefore essential that you should be cautious not to engage in very serious affairs: you should use your best endeavors to spread abroad exaggerated accounts of your numbers, so that these rumors should reach the King, puzzling him and causing him to divide his forces. My position to day is as follows – Russells Regt. moves to day to foot of Moinsi Hill: Woods Regt & Raits artillery to Ahquansraimu, in support: 200 of 2nd W.I. Regt. to Akrowfumu. A company of Woods Regt. is at Essiaman. In camp here I have Naval Brigade, one wing of Rifle Brigade and 130 of 2nd W.I. Regt. On the 20th the Naval Brigade crosses the river en route for Moinsi.

On 21st. Rifle Brigade do do do

On 22nd. – 42d Highlanders do do do

On 23rd. 100 men of 23rd Fuslrs. do do

together with reserve Ammunition Column & Field Hospital.

On 25th All will be concentrated at Moinsi and on 26th *all* move forward to Quisah and Fommanah. Negociations are now going on, so it is impossible to say what my movements may be after the 26th inst – but you shall be kept constantly informed of them. Having adopted strong measures I think I have now got over my transport difficulties, but feeding so many English soldiers at over a hundred miles from Cape Coast is no very easy matter when one has to depend upon untrustworthy carriers.

One missionary Mr. Kuhne is now in our camp, and I think it probable that the other prisoners may be sent back tomorrow or next day. If not sent back, the King will, I should say, fight. The general health is good. Weather warm but fine and everything looks well. I hope that a large number of your Eastern Allies may have joined you by this time, and that you are now as I write this, in Ashantee territory.

I have told the King that in communicating with us, his messengers are to carry a white flag, so please inform your men accordingly.

Wishing you every success.

CUL, RCMS 131/7, Glover MSS

134

Wolseley Journal, 18–24 January

[Copy]

Sunday 18 January

News in from Russell last night. He holds the Adansi or Moinse Hill, the Ashantees ran away without firing a shot: Lord Gifford in command of the scouts has done admirably. Russell speaks in the highest terms of the way in which he handled his men during this operation. Letter from Butler speaking very despondingly of his prospects. The curs of Kings won't move, they procrastinate from day to day, in fact they are afraid to cross the Prah. The same news comes from Dalrymple in Wassaw. I have written to all these cowardly Kings telling them I regard them as traitors & direct their appearing before me to answer for their conduct. I shall imprison & fine them severely the cowardly brutes. I think I shall flog them all round. If this was the beginning of the war I should try one of them & see what effect a sentence of death or of transportation would have on them. This has been the hottest day I have felt since I landed. Huyshe still holds his own.

Monday 19 January

The dysentery has entirely left Huyshe, but fever has flown to his brain. He is now quite delirious. This morning when the orderly of the A. H. Corps looking after him gave him a cup of tea to drink, Huyshe took it with one hand & struck him on the mouth with the other cutting his lip in two. He then bolted out of his hut, but was soon caught & brought back. He told Buller then that this man had been trying to kill him for weeks past etc etc. poor fellow I trust he may come round all right yet. News from Russell that Lord Gifford went within a few hundred yards yesterday of Quisah which is occupied by Ashantees. They beat their war drums & their scouts with arms reversed came forward & asked what we wanted: they said if we wanted to fight they were quite ready & only waited for their chiefs orders to do so. Gifford replied in the same strain & then retired. Russell says in his letter that he intends pushing on to-day to Quisah. If he does he will bring on a fight against my positive orders, & we shall have a row. He is rather impetuous & does not obey orders as strictly as I should like when he is near the enemy. He is one of those men who when they think they have a chance of having a fight on their own hook, almost invariably bring it on no matter what orders they may have received to the contrary. In the afternoon Huyshe began to sink. He knew the doctor but was not able to speak. His pulse went down & down. Everything was tried. He drank nearly a bottle of champagne during the day: He was blistered etc etc but without any effect & poor fellow he went to another & I trust a happier world at 7 p.m. It is a great blow to us all. There has always been a great deal of chaff amongst us at the number of times we sat down 13 to dinner. We sat down 13 at Liverpool & that began it. At Madeira again & Major Baker tells me that he made a note in his pocket book there of the circumstances because Huyshe kept us all waiting & he came in after we had all begun dinner & sat down making the thirteenth of the party.

Tuesday 20 January
I had a bad night's rest, thinking of Huyshe whose coffin was being made not far from me during the night & the noise of the carpenters sawing & hammering was not a pleasant thing to listen to for hours. I left Buller & Maurice behind to see him buried: his own Regt was in Camp, so he was carried by his own men to his grave. I started with the rest of the Staff at 6 a.m. & reached Essiaman at 10.30 a.m. It is a long eleven miles. The Naval Brigade started an hour before. I passed them at Atobiasi where they had halted for breakfast. They reached Essiaman about an hour after me. Two men fell out with fever & were sent back. A blackguard climate, I wish King Koffee was disposed of & that I had all the English troops back on board ship again. A strong stockade with a good clearance has been made here & is garrisoned by a company of Wood's Regt: the worst lot he has in his corps, so I intend leaving them here for good until we return. Several little Assin houses, very old stand inside the stockade. They are all of the same character everywhere in the Assin country. They are built on raised platforms of red earth about two feet high. No news from the front except that received last night that Baker Russell had pushed on & occupied Quisah with no opposition. Fommanah is also deserted.

Wednesday 21 January
Marched at 6 a.m. and reached Akrofumoo at 10.15 a.m. Road much better than yesterday. The scenery at the Fumusu River is very pretty, reminding me of a trout stream at home. Naval Brigade marched in

here very well. I left one A.D.C. down with fever at Prahsu (Wood 10th Hussars) & I had to leave my other (Lanyon 2nd W. I. Regt.) at Essiaman ill with dysentery. He goes back to-day to Prahsu & if he does not get better in a few days is to be sent to Cape Coast. Wood I expect to rejoin in a couple of days as he has only a slight fever. I am unfortunate in my ADC's. I cannot understand what King Koffee is about. It looks now as if he would fight. The Commodore overtook us in the afternoon & will go on with us to Coomassie. Dr. Mackinnon our new P.M.O. also came up.

Thursday 22 January
Marched at 6.15 a.m. A cool morning for marching. Reached Wood's Camp under the Adansi Hills a little before 10 a.m. So many men of the Rifle Brigade have fallen out that I have ordered on 200 men more of 23rd Regt, they should reach the Prah not later than 1st February. As things now look like fighting I have also ordered on 200 men of 1st W. I. Regt., to hold post along road etc etc. Rode a mile up to top of hills in the evening: the barometer showed the rise from our camp to be 620 feet, and our Camp is about 100 feet up the hill. We have been always told that this was only a hill & not a range, but it is a range, closely covered throughout with forest: the regular path up is very very steep, but we have zig-zagged a very fair road up it. There was a pleasant cool breeze on top where our fortified post is, but although vistas had been cut looking both north & south there was no view to be obtained to any great distance owing to the heavy haze that hangs over the tops of the trees in every direction. Our scouting parties report heavy firing in the direction of Fommanah but to the east of that place. The King is now evidently going to fight, & will do so most probably before we reach Amoaful as from thence lead to the east & west the roads to Becquah & Cocoofee from whence a large portion of his Army comes.

Friday 23 January
Sent on the Naval Brigade to Quisah: also Raits Artillery: Russells Regt. to Fommanah as I there intend making a post & collecting a magazine of stores; the Harmattan wind blew a little to-day. Rifle

Brigade marched in at 3.15 p.m. I was sitting on my bed not in very bright spirits when a messenger from the outposts brought me a letter from the King[20] dated Coomassie 21st inst saying that he sent me back all the white prisoners and would pay the indemnity I demanded. He again begs me to halt. I believe that he has been for some days between two opinions – at least his chiefs that belong to the war party have been at him to fight & his mother & those who want peace have been advising him the other way. Mr. Bonnat, Mr & Mrs Ramsayer & their two children[21] reached my Head Qtrs in the evening – poor devils they were rejoiced at getting free. They say that the Army that went back from the Prah was so demoralized that it will be next to impossible to collect it together again & that there is a regular scare throughout the country. The news of Butlers & Glovers advance had reached Coomassie & the people from the neighbourhood of Lake Echoy were running back north. They had applied to the King for assistance & he had sent them a few kegs of powder. Mr Bonnat is much the most intelligent of the party so I intend keeping him with me for a few days. He is a Frenchman & I don't like men of that nation.

Saturday 24 January
Fommanah: sent a cypher telegram down to Cape Coast last evening to be taken to Gibraltar or Lisbon to-day in a special steamer giving the Govt. the news. I hope it will reach England before the opening of Parliament so as to be in the Queen's speech. Marched on here this morning – quite a nice town. I have my Hd. Qtrs. in the King of Adansi's palace, a building consisting of many courtyards, ornamental as described in Bowdich's narrative,[22] & very Moorish in effect. The Naval Brigade & Rifle Brigade also marched in here & are quartered in the town. I sent back the Envoy to Coomassie with my answer to the King, couched in conciliatory but in very firm terms. I had him conducted through two ranks of British soldiers for a considerable distance.
TNA, WO 147/4

135

Wolseley to King Kofi Kakari

24 January

[Printed]

Your Majesty and all your chiefs know well, from past experience, that the promises of an English Governor are never broken. Whatever he says he will do, he does. I have in all my letters to your Majesty assured you that the Queen of England desires above all things to have peace firmly established between her subjects and yours; and I have told you that I wish only for your good. I am therefore surprised and grieved to find that you have not sent back all the prisoners that I demanded.

I intend to go to Coomassie. It is for your Majesty to decide whether I go there as your friend or as your enemy.

If I go there as your enemy, I shall march at the head of an irresistible English force, and I must again remind you of the consequences that this may have upon your Majesty's dynasty and upon the Ashanti kingdom.

If your Majesty sincerely wishes me to go to Coomassie as your friend, you must give me the following guarantees of your good faith:–

1st.   All the native prisoners still in your hands must be forthwith returned to me as demanded in my last letter; but as your Majesty wishes to retain Mr Dawson as an interpreter, whilst negotiations are going on, I have no objection to his remaining at Coomassie for the present.

2nd.   The following hostages[23] must be at once delivered up to me:–

1. Prince Mensa, your Majesty's heir.
2. Your Majesty's mother.
3. The heir to the King of Juabin.
4. The heir of the King of Kokofoo.
5. The heir of the King of Mampon.
6. The heir of the King of Becqua.

3rd.   One-half of the 50,000 ounces of gold to be paid by your Majesty as an indemnity must be sent to me immediately.

When these guarantees are given to me, I shall halt this army at the places where it may then happen to be, and I shall also send orders to halt to the armies now moving by the Wassaw path, and from Prahsu Akim, and from Eastern Akim.

I shall then proceed to Coomassie with an escort of only about 500 English soldiers, in order to make a treaty of peace with your Majesty. The sooner I receive these guarantees, the sooner will my armies halt; and in order to allow your Majesty to fulfil my demands without trouble, I shall only advance very slowly with this army during the next few days.

Your Majesty knows very well that you can safely rely upon the fulfilment of any promises that I may make.

I assure you that the hostages shall be well treated as becomes their position, and that they shall be sent back into Ashanti territory with due honour as soon as all the terms of peace offered by me have been complied with, and my armies have recrossed the Prah into Fanti territory, which they will do as soon as the treaty of peace has been signed. An officer of rank has conferred with your messengers, and I shall have much pleasure in conferring with your Majesty when I arrive at Coomassie.

PS. As Mr Dawson has asked for money, I send him £20 in silver by his servant.[24]

TNA, CO 879/6

136

Wolseley Journal, 25 January

[Copy]

Sunday 25 January

The mail for England closes to-night here & will leave Cape Coast on 27th for St. Vincent. Woods & Russell's Regts under Col. McLeod 42nd Regt. pushed on with Raits Artillery to Dompoassie. A close day threatening rain.

TNA, WO 147/4

137

Wolseley to Louisa Wolseley

[20–]25 January
[Holograph]
Camp Essiaman – in Ashantee

I begin this letter with sad feelings, for I have just been writing a letter to General Huyshe[25] informing him of his sons death – poor fellow. After what I mentioned to you in my letter – or perhaps it was in my journal – that I sent you yesterday, he sank and sank all day, being quite unconscious up to the moment of his death. This has cast a gloom over our usually merry party, but I shall not dwell longer on this painful subject. I move on tomorrow to Akrowfumu, and the following day to the foot of the Adansi Hill: Russell is now firmly established on the north side of the hill in the town of Quisah. I write this in what must once have been a nice little hut, but it is very old, rather dilapidated and the thatch swarms with rats. I am afraid that you would not enjoy a nights sojourn in such a place, but we are only too glad for any covering over our heads, rats or no rats. I have this moment had a note from Baker Russell – we have now four Russells out here – in which he deplores not having heard from your Pal by the mail of 24th ultimo. I shall write and tell him that I had none from you either. This will show him that both of you must have posted your letters too late for the mail. Not hearing from you was a very very great disappointment to me, but as I heard from Holmes I know you are all right, and I look forward to having the double enjoyment of reading two of your letters when the next mail arrives instead of only having one. I am in hourly expectation of having a despatch from Coomassie, and indeed I shall be very much disappointed if I do not have one before night. Thank God I am in excellent health, and things look well for my finishing this business one way or another before three weeks are over. And then, for England and you!!

Akrowful – 21st Janry. A little bush deer has just been brought me to look at. It is the size of a rabbit, and very prettily marked with spots and stripes. It would make such a nice plaything for Miss

Frances if I could only get it home, but that is out of the question. Our weather is very warm.

Fommanah – about 33 miles from Coomassie 24th January. As you will see by reading my journal I had another letter from the King yesterday, & he sent me back all the remaining white prisoners, Mrs Ramsayer, the wife of a Swiss missionary with her two children being of the party. The King says he will do all I ask, and begs of me to stop my armies. The indemnity he says shall also be paid, so after all we may not fire another shot, but I have to go on just as if I was certain of a fight, for these black ruffians are not to be trusted. I have just seen Baker Russell who is well and jolly, looking very well and as fit as a fiddle. He goes on to another town a few miles nearer Coomassie tomorrow, but I intend halting here for a few days until I collect sufficient supplies to feed my troops in advance. If all goes well I hope to have made my treaty and be on my return march before the end of first week in february & to be back again in Govt. House Cape Coast about the 20th of february, and perhaps to embark for England the first week in March. I shall take Baker Russell home with me in the ship I sail in, or perhaps if I am detained at all, he may go home before I can get away – please tell the Pal this. I write this in the King of Adansi's palace – It is really a nice place and the town generally is so very superior to anything in the Fantee country: All the towns here are deserted, and I believe there is a general scare throughout the Ashanti kingdom. – 25th January. The mail for England closes here to night and will leave Cape Coast on 27th. I have just read over what I wrote yesterday and the idea of getting back to you and England makes me quiver all over with joy and excitement. The next week will be the turning point in the war and I wish sincerely it was over. I hope that you and Miss Frances are enjoying yourselves. As you only have the house by the week you can easily get rid of it, for I shall be able to tell you at least a week beforehand when to expect me at home. God bless you my dearest little woman and praying that he may bless me by allowing me to return in safety to see you again, always believe me to be your very fondly devoted husband.
Hove, Wolseley, MSS W/P 4/6

138

Wolseley to Cambridge

25 January
[Holograph]
The King of Adansi's palace: Fommanah
I established my Head Quarters here on the 24th instant; the town is
a nice little place with a much better class of houses than anything
we have seen yet since we came to the Coast. The King has sent
me back all the white prisoners, and the natives [*sic*] captives will
be surrendered at once. My official dispatches contain copies of
my correspondence with him. Like all negroes, he is not to be
depended upon, so Your Royal Highness may be assured that until
I am well out of his territory, I shall omit no military precautions
for the safety of this Force. There is always the possibility of his
fighting at any period of the negociations, but if he does, I do
not imagine that his Army will be very numerous as the returned
Captives say that the Army that was lately in the Fanti country
came back to their own territory in a very demoralized condition,
and having dispersed throughout the Kingdom, cannot now be
easily collected together again. If the King fights at all, I expect
it will be about twelve miles on this side of Coomassie, where
according to our latest information he has now about 5000 men of
all sorts collected together. As I proceed I have to establish posts
behind me, fortifying them and leaving in them small garrisons
for their protection. This reduces my effective strength, but it
cannot be helped. The Adansi range of hills over which we passed
yesterday on our march to this place, is a very formidable obstacle.
I am very glad that I had not to force a passage over them, as for
a long time I believed I should have had to do: the native path
up them was exceedingly steep, and men at [the] top, might have
held the position with stones alone: we cut a zig-zag road up to
the crest which is about 620 feet above the surrounding country.
My official despatches to Lord Kimberley will inform your Royal
Highness regarding my recent correspondence with King Koffee.
I endeavored to write in a conciliatory tone, but at the same time
to word my letter so that he should see how determined I was to

make him feel that his Kingdom was a small affair when opposed to the Arms of England. I am anxious to make peace, but in order that the peace should be a lasting one, it is essential to make the King and his people feel that they are powerless when pitted against the strength of Great Britain. I hope Your Royal Highness may approve of the tone I have adopted in my dealings with the Court at Coomassie. Everything goes on well. We have slight fevers amongst the men, but nothing serious. I look forward to beginning to reembark the English troops about the 20th of next month, for once I have sufficient stores on this side of the Adansi Hills, I shall push on quickly to Coomassie and there end the war some-how or other. Colonel Colley has done wonders in the transport affair, and we have now a very fairly organized corps of carriers distributed throughout the line of communications. I cannot speak too highly of what he has done, and of the zeal & intelligence with which he has worked at this very uninteresting duty. Myself and Staff are in excellent health and spirits, and together with all around us, most confident of success. Everyone works hard and with a will: the behavior of the troops is admirable.

Cambridge MSS, RA VIC/ADD E/1/7309

139

Wolseley Journal, 26 January

Monday 26 January

Fommanah. This morning a reconnaissance in force was made by Col. McLeod 42nd Highdrs. who commands the advanced guard to the north & the west of his position at Dompoasi. That to the west came upon a party of the enemy at Atobiassi and surprising it took two prisoners. A little skirmish ensued in which two Ashantees were killed & two taken prisoners one being in command of the party and the chief scout of the King of Adansi. Col. McLeod had been ordered not to allow his men to fire unless the enemy fired first. He *says* the enemy fired first: the prisoners say that we fired first. At any rate McLeod very injudiciously burnt down the village as a punishment upon the Adansi people for having fired!! I sent back one of the prisoners with a letter to the King as I did not like the impression that the affair might have upon his mind. I told him *our* version of it and expressed my surprise that when he said he wished for peace he allowed my soldiers to be fired upon by his people, and asked him what he meant by collecting an armed force in my front. Our advanced guard moved on and occupied Essang Quantah. In the evening I rode to Quisah and inspected the 23rd & 42nd, the latter is a very fine Regt. I inspected the stockade constructed here. The enemy said to be collecting an army near Amoaful, about half way between this & Coomassie.

TNA, WO 147/3

140

Wolseley to King Kofi Kakari

26 January
[Printed]

When your messenger was leaving the day before yesterday, he was desired to tell Cobbina Obbin[26] that I could not permit him to remain with his armed followers so near the camp of my advanced guard, and that if he did not go back it would lead to trouble. This morning one of my scouting parties upon reaching the village of Adubiassie, was fired upon by Cobbina Obbin's men. In order to punish him for this unfriendly act, the village was set on fire.

Your Majesty tells me you wish for peace. Why, then, this collection of armed men between me and Coomassie? I have told your Majesty that, if you wish it, I am willing to go peacefully to Coomassie, as your friend, for the purpose of signing a lasting peace with you; and you know that an English Governor always speaks the truth. But if you collect an army before me, I shall defeat it and march through it; and then what will become of your Majesty's kingdom?

You know that your soldiers are powerless before an army of white men. Be wise and do not allow evil counsellors to advise you to adopt a line of conduct that must bring misery upon yourself and your people.

The Queen of England does not want to destroy the Ashanti kingdom. She wishes to have a lasting peace established with you, and to secure to you free access to the coast for purposes of trade.

355

This is the last time that I shall warn you. Decide quickly. I told you I would only advance slowly for a few days to allow your Majesty to send me the hostages and the prisoners, and the money which I demanded in my last letter. But if, when these few days have expired, you have not complied with my terms, I shall march straight to Coomassie.

I send this letter to you by the hands of a prisoner whom my scouts captured this morning, and whom I return to you as a proof of my good feeling towards you.

TNA, CO 879/6

141

Wolseley Journal, 27 January

Tuesday 27 January

Naval Brigade marched to the front to join Advanced Guard. Our scouting parties went to the Denkarau River where an old man was captured. He says all the Adansi people have been ordered to collect to the west of road somewhere near Bequah & there to await the Kings orders, also that an Army under Amanquartia (he says) is being assembled near Amoaful.

TNA, WO 147/3

142

Wolseley to Colonel John Sydney North, MP[27]

27 January

[Holograph]

King of Adansi's Palace,

Fommanah.

Your kind note of 24th Decmbr. reached me yesterday. You had not, when you wrote, heard of poor Alfred Charteris' death. It cast a sad gloom over us all, for I never knew a man more generally liked by everyone. He was a dear good fellow, the highest type of an English gentleman, and a first rate soldier. I never knew until after his illness that his constitution was delicate for he never spared himself any fatigue, and in some of our marches through the bush, the work was very hard, and too much for a man not strong by nature. I wrote to his father when he was invalided and although at that date he was very weak and ill, the Princpl. Medical Officer led me to believe that he would recover. When I bid him good bye on board the Simoom, he was quite collected, although the day before his mind had been wandering a little. When I told him that he would soon be in England, he brightened up, and the very idea of home seemed to have given him new strength. Colonel McNeill was with him when he died, and wrote to tell Lord Elcho the sad news. I did not hear it for over nearly three weeks, so as I knew that the news had been sent home, I thought it more merciful not to reopen the wound by writing on the subject to Lord Elcho. Perhaps I was wrong, but I did as I would be done by were I in Lord Elcho's grief.

It is difficult for me to say whether we are to have a battle or not, for although the King of Ashanti says he will accept my terms, he is *trying* to collect his Army, and if he succeeds it is quite possible that he may not keep his Royal word. However I am now only about 33 miles from Coomassie, and if all goes well I hope please God to be in that city ere many days go by. My difficulty is food: I have frequently to halt to bring it up from the rear. I am now over one hundred miles from the coast from whence all my supplies must come on the heads of men and women, and then I have to protect my line of communications by fortified posts every ten or twelve miles. I hope to have every white soldier re-embarked for England before the end of February and to follow them myself as soon as possible. I see no reason why I should not be in London by the 1ˢᵗ April. I shall leave this country with a pleasure that words fail me to describe, but I shall reserve my opinions regarding it until we next meet.

Gosford, Wemyss MSS, Drawer 39.

143

Wolseley Journal, 28–29 January

Wednesday 28 January
The Head Qtrs of 23rd Regt moved forward to Detchiasu – Colonel McLeod reports that Ahkanknassi is the only place in

his neighborhood fit for the encampment of the Europeans: I have ordered it to be cleared & intend moving there tomorrow, with 42nd & Rifle Brigade. I have just heard of poor Capt. Blakes death: he was a fine fellow and a rising naval officer. A report from McLeod in the afternoon saying that Gifford had reconnoitred to the village beyond Denkarau River. That it now appears all the Adansi people under their King have been collected at Borborassie. Gifford took two prisoners on the road between it & Bequah, they were carrying provisions for them. This is very annoying for our advanced guard has really gone beyond that place & must now hark back to attack it. I have ordered McLeod to go at it tomorrow. He is a little seedy I am sorry to say.

Thursday 29 January
Moved my Hd. Qtrs to Detchiasu; the Rifle Brigade & 42nd went on about a mile beyond it to Ahkanquassie. Just as I reached my halting place I received two letters from the King of 26th & 27th inst.[28] He begs me to halt, to halt, to halt, that is the burden of his song. I sent back his messengers within ten minutes of their reaching this place with my answer telling the King in it that I had halted at Fommanah for four days to please him – God forgive me the fib – & to allow him to make the necessary arrangements for carrying out the terms agreed upon, but I found that he had used it to collect an Army & that therefore I would halt no more. Mr. Dawson in a note acknowledging the money I had sent him said, see 2 Cor: 2. 11:. I looked at 2nd Corinthians 2nd Chapt accordingly & found it to be "*Lest Satan should get an advantage of us: for we are not ignorant of his devices*". This is evidently intended as a warning to us to beware of treachery. He evidently means to fight, so I fear that I shall not be able to get any indemnity out of him after all, and I would sooner have succeeded in getting it than in burning Coomassie, as I think it would have weakened him very seriously. I sent out Col. McLeod this morning to rout out some of the enemy who had collected on my left flank at a place called Borborassie he took with him a company of Russells Regt, the Naval Brigade & the 100 men of the 23rd who are in front. The distance was about 6 miles from

the main road. He had started before I heard from the King so I ordered him not to fire first & not to burn any villages. If I had had the Kings letter yesterday evening I should have reversed these orders. They took the village as usual by surprise, and Capt. Nicholl[29] of Russells Regt who was leading with his company of Anamaboes began to parley with the Ashantees and thereby allowing the greater portion to escape into the bush: a few shots were fired and then our men began. Poor Nichol was shot dead in the village simply through his humane feeling in restraining his men from firing as he thought the enemy would not fire – 12 barrels of powder much lead and a state umbrella were taken. The affair was very well managed. There were about 50 Ashantees killed. How many wounded it is hard to say: several prisoners taken. Amongst them a slave woman whom her master before he bolted had endeavored to shoot, he fired twice at her hitting her each time. She is now in camp, and the doctors have picked out all but one of the slugs. She was I may say quite naked when she reached my Head Quarters: for the sake of decency I had a cloth given to her. She says the King has promised his chiefs to come out to fight himself, and that he will move along the main road. Two sailors were hit: a couple of natives killed and a few wounded on our side. Poor Nichol was an old fellow: he is Adjutant of the Hampshire Militia & came here as a Volunteer, (he had been a soldier once) his inducement being to make a little money for a large family he now leaves behind him. At our Hd. Qtrs mess we got up a subscription for his family at dinner, and I think that about £70 was subscribed there and then. I gave £20 – more than I can afford, but I shall never miss it. We are now certainly in for a big fight, and I am glad that we now know that we are as this humbugging negociation on the part of the King complicated my position lest I should write or do anything that the Govt. at home might think was calculated to force on a battle. I have been however I think very cautious. I have always written to the King in a conciliatory but still in a firm tone. Report says that the Kings Army is only about 5000 men. If so, we shall make short work of them.

TNA, WO 147/3

359

144

Wolseley to King Kofi Kakari

29 January
[Printed]
I have received your Majesty's two letters, dated 26th and 27th instant.

In compliance with your Majesty's wishes, and in order to give you time to make arrangements for complying with my terms, I halted for a few days at Fommanah. Finding that neither the prisoners nor the hostages were sent to me, nor any part of the indemnity, I have advanced to this place.

I find that, instead of using the time I gave you in making peaceable arrangements, you have taken advantage of it to collect your armed men.

I cannot allow your soldiers to remain near my army. If you want peace, withdraw all your armed men at once behind Coomassie, and comply with my demands. If you really wish for peace, you have nothing to fear from me. This I promise you.

As I have already told your Majesty, I wish to visit you peacefully in Coomassie with an escort of white men, who shall only stay there one day while peace is being signed. As soon as peace is signed I shall order all my troops to go back as quickly as possible across the river Prah; and when they have done so, and when your Majesty has complied with the terms already agreed upon, all your hostages shall be sent back with honour to their own country. While under my care they shall be well treated.

I halted four days at Fommanah to please your Majesty. I cannot halt again until you have complied with my terms.
TNA, CO 879/6

145

Wolseley's Journal, 30–31 January

Friday 30 January
Insarfu. Moved on here to day with 42nd & Rifle Brigade: the 23rd and Naval Brigade coming on to Ahkanquassie. The country is

so close that I never can collect all together into one spot, and the water question has to be considered. Here the two Regts. are encamped along the side of the road, as the clearance made round the village is a plantain garden that would not do for a camp. The Advanced Guard, Russells & Woods Regts. under Col McLeod is in front at Quarman, the enemy's army being about half a mile again in front of their advanced piquets. We shall have our grand fight tomorrow so eagerly looked forward to by all here. I have left nothing undone to obtain a peaceable termination to this war, but Mr. Koffee in the folly of his barbarian pride has decided upon war. Upon his head be all the blood that may be spilt tomorrow.

Saturday 31 January
A hard fight that lasted all day, the enemy fought like men. After considerable trouble and delay their position was carried. Our list of casualties is rather heavy for my little force but I am glad to say that only one officer was killed: poor Buckle[30] of the Engineers, who was one of the most rising and one of the very best men in his Corps. Most of the wounds are slight. The enemy got round our rear and attacked a fortified post just in rear where they were well hammered: they then turned upon our baggage and of course a scare took place amongst the carriers, the result being that everyone was without his baggage for the night: this is tiresome as it retards my movements for tomorrow.
TNA, WO 147/3

6

Success (February to March 1874)

Following the success at Amoafo, Wolseley's advance towards the next obstacle of the Oda river was a methodical one, Bekwae being attacked and burned on 1 February and Agimmamu taken on the following day [**146**]. At Bekwae, Gifford's scouts had led the way as before, his pluck and energy fighting through an ambush on this occasion as well as his general dash throughout the campaign resulting in a recommendation for the VC, an award readily granted and presented to Gifford by the Queen at Windsor on 30 March 1874.[1] Asante resistance, however, was still evident with continuing attacks on the lines of communication back to the Pra. Indeed, Fomena was attacked on 2 February, the attack being beaten off by a hastily improvised defence organised by Captains Alexander Duncan, RA, and Dudley North of the 47th Foot, who was badly wounded [**157**]. While it was estimated that there had been about 1,000 Asante, the defence had amounted to just 34 Europeans – five officers, three surgeons, a commissary and a paymaster, and 24 sick and wounded – 38 West Indians and 102 levies.[2]

Though beaten off, the attack had serious consequences for the disruption to Colley's convoy system meant that there were now only five days' supplies remaining with the force still 16 miles short of Kumase. According to Butler in his later biography of Colley – there is no other record – Wolseley had held a council of war on the evening of 31 January, at which he proposed leaving much of the baggage at Agimmamu and forming a flying column to cut his way into Kumase and, if necessary, cutting his way out again in order to end the war swiftly: there had been 'some

362

at that council who held different views'. Nonetheless, Wolseley had made up his mind to go ahead on the morning of 1 February and, with the disruption to the convoys, on the following day he now asked his white troops if they would be prepared to make four days' supplies last for perhaps six, Colley having guaranteed that he could bring up fresh supplies as far as Agimmamu by 7 February. Colley certainly believed the decision the correct one: 'It was as plucky a thing as has ever been done in the world – but it was the right game – once you have licked a nigger keep him moving – any hesitation, or a day's halt, and I believe we should never have reached Coomassie.'[3] The men having readily agreed, the advance continued although, tents having been left behind, heavy rain on the night of 3 February soaked the force and added to the difficulties of Home's engineers improvising a bridge over the Oda.[4]

On 4 February, the flying column, comprising 118 officers, 1,044 white other ranks and 449 natives, crossed the Oda and advanced on Odaso at about 0630 [**150, 153**]. Wood's Opobos and the Rifle Brigade led the way as the 42nd had taken the lead at Amoafo. There was no square on this occasion, the column pushing up the main track and firing volleys into the bush, the track being effectively a sunken way that provided a natural breastwork for the troops advancing up it. Stanley noted that 'fire low, fire slow' had been abandoned with Wolseley happy to expend ammunition.[5] The Asante, whose resistance began to be encountered at about 0830, did not show quite the same spirit as previously, numbering perhaps 10,000 on this occasion, but it still proved a stiff engagement, Asamoa Nkwanta having used his considerable personal influence to effect in even gathering such a force together following the heavy losses at Amoafo.[6]

According to Wolseley and his adherents, difficulties arose from unsteadiness on the part of the levies, especially Wood's regiment, possibly due to the known presence of Kofi Karikari with his army. Bonnat, indeed, who had volunteered to stay on and was attached to the Naval Brigade, recognised the sound of the horns of two prominent palace officials, Bosommuro Dwira and Bosommuro Tia, denoting the king's attendance. To the dismay of Wood,

Lieutenant Eyre was mortally wounded by a slug through the bladder. When Eyre was buried later that day, Wood kissed his face for his mother, this sentimental attachment to Eyre being something of a precursor to that with Captain Ronald Campbell, who was to be killed in close proximity to Wood at Hlobane in Zululand in March 1879.[7]

At about 1100, the levies fell back on the Rifle Brigade, who 'did not do as well as they should have done', for which Wolseley largely blamed their commanding officer, Lieutenant Colonel Arthur Warren. Meanwhile Wolseley had ordered his baggage carriers brought up from the river between files of the 42nd, drawing them into the comparative safety of the main body, with the Naval Brigade closing the rear of the formation just as the Asante attacked it. At one point, Wolseley himself was bowled over by a slug hitting his helmet puggree and the Asante got near enough for Greaves to use his revolver on them. Initially, one of Rait's guns under Saunders had been unable to get forward and his crew had taken casualties but now Palmer brought forward the other. Wolseley once more summoned McLeod and the 42nd to head the stalled advance at about 1200. With pipers playing, the Highlanders moved forward in rushes up the road, brushing aside ambushes. News coming back that the 42nd was nearing Kumase at about 1345 resulted in a cheer among the troops still fighting at Odaso. This appeared to unnerve the Asante and they drew off. Pushing on himself on a mule, Wolseley reached Kumase at 1815, the troops raising three cheers for the Queen. The loss had been surprisingly small, just two dead – Eyre and one of Wood's men – with six officers and 60 men wounded.[8]

McLeod recommended VCs for four men from the 42nd, Captain Alexander Kidston, Lieutenants Nicholas Brophy and James McCallum (attached from the 79th Highlanders) and Private Thomas Adams. Adams in particular had distinguished himself at the forefront of the advance towards Kumase. Wolseley supported the recommendations for Kidston and Adams but neither received the award. Subsequently, however, a VC for Odaso was awarded to Lieutenant Mark Sever Bell RE, for inspiring leadership of his party of unarmed and unsupported Fante labourers in clearing the bush under fire. Bell's conduct was not brought to anyone's attention until April, and was initially rejected as falling outside the statutes but then reconsidered, and the award was finally granted in November. The Queen presented it to Bell at Windsor on 26 November 1874.[9] On 5 February, Wolseley also issued an Order of the Day congratulating his troops on their 'courage and devotion'.[10]

Reached as the light was rapidly failing since there had been a delay to bring up the supplies, Kumase was full of armed Asante returning from Odaso who passively observed the British arrival. Bizarrely, many repeated 'Thank you' over and over again, these being the only English words they knew. No one was impressed with the capital, Butler describing it as 'only a larger, a filthier, and far more blood-stained collection of mud and wattle hovels than any other village in the forest'. Fante captives were released and guards posted but not in sufficient numbers to prevent Asante removing arms and valuables while fires soon broke out, started, most assumed, by Wolseley's carriers though some pointed the finger at Rait's Hausa gunners. To stop the fires spreading in the absence of water supplies, Home's engineers pulled down houses while efforts were made to prevent looting, one Fante policeman being hanged summarily by McLeod.[11]

Kofi Karikari had fled and this presented immediate difficulties in terms of obtaining a settlement as, indeed, Kimberley had foreseen back in November. There had been attempted approaches by the Asante during the last days and hours of Wolseley's advance. Dawson, for example, had sent out two flags of truce on 3 February pleading for Wolseley to halt, or he and the other Fante captives would be killed. Kofi Karikari also offered one of his sons, Yao Berko, as an alternative hostage to his mother and brother. In reply, Wolseley had sent another message to Kofi Karikari refusing to halt until Afua Kobi and Mensa Bonsu were delivered up as hostages but also indicating that he would halt at the Oda in order to give the Asante time to reply: in fact it was necessary to do so to bring up his supplies. On 4 February, Dawson sent two more message trying to halt the advance. Wolseley ignored the first and McLeod, who received the second close to Kumase, also brushed it aside

[148, 149, 152]. Dawson duly appeared as the troops reached the outskirts and then led Gifford on such a roundabout route to the palace that Gifford threatened to shoot him: questioned as to Dawson's loyalty by Wolseley over a cup of tea, Bonnat vouched for him.[12] Once in Kumase, Wolseley immediately sent another message to Kofi Karikari, expressing his understanding that the king was reluctant to give up his mother and brother, and now offering to accept other hostages of rank instead, as well as concluding a treaty on the terms previously stated [151, 152].

From Wolseley's perspective, however, time was running short, the rain on the night before Odaso and more heavy rain on the three days following the action, suggesting that the weather was breaking. Indeed, it was reported by Baker Russell that the water was beginning to rise above the improvised bridge over the Oda. Messages were received from Kofi Karikari professing his intention of coming in on 5 February but he did not appear and his two envoys, Owusu Koko Kuma and Bosommura Dwira, were found trying to take weapons and ammunition out of Kumase, leading to their detention. Accordingly, Wolseley resolved to destroy Kumase and start his retreat to the Pra on 6 February [152, 153]. Subsequently, Wolseley admitted to Kimberley that he might have put more pressure on the Asante by staying longer in Kumase. Stanley was certainly critical of Wolseley for not doing more to disarm the Asante still in Kumase when he first arrived (thus encouraging Kofi Karikari to believe he could still muster an army), for retiring so precipitately, and also for failing to destroy the Asante royal mausoleum at Bantama a mile or so from Kumase, especially as the rain did not persist more than a few days. Reade, too, felt it a mistake to keep emphasising pacific intentions, for dropping the demand for hostages and not waiting at Kumase an extra day in order to destroy Bantama. Some later historians have also criticised Wolseley for withdrawing quickly 'to avoid the political complications which might otherwise detract from his clear military achievements'.[13]

In Wolseley's defence, Brackenbury subsequently echoed Wolseley's own despatches at the time in stressing that the rising water simply precluded any attempt 'to chase the king from one place to another' or to go to Bantama, from the destruction of which little could be gained, and that another action had to be avoided. In the latter context, Low, whose interviews with Wolseley were first published in the *United Service Journal* in 1874–75 before appearing in book form in 1878, argued that if another action had been fought it would have been difficult to bring away the sick and wounded. Maurice concurred in stressing the rain and the shortage of food as reasons for not destroying Bantama and that its destruction would also have hindered subsequent negotiations. Wolseley himself, who emphasised the problem of rain and lack of supplies in his memoirs, also suggested that destroying the stone palace at Kumase, built between 1817 and 1822, was worth more than a paper treaty as a demonstration of Asante weakness. Kimberley's view was that the destruction of the tombs at Bantama would have had 'a peculiarly repulsive character'.[14]

While Wolseley had been determined to stop indiscriminate looting at Kumase by the Fante, carriers or levies – even subsequently posting sentries at the bridge on the Pra to search all passing – officially sanctioned acquisition of legitimate prizes was another matter. However, the official prize agents headed by Buller, who was assisted by Bonnat, found relatively little of value at Kumase. Indeed, it was found that what was at first taken to be gold dust was largely brass dust used for defrauding recipients. Kofi Karikari's state umbrella was sent back for the Queen [**156, 163**], together with a carved stool for the Prince of Wales, in the care of Wolseley's ADC, the Hon. Henry Wood, who carried with him Wolseley's official despatch on the fall of Kumase and some of Prior's sketches. The prize sale subsequently held at Cape Coast from 23 February onwards saw inflated prices being given for items of little real value, Wolseley acquiring an umbrella, an old silver coffee pot, and an orb that his daughter used as a rattle. He was also presented by his staff with a sword once given to Kofi Karikari [**162, 163, 165**]. A particularly fine bronze was acquired by a visiting Russian prince, with whom Wolseley was burdened by the Duke of Cambridge and who otherwise arrived 'just in time to be too late' [**160, 162, 165**]. After the expedition's return to England, some of the gold items were displayed at Messrs Garrard in the Haymarket, and at the South Kensington Museum. Kofi Karikari's state umbrella and the orb both eventually ended up in the Royal United Service Institution in Whitehall, while a much fancied gold ram's mask went to the Royal Artillery Mess at Woolwich.[15]

The sword presented to Wolseley by his officers, the state umbrella, the rattle, the coffee pot, and a walking stick said to belong to Kofi Karikari, as well as the drum secured earlier in the campaign were all presented to the National Army Museum by the RUSI in 1963.[16] In all, items worth perhaps £2,000 fetched up to £6,000 but it was considered too little to distribute to the troops, who ultimately received instead 30 days' pay in lieu. Disraeli's Cabinet agreed on 25 April to provide £12–13,000 for the purpose 'which is not objected to on its own account, but there is a doubt as to the precedent it will create: however, the troops are to have it'.[17]

The wounded and sick having been sent off the day before, the palace at Kumase was blown up as the main column marched off at 0815 on 6 February, the rearguard leaving at 0900. As the available guncotton was damp and it was discovered that a vital component of the fuses had been kept by Buckle in his baggage and could not now be located, slow matches were improvised to ignite 160 lbs of captured Asante gunpowder. The bridge over the Oda was indeed already under water and, fearful of it giving way altogether, part of the Rifle Brigade and all of the 42nd had to strip and cross in fours holding hands while their clothes, rifles and ammunition were carried over on the carriers' heads. Wolseley halted at both Agimmamu and then Fomena to allow the sick and wounded to be sent back across the Adanse Hills. As they retired, the troops burned each village [152, 154, 155, 157].[18]

At Dechiasu on 9 February, however, Wolseley received a messenger from Kofi Karikari offering to negotiate. Wolseley replied by promising to halt at Fomena, which was necessary anyway, forgoing the hostages previously demanded, but indicating that a sum of 5,000 ounces of gold was still to be paid towards the indemnity, or he would continue to visit destruction on the Asante. The message was a verbal one as Kofi Karikari no longer had Dawson available to translate anything written in English. While halting at Fomena on 12 February, Wolseley then received a visit from the King of Adanse, Kwabina Oben, seeking to break away from the Asante kingdom and an indication that another of the principal tributary kings, Asafo Agyei of Dwaben, also wished to surrender. The following morning, an Asante delegation headed by a senior diplomat, Asabi Antwi, appeared with 1,040 ounces of gold – 40 of which were only disgorged after a search of the folds of their robes – and pleading Kofi Karikari's inability to pay more. In response to Wolseley's demands, Asabi Antwi also objected to the continuing size of the overall indemnity of 50,000 ounces of gold and to Adanse being allowed to detach itself from Asante sovereignty but otherwise accepting all other conditions [**157, 158**]. The draft Treaty of Fomena then taken back to Kofi Karikari specified the indemnity; the renunciation of the right to tribute and homage from Denkyira, Assin, Akyem, Adanse and others under British protection; the renunciation of any claim on Elmina; the withdrawal of remaining Asante forces in the coastal areas of the protectorate; the acceptance of free trade and free access between the coast and the interior; and a promise to prevent further human sacrifice [**159**].

In essence it was not so very different from the treaty of 1831 with the exception of the detachment of Adanse, since the potential dismemberment of Asante had not formed any part of the original aims of the expedition. Wolseley, however, argued that the Adanse feared retribution from Kofi Karikari and, allowing them to move en masse into Wassa territory as Kwabina Oben requested, would provide an additional buffer for the protectorate in the future. Wolseley had stressed that the British could offer no formal protection to the Adanse. Wolseley's assertion in his speech at the Mansion House on 31 March that his possession of military and civilian powers had been the key to successful negotiations was to be attacked, not least by Stanley, who felt diplomatic finesse had been distinctly lacking, but Wolseley's conduct was defended by Maurice. In response to the claim by some such as Henty that the treaty was not worth the paper on which it was written, as the indemnity would never be paid in full and there was no realistic means of enforcing it, Wolseley himself argued that the payment of some gold and the proof thereby of Asante submission was what really mattered. Subsequently, Asabi Antwi appeared with another delegation at Cape Coast Castle on 14 March after Wolseley's departure to sign the formal treaty, to which Kofi Karikari had already fixed his own mark. Objection was again raised to the size of the indemnity and the Asante were also to petition further against some of the terms such as the total suspension of human sacrifice. They did bring with them, however, Kofi Karikari's son, Kofi Nti, requesting that he be educated in England.[19]

What appears to have finally forced Kofi Karikari into negotiation was not so much the destruction of Kumase but the imminent arrival there of none other than Glover, whose advance the Asante messenger on 9 February had specifically asked Wolseley to halt [**157**]. Wolseley agreed to do so and asked the messenger to convey this to Glover though the message never actually reached Glover. Nothing had been heard of Glover since 17 January and no attempt had been made to ascertain his whereabouts. Thus, it was only when Captain Reginald Sartorius of the 6th Bengal Cavalry, attached to Glover's expedition, arrived in Wolseley's camp at Fomena on 12 February that anything was known of his progress [**157, 158, 160**]. By the end of January, though he had gathered some 4,500 men, Glover could count upon the reliability of only about 500 or so and all were reduced to subsisting on plantains and yams. Continuing to advance and having heard that Kumase had fallen, Glover was some 14 miles east of it on 8 February when he received a deputation from the *Dwabenhene*, Asafo Agyei, asking for terms. Dwaben had some kind of reciprocal treaty with the Akyem that made him reluctant to fight Glover though this applied equally to Glover's Akyem. Moreover, Glover's advance had prevented the Dwaben forces from joining the main Asante army to oppose Wolseley before Kumase, just as even Butler and Dalrymple's efforts had deterred men from Bekwae and Kokofo joining the main army. Accordingly, Sartorius had set out on a pony on 10 February with 20 Hausa as escort to try and contact Wolseley, riding through a deserted Kumase and crossing some 55 miles of hostile territory to reach Fomena.

When Sartorius did not return, Glover decided to enter Kumase himself on 12 February, though his original orders had been not to go beyond Dwaben. He remained only three hours, however, as he learned that the Asante intended to accept Wolseley's terms and that the envoys were on their way to Fomena. Halting at Moinsi on 15 February on his way down to Cape Coast, Glover received a gold dish and 14 ounces of gold as a gift from Kofi Karikari requesting that the Eastern Akyem desist from encouraging Asafo Agyei to defect. Glover returned the gift but did order the Akyem to return to their own territory. Making contact with Wolseley's rearguard, he crossed the Pra with his remaining disciplined Hausa and Yoruba on 17 February. The last West Indians were pulled back from Praso on 21 February and the bridge destroyed on 23 February.[20] Much was being made of Sartorius's ride through hostile territory and the VC was suggested but, as no other European had been present, there was doubt an award was covered by the statutes. In the event, although Sartorius and most others always considered the award for this ride, the VC was actually granted in October 1874 for saving the life of a Hausa in a skirmish at Abogoo on 17 January 1874. Sartorius's brother, Captain E. H. Sartorius of the 59th Foot, was also to win the VC for gallantry in Afghanistan in October 1879 though, again, only after the statutes had been amended in 1881 to allow for gallantry in performance of what was considered an act of duty.[21]

Wolseley had meanwhile returned to Cape Coast on 19 February to a rapturous reception from both his troops and the local Fante population. The Naval Brigade went back to its ships on that same day and, very quickly, the white battalions were embarked, the 2/23rd leaving on 20 February, the Rifle Brigade on 23 February, and the 42nd on 27 February [160, 161, 164]. Wood and Russell disbanded their levies and the 2nd West India Regiment then embarked on 19 March, leaving the 1st West India Regiment on the coast.[22] Wolseley was anxious to be gone himself but there was the question of handing over the administration. In turn, the succession to Wolseley with a salary of £4,000 a year was offered to Alison, Greaves, McLeod and Colley but all refused it [165, 168]. Colley suggested it was because he wished to return to his regiment but, as Kimberley noted, 'One & all replied – "not if we received £4000 a day!" The climate is our real enemy.'[23] Wolseley showed some irritation that George Berkeley was not apparently hurrying to assume overall charge [**158, 160, 161**]. Having persuaded a reluctant Lieutenant Colonel Maxwell of the 1st West India Regiment to succeed him in command at least temporarily, Wolseley paid a short trip to Accra on 1 and 2 March, penned some recommendations for the future defence of the protectorate by a Hausa police force and the West Indians, and then left Cape Coast for England on 4 March. He arrived back at Portsmouth on 18 March [**166, 168**]. A grievously ill Maxwell, who shortly after died at sea en route for England, then left the command in the hands of his second in command, Johnston, before Lees arrived to assume the government on 29 March 1874.[24]

The cost of the campaign had been a modest £767,093, of which the War Office share was £257,093 compared to the original estimate of £260,000. The Admiralty had spent some £280,000 and the Colonial Office £150,000. Within the overall total, Glover's expedition had cost £118,045. About £55,000 worth of arms and stores, however, had been left for Fante use and effectively written off, which would have raised the real cost to approximately £815,000.[25] Up to 31 May 1874, the cost in European lives, when taking into account those who died en route to England or died later at home, amounted to 18 officers and 53 other ranks, while the number of wounded and invalided totalled 95 officers and 628 other ranks. Low was quick to point out that the financial and human cost of Napier's expedition to Abyssinia in 1867–68 had been far higher.[26]

For the Asante, the 'Sagrenti War' was a heavy blow. Apart from the loss of life, most villages on the line of the British advance had been abandoned and even those off the main route were affected by rumours and the sheer 'seismic' shock of defeat.[27] Kofi Karikari was ousted in October 1874, the leading role being taken by his mother, Afua Kobi, and Amankwatia's successor as *Bantamahene*, his younger brother Kwabena Awua. Kofi Karikari was replaced as *Asantehene* by his brother Mensa Bonsu, Kwaku Dua Kuma again being rejected. Mensa Bonsu was faced not only with the defection of Adanse but also that of Dwaben. A war followed in which Asafo Agyei was defeated in October 1875 by an Asante army led by Adu Bufo and Asamoa Nkwanta, the latter being killed. Groups such as the Atebubu and Bron on the northern fringes of the Asante kingdom also soon broke into open revolt, as did the Gonja, Dagoma and Kwahu, with disaffection also spreading to parts of Kokofo, Mampon and Nsuta. In effect, Asante descended into chaos. Mensa Bonsu was also confronted with a rising challenge from a broad coalition of anti-government groups including disaffected traders, budding private entrepreneurs or *asikafo*, commoners or *akonkofo*, and the underprivileged. Mensa Bonsu was overthrown in turn in 1883 to be succeeded briefly by Kwaku Dua Kuma, who died after just 44 days, probably from smallpox. In the protracted civil war that followed, Kofi Karikari was murdered in June 1884, and Afua Kobi was driven out by her daughter, Yaa Kyaa, who eventually succeeded in having her son, Agyeman Prempeh, installed as *Asantehene* Kwaku Dua III in March 1888.[28]

As for the protectorate, though the Asante threat had been removed in 1874, the incoming Conservative government, which took office five days after news reached London that Kumase had fallen, was faced with the same dilemma as its Liberal predecessor in terms of whether to abandon the coast or not. The new Colonial Secretary, the Earl of Carnarvon, understood that what has been characterised as Wolseley's 'Palmerstonian blow' was such a popular success that the Gladstone government's intervention could not simply be condemned. Carnarvon, indeed, hoped to find some middle way by which moral obligation could be met without extending sovereignty, especially as Parliamentary opinion seemed to suggest that a retreat from perceived responsibility would be opposed. The Colonial Office itself undertook a searching review of the options in March 1874 and, on 12 May, Carnarvon announced that Lagos and the coastal forts would be combined to form a new Crown colony modelled on the Straits Settlement with an enhanced administration and a Hausa police force for its defence. A soldier appears to have been considered as Wolseley's natural successor, Henry Bartle Frere, the former Governor of Bombay, suggesting to Carnarvon a number of Indian army officers who might be suitable while the Duke of Cambridge once more recommended Bisset, whom he had originally wanted to take command the year before. In the event, Lees became administrator of Lagos and Strahan the Governor of the new Gold Coast Colony. While it was emphasised that British sovereignty would not be extended to the protectorate, the colony's new Legislative Council could legislate for it. Then, in August 1874 Carnarvon was pushed against his better judgement by the Aborigines Protection Society and by Strahan's own commitment, to declare domestic slavery illegal in the protectorate. It was a policy that, even though not really properly enforced in the interior, still had a damaging effect on the Fante economy, trade generally also being disrupted by the continuing chaos in Asante.

Policy towards Asante remained what has been described as 'political attrition' with the undoubted encouragement given to disaffection falling short of any real desire to intervene, though Mensa Bonsu did pay another part of the indemnity as a result of the Dwaben War. Ultimately, however, Agyeman Prempeh's restoration of authority and French interest in the region prompted concern and the revival of the issues of human sacrifice and the outstanding indemnity from 1874. Prempeh's decision to accept inclusion within the protectorate came too late to prevent a third Asante War, partly because a diplomatic mission he sent to London was deliberately delayed by the Gold Coast authorities. A new expedition marched to Kumase in December 1895, removing Prempeh and members of his household to Cape Coast in January 1896, with a protectorate proclaimed and a British Resident installed. The Resident's subsequent attempt to find the Golden Stool then provoked a siege of the British in Kumase in 1900. The garrison fought its way back to the coast in June 1900 to meet a relief force, which retook Kumase in September 1900, leading to total annexation in 1901. At the same time, the protectorate was also annexed.[29]

While Disraeli's new administration grappled with the political aftermath, the advent of that government seemed to suggest that Wolseley and his officers would not reap the rewards that they might have expected from the administration that had initiated the campaign. Certainly, the peerage for which Wolseley had been earlier considering possible titles now seemed distant [154, 157, 163]. Alison wrote that the election had taken the 'wind' out of the expedition's sails and, as Buller put it, had he remained in office with the campaign as 'his child', Cardwell would 'do more for us than anyone else'. Cardwell himself was somewhat apprehensive as to the rewards that might be offered.[30] Wolseley's new-found public popularity, however, and the enthusiastic welcome accorded the troops as they returned to Portsmouth between 19 and 26 March ensured that suitable honours would be conferred.[31]

The difficulty so far as the government was concerned was Wolseley's attitude towards what was on offer, especially a baronetcy which he regarded as devalued through its past conferment on 'common people' such as the 'Duke of Devonshire's gardener', a somewhat unwarranted aspersion on the designer of the Crystal Palace, Sir Joseph Paxton. Wolseley was also offered the GCB but felt this might unduly antagonise more senior officers [172]. The Duke of Cambridge thought Wolseley's objection to the GCB justified but that he should accept the baronetcy and the annual pension of £1,000 that went with it whether he liked it or not as the public would expect no less. It might be added that Wolseley's stated objection to the baronetcy, so far as the politicians knew, was that two already existed within the extended Wolseley family and he would likely inherit one, though the new Secretary of State for War, Gathorne Hardy, also thought that Wolseley would benefit by turning it down: 'My impression is that if it be understood that he prefers to be without the Baronetcy it will do him good.' Certainly, in his meetings with Disraeli and other ministers between 23 and 29 March, Wolseley was apt to suggest that he was being over-rewarded. Nonetheless, in meeting Disraeli on 23 March he kept repeating 'I am only a Colonel' – his substantive rank was only that of a half pay Major – and, of course, he was not a wealthy man as evidenced by his concern when the Colonial Office had earlier cut his allowances and his desire to have his pay and accounts settled quickly [115, 168]. In the event, therefore, Wolseley was happy to accept the KCB; the GCMG, for which according to Disraeli he was 'amazingly gratified'; promotion to Major General backdated to 6 March 1868; and a one-off sum of £25,000 in lieu of a smaller annual pension of £1,200 [172, 176, 178].[32]

Wolseley was presented to the Queen on 23 March and he and his troops were reviewed at Windsor on 30 March, the Naval Brigade being reviewed later at Gosport [167, 172]. There was a banquet at the Mansion House on 31 March, at which Wolseley rehearsed some of the arguments with regard to the transport crisis that were to become familiar in the subsequent work of Brackenbury and Maurice [173]. Wolseley also received the thanks of both Houses of Parliament. On 18 April Wolseley was caricatured by 'Ape' as 'The Man Who Would Not Stop' in *Vanity Fair*'s 'Men of the Day' series. There were also honorary degrees from Oxford and Cambridge, honorary freedoms from both the Clothworkers and the Grocers in the City, a banquet at the Royal Academy, and a sword of honour from the City of London presented at the Guildhall on 22 October.[33] There was also a more personal gift of porcelain from Gladstone, whose regard for Wolseley at this stage of his career was in marked contrast to their subsequent relationship [174, 177].[34] After a busy period in London Wolseley then escaped the cold weather by heading for Italy.[35]

The *London Gazette* on 31 March 1874 announced the awards for the campaign generally with the KCB for Commerell, Hewett, Alison, McLeod, and Anthony Home; 26 CBs including Buller, Greaves, Festing, Fremantle, Wood, Colley, Baker Russell, Robert Home, T. D. Baker, Rait, and Butler; promotion to Brevet Colonel for Wood and Colley; 14 promotions to Brevet Lieutenant Colonel, including Baker Russell and Robert Home, with an announcement that Baird would also have got one if he had survived; and 24 promotions to Brevet Major including Brackenbury, Lanyon, Buller, Rait and Dalrymple, with an indication that Buckle would also have got one if he had survived. Butler and Gifford also received half-pay promotions to Major and Captain respectively, and there were various promotions for members of the Control and Medical departments. Glover received the GCMG and he and Goldsworthy also subsequently received gratuities of £2000 and £500 respectively. After the intervention of Fremantle and the Queen, Festing was also elevated to KCMG.[36] For the ordinary servicemen, as indicated previously, there was a pay grant and, then, on 1 June it was announced that a medal would be awarded for the campaign. For the dependants of those who had not survived, Lady Wolseley had announced a fund in March 1874 – one 'amateur' performance at St James's Theatre on 20 March raised £107 3s. 6d. – and there was also a fund to relieve Scots suffering as a result of the war.[37]

The memory of the campaign was preserved in other ways. In July, Ackerman's Gallery in Regent Street displayed paintings by Orlando Norie based on sketches by Colley and others of incidents from the campaign. One of the burial of Huyshe was acquired by the Queen while Prince Arthur and Prince Leopold also made choices and the Queen presented a drawing of the Naval Brigade to the Duke of Edinburgh. There were also at least two marches and two polkas celebrating the campaign.[38] Then, of course, there was the rapid appearance of the books by Henty, Boyle, Stanley and Reade from among the correspondents and by Dooner, Maurice and Brackenbury from among the soldiers. As Wolseley had intended, it was Brackenbury's two-volume account that appeared first but it was to arouse immediate controversy. There was always potential for this on such matters as the relationship with Glover's expedition and the distribution of rewards and honours. Colley sensed this in turning down the invitation to lecture on the expedition at the RUSI for, 'There are so many little delicate questions to be touched on. And I like to keep out of hot water when I can.'[39] He suggested Brackenbury but, in the event, it was Wood who did so on 12 June, Glover having already done so on 15 May. One Colonial Office official noted in June that Wolseley 'never likes to commit himself too hastily to any approval of an officer not selected for his own expedition', but there were also those who felt their contribution not sufficiently recognised such as Arthur Warren of the Rifle Brigade, whose cause was taken up by Alison [**175**]. There was also the issue of the landing of the 42nd before the 2/23rd, Alison taking care to ensure that his version of events was understood at the highest level.[40]

As it happened, however, it was Warren and the Rifle Brigade that were to figure in the most significant of the controversies surrounding Brackenbury's book. As previously indicated,

Brackenbury had originally contacted Blackwood's in November 1873, Wolseley's desire to have an account from his own perspective published first being conveyed to Blackwood's in January 1874. Accordingly, Brackenbury set to work immediately on his return, engaging shorthand writers to whom he dictated for up to two hours a day while himself working ten to twelve hours a day. Brackenbury eschewed all exercise and, suffering from insomnia, took chloral every night for a fortnight despite his doctor saying he ran the risk of brain fever. The first chapter was ready by 13 April, the whole of the first volume by 30 April and the completed manuscript – running to 795 printed pages – on 23 May. Brackenbury had declined an offer for assistance from MacDougall's War Office Intelligence Branch; it produced its own précis of events. This may have contributed to the refusal of the Topographical Section to release the originals of maps sent them from Asante, Brackenbury turning to Lieutenant Harry Cooper of the 47th Foot to draw them for him anew. Utterly exhausted, Brackenbury took himself off to the continent to recover in the company of Lord Elcho.[41]

Reviews were generally favourable when the book appeared in June but officers of the Rifle Brigade were appalled by the assertion that the battalion had been unsteady at Odaso. Alison was equally annoyed at what he saw as inaccuracies in Brackenbury's account of the incident and even Baker Russell queried the implication that his regiment had been as unsteady as that of Wood. Alison was especially vexed that Brackenbury had reproduced hurried notes penned to Wolseley in the heat of action by both himself and McLeod, which he believed should have remained confidential. In his view, it was a 'direct violation of military confidence'. Alison, indeed, wanted all official despatches released in order to refute the charges, his complaints reaching not only Cambridge but also Prince Arthur.[42] It is not clear how far Alison may have detected a seemingly feigned concern for his health on Wolseley's part [**170, 171, 175**].

John Blackwood was not convinced that there had been any malicious intent on Brackenbury's part and felt no refutation in *Blackwood's Magazine* was justified, while Brackenbury excused himself on the grounds that, while writing, he had continued to feel the pressures of the 'horrid coast'.[43] The affair, however, was to have continued repercussions for Brackenbury, who was denied further promotion to a Brevet Lieutenant Colonelcy even after further service as Wolseley's military secretary in Natal in 1875 as a result of what Lord Elcho termed his 'literary indiscretion subsequent to the campaign'. After a struggle, however, Brackenbury secured his promotion in October 1875 [**179**].[44]

The issue did little to improve the relationship between Wolseley and Cambridge, which rapidly deteriorated after Wolseley's return from Asante. The Duke's welcome seemed gracious enough but Wolseley was warned by MacDougall that the Duke had greatly resented comments about 'Bow and Arrow' generals. Cambridge had also noted an article in the *Daily News* 'which is *very significant*', suggesting that Wolseley might succeed MacDougall at the Intelligence Branch and supporting the creation of an altogether larger Prussian-style organisation. The appointment of Adjutant General in India had been settled back in January 1874 and, though the Duke did consider Wolseley as a possible successor to MacDougall if the latter took the Canadian command, he now felt – as previously related – that Wolseley should get the Canadian command to remove him from the scene and so minimise any political damage to the Duke's conservative views. As also already noted, Wolseley was appointed instead as Inspector General of the Auxiliary Forces. Increasingly aware of what he regarded as the Duke's 'malice' towards anyone who had served in Asante, Wolseley was grateful to escape Horse Guards for Natal in March 1875.[45] It was a post for which Wolseley's dual civil and military experience in Asante appeared to have made him eminently suitable. In the eyes of the politicians and public, indeed, if not Horse Guards, Wolseley was fast becoming 'our only general'.

146

Wolseley's Journal, 1–2 February

Sunday 1 February

Thanks be to God, yesterday has been a brilliant affair. It has taught the enemy a very severe lesson. I suppose he will fight once more near his capital, but I don't again expect to meet with such a determined resistance. I sent out the Brigadier with the 42nd[,] Naval Brigade and Russells Regt to burn Bequa, a large town to the west of this place (Amoaful). It is the capital town of the King of Becquah one of the 6 great chiefs who go to make up the Kingdom of Ashanti. The service was well done and with but little loss, although the enemy were severely punished. We were most fortunate in our weather yesterday, as it was cloudy all day; today has been very warm. To-morrow we go on.

Monday 2 February

Marched at daybreak & reached Agemmamu about 12 or 13 miles from Koomassie. Pushed on my Advanced Guard about 2½ miles further to Adjuabim. Met with but little resistance. The enemy are demoralized & fled before us. Three officers hit slightly casualties few. Tomorrow I push on again. Unless I have to fight a very heavy battle I hope to sleep in Koomassie to-morrow night. If the resistance is as serious as the day before yesterday & I have to lose another 100 men, I do not expect to be there until the 4th instant.

Monday 2 February (continued)

Agemmamu. Marched here this morning from Amoaful, pushing the enemy before us in good style. Here the road to Coomassie bifurcates: I have chosen the western one as according to our maps it is least intersected by streams and is the one most generally used and therefore most likely to be the best road. I sent forward the advanced Guard under Col. McLeod to Adwabin which it reached without difficulty – fine day.

TNA, WO 147/3

147

Wolseley to Louisa Wolseley

[28 January–]2 February

[Holograph]

Fommanah

Your delightful letters of the 23rd and 28th Decbr both reached me the day before yesterday at this place, from which I dated my last letter to you that left by the mail starting from Cape Coast yesterday. I have read them over twice and did so slowly, so as to prolong the pleasure as much as possible: all your little affectionate bits afford me a pleasure that I shall not attempt to describe. Your account of Pal fully accords with the opinion I had formed of her character: it is all owing to the making up process, and I fully concur with you in thinking that for a married woman it pays better that the world should call her a very nice than a pretty woman. I cannot imagine what she would have done with herself if she had not had you to live with during Russells absence. I am very much afraid that I shall not be able to get you the feather flowers you wish for, as all vessels going from this coast to Madeira are now put in quarantine, no communication with the shore being allowed. I move on from this place tomorrow about nine miles more to Coomassie: I then halt for another day to collect supplies, and the day following if we are to have a fight at all, it will come off, and that will end the business – however this will not leave until after that date, so you will learn the result in the course of the letter. I wrote to Eyty yesterday. You did not say whether you took Miss Frances to Iwerne with you or not. I hope she may have completely recovered from her cold when this reaches you. Mrs Frosts pudding was excellent: it did not arrive until the middle of January having been detained for a couple of weeks on the road between Cape Coast and Prahsu. You mention having received an unpleasant letter from Mrs Hops. What was it about? I really do not think she is given to writing nasty things about people. I have not written to her however, as I do not approve of anyone saying a rude thing to my runteefoozle. I am very glad that so many people have called upon you. I think Pal ought to be very grateful to you for had she been alone I fancy that none of your *great* people would have sought her acquaintance. I am in great hopes that the cypher telegrams I sent to England by a special steamer may reach in time for the Queens speech. It will be a grand coup for the Government if they arrive in time. I am sorry to learn from your letter that you have given up keeping your journal, for when such is kept regularly nothing affords one greater pleasure in after years than looking over its pages. [Passage erased.] I recd. a letter of introduction the other day from Sir S. Northcot: I mentioned it at dinner, when Capt. Buller who comes from a place adjoining the Northcots place, said that he looked upon Lady N. as the *most charming* women he had ever met.[1] After that it is impossible to say what men may think charming; upon asking him for particulars, it turned out that he meant she was the best hearted & the least selfish and the kindest woman in the world. I had not even given her credit for those virtues, for I thought her the dullest of uninteresting women, and I cannot reallize that a woman with such an unsympathetic voice could ever have a heart such as he described her to possess. I am not surprised at the Macdougals[2] thinking of buying a house at Surbiton, for from several things he said to me I thought he found living in town in a large house where he could have relations staying with him rather too much for his income whilst he kept up a large stable of horses at the same time. He seems to think that he is to be a fixture in London, else purchasing a house at Surbiton would seem to be rather a dangerous experiment. He writes very nice letters to me, recounting the complimentary things said of my doings here by Mr Cardwell etc etc.

Insarfu – 30th January. Tomorrow we fight, and on the result of the action everything here depends – my trust in God is implicit, and I feel that we shall have a victory over these bloodthirsty and cruel people, but I do not much feel in the humor for letter writing. Yesterday we had a skirmish and we lost a poor old fellow named Nichol who was a Captain in Russells Regt. It was the old Duke[3] I think who said that next to losing a battle the greatest calamity was gaining one: there are always vacant places in ones mess, no matter how small may be the numbers belonging to it that make one's dinner stick in the throat. But I rejoice at the prospect of tomorrow for it must end the business one way or another. Please God I shall be in Coomassie on the 2ⁿᵈ or 3ʳᵈ February – stay there a day and if all goes well, get back to the River Prah about the 10ᵗʰ or 11ᵗʰ of that month, & to Cape Coast about the 18ᵗʰ or 19ᵗʰ. I have told you all this I know many times but I take so much pleasure in contemplating the idea of getting out of this horrid country that I cannot refrain from repeating the calculations over & over again. The fighting with a small number against great odds is all very well on the plains of India or China where you can see what you are about, but here in this interminable forest where one can never see a hundred yards it is nervous work, especially with the handful of troops I have, at such a distance from their base of operations. Goodbye my dearest child for to day. I shall now close this up and seal it in case of any unlucky shot tomorrow. Believe me that I am very very very fond of you, and that I look forward earnestly to seeing you again very soon, your devoted husband.

Sunday 1ˢᵗ Feby. I open this to say that we have had a brilliant victory yesterday, but not without loss unfortunately. Please God I shall be shortly in *and out* of Coomassie. My journal gives you all details: Our loss was heavy and my heart was sick as I stood on the road behind the fighting and each wounded man went past me. Every doctor looked like a butcher his hands & clothes covered with blood. In most of the fights I have hitherto been in in my life I have taken an active part, leading men & fighting myself, but yesterday, I had only to remain cool, keeping my wits about me and walk up and down looking as if I liked it. I had those horrid newspaper correspondents round me – most of them were in a blue funk all day, and whenever the enemy approached very near us and the firing around us became very hot, I used to catch their eyes watching mine to see if I was in a funk. I whistled, sang snatches of songs, sauntered again and I hope looked thoroughly unconcerned although in my heart I was anxious once or twice during the day in a manner that I have never felt before. I got messages constantly from all directions saying that they wanted support. I was very angry with Sir A. Alison for sending me messages of this sort, for he knew that my reserve was very small and that it could not be lightly engaged in an action in the bush. My child I have my ups and downs but I pray God that I may never again have such an anxious three weeks again as those just past by. I have no looking glass with me so I cannot tell whether I look much older. When I meet Baker Russell and see him jolly having no responsibility on his shoulders, I envy him.

Agemmamu – 2nd February, whilst on the march here to day I received your letter of the 8th Janury written from Iwerne: I read it whilst the booming of rifle fire was going on ahead of me. Certainly, my runteefoozle shall come down to meet me at the ship if she likes, but as the date of my arrival will be uncertain, it would necessitate your remaining at an hotel perhaps for two or three days: however if Russell & I go home together Pal and you could keep one another company: however even supposing that he & I do not go home together, I shall be delighted to see my little bullfinch when I land. But think it over for you could always meet me at the Railway Station in London as I could telegraph to you, but as I said before the sooner I see you the sooner & the more I shall be pleased. I have just had a note from Holmes saying we must go to No 2, but I know you would prefer going to an hotel – so you must settle that with him – please find out some Hotel in Dover Street or wherever you like best. I put myself entirely in your hands in this matter for I feel that Holmes may be offended if we don't go to him & I know that you hate having to do so, and I do not rellish B J much nor the glue pot either. I think you might ask Fanny[4] to take the creature for a few weeks, but if you can get off going to No 2 of course you take her with you to the hotel, as I know you would like to have her with you, and I should like you to be as happy as possible when I return: Tomorrow I leave this place for a run into Koomassie to destroy it: I am sorry to say that we must have another battle, and that grieves me, as I hate to think of fine fellows being killed in such a war as this. Please God I shall wind up this letter from Koomassie. I write this on my knee, so that must account for the very bad writing: of the spelling I shall say nothing. Goodbye for this evening.

Late in the evening 2nd Febr. I send this off under an escort for the mail of the 6th inst. Goodbye my own little whippersnapper – your fond husband.

Hove, Wolseley MSS, W/P 4/7

148

Wolseley's Journal, 3 February

Tuesday 3 February

Marched at daybreak. Our advanced Guard soon heavily engaged: a very large army of the enemy said to be in their front. Our prisoners taken lately say we have 10,000 men to beat before we reach Coomassie. Whilst on the march about three quarters of road between Agemmamu and the River Dah or Ordah, received a flag of truce from the King who begs me to halt & says that he will agree to all my terms if I will consent to do so. Also letter from Mr. Dawson to the same effect, saying that all the native prisoners will be murdered unless I halt at once.[5] Sent back an answer saying that at his request I would not go beyond Ordah River tonight (I was not in a position to do so well, and did not wish to begin a general action so late in the day. If a general action was to be fought as I believed it was, I wanted to have it so that it's wind up might be the taking of Coomassie and I could not accomplish that if I fought to-day). But that if his troops fired upon mine I would take his capital. The messengers with the flag of truce were sent back at once & we could hear them as they ran along calling out to the Ashantee troops not to fire. All skirmishing soon ceased in consequence, & we bivouaced on the Ordah River, the advanced Guard on the north bank: the Engineers were set to work at once to bridge the River, which is about 25 yds wide & 2½ feet deep. We had left all our baggage at Agemmamu: however as we are carrying over four days provisions with us and two reserves of ammunition (in all 100 rds. per man) our convoy is very long and difficult to protect.

TNA, WO 147/3

149

Wolseley to King Kofi Kakari

3 February
[Printed]
12.10 p.m. On the march
You have deceived me so before, that I cannot halt until the hostages are in my possession. As time presses, I will consent to accept for to-day your mother and Prince Mensah. Both shall be well treated by me. You can trust my word. If you send them to me this evening, I will halt my army this side of the river Ordah.

Unless you send them at once, my army shall march upon Coomassie.

TNA, CO 879/6

150

Wolseley's Journal, 4 February

Wednesday 4 February
We were flooded in our bivouac last night by a torrent of rain. A regular tornado. Bridge finished during the night. I gave the enemy two hours of daylight as law to send me in the hostages I require, and was induced to do so especially as all the men had had a bad night of it. Immediately as the Advanced Guard began it's march, the enemy were met with in force and a serious, a very serious [fight] I do not hesitate in this my Journal to say began. I had put the Rifle Brigade in front as the brunt of the last general action (that on the 31st ultimo at Amoaful) had fallen upon the 42nd. The enemy resisted stoutly, but did not come as near us as on the previous occasion, nor did they seem to fight with the same spirit – their fire was very heavy but very wild & consequently our losses were not nearly so heavy as on the 31st. Russells & Woods Regts had to be sent to the rear as they were so unsteady that no reliance could be placed upon them. The Rifle Brigade a splendid Battalion led by a man who always looked as if he was going to his own funeral, and with a manner sufficient to demoralize the best troops in the world: the major being very little better, did not do as well as they ought

to have done.[6] After about 5 or 6 hours we got into the village of Ordasu not much over a mile from the river. I then formed up in two lines along the road from the river to the village, and passed all my provisions and ammunition into the village between these two lines. We buried poor young Eyre in the village.[7] He knew he was dying & was conscious to the last. An only child and heir to a good fortune – but above all things as gallant a young soul as ever wore Her Majesty's uniform. We covered over his grave with rubbish to prevent its being desecrated. When I had all my impedimenta parked in the village I drew in my rear guard to it: and we were then attacked by the enemy from every direction. The roar of musketry with an occasional bang from our Guns was deafening in such a small space as that we were fighting over. The enemy barred all further advance beyond the village. Whilst Baker Russell was bending over me to receive an order – I was sitting on a stool – a heavy leaden, slug gave me a crack on the side of the head, striking me in a very slanting direction: it lodged in my Puggaree. My helmet & Puggaree saved my old nut. The Rifle Brigade was useless, so I ordered Raits guns to fire up the road for a few minutes & then sent forward the 42nd under Col. McLeod who soon cleared the way and without any serious loss. In an hour the firing in front became more distant, although the enemy still hammered away at the rear of the village. They were evidently at a loss to know what had become of our baggage that they had hoped to have pitched into. I soon heard from McLeod that the enemy were flying in every direction, that the road was strewn with the debris of their flight. I at once pushed on with the Rifle Brigade, leaving rear Guard under Lt. Col. Wood (Woods & Russells Regts & the Naval Brigade) to bring to on the wounded and the other impedimenta. I sent forward to Alison directing him to push on as quickly as possible into Coomassie, where I arrived myself nearly as soon as he did. He had drawn up the troops & gave me a general salute as I appeared before them: I ordered three cheers for the Queen. The town was swarming with armed men, who offered no resistance. A little after dark all the force was up & established in quarters. Mr. Dawson was met in the streets as our troops entered: all the other Fantee prisoners were found in irons & released. It was a brilliant days work. The King was himself present on the main road, but when our bullets began whistling near him he bolted & all soon followed his example. He did not return to the city. His mother bolted just before we entered the place.

TNA, WO 147/3

151

Wolseley to King Kofi Kakari

4 February

[Printed]

Coomassie

You have deceived me, but I have kept my promise to you.

I am in Coomassie and my only wish is to make a lasting peace with you. I have shown you the power of England, and now I will be merciful.

As you do not wish to give up your mother and Prince Mensa, send me some other hostages of rank, and I will make peace with you to-morrow on the terms originally agreed upon.

If either your Majesty, or your royal mother, or Prince Mensa, will come to see me to-morrow morning early, I will treat you with all the honour due to your royal dignity, and allow you to return in safety. You can trust my word.

TNA, CO 879/6

152

Wolseley's Journal, 5–7 February

Thursday 5 February

Sent back all the wounded under the escort of one Compy of Rifle Brigade, Woods & Russells Regts. I forgot to mention that Mr. Dawson had sent out two flags of truce during our advance upon the city trying to induce us to halt for "Heavens sake" saying that he and all the other prisoners would be murdered if we did not do so. I was too old a bird to do any such thing. Dawson I believe to be either a fool or a ruffian, perhaps a little of each. During the night there were numerous fires in the city, caused I believe by native followers searching for loot. I sent messengers to the King last night and again this morning asking him to make peace and warning him of the consequences unless he did so. During the day very heavy rain fell. I began to feel nervous about the many streams in our rear. Towards the evening I found the King was humbugging, so I determined upon falling back tomorrow; gave orders to have the Kings palace ruined, and every arrangement made for burning the city. Prize agents appointed who worked during the night at collecting a few valuables from the palace.

Friday 6 February
A succession of tornadoes during the night: very very heavy rain fell: had a wretched time of it trying to sleep under my umbrella. Began our return journey at 7 a.m. Found the road in a dreadful condition; one of the swamps was up to the mens armpits – I had intended moving all the Force to Agemmamu, but found it was impossible to do so. The Ordah river was swollen and rising when I got to it: a man of 5 ft. 6 inches in height could just ford it without his mouth being covered, and the current was very rapid: our bridge had two feet of water over it. Pushed the Naval Brigade over it as quickly as possible: they dined on the south side and then marched on to Agemmamu with all the reserves of ammunition. The bridge became worse and worse every hour, and it was touch and go whether it would last until night. It became so bad at last that more than half the Rifle Brigade and all the 42nd had to ford, their clothes etc being taken over by natives on their heads. I pushed on with a small escort and reached Agammanu just before dark.

Saturday 7 February
It rained again last night: I halted here (at Agemmamu) for the day to write despatches. I send them home by Wood my A.D.C.: he left with them about 5 p.m. The Rifle Brigade, Artillery & 42nd marched in, and the 23rd. and Naval Brigade marched to Amoaful. Not a shot fired since we left Coomassie.
TNA, WO 147/3

153

Wolseley to Frances Wolseley

7 February
[Holograph]
Agemmamu
13 miles south of Coomassie

I have been to Coomassie and as the King would not come to terms I burnt his palace & the whole city. I am now on my return to Cape Coast. I am in excellent health and spirits, thank God for all his mercies vouchsafed to me. I had a narrow shave in our last battle a large leaden slug struck my helmet and lodged in my pugree, giving me a good crack in the head. We have had some very hard fighting, and the Government at home cannot I think do too much for all the men who have fought in this horrid climate.

Please God I shall be home 1st April when I hope to find you my dearest and best of mothers looking as pretty and as well as usual.

Goodbye my dearest mother and always believe me to be your devoted & dutiful son.

Duke, Wolseley MSS, XVIII-H

154

Wolseley to Louisa Wolseley

7 February
[Holograph]
Agemmamu

I wrote to you last from this place on the 2nd instant, telling you that I was to march forward the following day. I shall not describe our operations. The telegraph from Lisbon will have told you of our success. We have had some hard fighting, but God has blessed us with success. I am now on my way back to Cape Coast Castle, my rear Guard being here to day. I am as fit as a fiddle: so was Russell when I last saw him a few days ago. He is on in front being a long days march nearer England at present than I am. We have all had very hard work and have had some trying hours of it owing to the heavy tornadoes and rains that accompanied them. I slept without my boots last night for the first time for several days, and I had a good roof over my head, having slept!! for two nights under my umbrella amidst torrents of rain. But these are trifles. We took Coomassie and it has now ceased to exist as a city. Mr. Wood, 10th Hussars, my A.D.C. goes home from this today with despatches: he will go down to Folkestone to see you and give you all the news of this place. He is a son of Ld. Halifax & is a charming fellow and a brave soldier. Remember Lord Trent and Viscount Cannock[8] in case you are asked any questions, not that I for an instant think there is a likelyhood of such places being so honored but although not probable it is possible and you know that please God it is to come off some day or other & the sooner it comes the better. I hope to have all the English troops on board ship and on their way to England by the 26th or 27th instant, and that I may be able to follow in the first week of March. It is most probable that I shall have to go and see the Queen when I return. I hope she will ask you also, so be prepared for such a contingency, also have my star & orders handy and sweep together my portmanteaux that are as well as I remember at Fannys. If I am fortunate in my arrangements D.V. I shall kiss you my dear little woman on or about the 27th of March, but I shall let you know more by and bye before then: do not write to me here any more after the receipt of this – with what pleasure I tell you all this I cannot describe. God has been so good to me throughout this war, and I am sure that I deserve nothing from him. I have no more time for writing as I am obliged to write long official letters & despatches. Goodbye my darling little woman.

Hove, Wolseley MSS, W/P 4/8

155

Wolseley to Cambridge

7 February

[Holograph]

Agemmamu

My official telegram and the despatches that will go home with Mr Wood, 10th Hussars will place Your Royal Highness in possession of all our news. I have desired Mr Wood to pay his dutiful respects to Your Royal Highness as soon as he reaches London, and he will be able to suplement the information contained in my Official reports. We have had very hard fighting, the brunt of which was borne by the 42nd Highlanders, by far the best Battalion here, and possessing much the best officers. Most of the wounds [are] slight, and all are going on well. The first batch of the men, (the Naval Brigade and the 23rd R.W. Fuslrs.) will I hope, reembark on the 21st instant, and unless something unforeseen takes place, I trust that all may be again on board ship and en route for England about the 26th of this month. The troops have undergone great exposure during the last few days, but as yet none have suffered from it, and all are as cheery as possible. I hope that Your Royal Highness will be pleased with all I have done here, for I shall esteem myself most fortunate should I succeed in obtaining Your Royal Highnesses approbation.

Cambridge MSS, RA VIC/ADD E/1/7320

156

Wolseley to Major General Henry Ponsonby[9]

7 February
[Holograph]
HeadQuarters
Agemmamu
13 miles south of Coomassie

Amongst the few articles of Interest taken from the King's Palace at Coomassie, is the Royal State Umbrella, which I have now the honor to forward to you for presentation to Her Most Gracious Majesty the Queen, as a humble tribute of dutiful respect and affection from Her Majesty's Military and Naval Forces that took part in this War.

It will be taken to England by my Aide-de-Camp – Lieut. the Honble H.J. Wood 10th Hussars.

RA, VIC/MAIN F/7/105

157

Wolseley's Journal, 8–13 February

Sunday 8 February

Cleared everything out of Agemmamu and burnt it – marched to
Amoaful, burning all intervening villages. Appointed Lord Gifford
to be my A.D.C. vice Lanyon invalided.

Monday 9 February

Marched to Detchiasu, the troops halting at Ahkanknassie a mile
in rear. A messenger came in from the King begging for peace.[10]
I sent him back saying that I would forego the question of hostages,
and that I would halt at Fommanah until the evening of the 12th
instant; and that if by that time the King sent me accredited Chief
to treat who would bring with him 5000 ounces of gold (£20,000)
I would make peace. If not I intended to destroy his country. I sent
by the messenger a letter to Glover, written in French telling him
the position of affairs, and requesting him to halt where he was,
if he could do so with safety until the 13th or 14th instant, when he
was to fall back behind the Prah.

Tuesday 10 February

Marched to Fommanah, clearing out everything in rear of us. The
enemy has been interrupting our line of communications to the
south of the Adansi Hills, but in a very feeble manner. Fine day.

Wednesday 11 February

Sending back all the sick and wounded. I find that our losses in
the five days fighting were, 3 officers killed, 13 men, including
labourers killed and 368 wounded. One or two wounded
Englishmen are dying. There was a sharp little fight at this place
on the 2nd inst, and we had some good men wounded: a Captain
North 47th Regt amongst the number.[11] I fear he must lose his arm.
We have destroyed everything in rear of this, burning most of the
places, and levelling to the ground the large places such as Amoaful
& this place. A little seedy.

Thursday 12 February

King Abim the King of Adansi came in to surrender, he is now in camp, I shall see him tomorrow morning. Captain Sartorius arrived in camp with an escort of 20 men from Captain Glovers camp that he left at 12.30 p.m. on the 10th inst. expecting to find me at Coomassie through which city he marched meeting no one: its ruins were still smoking. Nothing can prove more conclusively than this how thorough has been the thrashing the Ashantis have received. The King of Fuabin wants to surrender, so out of the six great feudatory Kings whose territory goes to make up Ashanti, one (Mampon) has been killed in battle; one is now a state prisoner in my camp and a third is anxious to join him there. Glover had some skirmishing on the 2nd instant on the banks of the Anoom river. He had heard of the fall of Coomassie on the 8th inst. Cleared out all the remainder of our sick & wounded. The messengers from the King came in, in the evening, saying that a chief was at a village near our outposts having been sent by the King to make a treaty and that he had brought the gold with him, ordered him to come into camp at daybreak. I am glad that all the newspaper correspondents have left for the coast so we can carry on negociations freed from their accursed presence. Received a telegram from the Judge at Cape Coast saying that Mr. Cleaver[12] had received a private telegram saying Mr. Gladstone had resigned and that his resignation had been accepted: I cannot believe that the Liberals have gone out. Mr. Gladstone may have retired from ill health or he may be determined at last to throw off the mask and go over to Rome openly. If Mr. Cardwell or Lord Granville[13] take the office of first minister it will not matter much to us, but if the Conservatives go in, it is all over I fear with the honors that all this little Army expects. The excitement of a general election will drive out of the peoples heads all remembrance of our services. If the news is true, it is a sad blow to us all. We shall not know anything positive until the mail of the 30th ultimo from England arrives – We have had the harmattan wind blowing for the last few days, so although the days are warm, the nights are cold.

Friday 13 February
Fommanah. The Kings messengers arrived in camp bringing 1040 ounces of gold. They said he could not pay up the 5000 I had demanded – a lie of course, but I am too anxious to get a treaty to stick out for money. The gold was nearly all ornaments of various descriptions. The government cannot do less than throw the amount into the prize fund. I gave the messengers the draft treaty and they raised objections only to the total amount to be paid by the King and to the Adansi people being allowed to leave the Ashanti territory. They went off promising to be back at Cape Coast in a fortnight from this date with the Kings answer. I then saw the King of Adansi and told him that if he was determined to leave Ashanti he must understand that I could not promise to protect him, and that he must make his own arrangements with the Wassaw people regarding the land he was to occupy. He said he was afraid to remain here lest the King should reak vengeance upon him, and begged to be allowed to come into the Protectorate. Fine day.

TNA, WO 147/3

158

Wolseley to Cambridge

13 February
[Holograph]
Camp Fommanah
When halting for the day at Detchiasu messengers from the King of Ashantee reached me, saying that the King wished for peace and expressing his regret at having fought with white men. As he had no one with him that could write English his message was verbal as also was my answer to him. I replied that I was quite prepared to make peace also, and that in order to prove the sincerity of my assertion, I would consent to forego the hostages whom I had previously demanded, but if I did so, the King must send me in five thousand ounces of gold (about £20,000) as a first instalment of the indemnity he had previously agreed to pay. I had a long train of wounded men to get over the Adansi Hills, so

I considered it would be advisable that I myself should halt north of them until I had seen all of the wounded safely over them. I therefore told the messengers that I would remain at Fommanah until the evening of the 12th instant to receive the Kings reply, but that unless they brought the Gold I would not allow them into my camp. About 7 p.m. yesterday evening a flag of truce was stopped by my rear piquet, and brought into me. The bearers said that a Chief deputed by the King was at a village a couple of miles in [the] rear: I ordered them to come into camp at daybreak this morning which they did accordingly. They only brought one thousand and forty ounces of gold but as I thought it was a sufficient guarantee of the Kings good faith and desire for peace, I consented to receive it as the first instalment of the indemnity. A copy of the treaty I drew up goes home to the Colonial Office, and as of course it will be sent to the Horse Guards, I do not send Your Royal Highness a copy. The envoy only made objection to the largeness of the sum demanded, but conceded that point when it was shown him that the King had already agreed to pay it. And to the Adansi people being included in the list of those over whom the King was henceforward to exercise nor to claim any authority. This difficulty was thrust upon me, as the King of Adansi had come into my camp and surrendered himself and all his people, saying that he had resolved upon withdrawing from the Ashanti Kingdom. He is of the same race as the Assins who had in former years emigrated into the protected territory renouncing all allegiance to the Ashanti King. He was anxious to follow their example and to join the Assins already located south of the Prah, but I did not consider it advisable to allow him to do so, and told him that if he was determined to cut himself and his people adrift from the Ashanti Kingdom, he might go into the old Denkira bush, an uninhabited district west of the Prah river, adding that he must make his own arrangements with the Kings of Wassaw regarding the land he was to occupy, and that under no circumstances could I hold him out any promises of protection. He said he was afraid to remain where he was, so go he would. I felt it to be therefore necessary to include the Adansi people in the list of those who having been formerly subjects of the King of

Ashanti and having left his Kingdom were to be free for ever from all claims on the King of Ashantis part. I know that this will be a very severe blow to King Koffee, but it will materially weaken him and render him less able to annoy us in future. I availed myself of the messenger returning to Coomassie to send a letter to Captain Glover who is near that city to the east of it. I wrote saying that he was upon receipt of my letter, to fall back behind the river Prah and thence upon his base at Accra. Captain Sartorius one of his officers marched into my camp yesterday with 20 men as an escort, having left Captain Glovers camp (then 18 miles east of Coomassie) on the 10th instant, and having marched through that city on his road to join me. The ruins of the city were in some places still smouldering as he came through, but he saw no one en route except a few fugitive slaves who came out of the bush to join him and leave the country. There could be no greater proof of how thoroughly the enemy's army has been beaten and dispersed than the fact of one white man with only 20 black soldiers being able to traverse the country in safety.

I have sent the draft treaty to the King for signature with a request that he will return it signed to me at Cape Coast on the 28th instant.

Tomorrow I leave this for the Prah, intending to make two marches to Prahsu. There I shall leave about 200 of the 1st West [Indians] in garrison, until all the stores collected there have been taken back to the Coast. It will be for my successor – Mr Berkeley, the Governor in Chief – to decide whether he will replace these men of the 1st W.I. Regt. by police or give up the post altogether when the stores have been removed. As soon as I have dispatched all the English troops to England, I intend collecting the 2nd W.I. Regt. and embarking it for the West Indies.

Russells Regt. marches without halting to Cape Coast, Woods Regt. to Elmina at which places both will be disbanded, the men being sent to their respective homes. Several of the companies of those Corps come from various places along the Coast from Sierra Leone to the Oil rivers: all those men must be provided with sea transport, also the foreign carriers that I obtained at various times from distant ports.

I think I may say that my mission here is now at an end, and I trust that the results obtained may be considered satisfactory by Your Royal Highness. I have been surrounded by a body of officers who have worked like Gentlemen of the best stamp, and who were never above doing anything required of them, no matter how disagreeable may have been the duty to be done. I know of nothing more repugnant to the feelings of a soldier than having to remain in the rear in charge of transport, yet I have had a large number of officers so employed, amongst whom are men whose abilities were really thrown away upon such work – but I had nothing else to give them to do, and my transport required the utmost care and nursing. I am convinced that a civil transport corps under civilians as ours is in England will never work in war: We should have had a serious break down here, had I not taken my transport away from the Control and given it over to combatant officers. I shall reserve all my views on this subject until I shall have the honor of waiting upon Your Royal Highness at home. I have gained a great deal of most valuable experience in this war, the least part of which is not that regarding the working of our present system of administration. I have taken part in most of the wars that we have had for the last twenty two years, but upon no previous occasion has any operation caused me the anxiety of mind that I have experienced here. In none have I met with a braver enemy, and the difficulties of fighting in this forest country when there are *no* openings at all free from bush, exceed anything I had anticipated.

I hope to leave Cape Coast for England in the first week of March with all my staff, and to be at home about the 23rd or 25th of that month.

I would here take the liberty of bringing to Your Royal Highnesses notice the high opinion I entertain of Captain Brabazon late of the Grendr Guards. He was at first with Captain Butler on his expedition with the Western Akims. Captain Butler speaks very highly of his zeal and other soldierlike qualities. He regrets extremely having left the Army, and would be most grateful if Your Royal Highness would be pleased to give him a Lieutenants commission in a Cavalry Regt. now serving in India, or if that was impossible, even to give him a Sub Lieutenancy in such a Corps. I hope that Your Royal Highness will pardon the liberty I have taken in thus bringing him to notice, but it is really a pity that so good a soldier should for ever be debarred from again serving Her Majesty.

Counting Captain Brabazon I have had four officers of the Household Brigade here, and I am sure that Your Royal Highness will be pleased to hear that in all good soldierlike qualities none have surpassed them. One poor Alfred Charteris was the making of as fine a soldier as ever wore Her Majestys uniform. So brave, so good, and so genial that it was a pleasure to be associated with him.

Cambridge MSS, RA VIC/ADD E/1/7327

159

Treaty of Peace between Wolseley and Saibee Enquie,[14] acting on behalf of King Kofi Kakari

13 February
[Printed]
Fommanah

Article I
There shall; be hereafter perpetual peace between the Queen of England and her allies on the Coast on the one part, and the King of Ashanti and all his people on the other part.

Article II
The King of Ashanti promises to pay the sum of 50,000 ounces of approved gold as indemnity for the expenses he has occasioned to Her Majesty the Queen of England by the late war; and undertakes to pay 1000 ounces of gold forthwith, and the remainder by such instalments as Her Majesty's Government may from time to time demand.

Article III
The King of Ashanti, on the part of himself and his successors, renounces all right or title to any tribute or homage from the

Kings of Denkera, Assin, Akim, Adansi, and the other allies of Her
Majesty formerly subject to the kingdom of Ashanti.

Article IV
The king on the part of himself and of his heirs and successors,
does hereby further renounce for ever all pretensions of supremacy
over Elmina, or over any of the tribes formerly connected with
the Dutch Government, and to any tribute or homage from such
tribes, as well as to any payment or acknowledgement of any kind
by the British Government in respect of Elmina or any other of
the British forts and possessions on the Coast.

Article V
The king will at once withdraw all his troops from Apollonia and
its vicinity, and from the neighbourhood of Dixcove, Secondee,
and the adjoining coast-line.

Article VI
There shall be freedom of trade between Ashanti and Her
Majesty's forts on the Coast, all persons being at liberty to carry
their merchandise from the Coast to Coomassie, or from that place
to any of Her Majesty's possessions on the Coast.

Article VII
The King of Ashanti guarantees that the road from Coomassie to
the river Prah shall always be kept open and free from bush to a
width of 15 feet.

Article VIII
As Her Majesty's subjects and the people of Ashanti are henceforth
to be friends for ever, the king, in order to prove the sincerity of his
friendship for Queen Victoria, promises to use his best endeavours
to check the practice of human sacrifice, with a view to hereafter
putting an end to it altogether, as the practice is repugnant to the
feelings of all Christian nations.

Article IX

One copy of this Treaty shall be signed by the King of Ashanti, and sent to the Administrator of Her Majesty's Government at Cape Coast Castle within fourteen days from this date.

Article X

This Treaty shall be known as the Treaty of Fommanah.

TNA, FO 93/6/4

160

Wolseley's Journal, 14–22 February

Saturday 14 February

Marched to Akrofoomu about 14 miles – weather fine – Tomorrow I intend marching to the Prah, 22 miles.

Sunday 15 February

Prahsu – marched from Akrofoomu this morning doing a double march of 22 miles. Halted at Essiaman for breakfast. Went round the hospital in the evening at Prahsu. 105 patients still there most of them wounded men. Two of [them] must die poor fellows. They all look clean and well cared for. They are to halt here tomorrow and then go down to the Coast in two batches. The Prah has fallen I should say 18 inches since we left and is now fordable at many places. Buller & Maurice very seedy.

Monday 16 February

Yancoomassie Assin. Reached this place at 12.30 p.m. having halted at Barraco for breakfast – found the 42nd there, all looking well and cheery. I have ordered that all the English soldiers going down the road are to have as much food as they can eat, and of all sorts of kind. A Russian prince Leonide Wiasemaky was waiting for me yesterday at the Prah.[15] He has letters of introduction from the Duke of Cambridge. He has come out to see the fighting but was too late. I heard of him when I was at Fommanah and sent back word to have him stopped if possible at the Prah as I did not want to be incumbered by him. Confound him, here he is, and I have now to be bored by his presence and to feed him until such time as it may seem to him agreeable to go away. I have impressed upon him the splendid hippopotimus shooting there is to be had on the Volta and I am in hopes of getting rid of him when Sartorius goes back to the Volta to join Glover. Amateurs in war are always in the way. This fellow belongs to the Hussars of the Guard & speaks English fluently. In the evening I received a telegram from Glover from Essiaman. He had marched through Coomassie on the 12th and had found the route we took both in going and returning. He goes on to Prahsu – from thence he sends back his Akims to their homes. They are he says the greatest cowards possible. Capt. Sartorius remains here to await his arrival.

Tuesday 17 February
Mansue. Arrived here at 3 p.m. A very long and fatiguing march of 23 miles. Received a great ovation here. Indeed I have received ovations everywhere on this side of the Prah, but here it was overcoming. I could scarcely get my mule along without killing some one as the women threw themselves shouting on the ground before him and under his legs. The Rifle Brigade turned out and gave some hearty cheers. A very warm day, as everything going on well.

Wednesday 18 February
Yancoomassie Fantee. A long tiring march of 22 miles. Found the 23rd here, also a convoy of sick & wounded. Went round the Hospital in the evening. The men all looking well. Of this batch those that were to die have gone off already, and I think the remainder will do well. Two officers of the Navy died here yesterday. One a fine young fellow who was badly hit in the head at the battle of Amoaful. I did not think that he could have lived so long. The other died of dysentery.[16] Water is becoming scare at all these places now as most of the small streams have dried up, and the larger sized ones have resolved themselves into a succession of stagnant pools.

Thursday 19 February
Governmt House Cape Coast. A march of 13 miles – reached Cape Coast at 11.30 a.m. having started at 7 a.m. Was received by the

whole population roaring and screaming, the women throwing themselves in heaps on the ground in front of me, triumphal arches, Guards of honor, the fleet dressed with flags, and a Royal salute fired from the flag ship and another from the Castle in honor of the fall of Coomassie. Of the large staff that came out with me, only one marched in with me, Capt. Brackenbury. Colonel Greaves ill: also Maurice & Buller all of whom I sent on here during the night – Read Gladstones address to his constituents in the papers of the 24th ultimo, the latest that have been received.[17]

Friday 20 February
Cape Coast. The 23rd Regt. embarked this morning. I went on board the Victor Emmanuel to see the sick. I never saw men better looked after or more comfortable: every appliance that art or money could provide has been supplied in her. The wounded are doing well.

Saturday 21 February
The climate here is much better than inland. Walked to Prospect House to see that it was ready for Russells Regt. Mail in from England of 30th ultimo.

Sunday 22 February
Held a Levée in the afternoon. Went to the Castle in the evening to examine the loot. Have finally settled upon going home on the 7th March. Whether that wretched little shirk Mr. Berkeley arrives or not. I hope to have the "Manitoban" to go home in: she ought to be here the end of this week. I can scarcely realize that I am going home next week myself. Hurrah.
TNA, WO 147/3

161

Wolseley to Cambridge

22 February
[Holograph]
Government House: Cape Coast
My official despatches contain all the news from this place. The

"Tamar" leaves this evening, and the "Himalaya" tomorrow: the "Sarmatian" is hourly expected, and as soon as she arrives the 42nd will go on board of her. I have halted that Regiment at Inquabim, 6 miles from this, to await her arrival. I am very much disappointed at Mr. Berkeley's being unable to be here by the 1st March as I had long since requested him to be, so that I might get away about that date. All my staff are more or less sickly, and I want rest myself. Europeans cannot work at the high pressure that all around me have done for the last four or five months, and retain their health and vigor in this climate. In addition to my desire to leave this place as soon as possible on the score of health, I have long thought that it would not be advantageous to the public service, that the winding up of all the political business of the country generally, should be undertaken by me, whose stay under no circumstances could be extended for more than a few weeks after the departure of the European troops, and who could not consequently go as thoroughly into all the varied and complicated questions outstanding previous to my arrival, or that may have cropped up during the war, as a Civil Officer whose connection with the Coast was to be of a more or less permanent character.

When first asked by Lord Kimberley and by Mr. Cardwell to come out here, I distinctly stated that I would do so with pleasure upon the understanding that I was not to remain on the Coast after the Military operations had been brought to a close. I have by this mail sent Lord Kimberley copies of my correspondence with Mr. Berkeley on this subject, informing his Lordship that I intend leaving this for England on the 7th March, whether Mr Berkeley arrives or not. If he is not here by that date, I shall hand over the Government to the Colonial Secretary pending the arrival of the Governor in Chief. I hope therefore to have the honor of paying my respects to Your Royal Highness about the 28th of that month.

Cambridge MSS, RA VIC/ADD E/1/7333

162

Wolseley's Journal, 23–25 February

Monday 23 February

The prize sale began. Everything fetched very very high prices.

Tuesday 24 February

Sale still going on – so much money has been spent in the town that everyone even the poorest looking nigger has plenty to spend. It is a great time for the merchants, into whose pockets eventually most of the money will go. Walked in the evening up Connors Hill to see Butler who has been very seedy from fever. He goes home in the Thames on Thursday.

Wednesday 25 February

The Sarmatian still overdue – it is very provoking as I do not like sending home the 42nd Highlanders in the Nebraska[18] on board of which they are at present, and yet I do not rellish the idea of keeping them here on the chance of her arrival as it is possible that she may have broken down at sea. Last night was the pleasantest I have ever experienced in this country. It was cold & delightful, so we all slept well under a blanket each. Greaves still seedy. Baker a little better but very weak. Irvine on his back again with bad fever. Buller nearly well. This Russian prince is an infernal nuisance. He lives with us, drinks our champagne and takes it all as a matter of course, never seeming the least grateful for what is done for him. He wants to go home in the ship with me, but there I mean to "put my foot down", for I will not be bored by him any longer. Their Royal Highnesses George and Alfred[19] are very easy in giving these sort of fellows letters of introduction, but if we sent them in a bill for feeding them I don't think we should have much chance of getting it paid. I have been looking over the "Wild North Land". It is not as interesting nor has it as many scenes of adventure as the "Great Lone Land" but it is very well written: there is more real poetry in it than in five sixths of the rhyming twaddle that passes for poetry now adays.[20] It is a little too much overloaded I think with Butlers enraptured feelings in gazing upon beautiful scenery, and there is a little repetition in consequence.

TNA, WO 147/3

163

Wolseley to Louisa Wolseley

[25–]26 February

[Holograph]

There is no change in my plans: D.V. I leave this on Saturday week next the 7th March, and if we are fortunate we might be home by 26th but at all events by the 28th of that month. Baker Russell goes home with me. We have been having a great sale of the loot taken, and I have I fear been squandering my money away, for I cannot tell you the prices things have fetched. Of one thing I am very proud – I have bought King Koffees Coffee-pot. It is an old English silver one, I should say of George II, but it is in such a battered condition that I dare say you will laugh at me for having bought it: I thought however that it would be a never ending subject for conversation at breakfast whenever we might have very stupid people with us. I have [passage erased] the gold rattle taken from the Kings nursery, and I have bought a few things for my runteefoozle, if she doesn't like them, I can give them away to someone else. I know you do not care for barbaric ornaments, so when I saw men giving £20 and £30 for hideous ornaments I thought how much better such a sum might be expended at home. Holmes asked me to buy a few things for him, for about £5 or £10 please tell him that I have not yet succeeded in getting anything for that price. I had set my heart upon a bronze group of about 50 little figures representing the King of Ashantee being carried in state & had ordered one of my staff to go as far as £16 for it. It went for £100!!!

My staff have purchased the Kings sword for me & presented it to me – very nice of them, is it not? It [is] a handsome General Officers sword & was presented by Her Majesty to the King many years ago. I presume that I can never be asked to revert to the rank of Colonel, so it will do me very well as my General's sword.

There are beads here called Agency beads. They are found in the ground somewhere in the interior, and must have been I should say, made by the Egyptians. No one here knows anything about them, but they are the only thing not gold that the natives care for. They sell by weight at once or twice their weights in gold – I have a few to show you but I fear you may think them hideous – please ask Holmes to look up their history for me, so that I may be able to talk learnedly on the subject to dinners out. The best things I have got for presents are carved stools: they are peculiar to the country & not like anything in any other place. I have nigh ruined myself in buying them. When I sent home Wood with despatches, I sent in the name of the force here, the Kings State Umbrella to the Queen and a very handsome stool to the Princess of Wales. One nearly as good as that I had hoped to have bought for you for about £10 – went for £36 – so I did not get it, but I have bought you another quite as good except that it has no silver ornaments. It has been broken a little: it came out of the Queens appartments. I have succeeded in buying one of the Kings state hats: the one I have got is supposed to be the one which he wore when he was present at the battle of Ordasu. If Holmes likes it he can have it – please tell him that it is possible that a case and a small barrel of curiosities may reach home before I do: if so they are to be sent to St Georges Place. He might have them unpacked and the things put out in one of the bedrooms. Only half belong to me, so they must be equally divided into two lots: will you see this done. Myself and staff bought a silver goblet which we have presented to the Commodore as a remembrance of our march to Coomassie. We gave £20. It was worth about £3 being of Dutch Silver. All the troops, & sick & wounded are now on board ship. I am waiting for the arrival of the Sarmatian now several days overdue to send home the last ships. As soon as she arrives, I am going with the Commodore for a few days cruize, to visit Accra and some other outstanding posts in "*my dominions*".

26th February. In nine days I embark for England – delightful to think of. This note goes today in the Wye.[21] Goodbye my own dear little perriewinkle and always believe in your fond husband.

PS Since writing the above the Sarmatian has arrived bringing with it your long nice letter written from the Macdougalls. It is bad news for us here this change of Ministry. I am very much amused by your account of Lady S – and her manner.[22] [Passage erased.]

Hove, Wolseley MSS, W/P 4/9

164

Wolseley's Journal, 27 February

Friday 27 February

Dined with Baker Russell yesterday evening. The 42nd changed ship this morning from the Nebraska to the Sarmatian and left in the evening for England. The roadsted that some few days ago was so full of shipping has now only the "Active" and a couple of transports in it.

TNA, WO 147/3

165

Wolseley to Cambridge

27 February

[Holograph]

Cape Coast

The "Sarmatian" with the 42nd Highlanders on board leaves this evening for England. All the remaining sick and wounded left yesterday in the "Victor Emmanuel" and in the "Thames".[23] The only English soldiers now ashore are a few Army Service Corps men, a small Detachment of the Engineers employed in the telegraph work and a few Army Hospital Corps men. I hope to get away about the 4th or 5th of March in the "Manitoban" and I hope to take all these odds and ends of men with me. I was on the point of sending off the 2nd W.I. Regt. to the West Indies, but have now halted them a few miles distant, in accordance with orders received yesterday from the Quartr. Mastr. General.[24]

As directed by Sir Richard Airey,[25] I endeavored to get some good officer to remain here as my successor in office, but no one would accept the post on any terms, I have therefore been obliged to fall back upon the officer who will be in Command when I leave: it will be Colonel Maxwell, 1ˢᵗ W.I. Regt formerly in the 34ᵗʰ so it is possible that Sir Richard may know something of him. He is a gentleman and is a sober man, qualities not very common upon the coast of Africa. He at once responded to my call when I asked him to convert his Regt. into carriers, and everything that I know of him is in his favor. My acquaintance with him is however so very slight, that I am unable to give any opinion as to his abilities. He is I fear a delicate man, and I do not think, judging from the very little I know of him that Lt. Colonel Johnson[26] of the same Regt. and the next senior officer would do well as administrator: however as I know so little of him I ought not perhaps to give an opinion. What this place wants now is an able man who will remain here for some years, as changes of Governors are most injurious, especially at a time when the transition from a state of war and the despotic rule necessarily attendant thereon to the order and laws of peace has to be effected. There is a fine opening here for an energetic man of administrative ability. I have failed to get any officer of known talent to accept the berth and I do not think that anyone, except a man who looks to the Colonial Service as a career would throw up his military duties and come out here from England to serve as Administrator on the Gold Coast. I am therefore decidedly of opinion that an able civilian from the Colonial Service should be sent out here with as little delay as possible, unless the Secretary of State for the Colonies approves of Captain Lees (late of 23ʳᵈ R.W. Fuslrs.) who is now Colonial Secretary being made Administrator. He has had considerable experience on the Coast, and would I think do well in that capacity. He was the first Adjutant the 2ⁿᵈ Batt. of the 23ʳᵈ ever had, and was very much liked in the Regt. I need scarcely add after what I have said above, that I have not been able to appoint any officers to succeed to the Govt. in the event of Colonel Maxwells death, and this renders it all the more necessary that a Civil Governor should be appointed as soon as possible.

On Sunday I am going down in the Commodores ship to Accra, as Lord Kimberley wished me to visit it before I returned to England. The prize property brought away from Coomassie has been sold here by public auction at very high prices with the exception of some very heavy Gold ornaments that will be taken home by the Prize Agents for sale in England. The total amount of the prize money, when everything has been sold will not exceed about £4000, so I am afraid the soldiers will not get much, unless the Govt. would generously add to it the one thousand and forty ounces of Gold paid by the King of Ashantee as the first instalment of the indemnity he has promised to pay. Its value to the English nation is very small, but if thrown into the Prize fund, it would just make each privates share worth their having. I have not made this proposal officially, as I should not feel justified in doing so, and I trust that Your Royal Highness will kindly pardon my having mentioned it here.

Prince L. Viascensky, the Russian officer that Your Royal Highness wished me to take care of, returns to England in the Sarmatian. He has lived with me during his stay here, and I have done everything I could to make his sojourn here as agreeable as possible to him.

I was rejoiced to find from Your Royal Highnesses' gracious letter to me of the 6th instant that Your Royal Highness approves of what I have done.

Cambridge MSS, RA VIC/ADD E/1/7336

166

Wolseley's Journal, 28 February–4 March

Saturday 28 February

By orders received from home by last mail, I am desired to select an officer to remain here as Governor & to select a second and a third man to succeed in case of the death of the first & second. I asked the Brigadier, who refused: then McLeod who took a night to consider & refused, Colley the same, so I have to hand over the Govt. to the senior officer of the 1ˢᵗ W. I. Regt. Lt. Col. Maxwell. He may be fit for it & he may not. I know nothing for or against him except that he looks painfully delicate and weak. This is a bad arrangement, for what this place wants at present above all things is [a] Governor who means to stay his time here, and he should be a man of great energy and tact. No good soldier would stay here, so the only chance there is for obtaining a good Governor is to appoint a man who has made the Colonial service his career.

Sunday 1 March

Embarked at 8 a.m. on board H.M.S. "Active" where we were entertained most hospitably by Commodore Hewett, by far the best fellow I have ever known in the Navy. We reached Accra about 3 p.m. having had a pleasant voyage.

Monday 2 March

Landed at 6 a.m. a salute of 17 guns being fired from the Active as I went ashore. The Collector of Customs, Mr. Paul[27] is a most beery fellow, dull and lethargic: evidently is a hard drinker. He seemed to know nothing about the place. Had a very bad breakfast at the hotel and reembarked, the Commodore being very seedy. Got back to Cape Coast (distance 70 miles) about 4 p.m. & went ashore.

Tuesday 3 March

Lt. Colonel Maxwell arrived. He looks more dead than alive and has begged of me to have him relieved as soon as possible.

Wednesday 4 March

Left Cape Coast at 4 p.m. Guard of Honor. Salute etc etc. & never did I leave any spot upon earth with such pleasure. The Active manned rigging and gave three cheers as I went out past her & she fired a salute, the last I shall receive for a long time, perhaps the last I shall ever receive until three vollies are fired over my grave.

TNA, WO 147/3

167

Wolseley to Frances Wolseley

23 March
[Holograph]
Flemings Hotel
Half Moon St
Monday morning
6 a.m.

I have been like a hunted man for the last 36 hours & have had no time for anything. I have to see so many officials & to dine at so many official places, that I have no moments for private letter writing: I have got up at this early hour to write letters, so I scribble you this before the din and noise of the day begins. I was sent for to Windsor yesterday where I was most graciously received. The Queen was looking so well, and was so very nice and sympathetic. I told her all sorts of amusing things about the Gold Coast that made her laugh: she thanked me warmly for what I had done etc etc. and said she was very anxious to see the Ashantee Force on friday next provided the doctors did not think the weather would injure the mens health – she is to give away Victoria Crosses to those whom I have recommended for them. I am longing to get away from this as I am afraid of the cold, so I want to get to a warm climate such as Italy as soon as possible and to stay there until we have summer weather in England.

I have lost all my goods and chattels in the great fire at the Pantechnicon[28] but although no money can compensate for my loss, still I am glad to say that the Govt. intend giving me some monied compensation. My best love to Matilda & Caroline[29] and always my darling mother believe me to be your devoted & dutiful son.

PS My best love to Aunt Wolseley. Loo is asleep – if awake I know that she would send you all her best love.

Hove, Wolseley MSS, 163/4/26i

168

Wolseley to the Earl of Carnarvon[30]

24 March
[Holograph]
Flemings Hotel
Half Moon St
London

I have the honor to report my arrival in this country on my return from the Gold Coast. I left Cape Coast Castle on the 4th instant and reached Liverpool [Portsmouth inserted by another hand as correction] on the 18th in the Steam Ship "Manitoban".

I have the honor to enclose a certificate relating to my pay as Governor of the Gold Coast Settlement.

As it will be convenient to me to close my account with the Crown Agents as soon as possible I should be much obliged if you would direct that orders should be issued for the payment of the balance of my salary to my Agents Messrs. Cox and Co. Craigs Court, Charing Cross who will apply to the Crown Agents for it.[31]

TNA, CO 96/114

169

Wolseley to Elcho

25 March
[Holograph]
Flemings Hotel,
Half Moon Street

I thank you most sincerely for your warm congratulations and good wishes. No pleasure in this world is ever nearly perfect, and in my case the satisfaction of feeling that people are contented with what we have done on the Gold Coast, is marred beyond description by a knowledge of the grief that the war has entailed upon the families of those who died at their posts there.

It is no humbug when I say that this feeling is ever present with me, and the very kindness of your letter makes it all the more intense.

I did not ever think that I should have to say that I "*feared*" to do anything that was right, but I confess that I shrank back from writing to you last November like a true coward. I many times sat down to write to you, but found it impossible to do so. What could I tell you? Who, than Lady Elcho and yourself knew as well the character and qualities of the gallant soldier you had lost, why therefore in the midst of your overwhelming sorrow should I intrude upon you repeating the sad news? As I think of him even now his handsome face, his gallant bearing and his soldierlike endurance of pain, suffering and hardship came before me, and I can judge from my own feelings what those of his parents must be. I was so glad that we had not to leave him behind in that accursed country. I had decreed that in any case I was killed or died near the shore, that I was to be buried at sea, and it was a sort of satisfaction to me that the remains of your poor dear son had found that same burial place.

I am sure it is needless for me to add how my heart sympathised with you and Lady Elcho in your sorrow for it was impossible that I should have failed to share in a feeling that was common to all, even to those who had no personal knowledge of him whom you had lost for ever.

I shall not send any messages to Lady Elcho, as I shrink from anything that might lead to reopen in her mind the recollection of her sorrow, especially as I know that she is now with dear Augustus Anson who cannot I hear, last much longer.

Gosford, Wemyss MSS, Drawer 39.

170

Wolseley to Alison

25 March
[Holograph]
Flemings Hotel,
Half Moon Street
Private

I think you may tell Capt. Despard[32] that owing to the manner in which you have reported upon him, that he may calculate upon his promotion with as great a certainty as any other officer late upon the Gold Coast.

I do hope most sincerely that your finger may soon be well.[33] It is surprising to me how you bore up against the suffering you endured during the march to Coomassie.

Bodleian, Alison MSS, MS. Eng. lett. c. 450

171

Wolseley to Alison

Wednesday morning [25 March]
[Holograph]
Flemings Hotel,
Half Moon Street

I was delighted to hear from Dormer[34] yesterday that you were quite well and that the sea voyage had completely set you up again. The doctors had spoken to me gloomily of your finger before you left, and I need scarcely say how delighted I was to hear that it is now well again.

I am not going to the Levée on Thursday, as I was told that it would not be the correct thing to do so, as Her Majesty urgently desired to see us all on Friday & to have the Senior Officer then presented to Her.

Bodleian, Alison MSS, MS. Eng. lett. c. 450

172

Wolseley to Frances Wolseley

30 March
[Holograph]
Windsor Castle

Here I am installed in this Royal Castle. I have just returned from the review, where I was made a great deal of. The Queen presented me with the Grand Cross of Michael & St George on parade also the Order of the K.C.B. I was offered the G.C.B but refused it, as I did [not] like giving offence to so many older officers who have deserved more than I did. I have also refused a Baronetcy, but I have accepted a pension, how much I do not know – much pressure has been put upon me to accept the baronetcy, but as it is now a reward reserved for common people – the Duke of Devonshires gardener[35] was lately made a baronet – I do not wish to have my name inscribed in the roll with such people. I am quite contented with what has been given me, and what I prize most is the gracious reception I have received from the Queen, whose manner is really perfect.

I am quite contented to wait until I next have the good fortune to command an army for the peerage that I was to have had, if there had not been any change of Governmt. The fact is I am absurdly rewarded as it is, but these tories were so rediculous in the manner in which they rewarded everyone after the bloodless campaign in Abyssinia, that now everyone expects to be promoted and to have distinctions showered upon them if they only do their duty.

As you may imagine my promotion to be a Majr. General and a pension suits me better than anything I could be given. We have had a very fine day for our parade and all has passed off well. Tomorrow I have to dine at the Mansion House and to make a great speech at the dinner, an ordeal that I dread very much.

My best love to Matilda & to Caroline & ever my dearest mother believe me to be your devoted and most dutiful son.

Hove, Wolseley MSS, 163/4/26ii

173

Wolseley's Speech at the Mansion House

[Printed]

31 March

May it please your Royal Highnesses, my Lord Mayor, my Lords, Ladies and Gentlemen, – Since my return to England I have had conferred upon me what I esteem, the greatest honour that can be awarded to a subject. I have received personally from Her Majesty the assurance that she has highly appreciated the manner in which her soldiers, sailors, and marines have performed their duty during the recent war on the Gold Coast. (Cheers.) This is an honour apart from all others, but among the many others I have had bestowed upon me so liberally there is none which I value more dearly than the privilege afforded me now of speaking in the name of that gallant little Army which has recently carried Her Majesty's standards from this country and planted them in the capital of the most powerful and most warlike of the nations in Western Africa. This honour, however, entails responsibility, a responsibility which I do not feel equal to, for I have always found that to a soldier it is far easier to act than to describe his actions afterwards, especially when called upon to do so, as I am at the present moment, in a standing position. (Cheers.) To dilate on the bravery of the troops engaged would be almost insulting when it is remembered that the Royal Welsh Fusiliers, the Black Watch, and the Rifle Brigade formed part of the Expeditionary Force, and that the Naval Brigade consisted of sailors and marines carefully selected from the Fleet serving on the station. When I make use of the term 'Naval Brigade' I wish it to be clearly understood that I refer both to the seamen and marines who composed it. To tell you that Her Majesty's soldiers and sailors fought well and bravely would be something like telling you that when the sun shines it is daylight, but I feel bound to remind you that at no previous period of our military history have British troops been called upon to vindicate their country's honour in so pestilential a climate. The hardships, privations, and exposure so cheerfully endured by all ranks would, under ordinary circumstances and in ordinary climates, be subjects to be remembered in after years only to be laughed at, but they remind us of fevers and of sickness which have left their mark indelibly upon many of us, and which during the progress of the war robbed us of gallant comrades, whose uncomplaining endurance can never be forgotten. (Hear, hear.)

I have no intention of wearying you by attempting to give you a history of the war. I am glad to see by the newspapers that its history is about to be written by an officer eminently qualified for the task, and I must refer all those who would wish for further particulars than I can promise to afford them this evening to its pages. The war was embarked upon most unwillingly by all. There can be no greater mistake than to imagine that it was accidental, or that it arose from any sudden freak of a barbarous and despotic Monarch.

I believe it to have been long planned, and that preparations for it had long been made. I have good reason for asserting that large stores of powder and munitions of war had been collected for several years previous to hostilities being commenced. It is well-understood Ashantee custom that each successive King should make his reign remarkable by some military exploit. The King who now rules in Ashantee had never had any previous opportunity for prosecuting any successful war. He had looked forward for a long time to the invasion of the Fantee territory as not only a feasible but a profitable operation. The unsuitableness of the climate for European troops was well known at Coomassie as it was to those doleful alarmists who inundated the newspapers of England with innumerable prognostications of disasters previous to our leaving that Coast. From time immemorial our military policy on the Coast of Africa had not been of a nature to impress a powerful and warlike nation with any high opinion of our military strength. This fact was encouraging to the enemy, and the King, who had been long seeking for what he considered to be a plausible cause of quarrel, thought he had found one in the cession of Elmina by the Dutch to the English nation. We had right and justice on our side; but such were the appalling accounts we had received from the Coast as to the heath of the few Marines who had been landed there, that it was thought desirable to seek for any other solution of the difficulty than by an appeal to arms. Although I received no positive instructions on the subject, I embarked fully impressed with the intention of avoiding war, if it was possible to do so, compatibly with honour.

Now, of all the Monarchs one has ever heard of – the man in the moon perhaps excepted – the King of Ashantee was the most difficult to get at. The only base of operations from which it was possible to act against him was about 4,000 miles from England. To land men or stores on that surf-bound coast was always difficult, oftentimes dangerous, and occasionally altogether impossible. As I have previously said, the climate was the worst in the world. We were told that no animals – not even asses (a laugh) – would live long there. All our beef and mutton had to be imported from abroad, and, in fact, I may say that all our stores had to be drawn from England. No draught animals would live there. There were no roads, and the few paths existing were unsuited for military operations. I have frequently been asked since my return home why I did not organise a land transport service. My answer is that even supposing I could have obtained the necessary carts and animals I should have required it would have been impossible for me in the short time available for military operations to construct a road that would have sustained the constant traffic either of pack animals or of carts over it. Although the engineers worked unremittingly and well, to have made a road of the required description was not within the bounds of possibility. Coomassie, that must have been, under any circumstances, the object we [the?] point to be arrived at, was known to be 140 or 150 miles from the seashore. The intervening space was known to be covered by a dense forest of lofty trees and tangled jungle; and the Fantees, from whom it was expected to obtain much assistance, were known to be as cowardly as the enemy were celebrated for their hardihood, bravery, and military discipline. I am sure it will amuse the ladies present to be informed that the Fantee women are far braver than the men. When I have read of the female army maintained by the King of Dahomey in former years, it afforded me much amusement; but I now appreciate the wisdom of that barbarous monarch in selecting women to be his soldiers.

No general ever embarked upon any military expedition more untrammelled by instructions than I was when I left England for Africa last September. I feel it incumbent on me therefore to express that whatever honour or success has been achieved under the war is to a great extent owing to the forethought of the military authorities in England who organised the expedition, and that I alone am responsible for any errors in execution that may have been discovered by the most critical of observers. The character of the expedition was novel as a military operation, and the organisation of the force was peculiar to itself. Owing to the gracious kindness of his Royal Highness the Field Marshal Commanding-in-Chief, I was allowed to select not only my own Staff, but the large number of officers that I considered necessary for the organisation of native levies. This concession having been acceded to me, it is perhaps unnecessary for me to add that I selected only those who I conceived to be the best officers for the work. A large proportion had passed through the Staff College; many were of tried ability in the field, and all were men whose zeal was only equalled by their military talents. I have to thank you, my Lord Mayor, for affording me this opportunity of expressing to his Royal Highness my grateful acknowledgement for his great kindness to me previous to my embarcation for the Gold Coast, and it affords me much pleasure to express to him, in the presence of this large and distinguished assembly, how much I am indebted to his Royal Highness for his numerous letters, containing valuable military advice and cheerful encouragement, that he sent me during the progress of the war.

Previous to our departure from England last autumn all the officers were engaged in collecting information regarding the history and topography of the country we were bound for. Although we had occupied forts on the coast for a very lengthened period, it was surprising how little was known regarding it. To this is attributable the fact that the English newspapers were led astray in their accounts of what was before us. The few men who had been previously to the coast, presuming on the little information their service there had afforded them, inundated the Press with doleful stories regarding the horrors of the climate and the general unsuitableness of the country for military operations. One daily paper terrified its readers by informing them that it was almost impossible to walk through the bush without treading at every step upon a snake and that pythons and boa-constrictors were to be seen hanging from every tree. (A laugh.) An officer whom I have great pleasure in seeing here this evening sought for information as to the kit he should take with him from one of the worst of these alarmists, and the answer he received was, 'My dear fellow, there is only one thing you will require to take with you, and that is your coffin.' (A laugh.) This same distinguished gentleman, when applied to officially for information as to the feasibility of using English troops in the interior, warned every one that to attempt such an operation was to court disaster. He also was pleased to state that it was impossible for English soldiers to march in such a climate, and that to take a thousand white men into the bush would require 6,000 black men to carry them. It was known out of the twelve months in the year that three were fit for military operations. Those months were January, February, and March. It was determined, therefore, in accordance with the recommendation of the highest medical authorities, that in the event of its becoming necessary to send out English troops for service there they should leave England so as to reach the Coast by the beginning of the year.

Before leaving England I made large demands for military stores of all descriptions, and I have great pleasure in stating that everything I demanded then and subsequently during the progress of the war was liberally supplied. Owing to the erroneous nature of the information I had obtained regarding the character of the country, I had been led to believe that the construction of a railway would have been a feasible operation. I therefore requested to be supplied with material for laying down 30 miles of railroad. I had not been, however, 48 hours on the Coast until I became aware that the construction of a railway was impossible in the limited time available for military operations. I have, therefore, to confess that I am responsible for the expense thus entailed upon the public. Shortly after my arrival at Cape Coast Castle I wrote home, requesting that I might be sent three English regiments, and they were despatched from Great Britain with a promptitude previously unknown in the history of our military administration. More than once during the progress of the first phase of the war I had longed for the assistance of British soldiers, for I felt at times, especially after the defeat of the enemy at Abrakrampa, by the gallant officer, Major Russell, whom I see opposite to me, that with their aid I should have been able to inflict a crushing blow upon the enemy before he could possibly recross into his own territory. This was a natural feeling for a British commander under the circumstances, but I was always well aware whatever troops I employed in the unhealthy months of November and December would so suffer from disease that I could not count upon their assistance for the subsequent advance upon Coomassie. In fact, if I had been able to use British troops during the first phase of the war I should have required two distinct English armies – one for the operations south of the Prah and the other for the invasion of the Ashantee kingdom.

I shall not weary you by any detailed account of the work of the civil departments of the army, but I cannot sit down without acknowledging the valuable services performed by medical officers of the expeditionary forces. (Cheers.) The arrangements made for the care of the sick and wounded were perfect, and the manner in which they were carried out by the whole medical department was beyond all praise. The military world has learnt many military lessons in recent years, but the most valuable to us as a nation that has been taught us by the Abyssinian and Ashantee Wars is that when you have to appoint an English General to command any military undertaking it is necessary to trust him; to supply him with all he asks for; and, above all things, to avoid the error committed during the New Zealand War of severing the military command from the diplomacy necessarily connected with the operations. (Hear, hear.) I have no hesitation in stating that had my operations been encumbered by the presence with me of a Civil Governor, or of an Ambassador authorised to give me orders I do not think I should ever have reached Coomassie.

Upon my arrival at Cape Coast Castle at the beginning of last October, I found it in a state of siege. A large Ashantee army threatened both it and Elmina; panic and demoralisation had seized upon all classes; the people from the surrounding districts had flooded into the towns on the Coast, where they soon suffered from disease, owing to their crowded condition; trade had almost ceased altogether, and a large proportion of the people depended upon the Government for their support. When I left Cape Coast Castle at the beginning of this month, I left there a prosperous population, enjoying the blessings of peace and the mercantile advantages attendant thereon. I found upon my arrival on the Coast the *prestige* of England at its lowest ebb, but before I departed I left our military fame firmly established on a secure base, consequent on the victories so gallantly won by the troops under my command. (Cheers.) My Lord Mayor, I have to thank you most sincerely for the manner in which you have alluded to me personally and to my military services, and I have to thank you, in the name of all ranks composing the expeditionary force, for the warm reception and the noble hospitality you have accorded to us this evening. (Renewed cheers.)

The Times, 1 April 1874

174

Wolseley to William Ewart Gladstone

2 April
[Holograph]
Flemings Hotel
Half Moon Street

My wife and I went to see Mr Benjamin[36] this morning and were presented by him with three handsome Sévres vases. I thanked him very much for it really seemed as if I was in some enchanted palace to have presents thus so very unexpectedly showered upon us, but I feel that our first thanks should be to you who were instrumental in having brought about an incident so very flattering to me.

Mr Benjamin is quite a character, and I really prize his present immensely for the manner it was bestowed as much as it is to be valued for its intrinsic worth.

Thanking you very much for all your kindness to me.

BL, Gladstone MSS, Add. MSS 44443, f. 123

175

Wolseley to Alison

13 April
[Holograph]
Venice

Your note of the 2nd instant with enclosure from Colonel Warren only reached me yesterday afternoon, hence the delay in replying to it.

Lt. Colonel Warren received the same reward that was given to the other officers commdg Battalions, including Colonel McLeod, and Lt. Colonel Webber 2nd W. I. Regt the latter officer having served on the coast during the war during much of what I may term the first and certainly the most disagreeable phase of it. I do not think that Colonel Warren can compare the work he has performed during the war to that done by either Colonel Wood or by Col. Colley.

In fact, Col. Warren has received the recognized reward that it has been the established custom in the Army to see given to the Officers Commdg Regts named in despatches. Promotion to the rank of Colonel is a very exceptional reward received for very peculiar cases of distinguished service rendered in the field.

Under these circumstances I do not feel justified in moving in the matter any further.

You do not say how your hand is but I trust that it [is] quite well again. The weather here is settled but by no means as warm as I would wish.

With kindest regards to Lady Alison in which my wife joins me.

Bodleian, Alison MSS, MS. Eng. lett. c. 450

176

Wolseley to Benjamin Disraeli

30 April
[Holograph]
2 St George's Place, Hyde Park Corner
Upon my return home yesterday evening, I read for the first time your speech in the House of Commons proposing the large grant so liberally bestowed upon me by the country.

I thank you very much for the flattering manner in which you there alluded to my military services and for the substantial manner in which they have been rewarded.

Bodleian, Dep. Hughenden MSS, 147/3 (B/XXI/W/504), ff. 234–5

177

Wolseley to Gladstone

1 May
[Holograph]
Flemings Hotel
Half Moon Street
Upon my return from the Continent I found yesterday a note from you dated the 22nd February that had been to the West Coast of Africa after I had left that place, and I presume upon your kindness to me since my arrival in England to thank you most sincerely for your letter and the many flattering things regarding myself contained in it. I have, during my military career had many rewards bestowed upon me, but indeed your expressions of approval at the manner in which I tried to do my duty at Cape Coast Castle, reward me in a degree far beyond any previously received distinction. A knowledge of the opinion you have formed of me, whilst acting as an incentive to further exertions on my part, will also I fear make me nervous lest I should at any time forfeit it. I shall always keep your letter and prize it as document to be handed down to those who come after me.

Hoping you will pardon my presumption in intruding upon you with this note all about myself.

BL, Gladstone MSS, Add. MSS 44443, f. 206

178

Wolseley to Major General H. G. Hart

26 October
[Holograph]
War Office
I am much obliged to you for your note, and on the other side of this page I have dotted down what I think should be inserted in the list of my services in your valuable Army List.

[Was Governor and Commander of the Forces on the Gold Coast during the Ashanti War of 1873.74: received the thanks of both houses of Parliament, promoted to be Major General for distinguished service, and nominated G.C.M.G. and K.C.B.]

TNA, Hart MSS, WO 211/71

179

Wolseley to Elcho

21 September 1875
[Holograph]
Private
The Lines, Mortlake

I start tomorrow evening, and as the absent are always wrong, I wish to place before you the following facts with reference to the promotion to which I believe Major Brackenbury is entitled. I am induced to do so because, I know that you take a great interest in him as all must do who know his worth and ability, and besides I wish to clear my own character of the untruth that I am forced to consider is now imputed to me when I told Major Brackenbury that H.R.H. had been good enough to promise him a Brevet Lt. Colonelcy for distinguished service whenever he obtained his Regimental Majority. I can assure you on my honor as a Gentleman, that that promise was conveyed to me in the most *distinct terms* by the officer then acting as Military Secretary,[37] and was confirmed by H.R.H. when I personally thanked him for his goodness in complying with my request in the matter.

Promotion is now withheld from Major Brackenbury on the grounds – 1st a denial of the promise, & 2nd that Major B. has incurred H.R.H.'s grave displeasure by publishing a written report made to me by Sir A. Alison during the battle of Ordahsu.

The first is nothing short of telling me that my word of honor is not to be believed, an accusation that the circumstances under which it is made – coming from the quarter it does – deprives me of all redress.

To the second I have merely to remark, that it is an *ex post facto* arrangement contrary to all principles of English practice, and that up to this present moment no communication has been addressed to Major Brackenbury conveying to him any expression of H.R.H.'s displeasure in this matter.

I shall never believe that this refusal to fulfil a promise made has emanated from H.R.H. and the conviction is unavoidably forced upon me that in this affair He has allowed His better judgement to be influenced by others. The result is sadly disappointing to me, as it shows me that no matter what others may think of my humble services, they are not much esteemed at the Horse Guards: indeed it would seem that it is determined to make me feel how small is my influence, by making me an exception to the rule of promoting the Military Secretary of any successful General Officer.

I am now about to start upon another most disagreeable and difficult service, and I am sorry that I have to confess to you that I shall leave England feeling that Major Brackenbury has been – to say the least – very harshly, and I myself very ungenerously dealt with in this affair.

I hope that should you ever hear the subject discussed that you will kindly state the facts as I have written them upon my authority, and I am vain enough to believe that others will give a credence to my word of honor that it does not seem to carry with it in high quarters at the Horse Guards.

NAS, Wemyss MSS, RH4/40/10

Appendix I

Military passengers on the *Ambriz*, September 1873[1]

Brevet Colonel (Temporary Major General) Sir Garnet Joseph Wolseley

Colonel John Carstairs McNeill VC, h.p., 48th Foot

Brevet Lieutenant Colonel Henry Evelyn Wood VC, 90th Foot

Major Thomas Durand Baker, *psc*, 18th Foot

Major Robert Home, *psc*, Royal Engineers

Brevet Major Baker Creed Russell, 13th Hussars

Captain Henry Brackenbury, Royal Artillery

Captain Charles James Bromhead, 24th Foot

Captain Redvers Henry Buller, 60th Rifles

Captain George Armand Furse, 42nd Foot

Captain Algernon Arbuthnot Godwin, 103rd Foot

Captain George Lightfoot Huyshe, Rifle Brigade (died, 19 January 1874)

Captain Hugh McCalmont, 7th Hussars

Captain Arthur John Rait, Royal Artillery

Lieutenant Henry Francis Somerset Bolton, 1st West India Regiment

Lieutenant the Hon. Alfred W. Charteris, Coldstream Guards (died, 23 November 1873)

Lieutenant William Toke Dooner, *psc*, 8th Foot

Lieutenant Arthur Hardolph Eyre, 90th Foot (killed, 4 February 1874)

Lieutenant Lord Gifford, 24th Foot

Lieutenant Robert William Thew Gordon, *psc*, 93rd Foot

Lieutenant James William Graves, 18th Foot

Lieutenant Arthur Fitzroy Hart, *psc*, 31st Foot

Lieutenant John Frederick Maurice, *psc*, Royal Artillery

Lieutenant Richard Oliffe Richmond, 50th Foot

Lieutenant Joshua Morris Saunders, Royal Artillery

Lieutenant Edward Hunter Townshend, 16th Foot (died, 29 December 1873)

Lieutenant Eardley Wilmot, Royal Artillery (killed, 3 November 1873)

Lieutenant Edward Robert Prevost Woodgate, 4th Foot

Acting Deputy Controller (Colonel) Matthew Bell Irvine, Control Department

Commissary (Major) Charles Davis O'Connor, Control Department

Commissary (Major) William Henry Ravenscroft, Control Department

Deputy Commissary (Captain) Robert Walsh, Control Department

Assistant Commissary (Lieutenant) Edwin Fitz-Stubbs, Control Department

Deputy Paymaster (Captain) Henry Potter, Control Department

Assistant Paymaster (Lieutenant) Charles Ward, Control Department

Surgeon Major (Major) Robert William Jackson, Army Medical Department

Surgeon (Captain) Charles Alfred Atkins, Army Medical Department

Appendix II

Glossary and gazetteer of persons, tribes and places

The various versions are those given in Wolseley's journal or correspondence. The modern title, where it can be identified, is in square parentheses.

Abamoo

Abonum

Abrah [Abura]

Abrakrampa; Abracampah [Abrakampa]

Accroful; Akroful [Akrofo]

Adansi [Adanse]

Addah [Adda]

Adjeampon; Adjiempong; Adjiempon [Akyampon Yaw]

Agemmamu [Agimmamu]

Ahkanknassi; Ahkanquassie [Ahkanknasie]

Ahoonas; Alroona; Alroonas; Alroonahs [Awuna]

Ahquansraimu

Akimfoo

Akrofumoo; Akrofoomu; Acrowfumu; Akrowfumu [Acrowfoomu]

Akukorbunnum Insue

Akyus; Akim [Akyem]

Amanquartier; Amanquatia [Amankwatia]

Amoaful [Amoafo]

Ampene [Ampinee]

Amponsi Quantah [Amponsie Quantah]

Anamaboe; Anamaboo [Anamabu]

Anoom [Anum]

Ansah [Ansa]

Apollonia [Appolonia]

Aquapim [Akwapim]

Ashantee; Ashantees; Ashanti; Ashantis [Asante]

Assanchi

Assayboo [Asebu]

Assin [Assin]

Atah Insu [Ata]

Atobiasi; Atobiassi

Bagora; Bagoro

Baraco; Barraco; Barroco [Beraku]

Battyan

Becqua; Becquah; Bequah [Bekwae]

Bernim

Beulah; Bulah

Bonny [Bonny]

Boosemprah; Bosumaprah [Bosempra]

Borborasi [Borborassie]

Coasu, Koosoos [Susu]

Cocoofee; Kokofoo [Kokofu]

Coffee; Coffee Calculi; Coffee Calcalli; Koffee [Kofi Kakari]

Commendah [Komenda]
Coomassie; Koomassie [Kumase]
Croboes [Krobos]
Damsamsue [Dansame]
Denkarau; Denkera; Denkiras; Denkerahs [Denkyira]
Detchiasu [Dechiasu]
Dix Cove; Dixcove [Dixcove]
Duabim; Fuabin; Juabim; Juabin [Dwaben]
Dunquah; Dungwah [Dunkwa]
Eduabin [Adjuabim; Adwabin]
Effotoo [Efutu]
Elmina [Elmina]
Escabio
Essaman [Esamano]
Faisoowaah; Faisuwah; Faysoo, Faysowah [Fesu]
Fantee; Fanti [Fante]
Fommanah [Fomena]
Fumusu
Gamacas [Marka]
Houssas [Hausa]
Inacodayo; Quacodayo
Inquabim
Insarfu [Insafu]
Janketty
Jooquah [Jukwa]
Kroos; Kroomen [Kru]
Mampon [Mampon]
Mansue [Manso]
Moinsey; Moinse [Moinsi]
Morree [Mouri]
Ordah, Dah [Oda]
Ordasu [Odaso]
Pong [Kpong]
Prah [Pra]
Prahsu; Prahsue [Praso]
Quarman [Kwaman]
Quisah [Kwisa]

Secondee [Sekondi]
Sherboro [Sherbro]
Sutah [Suta]
Swedru: Swaidroo [Swedru]
Wassaw [Wassa]
Whydah [Ouidah]
Winnebah; Winnebales [Winneba]
Yancoomassee [Nyankomase]
Yancoomassie Assin [Assin Nyankomase]
Yancoomassie Fantee [Fante Nyankomase]

Appendix III

Wolseley Asante letters not reproduced

Wolseley to Louisa Wolseley, 19 September 1873 (Hove, W/P 3/2)
Wolseley to Louisa Wolseley, 30 September 1873 (Hove, W/P 3/5)
Wolseley to Louisa Wolseley, 2 October 1873 (Hove, W/P 3/6)
Wolseley to Edmund Fremantle, 1 November 1873 (NMM, FR/109)
Wolseley to Louisa Wolseley, 7 November 1873 (Hove, W/P 3/12)
Wolseley to Louisa Wolseley, 27 November 1873 (Hove, W/P 3.15)
Wolseley to Louisa Wolseley, 15 January 1874 (Hove, W/P 4/4)
Wolseley to Louisa Wolseley, 19 January 1874 (Hove, W/P 4/5)
Wolseley to Augustus Anson, 5 April 1874 (Gosford, Wemyss MSS)

Appendix IV

Ships of the West Coast of Africa Division Squadron

The number given in square brackets is the ship's number in the Navy List.

HMS *Active* [5] (Captain William Nathan Hewett VC) [iron screw corvette, 10 guns]

HMS *Argus* [44] (Commander Percy Luxmore) [paddle-wheel sloop, 5 guns]

HMS *Barracouta* [57] (Captain Edmund Robert Fremantle) [paddle-wheel sloop, 6 guns]

HMS *Beacon* [60] (Commander Hamilton Dunlop) [double-screw gun vessel, 4 guns]

HMS *Bittern* [63] (Commander Prescot Stephens) [double-screw gun vessel, 3 guns]

HMS *Decoy* [610] (Lieutenant and Commander John Hext) [steam-screw-composite gun boat, 4 guns]

HMS *Druid* [160] (Captain William Hans Blake) [screw corvette, 10 guns]

HMS *Encounter* [175] (Captain Richard Bradshaw) [screw corvette, 14 guns]

HMS *Merlin* [655] (Lieutenant and Commander Edward Day) [screw-steam-composite gun boat]

HMS *Simoom* [452] (Captain Mountford Peile) [iron-screw troopship]

Appendix V

Biographical notes

Adu Bufo (*c.* 1818–83). *Gyassehene, c.* 1867–83.

Akyampon Yaw (*c.* 1855–73). *Debosohene.* Died of wounds, 1873.

Alison, Archibald (1826–1907). Brigadier General in Asante. Commissioned 72nd Foot, 1846. Service in Crimea; Mutiny (left arm amputated); Asante; Egypt, 1882. Military Secretary to Lord Clyde, 1857–58; Commandant, Staff College, 1877; Head of Intelligence Department, 1878–82; GOC, Highland Brigade, 1882; GOC, Egypt, 1882–83; GOC, Aldershot, 1883–89; Member of the Council of India, 1889–99. Succeeded to Baronetcy, 1867; KCB, 1874; GCB, 1887; General, 1889.

Amankwatia III (Amankwa Tenten) (*c.* 1832–74). *Bantamahene* and *Krontihene* (CinC) of the Asante Army, *c.* 1867–74. Much criticised as a drunkard. Killed at Amoafo.

Asamoa Nkwanta (*c.* 1839–75). *Anantahene* and experienced Asante general seen as the *srafokra* (guardian spirit) of the army. Loss of his 'war charm' in January 1873 seen as portent of the defeat against the British. Committed suicide during Asante's war against Dwaben, 1875. Seen by the British as the Asante 'Moltke'.

Baker, Thomas Durand (1837–93). Major and AAQMG in Asante. Commissioned 18th Foot, 1854. Service in Crimea; Mutiny; New Zealand, 1864–66; Asante; Afghanistan, 1879–80; Burma, 1886–87. Military Secretary to the Viceroy, 1878–79; GOC, 2nd Infantry Brigade, 1879–80; AG in India, 1884–88; GOC, Allahabad Division, 1887–90; QMG, 1890–93. KCB, 1881; Major General, 1886 (Temporary Lieutenant General, 1891).

Boyle, R. Frederick (1841–93). Correspondent of the *Daily Telegraph* in Asante. Traveller and writer. Author of *Adventures among the Dyaks of Borneo* (1865), *A Ride Across a Continent* (1868), *To the Cape for Diamonds* (1873) and *Camp Notes* (1874). Campaign account published as *Through Fanteeland to Coomassie* (1874).

Brackenbury, Henry (1837–1914). Captain and Assistant Military Secretary in Asante. Commissioned Royal Artillery, 1856. Service in Mutiny; Asante; South Africa, 1879; Sudan, 1884–85. Professor at RMA, 1868–70; Military Attaché, Paris, 1881–82; Director of Military Intelligence, 1886–91; Military Member, Viceroy's Council, 1891–96; President of the Ordnance Board, 1896–99; Director General of Ordnance, 1899–1904. KCB, 1894; KCSI, 1896; GCB, 1900; Lieutenant General, 1888. Semi-official campaign account published as *The Ashanti War: A Narrative* (1874).

Buller, Redvers Henry (1839–1908). Captain and DAAQMG in Asante; head of intelligence. Commissioned 60th Rifles, 1858. Service in China, 1860; Red River, 1870; Asante; South Africa, 1877–79 and 1881; Egypt, 1882; Sudan, 1884–85; South Africa, 1899–1900. DAAG, War Office, 1874–78; AAG, War Office, 1883–84; QMG, 1887–90; AG, 1890–97; GOC, Aldershot, 1898–99 and 1901; CinC, South Africa, 1899–1900. VC, 1879; KCMG, 1882; KCB, 1885; GCB, 1894; General, 1896.

Butler, William Francis (1838–1910). Captain and Special Service Officer in Asante. Commissioned, 69th Foot, 1858. Service in Red River, 1870; Asante; South Africa, 1875 and 1879; Egypt, 1882 and 1885–86; Sudan, 1884–85. GOC, Alexandria 1890–93; GOC, 2nd Infantry Brigade, 1893–96; GOC, South-Eastern District, 1896–98; GOC, South Africa, 1898–99; GOC, Western District, 1899–1905. KCB, 1886; GCB, 1906; Lieutenant General, 1900. Campaign account published as *Akim-Foo: The History of a Failure* (1876).

Cambridge, George William Frederick Charles, Duke of (1819–1904). CinC of the British Army in 1873–74. Cousin of Queen Victoria. Appointed to British Army as Brevet Colonel, 1837. Service in Crimea. Inspector General of Cavalry, 1852–54; CinC of the British Army, 1856–95; KG, 1835; KP, 1881; Field Marshal, 1862. Succeeded as 2nd Duke, 1850.

Cardwell, Edward (1813–86). Secretary of State for War in 1873–74. Liberal Conservative MP for Clitheroe, 1842–47 and for Liverpool, 1847–52; Liberal Conservative (to 1859) and Liberal MP for Oxford,

1853–74. Secretary of President of Board of Trade, 1852–55; Chief Secretary for Ireland, 1859–61; Chancellor of the Duchy of Lancaster, 1861–64; Secretary of State for the Colonies, 1864–66; Secretary of State for War, 1868–74. Created Viscount, 1874.

Charteris, The Hon. Alfred Walter (1847–73). Lieutenant, Coldstream Guards and ADC to Wolseley in Asante. Commissioned 71st Foot, 1869. Service in Asante. Son of Lord Elcho. Died of fever at sea en route to Ascension Island. Memorial tablet in Guards Chapel, Birdcage Walk (destroyed in 1944 by flying bomb).

Clarke, Andrew (1824–1902). Governor of the Straits Settlements in 1873–74. Commissioned, Royal Engineers, 1844. Service on Gold Coast, 1863–64. Surveyor-General of Victoria, 1853–58; Director of Works at Admiralty, 1864–73; Governor of the Straits Settlement, 1873–75; Member of the Viceroy's Council, 1875–80; Commandant, School of Military Engineering, 1881–82; Inspector General of Fortifications, 1882–86; Agent General of Victoria, 1897–1902. KCMG, 1873; GCMG, 1885; Honorary Lieutenant General, 1886.

Colley, George Pomeroy (1835–81). Brevet Lieutenant Colonel and Special Service Officer in Asante, responsible for reorganising the transport system. Commissioned 2nd Foot, 1852. Service in China, 1860; Asante; South Africa, 1879 and 1880–81. Professor at Staff College, 1871–73; Military and then Private Secretary to the Viceroy, 1876–80; GOC, Natal, 1880–81. KCSI, 1879; Major General, 1880. Killed at Majuba, 1881.

Commerell, John Edmund (1829–1901), Captain (RN) and Senior Naval Officer, Cape of Good Hope and West Coast of Africa in 1873. Entered Royal Navy, 1842. Service in Baltic and Black Sea, 1854–56; China, 1859; Ashanti. SNO, Cape of Good Hope and West Coast of Africa, 1871–73; CinC, North America, 1882–85; CinC, Portsmouth, 1888–89; Conservative MP for Southampton, 1885–88. VC, 1855; KCB, 1874; GCB, 1887; Admiral of the Fleet, 1892.

Disraeli, Benjamin (1804–81). Prime Minister in 1874. Conservative MP for Maidstone, 1837–41; Shrewsbury, 1841–47; Buckinghamshire, 1847–76. Chancellor of the Exchequer and Leader of the House of Commons, 1852–53, 1858–59 and 1866–67; Prime Minister, 1868 and 1874–80. Created Earl of Beaconsfield, 1876

Dooner, William Toke (1844–1926). Lieutenant and Special Service

Officer in Asante; attached to Russell's Regiment. Commissioned 8th Foot, 1863. Service in Asante. DAAG, Dublin, 1883–88; CO, 1st Royal Inniskilling Fusiliers, 1888–93; CO, 87th Regimental District, 1894–99; AAG, 1899–1902. Mayor of Rochester, 1905–6. Colonel, 1894. Campaign account published (as by 'An Officer') as *Jottings en route to Coomassie* (1874), re-issued as *To Coomassie and Back* (1895).

Earle, William (1833–85). Colonel, Grenadier Guards and Military Secretary to the Viceroy in 1873–74. Commissioned 49th Foot, 1851. Service in Crimea; Egypt, 1882; Sudan, 1884–85. Military Secretary to the CinC, North America, 1865–72; Military Secretary to the Viceroy, 1872–76; GOC, Alexandria, 1882–84. Major General, 1880. Killed at Kirbekan, 1885.

Festing, Francis Worgan (1833–86). Brevet Colonel commanding Royal Marine detachment in Asante. Commissioned Royal Marines, 1850. Service in Baltic and Black Sea, 1854–56; China, 1857–59; Asante. AAG, Royal Marines, 1876–79. KCMG, 1874; Colonel, 1886.

Fremantle, Edmund Robert (1836–1929). Captain (RN) and Senior Naval Officer, Cape of Good Hope and West Coast of Africa in 1873. Entered Royal Navy, 1849. Service in Burma, 1852; New Zealand, 1864–66; Asante. SNO, Cape of Good Hope and West Coast of Africa, 1873; CinC, East Indies Station, 1888–91; CinC, China Station, 1892–95; CinC, Devonport, 1896–99. KCB, 1889; GCB, 1899; GCVO, 1926; Admiral, 1896. Son of 1st Baron Cottesloe (but title created only in 1874).

Gifford, Edric Frederick, Lord (1849–1911). Lieutenant, 24th Foot and Special Service Officer in Asante. Commissioned 83rd Foot, 1869. Service in Asante; South Africa, 1879. Colonial Secretary, Western Australia, 1880–83; Colonial Secretary, Gibraltar, 1883–88. VC, 1874; Major, 1882. Succeeded as 3rd Baron, 1872.

Gladstone, William Ewart (1809–98). Prime Minister in 1873–74. Conservative MP for Newark, 1832, 1835, 1837, 1841–45; Liberal Conservative MP (to 1859) and Liberal MP for Oxford University, 1847–65; South Lancashire, 1865–68; Greenwich, 1868–80; Midlothian, 1880–95. President of Board of Trade, 1843–45; Secretary of State for War and the Colonies, 1845–46; Chancellor of the Exchequer, 1852–55, 1859–66; Prime Minister, 1868–74, 1880–85, 1886, 1892–94.

Glover, John Hawley (1829–85). Commander (RN) and Special
Commissioner to the Eastern Gold Coast in 1873–74. Entered Royal
Navy, 1841. Service in Burma, 1853; Baltic, 1854–56; Niger, 1857.
Transferred to Colonial Service, 1862. Administrator of Lagos, 1866–72;
Governor of Newfoundland, 1876–81 and 1883–85; Governor of the
Leeward Islands, 1881–83. Captain (RN), 1877; GCMG, 1874.

Goldsworthy, Roger Tuckfield (1839–1900). Deputy Commissioner to
Glover in 1873–74. Service in Mutiny with Havelock's Irregulars.
Commissioned 17th Lancers, 1859. Transferred to Colonial
Service, 1866. Inspector General of Police, Sierra Leone, 1868–70;
Commandant of Hausa Armed Police and District Magistrate, Lagos,
1870–73; Deputy Commissioner and Inspector of Customs, Gold
Coast, 1873–74; President of Nevis, 1876–77; Colonial Secretary,
Western Australia, 1877–80; Administrator of Sierra Leone, 1881–84;
Governor of British Honduras, 1884–91; Governor of the Falkland
Islands, 1891–97. KCMG, 1889.

Greaves, George Richard (1831–1922). Colonel and Chief of Staff in
Asante. Commissioned 70th Foot, 1849. Service in Mutiny; New
Zealand, 1860–66; Asante; Sudan, 1885. DAAG, War Office, 1870–73;
AAG, War Office, 1874–78; Administrator, Cyprus, 1879; AG in
India, 1879–84; GOC, Meerut Division, 1885–90; CinC, Bombay,
1890–96. KCB, 1885; GCB, 1896; General, 1896.

Harley, Robert William. Administrator, Gold Coast, 1872–73.
Commissioned 2nd West India Regiment, 1847. Service on Gold
Coast, 1863; Gambia, 1864; Yucatan, 1867. CO, 2nd WI Regiment,
1870–72; Governor, Honduras, 1871–72; Brevet Lieutenant Colonel,
1864.

Hart (Hart-Synnot from 1902), Arthur Fitzroy (1844–1910). Lieutenant
and Special Service Officer in Asante, serving with Russell's
Regiment. Commissioned 31st Foot, 1864. Service in Asante; South
Africa, 1879, 1881 and 1899–1902; Egypt, 1882. AAG, Belfast 1896;
GOC, 1st Infantry Brigade, 1897–99; GOC, 5th Infantry Brigade in
South Africa, 1899–1900. Major General, 1897.

Henty, George Alfred (1832–1900). Correspondent of *The
Standard* in Asante. Service in Army Commissariat Department,
1854–65 (including Crimea) reaching rank of Purveyor (Captain).
Correspondent of *The Standard*, 1865–76 covering the Abyssinian

expedition, 1867–68, Asante; the Spanish Civil War, 1875–76; and the Turco-Serbian War, 1876; Editor of *Union Jack*, 1880–83. Prolific children's novelist including *By Sheer Pluck: A Tale of the Ashanti War* (1897). Campaign account published as *The March to Coomassie* (1874).

Hewett, William Nathan Wrighte (1834–88). Commodore and Senior Naval Officer, Cape of Good Hope and West Coast of Africa in 1873–74. Entered Royal Navy, 1847. Service in Burma, 1852–53; Crimea; Asante; Sudan, 1884. SNO, Cape of Good Hope and West Coast of Africa, 1873–76; CinC, East Indies Station, 1882–84; CinC, Channel Fleet, 1886–88. VC, 1854; KCB, 1874; KCSI, 1883; Vice Admiral, 1884.

Home, Dr Anthony Dickson (1826–1914). Surgeon Major, Army Medical Department and Principal Medical Officer in Asante. Appointed to Army Medical Department, 1848. Service in Crimea; Mutiny; China, 1860; New Zealand, 1863–65; Asante. Principal Medical Officer to the Forces in India, 1881–85; Principal Medical Officer, Southern District, 1885–86. VC, 1857; KCB, 1874; Surgeon General, 1880.

Home, Robert (1837–79) Major and Commanding Royal Engineer in Asante. Commissioned Royal Engineers 1856. Service in Asante. Served with Intelligence Branch, War Office, 1871–79, latterly as AQMG, 1876–79. British Commissioner on Bulgarian Frontier Delineation Committee, 1878–79. Died of typhoid fever contracted in Bulgaria.

Huyshe, George Lightfoot (1839–74). Captain and DAAQMG in Asante. Commissioned 83rd Foot, 1856. Service in Mutiny, Red River, 1870; Asante. Historian of the Red River campaign. Died of fever at Praso.

Kimberley, John Wodehouse, Earl of (1826–1902). Secretary of State for the Colonies in 1873–74. Minister Plenipotentiary to St Petersburg, 1856–58; Lord Lieutenant of Ireland, 1864–66; Lord Privy Seal, 1868–70; Secretary of State for the Colonies, 1870–74 and 1880–88; Secretary of State for India, 1882–85, 1886, 1892–94; Foreign Secretary, 1894–95. Succeeded as Baron Wodehouse, 1846; created 1st Earl of Kimberley, 1866; KG, 1885.

Kofi Kakari (*c.* 1837–84). *Asantehene* (King) of the Asante, 1867–74. Elected, May 1867; destooled, October 1874. Murdered by rivals, 1884.

McCalmont, Hugh (1845–1924). Captain, 7th Hussars and ADC to
Wolseley in Asante until invalided. Commissioned 9th Lancers, 1865.
Service in Red River, 1870; Asante; South Africa, 1879–80 and
1881–82; Afghanistan, 1880; Egypt, 1882 and 1888; Sudan, 1884–85.
Military Attaché at Constantinople, 1877–78; GOC, Cork, 1898–1903.
MP for North Antrim, 1895–99. KCB, 1900; Major General, 1896.

McCarthy, Charles (1764–1824). Born Charles Guéroult; adopted
mother's maiden name. Commissioned 5th Regiment, Irish Brigade,
1794. Lieutenant Colonel, Royal African Corps, 1811, Colonel, 1821.
Service in Flanders, West Indies and Spain. Governor, Senegal and
Gorée, 1812–14; Governor of Sierra Leone and Cape Coast, 1814–24.
KCMG, 1820. Killed, 1824.

Maclean, George (1801–47). President of the Council of the Merchants
Committee at Cape Coast and self-styled Governor of the Gold
Coast, 1830–36, 1838–43. Commissioned 27th Foot, 1817. Retired
from army, 1821. Lieutenant, Royal African Colonial Corps, 1826–30.
Judicial Assessor, Gold Coast, 1843–47.

McLeod, John Chetham (1831–1914), Lieutenant Colonel commanding
42nd Foot in Asante. Commissioned 42nd Foot, 1846. Service in
Crimea; Mutiny; Asante. GOC, Ceylon, 1882–87. KCB, 1874; GCB,
1891; Lieutenant General, 1888.

McNeill, John Carstairs (1831–1904). Colonel, 48th Foot and Chief of
Staff in Asante until wounded at Esamano. Commissioned 12th Bengal
Native Infantry, 1850. Service in Mutiny; New Zealand, 1861–65;
Asante; Egypt, 1882; Sudan, 1885. Military Secretary to the Governor
General of Canada, 1869–72; Equerry to Queen Victoria, 1874–1901.
VC, 1864; KCMG, 1880; KCB, 1882; Major General, 1882.

Maurice, John Frederick (1841–1912), Lieutenant and Special Service
Officer in Asante; Private Secretary to Wolseley. Commissioned Royal
Artillery, 1861. Service in Asante; South Africa, 1879–80; Egypt,
1882; Sudan, 1884–85. Instructor at RMC Sandhurst, 1872–73;
Professor at Staff College, 1885–92. KCB, 1900; Major General,
1895. Campaign account published (as by the 'Daily News' Special
Correspondent) as *The Ashantee War: A Popular Narrative* (1874).

Methuen, The Hon. Paul Sanford (1845–1932). Captain and
Special Service Officer in Asante, serving in Wood's Regiment.
Commissioned Scots Fusilier Guards, 1864. Service in Asante; Egypt,

1882; Bechuanaland, 1884–85; Tirah, 1897; South Africa, 1899–1902.
Military Attaché, Berlin, 1878–81; DAG, South Africa, 1888–90;
GOC, Home District, 1892–97; GOC, 1st Division in South Africa,
1899–1900; GOC, Eastern Command, 1903–08; GOC, South Africa,
1908–12; Governor of Natal, 1910; GOC, Malta, 1915–19. KCVO,
1897; KCB, 1900; GCB, 1902; GCVO, 1910; GCMG, 1919; Field
Marshal, 1911. Succeeded as 3rd Baron Methuen, 1891.

Paget, Arthur Henry Fitzroy (1851–1928). Captain and Special Service
Officer in Asante. Commissioned Scots Fusilier Guards, 1869. Service
in Asante; Sudan, 1884 and 1888–89; Burma, 1887–88; South Africa,
1899–1900. GOC 20th Infantry Brigade, 1899–1901; GOC, 1st
Division, 1902–06; GOC, Eastern Command, 1908–11; CinC, Ireland,
1911–14. KCVO, 1906; KCB, 1907; Lieutenant General, 1906.

Pope Hennessy, John (1834–91). Governor of the Bahamas in 1873–74.
Governor of Labuan (Borneo), 1867–71; Governor in Chief of the
West African Settlements, 1872–73; Governor, Bahamas, 1873–74;
Governor, Windward Islands, 1875–76; Governor, Hong Kong,
1876–82; Governor, Mauritius, 1882–89. MP for King's County,
1859–65; for North Kilkenny, 1890–91. KCMG, 1880.

Prior, Melton (1845–1910). Artist of the *Illustrated London News* in
Asante. Worked for *ILN* from 1868 to 1904 and claimed to have
covered 26 wars, the first being that in Asante. Wars covered included
South Africa, 1878–79 and 1900–2; Egypt, 1882; Sudan, 1883 and
1884; Burma, 1887; Rhodesia, 1896; North-West Frontier, 1897; and
Somaliland, 1903.

Rait, Arthur John (1839–1902). Captain and Special Service Officer in
Asante, commanding 'Rait's Artillery'. Commissioned Royal Artillery,
1857. Service in India, 1859; New Zealand, 1863–64; Asante.
Lieutenant Colonel, 1877.

Reade, William Winwood (1838–75). Correspondent of *The Times* in
Asante. Traveller in West Africa, 1861–63 and 1868. Novelist, traveller
and writer, best known for *Savage Africa* (1863), *The Martyrdom of
Man* (1872) and *The African Sketch Book* (1873). Campaign account
published as *The Story of the Ashantee Campaign* (1874).

Russell, Baker Creed (1837–1911). Brevet Major, 13th Hussars and
Special Service Officer in Asante, commanding 'Russell's Regiment'.
Commissioned 6th Dragoon Guards, 1855. Service in Mutiny;

Asante; South Africa, 1879; and Egypt, 1882. GOC, Aldershot
Cavalry Brigade, 1890–94; GOC North-Western District, 1895–96;
GOC, Southern Command, 1898–1904. KCMG, 1879; KCB, 1882;
GCB, 1900; Major General, 1889.

Stanley, Henry Morton (1841–1904). Correspondent of the *New York
Herald* in Asante. Born in Wales, the illegitimate son of John Rowlands
and baptised as John Rowlands, taking the name of Stanley from a
benefactor who employed him soon after his arrival in the United
States in 1858. Service in Confederate Army, 1861–62 and Union
Navy, 1864–65. Correspondent for *Missouri Democrat*, 1865–67; for
New York Herald, 1867–78, including Abyssinian campaign, 1867–68
and Asante. 'Discoverer' of Livingstone, 1872; leader of Trans-Africa
Expedition, 1874–77; explorer of the Congo, 1879–84; leader of Emin
Pasha Relief Expedition, 1886–90. Re-naturalised as British subject,
1892; KCB, 1899. Campaign account published as *Coomassie and
Magdala: The Story of Two British Campaigns in Africa* (1874).

Victoria (1819–1901). Queen of the United Kingdom of Great Britain
and Northern Ireland, 1837–1901; Empress of India, 1877–1901.

Wauchope, Andrew Gilbert (1846–99). Lieutenant and Special Service
Officer in Asante; served with Russell's Regiment. Entered Royal
Navy, 1860; Commissioned 42nd Foot, 1865. Service in Asante;
Egypt, 1882; Sudan, 1884–85 and 1898; South Africa, 1881 and 1899.
GOC, 1st Brigade, 1898; GOC, Highland Brigade, 1899. Contested
the Midlothian seat against Gladstone in 1892. Major General, 1899.
Killed at Magersfontein, 1899.

Wolseley, Garnet Joseph (1833–1913). (Temporary) Major General
Commanding in Asante. Commissioned 12th Foot, 1852. Service in
Burma, 1852–53; Crimea; Mutiny; China, 1860; Red River, 1870;
Asante; South Africa, 1879–80; Egypt, 1882; Sudan, 1884–85. Governor,
Natal, 1875; High Commissioner, Cyprus, 1878–79; High Commissioner
in South Eastern Africa and Governor of Natal and the Transvaal,
1879–80; QMG, 1880–82; AG 1882–90; GOC, Ireland, 1890–95; CinC,
British Army, 1895–1900. KCMG, 1870; KCB, 1874; GCMG, 1874;
GCB, 1879; KP, 1885; Viscount, 1885; Field Marshal, 1894.

Wolseley, Louisa (née Erskine) (1843–1920). Illegitimate and brought
up as the niece and ward of Alexander Holmes, almost certainly her
natural father. Married Wolseley in June 1868.

Wolseley, Richard (1835–87). Surgeon and Major, Army Medical Department in 1873–74 attached to 2/5th Foot at Kilkenny. Commissioned Army Medical Department, 1854. Service in Crimea with 20th Foot. Deputy Surgeon General, 1883. Died as a result of a fall from his horse at Meerut, January 1887.

Wood, Henry Evelyn (1838–1919). Brevet Lieutenant Colonel, 90th Foot and Special Service Officer in Asante, commanding 'Wood's Regiment'. Entered Royal Navy, 1852; Commissioned 13th Light Dragoons, 1855. Service in Crimea; Mutiny; Asante; South Africa, 1877–79 and 1880–1; Egypt, 1882; Sudan, 1884–85. Sirdar, 1882–85, GOC, Eastern District, 1886–88; GOC, Aldershot, 1889–93; QMG, 1893–97; AG, 1897–1901; GOC, II Corps, 1901–05. VC, 1859; KCB, 1879; GCB, 1890; Field Marshal, 1903.

Woodgate, Edward Robert Prevost (1845–1900), Lieutenant and Special Service Officer in Asante. Commissioned 4th Foot, 1865. Service in Abyssinia, 1867–68; Asante; South Africa, 1879 and 1899–1900; Sierra Leone, 1898. GOC, 17th Regimental District, 1899; GOC, Lancashire Brigade, 1899–1900. KCMG, 1899; (Local) Major General, 1899. Mortally wounded at Spion Kop, 1900.

Notes

Notes to Introduction

1   Philip Curtin, *Disease and Empire: The Health of European Troops and the Conquest of Africa* (Cambridge: Cambridge University Press, 1998), p. 49.

2   Purchase, by which most but not all commissions in the infantry and cavalry could be obtained, had existed since the reign of Charles II though the most obvious abuses had been weeded out by the mid-nineteenth century. Sir Robert Biddulph, *Lord Cardwell at the War Office: A History of his Administration, 1868–74* (London: John Murray, 1904), p. 224. For the Cardwell reforms generally, see Edward Spiers, *The Late Victorian Army, 1868–1902* (Manchester: Manchester University Press, 1992), pp. 1–28; idem, *The Army and Society, 1815–1914* (London: Longman, 1980), pp. 177–205; A. V. Tucker, 'Army and Society in England, 1870–1900: A Reassessment of the Cardwell Reforms', *Journal of British Studies* 2 (1963), pp. 110–41; Brian Bond, 'The Effect of the Cardwell Reforms on Army Organisation, 1874–1904', *Journal of the Royal United Services Institution for Defence Studies* 105 (1960), pp. 515–24; Anthony Bruce, 'Edward Cardwell and the Abolition of Purchase', in Ian Beckett and John Gooch, eds, *Politicians and Defence: Studies in the Formulation of British Defence Policy, 1846–1970* (Manchester: Manchester University Press, 1981), pp. 24–46; T. F. Gallagher, 'Cardwellian Mysteries: The Fate of the British Army Regulation Bill, 1871', *Historical Journal* 18, 2 (1975), pp. 327–48.

3   Hew Strachan, *European Armies and the Conduct of War* (London: Allen & Unwin, 1983), p. 78; Curtin, *Disease and Empire*, p. 73.

444

4   Charles Rathbone Low, *General Lord Wolseley of Cairo*, 2nd edn (London: Richard Bentley & Son, 1883), p. 240.

5   J. E. Condua-Harley, *Sagrenti War: An Illustrated History of the Ashanti Campaign, 1873–74* (London: privately published, 1974), p. 7.

6   By the time *Pirates* was first performed, Wolseley had become a lieutenant general, his promotion dating from 25 March 1878. The first performances for copyright purposes took place at Paignton's Royal Bijou Theatre on 30 December 1879 and New York's Fifth Avenue Theatre on 31 December 1879, and the first performance on the London stage at the Opéra Comique on 3 April 1880.

7   T. C. McCaskie, 'Cultural Encounters: Britain and Africa in the Nineteenth Century', in Andrew Porter, ed., *The Oxford History of the British Empire: The Nineteenth Century* (Oxford: Oxford University Press, 1999), pp. 644–89 at p. 676.

8   W. D. McIntyre, *The Imperial Frontier in the Tropics, 1865–75* (London: Macmillan, 1967), p. 81.

9   Idem, 'British Policy in West Africa: The Ashanti Expedition of 1873–74', *Historical Journal* 5, 1 (1962), pp. 19–46.

10 An account of the history of Cape Coast Castle prior to 1807, intended for general readers, can be found in William St Clair, *The Grand Slave Emporium* (London: Profile Books, 2006).

11 A. G. Hopkins, 'Asante and the Victorians: Transition and Partition on the Gold Coast', in Roy Bridges, ed., *Imperialism, Decolonisation and Africa* (Basingstoke: Macmillan, 2000), pp. 25–64; Ivor Wilks, *Asante in the Nineteenth Century: The Structure and Evolution of a Political Order* (Cambridge: Cambridge University Press, 1975), pp. 8–13, 73, 80–2; idem, *Forests of Gold: Essays on the Akan and the Kingdom of Asante* (Athens, OH: Ohio University Press, 1993), pp. 41–2, 119, 129, 156, 170, 191–5; T. C. McCaskie, *State and Society in Pre-colonial Asante* (Cambridge: Cambridge University Press, 1995), pp. 10, 14, 39, 334 n. 33, 343 n. 60.

12 A. Adu Boahen, 'Asante and Fante, AD 1000–1800', and idem, 'Asante, Fante and the British, 1800–80', both in J. F. Ade Ajayi and Ian Espie, eds, *A Thousand Years of West African History* (Ibadan: Ibadan University Press, 1965), pp. 165–90, 346–63.

13 Two accounts of the Asante relationship with the British and the three main Asante Wars of 1824–26, 1873–74 and 1895–1900 intended

for a general readership can be found in Alan Lloyd, *The Drums of Kumasi: The Story of the Ashanti Wars* (London: Longmans Green & C, 1964), and Robert Edgerton, *The Fall of the Asante Empire* (New York: Free Press, 1995).

14 For the Bowdich and Dupuis missions, see Thomas Edward Bowdich, *A Mission from Cape Coast Castle to Ashantee* (London: John Murray, 1819); Joseph Dupuis, *Journal of a Residence in Ashantee*, 2nd edn (London: Frank Cass, 1966).

15 John Keegan, 'The Ashanti Campaign, 1873–74', in Brian Bond, ed., *Victorian Military Campaigns* (London: Hutchinson, 1967), pp. 161–98 at p. 171.

16 Wilks, *Asante*, p. 73.

17 The fullest account of the ceremonies, and the part of skulls such as McCarthy's in it, can be found in McCaskie, *State and Society*, pp. 144–66, 199–242.

18 The 1831 treaty is reproduced fully in J. J. Crooks, *Records Relating to the Gold Coast Settlements from 1750 to 1874* (Dublin: Browne & Nolan, 1923), pp. 262–4; and partially in G. W. Newbury, *British Policy towards West Africa: Select Documents, 1786–1874* (Oxford: Clarendon Press, 1965), pp. 293–4.

19 Douglas Coombs, *The Gold Coast, Britain and the Netherlands, 1850–74* (London and Ibadan: Oxford University Press, 1963), p. 8; Joseph Adjaye, *Diplomacy and Diplomats in Nineteenth Century Asante* (Trenton, NJ: Africa World Press, 1996), pp. 200–1.

20 Crooks, *Records*, pp. 320–2.

21 McIntyre, 'British Policy', p. 20; BPP, XLVI, 1874, Cmd. 941, *Return of Revenue and Expenditure, and Imports and Exports of the British Possessions in West Africa for Twenty Years*, p. 3.

22 G. L. Huyshe, 'The Topography of Ashanti and the Protectorate of the Gold Coast', in Henry Brackenbury and George Huyshe, *Fanti and Ashanti* (Edinburgh: William Blackwood & Sons, 1873), pp. 91–131 at p. 100.

23 C. C. Eldridge, 'Newcastle and the Ashanti War of 1863–84: A Failure of the Policy of Anti-imperialism', *Renaissance and Modern Studies* 12 (1968), pp. 68–90; G. E. Metcalfe, *Great Britain and Ghana: Documents of Ghana History, 1807–1957* (London: Thomas Nelson & Sons, 1964), pp. 291–301.

24 Crooks, *Records*, pp. 369–70; Newbury, *British Policy*, pp. 529–30.

25 J. D. Hargreaves, *Prelude to the Partition of West Africa* (London: Macmillan, 1963), pp. 136–95; W. D. McIntyre, 'Commander Glover and the Colony of Lagos, 1861–73', *Journal of African History* 4 (1963), pp. 57–79; idem, *Imperial Frontier*, pp. 112–16.

26 Coombs, *Gold Coast, Britain and Netherlands*, pp. 8–9.

27 See F. A. Ramseyer and J. Kühne, *Four Years in Ashantee* (London: James Nisbet & Co., 1875); A. Jones, 'Four Years in Ashantee: One Source or Several?' *History in Africa* 18 (1991), pp. 173–203; Claude-Hélène Perrot and Albert von Dantzig, eds, *Marie-Joseph Bonnat et les Ashanti: Journal, 1869–74* (Paris: Musée de l'Homme and Société des Africanistes, 1994).

28 McIntyre, *Imperial Frontier*, p. 126.

29 Coombs, *Gold Coast, Britain and Netherlands*, pp. 82, 98–108; Crooks, *Records*, pp. 400–1.

30 McIntyre, *Imperial Frontier*, p. 132; Coombs, *Gold Coast, Britain and Netherlands*, pp. 123–7.

31 Coombs, *Gold Coast, Britain and Netherlands*, p. 125.

32 Ethel Drus, ed., *A Journal of Events during the Gladstone Ministry, 1868–74 by John, First Earl of Kimberley* (London: Royal Historical Society, 1958: Camden Miscellany, 3rd series, XXI), p. 42; James Pope Hennessy, *Verandah: Some Episodes in the Crown Colonies, 1867–89* (London: George Allen & Unwin, 1964), p. 145; Hargreaves, *Prelude to Partition*, p. 168.

33 Wilks, *Asante*, p. 682; idem, *Forests of Gold*, p. 271; R. Frederick Boyle, *Through Fanteeland to Coomassie* (London: Chapman and Hall, 1874), p. 319; Henry Brackenbury, *The Ashanti War: A Narrative*, 2 vols (Edinburgh and London: William Blackwood & Sons, 1874), II, pp. 154, 332; Henry Morton Stanley, *Coomassie and Magdala* (New York: Harper, 1874), p. 200.

34 Wilks, *Asante*, pp. 175–89, 477–548, 666, 680–8; Bruce Vandervort, *Wars of Imperial Conquest in Africa, 1830–1914* (London: UCL Press, 1998), p. 86; Hopkins, 'Asante and the Victorians', pp. 25–64.

35 Wilks, *Asante*, pp. 387–8, 477–83, 495–509, 674–9; McCaskie, *State and Society*, pp. 189–98, 417 n. 171; idem, 'Death and the Asantehene: A Historical Meditation', *Journal of African History* 30, 3 (1989), pp. 417–44; David Kimble, *A Political History of Ghana*,

1850–1928 (Oxford: Clarendon Press, 1963), pp. 265–7; Agnes Aidoo, 'Order and Conflict in the Asante Empire: A Study in Interest Group Relations', *African Studies Review* 20, 1 (1977), pp. 1–36; W. W. Claridge, *A History of the Gold Coast and Ashanti*, 2 vols (London: John Murray, 1915), II, pp. 555–6.

36 Newbury, *British Policy*, p. 604.

37 TNA, WO 32/826, Minutes of WO conference, 10 May 1873.

38 TNA, CO 96/107, Minute by Kimberley, 28 May 1873.

39 Admiral Sir Edmund Fremantle, *The Navy As I Have Known It, 1849–99* (London: Cassell, 1904), pp. 194–7; Drus, *Journal of Events*, p. 40.

40 McIntyre, 'British Policy', p. 23.

41 TNA, Cardwell MSS, PRO 30/48/5/33, Kimberley to Cardwell, 30 July 1873.

42 Lady Glover, *Life of Sir John Hawley Glover*, ed. by Sir Richard Temple (London: Smith, Elder & Co, 1897), pp. 150–1; CUL, Glover MSS, RCMS 131/6, Account by Glover, n.d.; NMM, Fremantle MSS, FRE/109, Milne to Fremantle, 23 Sept. 1873. In 1875 Glover was still trying to obtain a copy of the minutes of the meeting of 29 July 1873, at which he had outlined his original proposals, since no copy appeared to have survived in either the War Office or the Colonial Office. See Bodleian, Kimberley MSS, Ms. Eng. c. 4470, Glover to Kimberley, 25 Oct. 1875.

43 Glover, *Life*, pp. 151–4; McIntyre, 'British Policy', p. 32; Angus Hawkins and John Powell, eds, *The Journal of John Wodehouse, First Earl of Kimberley, 1862–1902* (London: Royal Historical Society, 1997: Camden 5th series, IX), p. 281.

44 RA, VIC/MAIN F6/17 and 19, Cardwell to Ponsonby, 31 Aug. 1873, and Kimberley to Ponsonby, 5 Sept. 1873.

45 Glover, *Life*, pp. 154–5; McIntyre, 'British Policy', p. 31; TNA, Cardwell MSS, PRO 30/48/5/33, Cardwell to Kimberley, 1 Aug. 1873; BL, Gladstone MSS, Add. MSS 44120, Cardwell to Gladstone, 3 Sept. 1873.

46 Field Marshal Viscount Wolseley, *The Story of a Soldier's Life*, 2 vols (London: Archibald Constable & Co, 1903), II, p. 268; Duke, Wolseley MSS, XVIII-H, Wolseley to Fleetwood-Wilson, 22 Sept. 1902.

47 Hawkins and Powell, *Journal of Kimberley*, p. 282; McIntyre, 'British Policy', pp. 33–4; idem, *Imperial Frontier*, pp. 97–9; Drus, *Journal of Events*, p. 42; R. H. Vetch, *Life of Lieutenant-General the Hon. Sir Andrew Clarke* (London: John Murray, 1905), p. 115; Major General Sir Archibald Anson, *About Others and Myself* (London: John Murray, 1920), p. 324.

48 McIntyre, *Imperial Frontier*, p. 143; John Pollock, *Gordon: The Man Behind the Legend* (Oxford: Lion Publishing, 1993), pp. 131–2. According to Frederic Villiers, fellow war correspondent Archibald Forbes had some impact in advocating Wolseley's appointment over that of Gordon in the pages of *The Daily News*: see Frederic Villiers, *Peaceful Personalities and Warriors Bold* (London: Harper & Brothers, 1907), pp. 251–2.

49 BPP, XLVI, 1874, Cmd. 891, *Further Correspondence respecting the Ashantee Invasion* No 2, pp. 150–1, 186–7, 209; Richard Brooks, *The Long Arm of Empire: Naval Brigades from the Crimea to the Boxer Rebellion* (London: Constable, 1999), pp. 118–20.

50 Hawkins and Powell, *Journal of Kimberley*, p. 282; Drus, *Journal of Events*, p. 42; TNA, Cardwell MSS, PRO 30/48/33, Cardwell to Kimberley, 9 Aug. 1873. John Jarvis Bisset had been commissioned in the 68th Foot in 1840. Service in South Africa, 1835–36, 1842, 1846–47 and 1850–52. General, 1877; KCMG, 1877.

51 NMM, Fremantle MSS, FRE/105, Fremantle to Blake, 29 Aug. 1873; TNA, CO 96/102, Minutes of Meeting of Gold Coast Council, 12 Sept. 1873 (also in TNA, ADM 201/39); Crooks, *Records*, pp. 453–4; Fremantle, *Navy As I Have Known It*, pp. 192, 205, 212–13.

52 BL, Gladstone MSS, Add. MSS 44225, Kimberley to Gladstone, 18 Aug. 1873; Coombs, *Gold Coast, Britain and Netherlands*, pp. 132–4.

53 Hawkins and Powell, *Journal of Kimberley*, p. 282; H. C. G. Matthew, ed., *The Gladstone Diaries: VIII, 1871–74* (Oxford: Clarendon Press, 1982), pp. 364–5, 372, 391–2; R. A. J. Walling, ed., *The Diaries of John Bright* (London: Cassell, 1930), pp. 357–8; McIntyre, 'British Policy', pp. 36–7, 45.

54 Winwood Reade, *The Story of the Ashantee Campaign* (London: Smith, Elder & Co, 1874), p. 146.

55 The Marquis of Zetland, ed., *The Letters of Disraeli to Lady Bradford and Lady Chesterfield*, 2 vols (London: Ernest Benn, 1929), I, p. 65;

William Moneypenny and G. E. Buckle, eds, *The Life of Benjamin Disraeli, Earl of Beaconsfield*, 6 vols (New York: Macmillan, 1920), II, p. 645; G. E. Buckle, ed., *The Letters of Queen Victoria: A Selection from Her Majesty's Correspondence and Journal, 1862–78*, 2nd series, 3 vols (London: John Murray, 1926–28), II, p. 331; General Sir George Greaves, *Memoirs* (London: John Murray, 1924), p. 121.

56 The principal biographies of Wolseley are the hagiographical Sir Frederick Maurice and Sir George Arthur, *The Life of Lord Wolseley* (London: William Heinemann Ltd, 1924); the now outdated Joseph Lehmann, *All Sir Garnet: A Life of Field Marshal Lord Wolseley, 1833–1913* (London: Jonathan Cape, 1964); and, most recently, Halik Kochanski, *Sir Garnet Wolseley: Victorian Hero* (London: Hambledon Press, 1999), based upon her unpublished PhD thesis, 'Sir Garnet Wolseley and the Reform of the British Army, 1870–99' (University of London, 1996). Wolseley's own two-volume autobiography, *The Story of a Soldier's Life*, carried his career only to 1874.

57 See James A. Rawley, ed., *The American Civil War: An English View by Field Marshal Viscount Wolseley* (Charlottesville, VA: University Press of Virginia, 1964).

58 J. M. Bumsted, *The Red River Rebellion* (Winnipeg: Watson & Dyer, 1996), pp. 192–220.

59 G. L. Huyshe, *The Red River Expedition* (London: Macmillan, 1871). See also G. L. Huyshe, 'The Red River Expedition', *Journal of the Royal United Service Institution* 15, 52 (1872), pp. 70–85.

60 The War Office had been located at the Horse Guards building in Whitehall from 1683 until 1858, at which point it had moved to various buildings in Pall Mall. The office of the army's CinC, however, remained at Horse Guards. As a demonstration of his political authority over the military, Cardwell forced the Duke of Cambridge to quit Horse Guards for Pall Mall in the summer of 1871. Indeed, as Wolseley arrived, Buckingham House in Pall Mall was being prepared for the Duke – see *The Times*, 23 May 1871. The Duke insisted on a separate entrance to the building and on addressing his letters from 'Horse Guards, Pall Mall'.

61 Hove, Wolseley MSS, 163/iv, Wolseley to Richard Wolseley, 12 May and 27 July 1871.

62 BL, OIOC, Northbrook MSS, C/144/20, Wolseley to Northbrook,
   1 March 1872; Cambridge MSS, RA VIC/ADD E/1/6813 and 6814,
   Cambridge to Foster, and Cambridge to Airey, both 19 Aug. 1871.

63 Cambridge MSS, RA VIC/ADD E/1/7200, Napier to Cambridge,
   2 Oct. 1873; ibid., 7358, Cambridge to Airey, 9 April 1874;
   C. W. De Kiewiet and F. H. Underhill, eds, *Dufferin–Carnarvon
   Correspondence, 1874–78* (Toronto: Publications of the Champlain
   Society, No 33, 1955), pp. 17–18, 24–6.

64 Hove, Wolseley MSS, W/P 11/23, Wolseley to Lady Wolseley, 28
   Sept. 1882.

65 Hove, Wolseley MSS, W/P 13/31, Wolseley to Lady Wolseley, 24–27
   Nov. 1884; Kent Archives Office, Stanhope MSS, U1590, 0314,
   Stanhope to Cambridge, 26 April 1888 and Wolseley to Stanhope,
   27 April 1888.

66 Adrian Preston, 'Wolseley, the Khartoum Relief Expedition and the
   Defence of India, 1885–1900', in Adrian Preston and Peter Dennis,
   eds, *Swords and Covenants* (London: Croom Helm, 1976), p. 97.

67 SLCM, Wolseley Diaries, CAM.H.22, Diary entry, 31 Dec. 1877.

68 TNA, WO 147/7, Wolseley's South African Journal, 15 April 1880.

69 Adrian Preston, ed., *Sir Garnet Wolseley's South African Diaries
   (Natal) 1875* (Cape Town: A. A. Balkema, 1971), p. 13.

70 Hove, Wolseley MSS, 163/iv, Wolseley to Richard Wolseley, 18 Feb.
   1878.

71 SLCM, Wolseley Diaries, CAM.H.22, Diary entry, 4 June 1877.

72 Hove, Wolseley MSS, SSL. Notes for, and drafts of *Story of a
   Soldier's Life*.

73 Adrian Preston, ed., *In Relief of Gordon: Lord Wolseley's Campaign
   Journal of the Khartoum Relief Expedition, 1884–85* (London:
   Hutchinson, 1967); idem, *Wolseley's South African Diaries*; idem,
   Sir Garnet Wolseley's South African Journal, 1879–80 (Cape Town:
   A. A. Balkema, 1973); idem, 'Sir Garnet Wolseley and the Cyprus
   Expedition, 1878', *Journal of the Society for Army Historical Research*
   45, 181 (1967), pp. 4–16; Anne Cavendish, ed., *Cyprus 1878: The
   Journal of Sir Garnet Wolseley* (Nicosia: Cyprus Popular Bank
   Cultural Centre, 1991).

74 Preston, *In Relief of Gordon*, p. x; idem, *Wolseley's South African
   Diaries*, p. 9.

75 The batches run from 11 to 18 Sept. 1873; 19 to 26 Sept.; 27 Sept. to 2 Oct.; 2 to 8 Oct.; 10 to 25 Oct.; 26 to 30 Oct.; 30 to 4 Nov.; 5 to 21 Nov.; 22 Nov. to 4 Dec.; 4 to 15 Dec.; 19 Dec. to 7 Jan.; 26 Jan. to 2 Feb.; 2 to 14 Feb.; 15 to 22 Feb.; 23 to 25 Feb.; and 27 Feb. to 4 March 1874.

76 Hove, Wolseley MSS, W/P 13/33, Wolseley to Lady Wolseley, 29 Nov.–4 Dec. 1884.

77 Wolseley, *Story of a Soldier's Life*, II, pp. 369–70.

78 Hove, Wolseley MSS, W/P 5/5, Wolseley to Lady Wolseley, 23 March 1875.

79 Sir George Arthur, ed., *The Letters of Lord and Lady Wolseley, 1870–1911* (London: William Heinemann, 1922), pp. 9–19.

80 Marjory Pegram, *The Wolseley Heritage: The Story of Frances Viscountess Wolseley and Her Parents* (London: John Murray, 1939), pp. 265–8.

81 The diary for 1875 is in Hove, Wolseley MSS, M2/41/8/4, while those for 1877, 1878, 1880, 1881, 1882, 1883, 1885, 1900, 1902, 1903, 1904, 1905 and 1906 are to be found in South Lanarkshire Council Museum at Hamilton.

82 Hove, Wolseley MSS, Autobiographical Collection, Cardwell to Wolseley, 18 Nov. 1873.

83 Hove, Wolseley MSS, W/P 8/19, Wolseley to Lady Wolseley, 8–13 Aug. 1879; Autobiographical Coll., Cardwell to Wolseley, 18 Nov. 1873.

84 Colonel Willoughby Verner, *The Military Life of HRH George, Duke of Cambridge*, 2 vols (London: John Murray, 1905), II, pp. 63–88.

85 See, for example, TNA, CO 96/102, Wolseley to Kimberley, 2 and 9 Oct. 1873, both reproduced in BPP, XLVI, 1874, Cmd. 892, *Further Correspondence Respecting the Ashantee Invasion*, No 3, pp. 124–5, 162–6.

86 TNA, CO 879/5, Wolseley to Kimberley, 22 Feb. 1874, reproduced in Cmd. 922, *Further Correspondence Respecting the Ashantee Invasion*, No 8, p. 76.

87 The Parliamentary Papers containing Wolseley's despatches are BPP, XLVI, 1874, Cmd. 891, 892, 893, 894, 921 and 922, *Further Correspondence Respecting the Ashantee Invasion*, Nos. 2–5, 7 and 8; and Cmd. 907, *Despatches from Sir Garnet Wolseley*, No 6. Some

are also reproduced in Crooks, *Records*, pp. 460–516, and Newbury, *British Policy*, pp. 332–5, 606–9.

88 TNA, CO 96/108, Note by AWLH, 16. Oct. 1873; CO 96/103, Wolseley to Kimberley, 29 Dec. 1873, reproduced in Cmd. 894, pp. 49–50. Barrow's letters are reproduced in BPP, Cmd. 891, pp. 191–3, 139–40; and Cmd. 892, pp. 62–4, 225–6. An earlier Wolseley rejoinder is in BPP, Cmd. 892, p. 202.

89 TNA, CO 96/103, Notes by Herbert, 22 and 25 Feb. 1874.

90 Duke University, William Perkins Library, Wolseley MSS, XVIII-4, Wolseley to Fleetwood-Wilson, 22 Sept. 1902.

91 Reade, *Story of the Ashantee Campaign*, p. 133.

92 The 'Daily News' Special Correspondent [Frederick Maurice], *The Ashantee War: A Personal Narrative* (London: Henry S. King & Co., 1874; Brackenbury, *Ashanti War*; W. F. Butler, *Akim-Foo: The History of a Failure* (London: Sampson Low, Marston, Searle & Rivington, 1876).

93 Sir Henry Brackenbury, *Some Memories of My Spare Time* (Edinburgh: William Blackwood & Sons, 1909), p. 232; NLS, Blackwood MSS, 4300, Brackenbury to Blackwood, 23 Nov. 1873; ibid., 4313, Brackenbury to Blackwood, 28 Jan. 1874.

94 NLS, Blackwood MSS, 4313, Alison to Blackwood, 16 June 1874.

95 Sir John Glover, 'The Volta Expedition during the late Ashantee Campaign', and Evelyn Wood, 'The Ashanti Expedition of 1873–74', *Journal of the Royal United Service Institution* 18, 78 (1874–5), pp. 317–30, 331–57; Field Marshal Sir Evelyn Wood, 'The Ashanti Expedition, 1873–74', in idem, ed., *British Battles on Land and Sea*, 2 vols (London: Cassell & Co, 1915), II, pp. 680–703.

96 Wolseley, *Story of a Soldier's Life*, II, pp. 257–70.

97 An Officer [William Toke Dooner], *Jottings en route to Coomassie: With a Map* (London: W. Mitchell & Co, 1874), reprinted as *To Coomassie and Back (with a Map)* (London: Simpkin, Marshall, Hamilton, Kent & Co, 1895).

98 Copies of the War Office Intelligence Department, *Précis of Ashanti Expedition* (1874) and the *Journal of Engineer Operations on the Gold Coast during the Recent Expedition* (1874) can be found in TNA, WO 33/26, WO 106/285, 286 and 6390, and WO 147/27. For the medical report, see BPP, XV, 1875, Cmd. 1374, *Statistical, Sanitary*

and Medical Reports of the Army Medical Department, Report for the Year 1873, Appendix II: *The Ashanti Campaign*.

99 See, for example, Beatrice Hart-Synnot, ed., *Letters of Major General Fitzroy Hart-Synnot* (London: Edward Arnold, 1912); Ian Harvie, 'The Raid on Essaman, 14 October 1873: An Account by Lieutenant Edward Woodgate of an Operation during Wolseley's Ashanti Expedition', *Journal of the Society for Army Historical Research* 77, 309 (1999), pp. 19–27. The latter is from Woodgate's journal in the Museum of the King's Own Royal Regiment, Lancaster, KO LIB 137.

100 Edward Spiers, *The Victorian Soldier in Africa* (Manchester: Manchester University Press, 2004), pp. 20–34; idem, *The Scottish Soldier and Empire, 1854–1902* (Edinburgh: Edinburgh University Press, 2006), pp. 24–40. See also Frank Emery, *Marching Over Africa* (London: Hodder & Stoughton, 1986), pp. 42–50.

101 Reade, *Story of the Ashantee Campaign*; G. A. Henty, *The March to Coomassie* (London: Tinsley, 1874); Boyle, *Through Fanteeland*; and Stanley, *Coomassie and Magdala*.

1 Plans (August to September 1873)

Notes to introduction

1 Sir Evelyn Wood, *From Midshipman to Field Marshal*, 2 vols (London: Methuen & Co, 1906), I, pp. 254–5.

2 Wolseley, *Story of a Soldier's Life*, II, p. 262.

3 TNA, Cardwell MSS, PRO 30/48/5/33, Cardwell to Kimberley, 1 Aug. 1873, and Kimberley to Cardwell, 2 Aug. 1873.

4 Vetch, *Andrew Clarke*, p. 115; CUL, Glover MSS, RCMS 131/6, Memorandum by Clarke, 11 Aug. 1873; ibid., Thompson to Kimberley, 31 July 1873.

5 Charles Callwell, *Small Wars: Their Principles and Practice*, 3rd edn (London: HMSO, 1906), p. 40. See also Ian F. W. Beckett, 'Another British Way in Warfare: Charles Callwell and Small Wars', in Ian F. W. Beckett, ed., *Victorians at War: New Perspectives* (Society for

Army Historical Research Special Publication No. 16, 2007),
pp. 89–102.

6 Glover, *Life*, p. 155; CUL, Glover MSS, RCMS 131/6, Account by
Glover, n.d.; Wolseley, *Story of a Soldier's Life*, II, pp. 266–7; Butler,
Akim-Foo, pp. 49–50, 87–8.

7 Newbury, *British Policy*, pp. 330–1; McIntyre, 'British Policy', p. 31;
Glover, *Life*, pp. 167–8.

8 Wolseley, *Story of a Soldier's Life*, II, p. 268.

9 Cambridge MSS, RA VIC/ADD E/1/7184, 7187, 7188, Cambridge
to Airey, 25 Aug., Cardwell to Cambridge, 28 Aug., and Cambridge
to Airey, 30 Aug. 1873; TNA, Cardwell MSS, PRO 30/48/17,
Cambridge to Cardwell, 19 Aug. 1873.

10 TNA, Cardwell MSS, PRO 30/48/33, Cardwell to Kimberley, 8
Sept. 1873.

11 Reade, *Story of the Ashantee Campaign*, pp. 138, 163.

12 McIntyre 'British Policy', p. 20; idem, *Imperial Frontier*, pp. 273–4;
John Vincent, ed., *A Selection from the Diaries of Edward Henry
Stanley, Fifteenth Earl of Derby, 1869–78* Camden 5th series, IV.
(London: Royal Historical Society, 1994), p. 14.

13 Henry Brackenbury, 'The Relations between Great Britain, the
Protected Tribes, and Ashanti, with the Causes of the Ashanti War',
Pt II, in Brackenbury and Huyshe, *Fanti and Ashanti*, pp. 1–90 at
p. 89; Henty, *March to Coomassie*, pp. 12–13; Maurice, *Ashantee War*,
pp. 5–20.

14 TNA, CO 96/110, Thomson to Pennell, 1 Oct. 1873; ibid., Note by
Pennell, 30 Sept., and Note by Vivian, 1 Oct. 1873.

15 Though observers of the Asante since Bowdich in 1817 had emphasised
human sacrifice, to the Asante it was more a matter of mortuary
slayings and public executions. See Wilks, *Forests of Gold*, pp. 215–40.

16 Bodleian, Kimberley MSS, Ms. Eng. c. 4074, Ponsonby to
Kimberley, 8 Sept. 1873 and Kimberley to Ponsonby, 9 Sept. 1873;
ibid., Ms. Eng. c. 4112, for various drafts of Wolseley's instructions.
See also McIntyre, 'British Policy', pp. 35–6; Agatha Ramm, ed.,
The Gladstone–Granville Correspondence, 2nd edn (Cambridge:
Cambridge University Press for Royal Historical Society, 1998),
pp. 405, 412–13; Matthew, *Gladstone Diaries*, pp. 372, 379–80, 383–4,
389, 391–2.

17 Gavin White, 'Firearms in Africa: An Introduction', *Journal of African History* 12, 2 (1971), pp. 173–84; R. A. Kea, 'Firearms and Warfare on the Gold and Slave Coasts from the Sixteenth to the Nineteenth Centuries', *Journal of African History* 12, 2 (1971), pp. 185–213; Robert Smith, *Warfare and Diplomacy in Pre-colonial West Africa*, 2nd edn (London: James Currey, 1989), pp. 80–6.

18 NMM, Fremantle MSS, FRE/101, Orders of 11, 14, 29 Sept. 1873, 26 Oct., and 3 Nov. 1873; ibid., FRE/102, Fremantle to Harley, 8 Sept. 1873; ibid., Fremantle to Admiralty, 14 Sept., 16 Sept., 5 Oct., 9 Oct., and 26 Oct. 1873; ibid., FRE/105, Fremantle to Blake, 29 Aug., and Fremantle to Stephens, 29 Aug. 73; TNA, CO 879/6, Fremantle to Kimberley, 27 Nov. 1873, Wolseley to Hewett, 11 Dec. 1873, Swanzy to Kimberley, 15 Jan. 1874, and Fremantle to Hewett, 12 Jan. 74; Brackenbury, *Ashanti War*, II, pp. 306–14. The dispute can be traced in BPP, Cmd. 892, pp. 10–13, 20–1, 55–6, 61, 68–9, 81, 83–4, 100, 102–3, 152–4, 157, 190, 192–4; Cmd. 893, pp. 1–2; Cmd. 894, pp. 16–18; Cmd. 922, pp. 8–9; and Cmd. 1006, pp. 5–8, 32. See also Fremantle, *Navy As I Have Known It*, pp. 207–8, 243.

19 Low, *General Lord Wolseley*, p. 243; Henty, *March to Coomassie*, p. 28; Wolseley, *Story of a Soldier's Life*, II, p. 274–5.

20 RA VIC/MAIN F/6/17, Cardwell to Ponsonby, 31 Aug. 1873.

21 TNA, WO 147/27, Wolseley to Cardwell 18 Oct. 73; Brackenbury, *Ashanti War*, I, p. 127; Henty, *March to Coomassie*, pp. 24–35; Low, *General Lord Wolseley*, p. 245.

22 TNA, WO 33/26, Memo, 5 Oct. 1873, and undated Memo, *circa* Jan. 1874; ibid., WO 33/25, Wolseley to Cardwell, 30 Nov. 1873; ibid., WO 32/7638; BPP, Cmd. 893, pp. 43–4; Hove, Wolseley MSS, W/P 3/10, Wolseley to Lady Wolseley, 3–5 Nov. 1873; Henty, *March to Coomassie*, pp. 231–2; Brackenbury, *Ashanti War*, I, pp. 299–300.

23 Stanley, *Coomassie and Magdala*, pp. 26–8; Brackenbury, *Ashanti War*, I, p. 127.

24 TNA, Cardwell MSS, PRO 30/48/33, Cardwell to Kimberley, 15, 18 and 19 Sept. 1873; Kimberley to Cardwell, 14 Sept. and 17 Sept. 1873; ibid., CO 96/107, Note by Vivian 15 Sept. 1873; Storks to Under Secretary of State, 13 Sept. 1873; ibid., WO 33/25, Note by Nugent, 1 Oct. 1873; BPP, Cmd. 891, p. 146.

25 TNA, WO 147/27, 'Notes on War', Oct. 1873; ibid., *Journal of*

Engineer Operations (also in WO 33/26, WO 106/285 and 286); Keith
Cima, *Reflections from the Bridge* (Buckingham: Baron Birch, 1994),
pp. 69, 77, 108.

26 Reade, *Story of the Ashantee Campaign*, p. 194; Boyle, *Through
Fanteeland*, pp. 50–1; Henty, *March to Coomassie*, pp. 165–8; Butler,
Akim-Foo, p. 70; Stanley, *Coomassie and Magdala*, pp. 27–8.

27 Brackenbury, *Ashanti War*, I, p. 116; Boyle, *Through Fanteeland*,
pp. 48–9; TNA, CO 96/103, Wolseley to Kimberley, 29 Dec. 1873; ibid.,
WO 33/26, Undated Memo, *circa* Jan. 1874; ibid., CO 37/207/24.

28 TNA, WO 147/27, *Journal of Engineer Operations*; ibid., Wolseley to
Cardwell 7 Oct. 1873; ibid., CO 96/108, Barrow to Under Secretary,
21 Nov., 1873; ibid., CO 96/103, Wolseley to Kimberley, 29 Dec.
1873; Melton Prior, *Campaigns of a War Correspondent* (London:
Edward Arnold, 1912), p. 22; Cima, *Reflections*, p. 108.

29 TNA, CO 96/107, Storks to Under Secretary, 22 Aug. 1873;
Brackenbury, *Ashanti War*, I, p. 126; NMM, Fremantle MSS,
FRE/109, Milne to Fremantle, 23 Sept. 1873. Storks, the Surveyor
General, was advising Cardwell to a significant degree. See, for
example, TNA, Cardwell MSS, PRO 30/48/33, Cardwell to
Kimberley, 9 Aug., 13 Sept. 1873.

30 Wolseley, *Story of a Soldier's Life*, II, p. 201; Hove, Wolseley MSS,
W/P 10/38, Wolseley to Lady Wolseley, 23–29 Dec. 1884.

31 Sir William Butler, *An Autobiography* (New York: Charles Scribner's
Sons, 1911), pp. 143–4; idem, *Akim-Foo*, p. 3; Edward McCourt,
Remember Butler (London: Routledge & Kegan Paul, 1967), p. 91;
BPP, Cmd. 892, p. 96.

32 C. H. Melville, *Life of General the Rt. Hon. Sir Redvers Buller*, 2
vols (London: Edward Arnold, 1923), I, pp. 55, 58–9; Brackenbury,
Ashanti War, I, p. 106.

33 C. E. Callwell, ed., *The Memoirs of Major General Sir Hugh
McCalmont* (London: Hutchinson & Co, 1924), p. 69.

34 Ponsonby MSS, RA VIC/ADD A36, Ponsonby to his wife, 4 Nov.
1882; Wolseley, *Story of a Soldier's Life*, II, p. 278.

35 NLS, Blackwood MSS, 4312, Wolseley to Blackwood, 18 June 1873;
Brackenbury, *Ashanti War*, I, p. 85.

36 Wood, *Midshipman to Field Marshal*, I, p. 255; Gosford, Wemyss
MSS, Charteris journal, 12 Sept. 1873.

37 Hove, Wolseley MSS, W/P 2/2, Wolseley to Lady Wolseley, 27 Aug. 1872.

38 Wolseley, *Story of a Soldier's Life*, II, p. 282; Brackenbury, *Some Memories*, p. 223.

39 A Staff Officer [Wolseley], 'Military Staff-systems Abroad and in England', *Macmillan's Magazine* 37 (1878), pp. 323–35; A. R. Godwin-Austen, *The Staff and the Staff College* (London: Constable, 1927), pp. 207–8.

40 Hart-Synnot, *Letters*, pp. 4–5; Dooner, *Jottings*, pp. 1, 4.

41 Brackenbury, *Some Memories*, pp. 228–9; Brian Bond, *The Victorian Army and the Staff College* (London; Eyre Methuen, 1972), pp. 128–9; Bodleian, Alison MSS, MS. Eng. lett. c. 450, Herbert to Jane Alison, 24 Nov. 1873.

42 Verner, *Military Life*, II, p. 65; Cambridge MSS, RA VIC/ADD E/1/7184, Cambridge to Airey, 25 Aug. 1873; Greaves, *Memoirs*, pp. 121, 123.

43 TNA, CO 96/107; BPP, Cmd. 892, p. 96. Those requested were Captain Charles Burnett, 15th Foot; Captain William Butler, 69th Foot; Captain the Hon. Paul Methuen, Scots Fusilier Guards; Lieutenant the Hon. Henry Wood, 10th Hussars; Lieutenant Frederic Clowes, 30th Foot; Lieutenant Richard Hare, 22nd Foot; Lieutenant Thomas Irwin, 1st Foot; Lieutenant Ronald Lane, 1st Rifle Brigade; Lieutenant Francis Douglas, 7th Foot; Lieutenant Andrew Wauchope, 42nd Highlanders; Lieutenant Henry Aylmer, 103rd Foot; Lieutenant Arthur Pollock, 21st Foot; Lieutenant William Grant, 6th Foot; Lieutenant Walter Wynter, 33rd Foot; and Lieutenant Patrick Crosbie, 14th Foot. In the event, only Lane and Crosbie did not join the expedition.

44 Sir George Douglas, *The Life of Major General Wauchope* (London: Hodder & Stoughton, 1905), pp. 63–4, 74.

45 Hove, Wolseley MSS, W/P 3/6, Wolseley to Lady Wolseley, 2 Oct. 1873.

46 Devon County Record Office, Buller MSS, 2065M/SS4/9. Replies were received from 33 officers, one pointing out that the current absence of all three British battalions sent to Asante on overseas service would limit numbers. It is not clear whether the dinner went ahead, or became an annual event.

47 Preston, *Wolseley's South African Diaries*, pp. 88–9.

48 TNA, CO 96/114, Note by Hall, 4 June 1874.

49 Godwin-Austen, *Staff and Staff College*, p. 207.

50 Ian Harvie, 'The Wolseley Ring: A Case Study in the Exercise of Patronage in the Late Victorian Army', unpublished MA dissertation (University of Buckingham, 1993), pp. 115–56.

51 Maurice and Arthur, *Life of Lord Wolseley*, p. 183.

52 Callwell, *McCalmont*, p. 75.

53 TNA, WO 147/7, Wolseley's South African War Journal, 24 Aug. and 7 Sept. 1879.

54 Gosford, Wemyss MSS, Charteris to Lady Elcho, 8 Oct. 1873; ibid., Charteris journal, 4 Oct. 1873.

55 Preston, *Wolseley's South African Diaries*, p. 88; Brackenbury, *Ashanti War*, I, p. 305.

56 Sir John Fortescue, *Following the Drum* (Edinburgh: William Blackwood & Sons, 1931), pp. 131–2; TNA, WO 147/8, Wolseley's Sudan Journal, 22 Oct. 1884.

57 Jay Luvaas, *The Education of an Army* (London: Cassell, 1965), p. 215.

58 Ian F. W. Beckett, *The Victorians at War* (London: Hambledon, 2003), pp. 3–12; idem, 'Command in the Late Victorian Army', in Gary Sheffield, ed., *Leadership and Command: The Anglo-American Military Experience since 1861* (London: Brasseys, 1997), pp. 37–56; idem, 'Wolseley and the Ring', *Soldiers of the Queen* 69 (1992), pp. 14–25.

59 Brackenbury and Huyshe, *Fanti and Ashanti*, p. ix; Reade, *Story of the Ashantee Campaign*, p. 147; Low, *General Lord Wolseley*, p. 244. The publications in question were Bowdich, *Mission to Ashantee*; Dupuis, *Journal*; William Hutton, *A Voyage to Africa* (London: Longman, 1821); Major H. I. Ricketts, *Narrative of the Ashantee War* (London: Simpkin & Marshall, 1831); John Beecham, *Ashantee and the Gold Coast* (London: John Mason, 1841); A Fellow of the Royal Geographical Society [Richard Francis Burton], *Wanderings in West Africa* (London: Tinsley Brothers, 1863); and Windwood Reade, *Savage Africa* (London: Smith, Elder & Co, 1863).

60 Brackenbury and Huyshe, *Fanti and Ashanti*.

61 Hart-Synnot, *Letters*, p. 6.

62 C. Ballard, 'Sir Garnet Wolseley and John Dunn', in A. Duminy and C. Ballard, eds, *The Anglo-Zulu War: New Perspectives* (Pietermaritzburg: University of Natal Press, 1988), pp. 120–47 at p. 130; Ponsonby MSS, RA VIC/ADD A35, Ponsonby to his wife, 28 Oct. 1882.

63 Maurice, *Ashantee War*, pp. 32, 34; Henty, *March to Coomassie*, pp. 43–4; Brackenbury, *Ashanti War*, I, p. 147; Hove, Wolseley MSS, W/P 3/5, Wolseley to Lady Wolseley, 30 Sept. 1873.

64 Henty, *March to Coomassie*, p. 38; Gosford, Wemyss MSS, Charteris Order Book.

65 Wolseley, *Story of a Soldier's Life*, II, p. 276; Melville, *Buller*, I, p. 61; Maurice, *Ashantee War*, p. 30; Henty, *March to Coomassie*, pp. 19–21; Brackenbury, *Ashanti War*, I, p. 144; Dooner, *Jottings*, pp. 4, 11; Gosford, Wemyss MSS, Charteris journal, 12, 16 and 21 Sept. 1873.

66 Dooner, *Jottings*, p. 3; Gosford. Wemyss MSS, Charteris to Lady Elcho, 18 Sept. 73.

67 RA VIC/MAIN/F/6/41, Report on *Ambriz*, n.d.

68 Garnet Wolseley, *The Soldier's Pocket Book for Field Service* (London: Macmillan, 1886), pp. 178–80.

69 Stanley, *Coomassie and Magdala*, pp. 2–3, 22–4, 39, 136, 172–3.

70 Gosford, Wemyss MSS, Charteris journal, 22 and 23 Oct. 1873; Buller Family MSS, Buller to Lucy, 14 Nov. 1873.

71 Wolseley, *Story of a Soldier's Life*, II, p. 342.

72 Prior, *Campaigns*, p. 16.

73 Boyle, *Through Fanteeland*, p. 24; Prior, *Campaigns*, p. 2; R. J. Wilkinson-Latham, *From Our Special Correspondent: Victorian War Correspondents and Their Campaigns* (London: Hodder & Stoughton, 1979), p. 121. For examples of Prior's Asante work, see Pat Hodgson, *The War Illustrators* (London: Osprey, 1977), p. 110; and Condua-Harley, *Sagrenti War*.

74 RA VIC/MAIN/F/7/59, Ponsonby to the Queen [13 Feb. 1874].

75 Butler, *Akim-Foo*, pp. 136–7.

76 Brackenbury, *Some Memories*, p. 230; Gosford, Wemyss MSS, Charteris to Lady Elcho, 18 Sept. 1873; Author's Collection, George Colley to Henry Colley, n.d [March 1874]; WSRO, Methuen MSS, WSRO1742/RB 6335, Methuen to his father, 2 Jan. and 30 Jan. 1874. For Reade generally, see J. D. Hargreaves, 'Winwood Reade and the Discovery of Africa', *African Affairs* 56 (1957), pp. 306–16;

and Felix Driver, 'Distance and Disturbance: Travel, Exploration and Knowledge in the Nineteenth Century', *Transactions of the Royal Historical Society* 14 (2004), pp. 73–92.

77 Prior, *Campaigns*, pp. 9, 27; Henty, *March to Coomassie*, p. 453; Stanley, *Coomassie and Magdala*, pp. 172–3.

78 Stanley, *Coomassie and Magdala*, p. 39; Maurice, *Ashantee War*, p. 126.

79 BPP, Cmd. 892, pp. 14, 148–9; TNA, WO 147/27, Cardwell to Wolseley, 5 Nov. 1873; ibid., WO 33/25, Cardwell to Wolseley, 17 Nov. 1873, and Lushington to War Office, 8 Dec. 1873; ibid., CO 96/103, Wolseley to Kimberley, 27 Nov. 1873; CO 96/108, Legal opinion by Ashurst, 30. Dec. 1873; Hove, Wolseley MSS, W/P 3/15, Wolseley to Lady Wolseley, 27 Nov. 1873; D. R. Headrick, *The Invisible Weapon: Telecommunications and International Politics, 1851–1945* (New York: Oxford University Press, 1991), pp. 64–6.

80 Reade, *Story of the Ashantee Campaign*, pp. 133–4; Hart-Synnot, *Letters*, pp. 6, 12.

Notes to Documents 1–22

1 Wolseley's actual commission as Local Major General was dated 6 Sept. 1873.

2 Major General Daniel Lysons, GOC Northern District. Lysons (1816–98) was well known to Wolseley from his Canadian service. Commissioned, 1st Foot, 1834. Service in Canadian rebellion, 1837–8; Crimea. DAQMG, Canada, 1838–41; Brigade Major, Barbados, 1844–7; DQMG, Canada, 1862–7; GOC of Brigade at Aldershot, 1869–72; GOC, Northern District, 1872–4; Quartermaster General, 1876–80; GOC, Aldershot, 1880–3. KCB, 1877; GCB, 1886; General, 1879.

3 The main autumn manoeuvres for 1873 took place on Cannock Chase between 12 August and 12 September under the command of Lysons: see *The Times*, 13 Sept. 1873. There had also been a smaller subsidiary exercise on Dartmoor in August directed by Sir Charles Staveley. Wolseley had expressed particular support for annual manoeuvres, which he had analysed: see 'Our Autumn Manoeuvres', *Blackwood's Magazine*, 112, November 1872, pp. 627–44.

Manoeuvres had also been the subject of Wolseley's Wellington essay competition entry.

4 The Hausa inhabited the northern parts of what was to become Nigeria but it tended to be a term used to describe any soldier recruited from the Islamic north and, as a language, Hausa was also something of a lingua franca throughout West Africa.

5 The full contemporary name for the Pra.

6 Manya Krobos were a branch of the Adangbe people residing on the right bank of the Volta.

7 Pong was a Manya Krobo settlement on the Volta and a centre for the palm-oil trade.

8 Frances Anne Wolseley (nee Smith) (1811–83).

9 Canadian *voyageurs* were the trained boatmen, often French Canadians, Indians or half-breeds, upon whom Wolseley had relied to transport his expedition to Fort Garry on the Red River in 1870. Less happily, Wolseley was to recruit *voyageurs* for the Gordon Relief Expedition in 1884–5. See Julian Symons, *England's Pride: The Story of the Gordon Relief Expedition* (London: Hamish Hamilton, 1965), pp. 105–7, 142–4, 251.

10 Lieutenant General Lord of Napier of Magdala, CinC in India. Robert Cornelius Napier (1810–90), was commissioned in the Bengal Engineers, 1826. Service in Sikh Wars, 1845–6, 1848–9; Mutiny; China, 1860–1; Abyssinia, 1867–8. CinC, Bombay, 1865–70; CinC, India, 1870–6; Governor and CinC, Gibraltar, 1876–83; Constable of the Tower, 1887–90. KCB, 1859; GCB, 1868; GCSI, 1868; Baron, 1868; General, 1874; Field Marshal, 1883.
Brevet Colonel The Hon. Frederic Augustus Thesiger, Adjutant General in India. Thesiger (1827–1905) was commissioned in the Rifle Brigade, 1844. Service in Crimea; Mutiny; Abyssinia, 1867–8; South Africa, 1878–9. DAG, Bombay, 1861–3; Adjutant General in India, 1869–74; CinC in South Africa, 1878–9 until superseded by Wolseley; Lieutenant of the Tower, 1884–9. KCB, 1878; GCB, 1879; GCVO, 1902; General, 1888. Succeeded father as 2nd Baron Chelmsford, 1878.

11 Frederick York Wolseley (1837–99). Fred had gone to Australia in 1854 to seek his fortune, borrowing £1,000 from Garnet and a further £500 in 1861. Most of his business ventures there failed and,

by 1879, Fred was all but bankrupt and owed Garnet £8,500 though he had patented a sheep-shearing machine in 1877. Fred eventually tasted success with a second sheep-shearing machine patent in 1884, establishing the Wolseley Sheep Shearing Machine Company in Birmingham in 1889 in partnership with Herbert Austin. Fred resigned as managing director in 1894 and it was Austin who went on to produce the company's first Wolseley motorcar in 1895. Fred was then diagnosed with cancer, finally returning to England in 1898 and dying the following year, at which point Garnet had to make financial provision for Fred's widow. See Kochanski, *Wolseley*, pp. 33, 92, 210; J. O'Toole, *Frederick York Wolseley* (privately printed, 1995); and Ian Itter, ed., *Wolseley Letters concerning Fred* (Swan Hill, Victoria, Australia: Ian Itter Publishing, 2007).

12 The Hon. Augustus Henry Archibald Anson (1835–77), Liberal MP for Bewdley. Commissioned Rifle Brigade, 1853. Service in Crimea; Mutiny; China, 1860. MP for Lichfield, 1859–68; for Bewdley, 1869–74. VC, 1857; Lieutenant Colonel, 1866. Son of the Earl of Lichfield. Anson, who was Lady Elcho's brother, was an old friend of Wolseley, who had shared a tent with him in India and China: see Earl of Wemyss, *Memoirs, 1818–1911* (Edinburgh: David Douglas, 1912), I, pp. 286–7.

13 *Deo volente* ('God willing').

14 Presumably Captain William Bell McTaggart, 14th Hussars. Commissioned 1868.

15 Richard Wolseley was attached to the 2/5th Foot. In the event, no officers from the regiment served in Asante.

16 Francis Wemyss-Charteris-Douglas, Lord Elcho (1818–1914), Liberal Conservative MP for Haddingtonshire. MP for East Gloucester, 1841–6; Haddingtonshire, 1847–83. Lord of Treasury, 1852–5; Founder of Liberty and Property Defence League, 1882; Lieutenant Colonel commanding 15th Middlesex (London Scottish) Rifle Volunteer Corps, 1859–78; Honorary Colonel, 1878–1900. GVCO, 1909. Succeeded as 10th Earl of Wemyss, 1883. For Elcho's role in the rifle volunteer movement, see Ian F. W. Beckett, *Riflemen Form: A Study of the Rifle Volunteer Movement, 1859–1908* (Aldershot: Ogilby Trusts, 1982).

17 Evelyn Wood had lectured on mounted riflemen at the Royal United

Service Institution on 4 March 1873, Elcho acting as chairman. Subsequent correspondence on the issue was then published by Elcho as a pamphlet: see *Daily News*, 5 March 1873; *Pall Mall Gazette*, 22 Sept. 1873; and Stephen Manning, *Evelyn Wood VC: Pillar of Empire* (Barnsley: Pen & Sword, 2007), pp. 65–6. The lecture itself was published as Evelyn Wood, *Mounted Riflemen* (London: W. Mitchell & Co, 1873).

18 Hugh McCalmont.

19 Cornelius Johannes Marius Nagtglas, Governor of the Dutch Gold Coast, 1858–62, 1869–71. Nagtglas had first come out to the Gold Coast in 1837.

20 Lieutenant General Sir John Lintorn Arabin Simmons (1821–1903), Lieutenant Governor of the Royal Military Academy, Woolwich. Commissioned, Royal Engineers, 1837. Service in Danubian Provinces and Crimea. British Commissioner for the Delineation of the Russo-Turkish Frontier, 1857; British Consul at Warsaw, 1858–60; CRE, Aldershot, 1860–5; Director, School of Military Engineering, 1865–8; Lieutenant Governor, RMA, 1869–1875; Inspector General of Fortifications, 1875–80; Military Delegate to Congress of Berlin, 1878; Governor of Malta, 1884–8. KCB, 1869; GCB, 1878; GCMG 1888; Field Marshal, 1890.

21 There is no letter in the Royal Archives from Cambridge to Wolseley for this date.

22 HMS *Himalaya*, an iron screw troopship had arrived in July, bringing out the 2nd West India Regiment from Barbados and took on board sick marines for return to England in August.

23 BPP, LXX, 1872, Cmd. 670 *Correspondence Relative to the Cession by the Netherlands Government to the British Government of the Dutch Settlements on the West Coast of Africa* LXX, pp. 33–4. This also related to the 'Certificate of Apology' by which Kofi Karikari supposedly renounced his claim to Elmina: see ibid., pp. 39–40. See also Crooks, *Records*, pp. 399–401; and Brackenbury, *Ashanti War*, I, pp. 32–3. Herbert T. Ussher was Administrator of the Gold Coast, 1867–71. Service in the Crimea (Commissariat). Formerly Collector of Customs, Gold Coast. Ussher had a reputation as a serial womaniser: see Pope Hennessy, *Verandah*, p. 126.

24 Henry Ata Plange, Writer (Clerk) of the Dutch Government Office

at Elmina and envoy of the Dutch and British to Asante. It has
sometimes been claimed Plange forged the 'Certificate of Apology'
but it would appear genuine and, indeed, an attempt by the Asante
to deceive the British as to their real intentions: see Coombs, *Gold
Coast, Britain and Netherlands*, pp. 98–108.

25 Charles Spencer Salmon, Colonial Secretary at Cape Coast Castle.
Acting Administrator of the Gold Coast, 1871–2.

26 In 1831 the Asante had been asked to provide two young men of the
royal family as 'security' to be baptised and educated in England.
The Asante seemingly complied in 1836 by delivering up Owusu
Nkwantabisa (*c.* 1820–59), the son of the now deceased *Asantehene*
who had signed the treaty, Osei Yaw Akoto (ruled 1823–34), and
Owusu Ansa (*c.* 1822–84), the son of another former *Asantehene*,
Osei Tutu Kwame (ruled 1804–23). The British assumed that these
young men were potential future rulers but, under the matrilineal
system, while *adehyee* (nobles) they were not *ahenemma* (princes). Both
returned from England in 1841, working with the Wesleyan Methodist
missionaries established in Kumase though Owusu Ansa settled at
Cape Coast on a British government pension and only resided at
Kumase from 1867 to 1871. Owusu Ansa, indeed, played a significant
role in the negotiations between the British and Asante in the lead up
to the Asante incursion into Fante territory though he had distanced
himself from the missionaries since the 1860s: see McCaskie, *State
and Society*, pp. 138, 392–3 nn. 183–4; and BPP, Cmd. 891, pp. 160–2,
188–9. Suspected of collusion with the Asante, Owusu Ansa was
almost killed by a Fante mob at Cape Coast in 1873 and was sent to
Sierra Leone for safety: see Kimble, *Political History*, p. 269 n. 2.

27 No one beyond this official deputation turned out to see Wolseley and
his officers off as the expedition had excited no interest in Liverpool:
see Henty, *March to Coomassie*, p. 16. The Mayor of Liverpool for
1872–3 was Edward Samuelson. He was succeeded in November
1873 by Andrew Barclay Walker (1824–93), brewer and founder of
the Walker Art Gallery (1877).

28 The African Steam Ship Company, founded by Macgregor Laird,
had won the mail contract for West Africa in 1852, subsequently
agreeing to alternate sailings with the rival British and African Steam
Navigation Company, founded in 1868. The newly acquired *Ambriz*

(2,121 tons) had been the White Star Line's *Asiatic*, launched in 1871: it was sold off to a French company in 1896. The African Steam Ship Company became part of the Elder Dempster Line in 1891.

29 'Pal' was the nickname of Baker Russell's wife, Pauline Henrietta Russell (née Hunter) a close friend of Louisa Wolseley. She had married Baker Russell in 1866. The Grove was Wolseley's house in Kingston on Thames: see Document 3.

30 Sir Henry Knight Storks (1811–74), Surveyor General of the Ordnance. Commissioned, 61st Foot, 1828. Service in South Africa, 1846–7; Crimea. High Commissioner of the Ionian Islands, 1859–63; Governor of Malta, 1864–5; Governor of Jamaica, 1866–7; Head of Control Department, War Office, 1867–70; Surveyor General of the Ordnance, 1870–4; Liberal MP for Ripon, 1871–4. KCB, 1857; GCMG, 1860; GCB, 1864.

31 The letter from Cardwell to Storks, dated 9 Sept. 1873 is enclosed with that from Cardwell to Kimberley of 13 Sept. 1873 in TNA, PRO 30/48/33.

32 A rather typical Wolseley error. Heinty, of course, is Henty and is correctly spelled later in the same entry.

33 John Thadeus Delane (1817–79), Editor of *The Times*, 1841–77.

34 According to Charteris, the black had a business in Japan and was now hoping to set another up at Sierra Leone, while they suspected the trader was supplying arms to the Asante. See Gosford, Wemyss MSS, Charteris to his mother, 18 Sept. 1873; and Journal, 13 Sept. 1873.

35 William Carr Beresford, 1st Viscount Beresford (1768–1854). Commissioned 6th Foot, 1785. Marshal of the Portuguese Army, 1809–22. KB, 1810; Baron, 1814; Viscount, 1823; General, 1825.

36 Wolseley, of course, means the Tower of Babel, the story of which is recounted in Genesis, Chapter 11.

37 Sirocco is a wind originating in the Sahara that carries sand particles to southern Europe.

38 Madame Tussauds had opened at The Bazaar, Baker Street, in 1835. It moved to its present site in Marylebone Road in 1884.

39 So many wicker chairs were bought at Madeira that the decks of the *Ambriz* were littered with them: see Henty, *March to Coomassie*, p. 27.

40 There was no dismay on board at Commerell's wound. As Reade put it, 'most of us declared it was the reverse of a disaster for the expedition. Hitherto the British people had looked upon the war with languor and actual distrust … But the disaster on the Prah was a blow in the face of Europe, and it stirred the spirit of the Nation.' See Reade, *Story of the Ashantee Campaign*, p. 155.

41 James Lloyd Ashbury (1834–95), a well-known yachtsman, was Conservative MP for Brighton, 1874–80. According to Charteris, Ashbury hoped to see the 'fun': see Gosford, Wemyss MSS, Charteris journal, 19 Sept. 1873. The second named is possibly Lord George Montacute Nevill (1856–1920), second son of the 1st Marquis of Abergavenny. Nevill had held a commission as a lieutenant in the Royal West Kent Militia.

The third is presumably one of the three sons of Philip Henry Stanhope, 5th Earl of Stanhope (1805–75): Arthur Philip Stanhope, Viscount Mahon (1838–1905). Served Grenadier Guards, 1858–69. Conservative MP for Leominster 1868 and for East Suffolk, 1870–6; Junior Lord of the Treasury, 1874–6. Succeeded father, 1875. The Hon. Edward Stanhope (1840–93), Conservative MP for Mid-Lincolnshire, 1874–85, Hornchurch, 1885–93. President of Board of Trade, 1886; Secretary of State for the Colonies, 1886–7; Secretary of State for War, 1887–92. The Hon. Henry Augustus Stanhope (1845–1933). The latter seems the most likely candidate though he was to become a clergyman and this might not fit with the description of his character.

42 Captain George Cumine Strahan, Administrator of Lagos. Commissioned Royal Artillery, 1857; Captain, 1871. ADC to Gladstone as High Commissioner of the Ionian Islands, 1859; ADC to Governor of Malta, 1864–8; Chief Secretary of Malta, 1868–9; Colonial Secretary, Bahamas, 1869; Acting Governor of Bahamas, 1871–3; Administrator of Lagos, 1873–4; Governor of Gold Coast Colony, 1874–6; Governor of Windward Islands, 1876; Treasurer of Tasmania, 1880; Temporary High Commissioner in South Africa, 1880. KCMG, 1880. Wolseley is referring to the fraudulent bankruptcy of Messrs. Strahan, Paul & Bates, bankers in The Strand, and the subsequent trial between June and October 1855 of Sir John Dean Paul, William Strahan and Robert Makin Bates for unlawfully

and fraudulently disposing of securities to the value of £113,000. A dramatic early episode in the affair had been Sir John Dean Paul's initial escape from constables sent to arrest him. Each of the three men was sentenced controversially to fourteen years' transportation in October 1855: see *Daily News*, 21 June 1855, *Reynolds Newspaper*, 15 July 1855, *The Times*, 29 Oct. 1855, *Glasgow Herald*, 31 Oct. 1855, and *Lloyd's Weekly Newspaper*, 5 Oct. 1856.

43 The African Steamship Company's *Nigretia* (1,810 tons), launched in 1872, was lost on the Carpenter Rock off Sierra Leone on 14 June 1873. Apart from mails, it had also been carrying nine-pounder rockets and other arms and ammunition to equip the Fante: see *Liverpool Mercury* 2 Sept. 1873 and *Glasgow Herald* 11 July 1873. Stanley and Hart also noted the wreck: see Stanley, *Coomassie and Magdala*, p. 9; and Hart-Synnot, *Letters*, p. 13.

44 William Wilberforce (1759–1833), abolitionist. MP for Hull, 1780; Yorkshire, 1784–1812; and Bramber, 1812–25. Introduced bill to abolish the slave trade in 1791. The measure was passed by the Commons in 1804 but twice rejected in the Lords until passing onto the statute book in 1807.

45 Wolseley obviously means *en bloc*.

46 George Berkeley (1819–1905), Governor of the West African Settlements. Colonial Secretary, Honduras, 1845; Governor of St Vincent, 1864–72; Administrator of Lagos, 1872; Governor of the West African Settlements, 1873; Governor, Leeward Islands, 1874–81. KCMG, 1881.

47 Captain J. J. Kendall, Colonial Secretary at Sierra Leone, had acted as Administrator there from April to December 1869, in June 1871, and from January to February 1872. Moylan was Acting Treasurer at Sierra Leone.

48 Captain George Armand Furse, 42nd Foot. Commissioned 1855. Service in Mutiny; Asante; Sudan, 1884–5. Director of Transport, Gordon Relief Expedition; Brevet Colonel, 1885. Lieutenant Joshua Morris Saunders, Royal Artillery. Commissioned, 1860. Invalided and died after return to England.

49 James Craig Loggie, CMG, Collector of Customs at Sherbro. Service in Crimea with Royal Artillery. Loggie had previously been Inspector General of Police at Sierra Leone and had taken part in

the earlier fighting against the Asante at Elmina in June 1873. Most contemporary accounts refer to the Susu of northern Sierra Leone as Kossoo or Kossos rather than Coasu. Both Reade and Henty suggested that the real name was Mende or Menni but the Mende were a separate people who had fought against the Susu in the past. See Henty, *March to Coomassie*, p. 156; and Reade, *Story of the Ashantee Campaign*, p. 205.

50 Lieutenant Robert William Thew Gordon, 93rd Foot. Commissioned 1858. Service in Eusofzye and Umbeyla (North-West Frontier), 1863–4; Asante; Egypt, 1882; Sudan, 1884. Brevet Lieutenant Colonel, 1882.

51 Exeter Hall in The Strand was opened in 1831 and used as a meeting hall for a variety of religious and philanthropic organisations such as the Society for the Extinction of the Slave Trade. It was also a venue for concerts by the Sacred Harmonic Society. The building was taken over by the YMCA in 1880 and demolished in 1907.

52 Kroomen (Kru) are mentioned in all accounts as good labourers but too cowardly to be enlisted as soldiers: see Henty, *March to Coomassie*, pp. 43–4; Stanley, *Coomassie and Magdala*, pp. 10–11; Boyle, *Through Fanteeland*, pp. 20–2; and Brackenbury, *Ashanti War*, I, pp. 148–9.

53 Commissary (Major) Charles Davis O'Connor, Control Department. Commissioned 1854. Service in West Africa, 1854; Asante. Assistant Commissary General (Lieutenant Colonel), 1874.

54 Clearly, Wolseley errs here, having already correctly described the *Nigretia* as wrecked off Sierra Leone. Stanley identifies the Cape Palmas wreck as the African Steamship Company's *Monrovia* (1,019 tons): see Stanley, *Coomassie and Magdala*, p. 9. The *Monrovia*, however, had been refloated after running aground at the entrance to the Brass River: see *Derby Mercury*, 30 July 1873. Launched in 1873, the *Monrovia* would eventually be lost off Freetown in 1876. The wreck seen by Wolseley was actually that of the *Yoruba* (1,705 tons), launched in 1871, another African Steamship Company mail steamer, lost on 31 May 1873: see *Liverpool Mercury*, 26 June 1873; BPP, Cmd. 890, p. 176.

2 Assessment (October 1873)

Notes to Introduction

1   Low, *General Lord Wolseley*, p. 247; Maurice, *Ashantee War*, pp. 40–1.

2   Brackenbury, *Ashanti War*, I, pp. 151–2; Low, *General Lord Wolseley*, pp. 247, 250; Butler, *Akim-Foo*, p. 63.

3   Reade, *Story of the Ashantee Campaign*, p. 161; Wood, 'Ashanti Expedition', p. 336.Brackenbury, *Ashanti War*, I, p. 154, 171; Henty, *March to Coomassie*, pp. 55–7.

4   Henty, *March to Coomassie*, p. 67.

5   Crooks, *Records*, p. 469; BPP, Cmd. 892, p. 124; Wolseley, *Story of a Soldier's Life*, II, pp. 295–6.

6   CUL, Glover MSS, RCMS 131/12, McNeill to Glover, 7 Oct. 1873.

7   BPP, Cmd. 892, pp. 162–6; Crooks, *Records*, pp. 469, 472–3.

8   RA VIC/MAIN F/6/44, Cardwell to Ponsonby, 29 Oct. 73; Cambridge MSS, RA VIC/ADD E/1/7223, Cambridge to Wolseley, 30 Oct. 1873. See also TNA, WO 147/27, Meade to Lansdowne, 3 Nov. 1873.

9   TNA, WO 147/27, Cardwell to Wolseley, 6 Oct. 1873 (also in RA VIC/MAIN F/6/39); Cambridge MSS, RA VIC/ADD E/1/7233, Cambridge to Wolseley, 11 Nov. 1873.

10 NMM, Fremantle MSS, FRE/101, Fremantle to all captains, 13 Oct. 1873.

11 Maurice, *Ashantee War*, pp. 45–6; Brackenbury, *Ashanti War*, I, pp. 150, 164–7, 221–2; Low, *General Lord Wolseley*, p. 250; Butler, *Akim-Foo*, p. 63; TNA, WO 147/27, *Journal of Engineer Operations*.

12 Brackenbury, *Ashanti War*, I, pp. 170–1; Low, *General Lord Wolseley*, p. 251; Melville, *Buller*, I, pp. 62–3, 66, 78. Buller's intelligence notebook can be found in Devon County Record Office, Buller MSS, 2065M Add 2/SS5, while one of his reports is to be found in RA VIC/MAIN F/7/24. Rather similarly, in 1873, the Fante chiefs tended to refer to Wolseley as 'McCarthy': see Gosford, Wemyss MSS, Charteris journal, 6 Oct. 1873.

13 Callwell, *McCalmont*, p. 75; Low, *General Lord Wolseley*, pp. 248–9; Henty, *March to Coomassie*, pp. 60–6, 69–74; Maurice, *Ashantee War*, pp. 43–4, 47–54; Brackenbury, *Ashanti War*, I, pp. 156–60; Crooks,

Records, pp. 470–2; BPP, Cmd 892, pp. 125–6, Wolseley to Kimberley 5 Oct. 1873.

14 Percy Luxmore, 'Ashantee: Extracts from the Journal of a Naval Officer addressed to his Wife', *Blackwood's Edinburgh Magazine* 115 (1874), pp. 518–24; Henty, *March to Coomassie*, pp. 64, 69 ; Reade, *Story of the Ashantee Campaign*, p. 160; NMM, Fremantle MSS, FRE/102, Fremantle to Admiralty, 5 Oct. 1873.

15 Henty, *March to Coomassie*, pp. 70–4; Brackenbury, *Ashanti War*, I, pp. 162–3.

16 Maurice, *Ashantee War*, pp. 61–5; BPP, Cmd. 1892, pp. 61–5, 210–16; TNA, CO 96/102.

17 Low, *General Lord Wolseley*, pp. 249–50; Maurice, *Ashantee War*, pp. 67–8; Dooner, *Jottings*, p. 21; Hart-Synnot, *Letters*, pp. 24–5; Boyle, *Through Fanteeland*, p. 47; Henty, *March to Coomassie*, pp. 157–8, 163–4. The Queen was particularly amused by Wolseley's meeting with the 'ladies of colour': see Bodleian, Kimberley MSS, Ms Eng. c. 4074, Ponsonby to Kimberley, 23 Nov. 1873.

18 Maurice, *Ashantee War*, pp. 66–7; Crooks, *Records*, pp. 477–8.

19 Hearle's Asante journal can be found in the Royal Marines Museum, Gosport, 7/14/9(4).

20 NMM, Fremantle MSS, FRE/102, Fremantle to Admiralty, 5 Nov. 1873.

21 Maurice, *Ashantee War*, pp. 87–9; Brackenbury, *Ashanti War*, I, pp. 163, 208; Reade, *Story of the Ashantee Campaign*, p. 160.

22 Brackenbury, *Ashanti War*, I, pp. 206–7, 210–19, 250–1; Low, *General Lord Wolseley*, p. 258; BPP, Cmd. 892, pp. 244–5, 249; Crooks, *Records*, pp. 477–8.

23 Wood, *Midshipman to Field Marshal*, I, pp. 262–3; Henty, *March to Coomassie*, p. 173; Low, *General Lord Wolseley*, pp. 257–8; Reade, *Story of the Ashantee Campaign*, pp. 204–6; Wolseley, *Story of a Soldier's Life*, II, p. 293; Brackenbury, *Ashanti War*, I, pp. 209–10.

24 Dooner, *Jottings*, pp. 21, 37; Henty, *March to Coomassie*, pp. 122, 156; Hart-Synnot, *Letters*, p. 25; Wood, *Midshipman to Field Marshal*, I, p. 262.

25 Henty, *March to Coomassie*, pp. 80, 100; Reade, *Story of the Ashantee Campaign*, p. 173; Brackenbury, *Ashanti War*, I, pp. 178, 240; Ian Cross, 'The 7-pounder rifled muzzle-loading gun of 200 lbs, Mk. IV', *Soldiers of the Queen* 132 (2008), pp. 21–6.

26 CUL, Glover MSS, RCMS 131/12, McNeill to Glover, 3 Oct. 1873.
27 Glover, 'Volta Expedition', pp. 318–19; Glover, *Life*, pp. 156, 158–60, 172–4; John Parker, *Making the Town: Ga State and Society in Early Colonial Accra* (Oxford: James Currey, 2000), pp. 68–73; BL, Gladstone MSS, Add. MSS 44225, Kimberley to Gladstone, 15 Dec. 1873.
28 Maurice and Arthur, *Life of Lord Wolseley*, p. 66.
29 Brackenbury, *Ashanti War*, I, p. 172; Wood, 'Ashanti Expedition', p. 337; idem, *Midshipman to Field Marshal*, I, p. 258; Low, *General Lord Wolseley*, pp. 252–3; Maurice, *Ashantee War*, p. 69.
30 Maurice, *Ashantee War*, p. 71; Brackenbury, *Ashanti War*, I, p. 173; Gosford, Wemyss MSS, Charteris journal, 11 Oct. 1873; Harvie, 'Raid on Essaman', p. 22; Henty, *March to Coomassie*, p. 99.
31 BPP, Cmd. 892, pp. 195–200, Wolseley to Kimberley, 15 Oct. 1873, and Wood to Wolseley, 15 Oct. 1873; Crooks, *Records*, pp. 475–7; Brackenbury, *Ashanti War*, I, pp. 173–85; Maurice, *Ashantee War*, pp. 72–85; Low, *General Lord Wolseley*, pp. 253–5; Wood, *Midshipman to Field Marshal*, I, pp. 258–61; Reade, *Story of the Ashantee Campaign*, 168–83; Henty, *March to Coomassie*, pp. 94–117; Fremantle, *Navy As I Have Known It*, pp. 218–23; NMM, LOG/N/27, Luxmore journal, 14 Oct. 1873.
32 Wood, 'Ashanti Expedition', pp. 337–8; Gosford, Wemyss MSS, Charteris journal, 14 Oct. 1873; Wolseley, *Story of a Soldier's Life*, II, pp. 298–300; Manning, *Evelyn Wood VC*, pp. 71–4.
33 Maurice, *Ashantee War*, pp. 80–1; Crooks, *Records*, pp. 475–7; Harvie, 'Raid on Essaman', pp. 19–27; Melville, *Buller*, I, p. 64.
34 Wolseley, *Story of a Soldier's Life*, II, p. 279, 301; Fremantle, *Navy As I Have Known It*, p. 222–3. According to Fremantle, it was the doctors rather than he who regarded his wound as severe.
35 Maurice, *Ashantee War*, p. 84; Low, *General Lord Wolseley*, pp. 253–5; Brackenbury, *Ashanti War*, I, pp. 182–3.
36 An interesting sidelight of Cardwell conveying congratulations to Wolseley and commenting on the campaign was that he chose to do so in the name of the Queen. The Queen's Private Secretary, Sir Henry Ponsonby, drew the Queen's attention to the 'growing tendency on the part of Your Majesty's Ministers to assume a greater amount of independence both in language and in acts, which is especially remarkable among those who are less frequently brought

under the personal influence of Your Majesty'. Cardwell cited a Crimean precedent but the Queen rejected it on the grounds that 'when the sovereign's approval is given in a letter, no other expression of opinion should be stated in the same letter'. See RA VIC/MAIN F/6/58, Cardwell to Wolseley, 18 Nov. 1873; F/6/62, Ponsonby to the Queen, 20 Nov. 1873; F/6/74, Cardwell to Ponsonby, 27 Nov. 1873; F/6/75, Ponsonby to Cardwell 1 Dec. 1873.

37 NMM, Fremantle MSS, FRE/101, Fremantle to Peile, 17 Oct. 1873; ibid., FRE/102, Fremantle to Wolseley 16 Oct. 1873. Subsequently, Goschen as First Lord of the Admiralty took particular exception to Wolseley's despatch but, in the event, the offending passage was not removed. See TNA, PRO 30/48/33, Kimberley to Cardwell, 20 and 28 Jan. 1874; ibid., CO 96/111, Wolseley to Kimberley, 22 Feb. 1874.

38 Centre for Buckinghamshire Studies, Fremantle MSS, D/FR/136/20 (8), Note by Fremantle; Brackenbury, *Ashanti War*, I, pp. 178, 182–4; Harvie, 'Raid on Essaman', pp. 19–27; BPP, Cmd. 892, pp. 195–200, Wolseley to Kimberley, 15 Oct. 1873; Henty, *March to Coomassie*, pp 104, 106, 113–14.

39 Low, *General Lord Wolseley*, p. 257; Maurice, *Ashantee War*, p. 105; Brackenbury, *Ashanti War*, I, p. 400.

40 BPP, Cmd. 892, pp. 62–6, Wolseley to Kimberley, 9 Oct. 1873; McIntyre, 'British Policy', pp. 37–9.

41 Hawkins and Powell, *Journal of Kimberley*, pp. 282–83; Matthew, *Gladstone Diaries*, pp. 379, 399. Drafts of the instructions can be found in BL, Gladstone MSS, Add. MSS 44641, ff. 193–6. See also TNA, CO 96/108.

42 Cambridge MSS, RA VIC/ADD E/1/7241, Cardwell to Cambridge, 17 Nov. 1873; Hove, Wolseley MSS, Autobiographical Coll., Cardwell to Wolseley, 18 Nov. 1873; McIntyre, 'British Policy', p. 38; idem, *Imperial Frontier*, pp. 148–9; Walling, *Diaries of Bright*, pp. 357–8; Hawkins and Powell, *Journal of Kimberley*, p. 283; Drus, *Journal of Events*, pp. 42–3; BPP, Cmd. 892, p. 238, Cardwell to Wolseley, 18 Nov. 1873; BL, Gladstone MSS, Add. MSS 44641, ff. 218, 223, Gladstone to the Queen, 17 Nov. and Cabinet Minute, 21 Nov. 1873; Matthew, *Gladstone Diaries*, pp. 413–14.

43 RA VIC/MAIN F/6/61, Ponsonby to Queen 19 Nov. 1873; ibid., VIC/ADD A/36/692, Ponsonby to Lady Ponsonby, 20 Nov. 1873.

44 Cambridge MSS, RA VIC/ADD E/1/7243, Cambridge to Airey, 17 Nov. 1873; ibid., E/1/7233 and E/1/7255, Cambridge to Wolseley, 11 Nov. and 2 Dec. 1873; Sir William Butler, *The Life of Sir George Pomeroy-Colley* (London: John Murray, 1899), p. 90.

45 Brooks, *Long Arm of Empire*, p. 119; Fremantle, *Navy As I Have Known It*, p. 190.

46 Curtin, *Disease and Empire*, pp. 4–5, 11, 16, 18, 49, 52–3, 69–70; S. C. Ukpabi, 'West Indian Troops and the Defence of British West Africa in the Nineteenth Century', *African Studies Review* 18 (1974), pp. 33–50; Paul M. Ubaeyi, *British Military and Naval Forces in West African History, 1807–74* (New York: Nok, 1978), pp. 88–112.

47 Gosford, Wemyss MSS, Charteris journal, 4 Oct. 1873; ibid., Charteris to Lady Wemyss, 21 Oct. 1873; ibid., Bound Volume, 'Alfred', Charteris to Elcho, n.d.; Huyshe, 'Topography of Ashanti', p. 131; Henty, *March to Coomassie*, pp. 84–90; Dooner, *Jottings*, p. 18; Stanley, *Coomassie and Magdala*, pp. 30–3; Curtin, *Disease and Empire*, pp. 23–4, 65–6; WSRO, Methuen MSS, WRSO 1742/RB 6335, Methuen to his father, 17 Dec. and 26 Dec. 1873.

48 Henty, *March to Coomassie*, pp. 24–6; Dooner, *Jottings*, p. 23; Hart-Synnot, *Letters*, p. 23; Melville, *Buller*, I, pp. 66, 79; Wood, *Midshipman to Field Marshal*, I, p. 267.

49 BPP, Cmd. 892, pp. 140–6, Home to Logan, 12 Sept. 1873.

50 BPP, XV, 1875, Cmd. 1374 *Army Medical Department Report for the Year 1873*, pp. 206–15, 229, 243–4, 250, 258–9, 260–80; Cmd. 894, pp. 67–8, Wolseley to Kimberley, 8 Jan. 1874; TNA, MT 23/38; Curtin, *Disease and Empire*, pp. 60–1, 64–7; Maurice, *Ashantee War*, pp. 153–4, 203; NMM, LOG/N/E/1, McLeod Journal, 30 Oct., 17 Nov. and 23 Nov. 1873. Records compiled by naval surgeons attached to the Naval Brigade or on station off Cape Coast, which include detailed case notes and sketches, can be found in TNA, ADM 101/145, 146, 148 and 149.

51 Brackenbury, *Ashanti War*, I, p. 171; Reade, *Story of the Ashantee Campaign*, pp. 107, 223; Henty, *March to Coomassie*, p. 126; BPP, Cmd. 1374, pp. 228, 241; Curtin, *Disease and Empire*, pp. 51–2; Edgerton, *Fall of the Asante Empire*, p. 101; Wilks, *Asante*, p. 237.

52 Butler, *Autobiography*, p. 150; idem, *Akim-Foo*, pp. 65–6; Maurice, *Ashantee War*, p. 107; Henty, *March to Coomassie*, p. 128.

53 Reade, *Story of the Ashantee Campaign*, pp. 188–90; Crook, *Records*,
   pp. 479–80; Maurice, *Ashantee War*, pp. 118–19; Boyle, *Through
   Fanteeland*, pp. 46–7; Brackenbury, *Ashanti War*, I, pp. 248–9; BPP,
   Cmd. 892, pp. 229–30, 232. It was actually issued in Wolseley's name
   by Lanyon.

54 Ramseyer and Kühne, *Four Years*, pp. 214, 239, 241–2; Wilks, *Forests
   of Gold*, p. 272.

55 Henty, *March to Coomassie*, pp. 127, 158–9, 166–7; Brackenbury,
   Ashanti War, I, pp. 200–5; Crooks, *Records*, pp. 473–5; Wilks, *Forest
   of Gold*, p. 273; Maurice, *Ashantee War*, pp. 55–8; Buller Family
   MSS, Buller to Alice 'Lucy' Buller, 14 Nov. 1873; Melville, *Buller*, I,
   pp. 66–7; Ramseyer and Kühne, *Four Years*, pp. 245–7.

56 Keegan, 'Ashanti Campaign', p. 182; Wilks, *Asante*, pp. 8–10, 36, 39;
   idem, *Forests of Gold*, pp. 191–5.

57 Crooks, *Records*, pp. 480–2; Low, *General Lord Wolseley*, p. 261;
   Wolseley, *Story of a Soldier's Life*, II, pp. 303–4; Butler, *Autobiography*,
   pp. 151–3; idem, *Akim-Foo*, pp. 66–9; Reade, *Story of the Ashantee
   Campaign*, pp. 185–8; Maurice, *Ashantee War*, pp. 109–18; Boyle,
   Through Fanteeland, p. 45; Henty, *March to Coomassie*, pp. 135–53;
   Brackenbury, *Ashanti War*, I, pp. 232–52; Stanley, *Coomassie to
   Magdala*, p. 39.

58 BPP, Cmd. 892, pp. 229–30, Wolseley to Kimberley, 31 Oct. 1873.

Notes to Documents 23–58

1 Blackwood's printed them, of course, for general circulation: see
   Brackenbury and Huyshe, *Fanti and Ashanti*.

2 Wood's officers were Lieutenant James William Graves, 18th Foot,
   Lieutenant Arthur Hardolph Eyre, 90th Foot, Lieutenant Richard
   Oliffe Richmond, 50th Foot, and Lieutenant Edward Robert Prevost
   Woodgate, 4th Foot. Wood and his colleagues found six officers in
   Elmina already, three of whom were down with fever and two of whom
   'startled' Wood by offering trade gin rather than afternoon tea: see
   Wood, *Midshipman to Field Marshal*, I, p. 257. Wood's horse took a lot of
   getting ashore: see Gosford, Wemyss MSS, Charteris Journal, 2 Oct. 73.

3 LEL were the identifying initials of Letitia Elizabeth Landon
   (1802–38), whose grave was inside Cape Coast Castle next to that

of Maclean. A romantic poet and novelist, much of her work had appeared in the *Literary Gazette*. Major poetry collections included *The Improvisatrice and Other Poems* (1824), *The Troubadour* (1825), *The Golden Violet* (1827), and *The Venetian Bracelet* (1829), while her novels included *Romance and Reality* (1831). She was introduced to Maclean by John Forster, MP and married him in June 1838. She arrived at Cape Coast on 16 August 1838 but died on 15 October, being found dead with prussic acid close to her body. The verdict was an accidental overdose but Maclean was said to have had a mistress named Catherine Bannerman, who was probably half-caste, and it was rumoured this had played a factor in what was actually suicide. See Glennis Stephenson, *Letitia Landon* (Manchester: Manchester University Press, 1995), and St Clair, *Grand Slave Emporium*, pp. 171–82. Wolseley said he admired her poetry when he was a boy: see Wolseley, *Story of a Soldier's Life*, II, p. 290.

4   In 1826 it was rumoured Letitia had a child by William Jerdan, editor of the *Literary Gazette*, though this was always denied. In fact, she had at least one child by Jerdan and possibly others.

5   Edward George Earle Lytton Bulwer Lytton (1803–73), novelist and politician. Liberal MP for St Ives, 1831–2; Lincoln, 1832–41; Hertfordshire, 1852–66; Secretary of State for the Colonies, 1858–9; created Baron Lytton, 1866. Rosina Anne (nee Doyle), Lady Bulwer Lytton (1802–82), novelist. They married in 1826 and separated in 1836.

6   Donald Alexander Smith, Land Commissioner of the Hudson's Bay Company. Smith, later Baron Strathcona and Mount Royal (1820–1914), had begun work as a fur trader for the Company in 1838. Company Factor in Labrador, 1848–68; Chief Company Factor, Montreal, 1869; Dominion Commissioner to Inquire into the North West Rebellion, 1869; Company Chief Commissioner, 1871–3; Company Land Commissioner, 1874–9; Governor of the Company, 1889–1914; Canadian High Commissioner in London, 1896–1914. Raised Strathcona's Horse for South African War. KCMG, 1887; Baron, 1897.

7   Alexander Herman Adam Gordon, 98th Foot. Commissioned 1860. Promoted to Captain in 84th Foot as result of war services in Asante. Service in Asante; Afghanistan, 1878–79. Honorary Major General, 1885.

8   The Snider was the first breech-loading rifle issued for general
    use in the British army. The breech-loading mechanism designed
    by Jacob Snider, an American of Dutch extraction working in
    Philadelphia, was adopted in September 1866 and, initially, applied
    to the existing 1855 Pattern .577 Lancaster and 1858 Pattern .577
    Enfield percussion rifles converted for the purpose. Once the supply
    of Enfields was used up in 1869 the so-called Mark I and II Snider-
    Enfield rifles were replaced by an entirely new .577 Snider but its
    official designation of the Mark III Snider-Enfield persisted. The
    Mark I Martini-Henry replaced the Snider in 1874. A single shot
    breech-loader firing a rolled-brass cartridge designed by Colonel
    Edward Boxer of the Royal Laboratory, the Snider was capable of
    about ten rounds a minute up to a range of about 1,000 yards. See
    Peter Duckers, *British Military Rifles* (Princes Risborough: Shire
    Publications, 2005), pp. 19–20; and Charles Purdon, *The Snider-
    Enfield* (Alexandria Bay, NY: Museum Restoration Service, 1963).

9   Lieutenant Henry Francis Somerset Bolton, 1st West India
    Regiment. Commissioned 1863. Service in Asante. Honorary Major,
    1881.

10 Document **26**.

11 Surgeon General Sir William Mure Muir, Head of the Sanitary
    Branch, Army Medical Department. Commissioned 1842. Service in
    Crimea; Mutiny; China 1860. Director General of the Army Medical
    Department, 1874–82; KCB, 1873.

12 Captain Reginald William Sartorius (1841–1907), 6th Bengal
    Cavalry and Special Service Officer attached to Glover's Expedition.
    Commissioned 72nd Bengal Native Infantry, 1858. Service in
    Mutiny; Asante; Afghanistan, 1878–9. VC, 1874; Major General,
    1895.

13 BPP, Cmd. 892, p. 126, Glover to Wolseley, 4 Oct. 1873. Glover's
    request for blasting powder was rejected by Kimberley: see BPP,
    Cmd. 892, p. 176, Kimberley to Wolseley, 10 Nov. 1873.

14 James Marshall had been appointed Chief Magistrate on 14 May
    1873. Marshall was one-armed: see Dooner, *Jottings*, p. 15. Fremantle
    thought him able: see Fremantle, *Navy As I Have Known It*, p. 250.

15 John Barraclough Fell (1815–1902) designed a railway system for steep
    inclines with a raised centre rail between two running rails. It was

used, for example, at Whaley Bridge, 1863–4 and on the Mont Cenis railway, opened in 1868. Herbert Thompson had recommended a Fell railway as suitable for the Gold Coast while Robert Home also felt it the only kind of railway that might be practicable: see CUL, Glover MSS, RCMS 131/12, Thompson to Kimberley, 4 Aug. 1873; TNA, WO 147/27, *Journal of Engineer Operations*.

16 Thirty years later, Wolseley was still appalled by the pleasure and amusement the hanging afforded its African audience. The execution on a gallows in an embrasure of Fort William was botched, the drawn bolt not giving way with the result that the condemned man did not die for at least 13 minutes. Wolseley called the colonial engineer to account: see Wolseley, *Story of a Soldier's Life*, II, pp. 290–1; Henty, *March to Coomassie*, pp. 73–6; Gosford, Wemyss MSS, Charteris Journal, 8 Oct. 1873.

17 Alexander Erskine Holmes was supposedly Louisa Wolseley's uncle and she had been his ward when growing up. In reality, Loo was almost certainly illegitimate and Holmes her real father. See Pegram, *Wolseley Heritage*, pp. xii–xviii.

18 A note later added to the letter by Frances Wolseley indicates that the Bushby family was that of Commodore Commerell's wife.

19 The 'Baba' was Wolseley's daughter, Frances, born in September 1872. Frances Garnet Wolseley (1872–1936) became a well-known gardener, running the Glynde Gardening School for women. When Wolseley was made a viscount in 1885, the Queen requested that the title be inherited by Frances, who thus by special remainder became Viscountess Wolseley upon her father's death in 1913. She never married.

20 'Aunt' Wolseley was the Dowager Lady Wolseley of Mount Wolseley, Carlow.

21 It has not been possible to identify Major Stevens.

22 Goldsworthy had been appointed Collector of Customs on 6 June 1873, but was replaced in this post by Owen Lanyon on 22 September 1873 and then joined Glover's expedition.

23 The Asante had attacked King Kwamin Blay of the Ateabu in July 1873. See BPP, Cmd. 891, pp. 74–5, 92–3.

23 *Elmina* and *Roquelle* were both steamers owned by the African Steamship Company. The *Elmina* (1,018 tons) was built in 1873 and

sold on to a Cuban company in 1878, while the *Roquelle* (1,216 tons) was built in 1869 and sold on to a Spanish company in 1882. The *Roquelle* brought out Captain Richard Buckle and Lieutenants Mark Sever Bell and Gother Mann, all of the Royal Engineers, together with a sergeant and five enlisted men; Captain William Fowler of 2nd West India Regiment; various medical, commissary and control personnel; and 208 carriers from Sierra Leone and Cape Palmas. See BPP, Cmd. 892, pp. 208–10, Wolseley to Kimberley, 21 Oct. 1873.

24 Captain Charles Cameron Lees (1837–98), Acting Administrator at Lagos. Commissioned, 1854. Secretary of the Gold Coast, 1873–4; Administrator of Lagos and Lieutenant Governor of Gold Coast Colony 1874; Governor of Labuan, 1879–81; Governor of the Bahamas, 1881; Governor of the Leeward Islands, 1884; Governor of Barbados, 1885; Governor of Mauritius, 1989. KCMG, 1883.

25 Major Alexander Bravo, 2nd West India Regiment. Commissioned 1849. Retired as Lieutenant Colonel, 1874. The allusion is to Mr Mantalini in Charles Dickens's *Nicholas Nickleby*, a selfish, affected fop married to the dressmaker, Madame Mantalini, who lives off her earnings and ends by ruining her. By contrast to Wolseley's view of Bravo, Stanley found him well liked in the regiment, while Fremantle thought him intelligent: see Stanley, *Coomassie and Magdala*, pp. 118–19; Fremantle, *Navy As I Have Known It*, p. 187.

26 Glover had reported that 15,000 rounds drawn from the Colonial Stores at Cape Coast were unserviceable. See BPP, Cmd. 892, pp. 150–1, Wolseley to Cardwell, 10 Oct. 1873.

27 McCarthy's fatal foray into the bush in 1824 had been beset by supply difficulties, 'ammunition' boxes brought up during the engagement that cost his life containing only biscuit. McCarthy had also placed undue faith in the psychological effect on the Asante of both bright uniforms and the band of the Royal African Corps. See Lloyd, *Drums of Kumasi*, pp. 37–46

28 Fort St Iago was one of two forts at Elmina, St George della Mina having been constructed close to the sea by the Portuguese, with Fort St Iago further inland and commanding both Fort St George and the town.

29 The quarantine ordinance of 8 Oct. 1873 can be found in BPP, Cmd. 892, p. 217.

30 Captain Mounford Stephen Loviele Peile, RN (1824–85) commanded HMS *Simoom*. Captain, 1867; retired 1879.

31 Acting Deputy Controller Matthew Bell Irvine, Control Department. Commissioned, 1848. Service in Crimea; Red River; Asante. Deputy Commissary General, 1874.

32 Joseph Dupuis, Agent and Consul at Kumase, 1818–20.

33 Major Stephen John Hill, Governor of the British Settlements on the Gold Coast, 1851–4. Commissioned 1825. Service on the Gambia, 1849. Brevet Major, 1850.

34 Richard Pine, Governor of the British Settlements on the Gold Coast, 1862–5.

35 Charles H. T. B. de Ruvignès served in the Gold Coast Artillery Corps from 1857–61. He had forwarded a campaign plan to Kimberley in August 1873. See CUL, Glover MSS, RCMS 131/6, Meade to Kimberley, 13 Aug. 73.

36 Henry Bird, Acting Governor of the British Settlements on the Gold Coast, 1858–60. Bird had served in the Gold Coast Artillery Corps from 1851 to 1860, attaining the rank of Lieutenant Colonel in 1860.

37 Captain Herbert William Thompson (1842–74), 2nd Dragoon Guards (Queen's Bays). Commissioned 16th Foot, 1859. Thompson had been appointed Inspector General of Armed Police on 25 August 1873, having submitted a campaign plan to Kimberley in July. He also submitted road reports to Harley in September. In October he then changed his mind on the ability of Europeans to campaign on the Gold Coast, now believing it possible compared to his adverse assessment in July. Ironically, he died of disease off Cape St Vincent, 28 January 1874 and is commemorated by a memorial tablet and stained glass window in Brighton College Chapel. See CUL, Glover MSS, RCMS 131/6, Thompson to Kimberley, 31 July 1873; TNA, CO 96/102, Thompson to Harley, 4 Sept. 73; TNA, WO 147/27, Thompson to Wolseley, 8 Oct. 1873.

38 The *Warree* remains unidentified in terms of its shipping line and details.

39 Lieutenant Edward Barrington Stephens, Royal Marine Light Infantry. Commissioned 1868. Service in Asante. Brevet Major 1889.

40 Captain Lionel Lowdham Brett, 2nd West India Regiment.

Commissioned 1858. Service in West Africa, 1861; Asante. Colonel, 1881; retired on half pay, 1888. Received Royal Humane Society's Silver Medal for rescuing two people from drowning at Newquay, Cornwall in August 1867. Brett had been appointed an Assistant Magistrate at Cape Coast in July 1873.

Captain William Fowler, 2nd West India Regiment. Commissioned 1863. Service in Crimea with 21st Foot; invalided from Asante and retired.

41 John Sarbah was a merchant at Cape Coast. His son John Mensah Sarbah (1864–1910) founded 'Gold Coast People' in 1891 and the Gold Coast Aborigines Rights Society in 1897, serving on the Legislative Council, 1904–10. Following the disbandment of the Cape Coast Volunteers, Sarbah and other officers were attached to the 2nd West India Regiment: see BPP, Cmd. 907, p. 2.

42 *Bonny* (1,277 tons) was built for the African Steam Ship Company in 1869, and sold off to a French company in 1890.

43 See Brackenbury, *Ashanti War*, I, p. 204.

44 James Marshall. See note 14 above.

45 Possibly Colonel James Conolly, British Military Attaché in Paris. Commissioned, 1836; service in Crimea; Lieutenant General, 1880.

46 Lieutenant Colonel Arthur Frederick Warren (1830–1913), commanding 2nd Rifle Brigade. Commissioned, Rifle Brigade, 1847. Service in Crimea; Mutiny; Asante. CO, 32nd Regimental District, 1881–6. KCB, 1907; Major General, 1887.

47 Lieutenant Colonel the Hon. Savage Lloyd-Mostyn (1835–1914) commanding the 2/23rd Foot. Commissioned, 1853. Service in Crimea; Mutiny; Asante. CO Regimental District, 1880–5; KCB, 1907; Major General, 1885. Son of 2nd Baron Mostyn.

48 Major General Henry George Hart (1808–78) had started publishing his *Annual Army List* in 1840. Commissioned, 49th Foot, 1829; Lieutenant General, 1877.

49 Colonel Robert Biddulph (1835–1918), Private Secretary to the Secretary of State for War. Commissioned, Royal Artillery, 1853. Service in Crimea; Mutiny; China, 1860. Private Secretary to Secretary of State for War, 1871–4; AAG at War Office, 1874–8; High Commissioner, Cyprus, 1878–86; Inspector General of Recruiting, 1886–8; Director General of Education, 1888–93; QMG, 1893; CinC

and Governor, Gibraltar, 1893–1900. KCMG, 1880; GCMG, 1886; GCB, 1899; General, 1892.

50 Jessie Cruikshank's father, Brodie Cruikshank, had been Governor of Anomabu in the 1830s. Reade comments on how many of Wolseley's officers lusted after the half-caste Jessie while she sat sewing or ironing on her veranda, while Charteris remarked that she was 'spoiled' by wearing European clothes. Jessie, however, was engaged to a black or half-caste man in the Cape Coast Volunteers and married him just after the return of the expedition to the coast. See Reade, *Story of the Ashantee Campaign*, pp. 191–2; Gosford, Wemyss MSS, Charteris journal, 16 Oct. 1873.

51 According to a note by Wolseley's daughter, 'BJ' was Mrs Alexander Holmes.

52 McCort appears to have been a nurse for Frances Wolseley.

53 Major General the Hon. Robert Rollo. Commissioned 1832. Service in Crimea; AAG in Canada, 1855–60; Military Secretary to GOC, British North America, 1860–5; retired as General, 1880.

54 McCalmont had gone down with fever just before the Elmina affair and stayed on board HMS *Simoom* for another three weeks or so before going home. See Document **64** and Callwell, *Memoirs of McCalmont*, pp. 76–7.

55 See Document **57**.

56 Identified by Frances Wolseley as Rose Eyton, the daughter of a well-known antiquarian, Rev. Robert William Eyton (1815–81), author of *Antiquities of Shropshire* (1853–60).

57 Major General Frederick Charles Arthur Stephenson, Acting Inspector General of Auxiliary Forces, 1873–4 was always known as 'Ben': see F. C. A. Stephenson, *At Home and on the Battlefield* (London: John Murray, 1915), pp. 28–31. Wolseley still referred to him as Stevenson in his memoirs, having first made his acquaintance when en route to China in 1857: see Wolseley, *Story of a Soldier's Life*, I, p. 231. Stephenson (1821–1911) was commissioned in the Scots Fusilier Guards, 1837. Service in Crimea; China, 1857–61; Canada, 1861–2. Military Secretary to CinC in Crimea, 1855; AAG, China, 1857–60; DAG, China, 1860–1; GOC, Home District, 1876–9; GOC, Egypt, 1883–7; Constable of the Tower, 1898–1911. KCB, 1885; GCB, 1886; General, 1886.

58 Under the heading, 'Gold and Jewel', the entry in *Punch*, 65 (1873),

p. 130 on 27 Sept. 1873 read, 'Sir Garnet Wolseley, at the head of the expedition against the Ashantees, will doubtless prove himself worthy of his Christian name. A Garnet on the Gold Coast is as a precious stone with setting handy; but in sending our Garnet against those Niggers we are risking our gem.'

59 Princess Marguerite of Savoy (Margherita Maria Teresa Giovanna di Savola, 1851–1926) married Prince Humbert (Umberto) in 1868, Humbert succeeding to the Italian throne as Humbert I in 1878, reigning until his assassination by an anarchist in 1900.

60 *The Graphic* had shown an illustration of the 'late' Colonel Kenneth Douglas Mackenzie. 'Jock' Mackenzie (1811–73), AQMG at the Horse Guards, had died from syncope brought on by exhaustion after being swept away by the current in the River Meavy at Gratton Ford near Roborough when his carriage had overturned while he was attending the Dartmoor manoeuvres in August 1873: see *The Times*, 25 and 26 Aug. 1873. Commissioned in 1831. Service in Crimea; Mutiny; China, 1860–1. DAAG, Dublin, 1856–7; AAG, Bengal, 1858–9; AQAG at Horse Guards, 1870–3. CB, 1860; Brevet Colonel, 1869. Mackenzie had been chosen ahead of Wolseley as DQMG of the China expedition and Wolseley served under him both there and in Canada: see Wolseley, *Story of a Soldier's Life*, II, pp. 7, 103, 115.

61 Lieutenant George Pollard, HMS *Simoom*. Lieutenant, 1871. For a vivid description of 'Pollard's army' see Butler, *Akim-Foo*, pp. 73–4.

62 Captain Algernon Arbuthnot Godwin, 103rd Foot. Commissioned 1860. Service in Asante. Retired as Major, 1874; Honorary Lieutenant Colonel, 1881.

63 Captain John Frederick Crease (1837–1907) Royal Marine Artillery, appointed Colonial Surveyor, 26 Sept. 1873. Commissioned 1854. Service in China, 1857–61; Asante. Colonel Commandant of the Royal Marine Artillery, 1888; KCB, 1902; Honorary Major General, 1891. Invented the Crease filter, a detailed description of which can be found in Henty, *March to Coomassie*, pp. 81–2.

64 Kwasi Nakko, King of Abrakampa.

3 Marking Time (November 1873)

Notes to Introduction

1   Maurice, *Ashantee War*, pp. 121–2; Stanley, *Coomassie and Magdala*, p. 45; Wolseley, *Story of a Soldier's Life*, II, p. 304; Henty, *March to Coomassie*, pp. 174–5; Brackenbury, *Ashanti War*, I, pp. 255–6; Hart-Synnot, *Letters*, p. 46; TNA, Hart MSS, WO 211/71, Hart to his father, 1 Dec. 1873. Spiers, *Victorian Soldier*, p. 21 quotes Surgeon Major Gore's account of the retrieval of Wilmot's body from the *Evening Standard*.

2   Maurice, *Ashantee War*, p. 122; Henty, *March to Coomassie*, pp. 176–7; Reade, *Story of the Ashantee Campaign*, pp. 207–8; Brackenbury, *Ashanti War*, I, p. 256; Wood, 'Ashanti Expedition', p. 340.

3   Melville, *Buller*, I, pp. 66–7; Butler, *Autobiography*, p. 162.

4   Brackenbury, *Ashanti War*, I, pp. 223–5, 252–64, 267–8; Low, *General Lord Wolseley*, pp. 261–2; Reade, *Story of the Ashantee Campaign*, pp. 202–14; Maurice, *Ashantee War*, pp. 132, 151–2; Henty, *March to Coomassie*, pp. 179–84; Boyle, *Through Fanteeland*, pp. 53, 57–8, 77; Hart-Synnot, *Letters*, pp. 28–9, 33, 37; Dooner, *Jottings*, pp. 26–7; Hove, Wolseley MSS, W/P 3/12, Wolseley to Lady Wolseley, 7 Nov. 1873.

5   Low, *General Lord Wolseley*, pp. 261–2; Maurice, *Ashantee War*, pp. 126–7; Wolseley, *Story of a Soldier's Life*, II, pp. 204–7; Henty, *March to Coomassie*, pp. 184–5; Brackenbury, *Ashanti War*, I, pp. 263–6; Fremantle, *Navy As I have Known It*, pp. 225–7; NMM, Fremantle MSS, FRE/102, Fremantle to Admiralty, 8 Nov. 1873; BPP, Cmd. 893, p. 10, Wolseley to Cardwell, 7 Nov. 1873 (also in TNA, CO 96/107); BPP, Cmd. 1374, pp. 241–3; Wood, *Midshipman to Field Marshal*, I, p. 264.

6   Wood, *Midshipman to Field Marshal*, I, p. 265; idem, 'Ashanti Expedition;', p. 341; Low, *General Lord Wolseley*, pp. 263–4; Reade, *Story of the Ashantee Campaign*, pp. 217–18; Maurice, *Ashantee War*, p. 135; Boyle, *Through Fanteeland*, pp. 84–7, 94, 97; Henty, *March to Coomassie*, pp. 187–90, 198–9; Brackenbury, *Ashanti War*, I, pp. 267–75; Hart-Synnot, *Letters*, p. 3; Stanley, *Coomassie and Magdala*, p. 46. The drum passed to the National Army Museum in 1963, its catalogue number being NAM 1963–10–175–1.

7   Reade, *Story of the Ashantee Campaign*, pp. 218–19; Henty. *March
    to Coomassie*, pp. 191–5; Brackenbury, *Ashanti War*, I, pp. 276–9;
    Fremantle, *Navy As I Have Known it*, pp. 236–7.

8   Maurice, *Ashantee War*, pp. 155–8; Butler, *Akim-Foo*, p. 77;
    Brackenbury, *Ashanti War*, I, p. 281; TNA, WO 33/25, Wolseley to
    Cardwell, 21 Nov. 1873; ibid., WO 32/7638; Gosford, Wemyss MSS,
    Charteris to Lady Elcho, 8 Nov. 1873; ibid., Drawer 39, Irvine to
    Elcho, 2 Dec. 1873.

9   RA VIC/MAIN F/7/28, Home to Director General, Army Medical
    Department, 27 Nov. 1873; Brackenbury, *Ashanti War*, I, pp. 279–80;
    Maurice and Arthur, *Life of Wolseley*, p. 67; Low, *General Lord
    Wolseley*, p. 265; NMM, LOG/N/E/1, McLeod Journal, 8 and 23
    Nov. 1873; Fremantle, *Navy As I Have Known It*, pp. 238–9.

10 RA VIC/MAIN F/7/21 Home report on Wolseley, 13 Nov. 1873;
    BPP, Cmd. 893, pp. 15–16; Hove, Wolseley Autobiographical Coll.,
    Cardwell to Wolseley, 8 and 18 Dec. 1873; Wolseley, *Story of a
    Soldier's Life*, II, pp. 307–10; Low, *General Lord Wolseley*, p. 264;
    Wood, *Midshipman to Field Marshal*, I, p. 267; Maurice, *Ashantee
    War*, p. 146; Henty, *March to Coomassie*, pp. 221–2.

11 Henty, *March to Coomassie*, pp. 195, 218, 246–91; Stanley, *Coomassie
    and Magdala*, pp. 67–82, 88–102.

12 Glover, 'Volta Expedition', p. 319; BPP, Cmd. 893, p. 34; TNA, WO
    33/25, Wolseley to Cardwell, 27 Nov. 1873 (also in WO 32/7638);
    Butler, *Akim-Foo*, pp. 87–8; Boyle, *Through Fanteeland*, p. 159.

13 BPP, Cmd. 892, pp. 246–7; Brackenbury, *Ashanti Wa*r, I, p. 359; ibid.,
    II, pp. 111–22; Butler, *Autobiography*, pp. 153–63; idem, *Akim-Foo*,
    pp. 81, 87–8, 93–119, 201; Wood, *Midshipman to Field Marshal*, I,
    pp. 322–3; Boyle, *Through Fanteeland*, p. 159; Reade, *Story of the
    Ashantee Campaign*, pp. 366–7.

14 BPP, Cmd. 1374, pp. 245–8; Curtin, *Disease and Empire*, p. 64; Low,
    General Lord Wolseley, p. 267; Brackenbury, *Ashanti War*, I,
    pp. 308–28

15 Brackenbury, *Ashanti War*, I, pp. 308–16; TNA, WO 147/27, *Journal
    of Engineer Operations* (also in WO 33/26); ibid., WO 33/25, Home
    to Chapman, 26 Dec. 1873. Spiers, *Victorian Soldier*, pp. 23–4 quotes
    letters by Lieutenant Herbert Jekyll, RE from the *Royal Engineers'
    Journal*.

16 Wood, *Midshipman to Field Marshal*, I, pp. 268–72; idem, 'Ashanti Expedition', p. 343; Butler, *Akim-Foo*, pp. 132–6, 143–6; Boyle, *Through Fanteeland*, pp. 167–8; Ramseyer and Kühne, *Four Years*, pp. 249–5, 254–5; Perrot and Dantzig, *Bonnat*, pp. 52–3; Brackenbury, *Ashanti War*, I, pp. 282–97.

Notes to Documents 59–84

1 Actually the Union Steamship Company's *African* (2019 tons). Launched only in December 1872, she had completed her maiden voyage to Cape Town in April 1873. Sold to Stumore & Co. in 1885 and a total loss after running aground in the Red Sea in 1887.

2 Staff Surgeon Francis Hamilton Moore, RN. Staff Surgeon, 1868.

3 Lieutenant Eardley Wilmot (1846–73). Commissioned Royal Artillery, 1867. Third son of Sir John Eardley Eardley-Wilmot, Bt, Conservative MP for South Warwickshire, 1874–85.

4 Wolseley does not mention the incident in his memoirs, but it would appear he was sent on board the ship on 23 July 1855, remaining there for a little over a week. See Low, *General Lord Wolseley*, pp. 53–4.

5 McCalmont acquired the nickname of 'The King' because he talked so much on the voyage out of capturing Kofi Karikari. See Callwell, *McCalmont*, p. 73–4.

6 Captain William Owen Lanyon (1842–87), 2nd West Indian Regiment. Commissioned 6th Foot, 1860. Service in Ashanti; Egypt, 1882; Sudan, 1884–5. Private Secretary to Governor of Jamaica, 1868–73; Administrator of Griqualand West, 1875–79; Resident and Administrator, Transvaal, 1879–81. KCMG, 1880, Colonel, 1882.

7 Wolseley's recollection of Psalm 27 is correct but for one word, the King James text reading 'strengthen *thine* heart'.

8 From the Hindi, meaning a thrashing.

9 RA VIC/ADD E/1/7228, Fasting to Wolseley, 3 Nov. 1873.

10 Wolseley had a recurrence of his 'Burma fever' while on the Red River in 1870 and also on occasions in London: see Maurice, *Ashantee War*, p. 146. In Burma, apart from the serious wounds to his left leg, Wolseley had also survived a bout of what he described as 'a sort of cholera': see Wolseley, *Story of a Soldier's Life*, I, p. 73.

11 Mountford Peile.

12 Hewett arrived on HMS *Active* on 15 November.

13 It has not been possible to identify Mrs Bailiff.

14 Captain William Hans Blake, RN of HMS *Druid*. Service in New Zealand, 1860; Asante. Captain, 1867. Died 27 Jan. 1874 from fever and debility, aged 42. See TNA, ADM 101/145, Surgical Journal of Staff Surgeon Henry Fegan. Blake's own journal is in NMM, BLK/2, recording the onset of his fever on 17 January.

15 One of Glover's other requests was for 1,000 boxes of gin but, as the Colonial Office judged these were meant only for presents, he was restricted to 250. See BPP, Cmd. 92, p. 162, and Cmd. 1893, p. 3.

16 BPP, Cmd. 892, pp. 162–6, Wolseley to Kimberley, 9 Oct. 1873.

17 It has not been possible to identify this vessel.

18 In Bright's speech to his constituents at Bingley Hall in Birmingham on 22 October, he expressed the view that the time would come 'when Parliament, acting upon the opinion of one of its own committees [presumably the 1865 Select Committee] will consider that it would be wise to withdraw absolutely from the African coast', adding that he believed personally that 'the interests and the honour of the country at some not distant time would be best consulted by an entire withdrawal from that coast'. See *The Times*, 23 Oct. 1873.

19 Major General Edwin Beaumont Johnson (1825–93), Quartermaster-General in India. Commissioned Bengal Artillery, 1842. Service in Sikh War, 1845–6; Mutiny. Quartermaster-General in India, 1873–4; Adjutant General, India, 1874–77; Member of Council of India, 1874–77; Military Member of the Viceroy's Council, 1877–80; Director of Education, War Office, 1884–86. KCB, 1875; General, 1877. Both his brothers were also notable soldiers: Allen Bayard Johnson, with whom Wolseley had served in Burma, being Military Secretary at the India Office, 1877–80, and Charles Cooper Johnson being Quartermaster-General in India, 1878–80.

20 Thomas George Baring, 2nd Baron Northbrook (1826–1904), Governor-General and Viceroy of India, 1872–76. Liberal MP for Falmouth and Penryn, 1857–66; Civil Lord of Admiralty, 1857–58; Under Secretary of State for India, 1859–61 and 1861–64; Under Secretary of State for War, 1861 and 1868–72; Under Secretary of State, Home Office, 1864–66; Secretary to the Admiralty, 1866; First

Lord of the Admiralty, 1880–85. GCSI, 1869; created 1st Earl of Northbrook, 1876.
Captain Evelyn Baring (1841–1917), Private Secretary to his cousin, Lord Northbrook, 1872–76. Commissioned Royal Artillery, 1858. Service on Corfu, Malta and Jamaica; retired as Major, 1878. Controller-General, Egypt, 1879–82; Agent and Consul General, Egypt, 1883–1907; Chairman, Dardanelles Commission, 1916. KCSI 1883; OM, 1906; created 1st Baron Cromer, 1892; created 1st Earl of Cromer, 1901.

21 Sub Lieutenant Charles Windham RN, HMS *Active*. Sub Lieutenant, 1871. Wolseley refers possibly to Colonel William Wilby. Commissioned 4th Foot, 1836. Service in Crimea; Abyssinia, 1867–68. Retired as Lieutenant General, 1882.

22 Lieutenant Colonel George Daniel Webber, 2nd West India Regiment. Commissioned 17th Foot, 1855. Service in Crimea; Asante. Invalided in April 1874; retired on half pay, 1878. Cambridge was surprised at Webber's inefficiency as he had the *psc* qualification and was considered a good officer, but acknowledged that it was difficult to judge a man until he was tested in the field: see Cambridge MSS, RA VIC/ADD E/1/7272, Cambridge to Wolseley, 22 Dec. 1873. Stanley, however, praised Webber and his regiment: see Stanley, *Coomassie and Magdala*, pp. 118–19.

23 Wolseley's despatches to Cardwell on 27 and 30 November do not actually include such a request. See BPP, Cmd. 893, pp. 48–9.

24 Prince Charles Pepple of Bonny was the son of George Oruigbiji Pepple, King of Bonny, 1866–83 and 1887–88. George's father had been deported to Britain from 1854 to 1861 and George had been educated at Hall Place, Bexley. Both Wood and Boyle mention that Prince Charles had also been educated in England. See Wood, *Midshipman to Field Marshal*, I, p. 262; and Boyle, *Through Fanteeland*, pp. 176–7.

25 Lieutenant The Hon. Henry John Lindley Wood (1838–1903) arrived on 30 November in the *Volta* together with ten other special service officers from those Wolseley had requested back in October: see Brackenbury, *Ashanti War*, I, pp. 300–1. Wood was commissioned in the 10th Hussars in 1864. Service in Asante; South Africa, 1879. Honorary Lieutenant Colonel, 1883. Son of 1st Viscount Halifax.

4 Crisis (December 1873)

Notes to Introduction

1 Melville, *Buller*, I, pp. 68–9.

2 Henty, *March to Coomassie*, p. 237; Boyle, *Through Fanteeland*, p. 196; Stanley, *Coomassie and Magdala*, p. 118; J. E. Caulfield, *100 Years' History of the 2nd West India Regiment, 1795–1898* (London: Forster Groom & Co, 1898), p. 169.

3 Wood, 'Ashanti Expedition', p. 343.

4 Henty, *March to Coomassie*, pp. 304, 317; Brackenbury, *Ashanti War*, I, p. 345; ibid., II, pp. 84–5; report by Jekyll, 29 June 1874 in TNA, WO 147/27 and WO 33/26, *Journal of Engineer Operations*, pp. 43–57.

5 Brackenbury, *Ashanti War*, II, pp. 303–5; Henty, *March to Coomassie*, pp. 294–5; Boyle, *Through Fanteeland*, p. 225; Reade, *Story of the Ashantee Campaign*, pp. 258–61; Fremantle, *Navy As I Have Known It*, p. 203; NMM, LOG/N/27, Luxmore journal; BPP, Cmd. 894, 25 Wolseley to Kimberley, 26 Dec. 1873.

6 Buller Family MSS, Buller to Alice 'Lucy' Buller, 14 Nov. 73; Melville, *Buller*, I, p. 67.

7 Brackenbury, *Ashanti War*, I, pp. 335–6, 341, 353–4.

8 Low, *General Lord Wolseley*, p. 268; Brackenbury, *Ashanti War*, I, pp. 285, 333, 335; Maurice, *Ashantee War*, pp. 161–2.

9 Brackenbury, *Ashanti War*, I, p. 343.

10 Cambridge MSS, RA VIC/ADD E/1/7255, Cambridge to Wolseley, 2 Dec. 1873. Brackenbury, *Ashanti War*, II, p. 31 lists the officers allocated to Colley.

11 Butler, *Colley*, pp. 92–8, 111–12; Brackenbury, *Ashanti War*, II, pp. 30–1.

12 NAM, Cooper MSS, 6112–596–8–2 and 3 for examples of receipts for carriers' pay; Brackenbury, *Ashanti War*, I, pp. 369–72; ibid., II, pp. 90–7; G. Salis Schwabe, 'Carrier Corps and Coolies on Active Service in China, India, and Africa, 1860–79', *Journal of the Royal United Services Institution* 24, 107 (1880), pp. 815–46.

13 Spiers, *Scottish Soldier*, p. 29; Bodleian, Alison MSS, MS. Eng. lett. c. 450, Alison to his wife, 14–15 Jan. 1874.

14 Keegan, 'Ashanti Campaign', pp. 185–6; Brackenbury, *Ashanti War*, II, pp. 17–18, 24.

15 Boyle, *Through Fanteeland*, pp. 115–16; Henty, *March to Coomassie*, pp. 214–16; Brackenbury, *Ashanti War*, II, pp. 31–3.

16 TNA, CO 96/111 Report of Judicial Court of Assessors, 14 Nov. 1873, and Marshall to Wolseley, 29 Jan. 1874; BPP, Cmd. 922, pp. 17–18; Brackenbury, *Ashanti War*, II, pp. 20–1; Henty, *March to Coomassie*, p. 209.

17 TNA, CO 879/6, Wolseley to Kimberley, 26 Jan. 1874.

18 WSRO, Methuen MSS, WRSO 1742/6335, Methuen to his father, 26 Dec. 1873 and 2 Jan. 1874.

19 Bodleian, Alison MSS, MS. Eng. lett. c. 451, Alison to Greaves, 9 and 11 Jan. 1874; ibid., MS. Eng. lett. c. 450, Alison to his wife, 5–6 and 9–10 Jan. 1874; NAM, Cooper MSS, 6112–596–8–4, Colley to Cooper, 29 Jan. 1874; Brackenbury, *Ashanti War*, II, pp. 27–9, 36–7; Reade, *Story of the Ashantee Campaign*, pp. 239–40; Boyle, *Through Fanteeland*, p. 234; TNA, WO 33/26, *Journal of Engineer Operations*, p. 23–4; Curtin, *Disease and Empire*, p. 63; Lloyd, *Drums of Kumasi*, p. 91; Schwabe, 'Carrier Corps', pp. 815–46.

20 NAM, Cooper MSS, 6112–596, Colley to Cooper, 26 Feb. 1874.

21 Bodleian, Alison MSS, MS. Eng. lett. c. 450, Alison to his wife, 5–6 Jan. and 27–28 Jan. 1874; Dooner, *Jottings*, p. 35; WSRO, Methuen MSS, WRSO 1742/BR 6335, Methuen to his father, 26 Dec. 1873, and 2, 5, 18 and 30 Jan. 1874; NAM, Cooper MSS, 6112–596, Colley to Cooper, 26 Feb. 1874.

22 BPP, Cmd. 907, pp. 1–2; TNA, CO 879/6; ibid., WO 33/25; Crooks, *Records*, pp. 489–90.

23 Brackenbury, *Ashanti War*, II, p. 357.

24 Boyle, *Through Fanteeland*, p. 252; Stanley, *Coomassie and Magdala*, pp. 106, 110; Reade, *Story of the Ashantee Campaign*, pp. 229–44; Brackenbury, *Ashanti War*, II, pp. 9–10; Henty, *March to Coomassie*, pp. 209–10, 431–52.

25 Maurice, *Ashantee War*, pp. 53, 163, 251–60; Brackenbury, *Ashanti War*, I, p. 338; ibid, II, pp. 35–7.

26 Spiers, *Scottish Soldier*, pp. 26–7; Brackenbury, *Ashanti War*, I, pp. 342–3, 346.

27 Low, *General Lord Wolseley*, pp. 270–1; Brackenbury, *Ashanti War*, I, p. 352.

28 Low, *General Lord Wolseley*, pp. 269–70; Brackenbury, *Ashanti War*, I, pp. 346, 359; ibid., II, pp. 20–1; Henty, *March to Coomassie*, p. 317; Spiers, *Victorian Soldier*, p. 25; TNA, WO 147/27, *Journal of Engineer Operations*, p. 40.

29 Cavendish, *Cyprus 1878*, p. 58 (Wolseley's Cyprus journal entry for 22 Aug. 1878). On the tactical debate, see Howard Bailes, 'Patterns of Thought in the Late Victorian Army', *Journal of Strategic Studies* 4 (1981), pp. 29–45; idem, 'Technology and Tactics in the British Army, 1866–1900', in Ronald Haycock and Keith Neilson, eds, *Men, Machines and War* (Waterloo, ON: Wilfred Laurier University Press, 1988), pp. 23–47.

30 RA VIC/MAIN F/7/43, Ponsonby to the Queen, 20 Jan. 74; Bodleian, Alison MSS, MS. Eng. lett. c. 450, Alison to his wife, 6–18 Dec. 1873 and 27–28 Jan. 1874.

31 Bodleian, Alison MSS, MS. Eng. lett. c. 450; Alison to his wife, 6–18 and 21–26 Dec. 1873. See also Boyle, *Through Fanteeland*, pp. 228–32; Brackenbury, *Ashanti War*, I, pp. 361–7; Maurice *Ashantee War*, pp. 205–12.

32 Ian Knight, 'The Effectiveness of the Martini-Henry in Zululand', *Journal of the Anglo-Zulu War Historical Society* 11 (2002), pp. 1–5; idem, 'The Battle of Ulundi', in Adrian Greaves, ed., *Redcoats and Zulus* (Barnsley: Pen & Sword, 2004), pp. 206–15.

33 Low, *General Lord Wolseley*, p. 271; Callwell, *Small Wars*, pp. 28, 105, 111, 117, 187, 211, 350, 353–5, 358, 366, 396, 444, 475; W. C. G. Heneker, *Bush Warfare* (London: Hugh Rees, 1907), pp. 20–4, 34, 179–80; Beckett, 'Another British Way', pp. 89–102.

34 Crooks, *Records*, pp. 486–8; Cambridge MSS, RA VIC/ADD E/1/7284, Cambridge to Wolseley, 2 Jan. 1874; Verner, *Military Life*, II, p. 81.

35 Bodleian, Alison MSS, MS. Eng. lett. c. 450, Alison to his wife, 6–18 and 21–26 Dec. 1873.

36 Purdon, *Snider-Enfield*, p. 6.

37 Bodleian, Alison MSS, MS. Eng. lett. c. 450, Alison to his wife, 29 Dec. 1873–3 Jan. 1874; ibid., Hewett to Alison, 28 Dec. 1873; Brackenbury, *Ashanti War*, II, pp. 14–16.

38 Bodleian, Alison MSS, MS. Eng. lett. c. 450, Greaves to Alison, 28, 29 and 31 Dec. 1873; McLeod to Alison, 28 Dec, 1873;

Statement by Alison, 28 April 1874; Note of talk with Wolseley, 28 April 1874; Alison to Blackwood, 16 June 1874; Alison to his wife, 12–14 Jan. 1874; ibid., MSS. Eng. Lett. c. 451, Alison to Greaves 28 Dec. 1873; ibid., Report by Mackinnon, 28 Dec. 1873; WSRO, Methuen MSS, WRSO 1742/RB 6335, Methuen to his father, 5 Jan. 1874; BPP, Cmd. 1374, p. 254; TNA, WO 33/25, Wolseley to Cardwell, 8 Jan. 1874.

39 Cambridge MSS, RA VIC/ADD E/1/7319 and 7326, Cambridge to Wolseley, 6 and 13 Feb. 1874; Verner, *Military Life*, II, pp. 85–7.

40 Melville, *Buller*, I, pp. 69–70; Buller Family MSS, Buller to Henrietta, 31 Dec. 1873–1 Jan. 1874; Brackenbury, *Ashanti War*, II, p. 12; Maurice, *Ashantee War*, pp. 217–18; NMM, BLK/2, Blake journal, 27 Dec. 1873; ibid., LOG/N/27, Luxmore journal, 27 and 28 Dec. 1873.

41 CUL, Glover MSS, RCMS 131/6, Maurice to Glover, 4 Dec. 1873; TNA, CO 879/6, Wolseley to Kimberley 22 Dec. 1873.

42 CUL, Glover MSS, RCMS 131/6, Greaves to Glover, 24 and 31 Dec. 1873; TNA, CO 879/6, Wolseley to Kimberley, 26 Dec. 1873; ibid., Greaves to Glover, 31 Dec. 1873.

43 Wolseley, *Story of a Soldier's Life*, II, pp. 327–8; Low, *General Lord Wolseley*, p. 274; Brackenbury, *Ashanti War*, I, pp. 411–13.

44 Low, *General Lord Wolseley*, p. 274; TNA CO 96/111, Note by AWLH[emming], 3 Feb. 1874; Glover, 'Volta Expedition', pp. 320–3; Glover, *Life of Glover*, pp. 180–94; Brackenbury, *Ashanti War*, II, pp. 98–110.

Notes to Documents 85–111

1 Wolseley's letter to Robert Home appears to have arisen from Wood reporting that he had ordered Home detained on doctor's orders when he had tried to keep going despite sickness. Home then dictated a letter to Wolseley protesting that he should only receive orders direct from Wolseley. Wolseley replied that, as CRE, he received his orders from Wolseley but, as an officer, he was under the senior in whose camp he was on duty: see Wood, *Midshipman to Field Marshal*, I, p. 272. When he arrived in December, Methuen found Home the only one of Wolseley's officers who swaggered: 'I always though him a great ass, but he has done an immense amount of work

here.' See WSRO, Methuen MSS, WRSO 1742/6335, Methuen to his father, 26 Dec. 1873.

2 The Harmattan blows south off the Sahara, its sand and dust particles coating West Africa with yellow dirt and turning the nights cold.

3 Presumably Wolseley means the Marka, a Muslim tribe from Mali.

4 For the identification of the two 'sergeants' as Private Robert Fagan and Private Lewis, see Caulfield, *100 Years' History*, p. 168, and Stanley, *Coomassie to Magdala*, p. 118.

5 Lieutenant Richard Oliffe Richmond, 50th Foot. Commissioned 1858. Service in Asante. Promoted to Captain in 89th Foot, 1874; transferred to Army Pay Department as Paymaster, 1878; Staff Paymaster and Honorary Major, 1883.
Lieutenant Alwyn Shutt Bell, 2nd West India Regiment. Commissioned 1863; Lieutenant, 1867; invalided, 1874.

6 Literally a 'bridgehead', meaning in military parlance a fortified position guarding a bridge.

7 Conceivably, Wolseley means his strictures on the 2nd West India Regiment. For an extract of the despatch, see Brackenbury, *Ashanti War*, I, pp. 182–4. Cardwell's letter to Wolseley of 18 Nov. 1873 praising the moderate tone of his despatches can be found in Hove, Wolseley MSS, Autobiographical Coll.

8 HMS *Tamar* was an iron troopship.

9 Cambridge MSS, RA VIC/ADD E/1/7233 Cambridge to Wolseley, 11 Nov. 1873. The Duke had reminded Wolseley that he had been sent all the special service officers he had requested but that no more should be sent than actually needed.

10 For Wolseley to Cardwell, 15 Dec. 1873, see Crooks, *Records*, pp. 486–8; Brackenbury, *Ashanti War*, I, pp. 353–5.

11 Captain Robert Frederick Williamson, 2/23rd Foot. Commissioned 1861. Service in Asante; Burma, 1885–86; Hazara, 1891. Colonel, 1886; retired 1891.

12 The red-haired and deaf chaplain is most likely to have been Chaplain to the Forces (4th Class – Captain) Rev. Robert Stewart Patterson, who had previously served as a chaplain on Wolseley's Red River Expedition. Having been attached to the Ottoman forces in the Crimea, Patterson had also been a subaltern in the Canadian Volunteer Rifles, seeing service during the Fenian raids on Canada in

1866. He was only appointed a chaplain in the British army in 1872. Chaplain to the Forces (1st Class – Colonel), 1892.

13 Brackenbury, of course was Wolseley's Military Secretary.

14 Maurice was Wolseley's Private Secretary.

15 Matilda Wolseley tried her hand at being a novelist, publishing *Marley Castle: A Novel* (1877) and *Corafin* (1878). The former appeared as 'edited' by Wolseley himself to his intense embarrassment as he considered it 'rubbish': see SLCM, Wolseley Diaries, CAM.H.22, Entry for 8 Aug. 1877. Ironically, Matilda had reworked Wolseley's account of his visit to the Confederacy for publication in *Blackwood's* in January 1863: see Preston, *Wolseley's South African Diaries*, p. 26.

16 Captain HRH Prince Arthur William Patrick Albert, third son of Queen Victoria (1850–1942). Commissioned Royal Engineers, 1868. Service in Egypt, 1882. GOC, Rawalpindi Division, 1883–86; GOC, Bombay, 1886–90; GOC, Southern Command, 1890–93; GOC, Aldershot, 1893–98; GOC, Ireland, 1900–4; Inspector General of Forces, 1904–7; CinC, Mediterranean, 1907–9; Governor-General of Canada, 1911–16. KG, 1867; Field Marshal, 1902; created Duke of Connaught and Strathearn, and Earl of Sussex, 1874.

17 Captain Maurice FitzGerald, Extra Equerry to HRH Prince Arthur. Commissioned Rifle Brigade, 1869. Service in Asante as ADC to Alison, 1873–74; retired, 1881; CVO 1905. Succeeded as 2nd Baronet and 20th Knight of Kerry, 1880. Prince Arthur had written to Wolseley requesting that FitzGerald be placed on Alison's staff on 1 Dec. 1873: see Hove, Wolseley MSS, Autobiographical Coll., Arthur to Wolseley, 1 Dec. 1873.

18 *Sarmatian* (3647 tons), of the Allan Line, was launched in 1871 and scrapped in 1908.

19 Surgeon Valesius Skipton Goldsbury, African Medical Service. Commissioned 1863; Surgeon Major, 1876; retired as Honorary Brigade Surgeon, 1885.

20 Deputy Commissary Henry Frederick Blissett, African Branch, Control Department. Commissioned 1870. Service in Asante with Glover Expedition. Retired as Commissary, 1876.

21 The officer tasked with erecting the telegraph line was Lieutenant Herbert Jekyll, RE, until he was invalided on 30 January 1874. Jekyll

(1846–1932) was the brother of Gertrude Jekyll, the landscape gardener, and he was himself a noted woodcarver. Commissioned 1866. Service in Asante; Singapore, 1883–85. Private Secretary to Secretary of State for the Colonies, 1876–78; Secretary, Colonial Defence Committee, 1878–79; Secretary, Royal Commission on the Defence of British Possessions and Commerce, 1879–82; Private Secretary to Lord Lieutenant of Ireland, 1885–86 and 1892–95; Secretary to the Royal Commission for the Paris Exhibition, 1900–1; Chief, London Traffic Branch, Board of Trade, 1907–11; Chancellor of the Order of St John of Jerusalem, 1911–18. Brevet Colonel, 1896; retired, 1901; KCMG, 1901.

22 Lt Lewis F. Wells, RN. Lieutenant, 1869. The popular Wells had been due to take up the appointment of First Lieutenant on the Royal Yacht: see Henty, *March to Coomassie*, p. 203; Boyle, *Through Fanteeland*, p. 226; Reade, *Story of the Ashantee Campaign*, p. 262; NMM, LOG/N/E/1, McLeod journal, 16 and 23 Nov. 1873; WSRO, Methuen MSS, WSRO 1742/RB 6335, Methuen to his father, 26 Dec. 1873.
    Biafra (1487 tons) was owned by the African Steam Ship Co. It was launched in 1868 and sold to a French firm as *Energique* in 1889.

23 For Wolseley's official report on Sergeant Hughes, see BPP, Cmd. 894, p. 221.

24 *Ethiopia* (4005 tons) was an Anchor Line steamer launched in 1873 and scrapped in 1907. *Soudan* (1603 tons) was an African Steam Ship Co. steamer launched in 1870 and lost off Madeira in 1875. The latter had broken down at Tenerife while carrying £15,000 in specie: see Boyle, *Through Fanteeland* , p. 227; Stanley, *Coomassie and Magdala*, p. 105. *Ethiopia* arrived with yellow fever on board: see NMM, LOG/N/E/1, McLeod journal, 30 Oct. 1873.

25 Flag Lt Ernest Neville Rolfe, RN. Lieutenant, 1871. Rolfe acted as Wolseley's Naval ADC: see BPP, Cmd. 894, pp. 869–72, Hewett to Admiralty, 29 Jan. 1874; NMM, LOG/N/E/1, McLeod journal, 19 Jan. 1874.

26 Surgeon Major William Alexander Mackinnon (1830–97). Commissioned 1853. Service in Crimea attached to 42nd Highlanders; Mutiny; New Zealand, 1863–66; Asante. Surgeon-General, War Office, 1882–87; Director General, Army Medical Department (Major General), 1889–96; KCB, 1891.

27 Wolseley's buggy was left at Praso with Wolseley walking, being
carried in a Madeira wicker chair, or occasionally riding a mule
beyond the Pra: see Brackenbury, *Ashanti War*, II, p. 10; and Low,
General Lord Wolseley, p. 275.

28 Edmond Robert Wodehouse (1835–1914), Private Secretary to
Kimberley, 1864–66 and 1868–74. Successively Liberal and Liberal
Unionist MP for Bath, 1880–1906.

5 Advance (January 1874)

Notes to Introduction

1 WSRO, Methuen MSS, WSRO 1742/6335, Methuen to his father,
30 Jan. 1874.

2 TNA, WO 33/26, *Journal of Engineer Operations*, pp. 27–8, 41–2;
Cima, *Reflections*, p. 41.

3 Melville, *Buller*, I, pp. 72–3; Wolseley, *Story of a Soldier's Life*, II,
p. 338; Henty, *March to Coomassie*, p. 323; Stanley, *Coomassie and
Magdala*, pp. 135, 184; Spiers, *Victorian Soldier*, p. 24; Reade, *Story
of the Ashantee Campaign*, pp. 262–3.

4 NMM, LOG/N/E/1, McLeod journal, 17 Jan. 1874; ibid., LOG/
N/27, Luxmore journal, 1 Jan. 1874; Wolseley, *Story of a Soldier's
Life*, II, p. 319; Maurice, *Ashantee War*, pp. 289–90.

5 Prior, *Campaigns* p. 17; WSRO, Methuen MSS, WSRO 1742/6335,
Methuen to his father, 23 Jan. 1874; Bodleian, Alison MSS, MS.
Eng. lett. c. 451, Alison to Greaves, 21 Jan. 1874.

6 Low, *General Lord Wolseley*, p. 283; Bodleian, Alison MSS, MS. Eng.
lett. c. 450, Alison to his wife, 21–22 and 27–28 Jan. 1874; Greaves to
Alison 21 and 24 Jan. 1874.

7 Crooks, *Records*, pp. 490–2; Brackenbury, *Ashanti War*, II, pp. 64–81;
BPP, Cmd. 921, pp. 5–6; Maurice and Arthur, *Life of Lord Wolseley*, p. 68.

8 Captain Hans Garrett Moore, 88th Foot. Commissioned, 1855.
Service in Mutiny; Asante; Ninth Kaffir (Cape Frontier) War,
1877–78; Egypt, 1882. VC, 1877; Brevet Colonel, 1882.

9 Butler, *Autobiography*, pp. 166–70; idem, *Akim-Foo*, pp. 226, 246,
299; Brackenbury, *Ashanti War*, II, pp. 108–25.

10 Stanley, *Coomassie and Magdala*, pp. 183, 214–16, 243–44; Reade, *Story of the Ashantee Campaign*, p. 264; Low, *General Lord Wolseley*, p. 285; Brackenbury, *Ashanti War*, II, pp. 125–33, 249–56; Henty, *March to Coomassie*, pp. 197–8, 202–4; BPP, Cmd. 894, pp. 60–2; ibid., Cmd. 922, pp. 73–4; TNA, WO 33/25, Wolseley to Cardwell, 9 Nov. 1873; CUL, Glover MSS, RCMS 131/6, Baker to Glover, 10 Nov. 1873.

11 Douglas, *Wauchope*, p. 72; Wolseley, *Story of a Soldier's Life*, II, p. 331; Henty, *March to Coomassie*, pp. 357–8; Reade, *Story of the Ashantee Campaign*, pp. 281–2; Prior, *Campaigns*, p. 22; Dooner, *Jottings*, p. 45; Hart-Synnot, *Letters*, p. 70. There is some debate as to the influence of Muslim advisers over Kofi Karikari: see Wilks, *Asante*, pp. 238–9, 241, 256–61, 508; McCaskie, *State and Society*, pp. 135–42, 389 n. 170.

12 NMM, LOG/N/27, Luxmore journal, 17 Jan. 1874; Edgerton, *Fall of the Asante Empire*, pp. 130, 136–7; Boyle, *Through Fanteeland*, p. 274; Henty, *March to Coomassie*, p. 341; Stanley, *Coomassie and Magdala*, p. 182; Ramseyer and Kühne, *Four Years*, p. 293.

13 Stanley, *Coomassie and Magdala*, pp. 125–6. Brackenbury, *Ashanti War*, II, p. 45, and Maurice, *Ashantee War*, p. 240 variously name him as Sein Quaku and Essen Kueku, presumably meaning Esen Kwaku. On diplomacy, see Smith, *Warfare and Diplomacy*, pp. 7–23; Adjaye, *Diplomacy and Diplomats*, p. 9.

14 Maurice, *Ashantee War*, pp. 238–40; Brackenbury, *Ashanti War*, II, pp. 40–2; BPP, Cmd. 894, pp. 656–7; Dooner, *Jottings*, p. 44.

15 BPP, Cmd. 891, p. 191; NMM, BLK/2, Blake journal, 4 Jan. 1874; NMM, LOG/N/27, Luxmore journal, 4 Jan. 1874; Boyle, *Through Fanteeland*, pp. 99, 202, 217; Stanley, *Coomassie and Magdala*, pp. 127–8; Wolseley, *Story of a Soldier's Life*, II, p. 320; Brackenbury, *Ashanti War*, II, p. 44. Manning's suggestion in *Evelyn Wood VC*, p. 78 that Wood had decided on the demonstration and incurred Wolseley's displeasure as a result of the initial problems is not borne out by Wood's own account in *Midshipman to Field Marshal*, I, p. 273.

16 Wolseley, *Story of a Soldier's Life*, II, 320; Boyle, *Through Fanteeland*, pp. 248–9, 274; Henty, *March to Coomassie*, pp. 320–2; Maurice, *Ashantee War*, p. 248; Ramseyer and Kühne, *Four Years* pp. 262, 291; Brackenbury, *Ashanti War*, II, pp. 44–5.

17 Brackenbury, *Ashanti War*, II, pp. 52–3, 58; Maurice, *Ashantee War*, pp. 262–3; BPP, Cmd. 907, p. 6; Adjaye, *Diplomacy and Diplomats*, pp. 57–8, 110; Wilks, *Forests of Gold*, pp. 173–4; idem, *Asante*, p. 240; Ramseyer and Kühne, *Four Years*, p. 271; Perrot and Dantzig, *Bonnat*, pp. 58–62; Henty, *March to Coomassie*, p. 334; Stanley, *Coomassie and Magdala*, p. 149.

18 Brackenbury, *Ashanti War*, II, pp. 81–2, 135–6; Maurice, *Ashantee War*, pp. 294–5; BPP, Cmd. 907, p. 8; Reade, *Story of the Ashantee Campaign*, pp. 286–7; Perrot and Dantzig, *Bonnat*, pp. 565–6.

19 Preston, *Wolseley's South African Journal*, p. 272.

20 TNA, WO 33/25, Wolseley to Kimberley, 24 Jan. 1874; Reade, *Story of the Ashantee Campaign*, pp. 297–8; Stanley, *Coomassie and Magdala*, pp. 172–3; Henty, *March to Coomassie*, p. 368; Brackenbury, *Ashanti War*, II, pp. 83–4; Matthew, *Gladstone Diaries*, pp. 453–4; Low, *General Lord Wolseley*, pp. 281–2; McIntyre, *Imperial Frontier*, pp. 273–4; Ramm, *Gladstone–Granville Correspondence*, p. 439.

21 Reade, *Story of the Ashantee Campaign*, pp. 287–96.

22 W. E. F. Ward, *A History of Gold Coast* (London: Allen & Unwin, 1948), p. 273; McIntyre, *Imperial Frontier*, pp. 276–7; idem, 'British Policy', pp. 19–46.

23 Stanley, *Coomassie and Magdala*, p. 172.

24 Devon Country Record Office, Buller MSS, 2065 M add 2/SS/6, Horton to Home, 26 Dec. 1873. Assistant Surgeon Dr James 'Africanus' Beale Horton (1835–83), had received his medical education on a War Office-funded scholarship in London and Edinburgh, qualifying in 1859 when he was also commissioned. He had published *West African Countries and People* (1868) and *Letters on the Political Condition of the Gold Coast* (1870) and had also served in the Gambia expedition in 1866. Promoted Surgeon Major in 1875, he retired in 1880. See Adelola Adeloye, *Dr James Africanus Beale Horton* (Pittsburgh, PA: Durrance, 1992).

25 BPP, Cmd. 922, pp. 14–15, Wolseley to Kimberley, 2 Feb. 1874; Maurice, *Ashantee War*, p. 268; Adjaye, *Diplomacy and Diplomats*, pp. 111, 198.

26 Wolseley, *Story of a Soldier's Life*, II, pp. 334–5, 338; Brackenbury, *Ashanti War*, II, pp. 149–51; BPP, Cmd. 907, pp. 12–13.

27 NMM, LOG/N/E/1, McLeod journal, 29 Jan. 1874; ibid., LOG/N/27, Luxmore journal, 29 Jan. 1874; TNA, ADM 101/45; WSRO, Methuen MSS, WSRO 1742/6335, Methuen to his father, 30 Jan. 1874; Boyle, *Through Fanteeland*, p. 321; Henty, *March to Coomassie*, pp. 366–7; Stanley, *Coomassie and Magdala*, pp. 187–8; Reade, *Story of the Ashantee Campaign*, pp. 301–2; Maurice, *Ashantee War*, pp. 317–19; Brackenbury, *Ashanti War*, II, pp. 147–8, 152–4; Wood, 'Ashanti Expedition', pp. 346–7; Lloyd, *Drums of Kumasi*, p. 104; Spiers, *Victorian Soldier*, pp. 27–8.

28 *The Times*, 3 March 1874; Maurice, *Ashantee War*, p. 324; Stanley, *Coomassie and Magdala*, p. 158; Low, *General Lord Wolseley*, p. 283.

29 J. K. Fynn, 'Ghana-Asante (Ashanti)', in Michael Crowder, ed., *West African Resistance: The Military Response to Colonial Occupation* (London: Hutchinson, 1978), pp. 19–52 at p. 40; Edgerton, *Fall of the Asante Empire*, p. 137; Kwame Arhin, 'Ashanti Military Institutions', *Journal of African Studies* 7 (1980), pp. 22–30; Wilks, *Forests of Gold*, p. 272; idem, *Asante*, pp. 505–11; Boyle, *Through Fanteeland*, p,. 304; Wolseley, *Story of a Soldier's Life*, II, p. 337.

30 Wolseley, *Story of a Soldier's Life*, II, p 339.

31 For a schematic plan of the square, see Brackenbury, *Ashanti War*, II, p. 158; and Stanley, *Coomassie and Magdala*, p. 194.

32 Henty, *March to Coomassie*, p. 376.

33 BPP, Cmd. 922, pp. 66–8, Wolseley to Cardwell, 1 Feb. 1874; Crooks, *Records*, pp. 495–9; Stanley, *Coomassie and Magdala*, pp. 204–8; Brackenbury, *Ashanti War*, II, pp. 157–84.

34 Henty, *March to Coomassie*, p. 385; idem, 'Amoaful', in Archibald Forbes, G. A. Henty and Arthur Griffiths, eds, *Battles of the Nineteenth Century* (London: Cassell & Co, 1896), I, pp. 215–23.

35 Prior, *Campaigns*, p. 18. See also Wolseley, *Story of a Soldier's Life*, p. 341; Henty, *March to Coomassie*, p. 379; Reade, *Story of the Ashantee Campaign*, pp. 310–11; Spiers, *Victorian Soldier*, p. 29; NMM, LOG/N/E/1, McLeod journal, 31 Jan. 1874; ibid., LOG/N/27, Luxmore journal, 31 Jan. 1874.

36 NMM, LOG/N/E/1, McLeod journal, 31 Jan. 1874; ibid., LOG/N/27, Luxmore journal, 31 Jan. 1874; WSRO, Methuen MSS, WSRO 1742/6335, Methuen to his father, 7 Feb. 1874; Wood, *Midshipman to Field Marshal*, I, pp. 275–6.

37 Bodleian, Alison MSS, MS. Eng. lett. c. 450, Alison to his wife, 5 Feb. 1874.

38 Brackenbury, *Ashanti War*, II, pp. 163–5.

39 TNA, ADM 101/45; Wood, *Midshipman to Field Marshal*, I, pp. 275–6.

40 Captain Charles John Burnett. Commissioned, 1861. Service in Asante; Afghanistan, 1879–80. Chief Military Attaché with Japanese army in Manchuria, 1904–5. KCB, 1906; KCVO, 1909; General, 1909; retired, 1910.

41 Brackenbury, *Ashanti War*, II, pp. 157–84; Wolseley, *Story of a Soldier's Life*, II, pp. 242–5; Douglas, *Wauchope*, pp. 74–5; Lloyd, *Drums of Kumasi*, pp. 105–14; Spiers, *Scottish Soldier*, p. 31; Henty, *March to Coomassie*, pp. 374–92; Stanley, *Coomassie and Magdala*, pp. 191–208; Reade, *Story of the Ashantee Campaign*, pp. 308–29; Maurice, *Ashantee War*, pp. 327–39; Low, *General Lord Wolseley*, 287–93; Perrot and Dantzig, *Bonnat*, pp. 574–8; NMM, LOG/N/E/1, McLeod journal, 31 Jan. 1874; ibid., LOG/N/27, Luxmore journal, 31 Jan. 1874; Butler, *Colley*, pp. 99–101.

42 Brackenbury, *Ashanti War*, II, pp 182–4; Melville, *Buller*, I, p. 73; Douglas, *Wauchope*, p. 75; Maurice, *Ashantee War*, p. 332; BPP, Cmd. 1374, p. 255. Baird is commemorated by a memorial plaque in St Mary's Church, Whitekirk, Lothian.

43 TNA, WO 33/25, Wolseley to Cardwell 5 Feb. 1874; ibid., WO 32/7377, Whitmore to Vivian, 27 March 74; Brackenbury, *Ashanti War*, II, p. 225.

44 Wilks, *Asante*, pp. 505–6, 517, 532; NMM, LOG/N/E/1, McLeod journal 31 Jan. 1874; ibid., LOG/N/27, Luxmore journal, 31 Jan. 1874; Spiers, *Victorian Soldier*, p. 30; Boyle, *Through Fanteeland*, p. 332.

Notes to Documents 112–45

1 For the rest of Kofi Karikari's letters dated 25 November and 26 December 1873, see Maurice, *Ashantee War*, pp. 238–40; Brackenbury, *Ashanti War*, II, pp. 40–2; and BPP, Cmd. 894, pp. 656–7.

2 It can be noted that, while Wolseley claims to have completed the letter to Kofi Karikari on this day, all printed versions of the letter are dated 2 January.

3 Esen Kwaku.
4 Lieutenant Frank E. Hudson, HMS *Tamar*. Commissioned 1867. His
   brother(s) may have been either (Captain and) Lieutenant Colonel
   Joseph Henry Francis Harrington Hudson, Grenadier Guards,
   Assistant Military Secretary in Ceylon; and/or Lieutenant Colonel
   Joseph Hudson, late Grenadier Guards, Superintendent of Factory,
   Army Clothing Depot.
5 *De Imitatione Christi* ('The Imitation of Christ') (*c.* 1418) is
   traditionally ascribed to Thomas à Kempis (1380–1471), an
   Augustinian from the Mt St Agnes monastery near Utrecht.
6 A Canadian-pattern cribwork bridge was one made of logs formed
   into square cages and sunk into a riverbed as a basis for piers
   supporting a pontoon, on which a roadway could be laid. In this
   particular case, irregularities on the bottom between sand and rock
   caused the bridge to tilt: see Henty, *March to Coomassie*, pp. 324–5;
   and Brackenbury, *Ashanti War*, II, p. 59.
7 Lieutenant Colonel James Maxwell, 1st West India Regiment.
   Commissioned 34th Foot, 1841. Service in Crimea; Mutiny; Asante;
   Lieutenant Colonel, 1866. Acting Administrator of the Gold Coast in
   succession to Wolseley but died of fever in March 1874.
8 No drawing is extant.
9 The *ILN* correspondent, of course, was Melton Prior.
10 Major Joseph T. Brownell, Sub Collector of Customs at Saltpond.
   Formerly in the West India Regiment, Brownell had commanded a
   detachment of the Gold Coast Artillery in support of the Assin tribes
   against the Asante in 1852 and had been captured and held by them
   for two months. He had also served against the Krobos in 1858.
11 Captain William Liston Dalrymple, 88th Foot (1845–1938).
   Commissioned 44th Foot, 1863. Service in Ashanti; South Africa,
   1878–79. DAAQMG, Northern District, 1876–77; AAG, South
   Africa, 1878; Military Secretary to Viceroy, 1880; AQMG, India,
   1881–84; DAG, Ireland, 1888–90; DQMG, India, 1891–93. Major
   General, 1895; retired, 1903.
12 *Manitoban* (1810 tons) had been acquired by the Allan Line in 1868,
   having been launched in 1865 as *Ottawa*. It was scrapped in 1899.
13 John Palmer Brabazon (1843–1922). Retired Captain of the
   Grenadier Guards serving as a volunteer with Butler's mission in

Asante. Commissioned 16th Lancers, 1862. Resumed career, taking commission in 10th Hussars, 1874. Service in Asante; Afghanistan, 1878–80; Sudan, 1884–85; South Africa, 1899–1902. ADC to Viceroy, 1878–80; GOC, 2nd Cavalry Brigade, 1899–1900; GOC, Imperial Yeomanry, 1900. KCB, 1911; Major General, 1901. Methuen was glad that he had not been chosen to go with Brabazon and Arthur Paget on Butler's mission as they 'will go in for shooting niggers, which is not either my wish or [Francis] Russell's – as we hope in addition to fighting, to have some surveying to do'. See WSRO, Methuen MSS, WSRO 1742/6335, Methuen to his father, 17 Dec. 1873. Methuen was attached to Wood's regiment.

14 Captain Arthur Wybrow Baker. Commissioned in 66th Foot, 1862; retired from Army, 1865. He was the brother of T. D. Baker.

15 Assistant Commissary Joseph Marsh, African Branch, Control Department. Commissioned, 1863. Service in Spain with British Auxiliary Legion, 1836–37; South Africa, 1851–53; Crimea; Asante. Died on board hospital ship *Victor Emmanuel*, 2 Feb. 1874.

16 Johannes Kühne, a Silesian, had been in Africa since 1866 but had only joined Ramseyer at Anum two months before they were both seized.

17 Kofi Karikari's letter of 9 January can be found in Maurice, *Ashantee War*, pp. 262–3; Brackenbury, *Ashanti War*, II, pp. 52–3; and BPP, Cmd. 907, p. 6.

18 Joseph Dawson, son of an English father and a Fante mother, had worked for the Wesleyan Missionary Society before beginning to work for the colonial government on Fante confederation in 1872: see Ramseyer and Kühne, *Four Years*, p. 211.

19 Francis Chapman Grant (1825–1908) was a leading merchant who had helped organise the Fante Confederation and served several times on the Legislative Council. His father was Scottish and his mother African.

20 Kofi Karikari's letter of 21 Jan. is in Maurice, *Ashantee War*, pp. 294–5, Brackenbury, *Ashanti War*, II, pp. 81–2; and BPP, Cmd. 907, p. 8.

21 Marie-Joseph Bonnat (1844–81), the French trader seized in 1869, was to return to Asante in 1875 as an agent with a commercial monopoly: see TNA, CO 96/114, Hall to Bonnat, 21 Dec. 1874. Born in Ain, he had first come to Africa in 1867. The Swiss-born Friedrich August Ramseyer, who had been in Africa since 1864, may

not actually have been ordained: see Boyle, *Through Fanteeland*, p. 303. When seized, Ramseyer and his wife, Rose, had a ten-month-old son, who died within a month. However, two more children, Rose and Immanuel, were born to the couple during their captivity. The Ramseyers returned to Kumase to found a permanent mission and, indeed, participated in the forced evacuation of the British garrison from the besieged city in June 1900 during the Third Asante War.

22 Thomas Edward Bowdich (1790–1824) had published his *Mission from Cape Coast to Ashantee* in 1819.

23 The Queen Mother or *Asantehemaa*, Afua Kofi (*c.* 1815–1900), held the position from *c.* 1858 to 1883 when she abdicated. Mensa Bonsu (*c.* 1838–96), brother of Kofi Karikari, succeeded him as *Asantehene* in 1874 and ruled until deposed in 1883.

24 The postscript does not appear in the official printed version but does in Maurice, *Ashantee War*, p. 300; and Brackenbury, *Ashanti War*, II, p. 88.

25 Major General Alfred Huyshe, Inspector General for Artillery in India. Commissioned Bengal Artillery, 1827. Service in Gwalior campaign, 1843–44; 2nd Sikh War, 1848–49; Major General 1867.

26 Kwabina Oben, *Adansehene*.

27 Colonel John Sidney North of Wroxton Abbey (1804–94) was Conservative MP for Oxfordshire, 1852–85. Commissioned, 1821. Took name of North in 1838, his original surname being Doyle. Lieutenant Colonel of the Tower Hamlets Militia, 1836, and of the 2nd Administrative Battalion, Oxfordshire Rifle Volunteers, 1860. PC, 1886. North was an old friend of Wolseley and the first to tell him of the fire at the Pantechnicon: see Wolseley, *Story of a Soldier's Life*, II, p. 369 and note 28, p. 513.

28 Kofi Karikari's letters of 26 and 27 January are in Brackenbury, *Ashanti War*, II, pp. 149–51; and BPP Cmd. 907, pp. 12–13.

29 Captain James Nicol (1828–74), Adjutant of the Hampshire Militia since 1857. Originally commissioned in 13th Foot but retired 1853. Memorial tablet in Winchester Cathedral. Service in Crimea on private basis running despatch boat with his brother.

30 Captain Richard Nicolls Buckle. Commissioned RE, 1858. Service in Gibraltar; China; Japan; Asante. Captain, 1871. Memorial window in Rochester Cathedral.

6 Success (February to March 1874)

Notes to Introduction

1 TNA, WO 32/7377; Buller Family MSS, Buller to Lucy, 7 Feb.
74; Reade, *Story of the Ashantee Campaign*, p. 324; Henty, *March to Coomassie*, pp. 393–4; Brackenbury, *Ashanti War*, II, pp. 185–6; Stanley, *Coomassie and Magdala*, pp. 209–11.

2 TNA, WO 147/27, Report by Duncan; NAM, Cooper MSS, 6112–596–8–10, Grant to Cooper, 3 Feb. 74; Henty, *March to Coomassie*, pp. 491–2; Brackenbury, *Ashanti War*, II, pp. 187–9; Maurice, *Ashantee War*, pp. 195–6; Butler, *Colley*, pp. 102–3.

3 Butler, *Colley*, pp. 104–5; Wolseley, *Story of a Soldier's Life*, II, pp. 346–7; Brackenbury, *Ashanti War*, II, pp. 196–8; Low, *General Lord Wolseley*, p. 294; Reade, *Story of the Ashantee Campaign*, p. 332; NAM, Cooper MSS, 6112–596–8–5, Colley to Cooper, 26 Feb. 1874.

4 Reade, *Story of the Ashantee Campaign*, pp. 335–6; Henty, *March to Coomassie*, p. 400; Boyle, *Through Fanteeland*, p. 338; Brackenbury, *Ashanti War*, II, pp. 205–6; TNA, WO 147/27, *Journal of Engineer Operations*, p. 35.

5 Butler, *Colley*, p. 106; Stanley, *Coomassie and Magdala*, p. 218.

6 Wilks, *Asante*, p. 509.

7 Perrot and Dantzig, *Bonnat*, pp. 572–4, 584; Natal Archives Depot, Wood MSS, I–2–1 and I–2–2, Wood to Lady Eyre, 6 Feb. and Wood to Eyre's aunt, 13 Feb. 1874; Emery, *Marching Over Africa*, pp. 46–8; Wood, *Midshipman to Field Marshal*, I, pp. 277–80; Reade, *Story of the Ashantee Campaign*, p. 339; Stanley, *Coomassie and Magdala*, p. 219; Dooner, *Jottings*, p. 58. Subsequently, it was rumoured that the Asante had dug up Eyre's body: see WSRO, Methuen MSS, WSRO 1742/63365, Methuen to his father, 18 March 1874. On Campbell, see Manning, *Evelyn Wood VC*, pp. 116–17.

8 Wolseley, *Story of a Soldier's Life*, II, pp. 352–6; Maurice, *Ashantee War*, pp 347–50; Henty, *March to Coomassie*, pp. 401–3; Boyle, *Through Fanteeland*, pp. 339–41; Stanley, *Coomassie and Magdala*, pp. 217–23; Brackenbury, *Ashanti War*, II, pp. 207–23, 226–7; Low, *General Lord Wolseley*, pp. 297–9; Perrot and Dantzig, *Bonnat*, pp. 582–5.

9 Brackenbury, *Ashanti War*, II, pp. 225–6; TNA, WO 32/7377;
ibid., WO 32/7379; Crooks, *Records*, pp. 499–507; Bodleian, Alison
MSS, MS. Eng. lett. c. 451, Alison to Greaves, 10 May 1874; RA
F/8/153, Ponsonby to Hardy, 11 Nov. 1874; ibid., F/8/154, Hardy
to Ponsonby, 13 Nov. 1874.
10 Brackenbury, *Ashanti War*, II, p. 232; Dooner, *Jottings*, pp. 64–5.
11 Butler, *Colley*, p. 107–8; Wolseley, *Story of a Soldier's Life*, II, p. 358;
Melville, *Buller*, I, p. 76; Reade, *Story of the Ashantee Campaign*,
p. 348; Maurice, *Ashantee War*, p. 353; Henty, *March to Coomassie*,
pp. 405–11; Boyle, *Through Fanteeland*, pp. 357, 363; Stanley,
Coomassie and Magdala, pp. 227–9, 234; Brackenbury, *Ashanti War*,
II, pp. 223–4, 228–31; Low, *General Lord Wolseley*, p. 301; Dooner,
Jottings, p. 59; Perrot and Dantzig, *Bonnat*, p. 586; NMM, LOG/N/
E/1, McLeod journal, 4 Feb. 1874.
12 Reade, *Story of the Ashantee Campaign*, p. 343; Brackenbury, *Ashanti
War*, II, pp. 201–3; 219–21; Perrot and Dantzig, *Bonnat*, pp. 582, 585.
13 Stanley, *Coomassie and Magdala*, pp. 229–30, 236–40, 258–9; Reade,
Story of the Ashantee Campaign, pp. 350–4, 370; Perrot and Dantzig,
Bonnat, pp. 587–8.; McIntyre, *Imperial Frontier*, p. 277.
14 TNA, WO 33/25, Wolseley to Cardwell, 7 Feb. 1874; BPP, Cmd. 922,
pp. 19–20, Wolseley to Kimberley, 7 Feb. 1874; Brackenbury, *Ashanti
War*, II, pp. 237–9; Low, *General Lord Wolseley*, pp. 304–5; Preston,
Wolseley's South African Diaries, p. 93; Maurice, *Ashantee War*,
pp. 354–7; Wolseley, *Story of a Soldier's Life*, II, p. 359, 362–5; WSRO,
Methuen MSS. WSRO 1742/6335, Methuen to his father, 11 Feb.
1874; BL Add. MSS 44225, Kimberley to Gladstone, 27 May 1874.
15 Melville, *Buller*, I, p. 77; Buller Family MSS, Buller to Henrietta,
14 Feb. 1874; RA VIC/MAIN/F/7/112, Airey to Ponsonby, 9
March 1874; TNA, WO 33/25, Hardy to Wolseley, 11 March
74; Hove, Wolseley MSS, G4, Airey to Wolseley, 23 March 1874;
Maurice and Arthur, *Life of Lord Wolseley*, p. 71; Maurice, *Ashantee
War*, pp. 373–9; Boyle, *Through Fanteeland*, pp. 376–8, 380–90; Prior,
Campaigns, pp. 24, 27, 29; Brackenbury, *Ashanti War*, II, pp. 240–2,
246–7, 267; Low, *General Lord Wolseley*, pp. 305, 310, 320; Hart-
Synnot, *Letters*, p. 80; Perrot and Dantzig, *Bonnat*, p. 588.
16 NAM, 1963–10–172–1 and 2; 1963–05–17–1; 1963–10–295–1; 1963–
10–300–1; 1963–10–305–1; and 1963–10–175–1. For the delivery of

the umbrella, see Borthwick Institute, Hickleton MSS, Halifax/A2 and A4.

17 Vincent, *Derby Diary*, p. 172.

18 Brackenbury, *Ashanti War*, II, pp. 243–9; TNA, WO 147/27, *Journal of Engineering Operations*, p. 36; Henty, *March to Coomassie*, pp. 416–19; Maurice, *Ashantee War*, p. 358; BPP, Cmd. 1374, pp. 256–7; Dooner, *Jottings*, pp. 62–3.

19 Adjaye, *Diplomacy and Diplomats*, pp. 59, 109–14, 196; Crooks, *Records*, pp. 520–4; McIntyre, *Imperial Frontier*, p. 277; idem, 'British Policy', pp. 39–46; *The Times*, 1 April 1874; Stanley, *Coomassie and Magdala*, pp. 229–30, 241–3; Henty, *March to Coomassie*, p. 424; Low, *General Lord Wolseley*, p. 309; Brackenbury, *Ashanti War*, II, pp. 266–73, 317–19; Maurice, *Ashantee War*, pp. 385–6; Perrot and Dantzig, *Bonnat*, p. 590; BPP, Cmd. 922, p. 43, Wolseley to Kimberley, 13 Feb. 1874; ibid., pp. 45–6; Cmd. 1006, pp. 10–11. Kofi Nti went to Trinidad after schooling in Surrey to accept a colonial post but returned to Asante in the 1880s.

20 CUL, Glover MSS, RCMS 131/7, Greaves to Glover, 7 Feb. and 22 Feb. 1874; ibid., Butler to Glover, 3 Feb. 1874; Maurice, *Ashantee War*, pp. 339, 363–6; Reade, *Story of the Ashantee Campaign*, pp. 388–9; Henty, *March to Coomassie*, pp. 453–70; Stanley, *Coomassie and Magdala*, pp. 246–58; Brackenbury, *Ashanti War*, II, pp. 256–5; Low, *General Lord Wolseley*, p. 308; Glover, 'Volta Expedition', pp. 317–30; Glover, *Life of Glover*, pp. 195–215.

21 TNA, WO 32/7378; M. J. Crook, *The Evolution of the Victoria Cross* (Tunbridge Wells: Midas Books, 1975), pp. 158–9, 166, 221, 242–4. Only three other pairs of brothers have won the award before or since. Hugh and Charles Gough both won VCs during the Mutiny, Roland and George Bradford during the Great War, and Alexander and Victor Turner in the Great War and Second World War respectively: see Peter Duckers, *The Victoria Cross* (Princes Risborough: Shire Publications, 2005), pp. 56–7.

22 Brooks, *Long Arm of Empire*, p. 127; Caulfield, *100 Years' History*, p. 173.

23 Brackenbury, *Ashanti War*, II, p. 289; Butler, *Colley*, p. 109; Boyle, *Through Fanteeland*, p. 391; NAM, Cooper MSS, 6112–596–8–5, Colley to Cooper, 26 Feb. 74; Hawkins and Powell, *Kimberley Journal*, p. 287.

24 Brackenbury, *Ashanti War*, II, pp. 276–80, 286–9; Low, *General Lord Wolseley*, p. 310; Crook, *Records*, pp. 517, 528.

25 TNA, WO 147/27; ibid., WO 33/26; ibid., WO 87/6.

26 Crooks, *Records*, p. 538; Brackenbury, *Ashanti War*, II, pp. 340–4; Low, *General Lord Wolseley*, p. 311–16.

27 T. C. McCaskie, *Asante Identities: History and Modernity in an African Village, 1850–1950* (Edinburgh: Edinburgh University Press, 2000), pp. 63–4; Wilks, *Asante*, p. 98.

28 Wilks, *Forests of Gold*, p. 274; idem, *Asante*, pp. 367–8, 509–88; A. Adu Boahen, Emmanuel Akyeampong, Nancy Lawler, T. C. McCaskie and Ivor Wilks, eds, '*The History of Ashanti Kings and the Whole Country Itself' and Other Writings* (Oxford: Oxford University Press for the British Academy, 2008), pp. 3–20; Boahen, 'Asante, Fante and the British', pp. 346–63; Aidoo, 'Order and Conflict', pp. 1–36; Hopkins, 'Asante and the Victorians', pp. 25–64.

29 BL., Add. MSS 60763, Carnarvon MSS, Carnarvon to Disraeli, 6 March 1874; ibid., Add. MSS 60797, Frere to Carnarvon 2 May 74; RA VIC/ADD/E/1/7357, Carnarvon to Cambridge, 8 April 1874; Brackenbury, *Ashanti War*, II, pp. 345–53; Claridge, *Gold Coast and Ashanti*, II, pp. 170–82; Crook, *Records*, p. 530; McIntyre, *Imperial Frontier*, pp. 274–85; idem, 'British Policy', pp. 39–46; Ronald Robinson, John Gallagher and Alice Denny, *Africa and the Victorians: The Official Mind of Imperialism*, 2nd edn (London: Macmillan, 1967), pp. 31–2; C. C. Eldridge, *England's Mission: The Imperial Idea in the Age of Gladstone and Disraeli, 1868–80* (London: Macmillan, 1973), pp. 157–9; Kimble, *Political History*, pp. 274–300; Newbury, *British Policy*, pp. 534–6. For the Third Asante War, see Lloyd, *Drums of Kumasi*, pp. 155–9; and A. Adu Boahen, *Yaa Asantewaa and the Asante-British War of 1900–1* (London: James Currey, 2003).

30 Bodleian, Alison MSS, MS. Eng. lett. c. 450, Alison to his wife, 22 Feb. 1874; Buller Family MSS, Buller to Lucy, 7 Feb. 74; Hove, SSL.9 Pt II, Draft of unpub. Wolseley autobiography, pp. cdxxxiii–cdxxxvi; ibid., Wolseley Autobiographical Collection, Cardwell to 'General' (?), 15 March 1874.

31 For the reception of the 42nd, see Spiers, *Scottish Soldier*, pp. 33–7.

32 Verner, *Military Life*, II, p. 88; RA Cambridge MSS, VIC/ADD/E/1/7352, Hardy to Cambridge, 25 March 1874; ibid., VIC/MAIN/

F/8/18, Disraeli to the Queen, 25 March 1874; F/8/19, Ponsonby to the Queen, 25 March 1874; F/8/24, Carnarvon to the Queen, 27 March 1874; F/8/2, Cambridge to the Queen, 27 March 1874; F/8/32, Disraeli to the Queen, 28 March 1874; F/8/42, Disraeli to the Queen, 30 March 1874; D/4/28, Ponsonby to the Queen, 28 March 1874; Zetland, *Disraeli to Lady Bradford*, pp. 63–4; Vincent, *Derby Diaries*, p. 171. The two Wolseley baronetcies to which Wolseley referred were those of Wolseley of Staffordshire, the original created in 1628, and Wolseley of Mount Wolseley in Carlow, created in 1745, the brother of the 5th Baronet of Staffordshire being created the 1st Baronet of Mount Wolseley. While the original English baronetcy had continued to descend from father to son, the Irish baronetcy had several successions of brothers and cousins. Wolseley was the great grandson of the 1st Baronet of Mount Wolseley.

33 TNA, WO 32/7640 and 7642, Thanks of Parliament and Congratulatory Message to the Troops from the Queen respectively; Maurice and Arthur, *Life of Wolseley*, p. 73; Low, *General Lord Wolseley*, pp. 318–25; Mark Bryant, *Wars of Empire in Cartoons* (London: Grub Street Publishing, 2008), pp. 60–9; Crooks, *Records*, pp. 532–3.

34 Matthew, *Gladstone Diaries*, pp. 453–4, 466, n. 3, 645–6.

35 Gosford, Wemyss MSS, Wolseley to Anson, 5 April 1874.

36 Crooks, *Records*, pp. 528–34; Glover, *Life of Glover*, pp. 221–5; RA VIC/MAIN/F/8/89, Ponsonby to Disraeli, 22 April 1874; F/8/100, Carnarvon to the Queen, 24 April 1874; NMM, Fremantle MSS, FRE/109, Wilmot to Fremantle, 13 June 1874.

37 Crooks, *Records*, pp. 536–7; *The Times*, 1 and 9 March 1874; Notts County Record Office, Portland of Welbeck MSS, DD/4P/62/108/60. In the memory of some, there were suitable memorial plaques. Apart from those memorials already mentioned in the footnotes to Baird, Bradshaw, Buckle, Charteris, Eyre, Nicol, and Thompson, there are also plaques to the following: Lieutenant Henry Clough, 1st West India Regiment, who died at sea on passage home on 5 March 1874, in St Peter and St Paul Church, Bardwell (Suffolk); Sergeant George Sumner of the 2nd Rifle Brigade, killed at Odaso on 4 February 1874, in St George's Church, Beckenham; Lieutenant Edward Hunter Townshend, 16th Foot, who died at sea on 29 December 1873, at Rossall School, Fleetwood; officers and

men of the 2/23rd at St Giles Church, Wrexham; and officers of the Control Department at All Saints Royal Garrison Church, Aldershot.

38 *Daily News*, 27 July 1874; musical works by Azo de Ferrara, John Pridham, Henry Parker and R. W. Heney listed in BL, Integrated Catalogue.

39 NAM, Cooper MSS, 6112–596–8–7 and 8, Colley to Cooper, 19 April and 4 May 1874.

40 TNA, CO 96/114, Note by Hall, 4 June 1874; Bodleian, Alison MSS, MS. Eng. lett. c. 451, Alison to Wolseley, 2 April 1874; ibid., MS. Eng. lett. c. 450, Warren to Alison, 20 April 1874; Bodleian, Alison MSS, MS. Eng. lett. c. 450, Alison to his wife. 23 April and 24 April 1874; ibid,. Alison to Hope Grant, 7 May and 28 June 1874; Alison statement, 28 April 1874.

41 NLS, Blackwood MSS, 4300, Brackenbury to Blackwood, 23 Nov. 1873; ibid., 4313, Brackenbury to Blackwood, 28 Jan., 4 April, 9 April, 13 April, 17 April, 21 April, 22 April, 30 April, 4 May, 17 May, 23 May, and n.d., 1874; NAM, Cooper MSS, 6112–596–1, 1–2, 1–4, and 1–5, Brackenbury to Cooper, n.d., 6 May, n.d., n.d.; Brackenbury, *Some Memories*, pp. 232–35.

42 NAM, Cooper MSS, 6112–596–1–6 Brackenbury to Cooper, 11 July 1874; Bodleian, Alison MSS, MSS. Eng. lett. c. 450, Alison to Hawley, 13 June; Alison to Blackwood, 16 June; Hawley to Alison, 18 June; FitzGerald to Alison, 26 June; Warren to Alison, 28 June; Baker Russell to Alison, 3 July; Alison to Baker Russell, 3 July, Alison statement, 4 July; Alison to Horsford, 4 July; Baker Russell to Alison, 9 July; Alison to Baker Russell, 10 July; Alison to Lord Alexander Russell, 12 July; Armstrong to Alison, 23 Nov.; and Airey to Warren, 14 Nov. 1874; NLS, Blackwood MSS, 4300, Alison to Blackwood, 16 and 21 June 1874.

43 Bodleian, Alison MSS, MS. Eng. lett. c. 450, Blackwood to Alison, 19 June 1874; NLS, Blackwood MSS, 4315, Brackenbury to Blackwood, 27 Nov. 1874.

44 National Archives of Scotland, Wemyss MSS, RH4/40/10, Elcho to Cambridge, 12 Feb. 1875; ibid., Brackenbury to Elcho, 14 Feb. 1875; ibid,., Wolseley to Elcho, 15 Oct. 1875; Hove, Wolseley MSS, M2/41/8/4, Diary Entry, 20 Feb. 1875; Brackenbury, *Some Memories*, pp. 236, 242.

45 Hove, Wolseley MSS, Draft Autobiography, SSL.9 Pt II, cdxxxv; ibid., M2/41/8/4, Diary Entry, 22 Jan. 1875; RA VIC/ADD/ E/1/7306, Johnson to Cambridge, 23 Jan. 1874; ibid., E/1/7351, Cambridge to Airey, 25 March 1874; ibid., E//1/7358, Cambridge to Airey, 9 April 1874; *The Daily News*, 25 March 1874; Preston, *Wolseley's South African Diaries*, pp. 117–18.

Notes to Documents 146–79

1 Sir Stafford Henry Northcote, Bt (1818–87). Liberal Conservative MP for Dudley, 1855–57; Conservative MP for Stamford, 1858–66 and for North Devon, 1866–85. President of Board of Trade, 1866–67; Secretary of State for India, 1867–68; Governor of Hudson's Bay Company, 1869–74; Chancellor of the Exchequer, 1874–80; Foreign Secretary, 1886–87. Created Earl of Iddesleigh, 1885. Northcote had sent out a letter of introduction for Lieutenant Richard Frederick Thompson, Adjutant of the 2nd Rifle Brigade, who was brother-in-law to Northcote's son: see Hove, Wolseley MSS, W/P 4/5, Wolseley to Lady Wolseley, 19 Jan. 1874.

2 Major General Patrick Leonard MacDougall (1819–94), DQMG, Intelligence Branch at Horse Guards. Commissioned, 1836. Service in Crimea. Superintendent of Studies, Royal Military College, 1854; Commandant of Staff College, 1857–61; AG of Canadian Militia, 1865–69; Chairman, Localisation Committee, 1871; Head of Intelligence Branch, 1873–78; GOC, Canada, 1878–83. KCMG, 1877; General, 1883. His second wife was Marianne Adelaide MacDougall (nee Miles).

3 The allusion, of course, is to Arthur Wellesley, 1st Duke of Wellington (1769–1852). CinC of the British Army, 1827–28 and 1844–52, and Prime Minister, 1827–30.

4 Fanny was Mrs Frances Caldwell, another of Wolseley's sisters.

5 Dawson's letter accompanying that from Kofi Karikari is reproduced in Brackenbury, *Ashanti War*, II, pp. 201–3, though Brackenbury has the latter dated 4 Feb. 1874 rather than 3 February, which is clearly wrong.

6 Warren's second in command was Major Adolphus Haggerston Stephens. Commissioned 1851. Service in Crimea; Mutiny; Asante. Major General, 1889.

7 Lieutenant Arthur Hardolph Eyre, 90th Foot. Commissioned, 1869. Service in Asante. Memorial tablets in All Saints Church, Babworth (Notts), and All Saints Royal Garrison Church, Aldershot. His father was Sir William Eyre (1805–59). Commissioned 1823. Service in South Africa, 1847 and 1851–53; Crimea, commanding 3rd Division, 1854–55. GOC, Canada, 1856–59.

8 Lord Trent and Viscount Cannock are the titles Wolseley had in mind if elevated to the peerage.

9 Major General Henry Frederick Ponsonby (1825–95), Private Secretary to Queen Victoria, 1870–95. Commissioned, 49th Foot, 1842. Service in Crimea; Canada, 1861–62. KCB, 1879; PC, 1880; GCB, 1887; Major General, 1872.

10 The message was a verbal one only as Kofi Karikari had no one capable of writing English now Dawson had been released: see Document **158**.

11 Captain Dudley North, 47th Foot. Commissioned 1858. Service in Asante; Zhob Valley Expedition, 1884. Colonel, 1892.

12 Cleaver was presumably a trader at Cape Coast. The judge is Marshall.

13 Granville George Leveson-Gower, 2nd Earl of Granville (1815–91). Foreign Secretary, 1851–52, 1870–74 and 1880–85; Lord President of the Council, 1852–54 and 1859–66; Colonial Secretary, 1868–70 and 1886. Succeeded to title, 1846.

14 Asabi Antwi.

15 Actually Prince Wasemsky. While he was in Asante, Princess Wasemsky was attending a number of royal and state occasions in London with visiting Russian royalty. See *Pall Mall Gazette*, 9 March and 13 March 1874; *Leeds Mercury*, 14 March 1874; and *The Graphic*, 21 March 1874.

16 Sub Lieutenant Robert Leybourne Mundy, who had been commissioned in 1868, died of wounds on 17 February: see NMM, LOG/N/E/1, McLeod journal, 17 February. The other naval officer, however, Sub Lieutenant Victor Alexander Bradshaw of HMS *Encounter*, had died of dysentery on the previous day. Bradshaw, commissioned in 1869, is commemorated by a plaque in St Mary-the-Less, Durham: see Norman Emery, 'Durham City and a "Small War"', *Durham Archaeological Journal* 17 (2000), pp. 83–4.

17 Gladstone's address to his Greenwich constituents is reproduced in the *Pall Mall Gazette*, 24 Jan. 1874.

18 *Nebraska* (3,985 tons) had been built for the Guion Line in 1867 and had been laid up in 1872 before being used for Asante. Subsequently, it was chartered as *Victoria* by the Warren Line, being scrapped in 1887.

19 George, of course, is the Duke of Cambridge. Captain HRH Prince Alfred, Duke of Edinburgh (1844–1900), second son of Queen Victoria. Commissioned RN, 1858. CinC, Mediterranean, 1886–89; CinC, Devonport, 1890–93; Admiral of the Fleet, 1893. Created Duke of Edinburgh, Earl of Ulster and Kent, 1866; succeeded as Duke of Saxe-Coburg, 1893.

20 Butler's books, *The Great Lone Land* (London: Sampson Low, 1872) and *The Wild North Land* (London: Sampson Low, 1873) covered his exploits in Canada. The former dealt with his journey from Fort Garry along the Saskatchewan to the Rockies in 1870–71, and the latter with his journey from Fort Garry to the Pacific coast in 1873.

21 It has not been possible to identify the *Wye*, a Royal Mail Steam Packet Company vessel of that name having been wrecked in the West Indies in 1867.

22 It has not been possible to identify Lady S.

23 *Thames* (1,364 tons) was a British Colonial Steamship Line vessel, launched in 1864.

24 Lieutenant General Sir Charles Hay Ellice (1823–88), Quartermaster-General. Commissioned, Grenadier Guards, 1839. Service in Mutiny. QMG, 1871–76; Adjutant General, 1876–82. KCB, 1873; General, 1882.

25 General Sir Richard Airey (1803–81), Adjutant General. Commissioned, 34th Foot, 1821. Service in Crimea as QMG, 1854–55. AAG and DAG at Horse Guards, 1851; Military Secretary, 1852; QMG, 1855–55; GOC, Gibraltar, 1865–70; AG, 1870–76. KCB, 1855; GCB, 1867; General, 1871. Created Baron Airey of Killingworth, 1876. Airey died while on a visit to Wolseley's home.

26 Lieutenant Colonel William Walter Whitehall Johnson, 1st West India Regiment. Commissioned 1854; Lieutenant Colonel, 1873.

27 W. F. B. Paul, Civil Commandant and Collector of Customs at Accra. Previous service in Sarawak with Rajah James Brooke, 1860.

28 The Pantechnicon occupied a two-acre site fronting on Motcomb Street and Belgrave Square and extending to Lowndes Square at the rear. Erected in 1839, it was supposedly the largest and safest fireproof warehouse in the capital: see *The Times*, 14 and 16 Feb. 1874; Hawkins and Powell, *Journal of Kimberley*, p. 284.

29 Caroline was Wolseley's youngest sister.

30 Henry Howard Molyneux Herbert, 4th Earl of Carnarvon (1831–90), Colonial Secretary in Disraeli's new administration. Under Secretary for the Colonies, 1858–59; Colonial Secretary, 1866–67 and 1874–78; Lord Lieutenant of Ireland, 1885–86. Succeeded to title, 1849.

31 Wolseley's salary was paid up to 3 April 1874: see TNA, CO 96/114, Hall to Wolseley, 8 April 1874.

32 Captain William Edward Despard, RMLI. Commissioned, 1855. Service in Asante. Lieutenant Colonel, 1887.

33 Though Prior suggested that Alison had been wounded in the hand – he had seen him ride a mule with the reins between his teeth – Alison was actually troubled by severe boils and a whitlow that necessitated removal of a small bone near the upper joint of one finger: see Prior, *Campaigns*, p. 23; Bodleian MSS. Eng. lett. c. 450, Alison to his wife, 27 Jan., 5 Feb., 13 Feb. and 22 Feb. 1874.

34 Lieutenant Colonel The Hon. James Charlemagne Dormer (1834–93), DAQMG at Horse Guards. Commissioned 13th Foot, 1853. Service in Crimea; Mutiny; China, 1860; Egypt, 1882–85. DAQMG, Horse Guards, 1869–74; AAQMG Dover, 1874–78; AAQMG Malta, 1878–79; DAG, Egypt, 1882; Major General, Egypt, 1884–85; DAG, Horse Guards, 1885–86; GOC, Dublin District, 1886–87; GOC, Egypt, 1888–90; CinC, Madras, 1891–93. KCB, 1889; Lieutenant General, 1890. Dormer died at Ootacamund after being mauled on a tiger hunt. He was married to Alison's daughter, Ella.

35 Sir Joseph Paxton (1803–65), Head Gardener at Chatsworth, 1826–58; designer of the Crystal Palace, 1850–51, and of Mentmore House, 1850–55; Liberal MP for Coventry, 1854–65. Paxton received a knighthood in 1851 for his work on the Crystal Palace rather than being made a baronet.

36 Mr Benjamin's premises were in Glasshouse Street, London. He died in December 1874, whereupon his works of art were sold off: see *The Times*, 19 Dec. 1874.

37 Major General Sir Alfred Horsford (1818–85), Military Secretary. Commissioned, Rifle Brigade, 1833. Service in South Africa, 1847–48 and 1852–53; Crimea. DAG at Horse Guards, 1860–66; Brigadier General, Aldershot, 1866–69; Major General, Malta, 1869–71; GOC, SE District, 1872–74; Military Secretary, 1874–80. KCB, 1860; GCB, 1875; General, 1877.

Notes to Appendix I

1 Brackenbury lists correctly 36 officers as accompanying Wolseley in his official history, as does Maurice in his appendix, though Maurice actually miscounts the total as 35. Henty also suggests 35, but omits Brackenbury and substitutes Staff Surgeon Irvine for Atkins. Brackenbury and Huyshe correctly give 36 in *Fanti and Ashanti* and Huyshe also listed the original party for the benefit of *Hart's Army List*. See Brackenbury, *Ashanti War*, I, pp. 113–14; Maurice, *Ashantee War*, p. 406; Brackenbury and Huyshe, *Fanti and Ashanti*, p. v; Henty, *March to Coomassie*, pp. 18–19; TNA, Hart MSS, WO 211/71, Huyshe to Hart, 11 Sept. 1873.

Appendix VI

Wolseley's correspondence with Commodore William Hewett VC

It is clear that Wolseley had a warm regard for Hewett and greatly appreciated his willingness to make every effort to assist in the prosecution of the campaign. Subsequently, however, Hewett told Wolseley he would never again land sailors as infantrymen, only as artillerymen. Fremantle had also co-operated willingly, but there is a different tone to Wolseley's exchanges with Hewett, whom Wolseley had first met in the trenches before Sebastopol in the Crimea. Hewett, indeed, had won the VC defending his battery against a Russian sortie in October 1854.[1]

On 28 November 1873 Wolseley indicated that he proposed sending the Naval Brigade across the Pra first. He invited Hewett to accompany him on his coming tour of inspection of the proposed halting places for white troops when Wolseley intended 'rousing up the officers' commanding these posts as they 'seem to have gone asleep'.[2] In three subsequent letters in January 1874, Wolseley's concerns for the health and supply of his force are again evident [**180, 181, 182**] The campaign over, Wolseley sent his sincere appreciation to Hewett for the welcome he had received from a naval guard of honour when he returned to Cape Coast Castle, as well as for the 'complete cordiality' that had characterised the relations between soldiers and sailors. Wolseley hoped the bluejackets would not suffer subsequently from their exertions ashore and promised to do justice to them in his despatches.[3] Wolseley's desire to be away as soon as possible led him to ask Hewett on 21 February to send a fast ship to bring George Berkeley to Cape Coast in order to relieve him as soon as possible.[4] Similarly, six days later, Wolseley was telling the Control

Department 'to crack on every man and boat available' to load up the *Manitoban* when it arrived. Wolseley was expecting Colonel Maxwell to arrive shortly to take over from him, no one else having been prepared to remain even for £4,000 per annum and an additional allowance of three guineas a day whenever they travelled out of the town.[5]

Having left London for his period of leave in Italy, Wolseley was particularly exercised in April 1874 by the way in which the Admiralty had dispensed honours and rewards for the campaign, subsequently returning to the theme when back in London in August. Wolseley felt Glover and Festing had been over-rewarded and that the pressure being brought to bear on the latter's behalf by fellow marines was unseemly. Just as Hewett did not wish to put seamen ashore again as riflemen, Wolseley evidently had no wish to employ marines again. He also commented upon the controversy regarding Brackenbury's claims about the Rifle Brigade at Odaso [**183, 184**]. Wolseley and Hewett were to serve together again in Egypt in 1882, and in the Sudan in 1885. In 1882 Wolseley did employ marines once more, and Hewett did land seamen as riflemen in Egypt in 1882 and at Suakin in 1884.

180

Wolseley to Hewett

1 January 1874
[Holograph]
Camp Barraco

Your note of 30th ultimo just to hand. At present I do not expect anything to take place before the 15th instant, or at least anything worth seeing. However believe me that the sooner you come the more we shall all be pleased. Many thanks for the short rifles & cutlasses. I believe that before we are done, we shall leave you nothing but bare poles on board your ships. I am always asking for something, and the more you give me, the more I seem to want.

I do not understand what you mean in your note about "waiting for an Official about the departure of steamer for St Vincent".[6] Is it from me you expect it? & if so, to what effect? The Control at Cape Coast have orders to comply with your wishes regarding cots bearers carriers etc etc etc when you intend coming up & I shall have orders given at all intermediate posts so that you can travel as fast as you like. Upon Homes urgent representation I am writing to you today requesting you to be good enough to place *all* the mail steamers coming from Southern ports in quarantine whether their bill of health is clear or not. It is worth our while to do so, as for the next six weeks the quarantine *cannot be too strictly carried* out. Would you kindly impress this upon the officer you leave behind in command. I don't care what merchants may say, as the success of our expedition might at any moment be compromised by the lying of a Captain, and we know that the masters & doctors of these vessels do lie from the Biafra case.[7] The people of Adjuah & Secondee are begging for terms. I am going to pardon their political offences if they will give carriers. I have written to the Colonial Secretary to get Dr Gouldsbury or Dr O'Reilly[8] to go down there and tell them so in answer to the petition they have sent me. Can you kindly send down some vessel on this service to bring back whatever carriers can be obtained? I am sure you must "confound" me many times a day for writing as if you had the whole British fleet at your disposal, but this carrier question is too vital a one to stick at trifles. Lees will communicate with you on the subject. All your men here are healthy, one man only having diarrhoea two others being on the sick list one with swollen testicle the other with a thorn in his leg.

Wishing you many happy new years and hoping soon to see you at Prahsu.

PS What about the Barracouta?
NMM, Hewett MSS, HEW/4 (11)181

181

Wolseley to Hewett

4 January 1874
[Holograph]
Camp Prahsu
Yours of 2nd just arrived: many thanks for all that you have done to Windward Leeward and indeed in every direction to help us. It has now been reported to me that the blackguard steamers land men & stuff at Anamaboe (only 9 miles from Cape Coast Castle) & at Accra. I am

writing to ask you if you [can] stop this. I presume you can certainly as regards the former place. I am sending [an] order to the commandants of those places to prohibit the landing of all merchandize & passengers at those places; also to the Governor of Lagos requesting him to inform the agents of all steamers coming from the South that all those vessels are prohibited from landing goods or people at any port under Gold Coast jurisdiction & that anyone contravening this order will be guilty of a breach of our quarantine laws. We must leave no stone unturned to guard ourselves from having this horrid fever imported into Cape Coast, and if anything suggests itself to you as a further precaution that might be taken I should be very much obliged if you would kindly take it. I have just heard from Colonel Colley that all the carriers he had collected for the 23rd Regt have deserted. It is therefore just possible that the landing of that Battaln may be postponed for some days to come.

Will you kindly arrange that a mail shall go to England in Manitoban as you say she leaves on the 10th inst. direct for Spithead. A few hours after arriving here on the 2nd messengers came in from King Koffee. He writes evidently in ignorance of all that has recently taken place in his country, & I have ascertained that no one in Koomassie has the least idea of the impending invasion nor of the arrival of white troops on the coast. The Ashantee Army have dispersed to the mens homes and with the exception of half a dozen Ashantee scouts there is not a human being (alive for the road is said to be strewn with dead bodies) between this and Quisah where there are a few inhabitants so that all chance of a fight on this side of the Adansi Hill is at an end, & this is a sad blow to me, for with my transport difficulties before me every march I shall be forced to make inland to find my enemy encreases [sic] my difficulties. I am sending back the Kings messengers on the 6th. I have kept them here so that they might cross back over the river on my bridge which will be finished tomorrow morning. Your bluejackets are working away hard at it. I shall cross the Naval Brigade before I let these messengers go, and I have arranged so that they shall pass through the Naval Brigade *seemingly* on the march to Coomassie, but as soon as the messengers are well clear of your men, I shall bring back the Naval Brigade to this side where they are well housed. Tomorrow I mean to push Russells Regt forward to Atobiasi with an advanced party at Essiaman. His men will also be seen by the messengers, and I hope by this means to convince them that our invasion is not only contemplated, but begun. I may then induce Mr Koffee Kalcali either to make peace, accepting the terms that I now offer him, or to collect his Army and come down to meet me. This is a hard task before me; dangers and difficulties crop up on every side, and as one has been tolerably met, another starts up to trouble me.

Your people are all jolly and well. Your tent marked in large letters "The Commodore" is still vacant, and will be ready for you whenever you can join us. We celebrated New Years day at our mess last night: Captns Blake & Luxmore[9] dined with us and we had a merry dinner on the high bank of the river. I wish you had been with us.

NMM, Hewett MSS, HEW/4 (12)

182

Wolseley to Hewett

8 January 1874
[Holograph]
Camp Prahsu

I have again to thank you for all you have lately done for us. We shall all be delighted to see you here whenever you come. I am very glad you are bringing up some more Kroomen. The more you can bring the better as they are such reliable carriers. I would willingly give £5000 for 1000 of them. As regards mules from St Helena they would not be of any use by the time they could be brought, and besides the road and its bridges are not suited for mule transport, nor have I at my disposal the machinery for taking care of a four legged transport. If however you think that within twenty days at furthest you could obtain any more Kroomen or other *foreign* carriers from any place on the Coast, I think it would be well worth our while sending a ship for them, the officer who went for them offering fifteen or twenty dollars a head as bringing money to those who brought any. If you think this feasible, pray carry it out, for a few thousands pounds more or less is of no consequence and every day that we are delayed from want of carriers is of vital importance. My scouting party is now at Ansah and will be on the Fumusu River tomorrow. Only four of all ranks on the sick list this morning in your Brigade. They are still the only white troops I have here, as I have halted everyone where they are for the present. The nights are very cold here, so bring up a couple of blankets when you come. The weather is delightful. Out of 414 white men in camp to day, there are only 14 on the sick list, nearly all being slight cases.

Hoping soon to see you here believe me to [be] sincerely yours

PS The canvas tub you had so kindly made for me is of the greatest use in camp.

NMM, Hewett MSS, HEW/4 (13)

183

Wolseley to Hewett

16 April 1874
[Holograph]
Venice

Better late than never, so I sit down to scribble you a line of congratulation upon your well earned promotion. No one was more pleased at it than I was. I was asked to go over the list of the Bath promotions when I returned and was delighted to find that without anything from me it was proposed to make you a K.C.B. I hope and trust that your fever may have soon left you, for you were far from well when I started. We had a very pleasant voyage home, and all liked the ships you gave us very much. I have come abroad for a little quiet for I never had a moment to myself whilst at home.

I return on the 1st of next month, when I have looming before me a number of public dinners and the misery of having to make a speech at each.

I was very much annoyed at the Admiralty promoting Allnutt[10] of the Marines. When I read his name in the list several days before the Gazette appeared I told H.R.H. that I considered him unworthy to be an officer in Her Majestys Service and I frankly gave him my reasons, but I was told that the Admiralty were determined on this point, and that the Military authorities had nothing to do with the matter. The Marines have been writing letters in the newspapers complaining that I have not praised them sufficiently in my despatches. The whole corps seems to be off its head, and put forward Col. Festing as their hero. They are an ungracious lot to have anything to do with & I do not want ever again to serve with them. I met Commerell before I left home: he is all right again and looks as if he had never been unwell. Many of those who came home with me have had fever constantly, but on the whole their health is good. When I left England poor Butler was seriously ill as his brain had been attacked and some mad-doctors said he would not be all right again for a year or perhaps two – very sad is it not? I have done all I could to back up Glover, and gave Mr Disraeli such an account of his services that the old man in moving the thanks in parliament ran away with the subject, and made it appear that it was Glovers force that compelled King Koffi to make terms.

The Tories are now well in the saddle and I cannot see anything in the future that should disturb their seat – indeed there is no reason why they should not remain for years in office now. Tory as I am I regret my former masters at the War Office and have rather a dread that military progress may not be as certain under our new rulers as it was under those who are now in opposition. Please remember me most kindly to Rolfe and to doctor Fagan[11] and tell the latter that I believe it is arranged that the indemnity money is to be thrown into the prize fund. Hoping we may meet ere long – if on active service, so much the better, and congratulating you most sincerely on your knighthood always believe me to be my dear Commodore

NMM, Hewett MSS, HEW/4 (21)

184

Wolseley to Hewett

16 August 1874
[Holograph]
War Office letterhead
Before I had received your very nice letter of 25th June, I had spoken to Sir A. Milne about Rolfe, and he said that although too junior to be promoted now he should not be forgotten or words to that effect. Upon receipt of your letter I wrote to him, and yesterday I had his answer. I pointed out to him in my note that all my military A.D.C.s had been promoted, and that it was curious that my naval A.D.C. had been forgotten. His answer was the same as before but less satisfactory. I fear that I don't find favor with those in power at the Admiralty. What a fortunate man Commerell

has been. I never dreamt that he had a chance of being made a K.C.B.
I have no idea of what they go upon in determining who is & is not to
be rewarded. Glovers and Festings rewards have in my opinion been
beyond all bounds especially the latter whose speech at Portsmouth[12]
was ridiculous and in my opinion positively indecent where he upraided
[sic] the Navy for their treatment of the Marines. A Sir E. Wilmot[13] has
been moving heaven and earth to get Festing the V.C. for something he
is supposed to have done with reference to young Wilmots body in the
skirmish near Dunquah, when that poor fellow was killed. As there are
several who claim to have done the same thing I don't think that Festing
will ever have V.C. after his name.

I have not yet seen any of the books about the late war – but I am sorry
to say there is a bother about that brought out by Brackenbury owing to
his having imprudently inserted in it, one of the reports sent by Alison to
the rear during our last days fight, in which he talked of the unsteadiness
of the Rifle Brigade. All those who talk such nonsense ought to have seen
what you and I did the first moment we reached the village of Ordasu. I
think they would have reallized [sic] that the report was true. I hope this
will find you all right again. Pray remember me kindly to Rolfe and to Dr
Fagan and believe me to be always very sincerely yours
NMM, Hewett MSS, HEW/4 (17)

Notes to Appendix VI

1 Wolseley, *Story of Soldier's Life*, I, pp. 4, 7; ibid., II, pp. 344, 368.
2 NMM, Hewett MSS, HEW/4 (10), Wolseley to Hewett, 28 Nov.
   1873.
3 Ibid., HEW/4 (14), Wolseley to Hewett, 20 Feb. 1874.
4 Ibid., HEW/4 (15), Wolseley to Hewett, 21 Feb. 1874. See
   Documents 158, 160, 161.
5 Ibid., HEW/4 (16), Wolseley to Hewett, 27 Feb. 1874.
6 HMS *Simoom* left for St Vincent on 11 January. See BPP, Cmd. 894,
   pp. 42–3, Hewett to Admiralty, 10 Jan. 1874.
7 See Document 102. Hewett complied immediately with Wolseley's
   wishes with regard to the quarantine: see BPP, Cmd. 894, pp. 47–8,
   Hewett to Admiralty, 3 Jan. 1874.
8 Dr H. T. O'Reilly, Acting Civil Commandant at Elmina.
9 Commander Percy Luxmore of HMS *Argus*, raised to that rank in

1867, was second in command of the Naval Brigade under Hans Blake. He took part in the action at Amoafo but was then taken ill and did not go on to Kumase. Later in his career, Luxmore was deprived of his command after running the troopship, HMS *Malabar*, aground in February 1879, and again superseded after another ship under his command, HMS *Devastation*, collided with HMS *Ajax* at Spithead in July 1887: see *Freeman's Journal* and *Daily Commercial Advertiser*, 10 Feb. 1879, and *Aberdeen Weekly Journal*, 27 July 1887. As previously indicated, Luxmore's campaign journal is to be found at NMM, LOG/N/27, and extracts from a campaign account written for his wife appeared in *Blackwood's Magazine*.

10 Captain William Winkworth Allnutt, Royal Marine Light Infantry, was promoted Brevet Major on 1 April 1874. Commissioned 1855; service in China, 1858; Asante. Retired as Colonel, 1884.

11 Staff Surgeon Henry Fegan, RN of HMS *Active*. Fegan was promoted from Staff Surgeon 2nd Class to Staff Surgeon and awarded the CB for his services in Asante. According to Winwood Reade, Fegan discovered a 'very curious document, the journal of a Fante prisoner' at Kumase. See Reade, *Story of Ashantee*, p. 426. Fegan's campaign medical journal is in TNA, ADM 101/145.

12 Wolseley, Glover, Commerell, Fremantle, Festing and many others attended a civic banquet at Portsmouth on 12 May 1874, and this is presumably the occasion to which Wolseley refers. Press reports indicate that, after Wolseley made the main speech, both Glover and Festing also spoke but, unfortunately, there appears no record of what Festing said: see *Hampshire Telegraph* and *Sussex Chronicle*, 13 May 1874; and *Birmingham Daily Post*, 13 May 1874. Among letters in support of Festing and the Marines, see those of 'Semper Fidelis' in *The Times* on 17 March and 4 June 1874; and by 'PH' in the *Daily News*, 26 May 1874. Festing had been knighted on 8 May, while a sketch showing his rescue of Wilmot's body had appeared in *The Graphic* on 2 May. At the time of Wilmot's death on 3 November, Wolseley had accepted that Festing had carried the body to safety: see Documents 61, 64. Brackenbury's account also accepted that Festing had rescued the body but one who had claimed since to have done so was Surgeon Major Albert Gore: see *Hampshire Telegraph* and *Sussex Chronicle*, 17 June 1874. Commissioned in 1860, Gore had seen previous service in Sierra Leone in 1861 and had also been wounded on 3 November 1873. He was promoted Brigade Surgeon in 1886.

13 Presumably Wolseley means Wilmot's father, Sir John Eardley Wilmot Bt, MP.

Bibliography

Manuscript sources

Bodleian Library, Oxford: Alison MSS, Hughenden MSS, Kimberley MSS
Borthwick Institute of Historical Research, York: Hickleton MSS
British Library, London: Carnarvon MSS, Gladstone MSS,
    Northbrook MSS
Cambridge University Library: Glover MSS
Centre for Buckinghamshire Studies, Aylesbury: Fremantle MSS
Devon County Record Office, Exeter: Buller MSS
Downes House, Crediton: Buller Family Papers
Duke University (William Perkins Library), Durham, North Carolina:
    Wolseley MSS
Gosford House, Longniddry: Wemyss MSS
Hove Reference Library: Wolseley MSS
Kent Archives Office, Maidstone: Stanhope MSS
Killie Campbell Africana Library, Durban: Wood MSS
Kwazulu Natal Archives Depot, Pietermaritzburg: Wood MSS
National Archives, Kew: Admiralty Papers, Cardwell MSS, Colonial
    Office Papers, Hart MSS, War Office Papers, Wolseley MSS
National Archives of Scotland, Edinburgh: Wemyss MSS
National Army Museum: Cooper MSS, Warre MSS
National Library of Scotland, Edinburgh: Blackwood MSS
National Maritime Museum, Greenwich: Blake MSS, Fremantle MSS,
    Hewett MSS, Luxmore MSS, McLeod MSS
Nottinghamshire County Record Office, Nottingham: Portland of
    Welbeck MSS
Royal Archives, Windsor: Cambridge MSS, Ponsonby MSS, Victorian
    MSS

Royal Marines Museum, Gosport: Hearle MSS
South Lanarkshire Council Museum, Hamilton: Wolseley Diaries
Wiltshire and Swindon Record Office, Trowbridge: Methuen MSS

Parliamentary Papers

LXX, 1872, Cmd. 670 *Correspondence Relative to the Cession by the Netherlands Government to the British Government of the Dutch Settlements on the West Cast of Africa*

XLVI, 1874, Cmd. 941, *Return of Revenue and Expenditure, and Imports and Exports of the British Possessions in West Africa for Twenty Years*

XLVI, 1874, Cmd. 891, 892, 893, 894, 921 and 922, *Further Correspondence Respecting the Ashantee Invasion*, Nos. 2–5, 7 and 8

Cmd. 907, *Despatches from Sir Garnet Wolseley*, No 6

XV, 1875, Cmd. 1374, *Statistical, Sanitary and Medical Reports of the Army Medical Department, Report for the Year 1873*, Appendix II: *The Ashanti Campaign*

Contemporary works, memoirs and biographies

Adeloye, Adelola, *Dr James Africanus Beale Horton* (Pittsburgh, PA: Durrance, 1992)

Adu Boahen, A., Emmanuel Akyeampong, Nancy Lawler, T. C. McCaskie and Ivor Wilks, eds, '*The History of Ashanti Kings and the Whole Country Itself*' *and Other Writings* (Oxford: Oxford University Press for the British Academy, 2008)

Anson, Major General Sir Archibald, *About Others and Myself* (London: John Murray, 1920)

Arthur, Sir George, ed., *The Letters of Lord and Lady Wolseley, 1870–1911* (London: William Heinemann, 1922)

Beecham, John, *Ashantee and the Gold Coast* (London: John Mason, 1841)

Biddulph, Sir Robert, *Lord Cardwell at the War Office: A History of his Administration, 1868–74* (London: John Murray, 1904)

Bowdich, Thomas Edward, *A Mission from Cape Coast Castle to Ashantee* (London: John Murray, 1819)

Boyle, R. Frederick, *Through Fanteeland to Coomassie* (London: Chapman and Hall, 1874)

Brackenbury, Henry, 'The Relations between Great Britain, the Protected Tribes, and Ashanti, with the Causes of the Ashanti War', Pt II, in Henry Brackenbury and George Huyshe, *Fanti and Ashanti* (Edinburgh: William Blackwood & Sons, 1873), pp. 1–90

Brackenbury, Henry, *The Ashanti War: A Narrative*, 2 vols (Edinburgh and London: William Blackwood & Sons, 1874)

Brackenbury, Sir Henry, *Some Memories of My Spare Time* (Edinburgh: William Blackwood & Sons, 1909)

Brackenbury, Henry and George Huyshe, *Fanti and Ashanti* (Edinburgh: William Blackwood & Sons, 1873)

Buckle, G. E., ed., *The Letters of Queen Victoria: A Selection from Her Majesty's Correspondence and Journal, 1862–78*, 2nd series, 3 vols (London: John Murray, 1926–28)

[Burton, Richard Francis] A Fellow of the Royal Geographical Society, *Wanderings in West Africa* (London: Tinsley Brothers, 1863)

Butler, W. F., *Akim-Foo: The History of a Failure* (London: Sampson Low, Marston, Searle & Rivington, 1876)

Butler, Sir William, *The Life of Sir George Pomeroy-Colley* (London: John Murray, 1899)

Butler, Sir William, *An Autobiography* (New York: Charles Scribner's Sons, 1911)

Callwell, Charles, *Small Wars: Their Principles and Practice*, 3rd edn (London: HMSO, 1906)

Callwell, C. E., ed., *The Memoirs of Major General Sir Hugh McCalmont* (London: Hutchinson & Co, 1924)

Cavendish, Anne, ed., *Cyprus 1878: The Journal of Sir Garnet Wolseley* (Nicosia: Cyprus Popular Bank Cultural Centre, 1991)

Crooks, J. J., *Records Relating to the Gold Coast Settlements from 1750 to 1874* (Dublin: Browne & Nolan, 1923)

De Kiewiet, C. W. and F. H. Underhill, eds, *Dufferin–Carnarvon Correspondence, 1874–78* (Toronto: Publications of the Champlain Society, No 33, 1955)

[Dooner, William Toke] An Officer, *Jottings en route to Coomassie: With a Map* (London: W. Mitchell & Co, 1874)

[Dooner, William Toke] An Officer, *To Coomassie and Back (with a Map)* (London: Simpkin, Marshall, Hamilton, Kent & Co, 1895)

Douglas, Sir George, *The Life of Major General Wauchope* (London: Hodder & Stoughton, 1905)

Drus, Ethel, ed., *A Journal of Events during the Gladstone Ministry, 1868–74 by John, First Earl of Kimberley*, Camden Miscellany, 3rd series, XXI (London: Royal Historical Society, 1958)

Dupuis, Joseph, *Journal of a Residence in Ashantee*, 2nd edn (London: Frank Cass, 1966)

Fremantle, Admiral Sir Edmund, *The Navy As I Have Known It, 1849–99* (London: Cassell, 1904)

Glover, Sir John, 'The Volta Expedition during the late Ashantee Campaign', *Journal of the Royal United Service Institution* 18, 78 (1874–75), pp. 317–30

Glover, Lady, *Life of Sir John Hawley Glover*, ed. Sir Richard Temple (London: Smith, Elder & Co, 1897)

Greaves, General Sir George, *Memoirs* (London: John Murray, 1924)

Hart-Synnot, Beatrice, ed., *Letters of Major General Fitzroy Hart-Synnot* (London: Edward Arnold, 1912)

Hawkins, Angus and John Powell, eds, *The Journal of John Wodehouse, First Earl of Kimberley, 1862–1902*, Camden Miscellany, 5th series, IX (London: Royal Historical Society, 1997)

Heneker, W. C. G., *Bush Warfare* (London: Hugh Rees, 1907)

Henty, G. A., *The March to Coomassie* (London: Tinsley, 1874)

Henty, G. A., 'Amoaful', in Archibald Forbes, G. A. Henty and Arthur Griffiths, eds, *Battles of the Nineteenth Century*, 2 vols (London: Cassell & Co., 1896), I, pp. 215–23

Hutton, William, *A Voyage to Africa* (London: Longman, 1821)

Huyshe, G. L., *The Red River Expedition* (London: Macmillan, 1871)

Huyshe, G. L., 'The Red River Expedition', *Journal of the Royal United Service Institution* 15, 52 (1872), pp. 70–85

Huyshe, G. L. 'The Topography of Ashanti and the Protectorate of the Gold Coast', in Henry Brackenbury and George Huyshe, *Fanti and Ashanti* (Edinburgh: William Blackwood & Sons, 1873), pp. 91–131

Itter, Ian, ed., *Wolseley Letters concerning Fred* (Swan Hill, Victoria, Australia: Ian Itter Publishing, 2007)

Kochanski, Halik, *Sir Garnet Wolseley: Victorian Hero* (London: Hambledon Press, 1999)

Lehmann, Joseph, *All Sir Garnet: A Life of Field Marshal Lord Wolseley, 1833–1913* (London: Jonathan Cape, 1964)

Low, Charles Rathbone, *General Lord Wolseley of Cairo*, 2nd edn (London: Richard Bentley & Son, 1883)

Luxmore, Percy, 'Ashantee: Extracts from the Journal of a Naval Officer addressed to his Wife', *Blackwood's Edinburgh Magazine* 115 (1874), pp. 518–24

McCourt, Edward, *Remember Butler* (London: Routledge & Kegan Paul, 1967)

Manning, Stephen, *Evelyn Wood VC: Pillar of Empire* (Barnsley: Pen and Sword, 2007)

Matthew, H. C. G., ed., *The Gladstone Diaries: VIII, 1871–74* (Oxford: Clarendon Press, 1982)

[Maurice, Frederick] The 'Daily News' Special Correspondent, *The Ashantee War: A Personal Narrative* (London: Henry S. King & Co., 1874)

Maurice Sir Frederick, and Sir George Arthur, *The Life of Lord Wolseley* (London: William Heinemann Ltd, 1924)

Melville, C. H., *Life of General the Rt. Hon. Sir Redvers Buller*, 2 vols (London: Edward Arnold, 1923)

Metcalfe, G. E., *Great Britain and Ghana: Documents of Ghana History, 1807–1957* (London: Thomas Nelson & Sons, 1964)

Moneypenny, William and G. E. Buckle, eds, *The Life of Benjamin Disraeli, Earl of Beaconsfield*, 6 vols (New York: Macmillan, 1920)

Newbury, G. W., *British Policy towards West Africa: Select Documents, 1786–1874* (Oxford: Clarendon Press, 1965)

O'Toole, J., *Frederick York Wolseley* (privately printed, 1995)

Pegram, Marjory, *The Wolseley Heritage: The Story of Frances Viscountess Wolseley and Her Parents* (London: John Murray, 1939)

Perrot, Claude-Hélène and Albert von Dantzig, eds, *Marie-Joseph Bonnat et les Ashanti: Journal, 1869–74* (Paris: Musée de l'Homme and Société des Africanistes, 1994)

Pollock, John, *Gordon: The Man Behind the Legend* (Oxford: Lion Publishing, 1993)

Pope Hennessy, James, *Verandah: Some Episodes in the Crown Colonies, 1867–89* (London: George Allen & Unwin, 1964)

Preston, Adrian, ed., *In Relief of Gordon: Lord Wolseley's Campaign Journal of the Khartoum Relief Expedition, 1884–85* (London: Hutchinson, 1967)

Preston, Adrian, ed., *Sir Garnet Wolseley's South African Diaries (Natal) 1875* (Cape Town: A. A. Balkema, 1971)

Preston, Adrian, *Sir Garnet Wolseley's South African Journal, 1879–80* (Cape Town: A. A. Balkema, 1973)

Prior, Melton, *Campaigns of a War Correspondent* (London: Edward Arnold, 1912)

Ramm, Agatha, ed., *The Gladstone–Granville Correspondence*, 2nd edn (Cambridge: Cambridge University Press for the Royal Historical Society, 1998)

Ramseyer, F. A., and J. Kühne, *Four Years in Ashantee* (London: James Nisbet & Co., 1875)

Rawley, James A., ed., *The American Civil War: An English View by Field Marshal Viscount Wolseley* (Charlottesville, VA: University Press of Virginia, 1964)

Reade, Windwood, *Savage Africa* (London: Smith, Elder & Co, 1863)

Reade, Winwood, *The Story of the Ashantee Campaign* (London: Smith, Elder & Co, 1874)

Ricketts, Major H. I., *Narrative of the Ashantee War* (London: Simpkin & Marshall, 1831)

Stanley, Henry Morton, *Coomassie and Magdala* (New York: Harper, 1874)

Stephenson, F. C. A., *At Home and on the Battlefield* (London: John Murray, 1915)

Stephenson, Glennis, *Letitia Landon* (Manchester: Manchester University Press, 1995)

Verner, Colonel Willoughby, *The Military Life of HRH George, Duke of Cambridge*, 2 vols (London: John Murray, 1905)

Vetch, R. H., *Life of Lieutenant-General the Hon. Sir Andrew Clarke* (London: John Murray, 1905)

Villiers, Frederic, *Peaceful Personalities and Warriors Bold* (London: Harper & Brothers, 1907)

Vincent, John, ed., *A Selection from the Diaries of Edward Henry Stanley, Fifteenth Earl of Derby, 1869–78*, Camden Miscellany, 5th series, IV (London: Royal Historical Society, 1994)

Walling, R. A. J., ed., *The Diaries of John Bright* (London: Cassell, 1930)

Wemyss, Earl of, *Memoirs, 1818–1911* (Edinburgh: David Douglas, 1912)

[Wolseley, Garnet], 'Our Autumn Manoeuvres', *Blackwood's Magazine*, 112 (November 1872), pp. 627–44

[Wolseley, Garnet] A Staff Officer, 'Military Staff-systems Abroad and in England', *Macmillan's Magazine* 37 (1878), pp. 323–35

Wolseley, Garnet, *The Soldier's Pocket Book for Field Service* (London: Macmillan, 1886)

Wolseley, Field Marshal Viscount, *The Story of a Soldier's Life*, 2 vols (London: Archibald Constable & Co, 1903)

Wood, Evelyn, *Mounted Riflemen* (London: W. Mitchell & Co, 1873)

Wood, Evelyn, 'The Ashanti Expedition of 1873–74', *Journal of the Royal United Service Institution* 18, 78 (1874–75), pp. 331–57

Wood, Sir Evelyn, *From Midshipman to Field Marshal*, 2 vols (London: Methuen & Co, 1906)

Wood, Field Marshal Sir Evelyn, 'The Ashanti Expedition, 1873–74', in idem, ed., *British Battles on Land and Sea*, 2 vols (London: Cassell & Co, 1915), II, pp. 680–703

Zetland, The Marquis of, ed., *The Letters of Disraeli to Lady Bradford and Lady Chesterfield*, 2 vols (London: Ernest Benn, 1929)

Secondary sources

Adjaye, Joseph, *Diplomacy and Diplomats in Nineteenth Century Asante* (Trenton, NJ: Africa World Press, 1996)

Adu Boahen, A., 'Asante and Fante, AD 1000–1800', in J. F. Ade Ajayi and Ian Espie, eds, *A Thousand Years of West African History* (Ibadan: Ibadan University Press, 1965), pp. 165–90

Adu Boahen, A., 'Asante, Fante and the British, 1800–80', in J. F. Ade Ajayi and Ian Espie, eds, *A Thousand Years of West African History* (Ibadan: Ibadan University Press, 1965), pp. 346–63

Adu Boahen, A., *Yaa Asantewaa and the Asante–British War of 1900–1* (London: James Currey, 2003)

Aidoo, Agnes, 'Order and Conflict in the Asante Empire: A Study in Interest Group Relations', *African Studies Review* 20, 1 (1977), pp. 1–36

Arhin, Kwame, 'Ashanti Military Institutions', *Journal of African Studies* 7 (1980), pp. 22–30

Bailes, Howard, 'Patterns of Thought in the Late Victorian Army', *Journal of Strategic Studies* 4 (1981), pp. 29–45

Bailes, Howard, 'Technology and Tactics in the British Army, 1866–1900', in Ronald Haycock and Keith Neilson, eds, *Men, Machines and War* (Waterloo, ON: Wilfred Laurier University Press, 1988), pp. 23–47

Ballard, C., 'Sir Garnet Wolseley and John Dunn', in A. Duminy and C. Ballard, eds, *The Anglo-Zulu War: New Perspectives* (Pietermaritzburg: University of Natal Press, 1988), pp. 120–47

Beckett, Ian F. W., *Riflemen Form: A Study of the Rifle Volunteer Movement, 1859–1908* (Aldershot: Ogilby Trusts, 1982)

Beckett, Ian F. W., 'Wolseley and the Ring', *Soldiers of the Queen* 69 (1992), pp. 14–25

Beckett, Ian F. W., 'Command in the Late Victorian Army', in Gary Sheffield, ed., *Leadership and Command: The Anglo-American Military Experience since 1861* (London: Brasseys, 1997), pp. 37–56

Beckett, Ian F. W., *The Victorians at War* (London: Hambledon, 2003)

Beckett, Ian F. W., 'Another British Way in Warfare: Charles Callwell and Small Wars', in Ian F. W. Beckett, ed., *Victorians at War: New Perspectives* (Society for Army Historical Research Special Publication No. 16, 2007), pp. 89–102

Beckett, Ian F. W., ed., *Victorians at War: New Perspectives* (Society for Army Historical Research Special Publication No. 16, 2007)

Bond, Brian, 'The Effect of the Cardwell Reforms on Army Organisation, 1874–1904', *Journal of the Royal United Services Institution for Defence Studies* 105 (1960), pp. 515–24

Bond, Brian, *The Victorian Army and the Staff College* (London; Eyre Methuen, 1972)

Brooks, Richard, *The Long Arm of Empire: Naval Brigades from the Crimea to the Boxer Rebellion* (London: Constable, 1999)

Bruce, Anthony, 'Edward Cardwell and the Abolition of Purchase', in Ian F. W. Beckett and John Gooch, eds, *Politicians and Defence: Studies in the Formulation of British Defence Policy, 1846–1970* (Manchester: Manchester University Press, 1981), pp. 24–46

Bryant, Mark, *Wars of Empire in Cartoons* (London: Grub Street Publishing, 2008)

Bumsted, J. M., *The Red River Rebellion* (Winnipeg: Watson & Dyer, 1996)

Caulfield, J. E., *100 Years' History of the 2nd West India Regiment, 1795–1898* (London: Forster Groom & Co, 1898)

Cima, Keith, *Reflections from the Bridge* (Buckingham: Baron Birch, 1994)

Claridge, W. W., *A History of the Gold Coast and Ashanti*, 2 vols (London: John Murray, 1915)

Condua-Harley, J. E., *Sagrenti War: An Illustrated History of the Ashanti Campaign, 1873–74* (London: privately published, 1974)

Coombs, Douglas, *The Gold Coast, Britain and the Netherlands, 1850–74* (London and Ibadan: Oxford University Press, 1963)

Crook, M. J., *The Evolution of the Victoria Cross* (Tunbridge Wells: Midas Books, 1975)

Cross, Ian, 'The 7-pounder rifled muzzle-loading gun of 200 lbs, Mk. IV', *Soldiers of the Queen* 132 (2008), pp. 21–6

Curtin, Philip, *Disease and Empire: The Health of European Troops and the Conquest of Africa* (Cambridge: Cambridge University Press, 1998)

Driver, Felix, 'Distance and Disturbance: Travel, Exploration and Knowledge in the Nineteenth Century', *Transactions of the Royal Historical Society* 14 (2004), pp. 73–92

Duckers, Peter, *British Military Rifles* (Princes Risborough: Shire Publications, 2005)

Duckers, Peter, *The Victoria Cross* (Princes Risborough: Shire Publications, 2005)

Edgerton, Robert, *The Fall of the Asante Empire* (New York: Free Press, 1995)

Eldridge, C. C., 'Newcastle and the Ashanti War of 1863–84: A Failure of the Policy of Anti-imperialism', *Renaissance and Modern Studies* 12 (1968), pp. 68–90

Eldridge, C. C., *England's Mission: The Imperial Idea in the Age of Gladstone and Disraeli, 1868–80* (London: Macmillan, 1973)

Emery, Frank, *Marching Over Africa* (London: Hodder & Stoughton, 1986)

Emery, Norman, 'Durham City and a "Small War"', *Durham Archaeological Journal* 17 (2000), pp. 83–4

Fortescue, Sir John, *Following the Drum* (Edinburgh: William Blackwood & Sons, 1931)

Fynn, J. K., 'Ghana-Asante (Ashanti)', in Michael Crowder, ed., *West African Resistance: The Military Response to Colonial Occupation* (London: Hutchinson, 1978), pp. 19–52

Gallagher, T. F., 'Cardwellian Mysteries: The Fate of the British Army Regulation Bill, 1871', *Historical Journal* 18, 2 (1975), pp. 327–48

Godwin-Austen, A. R., *The Staff and the Staff College* (London: Constable, 1927)

Greaves, Adrian, ed., *Redcoats and Zulus* (Barnsley: Pen & Sword, 2004)

Hargreaves, J. D., 'Winwood Reade and the Discovery of Africa', *African Affairs* 56 (1957), pp. 306–16

Hargreaves, J. D., *Prelude to the Partition of West Africa* (London: Macmillan, 1963)

Harvie, Ian, 'The Wolseley Ring: A Case Study in the Exercise of Patronage in the Late Victorian Army', unpublished MA dissertation, University of Buckingham, 1993

Harvie, Ian, 'The Raid on Essaman, 14 October 1873: An Account by Lieutenant Edward Woodgate of an Operation during Wolseley's Ashanti Expedition', *Journal of the Society for Army Historical Research* 77, 309 (1999), pp. 19–27

Haycock, Ronald and Keith Neilson, eds, *Men, Machines and War* (Waterloo, ON: Wilfred Laurier University Press, 1988)

Headrick, D. R., *The Invisible Weapon: Telecommunications and International Politics, 1851–1945* (New York: Oxford University Press, 1991)

Hodgson, Pat, *The War Illustrators* (London: Osprey, 1977)

Hopkins, A. G., 'Asante and the Victorians: Transition and Partition on the Gold Coast', in Roy Bridges, ed., *Imperialism, Decolonisation and Africa* (Basingstoke, Macmillan, 2000), pp. 25–64

Jones, A., '*Four Years in Ashantee*: One Source or Several?', *History in Africa* 18 (1991), pp. 173–203

Kea, R. A., 'Firearms and Warfare on the Gold and Slave Coasts from the Sixteenth to the Nineteenth Centuries', *Journal of African History* 12, 2 (1971), pp. 185–213

Keegan, John, 'The Ashanti Campaign, 1873–74', in Brian Bond, ed., *Victorian Military Campaigns* (London: Hutchinson, 1967), pp. 161–98

Kimble, David, *A Political History of Ghana, 1850–1928* (Oxford: Clarendon Press, 1963)

Knight, Ian, ' The Effectiveness of the Martini-Henry in Zululand', *Journal of the Anglo-Zulu War Historical Society* 11 (2002), pp. 1–5

Knight, Ian, 'The Battle of Ulundi', in Adrian Greaves, ed., *Redcoats and Zulus* (Barnsley: Pen & Sword, 2004), pp. 205–16

Kochanski, Halik, 'Sir Garnet Wolseley and the Reform of the British Army, 1870–99', unpublished PhD thesis, University of London, 1996

Lloyd, Alan, *The Drums of Kumasi: The Story of the Ashanti Wars* (London: Longmans Green & C, 1964)

Luvaas, Jay, *The Education of an Army* (London: Cassell, 1965)

McCaskie, T. C., 'Death and the Asantehene: A Historical Meditation', *Journal of African History* 30, 3 (1989), pp. 417–44

McCaskie, T. C., *State and Society in Pre-colonial Asante* (Cambridge: Cambridge University Press, 1995)

McCaskie, T. C., 'Cultural Encounters: Britain and Africa in the Nineteenth Century', in Andrew Porter, ed., *The Oxford History of the British Empire: The Nineteenth Century* (Oxford: Oxford University Press, 1999), pp. 644–89

McCaskie, T. C., *Asante Identities: History and Modernity in an African Village, 1850–1950* (Edinburgh: Edinburgh University Press, 2000)

McIntyre, W. D., 'British Policy in West Africa: The Ashanti Expedition of 1873–74', *Historical Journal* 5, 1 (1962), pp. 19–46

McIntyre, W. D., 'Commander Glover and the Colony of Lagos, 1861–73', *Journal of African History* 4 (1963), pp. 57–79

McIntyre, W. D., *The Imperial Frontier in the Tropics, 1865–75* (London: Macmillan, 1967)

Parker, John, *Making the Town: Ga State and Society in Early Colonial Accra* (Oxford: James Currey, 2000)

Preston, Adrian, 'Sir Garnet Wolseley and the Cyprus Expedition, 1878,' *Journal of the Society for Army Historical Research* 45, 181 (1967), pp. 4–16

Purdon, Charles, *The Snider-Enfield* (Alexandria Bay, NY: Museum Restoration Service, 1963)

Robinson, Ronald, John Gallagher and Alice Denny, *Africa and the Victorians: The Official Mind of Imperialism*, 2nd edn (London: Macmillan, 1967)

St Clair, William, *The Grand Slave Emporium* (London: Profile Books, 2006)

Salis Schwabe, G., 'Carrier Corps and Coolies on Active Service in China, India, and Africa, 1860–79', *Journal of the Royal United Service Institution* 24, 107 (1880), pp. 815–46

Smith, Robert, *Warfare and Diplomacy in Pre-colonial West Africa*, 2nd edn (London: James Currey, 1989)

Spiers, Edward, *The Army and Society, 1815–1914* (London: Longman, 1980)

Spiers, Edward, *The Late Victorian Army, 1868–1902* (Manchester: Manchester University Press, 1992)

Spiers, Edward, *The Victorian Soldier in Africa* (Manchester: Manchester University Press, 2004)

Spiers, Edward, *The Scottish Soldier and Empire, 1854–1902* (Edinburgh: Edinburgh University Press, 2006)

Strachan, Hew, *European Armies and the Conduct of War* (London: Allen & Unwin, 1983)

~ Symons, Julian, *England's Pride: the Story of the Gordon Relief Expedition* (London: Hamish Hamilton, 1965)

Tucker, A. V., 'Army and Society in England, 1870–1900: A Reassessment of the Cardwell Reforms', *Journal of British Studies* 2 (1963), pp. 110–41

Ubaeyi, Paul M., *British Military and Naval Forces in West African History, 1807–74* (New York: Nok, 1978)

Ukpabi, S. C., 'West Indian Troops and the Defence of British West Africa in the Nineteenth Century', *African Studies Review* 18 (1974), pp. 33–50

Vandervort, Bruce, *Wars of Imperial Conquest in Africa, 1830–1914* (London: UCL Press, 1998)

Ward, W. E. F., *A History of the Gold Coast* (London: Allen & Unwin, 1948)

White, Gavin, 'Firearms in Africa: An Introduction', *Journal of African History* 12, 2 (1971), pp. 173–84

Wilkinson-Latham, R. J., *From Our Special Correspondent: Victorian War Correspondents and Their Campaigns* (London: Hodder & Stoughton, 1979)

Wilks, Ivor, *Asante in the Nineteenth Century: The Structure and Evolution of a Political Order* (Cambridge: Cambridge University Press, 1975)

Wilks, Ivor, *Forests of Gold: Essays on the Akan and the Kingdom of Asante* (Athens, OH: Ohio University Press, 1993)

Index

537